programming.java

programming.java

An Introduction to Programming Using Java

Rick Decker
Stuart Hirshfield

Hamilton College

PWS PUBLISHING COMPANY

I(T)P *An International Thomson Publishing Company*

Boston • Albany • Bonn • Cincinnati • Detroit • London • Madrid
Melbourne • Mexico City • New York • Pacific Grove • Paris
San Francisco • Singapore • Tokyo • Toronto • Washington

PWS PUBLISHING COMPANY
20 Park Plaza, Boston, MA 02116-4324

I(T)P ™

International Thomson Publishing
The trademark ITP is used under license.

Sponsoring Editor: *David Dietz*
Editorial Assistant: *Katie Schooling*
Technology Editor: *Leslie Bondaryk*
Market Development Manager: *Nathan Wilbur*
Production Manager: *Elise S. Kaiser*
Production: *Publishers' Design and Production
    Services, Inc.*
Cover Designer: *Cyndy Patrick*
Manufacturing Buyer: *Andrew Christensen*
Text Printer: *R.R. Donnelley/Crawfordsville*
Cover Printer: *Phoenix Color Corp.*

 *This book is printed on
recycled, acid-free paper.*

Printed and bound in the United States of America.
97 98 99 00 01 — 10 9 8 7 6 5 4 3 2 1

*Library of Congress
Cataloging-in-Publication Data*

Decker, Rick.
  Programming.Java: an introduction to
programming using Java/ Rick Decker, Stuart
Hirshfield.
    p.   cm.
  Includes index.
  ISBN 0-534-95588-6 (alk. paper)
  1. Java (Computer program language)
I. Hirshfield, Stuart.   II. Title
QA76.73.J38D44 1997
005.13'3—dc21   97-29138
                                  CIP

For more information, contact:
**PWS Publishing Company
20 Park Plaza
Boston, MA 02116**

International Thomson Publishing Europe
Berkshire House 168-173
High Holborn
London WC1V 7AA
England

Thomas Nelson Australia
102 Dodds Street
South Melbourne, 3205
Victoria, Australia

Nelson Canada
1120 Birchmont Road
Scarborough, Ontario
Canada M1K 5G4

International Thomson Publishing GmbH
Königswinterer Strasse 418
53227 Bonn, Germany

International Thomson Editores
Campos Eliseos 385, Piso 7
Col. Polanco
11560 Mexico D.F., Mexico

International Thomson Publishing Asia
221 Henderson Road
#05-10 Henderson Building
Singapore 0315

International Thomson Publishing Japan
Hirakawacho Kyowa Building, 31
2-2-1 Hirakawacho
Chiyoda-ku, Tokyo 102
Japan

· ·

For Mike, David, Elise, Nathan, Leslie, and Liz

May you never leave us but to better yourselves,
and may your success among us be such as to
render bettering yourselves impossible.
—Charles Dickens *(more or less)*

CONTENTS

CHAPTER ONE BACKGROUND   **1**

1.1   The Evolution of Programming   1
      The Not-So-Good Old Days **2** ❦ Help Arrives **5**
1.2   The Internet and the Worldwide Web   7
      The Worldwide Web **9** ❦ HTML **10**
1.3   Along Comes Java   12
      Smart Toasters **12** ❦ Java, Meet Web; Web, Meet Java **13** ❦
      Applications and Applets **14**
1.4   An Overview of Java   19
      Syntax **19** ❦ Objects and Classes **20** ❦ Inheritance **21** ❦ Libraries **22**
1.5   Hands On   24
1.6   Resources Online   26
1.7   Summary   27
1.8   Exercises   27

CHAPTER TWO APPLETS   **31**

2.1   The `Applet` Class   31
      Learning from a Simple Applet **32**
2.2   Methods, Inheritance, and Overriding   35
      Java Methods **35** ❦ Inheritance and Overriding **38**
2.3   Graphical Programming   39
      The `Graphics` Class **39** ❦ Using the `Graphics` Class **42** ❦
      The `Color` Class **45** ❦ The `Font` Class **46** ❦ Positions and Sizes:
      The Classes `Point`, `Dimension`, and `Rectangle` **47**
2.4   Hands On   52
2.5   Summary   59
2.6   Exercises   61

CHAPTER THREE WIDGETS   **66**

3.1   Components   66
       Component's Graphical Methods **67**
3.2   Textual Widgets   71
       The `Label` Class **72** ❦ The `TextComponent` Class **73** ❦
       The `TextField` Class **74** ❦ The `TextArea` Class **76** ❦
       Widget Musings **78**
3.3   Active Widgets   81
       The `Button` Class **81** ❦ The `Checkbox` Class **82** ❦
       `CheckboxGroups` **84** ❦ The `Choice` Class **85** ❦
       The `List` Class **87**
3.4   Hands On   90
3.5   Summary   95
3.6   Exercises   96

CHAPTER FOUR VISUAL DESIGN   **100**

4.1   Containers   100
       Container Organization Methods **101** ❦ The Containment
       Hierarchy **103** ❦ The `Panel` Class **104**
4.2   Layouts   105
       Container Layout Methods **105** ❦ The `FlowLayout` Class **106** ❦
       The `BorderLayout` Class **108** ❦ The `GridLayout` Class **110** ❦
       The `CardLayout` Class **112** ❦ No Layout **115**
4.3   Other Containers, Other Details   117
       The `Canvas` Class **117** ❦ Windows **121** ❦ Frames **121** ❦
       Dialogs **124** ❦ Menus **130**
4.4   Hands On   138
       Designing the Lablet **139** ❦ The Lablet Code **141**
4.5   Summary   146
4.6   Exercises   148

CHAPTER FIVE JAVA LANGUAGE BASICS   **154**

5.1   Primitive Types   154
       Integers **155** ❦ Floating-Point Numbers **156** ❦ Characters **157** ❦
       The `boolean` Type **158**
5.2   Identifiers, Keywords, and Variables   158
       Variables **159** ❦ Scope **160** ❦ The Modifiers `static`
       and `final` **162** ❦ Brief Interlude: Packages **164** ❦ Access Modifiers **165**

5.3   Operators and Expressions   171
       Numeric Operators **171** ❦ The `Math` Class **175** ❦
       Bitwise Operators* **177** ❦ Boolean Operators **181**

5.4   Assignments and Statements   187
       Assignments **188** ❦ Class Variables vs. Primitive Variables **190** ❦
       Miscellaneous Operators **193** ❦ Statements **194**

5.5   Hands On   196
       Designing the Lablet, I **197** ❦ Designing the Lablet, II **198** ❦
       The Lablet Code **199**

5.6   Summary   205
5.7   Exercises   208

CHAPTER SIX EVENTS AND ACTIONS   **216**

6.1   More Java Programming   216
       The `if` Statement **217** ❦ Common Problems with `if` **220** ❦
       The `switch` Statement **224** ❦ Abstract Classes and Interfaces **227**

6.2   Event-Driven Programming   231
       The `Event` Class **232** ❦ The Event Hierarchy **233**

6.3   Event Handling   235
       Helper Methods **237** ❦ Deciphering the Event **238**

6.4   Other Events   239
       Masks, Key Modifiers, and Mouse Buttons **239** ❦ Focus Events **241** ❦
       Scroll Events **241**

6.5   The Java 1.1 Delegation Model   242
6.6   The `AWTEvent` Hierarchy   247
       Upper Level Event Classes **247** ❦ Action Events **249** ❦
       Input Events **249** ❦ Item Events **250** ❦ Key Events **251** ❦
       Mouse Events **252** ❦ Text Events **253**

6.7   Handling Events in Version 1.1   253
       Listener Interfaces **254** ❦ Adapters **257**

6.8   Hands On   257
       The `GalaEvents` Lablet **257** ❦ The `SketchPad` Lablet **260**

6.9   Summary   264
6.10   Exercises   269

CHAPTER SEVEN METHODICAL PROGRAMMING   **276**

7.1   Method Recap   277
       Method Signatures **277** ❦ Calling Methods **278** ❦ Arguments **280** ❦
       Value Arguments and Reference Arguments **283**

7.2   Step 1: Specification   285
       Look and Feel **286**

7.3   Step 2: Determine the Classes   288
       Layout **289** ❦ Filling in the Details **293**

7.4   Step 3: Determine the Methods   294
       Top Level Decomposition **294** ❦ Filling in the Details, Again **298**

7.5   Step 3, Continued   300
       A New Class **302** ❦ Cleanup **311**

7.6   The ATM Applet   314
7.7   Hands On   320
7.8   Summary   321
7.9   Exercises   323

CHAPTER EIGHT COLLECTIONS   **330**

8.1   Loops   330
       The do Loop **332** ❦ The while Loop **332** ❦ The for Loop **333** ❦
       Common Problems with Loops **335**

8.2   Arrays   337
       Declaring Arrays **338** ❦ Accessing Array Elements **339** ❦ Arrays and
       Loops **340** ❦ Multidimensional Arrays **344** ❦ Heterogeneous Arrays **346**

8.3   Sorting   348
       Selection Sort **348** ❦ Insertion Sort **350** ❦ Shellsort **352**

8.4   Strings   355
       The String Class **356** ❦ Access and Comparison **357** ❦
       Builders **360** ❦ Using Strings for Conversion **361**

8.5   Hands On   363
       Designing the Lablet **363** ❦ Exploring the Lablet **365**

8.6   Summary   372
8.7   Exercises   375

CHAPTER NINE EXCEPTIONS   **384**

9.1   Exceptional Conditions   384
       Exception Subclasses **385** ❦ Methods That Throw Exceptions **388**

9.2   Handling Exceptions   389
       try and catch **390** ❦ Exception Propagation **392** ❦ Throwing
       Exceptions **393** ❦ Prophylactic Programming **397** ❦ Finally, finally **399**

9.3   Your Very Own Exceptions   400
9.4   Hands On   402
       Designing the Lablet **403** ❦ Exploring OrderPlease **404**

9.5   Summary   412
9.6   Exercises   413

CHAPTER TEN INPUT/OUTPUT   **418**
. . . .

10.1   Streams   419
        The Classes `InputStream` and `OutputStream` **419** ❦ The Classes
        `DataInputStream` and `DataOutputStream` **422**

10.2   File I/O   425
        The `FileInputStream` and `FileOutputStream` Classes **426** ❦
        I/O for Primitive Types **427** ❦ I/O for Class Types **430** ❦ Headers **431**

10.3   Advanced File I/O   434
        Filtering File Names **434** ❦ The `File` Class **435** ❦ The `FileDialog`
        Class **438**

10.4   Security, Applets, and Applications   441
        Java Security **442** ❦ Applet Security **443** ❦ Security of Java
        Applications **444**

10.5   Hands On   447
        Designing the Lablet **447** ❦ Exploring `WordPro` **450**

10.6   Summary   456
10.7   Exercises   458

CHAPTER ELEVEN THREADS   **462**
. . . .

11.1   Threaded Execution   463
        The Basics of the `Thread` Class **466** ❦ The `Runnable` Interface **469** ❦
        Grouping Threads 472

11.2   Threads and Applets   475
11.3   Synchronizing Threads   479
        Synchronization and Mutual Exclusion **480** ❦ The `wait( )` and `notify( )`
        Methods **482** ❦ Priorities **487**

11.4   Summary of the `Thread` Class   488
        Class Constants **488** ❦ Constructors **489** ❦ Class Methods **489** ❦
        Instance Methods **490** ❦ Methods from `Object` **490**

11.5   Hands On   491
        Designing the Lablet, I: The `TickTock` User's Manual **491** ❦ Designing the
        Lablet, II: Meeting the Specifications **493** ❦ Exploring `TickTock` **495**

11.6   Summary   501
11.7   Exercises   503

CHAPTER TWELVE APPLETS IN CYBERSPACE 508

12.1 Setting the Scene 508
URLs **509** ❦ The `Applet` Class, Revisited **512** ❦ The `AppletContext`
Interface **515** ❦ Applet Parameters, Applet Attributes **516**

12.2 Lights, Camera, . . . 517
Audio Clips **517** ❦ Image Basics **518** ❦ Drawing Offscreen **522** ❦
Image Processing Prerequisites **524** ❦ Image Processing, Behind the
Scenes **528** ❦ Image Filters **532**

12.3 Action! 535
Preliminaries: Drawing on a Canvas **535** ❦ Animation Preamble **538** ❦
Loading Images: The `MediaTracker` Class **538** ❦ Animation I: Starting
Out **540** ❦ Animation II: Better Design **542** ❦ Animation III: Moving
the Ship **544** ❦ Animation IV: Clipping **547**

12.4 Hands On 549
Designing the `Lablet` **549** ❦ Exploring the `OldButtoner`
Applet **550** ❦ Exploring the `GraphicButton` Class **555** ❦
Exploring the `AnimatedButton` Class **559** ❦ Finally, the HTML **561**

12.5 Summary 562
12.6 Exercises 564

INDEX 568

PREFACE

ABOUT *programming.java*

"Programming dot Java" is intended to be used in a one-semester introduction to programming, suitable for a Computer Science I (CS1) course. We assume no prior programming experience on the part of our audience. We use the Java language, for reasons we explain, but this is much more than a Java programming book. Although it might be possible for a novice to "learn just Java in *x* days" by concentrating solely on the language and its libraries, we feel that the result wouldn't be worth the effort. Effective programming involves far more than mastery of the syntactic rules of a language and the actions of its elements. Knowing how the `if` statement works and the methods of the `Button` class will no more make you a master of the programming craft than knowledge of what a whisk is and how to operate a stove would make you a chef. As with all crafts, programming involves more than mastery of the tools. In addition, programmers must understand principles and practices before they can confidently design and produce a program that is correct, efficient, robust, easy to understand, and easy to maintain and modify. If you just want an apprentice-level introduction to Java, go elsewhere; if you want a book that teaches what a program is and how to build one with style, verve, and efficiency, then you've come to the right place.

HOW WE GOT HERE

This is our third CS1 text. Each time, the reason we took up the arduous task of writing a book was the same as that which, we suspect, motivates many of our colleagues—we identified problems with our CS1 course, looked unsuccessfully for solutions in other texts, and reluctantly decided that we had to write one of our own.

Pascal's Triangle came from our positive experience teaching beginning programmers using hands-on exploration in a lab. Over nearly a decade of teaching, we came to realize that programming was a contact sport—the best way to learn about a language and the principles of programming was to dig into example programs, trying to read and modify them, and to learn the features of a language by exploring them. The integration of directed and exploratory laboratory work, linked to the text by engaging sample programs, still seems to us to be the best way to make any programming material come alive. We even made explicit and repeated mention of code reuse, and tried (as best we could, given the language and the paradigm) to supply students with code "building blocks."

By the end of the 1980s Pascal was beginning to show its age. In the twenty years since the invention of the language, we had learned a lot about efficient programming. It seemed that our students would benefit from a different approach. Pascal is a *procedural language*—the basic building block of a Pascal program is the procedure or function, and a Pascal program is organized into a collection of procedure calls. A different way of thinking about a program is to consider it as a collection of cooperating *objects*—higher level units that contain both information and procedures for acting on that information. *The Object Concept* was our attempt to introduce object-oriented programming, using the C++ language.

Our teaching experience convinced us that object-oriented programming was a viable approach for novice programmers. For all its power and expressiveness, though, C++ is a big, baggy-monster of a language. It's hard enough to get a C++ program to compile, but even more distressing for novices was the fact that the language was so expressive that it allowed the programmer to produce code that compiled correctly but didn't act at all as expected. In the words of the title of Allen Holub's delightful little book, C++ gives you *Enough Rope to Shoot Yourself in the Foot* (McGraw-Hill, 1995). After a few years of teaching object-oriented programming in CS1 using C++, we realized that we would switch languages in an instant if we could find an object-oriented language that embodied the object orientation of C++ and the simplicity of Pascal.

JAVA? JAVA!

Almost as soon as we finished whining about the lack of a suitable language for CS1, we found what we needed. Java, a language developed by Sun Microsystems, Inc., gave us what we were looking for. It was object-oriented, its syntax was very similar to that of C++, but simpler, and it came with a collection of platform-independent libraries that we could use to have our students make visually interesting applications.

Java became one of the CS buzzwords of the 1990s. It was hot, certainly, but was that a sufficient justification for jumping on the bandwagon? No, of course not. A number of astute observers raised questions about Java from the start. In a newsgroup post, for example, Ketil Z. Malde posed the following definition.

```
Java: A simple, easy to learn language, where *everybody*
can, just by copying other's code, make neat "applets"
that make everything on a WWW-page jump, skid, skitter,
twist, turn and flash, thereby drawing attention from all
that boring information embedded in the text, which isn't
very user-friendly anyway, so who needs it. The greatest
invention since the <blink> extension in HTML.
```

Admittedly, quite a few of the Java applets that first appeared were little more than eye candy, but that says more about the applet designers than the language itself.

After all, a programmer can write silly programs in any language. The fact remained that Java seemed to us to be an excellent vehicle for a first course in programming for a number of reasons.

C++(− −)

Java is syntactically similar to C++, but it discards many of the dangerous and confusing features of its parent. There are no apparent pointers in Java—all the pointer manipulation is done automatically, behind the scenes. All array references are checked at run-time, and memory management is done by the run-time system, freeing the user from having to deal with potential memory leaks. Java gave us a language that was easier to teach and also gave us the option of introducing C++ in a subsequent course, if we wanted to.

Object Orientation

It's almost impossible to avoid classes, objects, and inheritance in a Java program. Thus we could build in an object-oriented approach from the very beginning, rather than just tacking it on later. Of course, object-oriented programming (OOP) is just one of many programming paradigms, but we found it to be an excellent starting point. As we said in the preface to *The Object Concept:*

> The advantages of this approach to teaching novices are numerous and tangible. First, introducing the object-oriented paradigm from the beginning allows us to exploit it as a design medium. Second, doing so puts the procedural paradigm (along with the ideas of top-down design and stepwise refinement) into a meaningful and useful problem-solving context. Third, it eliminates (at least, for the student!) the dreaded paradigm shift from procedural programming to object-oriented programming. Finally, and most importantly, it helps students to develop their problem-solving skills in conjunction with their programming skills.

Graphical Orientation

Java contains a rich class library containing complete, platform-independent support for event-driven, graphically oriented programming. That is, users can interact with Java programs in a modeless way by means of a contemporary graphical user interface, rather than by responding to program prompts by typing text into a console window. Just as the language dictates a reliance on object-oriented design, the class library makes avoiding an approach that emphasizes code reuse virtually impossible. The instructor gains a natural context for discussing important principles of software design, and students can build visually interesting programs from the very start. After all, students have been raised on programs that have a rich graphical user interface and Java allows them to build the kind of programs they're used to seeing.

OUR APPROACH

This reliance on existing code, both at the applet and class levels, has convinced us that Java has the potential to fulfill what software engineers (and OOP practitioners, in particular) have been predicting for years: that Java represents a giant step toward the age of reusable software. Interesting Java programs can be built by assembling off-the-shelf software components. The keys to doing so lie in understanding the fundamental concepts of object-oriented programming, not in the details of operator precedence and complex control structures. In fact, programmers can easily write applets that produce very interesting graphical output by using only straight-line code (with no explicit control structures). This approach—as many computer science educators have recently and rightly predicted—signals a profound change in how students learn to program. Students seem to have already embraced this paradigm shift. The only ones who appear to be dreading this shift are those of us who are being asked to teach it.

OOP and the Abstract Windows Toolkit

What we decided, then, was that we should revise our approach to teaching novice programmers. Just as Java is an OOP language that has been freed substantially from the procedural underpinnings of C++, we decided that we should exploit Java's most attractive and powerful features—those that support most directly code reuse, graphical programming, and interactive learning. Indeed, these three features are the keys to our pedagogical approach.

Specifically, we introduce students to Java and OOP from the top down. That is, we start by presenting the empowering features of Java and OOP—classes, packages, and inheritance—and defer until later the algorithmic details. Essentially, we take our "classes first" approach from *The Object Concept* one step further: We initially emphasize *using* classes, as opposed to writing them. After a quick generic introduction to computers and programming, we devote roughly the first third of the text to using and experimenting with Java's Abstract Windows Toolkit (AWT). Doing so allows us to provide students with lots of algorithmically simple code to read and use, all of which emphasizes basic OOP notations and ideas while providing tangible graphical output. Our overriding motivation is to introduce students to object-oriented design early, before they develop any bad programming habits. By the end of this part of the course, students will be able to use the AWT to describe arbitrarily complex graphical user interfaces. More important, they will be completely conversant with the basics of OOP and the use of Java packages. Thus, by the end of the first third of the course, students can confidently design and lay out the visual aspect of a calculator, for instance, and are itching to make it work. Then, and only then, do we introduce the language features that students need to make a fully functional program.

Lablets

Another source of continuity between the two main parts of the text is that both rely critically on lab exercises for conveying programming essentials. In a separate lab manual we provide students with detailed and directed experimental exercises to help them explore firsthand the principles of OOP and Java in a controlled way. These exercises have been integrated with the text and serve to bring static text material to life. We've used a lab-based approach in teaching programming for ten years for one main reason—it works. Students are introduced to new concepts in the text. In the process of reading the text, students encounter sample programs that are used to illustrate the new concepts. Then, in the laboratory, they use a "Lablet" program, experiment with it, and extend it by using what they have learned from the text. All the sample programs are provided on a disk that accompanies the lab manual.

Our goal, then, is to incorporate the best and most enduring features of our previous texts into a pedagogically sound, state-of-the-art package for teaching a first course in computer programming. It takes advantage of Java to address program specification, program design, algorithm development, coding, testing, and interface development—all from within the object-oriented paradigm.

We don't cover all of Java—that would be impossible in a semester. We've omitted much of the networking capabilities and almost all the data structures, reserving them for the next course. We also had to decide on how to allocate coverage of versions 1.0 and 1.1 of Java. Version 1.1 was introduced as we were writing this book, which presented us with something of a quandary. Java 1.1 is supposed to be downward compatible with version 1.0, but version 1.1 introduced a number of new classes and quite a few new methods in existing classes. We decided to cover the important features of version 1.1 but to cast all of our sample code in version 1.0. Hence, this book should be usable regardless of the platform being used. A word of caution, however, is in order here. Because Java is so new, some run-time systems aren't as solid as we'd like them to be. We tested all our sample code on several computers, using several applet runners and Web browsers. Because of the platform-independence of Java, we expected the same applet or application to look different on different platforms, but we did find some cases where the same program *ran* differently on different platforms. We've indicated some of the differences in the text, but don't be surprised if you discover a few inconsistencies we've missed.

COVERAGE

You won't find the traditional CS1 chapters "Loops" or "Selection Statements" here. As indicated, our approach is to cover object-oriented design and programming from the beginning and adopt a "just in time" approach to the algorithmic language features. **Chapter 1** provides background, in which we discuss the evolution of programming, the Internet and the World Wide Web, and providing an overview of Java.

The next three chapters introduce AWT fundamentals. In **Chapter 2** we discuss the `Applet` class and graphical programming. In **Chapter 3** we introduce the basic graphical user interface components, like buttons, labels, textfields, and checkboxes. The Lablet for this chapter uses all the components in the front end of an online ordering program. In **Chapter 4** we continue the investigation of AWT classes by talking about containers, layouts, windows, frames, dialogs, and menus.

In **Chapter 5** we begin the transition from using AWT classes for visual design to writing programs that actively interact with the user. In this chapter we introduce the Java language features that will be needed, discussing primitive types, identifiers, scope, access, expressions, and statements. In **Chapter 6** we introduce event-driven programming and, now that they're necessary, the Java selection statements. In **Chapter 7** we recapitulate everything that we've introduced so far. In this chapter we explore the design process in detail, going from a vaguely worded description of a problem to a fully functional simulation of an automatic teller machine. In **Chapter 8** we discuss arrays and the `String` class, introducing loops. We begin discussing algorithmic programming by producing a visual sorting demonstration.

In the remaining four chapters we cover the other classes needed to produce all but the more arcane Java programs. In **Chapter 9** we introduce exceptions and in **Chapter 10** discuss file input and output, culminating with design and exploration of a word processor. In **Chapter 11** we introduce threads and conclude with **Chapter 12**, where we describe how to make an applet interact with the Web, using sounds, images, and animation.

THANKS

This book wouldn't exist were it not for the efforts of a number of diligent and helpful people, many of whom we're proud to count among our friends. Our heartfelt thanks go out to the people at PWS: David Dietz, our editor, and Elise Kaiser, head honcha of production, Nathan Wilbur, Liz Clayton, and the Big Guy himself, Mike Sugarman, who watched over the entire process and who should give raises to everyone involved. Thanks also go to Jerrold Moore, for editing the manuscript, in the process smoothing our slightly different writing styles and holding us to accepted standards of punctuation, grammar, and orthography; to Ben Norman who checked each scrap of Java code; and to Shawn Swistak and Brian Stedman for slogging their way through all the exercises. Special thanks, finally, go out to our families for putting up with frequently absent and always bemused husbands and fathers. Writing and producing a book is a process that ranks right up there on the misery scale with cholera, except that it takes longer. It can never be called a pleasant experience, but the help, support, and warmth of all involved make it bearable and the result magical.

Rick Decker
Stuart Hirshfield

CHAPTER ONE

Background

So what's all this fuss about Java? In this chapter, we'll put Java in historical and technological contexts. We'll describe briefly what programming languages are, how they evolved in the past fifty years, how they work, and what sets Java apart from the scores of other programming languages, both ancient (well, as ancient as anything can be in the short history of computers) and modern. Along the way, we'll touch on the development of graphical user interfaces and describe the burgeoning of the Worldwide Web, an aspect of modern computer use that is closely tied to the growing popularity of Java.

OBJECTIVES

In this chapter, we will
- Discuss the history of programming, from the earliest days to the development of Java.
- Learn about the development of the Internet and the Worldwide Web, and see how Java came to be associated with Web pages.
- Take you through the development process of making a Java program and placing it in a Web page.
- Explore the nature of Java, and see what makes it different from other programming languages.

1.1 THE EVOLUTION OF PROGRAMMING

In simplest terms, programming is the process of designing a collection of instructions that a computer can execute to solve a problem. This sounds like a straightforward exercise—if we replace the word "computer" with "person," we do this sort of thing every time we give a passing motorist directions to the local post office. All we have to do is provide an unambiguous list of commands that the recipient can perform, like "Go down this road for three miles, turn left at the first light, and keep going until you see the school. The post office is just past the school on the left." The difference—and the real problem, in fact—is that the person to whom you give these directions speaks the same language you do. Computers don't. In fact, the only language a computer "understands" (in the sense of being able to execute statements in that language) is about as far as we can imagine from a natural language like English. Indeed, you could hardly invent a language more difficult for people to understand than the machine language used by a computer. It's not unreasonable to view the entire history of programming as a series of attempts to facilitate the process of communicating with computers. Let's take a look at the problems of communicating with computers and the solutions that have evolved.

The Not-So-Good Old Days

Electronic computers were invented independently in the United States, Germany, and England during the 1930s and 1940s. The first successful computers were huge and expensive, and had roughly the same computational power as a modern digital watch. Still, for all their disadvantages from today's perspective, the computers available by the end of World War II were thousands of times faster than human calculators, and these "giant brains," as they were called, found many eager buyers at research centers, government facilities, and the private corporations that could afford the million-plus-dollar price tag. Programming in those days was very different from what we do today—the instructions for the computer were written in the language of the machine itself. As a result, the only people who could write programs were those few who had mastered the daunting task of speaking directly in the machine's own dialect.

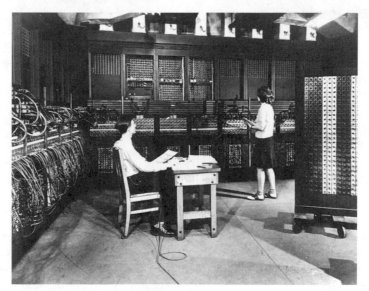

FIGURE 1.1 ENIAC[1] (circa 1945), an early computer. (Courtesy of International Business Machines Corporation)

---

[1]ENIAC stands for Electronic Numeric Integrator and Computer. It was designed at the University of Pennsylvania's Moore School of Electrical Engineering and was first used to produce artillery firing tables. It was recently restored to working condition to celebrate its fiftieth birthday.

The language of a computer is determined by the way the computer is designed. In essence, a computer—ancient or modern—is nothing more than an enormous collection of on–off switches connected to each other. Everything a computer handles, whether data or instructions, must be represented internally in a collection of these switches. For example, if we wanted to build a computer that was capable of performing arithmetic on whole numbers, we would have to design it so that each number we wanted to manipulate was represented by a suitable collection of "on" and "off" values. Such a two-value encoding of information is known as *binary* representation.

We might, for instance, decide to represent zero as "off, off," one as "off, on," two as "on, off," and three as "on, on." To simplify the description, let's use "0" to represent "off" and "1" to represent "on." Then, with this two-switch system, we might decide on the representation $00 \rightarrow 0, 01 \rightarrow 1, 10 \rightarrow 2, 11 \rightarrow 3$. Of course, this is a pretty limited coding scheme, since only four values can be represented by the on–off combinations of two switches. We would probably design our computer using groups of eight or sixteen switches, but the principle would be the same.

Having decided how to represent numbers, we would then have to design a collection of other switches that would take these values and perform operations, like addition, on them. We would have to put together a circuit that would have four wires coming in (for the two pairs of numbers) and three coming out (for the two digits of the sum, plus one more for the carry), as we illustrate in Figure 1.2. The details of what goes on in the adder circuit are unimportant here (though, of course, vitally important to the computer engineers). What is important is that we would design circuits to provide all the operations we deemed necessary, like subtraction, multiplication, and comparison. We would also have to set aside a collection of groups of switches for storage of incoming, intermediate, and final data values, to serve as the memory of our computer.

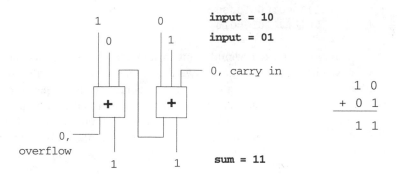

FIGURE 1.2 A simple addition circuit, computing $1 + 2 = 3$.

To complete our design, we would include some more switches to control which of the possible operation circuits would be activated on which values in memory. In our simple example, for instance, we might decide to use three control switches arranged so that "off, off, on" would turn on the adder, "off, on, off" would turn on the subtracter, and so on. These design choices, then, would dictate the language of our machine. A machine language instruction might take the form illustrated in Figure 1.3, using three binary values to determine the operation, four each for the memory locations to be used, and four more for the memory location where the result will be stored. With this representation, we could refer to any of eight instructions acting on any of sixteen memory locations (do you see why?). For example, the machine instruction 001 0000 0001 0010 would add (the 001 code) the values in memory locations 0 (0000 code) and 1 (0001 code) and place the result in memory location 2 (0010 code).

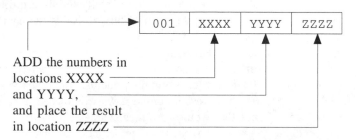

FIGURE 1.3 A (highly simplified) machine language instruction format.

Finally, we'd be ready to write a program for our computer. Here's what it might look like, in part:

```
001000000010010
110001000011010
011101000010000
111000100010000
001000010100010
```

Obviously, no one would want to instruct a computer in this language if given any other choice. First, we have the problem that stems from the fact that a computer only has a very small collection of operations it can perform. There were only eight possible operations in our sample computer and even modern computers are limited to a few score fundamental operations, simply because it is costly and difficult to design and build a computer with any more. This means we have to express a problem like "sort a list of numbers stored in memory locations 0 to 1000" using only the few simple operations, like COMPARE and MOVE, that have been provided for us.

If that weren't bad enough, imagine how unlikely it would be—even if you correctly figured out which instructions to employ and the order they should be used—that you would be able to produce the hundreds of necessary machine language instructions without once mistakenly placing a "1" where a "0" should be or vice versa. Not only would it be a near certainty that your program had a host of such small errors, each potentially fatal to its success, but it would also be almost impossibly difficult for you to track down the errors you had made among such a sea of 1s and 0s.

Finally, and most important in the long run, the fact that machine language is dictated by the computer's design implies that a machine language program is no more portable than a set of dentures. Different machines use different languages, and there's nothing we can do about it. If a company were to buy a new computer, all its old programs would have to be rewritten from scratch to run on the new machine, and if the Des Moines office had a different model than the one used in Philadelphia, there wouldn't be a prayer of cutting costs by sharing programs. This pretty well describes the state of the programming art in the 1950s, a sorry state indeed. There *had* to be a better way to get the job done, and there was. The solution was right there in the building, downstairs in the big air-conditioned room.

Help Arrives

In those early days, writing programs required a near-inhuman precision, flawless mastery of a host of details, and a powerful resistance to boredom and frustration. Hmm—computers are inhumanly precise; properly programmed, they have no difficulty keeping track of far more details than we can; and they are innately immune to boredom and frustration. It wasn't long before computer scientists came up with the idea of enlisting the help of the very machines that were responsible for the problem.

Since the instructions that make up a program can be stored in memory just like any other data,[2] the computer can manipulate program instructions just as it manipulates numbers, strings of characters, pictures, sounds, and anything else that can be represented in binary. With this insight, we can free ourselves from the tyranny of the machine's architecture-dictated language and can design a language that is far easier for human programmers to work with.

The earliest steps in making the programming process easier were simple extensions of some of the techniques that machine language programmers did manually. Imagine for a moment that you were faced with the task of writing a machine language program. Just as we used 0s and 1s to symbolize OFF and ON switches, you could develop simple mnemonics to replace the binary notation, saying something like "I'll represent memory locations 0000, 0001, and 0010 by 'A', 'B', and 'C.' What I want to do here is ADD A and B and store the result in C." In fact, you might actually write that down, producing a representation of a program that looked like the following, complete with notes to yourself.

```
ADD  A  B  C
MUL  C  C  D; now D contains (A + B) * (A + B)
```

---

[2]The notion of the *stored-program computer* is credited to John von Neumann. The original ENIAC didn't store its programs in memory and was "programmed" by plugging in wires and setting switches.

Certainly, this is much easier to understand than the binary version. Now we can write a (machine language) program that takes as its input a collection of characters like the preceding ones and translates it line-by-line into the corresponding binary instructions. If this *assembler* program, as it is called, sees "ADD" it produces the operation code "001." Seeing "A" for the first time, it would find a memory address it hadn't used, like "0000," append that to the operation code it had produced, and continue similarly. We could even write our assembler so that everything from the semicolon to the end of the line would be recognized as a *comment* and ignored in the translation process.

The task of programming now becomes simultaneously simpler for the machine and more complex for the machine: You would program in the easier *assembly language,* feed the program into the assembler and get out executable machine language as output, which the computer could then run. This process would be more or less invisible to you; in fact, you could think as if the assembly language program was actually running on a *virtual machine* that somehow was wired to execute assembly language, rather than binary.

The next step in the evolution of programming languages, and one that continues to this day, was to invent languages that were even easier for human beings to use. Obviously, people are happier working at much higher conceptual levels than a machine is capable of. Our earlier example, for instance, could be captured in the single instruction D = (A + B)**2, where the algebraic symbols "(", ")", and "+" have their customary meanings, "**" denotes raising to a power, and "=" is interpreted as "evaluate the expression on the right and store it in the location named on the left."

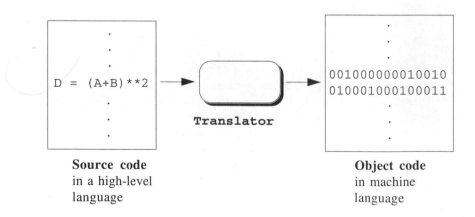

Source code
in a high-level
language

Translator

Object code
in machine
language

FIGURE 1.4 Using a program to translate programs.

Of course, the translation from high-level *source code* into machine language *object code* is much more complicated, since one statement in source code might very well translate into a dozen or more instructions in object code. For example, the FORTRAN (FORmula TRANslator) language, introduced in 1954, was among the first high-level languages invented and it took 18 person-years to complete the translator program. We've learned enough since then about language design and the translation process that the design of a translator for a high-level language is now a common semester-length project in computer science graduate schools.

Since we'll be using the terms frequently in what follows, it's worth mentioning that the translation process from high-level language to machine code comes in two forms. On the one hand an *interpreter* translates a single source code statement into its machine code equivalents, executes the machine code, and then goes on to the next source code statement, translates and runs it, and so on. A *compiler,* on the other hand, translates the entire source code program, producing an object code file which can then be executed. Interpreted programs tend to run slower than their compiled equivalents, since execution is interleaved with the translation process. However, it is generally easier to write an interpreter than a compiler, and, all other things being equal, it is easier to *debug* a program (find and fix errors) in an interpreted environment than when using a compiler. Languages like LISP and BASIC are often interpreted, while more complex languages like C++ are generally compiled. Java, as you will see, is compiled and then interpreted.

Using a high-level language frees us from the dictates of the underlying machine. A language designer can concentrate on designing a language that is as easy as possible to use, subject only to the constraint that it can be translated into machine code (which is why, at least at present, we can't write programs in English). Studies have shown that the number of lines of debugged code a programmer can produce in a day is pretty much independent of the language used. So working at a high conceptual level—where a single instruction can describe a complex task—tends to be more efficient, since a 200-line Java program might very well translate into a thousand or more machine code instructions. We get another benefit, as well, when using a high-level language. While the machine languages used in a Sun workstation, a Pentium-based IBM PC, or a PowerPC Macintosh are completely different, the same Java source code will run on all three, as long as each has a suitable translator program installed. As far as the programmer is concerned, all three computers are just Java machines with different logos on the box.

1.2 THE INTERNET AND THE WORLDWIDE WEB

By the 1960s, computers were commonplace in government installations and scientific laboratories throughout the United States. While computers were growing more powerful and programming languages were growing more sophisticated, developments of interest to us were taking place on another front. Recognizing the importance of computers, both for research and for what is known in the jargon as "C3" (command, control, and communication), the U.S. Department of Defense proposed a network connecting computers at government facilities, research labs, and universities. As a result, what we now call the Internet was born on Labor Day,

1969, connecting host computers at UCLA, the Stanford Research Institute, the University of California at Santa Barbara, and the University of Utah at Salt Lake City.

The Internet was designed from the beginning with security and robustness in mind. The Department of Defense required that the network be resistant to what was known as a "point of failure attack," meaning that in the event of a nuclear attack the destruction of a few host computers would not compromise the communications capabilities of the remainder of the network. This requirement had important and unforeseen consequences. First, it meant that the network could not be designed like the existing telephone network, with a few centralized switching centers responsible for routing all messages. Instead, the proposed network had to be *decentralized,* with each host computer responsible for routing any messages it received, whether the message was for use by a computer in a local network connected to the host site, or was to be passed along to another location.

This decentralization implied that it was quite simple to add other sites to the network. A location with its own local network could simply designate one of its computers as an Internet host, install the necessary routing software, and connect the host computer to one or more routing computers at other sites that had agreed to the connection. This connection was more or less transparent to the local computers; even though the Internet is in fact a network of local networks connected by routing computers, it appears to the local machines as if each is connected directly to all others anywhere on the net.

Since the routing computers were responsible for managing network traffic, another consequence was that every communication over the Internet was in effect a local call. Distance over the Internet was a meaningless concept from the very beginning. To send a message from San Francisco to Pasadena, the routing computers may decide that the most efficient path in terms of current net traffic would be from San Francisco via satellite to Norway, then over land lines to London, by satellite again to West Virginia, and finally by wire and microwave to Pasadena.[3]

The fact that it was so easy to connect to the Internet, no matter where you were located, led to an amazing and completely unexpected growth. Fired by the desire for electronic mail (another unexpected use of a network that was originally designed with collaborative projects in mind), the number of hosts doubled each year, reaching 1024 in 1984, 28,174 in 1987, and more than one million by 1992. Today, as this is written, there are more than eight million host computers serving fifty million users worldwide with a total traffic of well over thirty trillion bytes per month. (A *byte* is a group of eight binary digits, the amount needed to encode a single character.) To put it in perspective, this traffic is roughly equivalent to transmitting the entire contents of the Library of Congress electronically each month. That's pretty impressive, especially when you consider that in 1973 the designers of the Internet anticipated a maximum of 256 sites.

---

[3]This is not a far-fetched example. It is, in fact, the path used for an early demonstration of the network.

The Worldwide Web

In its early years, the Internet was used primarily for electronic mail, newsgroups, remote log-in to computers, and access to information stored in files at other sites. Using the Internet was a fairly technical and somewhat daunting process back then. Not only did transferring information from one computer to another require mastery of one or more software packages, but even locating the information in the first place was by no means easy, even with the help of programs designed to search out the needed data. The anarchic, decentralized nature of the Internet meant that there was no central directory you could use to look up information on, for instance, colobus monkeys.

Partly to address these problems, researchers at CERN, the European laboratory for particle physics, proposed the notion of *distributed hypermedia* in 1989. A hypermedia system is one that mixes text, graphics, animation, and sound in a single document. A *hypertext* document (as it is also known) about colobus monkeys might contain a textual description of their habitat, physical character- istics, social behavior, and the like, along with pictures of a family group, the sounds of their calls, and an animated video clip of their threat behavior. You may be familiar with hypermedia if you have ever seen a computer-based encyclopedia, for example. Of course, the concept of hypermedia originated long before 1989; what made the CERN proposal so important was that it included the idea of having a hypertext document include *links* to others, even those stored at other computers. This is why we use the term *distributed* hypermedia: a Web page may appear as a single visual entity, but the information it contains may come from a number of files, stored on computers spread around the world.

Such a project was clearly a substantial undertaking. Not only did there have to be standards for the way text, pictures, sounds, and the like were to be represented in binary, but there also had to be programs, known as *browsers,* to support the display of all this information and to handle the process of calling up hypertext documents from other computers on the Internet. By 1993 the first browsers had been developed and the Worldwide Web was born, with some fifty sites supporting these linked hypertext documents by January of that year. Within just nine months, Web messages represented one percent of all Internet traffic. By June, 1994 there were about fifteen hundred Web sites, and today the number is approaching one hundred thousand.

It's important to realize that, unlike the Internet or a purely local network (known as an *intranet*), the Worldwide Web is not a physical entity. Rather, it is a concept we use to refer to the documents, their links, and the browsers used to view and interact with this collection. In a sense, the Web lives on top of a computer network such as the Internet.

It would be difficult to overestimate the impact of the Worldwide Web. Suddenly, it became possible for every user to become an information source. All you need is access to a *Web server* (that is, a computer with the appropriate soft- ware and Internet connections), and anyone in the world with a connected browser can access your Web pages. The ease with which Web pages can be generated and accessed has led to hundreds of thousands of pages across the global network, all densely interconnected. Information access has become far easier, as well, with the invention of *search engines*. These programs, like Yahoo, Lycos, and Excite, spend their free time jumping from one link to another and recording references to what they find in a database that is used to handle user queries. To find information on colobus monkeys, again, you no longer need to know where the information is located. Instead, you can point your browser to one of these search engines and tell it to look for the keyword "colobus." The engine then looks in its database and returns the Net addresses of all the locations where it had found the word "colobus." Just for fun, we tried this with several search engines and the results ranged from a low of 50 sites to a high of 709. We found enough text, photographs, video clips, and sounds in the space of a few minutes to satisfy anyone's curiosity about *colobus abyssinicus*.

HTML

One of the nicest features of the Worldwide Web is that to make a Web page, all that is required is a computer, a text editor, and a browser (and you can even dispense with the browser if you don't care to see what your creation looks like when displayed). Web browsers are all designed to recognize a purely text-based language, known as *Hypertext Markup Language,* or HTML, for short. The elements of HTML are known as *tags,* consisting of keywords and other information enclosed between pointy brackets, "<" and ">".[4] Anything that's not a tag is considered to be plain text, and is displayed appropriately by the browser.

One important feature of HTML is that it is exceedingly easy to learn. There are only a few score tags to learn and most of them are simple enough to be almost self-explanatory. For example, if you enclose text between the paired tags <B> and </B>, the enclosed text will be displayed in boldface. So, if you were to write

```
This is <B>really</B> easy.
```

the browser would see the tags and display

This is **really** easy.

Statistics indicate that there's a good chance you've already used a browser like Netscape Navigator or Microsoft's Internet Explorer to wander around the Web. When you do, what happens is both very simple and very complex. If you instruct your browser to go to a location like the following (which happens to be one of our home pages)

---

[4]Technical term alert. The characters "<" and ">" were originally placed on computer keyboards to represent the mathematical operators "less than" and "greater than," but for us they're just special angular forms of parentheses. In geekspeak, they're known as "brockets," for "broken brackets."

```
http://www.hamilton.edu/html/academic/compsci/rdecker/
```

the browser sends a message over the network to the *Web server* computer www, located at the domain `hamilton` (our school), in the wider domain `edu` of all educational institutions. The message tells the host computer to find the HTML document in the location `html/academic/compsci/rdecker` and send a copy back to your computer. Once there, your browser reads the document, interprets the tags, and displays the result, all nicely formatted, on the monitor of your computer, as we indicate in Figure 1.5. The concept, at least, is quite simple.

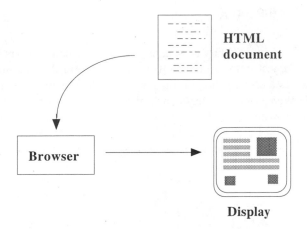

FIGURE 1.5 An HTML document displayed by a Web browser.

The actual process of getting the document, interpreting the tags, and displaying the result is, of course, quite complicated. For example, decisions about which font to use for displaying plain text, or how to size a page to fit the monitor on which it is to be displayed are left to the programmers who write Web browsers. This complexity stems in part from the fact that HTML is a *platform independent* standard. As we mentioned when we were discussing language translation, as long as you have a Web browser that is designed for use on your computer, it doesn't matter who makes the computer; the web page is guaranteed by the HTML standards to communicate the same information, even if it might look a little different from one browser to another.

Most browsers have an option to inspect the underlying HTML code of any document. You can use this feature to inspect the HTML source code Rick used to make his Web page. Try it—find a Web-connected browser, try opening Rick's page, and explore the code.

Pay particular attention to the tag in the seventh line,

```
<IMG src = "common/graph.gif" align = right>
```

This line instructs the browser to go to the computer where the original HTML document is stored, find the image `graph.gif` in the directory `common`, and draw the image aligned to the right side of the browser window. If you wanted to, you could even copy this image for use in an HTML document of your own.[5] The point of all this is to illustrate how easy it is in the Worldwide Web to find information on other computers and download it for use by a browser. We'll use this feature quite a lot in the chapters to come, both for searching for online Java information and for looking at Java programs that other people have written.

1.3   ALONG COMES JAVA

For all its visual and auditory appeal, an HTML document appears in a browser as a fairly static object with limited functionality, beyond the (admittedly important) ability it gives a user to click on links and see documents stored elsewhere. The Worldwide Web provides access to an unimaginably vast storehouse of information, but the fact remains that Web pages, at least as originally conceived, don't offer much in the way of user interactivity. That's all changing now, largely as a result of a project that began at about the same time as the Web, nearly half a world away.

Smart Toasters

In 1990, at Sun Microsystems in California, James Gosling was working on the design of a new programming language. Unlike many traditional languages, this one was designed for use in control systems of consumer electronics devices like toasters, microwave ovens, and television sets. Because of the nature of such appliances and the economics involved, languages that were standards in data processing and scientific use, like C++, were inappropriate choices. Simply speaking, they were too large for the problem at hand. Most of the languages current at the time were designed for industrial-strength programming and so were intended to make the programmer's life easier, regardless of the computational costs involved. For many, the memory and processing chips needed to run them might have exceeded the cost of the appliance itself. While they certainly could have handled tasks like setting a microwave to cook at full power for three minutes and then switching to half power until the temperature probe measured a heat of 185°,

---

[5] A word of caution is in order here. In spite of the open nature of the Web, it's still true that *everything* you see while browsing is owned by someone and that copyright laws do indeed apply in cyberspace. While you can legally copy anything you find for your own personal use, it's both immoral and illegal to copy and publish someone else's work without their permission.

doing so would have been the equivalent of chartering a nuclear-powered aircraft carrier for a day's fishing trip. What was needed was a language that was designed from the start to be fast, small, reliable, and universal.

The traditional solution to this problem had been around for two decades, in digital watches and electronic calculators.[6] A manufacturer of microwave ovens, for instance, would decide on an inexpensive processor chip, build it into the appliance, and hire someone to write its program in machine code. There were several problems with this approach, though. First, machine language, as we mentioned earlier, is machine-specific. If the manufacturer were to change brands of control processors, they would have to pay for new machine code, since the older code would almost certainly be incompatible with the new processors. This would also make upgrading or repairing the old appliances more difficult, since the manufacturer would have to keep a stock of the old control processors and, by and large, microprocessors are superceded by new models far faster than appliances wear out.

Gosling and his team decided that the solution would be to make a small language, but not as small or hard to use as machine language, that would run on any kind of computer chip. As you saw in Section 1.1, the only way to do that would be to make the new language easy to compile. With such a language, the hardware would no longer be an issue. A manufacturer upgrading to a new control processor could use exactly the same programs it had on hand, and only spend the money to buy or design a new complier to translate its programs into the machine code for the new model chips. In effect, the programmers could write the control code once and be done with it, never giving a thought to what kind of chip the code would eventually run on.

Java, Meet Web; Web, Meet Java

The first use of this new language[7] was in a device designed to act as a master control for a number of household appliances like TV, lights, telephone, and so on. That product never made it to store shelves, but shortly thereafter the design team hit upon a "virtual appliance" that seemed to provide a perfect match for Java's speed, simplicity, and robustness: a Web page. Why not embed Java code in HTML documents? Web pages were designed to be device-independent, Java was designed to be device independent—to view a Web page on an Intel-based PC, a Macintosh, or a Sun workstation, all one needed was the right browser, and Java was simple enough to be embedded in a browser. All that was needed was to get a browser

---

[6] In fact, the first microprocessor, or computer-on-a-chip, the Intel 4004 chip, was developed for use in electronic calculators.

[7] Trivia: The language was originally named Oak, but the design team learned that that name was already taken by another language. The more or less official story about the final name, Java, was that it was selected during a visit to a local coffee shop.

developer to agree, and in 1995 that happened when it was announced that Netscape Navigator 2.0 would support Java. If you want to see the difference that made, take a look at

```
http://www.acm.uiuc.edu/webmonkeys/juggling/index.html
```

With Java, you can make a Web page come alive with animation and user interactivity. Properly designed, the Java portion of a page can instruct, inform, amuse, explain, entertain, and emphasize. Of course, as with all design decisions, you can also make a Java program that will bore, irritate, or outrage your audience. We would encourage the former choices, naturally, but we'll point you to enough of the latter that you'll at least be able to make an informed decision about what to do.

Applications and Applets

Java programs come in two flavors, depending on their eventual use. *Applications* are traditional stand-alone programs, like

```
public class Hello
// Just about the simplest Java application anyone can write.
{
    public static void main(String argv[])
    {
        System.out.println("Hi!");
    }
}
```

The heart of this program is the line containing `main`. That line and the three below it is known as a *method,* which is nothing more than jargon for "a named section of a program that contains code instructing the computer to take some action." In this example, the action that takes place is the single statement

```
System.out.println("Hi!");
```

which, in turn, causes the message "Hi!" to be displayed. Every Java application must have a main method, called, appropriately enough, `main`. The rest of this application is easy enough to understand; the braces have the same punctuation purposes for the compiler as they do for people—they serve to collect the code into groups.

The line starting with two slashes[8] (/ /) is a *comment*—it's ignored by the compiler and is solely for the edification of the human being (that's you) reading the

---

[8]The character '/' is also known as *virgule* or *solidus,* though no programmer calls it by those names.

code. Finally, looking at the top line you can see that the whole thing is part of a *class* because, . . . well, that's the way things have to be in Java. As with any language, human or computer, there are rules for correct grammar that appear to make little sense when you first see them (and sometimes make little sense even when you've heard the explanation for their existence).

For applications, Java is just one choice among many. We could write the same program in any of a number of languages. Here's what it would look like in Pascal:

```
program Hello(output);
{Just about the simplest Pascal program anyone can write.}
begin
    writeln("Hi!");
end.
```

And here's what it would look like in C (or in C++, with some minor changes):

```
main()
/* Just about the simplest C program anyone can write */
{
    printf("Hi!\n");
}
```

Although Java is just one of many language choices for writing applications (and a pretty good one, we feel), it is at present the *only* choice available if you want to embed a program in a Web page. A Java *applet* is a program that's not intended to be run on its own, but rather is supposed to live at some location in a Web page, in much the same way as a graphic image might. Applets are a trifle more complicated to write than applications, but not much more. Here's an applet that does the same thing as the application we just listed:

```
import java.applet.*;
import java.awt.*;

public class Hello extends Applet
// Just about the simplest Java applet anyone can write.
{
    public void paint(Graphics g)
    {
        g.drawString("Hi!", 20, 10);
    }
}
```

The applet looks a lot like the application, which isn't too surprising since they do just about the same thing in different contexts. There's a class, `Hello`, containing all the code for the applet, which in this case is the single method `paint`. The body of the `paint` method contains the single statement

```
g.drawString("Hi!", 20, 10);
```

which causes the "Hi!" message to be displayed. We could even have used the same

```
System.out.println("Hi!");
```

here that we did in the application—it would have just placed the message in a different location in the browser window (down in the status bar at the bottom, for some browsers). The two import statements at the top are instructions for the system to look up two *packages* of additional code, where the definitions of Applet and Graphics, respectively, are stored.

To use this applet in a Web page, we have two tasks to perform. One task is to compile the text-based Java *source code* into Java *bytecode*. Bytecode is an easy to translate, low-level language that can be interpreted by any Java-aware browser, like Netscape Navigator or Internet Explorer. The other task is to prepare an HTML document which describes the Web page in which the applet will live. Figure 1.6 illustrates what we have to do to display an applet in a Web page.

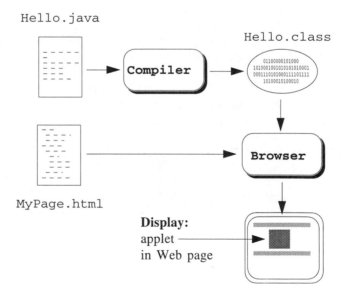

FIGURE 1.6 Applets, from source code to display.

Let's make the HTML document first, since it's the easier of the two tasks. For this part, you'll need a text editor. Any word processor will do; it doesn't have to be fancy or expensive, since all you need is to produce raw text, without any style information. You can even use the one that came with your computer, like SimpleText for the Macintosh or Write for a Windows environment. You would type the following HTML, without the italicized comments.

```
<HTML>                                    The HTML code starts here.
   <HEAD>                                 Nothing in the HEAD is displayed,
      <TITLE>
         My Applet Page                   except for the title, which will show
      </TITLE>                            up in the window's title bar.
   </HEAD>

   <BODY>                                 The BODY part will be displayed:
      Here's my applet...                 Ordinary text,
      <HR>                                A horizontal rule, for separation
      <APPLET    code = "Hello.class"     The applet comes next,
                 width = 60               with specified width and height
                 height = 60>
      </APPLET>
      <HR>                                Another horizontal rule
   </BODY>                                The end of the BODY part
</HTML>                                   The HTML code ends here.
```

You can be pretty careless when typing HTML. Although misspellings can hurt you (browsers will ignore any tag they don't recognize, like <BIDY>), HTML is *case-insensitive,* so <BODY>, <body> and even <bOdY> all represent the same tag. In addition, browsers will ignore any repeated *whitespace* (spaces, tabs, and returns), so you can format your HTML in any way that you find makes it easier to read.

When you're done, you would save the document as text (your editor might also call this format ASCII) and save it under the name MyPage.html. (The last dot is a period at the end of the sentence, and shouldn't be used in the file name.) You can name the document anything you wish, as long as it ends with the .html extension. You'll have to be more careful here than you were when typing the HTML. Although Java compilers, like Web browsers simply ignore repeated whitespace, Java treats upper- and lowercase letters as being different things.

Caution:

Java is a *case-sensitive* language: "aName" and "aname" are treated as different names.

The next step is to produce the compiled applet code. We'll have to use general terms here, since the actual steps involved vary quite a bit from one Java environment to another. Whatever the details might be, your job here is simple enough—you will make a source code document containing exactly the applet text we listed two pages ago and then invoke your compiler to produce the file Hello.class. As with the .java and .html extensions, a Java object code file (which is to say, the compiled bytecode) must be identified with the extension .class. In addition, you should make sure that the part of the file name before the extension is the same as the corresponding name in the .java file, as we did with the Hello.java source code and its corresponding Hello.class object code. While failure to follow these guidelines won't be fatal in all Java development environments, it's better to adopt a course that is guaranteed not to cause problems. Finally, at this stage you should make sure that the MyPage.html and Hello.class files are stored in the same directory or folder. There are ways to avoid this, but you'll have to wait a bit before we're ready to describe them.

You're done. If you've typed everything in correctly, you should now be able to start your Web browser and use it to open the file MyPage.html. The result should appear as illustrated in Figure 1.7 (though, of course, it may look somewhat different if you're using a different browser than the one we used to generate the picture).

FIGURE 1.7 Your first applet.

1.4   AN OVERVIEW OF JAVA

Java represents an evolutionary change from earlier programming languages, rather than a radical departure. In many ways, Java is like its predecessors Pascal, C, and, especially, C++. In this section we'll explore the important features of Java and show how these features make it similar to, and different from, other programming languages that came before it.

Syntax

The syntax—the rules of grammar—of Java is extremely close to that of its big brother, C++. Originally known as C with Classes, C++ was conceived in 1979 by Bjarne Stroustrup, of Bell Laboratories. Designed as an improved successor to the language C, it had substantially attained its present form by 1986.[9] It was adopted rapidly and enthusiastically by industry, and somewhat less rapidly and enthusiastically by educational institutions. The reason for the difference has a lot to do with the invention of Java.

C++ is a very good choice for a wide variety of real-world programming projects. It is a very high-level language, allowing programmers to design programs without initially having to keep track of a host of minor details. At the same time, it is also a highly expressive language, allowing a programmer to think in very low-level terms (that is, think about what the underlying machine is doing) when necessary. It has a rich set of features, which provide many different ways of performing the same task.

The features that made C++ so suitable for large-scale work by teams of experienced programmers also made it a very large and complex language and a rather daunting prospect for compiler designers (which is why Gosling's team at Sun discarded it as a choice for their embedded systems project). In addition, because of C++'s expressiveness, it is fairly easy for a novice programmer to write code in C++ that compiles without error but which actually runs in a way that the author never intended. In the words of the title of Allen I. Holub's delightful book, C++ gives you *Enough Rope to Shoot Yourself in the Foot* (McGraw-Hill, New York, 1985).

Java was designed from the start to keep the core parts of C++ syntax, while trimming away as much of the rest as possible. Many of the powerful but nasty features of C++ (like pointers, for those of you who have a background in Pascal, C, or C++) were axed, along with some (like templates) that were elegant but gave compiler designers nightmares. The result was a language that should look familiar to those experienced in C++ but that is far leaner and smaller.

---

[9]The name C++ was chosen in 1983 and is something of an inside joke, as you'll see in a later chapter.

Objects and Classes

The essence of Java, like that of C++ and Smalltalk, is that it is an *object-oriented* language. In such languages, the basic conceptual building block is the *object,* an entity that has its own data and its own methods for manipulating that data and interacting with the world around it. In programming terms, for example, we might consider a `Circle` object. Such an object would need data to describe its center (two numbers would suffice, for the *x*- and *y*-coordinates) and its radius (one number). A `Circle` object might need to be able to set its center coordinates or its radius and a method to report its radius to another object. It might need methods to determine whether it intersected with another circle, whether another circle was contained wholly within it, or whether a `Line` object intersected it. The description of a Circle object might look like

DATA
    `ctr_x`   *the x-coordinate of the center (a number)*
    `ctr_y`   *the y-coordinate of the center (a number)*
    `radius`   *the radius (a number)*
METHODS
    `setCenter`   *Take in two numbers and set the coordinates to them.*
    `setRadius`   *Take in one number and set the radius to it.*
    `radius`   *Report back what this Circle's radius is.*
    `intersects`   *Take in a Circle and report 'true' if it intersects this circle.*
    `contains`   *Take in a Circle and report "true" if it is contained in this circle.*
    `intersects`   *Take in a Line and report 'true' if it intersects this circle.*

In Java, everything is an object, with the exception of the *primitive types* of information like integers (whole numbers, like 0, 4809, and −13). You should think of every Java program as being a collection of cooperating objects, passing requests to others to perform their methods, and responding to similar requests from other objects.

When we spoke of `Circle` objects, we were operating under the assumption that a program might have more than one object. It would be a waste of effort to redo all the descriptions shown for each such object, so Java, like other object-oriented languages, provides us with the notion of the *class*. A class is nothing more than a collection of objects or, equivalently, every object is a single instance of a class. If you wish, you can think of a class definition as providing a prototype for all of its objects.

A class is a set of objects that share a common structure and a common behavior.
                 —Grady Booch, *Object-Oriented Analysis and Design*

Two `Circle` objects might have different values for their center coordinates, but they—along with all other `Circle` objects—would still have three numbers for data and the six methods listed above, as we illustrate in Figure 1.8.

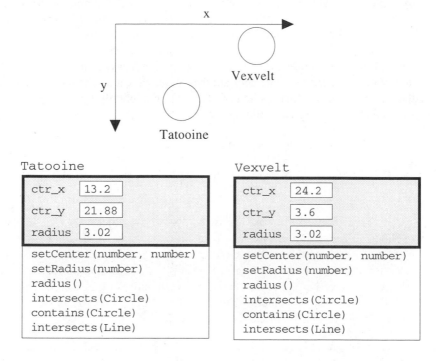

FIGURE 1.8 A conceptual view of two `Circle` objects, along with their descriptions.

The notion of classes of objects provides us with a natural way of solving problems by extending the programming language we're using. The designers of Java—or any other programming language, for that matter—obviously couldn't possibly have anticipated all the possible needs of all programmers. Thus, making our own classes allows us to pretend, at least for the life of the program, that the language has the features we need. For example, Java doesn't have a built-in class for representing circles, but it allows us to design our own and use it, just as if it had been part of the language right from the start.

Inheritance

Even if Java had its own `Circle` class, there's no guarantee it would meet our needs. We might, for instance, have to write a graphic arts program that would require circles to be drawn on the screen. The `Circle` class we described, however useful it might be for other applications, simply won't satisfy our needs because it lacks a method that instructs a `Circle` object to draw itself. Fortunately, object-oriented languages like Java have just the capability we require.

We can define a class in such a way that it *inherits* all or most of the definition of another, and then go on to add whatever features we need. In our example, we might define a new class, GraphicCircle, that has the three data members ctr_x, ctr_y, and radius of the Circle class, along with the six Circle methods. We could then add two new data members, fillColor and borderColor and some graphical methods like draw() and erase(). A particularly nice feature of inheritance is the typing it saves. In Java, if we say in the definition of a class that it *extends* another class, we get all the methods and data of the original class for free, without ever having to explicitly mention them.[10] In Java we do that by starting the definition of GraphicCircle as follows:

```
class GraphicCircle extends Circle
{
// The rest of the definition goes here.
}
```

Then, if myCirc was a GraphicCircle object, we could invoke its methods draw() and erase(). In addition, we could also have it perform a setRadius() method, since a GraphicCircle "is-a" Circle, under the rules for inheritance. In one sense, "extends" is a less than perfect word choice: Although GraphicCircle extends the functionality of Circle, it could equally well be argued that we should write GraphicCircle **restricts** Circle, since the GraphicCircle objects form a subset of the Circle objects.

To say class B *extends* class A is to say, roughly speaking, that

1. Every B object is also an A object.
2. B objects may have information and abilities that A objects don't.

Libraries

We might, after lots of arduous effort, put together a whole collection of graphics-related classes for our graphic arts program. We might have a "base" class of GeometricObjects, along with a hierarchy of classes that extend from the base class, as illustrated in Figure 1.9. If we wanted to make efficient use of our time, we might consider saving these classes for later use, in case we were ever called upon to design a landscape-planning program, for example. As you'll see later, Java provides a mechanism to group a collection of logically related classes into a *package,* so the classes in the package can be invoked by using the import statement.

---

[10]That's not entirely true, as you'll see when we discuss *access.* It is possible to tag some of the data and methods of a class so that they are not available to any inheriting class.

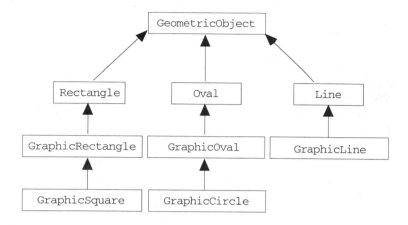

FIGURE 1.9 An example class hierarchy.

This is just what we did when we wrote `import java.applet.*` at the start of our `Hello` applet. In doing so, we instructed Java to make available to our program all the classes in the `java.applet` package (there are four of them, including the `Applet` class).

Java provides a rich collection of library packages. While none of them are, strictly speaking, parts of the language itself, they contain such useful extension classes that it is a rare Java program indeed that doesn't use at least some of them.[11] The packages that come with Java are

- `java.applet`, which we've already mentioned.
- `java.awt`, containing loads of useful classes, like `button` and `textfield`, for making graphical user interfaces.
- `java.io`, with twenty-three classes for file reading and writing.
- `java.lang`, which has classes like `Object`, `Math`, and `String`, that are of general use.
- `java.net`, with eight classes for working with networks.
- `java.util`, containing utility classes such as `Date` and `Random`, along with data containers like `Hashtable` and `Vector`.

We'll spend much of the first third of this book discussing the classes in `java.awt` and will eventually cover most of the classes in the other packages.

---

[11]No useful applet can be written without importing `java.applet`. The sample application we gave in Section 1.2 is just about the limit of what can be accomplished without importing some package.

1.5   HANDS ON

We'd be the first to admit that the Hello applet we gave you is pretty silly. What's the point, after all, of taking the time to write, debug, and error-test it when all it does is display the string "Hi!"? We could have saved a lot of time by simply typing the message in the original HTML, rather than have the computer do it for us. In this, our first *lablet,* we'll walk you through a simple applet that actually *does* something.

Don't expect to understand all the Java code you'll see—we explore Java's vocabulary and rules of grammar in the chapters to come. We present here a sample that demonstrates some of the things a Java applet can do, and which you can use to explore your particular Java development environment.

On the screen, our lablet takes the following form.

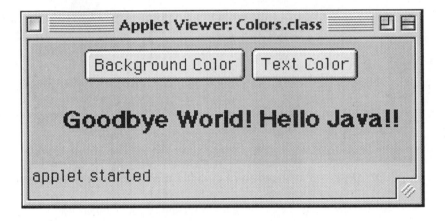

Clicking on the buttons will cause the colors of the background or text to be changed. In the lab manual, we take you through some exercises to give you practice in entering, compiling, running, and correcting a Java applet. This would be a good time to turn to the lab manual and work through the exercises. If you can't spare the time right now, the following is what the Java source code looks like. Read through it and look first at the overall structure: The applet subclass Colors contains six data members—a Font, f, two integers, colorOfBackground and colorOfText, two buttons, backButton and textButton, and a Dimension object named myAppletDim—and three methods—init(), action(), and paint(). Once you've detected the structure, see if you can deduce what some of the statements, like if or switch, are accomplishing.

```
// My First Applet
// Watch the colors change as you click the buttons

import java.awt.*;
import java.applet.*;

public class Colors extends Applet
{
    Font f = new Font("Helvetica",Font.BOLD,18);
    int colorOfBackground = 0;
    int colorOfText = 0;
    Button backButton,textButton;
    Dimension myAppletDim;

    public void init()
    {
        backButton = new Button("Background Color");
        add(backButton);

        textButton = new Button("Text Color");
        add(textButton);
    }

    public boolean action(Event e, Object o)
    {
        if(e.target == backButton)
            colorOfBackground = ++colorOfBackground % 4;

        if(e.target == textButton)
            colorOfText = ++colorOfText % 3;

        repaint();

        return true;
    }

    public void paint(Graphics g)
    {
        switch (colorOfBackground)
        {
            case 0: setBackground(Color.cyan); break;
            case 1: setBackground(Color.orange); break;
            case 2: setBackground(Color.red); break;
            case 3: setBackground(Color.black); break;
            default: setBackground(Color.cyan); break;
        }

        switch (colorOfText)
        {
```

(continued)

```
              case 0: g.setColor(Color.blue); break;
              case 1: g.setColor(Color.magenta); break;
              case 2: g.setColor(Color.green); break;
              default: g.setColor(Color.blue); break;
        }

        g.setFont(f);
        myAppletDim = size();
        g.drawString("Goodbye World! Hello Java!!",
                     (myAppletDim.width/2) - 120,
                     (myAppletDim.height/2) + 20);
    }
}
```

1.6   RESOURCES ONLINE

Because of the intimate connection between Java and the Worldwide Web, you'll discover that there are abundant Java resources available on the Web. Here are some of the most important and useful ones. Crank up your browser and check them out.

- ❧ http://java.sun.com/ Sun Microsystem's Java home page. May as well go to the source, after all.

- ❧ http://www.javasoft.com/nav/read/tutorial.html Sun's own Java tutorial.

- ❧ http://www.javasoft.com/products/jdk/1.1/docs/api/packages.html Index of all Java packages. If you need the official word on any of the Java classes, this is where you should look.

- ❧ http://www-a.gamelan.com/index.shtml The Gamelan home page. A *huge* collection of links to Java sources.

- ❧ http://sunsite.unc.edu:80/javafaq/links.html Java links. Very nicely done.

- ❧ http://www.javasoft.com/applets/ Java Applets. Javasoft is Sun's Java promotional arm. This is their source for applets. You can try them out (with a Java-enabled browser) and inspect the source code.

- ❧ http://www.yahoo.com/Computers/Languages/Java/ Yahoo's Java sources.

- ❧ http://infoweb.magi.com:80/~steve/java.html The Programmer's Source. Another nice collection of Java links.

1.7 SUMMARY

❧ A computer can execute programs only in its own *machine language.* Machine language is unsuitable for human beings, to say the least.

❧ A *high-level language* is designed for ease of use by programmers. To run a high-level language on a computer, we employ a translator program to translate the high-level *source code* into machine-excutable *object code.*

❧ There are two forms of program translators: a *compiler* translates all of the source code into object code, which then can be executed. An *interpreter* interleaves translation with statement-by-statement execution. Compilers are generally harder to write than interpreters, but a compiled program generally runs faster than an interpreted one, since translation is separated from execution.

❧ Worldwide Web pages are produced by making a *HTML* text document and then having the document displayed by a Web browser.

❧ A Java *applet* is a program that is designed to be embedded in a Web page. A Java *application* is an ordinary stand-alone program.

❧ A Java applet is first compiled into *bytecode,* a simple intermediate language, and the bytecode is then interpreted by the browser.

❧ A Java source file's name is given a `.java` extension; the compiled bytecode file has the same name, but has a `.class` extension.

❧ An applet is marked in an HTML document by using the `APPLET` tag, which provides the location of the `.class` file.

❧ HTML is not case-sensitive; Java source code is.

❧ The fundamental unit of a Java program is the *class.* A class is a collection of *objects,* or entities with data and methods for manipulating their data.

❧ In an *object-oriented language* like Java, a program is considered as a collection of cooperating objects.

❧ One class can *inherit* the data descriptions and methods from another. In Java, inheritance is indicated by the `extends` keyword.

❧ The Java language may be augmented by including *packages* of classes. A programmer can create packages, and Java provides a collection of useful packages like `java.awt`.

1.8 EXERCISES

1. What is a computer? According to your definition, which of the following are "computers"?

   a. A dog.

   b. A toaster.

   c. The solar system.

   d. You.

   e. "Malzel's Chessplayer," a nineteenth-century automaton shaped like a man sitting at a chessboard, purportedly constructed of clockwork gears, rods, cams, and levers, and which was reliably reported to be able to play chess as well as most people. Edgar Allan Poe wrote an essay about The Turk, as it was also known, but it was a real device (now lost), and not one of Poe's fictions.

f. A newborn baby.

2. We mentioned at the beginning of this chapter that using three binary digits to represent the operation of a machine language statement would allow us to have as many as eight operations.

a. Why?

b. How many different sequences of ten binary digits can we make?

c. Many modern computers access memory locations by using thirty-two binary digits for the addresses. How many memory locations could a computer have if it used 32-bit addresses? How does this compare with the amount of memory in the computer you use?

3. We concentrated on two-value binary notation because modern electronic computers have two states their hardware components can take: "on" and "off." Suppose someone were to discover a practical method for making hardware with three states, "foo," "bar," and "baz." Call a three-value digit a *trit*.

a. If we used three trits to encode operations, how many different operations could our new computer have?

b. How many trits would we need to provide at least as many sequences as we could make with ten binary digits? (See Exercise 2.)

c. With off-the-shelf components available today we could build three-value hardware. We might decide that 0–2 volts would represent one state, 3–5 volts would represent another and 7–9 volts would represent the third (assume that the hardware could be designed so that there would be no ambiguous voltages, like 4 volts). What would be the advantages and disadvantages of such a three-value computer?

4. Java represents characters, like 'q' or 'Æ' using a 16-bit code called *unicode*. Using 16 bits gives unicode the ability to encode any of 65,536 different characters. If you look at a keyboard, you'll see that even accounting for characters modified by shift or control-shift combinations, we still come up with under 300 possible characters. Explain why unicode seems to permit almost 200 times as many characters as we'll ever need.

5. Digital encoding of information is particularly useful for the Internet, since the same net hardware can be used for anything that can be encoded with 1s and 0s. Invent a protocol for encoding graphical information in binary form. Using your protocol, how true is the statement "a picture is worth a thousand words?"

6. What is the difference between a compiler and an interpreter?

7. Java differs from many languages because it is compiled and then interpreted. Describe the translation and execution involved in going from Java source code to a running applet.

8.   What is a program? Under your definition, which of the following (if any) could be made into programs? Why or why not?

   a.   1. Go to Hollywood.
   2. Get a contract with a movie studio.
   3. Star in a hit movie.
   4. Become rich and famous.

   b.   Given a list of numbers, do the following.
   1. Start with a number, *sum,* initially 0, and start at the beginning of the list.
   2. Add the current number in the list to *sum.*
   3. If there are any more numbers in the list, move to the next one and go back to step 2. Otherwise, go to step 4.
   4. Divide *sum* by the number of numbers in the list.

   c.   Given a whole number, *n,* greater than 0, do the following.
   1. If *n* is even, divide it by 2. If *n* is odd, multiply it by 3 and add 1 to the result. In either case, replace *n* by the result.
   2. If the result isn't 1, go back to step 1.

9.   There are dozens of computer languages in use today, ranging from the popular ones like COBOL, FORTRAN, BASIC, Pascal, C, and C++, to "niche" languages like Prolog and FORTH. How do you account for this multiplicity of languages? If you became King or Queen of the World and dictated a single language for all programs, how might your subjects respond?

10.   What is a·high-level language? Why do we have them?

11.   Here is the syntax for braces, { and } in Java. A *brace expression* is defined by these and only these rules.

   (1) { } is a brace expression.
   (2) If *B* is a brace expression, so is { *B* }.
   (3) If *A* and *B* are brace expressions, so is *A B.*

   Which of the following are brace expressions?

   a.   { { } { } }
   b.   { { { } { }
   c.   } { { { { } } }
   d.   { { { } { } { { } } } }

12.   Why is it redundant to say "Java applet?"

13.   Can you write a Java applet or application without using classes?

14.   Consider two classes of a single model of cars, `Standard` and `Loaded`. Cars in the Standard class are the cheap versions and Loaded cars are the fancy ones, with six-way power seats, computerized navigation systems, walnut burl veneer, and so on. Which class would be an extension of the other?

15. Design a class hierarchy for motor vehicles, as we did for geometric objects.

    In Exercises 16–21, describe the classes you would use in programs that would perform the indicated tasks. These descriptions are very much like the ones you might get at the start of a programming job—vague and open ended—so feel free to make any reasonable assumptions you want.

16. Control a conventional soda machine.

17. Implement an on-screen calculator. The user would "press" the buttons by moving the pointer to the necessary location and clicking the mouse button.

18. Control the action of a bank of elevators.

19. Manage the inventory of a fast food restaurant.

20. Manage the payroll of a fast-food restaurant.

21. Operate a traffic light attached to sensors that could tell whether a car was waiting at the light.

CHAPTER TWO

Applets

If you've had some experience with programming languages like BASIC, C, or Pascal, you'll discover that programming in Java is somewhat different than you're used to. First, as we mentioned earlier, Java is an object-oriented language. This means that we think of a Java program as a collection of cooperating classes, rather than primarily as a list of instructions to be executed in some clearly defined order. In addition, Java comes with a rich collection of classes that we can use to make our programs visually interesting. We'll explore these two themes in this chapter.

OBJECTIVES

In this chapter, we will
- Use the `Applet` class to illustrate the properties common to all Java classes.
- Discuss the way we use classes and their methods to design object-oriented programs.
- Begin our discussion of the classes in the `java.awt` package.
- Introduce several of the Java classes that we can use to produce graphic images.

2.1   THE APPLET CLASS

As we mentioned in Chapter 1, an applet is a kind of program that is designed to be run within a Java-aware environment like a Web browser. An applet, unlike a Java application, isn't a traditional stand-alone program, but rather is a class that is loaded and executed by another program. We begin our discussion of Java programming by talking about applets—first, because they serve as the "entry point" for every Java Web program and, second, because applets serve to illustrate the fundamental properties of all Java classes. In what follows, we'll build several applets, explaining what we've done and gradually adding features.

Learning from a Simple Applet

We'll begin by recalling the ultra-simple applet we used in Chapter 1.

```
import java.applet.*;
import java.awt.*;

public class Hello extends Applet
// Just about the simplest Java applet anyone can write.
{
    public void paint(Graphics g)
    {
        g.drawString("Hi!", 20, 10);
    }
}
```

Obviously, all this does is display the string "Hi!" in the space the browser has reserved for the applet. This is something of an abuse of the power of Java, we'll admit. It's completely static and it doesn't do anything (except consume computer resources) that we couldn't do far easier with basic HTML. It does, though, illustrate quite a lot about Java classes, and so it's worth studying for that reason alone. Let's go through it line-by line.

The first two lines,

```
import java.applet.*;
import java.awt.*;
```

inform the Java compiler that we will be using classes from the packages `java.applet` and `java.awt`. The first package contains the definitions for the `Applet` class, along with some other definitions (`AppletContext`, `AppletStub`, and `AudioClip`) that will be of no concern to us here. We need this for a somewhat subtle reason—since a Java program is composed of a collection of separately compiled files, there would be no reason to expect that the compiler would recognize any of the externally defined names, like `Applet`, while translating our program. All we're doing here is saying to the compiler, "if you come across a name in this file you don't recognize, try looking for its definition in the `java.applet` package before you yell at me."

The star (*) at the end of the package name is simply a "wild card" marker, telling the compiler to look for names among all the classes in the package. Since our sample never used any of the names from `AppletContext` or the other definitions, we could have made the `import` statement clearer by writing

```
import java.applet.Applet;
```

Some people prefer this form; the only downside is that in a big package like `java.awt`, with its forty-four classes (and classlike things known as *interfaces*, which we'll discuss later), it's easy to leave out a class name inadvertently, thereby confusing the compiler. We prefer the wildcard form because it doesn't add any overhead to the running of the applet and makes mistakes less likely.

The `import` statement allows you to use names of classes and methods defined in other packages. It takes the form

`import packageName.*;`

or

`import packageName.className;`

The semicolons at the end are required, and the `import` statement must appear before any of the names defined in the package are used (which is why we always place all `import` statements at the beginning of the file).

The next line in our program,

`public class Hello extends Applet`

is the beginning of the definition of our `Hello` class, the rest of which is enclosed in the pair of braces { and }. The keyword `public` allows access to this class from outside the file. We'll have more to say about access control later. The remainder of that line indicates that what follows is the definition of a class of our own, named `Hello`, which is an extension of the library `Applet` class. This means that our `Hello` class is in fact an `Applet` and inherits all twenty-one of the `public` methods of the `Applet` class, along with any additional ones we decide to define.

We named our class Hello, though we could have chosen any legal Java name we wanted to, as long as it hadn't already been defined. For example, we could have called our class `Fred`, though that's somewhat non-descriptive, but we would have gotten into big trouble with the compiler if we had chosen to call our class `Panel`, `false`, or `if`, since those names have predefined meanings in Java.

Names of Java classes, methods, and variables (collectively known as *identifiers*) can be any strings of letters, digits and the underscore character, as long as they start with a letter.

For example, `limitValue`, `x`, `switch72b`, `a_long_name` are all legal identifiers, while `2wayStreet`, `my variable`, `#*&!!` are not.

Java identifiers, recall, are case-sensitive, so `limitValue`, `LIMITVALUE`, `limitvalue`, `lImItVaLuE` are all considered to be different names.

The next line,

```
// Just about the simplest Java applet anyone can write.
```

is a *comment*. The Java compiler ignores everything from the two slashes to the end of the line, which gives us a way to put in explanatory notes. Remember, every program has two audiences: the compiler and the person reading the source code. The compiler quite literally is blind to comments, but they are invaluable to people reading your code (including yourself a week or more later—it's amazing how often you can find yourself saying, "Now what in the world did I intend here?").

Comments in Java come in two flavors.[1] A single-line comment begins with two slashes, //, and extends to the end of the line, as in

```
// Set up the initial values
height = 0.0;  // Measured in meters above sea level
```

Note in the second line how we follow a statement with an explanation. For longer comments, Java will also ignore anything between the pair /* and */, no matter how far apart the markers are. Here's an example:

```
/*  This method will return the maximum of the
    values of its three arguments x, y, and z. */
```

Style Tips:

1. While it's possible to go overboard with comments, it's far better to err on the side of too many, than too few.
2. Some comments, like this one, however, are not worth including:

   ```
   x = 0;     // set x to zero
   ```

   Well-written programs should be *self-documenting* as much as possible, which means that the code should explain itself.
3. Get in the habit of including comments while you're writing code. This way, you don't run the risk of later forgetting what you intended to say.

You can't nest comments within comments of the same type, but you can enclose a // comment within a /* */ pair. This is useful if you want to remove code from your program temporarily for test purposes. Rather than deleting the questionable lines, simply enclose them between /* and */, as long as the lines you enclosed didn't contain those delimiters.

---

[1] There is a third type, known as the *documentation comment,* which we won't cover here.

2.2 METHODS, INHERITANCE, AND OVERRIDING

Having completed the `import` portion, the head of the `Hello` class definition, and a comment line, we come to the body of the class itself:

```
{
    public void paint(Graphics g)
    {
        g.drawString("Hi!", 20, 10);
    }
}
```

In this simple example, the class definition consists of a single method definition, for the `paint()` method. What's going on here? In simple terms, we're providing our applet with a method that will control what appears whenever the browser or applet viewer decides that the applet needs to be drawn. To do that, our `paint()` expects to be given a `Graphics` object named `g` and invokes `g`'s `drawString()` method to draw the appropriate message on the screen at the coordinates provided.

Yeah, we thought that would be confusing. If you're thinking of any of the following questions, pat yourself on the back for diligence and rest assured we'll explain everything shortly.

- What's the purpose of the parentheses?
- What's a `Graphics`?
- What's a `void`?
- What's with the braces?
- What's the `g.` doing before the `drawString()`?
- Is it too late to drop this course?

Java Methods

Recall that a method in Java is a named sequence of statements that perform some task. A method takes in a (perhaps empty) collection of information and uses that information to do its job, optionally sending back a piece of information. Think of a method as a small factory: In the right end (the *arguments,* that part enclosed in parentheses) you put some raw materials and some money, the factory grinds away noisily, and out of the left end comes a custom-built toaster.

There are two slightly different forms of methods in Java. In the first kind, the method is intended to take in whatever arguments it needs, do the statements in its *body,* and then return control to that part of the program where it was first invoked.

Such a method is characterized by the fact that its header begins with the keyword `void`. Such a method is defined in the form

```
void methodName(list of arguments)
// Nothing comes out the left end--we're interested only in the
// noise the factory makes
{
     list of statements, enclosed by braces
}
```

The second kind of method acts almost exactly as the first. The only difference is that this kind of method returns to its point of invocation with some information. The type of information it returns is indicated by placing a type name at the start of the method head, such as

```
returnTypeName methodName(list of arguments)
// Something comes out the left end, which we'll use later.
{
     list of statements, enclosed by braces
}
```

For the moment, we'll devote our attention to the first form, the one with the void return type. Such a method is called into action by telling an object to perform that method, using the object's name, a dot, and the name of the method, along with any arguments the method needs to do its job. That's what we're doing in the line

```
g.drawString("Hi!", 20, 10);
```

Every method is defined in some class. To *call* a method into action, we must specify the object whose copy of the method we'll use by using

```
objectName.methodName(argument list);
```

The arguments used in the call have to match those in the method definition in order, number, and type.

---

drawString() is a method that belongs to the Graphics class (part of the java.awt package). Since g is a Graphics object, we are requesting g to execute its own drawString method. In doing so, we're giving the method the string we want it to draw on the screen, along with two integers that tell the method how many *pixels*[2] from the left and top edges of the applet we want the drawing to start.

---

[2]A pixel (from *pic* ture *el* ement) is one dot on the screen. The size of a pixel varies from monitor to monitor, but is generally about 1/72 of an inch (or 0.39 mm.).

In Figure 2.1 we provide an illustration of (roughly speaking) the interaction between a method call and its definition in a class. When we call a method, execution jumps from the place of calling to the place where the method is defined. As this happens, the *actual arguments* are sent to fill in the placeholder *formal arguments* in the method definition. Then the method code is executed, and, upon completion, execution returns to the statement immediately following the method call.

In Java, every method definition consists of a collection of calls to other methods, along with some other statements that are invoked in place, without hopping out to another method.

```
class Hello extends Applet
{
    public void paint(Graphics g)
    {
        g.drawString("Hi!, 20, 10);        1. Call the function.
    }
}
```

2. Fill in arguments.

```
class Graphics
{
    ...
    public void drawString(String s, int x, int y)
    {
        3. Execute the function code.
        Lots of esoteric code about how to
        draw s on the screen, at location (x, y).
    }
}
```

4. Return back to the calling location.

Figure 2.1 What happens when a method is called.

We've answered all the questions we posed earlier, but there's still one we've avoided until now. Where is paint() called? You'll come to see that a lot of action in a Java program takes place behind the scenes. Unlike the situation in many other languages, much of object-oriented programming consists of providing the necessary functionality (the methods) without worrying too much about when these methods will be called. In our sample applet, it's the responsibility of the browser or applet runner to decide when paint() should be called. It might be when the applet first appears or when the user decides to scroll or resize the browser window—the applet doesn't know and we shouldn't care. All we have to do is understand that there will be times when a method named paint() will be called and to take steps to make sure that when it is it will do the right thing. We leave it to the applet runner to decide when to call `paint()` and to provide the necessary `Graphics` object as the argument.

Inheritance and Overriding

While it's confusing enough at first to think of programming in terms of providing the needed functionality by writing appropriate method definitions, that confusion passes quickly. To further complicate things, though, we'll let you in on a secret: `paint()` isn't even an Applet method! You'll search through the documentation of the Applet class in vain trying to find the `paint()` method—it's just not there.

If you look through the documentation, though, you'll discover that the `Applet` class extends the `Panel` class, whatever that is. We'll describe the `Panel` class in Chapter 4; is `paint()` defined there? No. Continuing our search, we find that every `Panel` object is also a member of the `Container` class but, sad to say, `paint()` isn't among the `Container` methods, either. Finally, we find that the `Container` class extends `Component`, and *that's* where we find the first mention of `paint()`.

If you think about it, that's where we'd expect `paint()` to be, way up near the top of the class hierarchy, part of which we illustrate in Figure 2.2.

Since drawing an object to the screen is such a fundamentally important task, it makes good sense that it should be in a method that would be inherited by all the classes that contain drawable objects, like buttons, fields to hold text, panels to hold other components, and, finally, applets.

Each of these "paint-able" objects, though, has to be drawn in an entirely different way, so we can't expect there to be an ultraclever `paint()` method up in `Component` that knows how to draw everything. Instead, what we have to do is *override* Component's `paint()` method, describing what it is expected to do for our particular class, `Hello`. That's exactly what we did—and, in fact, that's all we did—in the definition of our `Hello` class. That way, when our applet is asked to draw itself, the call will be to `paint()`, but it will be our own `paint()` method that's invoked.

In what is to come, we'll be doing a lot of this overriding of methods from superclasses. As a matter of fact, for the first four chapters, this activity will occupy a considerable portion of our time. Rest assured that we won't expect you to memorize several dozen classes and their several hundred methods. A lot of the methods out there are never overridden and are called behind the scenes, so the methods you'll actually have to deal with are fairly few in number. To give you a sample of what's to come, in the next section we'll introduce a few of the classes we'll use just as they come "out of the box."

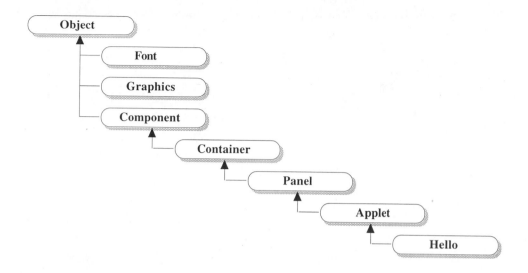

Figure 2.2 A portion of Java's class hierarchy.

2.3 GRAPHICAL PROGRAMMING

The `java.awt` package contains, as we mentioned, forty-four classes and interfaces (in version 1.0; there are sixty-one in version 1.1, the latest version of the language), all of which are devoted in one way or another to producing applets and applications with graphical user interfaces (GUIs, in the jargon). In this section, we'll introduce some of the classes that can be used in an applet's `paint()` method to spruce up the applet's look.

The `Graphics` Class

This class consists of objects that know how to draw on the display. As we mentioned before, an applet will have a `Graphics` object associated with it, which you can access within `paint()` since it's provided as an argument. Once you have the `Graphics` object, you can use its methods to draw anything you want, limited only by your creativity (and, to be fair, your patience). The following are some of the more useful `Graphics` methods. We've omitted several, either because they're not often used or because we have to lay some additional groundwork before we can fully explain them.

`void` **`clearRect`**`(int x, int y, int width, int height)`
    This method clears a rectangle by painting it in the background color. The

arguments are integers, like 2 and 450, and represent the coordinates of the upper left corner of the rectangle and the width and height of the rectangle.

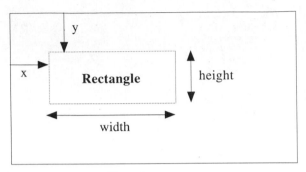

Drawing area

void **draw3DRect**(int x, int y, int width, int height,
                    boolean raised)
　　This method draws a rectangular border of the specified dimensions, shaded in the background color to look three-dimensional. A boolean type has either of two values, called true and false. If the argument raised has the value true the border is painted as if it were raised out of the surface and if it has the value false, it appears as if it is depressed.

void **drawArc**(int x, int y, int width, int height,
                 int startAngle, int arcAngle)
　　This method draws an unfilled arc within the rectangle specified by x, y, width, and height. The arc begins at the angle, in degrees, specified by the argument startAngle, and extends to arcAngle. Angles are measured counterclockwise from 3:00 o'clock and extend from the center of the bounding rectangle. A call to drawArc(10, 10, 160, 80, 45, 210) might look like this.

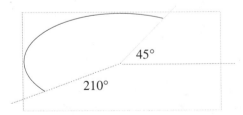

void **drawLine**(int x1, int y1, int x2, int y2)
　　This draws a line from the point with coordinates (x1, y1) to the point with coordinates (x2, y2).

void **drawOval**(int x, int y, int width, int height)

This draws an unfilled oval within the bounding rectangle specified by the arguments. Observe that `drawOval(x, y, width, height)` has the same effect as a call to `drawArc(x, y, width, height, 0, 360)`.

`void` **`drawRect`**`(int x, int y, int width, int height)`
    This draws an unfilled rectangle with position and size given by the arguments.

`void` **`drawRoundRect`**`(int x, int y, int width, int height,`
                    `int arcWidth, int arcHeight)`
    This draws an unfilled rounded rectangle with position and size given by the first four arguments. The last two specify the width and height, respectively, of the rounded corners.

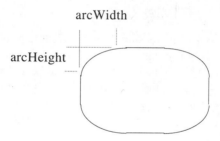

`void` **`drawString`**`(String s, int x, int y)`
    This draws a string of characters with its *baseline* (the lower edge of letters like "m" and "A" that have no descenders) starting at coordinates x and y.

`void` **`fill3DRect`**`(int x, int y, int w, int h, boolean raised)`
`void` **`fillArc`**`(int x, int y, int w, int w, int stA, int arcA)`
`void` **`fillOval`**`(int x, int y, int w, int h)`
`void` **`fillRect`**`(int x, int y, int w, int h)`
`void` **`fillRoundRect`**`(int x, int y, int w, int h, int aW, int aH)`
    These five work just like their "draw" counterparts except that they also fill the enclosed region in the current drawing color.

`void` **`setColor`**`(Color c)`
    This sets the current drawing color to the color specified in the argument. The drawing color stays fixed until it is changed by another call to `setColor()`. You'll see shortly how the `Color` class is defined.

Using the `Graphics` Class (and Learning Some Programming in the Process)

Here's a simple example of what we can do with the Graphics methods. One drawback to the drawing routines is that they don't provide us with any way of changing the line width. Suppose we want to make an applet that draws a logo consisting of three squares like this:

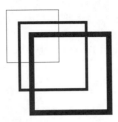

A clever way of increasing the line width is to draw several rectangles, one inside the other. To do so, all we have to do is increase the *x* and *y* coordinates by one at each stage, while reducing the width and height by two. We do this as many times as we need to make the desired thicknesses of lines. For example, to draw a 100 by 100 pixel square with its upper left corner at (50, 80) with line thickness three, all we'd have to do is use the following three method calls

```
g.drawRect(50, 80, 100, 100);
g.drawRect(51, 81, 98, 98);
g.drawRect(52, 82, 96, 96);
```

On this page and the next, we show what the complete applet would look like. We encourage you to start up your Java compiler and try it.

```
/* ***************************************************
    This is a sample applet for trying some of the
    Graphics methods. It draws a sequence of three
    squares with increasing sizes and border
    thicknesses.
    *************************************************** */
import java.applet.*;
import java.awt.*;

public class Logo extends Applet
{
    public void paint(Graphics g)
    {
        // Draw the first square
        g.drawRect(50, 80, 100, 100);
```

```
        // Draw the next square, offset from the first
        // by 25, 50 pixels larger, with line width 2.
        g.drawRect(75, 105, 150, 150);
        g.drawRect(76, 106, 148, 148);
        // Draw the last square, offset from the second
        // by 25, 50 pixels larger, with line width 3.
        g.drawRect(100, 130, 200, 200);
        g.drawRect(101, 131, 198, 198);
        g.drawRect(102, 132, 196, 196);
    }
}
```

This certainly does what we need, but there's a wide gulf between a program that merely works and one that's easy to read and modify. One problem with this program is that it has entirely too many "magic numbers"—numbers with no immediately obvious meaning. Observe that the second and third squares are offset from the first and second by a common amount, 25, and that the sizes likewise increase by a common amount, 50. We can provide named storage for these two numbers. While we're at it, let's also use three more *variables* (as they're called) to hold the x and y coordinates of the upper left corner of the first square and the initial size. Our paint() routine would now look like this:

```
public void paint(Graphics g)
{
    int x = 50;         // x coord. of first square
    int y = 80;         // y coord. of first square
    int size = 100;     // size of first square
    int OFFSET = 25;    // x, y offsets of squares
    int INCREMENT = 50; // size increases of squares

    // Draw the first square
    g.drawRect(x, y, size, size);
    // Increment the start coordinates and size
    // and draw a border-width-2 square.
    x = x + OFFSET;
    y = y + OFFSET;
    size = size + INCREMENT;
    g.drawRect(x, y, size, size);
    g.drawRect(x + 1, y + 1, size - 2, size - 2);
    // Do it again, for the third square
    x = x + OFFSET;
    y = y + OFFSET;
    size = size + INCREMENT;
    g.drawRect(x, y, size, size);
    g.drawRect(x + 1, y + 1, size - 2, size - 2);
    g.drawRect(x + 2, y + 2, size - 4, size - 4);
}
```

Sure, it's quite a bit longer than the original, but it's a heck of a lot easier to read and modify. To change the start coordinates, size, offset, and increment would require modifying five numbers and almost no thought, whereas in the original version we would have to carefully modify twenty-four different numbers!

Programming Tip:

Avoid magic numbers as much as possible. It's generally much better to devote a variable to the task of storing a value, rather than "hard-wiring" it in.

All we're doing is providing five integer variables within the `paint()` method to hold the numbers we need. We'll talk more about variables in Chapter 5; for now all we need to do is mention that we must *declare* a variable before we use it. Declaring a variable requires us to specify the type of information it will hold, which is why we preface each variable with the type name `int`: (whole numbers in Java are called `int`s.). If we want, we can set the initial value stored in the variable, too, as we did in the preceding routine, by using = and the initial value at the end of the declaration.

A variable declaration looks like

```
typeName identifier;
```

or

```
typeName identifier = initialValue;
```

Variables must be declared before they are used, and a variable declared in a method has meaning only within that method (so wouldn't be recognized in some other method).

Notice that Java allows you to perform arithmetic operations, like `x + 2`, and that the *assignment* operator, =, evaluates whatever expression is on the right and stores the result in the variable on the left. In our example, the statement

```
x = x + OFFSET;
```

computes the value of `x + OFFSET` and then places that value in the variable `x`. In simple terms, this statement increases the value of `x` by the amount `OFFSET`.

Before we leave this example, we'll mention in passing that you'll soon see how we can make it even better and more general purpose. Finally, note how we used all lowercase names for the variables `x`, `y`, and `size`, which changed during the method's execution, and uppercase names for INCREMENT and OFFSET, which didn't. This is a fairly common convention.

Style Tip:

Build in as much information as you can in your program by adopting consistent standards of naming. Many programmers use ALL_CAPS for variables that are not going to change their values during execution and lowerCase or lower_case_with_underscores for variables whose values might change.

The Color Class

This class's objects represent colors. It contains thirteen constant values that can be used when you want black, blue, cyan, darkGray, gray, green, lightGray, magenta, orange, pink, red, white, or yellow. To use one of these constants, you need to inform the compiler that the identifier belongs to the Color class, so you attach the class name to the front of the color name, along with a dot. In other words, to draw a green rectangle, we could use Graphics' setColor() method, along with the color name, and then make a call to fillRect():

```
g.setColor(Color.green);          // assuming g is a Graphics object
g.fillRect(10, 20, 100, 200);
```

Colors in Java are described by a model that specifies the amount of red, green, and blue, as if the color were made by shining lights of the three base colors on a spot. To specify a color, you can specify the brightness of each of the components as an integer between 0 and 255, with 0 representing none of the component (the light is off). The color 0, 0, 0 in this *RGB model,* then, is black, 128, 128, 128 is a medium gray, and 255, 0, 128 is fuchsia, a red with a bit of blue in it. For reasons that will be clear in the next chapter, you declare a Color variable by using the operator new. In our example, for instance, we could have painted a fuchsia rectangle by using a Color variable myColor:

```
Color myColor = new Color(255, 0, 128);      // a new Color object,
g.setColor(myColor);                         // used here
g.fillRect(10, 20, 100, 200);
```

We could have accomplished the same thing, by the way, by defining the color "on the fly," just as we sent it into the argument of setColor():

```
g.setColor(new Color(255, 0, 128));
```

The `Font` Class

Just as the `Color` class is used to represent colors, objects in the `Font` class represent the fonts used for textual displays. There are five basic fonts that should be supported on any platform on which Java is running. In Java, their names are "Helvetica," "TimesRoman," "Courier," "Dialog," and "DialogInput." Because of copyright considerations, version 1.1 of Java has changed the names of some of the fonts: "Helvetica" is now "SanSerif," "TimesRoman" is "Serif," and "Courier" is now called "Monospaced." Although the older names are still supported, they have become what is called "deprecated," meaning that they may not be recognized in future versions of the language. Since installed fonts vary from computer to computer, you shouldn't expect a particular font to look exactly the same on all systems, but they should be close to the following.

Java Name	Appearance	v.1.1 Name Change
Helvetica	Helvetica	SanSerif
TimesRoman	TimesRoman	Serif
Courier	Courier	Monospaced
Dialog	Dialog	
DialogInput	**DialogInput**	

As there are with colors, there are some `Font` class constants, in this case used to specify the style of the font. These are `Font.BOLD`, `Font.PLAIN`, and `Font.ITALIC`. Also as with colors, you make a `Font` object by using the `new` operator and a `Font` *constructor,* to which you send as arguments the font name, style, and size. Newly constructed `Font` objects are often used with `Graphics'` `setFont()` method as in

```
g.setFont(new Font("Helvetica", Font.BOLD, 12));
g.drawString("This is Helvetica bold-12", 10, 20);
```

You can combine styles by adding them, so if you used the expression `Font.BOLD + Font.ITALIC` as the second argument in a `Font` constructor, the text would be displayed as ***bold italic.*** The size argument is (more or less) the height in pixels. Finally, if you specify a font name that isn't installed, Java will choose a default font on its own. Unfortunately, there is no way for an applet to determine what fonts are resident on the machine on which it is running.[3]

---

[3]However, you could test for the presence of a particular font name by using the `Font` method `getFont()`.

Positions and Sizes: the Classes `Point`, `Dimension` , and `Rectangle`

Since drawing a graphical user interface requires a considerable amount of coordinate calculations, Java provides three classes that are useful for manipulating collections of dimension values. These are the classes `Point`, `Rectangle`, and `Dimension`.

The `Point` class is the simplest of the three. A `Point` object contains two integers, `x` and `y`. As with the rest of the dimensional classes, the purpose of the `Point` class is to allow us to make a single object that contains several pieces of information. There are three constructors, used with the `new` operator to make a new `Point` object.

Point`() // version 1.1 only`
This constructs a new `Point` object with both `x` and `y` coordinates equal to zero.

Point`(int x, int y)`
This constructs a new `Point` object by specifying the *x* and *y* coordinates.

Point`(Point p) // version 1.1 only`
Known as a *copy constructor,* this method makes a new `Point` object with coordinates equal to those of the argument, `p`.

There are a few methods that we can use to manipulate points.

`boolean` **equals**`(int x, int y)`
This returns the `boolean` value `true` if this point has coordinates `x` and `y` and returns the value `false` if either or both of this point's coordinates fail to match those of the argument. Note: You'll have to wait a little while to understand how to use this function.

`void` **move**`(int x, int y)`
This changes the point's coordinates to those given by the arguments. In version 1.1, there's an equivalent method named **setLocation**().

`void` **translate**`(int dx, int dy)`
This changes the point's coordinates by adding `dx` and `dy` to its `x` and `y` coordinates, respectively. For example, if a `Point` object `myPoint` originally had the coordinates `x = 0` and `y = 3`, after calling `myPoint. translate (2, -4),` `myPoint` would have `x = 2` and `y = -1`.

In one respect, the `Point` class is somewhat unusual. As you'll see when we talk about access in more detail, we almost always make an object's data `private`, so that it can be modified only by an object in the same class. In the case of Point's `x` and `y` data, though, Java has departed from this rule and made both data members `public`. This means we can write code like

```
Point myPoint = new Point(0, 3);
myPoint.x = 2;      // unusual--we can get to the data directly
myPoint.y = -1;
```

The Dimension class is very much like the Point class in that it contains two integer data members, both of which are publicly accessible. The only real difference between the two classes is in their intent: The two integers in Point are supposed to represent coordinates of a point, whereas the integers in a Dimension object, named width and height, are intended to represent the horizontal and vertical extent of some geometric object. In Java 1.1, like the Point class, the Dimension class has three constructors:

Dimension()
This constructs a new Dimension object with both width and height equal to zero.

Dimension(int w, int h)
Constructs a new Dimension object with data members width = w and height = h.

Dimension(Dimension d)
Another copy constructor, this method builds a new Dimension object having the same width and height values as that of the argument d.

This class has even fewer methods than Point. The ones of interest exist only in Java 1.1:

boolean **equals**(Dimension d)   // version 1.1 only
As with the method of the same name in Point, this method returns true if this object has the same width and height as d, and returns false otherwise.

void **setSize**(int w, int h)   // version 1.1 only
This sets the width and height of this object to w and h, respectively.

void **setSize**(Dimension d)   // version 1.1 only
This sets the width and height of this object to those of the argument.

The Rectangle class is a combination of the two we've already discussed. A Rectangle object is described by a point (the x and y coordinates of the upper left corner) and a dimension (its width and height). These four member data are named x, y, width, and height, and all are publicly accessible by using the usual dot notation. Figure 2.3 illustrates how these four member data combine to describe a Rectangle object.

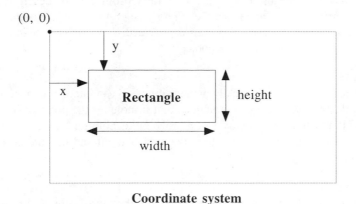

Coordinate system

Figure 2.3 Member data describing a `Rectangle`.

There are six constructors for `Rectangles` (version 1.1 adds another, bringing the total to seven), providing a good deal of flexibility in how we can make a new `Rectangle` object.

`Rectangle()`
Constructs an "empty" rectangle located at (0, 0) and having width and height zero.

`Rectangle(int w, int h)`
Constructs a `Rectangle` at (0, 0) with `width` = w and `height` = h.

`Rectangle(int x, int y, int w, int h)`
Constructs a `Rectangle` from four `ints`, specifying the upper left corner (x and y), the width (w) and height (h).

`Rectangle(Point p)`
Constructs an empty `Rectangle` (width and `height` both zero) anchored at the `Point` given by p.

`Rectangle(Dimension d)`
Constructs a `Rectangle` anchored at (0, 0) with `width` and `height` given by the argument d.

`Rectangle(Point p, Dimension d)`
Constructs a `Rectangle` anchored at the `Point` given by p and having `width` and `height` given by d.

`Rectangle(Rectangle r)   // version 1.1 only`
Make a new `Rectangle` having the same anchor and dimensions as r.

Rectangles are used quite a lot in Java programs, to describe bounding regions of many objects and to set the *clipping region* in which drawing is allowed to take place. For that reason, this class is provided with a rich collection of methods for inspecting and manipulating its objects.

void **add**(int x, int y)

This, and its two identically named siblings, is an interesting method. add() expands this rectangle by just enough so that it includes the point with coordinates *x* and *y*. If the point is already in this rectangle, nothing happens. Note that in general this method may change both the anchor point and the dimensions of this rectangle.

void **add**(Point p)

Acts like the preceding method, except that the point to be enclosed is specified by a Point object.

void **add**(Rectangle r)

Expands the rectangle enough to include all of rectangle r.

boolean **contains**(int x, int y)   // version 1.1 only

Tests whether the point (x, y) is in this rectangle. If it is, returns true, otherwise returns false.

boolean **contains**(Point p)   // version 1.1 only

Behaves like the preceding method, except that a Point is used as the argument.

boolean **equals**(Rectangle r)

Returns true if and only if this rectangle has the same anchor point and dimensions as r.

Point **getLocation**()   // version 1.1 only

Returns a Point with the same coordinates as the anchor of this rectangle.

Dimension **getSize**()   // version 1.1 only

Returns a Dimension object with the same width and height of this rectangle.

void **grow**(int h, int v)

Changes the size of this rectangle by expanding the width by h on both sides and expanding the height by v on top and bottom. Note that "expanding" isn't quite accurate: If either h or v is negative, this rectangle will contract in the appropriate direction.

boolean **inside**(int x, int y) // may vanish in future releases

Returns true if and only if the point (x, y) is in this rectangle. In the future, this method may be eliminated and replaced by contains().

Rectangle **intersection**(Rectangle r)
Returns Rectangle, consisting of all the points in this rectangle that are also in r.

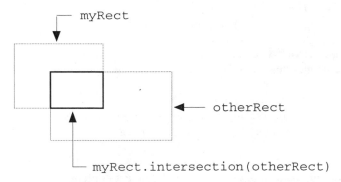

Rectangle **intersection**(Rectangle r)
Returns Rectangle, consisting of all the points in this rectangle that are also in r.

boolean **intersects**(Rectangle r)
Returns true if and only if this rectangle contains any points of r.

boolean **isEmpty**()
Returns true if and only if this rectangle is empty; i.e., either width or height are zero or less.

void **move**(int x, int y) // may vanish in future releases
Changes this rectangle's anchor point to (x, y). May eventually be replaced by setLocation().

void **rehape**(int x, int y, int w, int h)   // may vanish
Changes this rectangle's anchor and dimensions to those specified by the arguments. May eventually be replaced by setBounds().

void **resize**(int w, int h)   // may vanish
Changes this rectangle's dimension to that given by the arguments. May be replaced by setSize().

void **setBounds**(int x, int y, int w, int h) // only in v.1.1
Changes this rectangle's anchor and dimensions to those specified by the arguments.

void **setBounds**(Rectangle r)   // only in v.1.1
Changes as in the preceding method, except that the new bounds are given by a Rectangle argument.

void **setLocation**(int x, int y)   // only in v.1.1
Changes this rectangle's anchor to (x, y).

```
void setLocation(Point p)              // only in v.1.1
```
Changes this rectangle's anchor to the point p.

```
void setSize(int w, int h)             // only in v.1.1
```
Changes this rectangle's dimensions to w by h.

```
void setSize(Dimension d)              // only in v.1.1
```
Changes this rectangle's dimensions to those given by d.

```
void translate(int dx, int dy)
```
Changes this rectangle's anchor by adding dx to its x datum and dy to its y datum. In other words, shift this rectangle in the direction (dx, dy).

```
Rectangle union(Rectangle r)
```
Returns the smallest Rectangle object containing both this rectangle and the argument r.

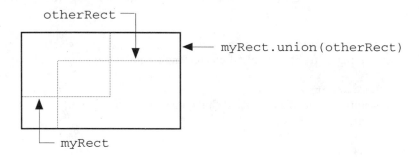

2.4   HANDS ON

In the Lablet for this chapter, we'll use some of the classes we've discussed (and some we haven't) to build an applet that will tell us about the environment in which it is running.

As always, we begin with a documentation block, describing the purposes of the class definitions it contains (in this case, the single class, Snapshot).

```
/* ************************************************************
              CHAPTER 2 LABLET: SNAPSHOT

 This class uses some of Java's built-in classes to identify
 and report on some of the properties of the machine and the
 Java programming environment being used.
 ************************************************************ */
```

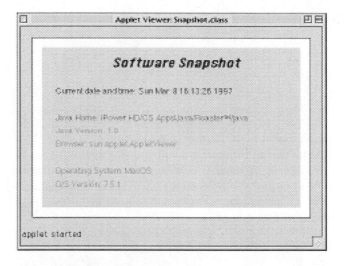

Figure 2.4   The Snapshot applet in action

The customary collection of `import` statements refers to the ones we expect, as well as two classes we haven't seen so far, the `Date` and `Properties` classes defined in the `java.util` package.

```
import java.applet.Applet;
import java.awt.*;
import java.util.Date;
import java.util.Properties;
```

Next, we come to the beginning of the definition of the only class in this file, the subclass `Snapshot` of `Applet`. It's worth pointing out here that we've decided to adopt the same naming convention that Java does, namely, that class names have initial capitals but that other identifiers, like variable and method names, do not.

```
public class Snapshot extends Applet
{
    // Construct fonts for the header and the body of the display.
    Font f1 = new Font("TimesRoman",Font.ITALIC,18);
    Font f2 = new Font("Helvetica",Font.PLAIN,12);
```

Immediately after the class header, we come to what are obviously two variables, `f1` and `f2`, of `Font` type. This is no surprise, but the location of the declaration should be. These two variables are not declared in any method, but instead are declared at the class level. Declaring `f1` and `f2` that way makes them *instance variables,* like `x` and `y` in `Point`, rather than the *local variables* they would be if they had been declared in some method.

These are the only choices we have for variables—either they're declared "globally" in a class or they are local variables. Instance variables can be accessed by any method in the class (and, in this example, by other classes, as well, since we didn't put the `private` modifier in front of their declarations). Local variables are—at best—only valid within the method in which they are declared.

Every variable must be declared within some class. If a variable is declared within some class method, it is called a *local variable* and only has meaning within the nearest pair of enclosing braces, { and }. If a variable is declared within a class but not within any of the class's methods, it is an *instance variable* and may be accessed by any method in the class. Of course, no variable may be used before it has been declared.

In this example, we deliberately departed from good programming practice so that we would have an excuse to talk about instance variables. As a matter of fact, there's no reason to make `f1` and `f2` instance variables, since a quick look at the class definition shows that they're only used within the `paint()` method. Seeing this, it would make more sense to declare `f1` and `f2` locally to `paint()`, as we did with the variables in the Logo applet in the previous section. This would be particularly important in a large class with many methods—it's very irritating to come across what is clearly a variable and have to scroll several screens away to discover how it was declared.

Programming Tips:

1. Declare variables as locally as possible.
2. Unless there's a *very* compelling reason to make an instance variable publicly available, make it `private`.

We next come to a method we haven't seen so far, `init()`.

```
public void init()
// The only initialization required is to resize the applet.
{
      resize(450,300);
}
```

It looks like this method is somewhat like `paint()` in that it's not called by any method in our class. We can conclude that this is probably an override of a method that belongs to `Applet` or one of its superclasses, like `Panel`,

`Container`, `Component`, or `Object`. This is exactly right—the `init()` method belongs to the `Applet` class and is called when the applet is first loaded by the browser or applet runner. This is the place where we do any one-time initialization, and that's exactly what's happening in `init()`'s code body. We're not trusting the HTML <APPLET> tag to set the size of the applet; instead, we're setting its size ourselves by using the `Component` method `resize()`.

Oops! It looks as if there's an error here, though. So far, every method call we've seen has begun with a reference to some object, like the `Graphics` object g in `g.setColor(Color.red)`. Here, though, the method call is simply the naked `resize(450, 300)`. What object's `resize()` method is being called here? Well, it's clearly the Snapshot applet itself, since the intent of the method call is to have the applet resize itself, but how do we get an object to call one of its own methods—by using something like `this.resize(450, 300)`? How about that—that's *exactly* what we can do!

An object can call one of its own methods, or any inherited method of one of its superclasses, by either (1) not having any object name in front of the method or (2) by having the name `this`, which always is understood by Java to mean the object itself.

Continuing on, we return to familiar territory, the `paint()` method. We know the browser or applet runner will call `paint()` when it needs to and will provide a `Graphics` object g that will be responsible for doing the actual display. The job of `paint()` is to make the appropriate calls to g's methods.

```
public void paint(Graphics g)
{
    // Draw the enclosing boxes and the title
    // Use the current applet dimensions to determine
    // their sizes
    Dimension myAppletDim = size();
```

Hmm. There's another method here we haven't seen yet, the `size()` method. We've just seen one of those naked method calls, so it's obvious that the applet itself is making this call. Looking up the class hierarchy we find `size()` among the methods of—guess what?—`Component`, again. "When in doubt about who owns an `awt` method, look at `Component` first" is evidently good advice.

If we look it up we see that the *signature* (the return type, name, and arguments) of this method is `public Dimension size()`. This is one of those methods that has a non-`void` return type. In this case it returns an anonymous `Dimension` object after it has been called. We then use that object to initialize our variable `myAppletDim`, just as we would initialize an integer variable like x by writing the declaration `int x = 3;`.

If a method has a non-`void` return type of T, the method call can be used anywhere
a value of type T could.

With this in mind, we see that the declaration is just storing the current size of the
applet in the local `Dimension` variable `myAppletDim`.

We use this variable in the next few statements:

```
g.setColor(Color.black);
g.drawRect(15,15,myAppletDim.width      - 30,
                 myAppletDim.height     - 30);
g.setColor(Color.white);
g.fillRect(16,16,myAppletDim.width      - 32,
                 myAppletDim.height     - 32);
g.setColor(Color.lightGray);
g.fillRect(30,30,myAppletDim.width      - 60,
                 myAppletDim.height     - 60);
```

First, we have g set its drawing color to black and draw a rectangle, anchored
at (15, 15) and having dimensions just 30 pixels less than the entire applet. Aha! —
we're drawing a rectangle that is uniformly inset 15 pixels from the edges of the
applet, and this will work even if we resize the applet window manually. We then
inset one pixel farther and fill a rectangle with white; finally we inset 14 more pixels
and fill in the rectangle with light gray. We're left with a tidy border that, in part,
looks like this:

The next part is, finally, completely familiar—we set g's font to f1 (18-
point TimesRoman italic, which we have to look for among the instance variables,
since it's not declared locally, where it should be), set the drawing color to black,
and draw the title string.

```
// Draw the heading
g.setFont(f1);
g.setColor(Color.black);
g.drawString("Software Snapshot", 135, 60);
```

After that, we change fonts, set the drawing color to blue and draw another string. This time, we're using another variable, thisDay, of type Date. Date objects contain information about years, months, days, hours, minutes, and seconds, along with methods for setting, extracting, and comparing dates. The new Date object we construct on the right side of the declaration generates an object initialized to the current date and time, which we then store in the variable thisDay.

```
// Display date and time information as available
// in class Date
g.setFont(f2);
Date thisDay = new Date();
g.setColor(Color.blue);
g.drawString("Current date and time: " + thisDay,
             50, 100);
```

In the drawString() call, we provide a string that is partly our own (the "Current date and time:" portion) and partly from thisDate. The + operator in this context isn't addition; rather, it's string *concatenation*. When we concatenate two strings, we make a new string of characters that results from appending the right one to the end of the left one. For example, "dog" + "food" is the string with value "dogfood." There's a bit going on behind the scenes here—Java is converting the Date-type variable thisDay to a string of characters so that it can be used as the right-hand operand of the + operator. Unseen by us, Java is calling Date's toString() method to perform the conversion. Most classes have a toString() method, and we'll talk about the String class in Chapter 9.

We're almost at the end of the paint() method, which in this Lablet means we're almost finished with the applet definition. There are only two new classes to introduce here: System, from the java.lang package and Properties, found in java.util. We didn't have to import java.lang, since the compiler will look for names there without any special instructions by us.

The code begins by setting g's drawing color to red and then declares another variable, myProperties, of type Properties. This variable is initialized, much as we did above with thisDate, by setting it to the Properties object we get when we call the getProperties() method of the class System.

```
// Display some of the Java system properties available
// from class Properties
g.setColor(Color.red);
Properties myProperties = System.getProperties();
g.drawString("Java Home: " +
         myProperties.getProperty("java.home"),
             50, 140);
```

The System class contains data and members that allow us access to the system on which a Java programming is running. Along with input and output objects, the System class contains the getProperties() method, which allows a program to find out some information about the system. The Properties class is somewhat of a queer duck—in essence a Properties object is nothing more than a matching between strings. A typical Properties object, for example, might match the key "name" to the value "Joe Smith" and the key "address" to "9 S. Main St." When you call System.getProperties(), you're guaranteed to get back a Properties object with matches for at least the following keys (and some others, like the character being used on the System's files to separate lines, which we've omitted):

"java.home"   the directory where Java is located
"java.version"   the version number of the running Java system
"java.vendor.url"   the URL of the vendor of this version of Java
"os.name"   the name of the operating system being used
"os.version"   the version of the operating system"

All we need, once we've initialized myProperties to hold the System properties, is to call its getProperty() method, which takes a key string as argument and returns the corresponding value as a string, which we concatenate to a message of our own and display on the screen, very much as we did to get the current date.

```
g.drawString("Java Version: " +
            myProperties.getProperty("java.version"),
            50, 160);
g.drawString("Browser: " +
            myProperties.getProperty("browser"),
            50, 180);

// Display the operating system information, also from
// class Properties
g.setColor(Color.magenta);
g.drawString("Operating System: " +
            myProperties.getProperty("os.name"),
            50, 220);
g.drawString("O/S Version: " +
            myProperties.getProperty("os.version"),
            50, 240);
    }
}
```

2.5 SUMMARY

❧ We discussed the following classes:

```
Applet
Color
Component
Date
Dimension
Font
Graphics
Point
Properties
Rectangle
System
```

❧ The `import` statement is used to indicate to the compiler that a file may contain names of classes, methods, and data that were defined in packages located in other files. We discussed the packages `java.applet`, `java.awt`, and `java.util`.

❧ Comments in Java come in two forms. Any text from `//` to the end of the line are ignored, as is anything between the pairs `/*` and `*/`. Comments of the same type cannot be nested within each other, though any `//` comments within a `/*...*/` pair are ignored. Comments are Good Things; use them.

❧ An identifier is a class, variable, or method name. Java identifiers must start with a letter and after that may contain any combination of letters, digits or underscore characters.

❧ Java identifiers are case-sensitive: Lower- and uppercase letters are considered different by the compiler when looking up names.

❧ A class definition always looks like

```
class Name extends OtherClassName
{
     Instance variable declarations

     Method definitions
}
```

Although we often derive a class from a superclass, the `extends` part of the header is optional—classes do not necessarily have to be derived from other classes.

❧ When we declare a variable, we are indicating to the compiler that it should remember the variable name and should associate that name with a type, either a *primitive type* like `int` or `boolean`, or a *class type*.

❧ Variable declarations take one of two forms:

```
TypeName variableName;
TypeName variableName = expression of the correct type;
```

❦ Any variable must be declared in some class. The *scope* of a variable—the locations in the program where the compiler will recognize its name—is limited to the portion of the program between the nearest pair of braces that enclose the declaration. In addition, a variable has meaning only in that part of its scope that occurs after its declaration.

❦ When we construct an object for use in a declaration, we must use the `new` operator in front of the constructor:

```
ClassName variableName = new ClassName(argument list);
```

❦ Declaring a non-class–type variable, like an `int` or `boolean`, does not use the `new` operator.

❦ A method definition takes one of two forms, depending on whether or not it returns a value to the location it was called:

```
void methodName(formal argument list)
{
     list of statements
}
```

or

```
TypeName methodName(formal argument list)
{
     list of statements
}
```

❦ The argument list of a method is a (possibly empty) list, separated by commas, of terms of the form `TypeName  formalArgument`. When a method is called, the formal arguments are set equal to the actual arguments provided by the method call. Formal arguments are local to the function.

❦ If a `void` method belonging to class `T` is called, the call forms a single statement and looks like

```
T-typeObjectName.methodName(actual arguments);
```

In all method calls, regardless of return type, the actual arguments must match the formal arguments of the method definition in order, type, and number.

❦ If an object calls one of its own methods or an accessible method from one of its superclasses, the call can take one of two forms:

```
methodName(actual arguments)
```

or

```
this.methodName(actual arguments)
```

The keyword `this` is a synonym for "the object itself."

❦ You have learned two kinds of statements so far: declarations and `void` method calls (technically, `import` is classed as a declaration).

2.6 EXERCISES

1. In terms of the number of characters (counting spaces and carriage returns, too) what is the smallest possible Java applet? It needn't do anything, but it should compile correctly.

2. Which of the following are legal choices for the name of a variable of your own? For those that aren't syntactically correct (i.e., those that would cause problems during compilation), explain briefly what's wrong with them.
   a. `FOO`
   b. `version1.1`
   c. `two`
   d. `2`
   e. `Supercalifragilisticexpialidocious`
   f. `O.K.`
   g. `_temp1`
   h. `applet`
   i. `w_i_e_r_d_n_e_s_s`

3. Since comments are ignored in Java, is the following a legal declaration? Explain why or why not. Note that we've moved the semicolon.

   ```
   int x = 3 // 0, 1, and 2 are disallowed;
   ```

4. Each of these variable declarations is fatally flawed. Explain what's wrong with each one.
   a. `x = 21;`
   b. `Color c = Color.blue;`
   c. `int x`
   d. `Dimension = new Dimension(200, 100);`
   e. `Point origin = new Point(200);`
   f. `Font titleFont = Font("Dialog", Font.BOLD, 24);`
   g. `int x = new int(145);`
   h. `rectangle r = new rectangle(5, 10);`

5. In some applet method, could you make the following method call?

   ```
   this.drawRect(29, 37, 113, 84);
   ```

   Explain why or why not.

6. (You'll have to do some digging for this one.) Can an applet make the call `add()`? Why or why not?

7. What classes lie between `Object` and `Applet` in the inheritance hierarchy?

8. Describe what would be displayed if the `Graphics` object `artist` was used to make the following calls. You may assume that `artist` would be capable of drawing on the screen.
    a. This sequence:

    ```
    artist.setColor(Color.red);
    artist.drawOval(20, 30, 40, 50);
    artist.setColor(Color. black);
    artist.fillRect(20, 20, 100, 70);
    ```

    b. This sequence:

    ```
    artist.drawOval(20, 30, 150, 60);
    artist.setFont(new Font("Helvetica", Font.PLAIN, 9));
    artist.drawString("Cool!", 35, 55);
    ```

9. The following applet is a complete mess. Identify all the errors you can. Don't concern yourself with stylistic problems—just pick out and explain the potential compiler errors. Depending on how you count, there are at least a dozen errors here.

    ```
    /*******************************************
          My First Applet--I'm sooo proud!
     *******************************************
    import Java.applet;

    public class MyFirstApplet
    {
          this.resize();
          private void panit(graphics theGraphics);
          {
                theGraphics.drawstring('Hi, dummy!', 20)
    }
    ```

10. Come up with a strategy that would make Exercise 9 a fairly easy problem.

11. Java is a *free-form* language: Like C and C++, it ignores spaces, tabs, and carriage returns, except where necessary to separate linguistic elements. This means we have a considerable amount of flexibility in the way we lay out our programs. Comment on the readability of the following conventions for program layout, some of which are used in actual practice.
    a. The layout we use in this book, with braces tab-aligned on separate lines and interior elements one tab to the right of the enclosing braces.

```
public class Hello extends Applet
{
    public void paint(Graphics g)
    {
        g.drawString("Hi!", 20, 10);
    }
}
```

b. A layout like (a), but with opening braces on the line above.

```
public class Hello extends Applet {
    public void paint(Graphics g) {
        g.drawString("Hi!", 20, 10);
    }
}
```

c. An extension of (b), with the closing braces also moved up.

```
public class Hello extends Applet {
    public void paint(Graphics g) {
        g.drawString("Hi!", 20, 10); } }
```

d. Like (a), but with a broken Tab key.

```
public class Hello extends Applet
{
public void paint(Graphics g)
{
g.drawString("Hi!", 20, 10);
}
}
```

e. Java is enough like C and C++ that they share many stylistic conventions. Look at several C or C++ texts for a different style and comment on it. Another good source is the Net—crank up your browser and go looking for Java sources to critique.

12. There's a difference between the way we must make method calls. Some method calls need the name of an object in front of the method name, like `g.setColor(Color.lightGray)` or `resize(250, 300)`, where the object (`this`) is implicit. Other calls, though, require the name of a class, as we showed in the Lablet when we called `System.getProperties()`. This is because methods can either be *instance methods,* belonging to each object in a class, or *class methods,* which belong to the class rather than to its objects. We'll explore this difference in detail later; for now, see if you can find examples of a similar distinction among class-level (nonlocal) variables.

13.   Give a sequence of statements that would draw a yellow "smiley face."

14.   Modify the Logo applet we wrote in Section 2.3 so that it draws one of the following images. Pick your favorite colors.

a.    **b.**

15.   What are the RGB values of bright yellow? Hint: If you're not a professional colorist, you might want to write a tiny applet that draws a filled rectangle in colors you choose.

16.   What color has RGB values 40, 80, 160?

17.   Given a `Rectangle` object `r`, how would you compute the coordinates of its lower right corner?

18.   There's a lot going on behind the scenes in the `Rectangle` class. Provide complete descriptions of what the following methods have to do to perform their tasks. For example, in part (a), a portion of the answer is "if `p.x` is greater than `x + width`, then set `width` to `p.x - x`."
   a.   `add(Point p)`
   b.   `intersection(Rectangle r)`

If you need to, you can define your own methods, rather than just overriding some existing method. Exercises 19–24 form a multipart exploration to get you to the stage where you can do just that.

19.   Suppose you had been given a `Graphics` object, `g` (as you would if you were in a `paint()` method, for example). Show the calls to `g`'s methods you would use to draw a shaded ball like the one shown.

20.   In Exercise 19, did you use any "magic numbers?" How about for the radius or center? Rewrite those calls, assuming that you had local `int` variables `x` and `y`

for the coordinates of the center and `size` for the radius of the outer ball. You should have code that looks like

```
int x = 20;
int y = 40;
int size = 15;
// ... Some code follows that uses g, x, y, and size
// to draw the ball.
```

21. If you haven't tried it yet, put your code in the `paint()` method of an applet and see whether it draws as it should.

22. Now comes the fun part. In your applet, define a new method with signature

```
void drawBall(Graphics g, int x, int y, int size)
```

that would, when called, draw a ball of radius `size`, centered at (x, y), using the `Graphics` object g to do the necessary drawing. Basically, all you have to do is pull out the code you had in part (c) from the `paint()` method and place it in your `drawBall()` method. You won't need the declarations of x, y, and size, of course, since they are formal arguments in your new method, so they're already declared.

23. Try it. Make your `paint()` method look like the following and run the applet.

```
void paint(Graphics g)
{
      drawBall(g, 20, 40, 15);
}
```

24. That was a lot of work, and hardly worth it. Or so it seems. Modify your applet to draw ten balls at various locations and sizes. Comment on what the `paint()` method would look like if you hadn't made a helper method.

CHAPTER THREE

Widgets

Modern graphical user interfaces (GUIs) are built from an increasingly common set of parts, like buttons for user response, regions for displaying and entering text, drop-down menus, and so on. These parts are called *widgets* in computerspeak. The `java.awt` package (AWT stands for "Abstract Window Toolkit") provides a platform-independent collection of classes that implement a wide variety of widgets. Using the AWT classes, you can design a useful and visually effective program without having to worry about the low-level details associated with graphic objects. A menu in a Java program, for example, will look like a Windows menu on a PC running Windows, a Mac menu on a Macintosh, and a Motif menu on a Unix machine—all with the same code.

OBJECTIVES

In this chapter, we will
- ❦ Continue our discussion of the `Component` class that is the parent class for all the Java widget classes.
- ❦ Investigate the look and actions of the most important `Component` subclasses, like `Label`, `TextField`, `TextArea`, `Button`, `Checkbox`, and `Choice`, to name just a few.
- ❦ Begin an exploration of GUI programming, which we'll continue over the next four chapters.

3.1   COMPONENTS

The `Component` class is unquestionably the most important class in the `java.awt` package. With 129 methods, it is also by far the largest. `Component` is the superclass of all the widget classes, with the exception of menus, and serves as the repository of all the methods that are common to the widgets. We'll talk about some of these methods, especially the ones dealing with the way components look on the screen, in this chapter, and we'll return to `Component` in Chapter 6 when we talk about making our widgets take action in response to user input.

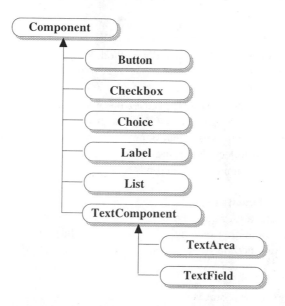

Figure 3.1 A portion of the class hierarchy derived from `Component`.

For all its importance, you'll never see a direct instance of a `Component` object in a Java program. That's because `Component` is an *abstract class,* meaning that it is intended as a repository of methods and data and can never be *instantiated* into an object. The notion of an abstract class arises quite naturally when we take an object-oriented view of the world. It's reasonable to think of a class `Car`, for instance, since cars all have features like engines and seats in common, along with common behaviors like accelerating, braking, and turning left. In the real world, though, you'll never see a generic `Car` object—instead, you'll see instances of `Car` subclasses, like the Universal Motors Belchfire 5000.

`Component`'s Graphical Methods

We have no intention of dumping all the `Component` methods on you at once, but there's a fairly long list we have to discuss. This is due in part to the current multiplicity of differently named methods that do the same thing, thanks to the transition between versions 1.0 and 1.1 of Java. At any rate, after some practice, you'll come to learn the most useful methods and will use them more or less automatically, often not even thinking about the class to which they belong. After having built a few applets, for example, you'll get used to putting in an override of the `paint()` method and won't need to think much about the fact that `paint()` is in truth a method that belongs to a class several levels up the hierarchy from

`Applet`. About the only time you need to worry about the hierarchy is when you need a method that you think *should* belong to a class and can't find it in the class documentation. If it should be there, but isn't, there's a good chance that it belongs to some superclass.

When in doubt about where to find a method, look it up (in the class hierarchy).

Let's get the constructor out of the way first. In version 1.0, `Component` doesn't even have a constructor.[1] The list that follows includes those `Component` methods having to do with what appears on the screen, like the position, size, and visibility of an object. Here and in the chapters that follow, we use ❦ to mark important or commonly used methods.

Rectangle **bounds**()   `// may vanish`
Returns a `Rectangle` object that describes the *bounding rectangle* of this object. The bounding rectangle will be at least large enough to contain the entire object. This method will probably be replaced by the version 1.1 method, `getBounds()`.

Color **getBackground**()
Returns the `Color` object used for the background color of this `Component`. This is a companion method to `getForeground()`. A `Label` object, for example, appears as a line of text in the foreground color, painted over a rectangle of the background color.

Rectangle **getBounds**()   `// version 1.1 only`
Does exactly the same thing as the version 1.0 method `bounds()`.

Font **getFont**()
Returns the `Font` object that is currently being used by this `Component`. You can use `setFont()` to change the font.

Color **getForeground**()
Returns the `Color` used for the foreground of this `Component`. As with many of the "get-" methods (known as *accessors*), there's a corresponding "set–" method (a *mutator*), `setForeground()`, that can be used to change the foreground color.

❦   Graphics **getGraphics**()
This useful method returns the `Graphics` object that is associated with this `Component`. Using this method, you can retrieve the `Graphics` object and use it for drawing on the component.

---

[1]There's one in version 1.1, but its use is beyond the scope of this book.

Point **getlocation**()   // version 1.1 only
     Returns the *anchor point* of this Component, namely the upper left corner
of the bounding rectangle. It replaces the version 1.0 method location().

Dimension **getMinimumSize**()   // version 1.1 only
Dimension **getMaximumSize**()   // version 1.1 only
Dimension **getPreferredSize**()   // version 1.1 only
     Each Component has a collection of three sizes that are determined in part
by the needs of the system environment. When laying out a Component object on
the screen, the system will try to use the object's preferred size, but will never make
the object smaller than the minimum, nor larger than the maximum, size.
These methods replace the version 1.0 methods minimumSize() and
preferredSize(); there is no 1.0 equivalent for getMaximumSize(). We'll
have much more to say about laying out components in Chapter 4.

Dimension **getSize**()   // version 1.1 only
     Returns the current width and height of this Component. This method
replaces the version 1.0 method size().

void **hide**()   // may vanish
     Makes this Component invisible. Replaced in version 1.1 by the method
setVisible(false). This is the companion method to show().

boolean **isShowing**()
boolean **isVisible**()
     On the one hand, isShowing() returns true if and only if this
Component can currently be seen on the screen. On the other hand,
isVisible() tests for the *property* of visibility. It is possible for a component
to be visible but not showing—this would happen, for instance, when a Button
object had been created but not yet painted or when a Component was in an
invisible Container (which we'll talk about in Chapter 4).

Point **location**()   // may vanish
     Returns the anchor point of this Component. In future releases, this method
may be replaced by the 1.1 version getLocation().

Dimension **minimumSize**()   // may vanish
     Returns the minimum size this Component can be. This method is replaced
in version 1.1 by getMinimumSize().

void **move**(int x, int y)   // may vanish
     Moves this Component so that its anchor is at the coordinates given by the
arguments. This method is replaced in version 1.1 by setLocation().

❦ void **paint**(Graphics g)
     You've seen this one. This method causes this Component to be painted,
using the Graphics object in the argument. In Component, this is an empty

method that does nothing. It is intended to be overridden in a subclass, as we did in our applets in Chapter 2. You cannot call this method—the system will call it when needed. You can, however, cause it to be called by calling `repaint()`.

Dimension **preferredSize**()   // may vanish

     Returns the preferred size of this `Component`. The version 1.1 equivalent of this method is `getPreferredSize()`; see the description of that method for details.

☽ void **repaint**()
void **repaint**(int x, int y, int width, int height)

     You'll use these methods a lot. They tell the system that this `Component` needs to be redrawn as soon as possible. The second version specifies a rectangular region within which redrawing should take place, for those instances when you don't need to redraw the entire `Component`.

     These methods instruct the system to schedule a call to `update()` on what we might call its "to do" list, along with things like responding to keyboard input and handling requests for access to the disk drive. You can't count on a call to `repaint()` to result in an immediate screen update—most times the update will happen quickly, but if you're doing something very time-sensitive like animation, you will have to employ some special techniques.

void **reshape**(int x, int y,
                int width, int height)   // may vanish

     Changes the size and location of this `Component`. This is the 1.0 version of the 1.1 method `setBounds()`.

☽ void **resize**(int x, int y)   // may vanish
void **resize**(Dimension d)   // may vanish

     Change the size of this `Component`, keeping the current anchor. These methods are replaced in version 1.1 by `setSize()`.

void **setBackground**(Color c)

     Sets the background color of this `Component`. This method is the companion to `getBackground()`.

void **setBounds**(int x, int y,
              int width, int height)   // version 1.1 only
void **setBounds**(Rectangle r)   // version 1.1 only

     Change the size and location of this `Component`. These methods will probably replace the 1.0 method `reshape()`.

void **setFont**(Font f)

     Sets the font of this Component to f.

void **setForeground**(Color c)

     Sets the foreground color of this `Component`. This method is a companion to `getForeground()`.

```
void setLocation(int x, int y)        // version 1.1 only
void setLocation(Point p)             // version 1.1 only
```
Move this Component so that its anchor is at the coordinates given by the arguments. These methods are intended to replace the version 1.0 move() method.

```
void setSize(int w, int h)            // version 1.1 only
void setSize(Dimension d)             // version 1.1 only
```
Change the size of this Component, keeping the current anchor. These methods may eventually replace resize().

```
void setVisible(boolean isVisible)      // version 1.1 only
```
If the argument is true, makes this Component visible on the screen, otherwise makes it invisible. For more details, see the preceding discussion of isVisible().

```
void show()                             // may vanish
```
Makes this Component visible. In version 1.1 we can do the same thing by calling setVisible(true).

```
Dimension size()                        // may vanish
```
Returns the height and width of this Component. This method may eventually be replaced by getSize().

```
☙ void update(Graphic g)
```
Like paint(), you can't call this method. It is called by the system when the screen needs to be redrawn. If you don't override it, this method will erase this Component (by painting over it in the background color) and then call the Component's paint() method. The erase–redraw combination may cause an annoying flicker unless you override this method.

3.2   TEXTUAL WIDGETS

There are three widgets that you can use to deal with the display of text: Label, TextField, and TextArea. Along with these three, there's one more or less abstract one, TextComponent, that contains many of the methods common to TextField and TextArea. All are Components by inheritance, so they have access to the Component methods, as well as to their own.

The `Label` Class

This is a simple class. A `Label` is a `Component` that displays a line of text on the screen. The text can't be altered by the user once it has been painted, though it can be modified by the program during execution.

The `Label` class has three constructors.

`Label``()`

Creates a `Label` object with center alignment and no text.

`Label``(String label)`

Creates a center-aligned `Label` object displaying the `label` text given in the argument.

`Label``(String label, int alignment)`

As does the preceding constructor, this method creates a `Label` with the given text. In addition, the alignment of the text is specified by using one of the three class constants `Label.LEFT`, `Label.CENTER`, or `Label.RIGHT`. For example, if you wanted to construct a `Label` with the text "Future value" aligned to the right, you could use the declaration

```
Label fvLabel = new Label("Future value", Label.RIGHT);
```

There are four `Label` methods (out of a total of six) that are of interest to us here.

int **`getAlignment`**`()`

Returns an integer corresponding to the alignment of this `Label`. This integer could then be compared to one of the three class constants to determine the current alignment of this object, for example.

String **`getText`**`()`

Returns a `String` object whose value is the same as that of this `Label`'s text.

void **`setAlignment`**`(int alignment)`

Sets the alignment of this `Label` to the one given by the argument. For example, `myLabel.setAlignment(Label.LEFT)` would align the text of `myLabel` to the left edge.

void **`setText`**`(String label)`

Sets the text of this label to the `label` string given in the argument.

The `TextComponent` Class

Since `TextFields` and `TextAreas` are so similar in their purposes, the data and methods common to both were "factored out" and placed in the `TextComponent` class, and both `TextField` and `TextArea` were then defined to be subclasses of `TextComponent`. This is a class that does its work behind the scenes; it has no constructors, so you can't initialize a `TextComponent` object, even if for some bizarre reason you'd ever want to use one in a program.

This class, however, does contain quite a few useful methods that are inherited by both `TextField` and `TextArea` objects.

int **getCaretPosition**()   // version 1.1 only
    Returns the position, measured in number of characters, of the text cursor (that thing that might be a vertical bar, blinking bar, "I-beam," or whatever else the system uses for editing text).

Java prefers to count from 0.[2] In all `TextComponent` and `TextArea` methods that measure positions of characters, the first (or leftmost) character is always in position 0.

String **getSelectedText**()
    Returns a copy of the part of the text that has been selected. Such text is often highlighted on many systems—think of the way your favorite word processor works, for instance.

int **getSelectionEnd**()
int **getSelectionStart**()
    These two methods return the position, in characters, of the end and start, respectively, of the selected text.

☙ String **getText**()
    As does the method of the same name in `Label`, this method returns a copy of the current contents of the component.

boolean **isEditable**()
    Returns `true` if the user can modify the text and `false` otherwise.

void **select**(int start, int end)
    Selects all characters in the text, from position `start` to position `end`, highlighting the selected area in whatever way is appropriate for the system in which it is running.

---

[2]This "start counting from 0" convention is common to many programming languages, new and old. It seems odd at first, but you get used to it eventually.

`void` **`selectAll`**`()`
> Selects and highlights all characters in the text.

`void` **`setCursor`**`(int position)`   `// version 1.1 only`
> Moves the cursor to the indicated position in the text. The position argument must be greater than or equal to 0.

`void` **`setEditable`**`(boolean canEdit)`
> If the argument is `true`, the user can modify the text; if it is `false`, the user can't edit the text.

`void` **`setSelectionEnd`**`(int position)`   `// version 1.1 only`
`void` **`setSelectionStart`**`(int position)`   `// version 1.1 only`
> These methods allow the program to set the end and start of the selected portion of the text.

☙ `void` **`setText`**`(String text)`
> Sets the current text to be that given by the argument.

The `TextField` Class

A `TextField` object looks like a box into which you can place a single line of text. You can change the text in the field (by clicking and typing) or by the program (using the following methods). Here's a sample of what a `TextField` object might look like on the screen.

This is a very common and useful class. It is used in many instances where a small amount of text is needed for input or output.

The `TextField` class has four constructors.

`TextField``()`
> Creates a `TextField` object with empty text (that is, containing no characters) and a default width determined by the system.

`TextField``(int columns)`
> Creates a `TextField` with empty text, wide enough to hold `columns` characters.

TextField(String text)
   Creates a `TextField` object with content given by the argument string.

TextField(String text, int columns)
   Creates a `TextField` object with content and width given by the arguments.

   Along with the methods `TextField` inherits from `TextComponent` and other classes above it in the class hierarchy (like `Component`), this class has the following methods, among others.

boolean **echoCharIsSet**()
   Returns `true` if this `TextField` has an *echo character* and returns `false` otherwise. An echo character is one that will appear in place of what you type. If you've ever been asked to provide a program with a password, you'll understand what we mean. For example, if the echo character had been set to '*' and you typed in "booGeymAn," the text "*********" would appear in the field.

int **getColumns**()
   Returns the current width, in columns, of this `TextField`.

char **getEchoChar**()
   Returns the current echo character, if any has been set. See the discussion under `echoCharIsSet()` for details.

Dimension **getMinimumSize**()   // version 1.1 only
Dimension **getPreferredSize**()   // version 1.1 only
   These methods return a `Dimension` object with width and height set to the minimum or preferred size, respectively of this `TextField`. They are overrides of the `Component` methods of the same name. See the `Component` method list in Section 3.1 for details on minimum and preferred sizes.

Dimension **minimumSize**()   // may vanish
Dimension **preferredSize**()   // may vanish
   These methods are "deprecated" versions of `getMinimumSize()` and `getPreferredSize()`. They are supported in Java versions 1.0 and 1.1, but they may not exist in future releases.

int **setColumns**(int columns)   // version 1.1 only
   Sets the width of this `TextField` to be enough to hold `columns` characters. The argument must be greater than or equal to 0.

void **setEchoChar**(char c)
   Sets the current echo character to that provided in the argument. See the discussion under `echoCharIsSet()` for details.

The `TextArea` Class

If you need more than a single line of text for input or output, you can use a
`TextArea` object. As is the case with all Java widgets, you can be sure about how
a `TextArea` object will work, but you can't guarantee precisely what it will look
like. Here's an example from one environment.

There are four `TextArea` constructors available in versions 1.0 and 1.1 of
Java, and one that's only in version 1.1.

TextArea()
Creates a `TextArea` of default size, with empty text (i.e., no characters).

TextArea(int rows, int columns)
Creates a `TextArea` with empty text, with room for `rows` rows of text,
each of which has room for `columns` characters.

TextArea(String text)
Creates a default-sized `TextArea`, containing the argument string.

TextArea(String text, int rows, int columns)
Creates a `TextArea` containing the argument string, of size specified by the
`rows` and `columns` arguments.

TextArea(String text, int rows,
          int columns, int scrollbars)   // version 1.1 only
Acts just like the preceding constructor, but in addition it allows the program
to specify whether the `TextArea` will have horizontal and/or vertical scrollbars.
The class constants that can be used as arguments are pretty much self-explanatory:

```
TextArea.SCROLLBARS_BOTH
TextArea.SCROLLBARS_NONE
TextArea.SCROLLBARS_HORIZONTAL_ONLY
TextArea.SCROLLBARS_VERTICAL_ONLY
```

The `TextArea` methods are, as you might expect, somewhat similar to those in `TextField`, though they're more heavily oriented to editing here than in `TextField`.

```
void append(String str)              // version 1.1 only
void appendText(String str)          // may vanish
```
These two methods do the same thing—change the text of this object by appending the characters in the argument to the end of the current text. This is the `TextArea` version of string concatenation. For example, if the `TextArea` object `myDisplay` contained the text "In", the call

```
myDisplay.appendText("credible!");
```

would make the current text in `myDisplay` "incredible!" (without the quotes, of course).

```
int getColumns()
```
Returns the current width, in columns, of this `TextArea`.

```
Dimension getMinimumSize()           // version 1.1 only
Dimension getPreferredSize()         // version 1.1 only
```
These methods return a `Dimension` object with width and height set to that of the minimum or preferred size, respectively, of this `TextArea`. They are overrides of the `Component` methods of the same names. See the `Component` method list in Section 3.1 for details on minimum and preferred sizes.

```
int getRows()
```
Returns the current height, in rows, of this `TextArea`.

```
int getScrollbarVisibility()         // version 1.1 only
```
Returns one of the four class constants, indicating which of the scrollbars are visible.

```
void insert(String str, int position)    // version 1.1 only
void insertText(String str, int position)   // may vanish
```
These two methods do the same thing—insert the argument string into the current text, at the location given by the position argument. The text is shifted to make room for the new characters. For example, if the `TextArea` `myDisplay` originally contained "mud," after the call

```
myDisplay.insertText("star", 2);
```

`myDisplay` would contain the text "mustard." As in all the `TextComponent` methods, positions are counted from the left, beginning with 0. Thus a `position` argument of 0 will result in the argument string being concatenated to the front of the current text. If the position argument is greater than the number of characters in the current text, the additional text will be appended to the immediate right.

```
Dimension minimumSize()                    // may vanish
Dimension preferredSize()                   // may vanish
```
These methods do the same things as getMinimumSize() and getPreferredSize(). Supported in versions 1.0 and 1.1, both may not be part of later releases of Java.

```
void replaceRange(String str,
                  int start, int end) // version 1.1 only
void replaceText(String str,
                 int start int end)   // may vanish
```
These methods do the same thing—they replace the current text between positions start (included in the replacement) and end (*not* included) with the argument string. For example, if the TextArea myDisplay originally contained "abcdefghi," after the call

```
myDisplay.replaceText("**", 2, 6);
```

myDisplay would contain the text "ab**ghi." You can use this to delete a range of the current text, by using as argument the *empty string,* "". There are certain conditions on the arguments you should try to satisfy: $0 \leq$ start $\leq$ end $\leq$ *length of current text.* If you violate any of them, you may get strange results in some Java environments.

```
void setColumns(int columns)               // version 1.1 only
```
Changes the number of columns in this TextArea. There is no companion method to set the number of rows.

Widget Musings

Here's an applet that includes some of the features we've discussed in this section.

```
import   java.awt.*;
import   java.applet.*;

public  class  WidgetSample  extends  Applet
{
    // Declare  and  initialize  a  pair  of  text  widgets.
    TextArea  myArea  =  new  TextArea(4,  12);
    TextField  myField  =  new  TextField(15);
```

```
public void init()
{
      // Put some text into the TextArea.
      myArea.appendText("Here's some text, just for practice.");
      myArea.appendText("Here's some more text.");
      // Select the text from position 18
      // up to (but not including) 35.
      myArea.select(18, 35);
      // Declare a string for moving text from the TextArea to
      // the TextField and initialize it to the selected text.
      String transferText = myArea.getSelectedText();
      // Use the string to set the text in the TextField
      myField.setText(transferText);

      // Add the area and the field to this applet.
      add(myArea);
      add(myField);
}
}
```

Let's take a close look at it and see what we can learn. First, we see that the structure is simple and familiar—the class definition begins with the declaration of two new instance variables, `myArea` and `myField`, and includes an override of the Applet method `init()`.

_____

Programming Tip:

When reading a program, concentrate first on the Big Picture and put the details aside for later. This is excellent advice for writing programs, too—get the structure right before you start filling in code.

_____

Looking at the body of `init()`, we see that it begins by using two calls to `appendText()` to put some text into `myArea`. Next, we see a call to `select()`. The documentation reminds us that `select(18, 35)` will select the text in positions 18 .. 34. Recalling that character positions in `TextArea`s and `TextField`s begin at 0, we count characters in `myArea` and see that the selected text should be "just for practice". Now that we know what to expect, we run the applet.

Programming Tip:

Running a program just to spot potential compile errors is a very useful technique. Even better is to predict what the program should do before you run it. A common source of error is caused by having the wrong mental model of what a language feature does.

When we were writing this, we ran the applet as listed and nothing appeared in the applet runner window until we manually resized the window. We were used to the problem, having encountered it countless times in the past. The code was correct; the fault was with the applet runner. We tried the same code in two other environments and it ran perfectly.

Java Programming Tip:

Java is a new language and the programming tools aren't entirely bulletproof yet. If you run a program and it doesn't work as expected, the odds are that you've made a mistake. However, there is also a slim chance that the error resides in the Java environment itself. You can test this possibility by running your program in a different environment or on a different computer.

The next statements,

```
String transferText = myArea.getSelectedText();
myField.setText(transferText);
```

are supposed to transfer a copy of the selected text from `myArea` into `myField`. It seems straightforward enough at first—use `getSelectedText()` to return a `String` containing the text and then use `setText()` to put the text into `myField`. We declare a local `String` variable to hold the text, but where's the new operator we're used to?

It's not there because we don't need it. A new `String` is being constructed, but it is constructed by `getSelectedText()`, so we don't have to do anything but use the returned string to initialize `transferText`. We could have done the same thing, by omitting any explicit mention of the `String` being used for the transfer, combining the two statements into one:

```
myField.setText(myArea.getSelectedText());
```

In declaring a class-type variable (as opposed to a nonclass type, like `int` or `boolean`), you can make the right-hand side a method call, a variable, or a constructor call. If you use a method call or variable on the right, don't use the `new` operator; if you use a constructor, `new` is required.

   In either case, of course, the type returned by the expression on the right must match the type declared on the left.[3]

   There are still one or two things about this applet (like that `add()` method call) that need to be explained, but we don't want to spoil the surprises we have in store for you in Section 3.4.

3.3   ACTIVE WIDGETS

As useful as `Textfields` and `TextAreas` are, a program almost always needs to do more than serve as a repository of text. In particular, one of the consequences of modern GUI design is that a program typically spends most of its time sitting around waiting for you to communicate your intent. Think of your favorite application and you'll see what we mean: In many cases, nothing apparently happens until you click a button or pull down a menu and make a choice. Once you do, the program then recognizes that you've done something and takes appropriate action. In Chapter 6 we'll talk in detail about how a Java program recognizes and responds to a user-generated event, but we can start by describing the `Components` that are provided for user interaction.

   The "active widgets" classes include `Button`, `Checkbox`, `Choice`, and `List`.[4] As with the text widgets, all are subclasses of `Component`, so they all have access to the `Component` methods to change their size, position, color, visibility, and so on.

The `Button` Class

This class is designed solely to give you a place to click (and, as we'll see in Chapter 6, provide the program with a way to recognize that a mouse click has occurred on the button). A `Button` object can have an optional label string and, since it is a `Component`, it will have a size, location, font, foreground and background colors, and an appearance on the screen.[5] As with the other widgets,

---

[3]There are some subtleties at work here that we'll explain in Chapter 5.

[4]We left out only the `Dialog`, `Menu`, and `Scrollbar` classes. We'll discuss `Dialog` and `Menu` in Chapter 4 and Scrollbar in Chapter 6.

[5]Actually, a `Button` object will in all likelihood have two appearances on the screen, its normal appearance and the highlighted look it takes when it is clicked.

the appearance of a Button object will depend on the system in which its program is running. Here are two examples, taken from screen shots of the Lablet for this chapter, running in two different environments.

There are just two constructors for Buttons, which let you specify a label string or not.

Button()
Button(String label)

The Button class has four methods in version 1.0 and six more in version 1.1. In both versions, there are only two that are of interest to us at present.

String **getLabel**()
void **setLabel**(String label)

These methods are a now-familiar get/set pair. The former method returns a copy of the label text, and the latter allows you to change the label text. setLabel() is often used for *toggle buttons.* A toggle button can be in two or more states and changes its state each time it is clicked. A START/STOP button is a good example—the first time it is clicked it sends a message to the program to start something and on the next click sends a message to stop something. We could provide visual feedback to the user by altering the label text on each click between the strings "On" and "Off."

Design Tip:

Keep the user informed about what your program is doing and what state it's in. Users get very grumpy when a program surprises or confuses them.

The Checkbox Class

A Checkbox object is a specific kind of toggle button with visual feedback. It has a boolean member datum indicating its state and, like a Button, has an optional text label. The object has a different look, depending on whether its state is true or false. The following illustrations are typical of the look of a CheckBox object. The one on the left is in a true state and the one on the right is in a false state.

☒ Super Size?   ☐ Super Size?

There are three version 1.0 Checkbox constructors and version 1.1 includes two more.

Checkbox()
This *default constructor* (that is, a constructor with no arguments) creates a Checkbox with no label and false state.

Checkbox(String label)
Constructs a Checkbox with the given label and an initial false state.

Checkbox(String label, boolean state)   // version 1.1 only
Constructs a Checkbox with the specified label and state.

Checkbox(String label, boolean state,
        CheckboxGroup group)   // version 1.1 only
Checkbox(String label, CheckboxGroup group,
        boolean state)
For some reason, the version 1.1 design crew decided to provide another constructor that differs from the original one only in the order of its arguments. Go figure. At any rate, both of these set the label and state, and in addition specify the group of Checkboxes to which this one will belong. We'll talk about the class CheckboxGroup in a moment.

There are six Checkbox methods we'll discuss now.

CheckboxGroup **getCheckboxGroup**()
Returns the CheckboxGroup, if any, to which this Checkbox belongs. Patience! We'll get to CheckboxGroup very soon.

String **getLabel**()
Paired with setLabel(), returns a string containing the label text of this Checkbox.

☙ boolean **getState**()
Returns the current state (true or false) of this Checkbox.

void **setCheckboxGroup**(CheckboxGroup group)
Sets the CheckboxGroup to which this object belongs.

void **setLabel**(String label)
Sets the label of this Checkbox.

```
void setState(boolean state)
```
Sets the state of this Checkbox.

CheckboxGroupS

You may have seen electronic devices with a row of buttons, only one of which can be down at any time; pushing one down will cause any other that is down to pop up. That's just what a CheckboxGroup is: a collection of Checkboxes, only one of which in in a true state at any time. These are often called "radio buttons" (since many old radios had such buttons for station selection), and they usually have a distinguishing look, like the following.

This class is *not* a subclass of Component. It's a subclass of the top level class, Object. CheckboxGroup has no visual appearance; all it does is provide a way to collect Checkboxes into a related group. You can have as many CheckboxGroups in a program as you wish.

There is a single default constructor for this class,

CheckboxGroup()

and two sets of paired get/set methods,

```
Checkbox getCurrent()                    // may vanish
void setCurrent(Checkbox c)              // may vanish
```
The getCurrent() method returns the Checkbox in this group, if any, which is in the true state. The setCurrent() method has the same effect as if the user had clicked on the Checkbox in the argument—it sets the state of c to true and turns off any other true Checkbox in this group.

```
Checkbox getSelectedCheckbox()           // version 1.1 only
void setSelectedCheckbox(Checkbox c)     // version 1.1 only
```
These methods are just the 1.1 versions of getCurrent() and setCurrent().

Just for fun, here's an applet you can try. We'll explain the add() method in the next section.

```
import java.awt.*;
```

```
import java.applet.*;

public class RadioButtonTest extends Applet
{
    Checkbox fee = new Checkbox("fee");
    Checkbox fie = new Checkbox("fie");
    Checkbox foe = new Checkbox("foe");
    CheckboxGroup giant = new CheckboxGroup();

    public void init()
    {
        fee.setCheckboxGroup(giant);
        fie.setCheckboxGroup(giant);
        foe.setCheckboxGroup(giant);
        // The add() method of Container adds a Component to
        // the Container. In this case, the three Checkboxes
        // will appear when the applet does.
        add(fee);
        add(fie);
        add(foe);
    }
}
```

The Choice Class

When a Choice object is quiescent, it looks like this:

When you click on it and hold down the mouse button, a list of items drops down, from which you can make a selection. Here are two samples.

The items in the list highlight as the pointer moves over them and when the mouse button is released, the label changes to the text of the selection. A Choice object has methods that allow you to add new items, determine the number of items and the currently selected item, and inspect the label of the item in a given position.

The Choice class has one constructor,

```
Choice()
```

and quite a few methods you can use, some of which we list here.

❦ void **add**(String item)   // version 1.1 only
❦ void **addItem**(String item)   // may vanish
     Add a new item with the given label to the list of this `Choice` object. Items are added to the list from top down; in version 1.0 of Java there is no easy way to add an item to the interior of the list.

int **countItems**()   // may vanish
int **getItemCount**()   // version 1.1 only
     Return the number of items currently in this `Choice` object.

String **getItem**(int index)
     Returns the text of the item in position `index` in the list. As expected, positions are enumerated top-to-bottom, starting at 0. The `index` argument must be in the range 0 .. *itemCount* − 1.

int **getSelectedIndex**()
     Returns the index of the current selection.

❦ String **getSelectedItem**()
     Returns the text of the current selection.

void **insert**(String item, int index)   // version 1.1 only
void **remove**(int index)   // version 1.1 only
     The first of these methods inserts a new item string in the list in the given position, and the second removes the item at the given position. In both, the `index` argument must be valid, which is to say that for `insert()` you must have 0 ≤ index ≤ *itemCount* and for `remove()` you must have 0 ≤ index < *itemCount*.

void **removeAll**()   // version 1.1 only
     Removes all items from this `Choice`.

void **select**(int index)
void **select**(String item)
     Both methods can be used to change the currently selected item (and hence the text that appears in the object when the mouse is not clicked). In the first version, the item is selected by position (which must be from 0 to *itemCount* − 1) and in the second the selected item is the one, if any, that matches the string given in the argument.

The `List` Class

A `List` is somewhat like a permanently expanded `Choice`. A `List` object appears as a `TextArea` with a collection of items, one per line, like this:

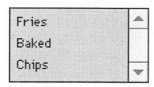 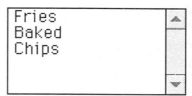

When you click the mouse on one of the lines, it becomes highlighted and serves as the current selection. A `List` object may behave in one of two ways: A click on the item may highlight it without influencing any already highlighted rows (*multiple-selection* mode) or a click on an item may turn off any currently highlighted rows (*single-selection* mode). As with `Choice`, the items are enumerated from top down, with the topmost item having index 0.

There are three `List` constructors. All construct an initially empty `List` object (that is, one with no items).

List ()
    Creates a default-sized `List` object in single-selection mode.

List (int rows)   // version 1.1 only
    Creates a `List` object in single-selection mode, with a number of rows given by the argument.

List (int rows, boolean multipleSelections)
    Creates a `List` object with the specified number of rows. If the boolean argument is `true`, the `List` is in multiple-selection mode, and if the argument is `false`, the created `List` is in single-selection mode.

As you might expect, there's a strong similarity between the `List` methods and those of `Choice`. Unfortunately, you'll have to wait until we talk about arrays in Chapter 8 to see the methods specific to the multiple-selection mode.

```
❦ void add(String item)                // version 1.1 only
  void add(String item, int index)      // version 1.1 only
❦ void addItem(String item)            // may vanish
  void addItem(String item, int index)  // may vanish
```

All add a new item with the given label to this `List` object. If the index is not specified, the item is added to the bottom; otherwise the existing items at and after position `index` are shifted down one row to make room for the new item.

boolean **allowsMultipleSelections**()   // may vanish

Returns `true` if this `List` is in multiple-selection mode. Replaced by the version 1.1 isMultipleMode().

void **clear**()   // may vanish

Removes all items from this `List` object. Replaced by the version 1.1 removeAll().

int **countItems**()   // may vanish

Returns the number of items in this `List`. Replaced by the version 1.1 getItemCount().

void **delItem**(int index)   // may vanish

Removes the item at position `index`, shifting the elements below that position up one row to fill the "hole." In version 1.1, this is replaced by the two remove() methods.

void **delItems**(int start, int end)

Removes a range of items from this `List`. The removed items are those in the range `start .. end`, inclusive. For example, if the `List` object `myList` contained the items

        A
        B
        C
        D
        E

after the call `myList.delItems(2, 3)`, `myList` would contain

        A
        B
        E

(remember, positions are counted from 0).

void **deselect**(int index)

Turns off the selection of the item in position `index`.

String **getItem**(int index)

Returns the text of the item in position `index` in the `List`. The index argument must be in the range 0 .. *itemCount* – 1.

int **getItemCount**()   // version 1.1 only

Returns the number of items in this `List`.

```
Dimension getMinimumSize()              // version 1.1 only
Dimension getMinimumSize(int rows)      // version 1.1 only
Dimension getPreferredSize()            // version 1.1 only
Dimension getPreferredSize(int rows)    // version 1.1 only
```
These methods return a Dimension object with width and height set to that of the minimum or preferred size, respectively, of this List. These are overrides of the Component methods of the same name. See the Component method list in Section 3.1 for details on minimum and preferred sizes. The two methods with int arguments return the minimum or preferred size of a List object with the specified number of rows.

```
int getRows()
```
Returns the number of rows in this List object.

```
❦ int getSelectedIndex()
```
Returns the index of the current selection. This method returns −1 if no item is currently selected or if more than one item is selected.

```
int getVisibleIndex()
```
Returns the argument that was used in the last call to makeVisible() or −1 if no call to makeVisible() has been made previously. See the discussion of makeVisible() for details.

```
boolean isIndexSelected(int index)      // version 1.1 only
```
Returns true if the item in position index is selected; otherwise returns false. This method replaces isSelected().

```
boolean isMultiple Mode()               // version 1.1 only
```
Returns true if this List is in multiple-selection mode; otherwise returns false.

```
boolean isSelected(int index)           // may vanish
```
Returns true if the item in position index is selected; otherwise returns false. This method may eventually be replaced by isIndexSelected().

```
void makeVisible(int index)
```
A List object is displayed as a scrollable text area, since the number of items in the List may be larger than the number of rows displayed. This routine scrolls the List display so that the item in position index is visible.

```
Dimension minimumSize()                 // may vanish
Dimension minimumSize(int rows)         // may vanish
Dimension preferredSize()               // may vanish
Dimension preferredSize(int rows)       // may vanish
```
These methods are the 1.0 versions of the 1.1 "get..." methods. See the discussion under getMinimumSize() for details.

```
void remove(int index)                  // version 1.1 only
void remove(String item)                // version 1.1 only
```
These methods remove an item from the `List`. In the first, the item in position `index` is removed. The `index` argument must be valid, which is to say that you must have 0 ≤ index < *itemCount*. The second form searches for an item matching the `String` argument, and, if there is one, it is removed. These methods replace the 1.0 method `delItem()`.

```
void removeAll()                        // version 1.1 only
```
Removes all items from this `List`.

```
void replaceItem(String newItem, int index)
```
Replaces the item in position `index` with the text given by the argument `newItem`.

```
void select(int index)
```
Selects the item in position `index`.

```
void setMultipleMode(boolean m)         // version 1.1 only
void setMultipleSelections(boolean m)   // may vanish
```
Both methods turn the multiple-selection mode on if the argument is `true` and set the mode to single-selection if the argument is `false`.

3.4 HANDS ON

This chapter's Lablet lays out a screen for on-line ordering from a fast-food restaurant we've invented. It's not what you'd see from a professional site, but we've designed it to use all the widgets we've talked about in this chapter.[6]

As usual, we begin with a comment block and a collection of `import` declarations.

```
/* ****************************************************
            CHAPTER 3 LABLET: GIGOBITE

  A simple order form that illustrates the use of Java's
  built-in graphical widgets.

  **************************************************** */

import java.awt.*;
import java.applet.*;
```

---

[6]An example of professional food ordering is the Web site that Pizza Hut has set up. Start at `http://www.pizzahut.com/` and go to its demo area. It's not a Java-based site, but it's easy to see how you could design an applet to do what the Pizza Hut site does.

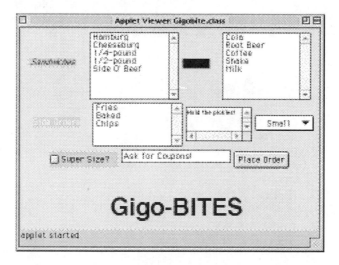

Figure 3.2 The appearance of the GigoBites applet.

We continue with the applet class definition, first declaring all the widget variables that we'll use.

```
public class Gigobite extends Applet
{
    // Declare all the widgets that make the applet's interface.
    Checkbox superSize = new Checkbox("Super Size?");

    TextField reminder = new TextField("Ask for Coupons!",18);

    List sandwiches =   new List(5,true);
    List drinks =       new List(5, true);
    List sides =        new List(3, false);

    Choice sizes = new Choice();

    TextArea comments = new TextArea("Hold the pickles!", 2, 10);

    Button order = new Button("Place Order");

    Label label1 = new Label("Sandwiches");
    Label label2 = new Label("Drinks");
    Label label3 = new Label("Side Orders");
    Label title = new Label("Gigo-BITES");

    Font myFont1 = new Font("Helvetica",Font.BOLD,36);
    Font myFont2 = new Font("Helvetica",Font.ITALIC,12);
```

Now we come to Applet's init() method. You can see from the declaration above that sandwiches is a List instance variable. In the first few lines we call its method `add()` to add five items to it. We then do the same thing to the other two `List` objects, `sides` and `drinks`.

```
public void init()
{
    // Build the sandwich list
    sandwiches.addItem("Hamburg");
    sandwiches.addItem("Cheeseburg");
    sandwiches.addItem("1/4-pound");
    sandwiches.addItem("1/2-pound");
    sandwiches.addItem("Side O' Beef");

    // Build the side order list
    sides.addItem("Fries");
    sides.addItem("Baked");
    sides.addItem("Chips");

    // Build the drinks list
    drinks.addItem("Cola");
    drinks.addItem("Root Beer");
    drinks.addItem("Coffee");
    drinks.addItem("Shake");
    drinks.addItem("Milk");
```

Next, we add some items to the `sizes` object, using the `Choice` method `addItem()`.

```
    // Build the size choices
    sizes.addItem("Small");
    sizes.addItem("Medium");
    sizes.addItem("Large");
```

We're just about finished with the setup. All we need to do now is a bit of miscellaneous tweaking, more to show that we can than for any real purpose. We resize the applet and set its background color, we call `sizes`' inherited `resize()` method (from `Component`, recall), and we set the fonts and colors of the four `Label`s, again using methods `Label` inherits from `Component`.

```
    // Set the applet's background color.
    resize(450,300);
    setBackground(Color.yellow);
    // Adjust the properties of individual widgets.
    sizes.resize(90,100);
    label1.setFont(myFont2);
    label2.setBackground(Color.blue);
    label3.setForeground(Color.white);
    title.setFont(myFont1);
    title.setForeground(Color.blue);
```

At this stage, we've initialized all twelve widgets and the applet itself. We could end the `init()` method here and run the applet. If we did, though, we wouldn't see any of the widgets we've spent so much time designing. They would be instance variables of our applet, but they would never appear, since we hadn't indicated that they should. To make them visible when the applet is drawn, we need to apply the method `add()`. This method, belonging to `Container`, associates a `Component` with the `Container` for graphical purposes.

In Chapter 4, we'll show that a `Container` object (which is what an applet is, by inheritance) can be used to group other `Components` together. We've demonstrated this sort of behavior already—a `CheckboxGroup` is a way of collecting logically related `Checkboxes` into a single entity. In the case of `Container`, we use `add()` to indicate that when the `Container` is drawn, the part added should also be drawn.

```
        // Add all of the widgets to our applet
        add(label1);
        add(sandwiches);
        add(label2);
        add(drinks);
        add(label3);
        add(sides);
        add(comments);
        add(sizes);
        add(superSize);
        add(reminder);
        add(order);
        add(title);
    }
}
```

The twelve `Component` widgets are added to our applet in the order they appear in the code—altering the order in which we add the widgets would produce a corresponding visual shuffling when the applet was finally drawn.

If you run the applet, it should look more or less like Figure 3.2 (page 91). We say "more or less" because the actual look will depend on how large the widgets are in the screen and how well they fit in the 450 by 300 pixel dimension we've set for our applet. Recall, in the discussion of the `Component` class we mentioned that the minimum and preferred sizes of a `Component` object were determined by the system. In our applet, we haven't specified how the widgets will be laid out on the screen; we really can't in this case, since we have no idea about how large they are.[7] We ran this applet on two different systems on the same computer, for instance, and found that in one system the `sides List` was 144×72 pixels, while on another it appeared as 108×54 pixels.

---

[7]We could, though, have used their `Component` methods `reshape()`, `resize()`, or `move()` to place them precisely where we wanted them. We'll show how to do this in Chapter 4.

In Chapter 4, we'll discuss the LayoutManager classes and show how you can have control over the way Components are placed on the screen. Since we haven't specified any layout here, the default is to "flow" the widgets within the applet frame, from left to right and top to bottom. If you run the applet in an applet viewer and manually resize the window, you'll see that the widget Components change their positions. In Figure 3.3, we show how the widgets might be arranged in two different applet frames. Note that in both cases the overall order is the one in which they were added, but the final result will depend on how they fit the applet.

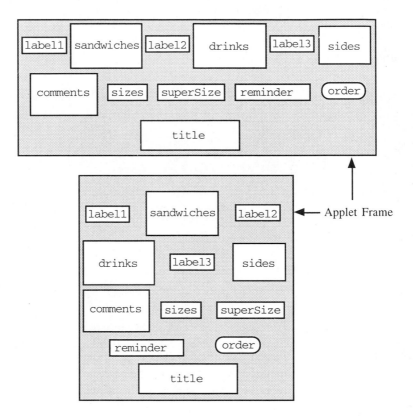

Figure 3.3 Same applet, different dimensions.

That's it—we're done with this applet. Almost. Do you notice anything peculiar about its structure? *There's no* paint() *method!* What's going on here?

You don't have to paint() widgets—the system will do it for you.

All of the `Components` in the AWT library "know" how to paint themselves. The only time you need to worry about painting `Components` is when you design a custom widget of your own. Since we weren't doing any `Graphics`-related drawing on the applet frame, we didn't need a `paint()` method here.

3.5 SUMMARY

❦ We discussed the following classes:
>   Button
>   Checkbox
>   CheckboxGroup
>   Choice
>   Component
>   Container (briefly)
>   Label
>   List
>   String (briefly)
>   TextArea
>   TextComponent
>   TextField

❦ Among other data, a `Component` object has information about its bounding rectangle, foreground and background colors, font, and its minimum and preferred sizes, along with methods for inspecting and modifying most of these features.

❦ `Component` is a superclass of `Button`, `Checkbox` (but not `Checkbox-Group`), `Choice`, `Label`, `List`, `TextArea`, `TextComponent`, and `TextField`. These subclasses have access to all the methods we've mentioned in the discussion of `Component`.

❦ `Component` is an abstract class, meaning that it is impossible to declare and initialize a `Component` object. It is, of course, perfectly legal to declare and construct any of the `Component` subclasses we've mentioned.

❦ A `Button` is designed to respond to mouse clicks.

❦ A `Checkbox` is a two-state `Button` with a particular look. A `Checkbox` has an internal state (`true` or `false`), which is mirrored by its visual appearance.

❦ Checkboxes can be grouped into "radio buttons" by making them part of a `CheckboxGroup`. At most one `Checkbox` in a group can be in the `true` state at any time.

❦ A `Choice` object is a drop-down menu, used for selecting one of a list of items.

❦ A `List` generally looks like a `TextArea`, containing a collection of items, one per row. You can select one or more items from the list by clicking on them. A `List` can be in one of two modes: single-selection, in which at most one item can be selected at a time, and multiple-selection, in which several items can be selected (and hence highlighted).

- ❦ `TextComponent` is the superclass of `TextArea` and `TextField`. You cannot construct a `TextComponent`—like `Component`, the `TextComponent` class is designed to serve as a repository of methods to be used by its subclasses.

- ❦ A `TextField` is a holder for an (optionally) editable single line of text.

- ❦ A `TextArea` can contain several lines of text for input by the user or output by the program.

- ❦ When declaring and initializing an object in Java, use the `new` operator if the right side of the declaration calls a constructor. You don't need `new` if the right side of the declaration uses a method that returns an object.

- ❦ Constructors in Java always have the same name as the type of object they construct.

- ❦ Java counts from 0. If there is a linear collection of things in Java (like items in a `List` or `Choice`), they are almost always indexed from 0.

- ❦ The AWT classes are platform-independent, meaning that the look of a widget will generally differ from one implementation to another.

- ❦ A `Container` is a `Component` that is used to contain other `Components`.

- ❦ To make a `Component` a visual part of an applet (or any other `Container`, for that matter, you must use `Container`'s `add()` method.

- ❦ You do not need to write code to paint a widget. All the AWT widgets "know" how to paint themselves. The only time you need a `paint()` override in a `Component` is if you are going to perform any `Graphics` drawing methods in the `Component`.

3.6   EXERCISES

1. If you were presented with an unfamiliar applet, how could you tell whether an object on the screen was a `List` or a `TextArea`, without inspecting the underlying code? Hint: Run the `Gigobite` Lablet and see.

2. Think about how an applet is displayed and try to guess what the effect would be of calling `this.move(100, 200)` in an applet's `init()` method. After you've made your guess, add the line at the start of the Lablet's `init()` (don't forget that the statement will need a semicolon at the end), run the Lablet and correct your guess, if necessary, explaining what you observe.

3. Where is the anchor point of a `Component`?

4. Name eleven pieces of information that each `Component` contains.

5. How could an applet test whether two of its components overlap?

6. Can an applet change the size of one of its components while it is running?

7. Can you change the font of just a part of the text in a `TextField`; for example, making just one word italic out of a total of ten?

8. After executing this code fragment, what text would be in `result`?

```
TextArea entry = new TextArea("Are these");
entry.appendText(" the shadows of things that must be?");
entry.select(1, 21);
TextField result = new TextField(entry.getSelectedText);
```

9. **a.** Write the code that would delete all but the first and last characters in a `TextArea` named `display`. Hint: the `String` class has a method,

```
int length()
```

that returns the number of characters in the `String`. You may assume that `display` contains more than two characters.
   b. Do part (a) under the assumption that `display` is a `TextField`.
   c. Which of (a) or (b) is easier? Why?

10. Two-state devices are so common that the AWT contains a class, `Checkbox`, specifically for that purpose. Come up with a reasonable situation in which a *three*-state device would be useful.

11. What consumer electronic product commonly contains parts that act like a `CheckboxGroup`?

12. Can a `Checkbox` be in two `CheckboxGroups` simultaneously?

13. In the Lablet, we used a `TextField` for the title, "Gigo-BITE," that appeared at the bottom. We could have used `drawString()` in a `paint()` override to place the title, but didn't. We wanted to make a point by showing you an applet without a `paint()` override, but that wasn't the only reason.
   a. Why would it not be a good idea, *in general,* to have painted the title directly on the applet frame?
   b. Ignore the reason or reasons you came up with in part (a). What would the `paint()` override for the Lablet look like if you were to eliminate the `title` variable and draw the title string directly on the applet?

14. Write an applet that contains a single `Button`, 20 pixels high and 36 pixels wide, containing the label text "Plonk," centered vertically and horizontally in the applet frame. Your code should work correctly regardless of the applet's dimensions. Hint: Look at Chapter 2.

15. Run the Lablet in a Java-aware Web browser, like Netscape Navigator or Internet Explorer, and then run it again in the applet runner in your Java development environment. Record the differences in appearance you notice.

16. In the Lablet, do the twelve widget objects need to be instance variables, or could we have made them local variables within the `init()` method?

17. Write a declaration and any other code you would need to make a `TextField` named myLCD appear in an applet with the text "Status set" in green on a black background.

18. Which of the following variable declarations are legal Java? For those that would cause compile errors, explain what's wrong with them. You may assume that any other variables have already been declared to be the right type and initialized to some appropriate values.
   a. `Dimension theSize = new myButton.minimumSize();`
   b. `Choice options = new Choice();`
   c. `String contents = theField.getText();`
   d. `TextField field2 = theField;`
   e. `Component myWidget = new Component();`
   f. `int start = new int(theField.getSelectionStart());`
   g. `int end = theField.getSelectionEnd();`

19. The following is a screen shot of an applet we wrote, with two `Buttons`, two `Lists`, a `Textfield`, and a `Choice`. Write an applet that will lay out these items, with their contents as indicated. You may have to adjust the applet size to make it look (more or less) like this.

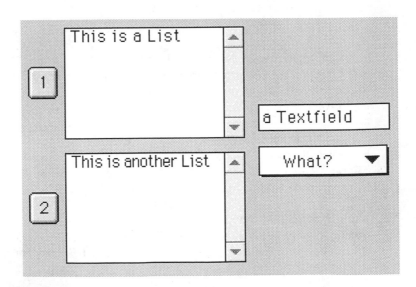

20. Write an applet that contains this calculator, with eighteen `Buttons`, a `TextField` and a 2-pixel-wide drop shadow below and to the right of the `TextField`, all on top of an enclosing round rectangle.

Try to make your applet appear as close to this as possible (get out your ruler and assume that there are 72 pixels per inch). The font for all the button labels is 14-point courier bold and the background is medium gray with a black border. We understand that you have no control over exactly how the buttons will appear on your system, so don't worry about that part. Do this exercise with the requirement that the calculator should not change its look if the applet frame is resized—in other words, you'll have to anchor the `Components` in place.

     Note: To do this, you'll need to include the following statement at the start of your `init()` method. We'll explain why in the next chapter.

```
setLayout(null);
```

21. Can a `Container` contain another `Container`?

CHAPTER FOUR

Visual Design

In Chapter 3 we discussed how to build an applet by using a collection of buttons, text displays, checkboxes, and other widgets. As you saw, simply adding widgets to an applet gives you very little control over the look of the interface—what looks good in one environment might be completely unacceptable in another. In this chapter, we'll conclude our discussion of the visual design of a Java program by discussing two features that give us the ability to make a GUI look the way we want, regardless of the system in which our programming is running. The Container subclasses permit us to think of visual design in terms of a hierarchical organization, and the layout classes allow us to specify how our hierarchy of Containers and their Components will appear.

OBJECTIVES

In this chapter, we will
- ❧ Discuss the Container class and its subclasses Panel, Window, Dialog, and Frame.
- ❧ Show how to make a Java application.
- ❧ Introduce the Canvas subclass of Component.
- ❧ Discuss four of Java's layout classes: BorderLayout, CardLayout, FlowLayout, and GridLayout.
- ❧ Use what we've presented to produce a complicated user interface.

4.1   CONTAINERS

A Container object is used to group Components for display purposes. There is no limit to the number of Components a Container may hold. The Container class is a subclass of Component, which means, first, that any

100

Container object has access to all the Component methods we listed in Chapter 3. In addition, since a Container is a Component, we can put Containers within other Containers. In fact, there's no limit to the number of Components a Container may hold. A Container has references to each Component it contains, and each Component also has a reference to its *parent,* the Container to which it belongs. A Container has a local coordinate system, measured from the anchor point of its bounding rectangle. This local coordinate system is independent of where the Container is located on the screen.

Every Container has its own LayoutManager that determines how its Components will be arranged within the Container when it is displayed. We'll describe the LayoutManager classes in the next section.

As with Component, Container is an abstract class. You can never have a generic Container object in a Java program—you must use one of its subclasses (or create your own class that extends Container).

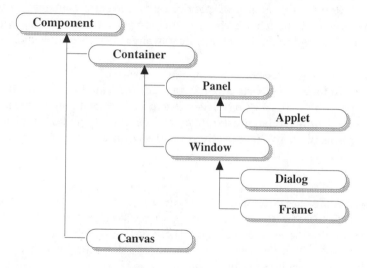

Figure 4.1 Most of the Container classes and Canvas.

Container Organization Methods

As you might expect, Container is a fairly large class. It has a single *default* constructor with no arguments, which is invoked automatically (and invisibly) whenever we create a specific type of Container object. We'll discuss the methods that apply to the Components a Container holds and defer discussion of methods dealing with layout until the next section.

```
void add(Component c)
void add(Component c, int position)
void add(String name, Component c)
```

These three methods are among the most important and commonly used of the Container class. Each method adds a new Component to those in this

Container. The first method simply adds the argument to the end of the list of Components already in this Container. The second method allows you to specify the position in the list where the new Component will be added. In this version, the position must be valid, meaning that it must be between 0 and the number of Components currently in this Container. If you don't want to bother counting the Components, a position argument of −1 will always just add the Component argument to the end of the current list. The final add() method has a String argument for the convenience of some LayoutManagers, like BorderLayout and CardLayout.

You cannot add a Container to itself, and if you attempt to add a Component that's already there, it will be removed and reinserted, generally in a different position.

int **countComponents**()   // may vanish

Returns the number of Components currently contained in this object. It may eventually be replaced by getComponentCount(). This counts only the top-level components, not those present in any Containers within this object.

Component **getComponent**(int position)

Returns the Component in the indicated position in the list of Components in this Container. The position argument must be valid, i.e., position must be greater than or equal to 0 and less than the current Component count (since the list is indexed from 0, the last element is in position *count* − 1).

Component **getComponentAt**(int x, int y) // version 1.1 only
Component **getComponentAt**(Point p)   // version 1.1 only

Return the Component in this Container that holds the given point, measured in the local coordinates. These methods replace the version 1.0 method locate(). You might want to use them to determine which object the mouse pointer is currently over, for example.

int **getComponentCount**()   // version 1.1 only

Returns the number of Components currently contained in this object. This is the version 1.1 equivalent of countComponents().

Container **getParent**()

This is *not* a Container method. It is a Component method that returns the Container that holds this Component. In the containment hierarchy of Figure 4.2, for instance, choice.getParent() would return panelB.

boolean **isAncestorOf**(Component c)   // version 1.1 only

Returns true if this Container is the parent of c (or is the parent of the parent, and so on). Returns false if c isn't below this Container in the containment hierarchy. In Figure 4.2, for example, the method call `panelA.isAncestorOf(list1)`

would return `true` and

`panelB.isAncestorOf(panelA)`

would return `false`.

```
void remove(int index)                    // version 1.1 only
void remove(Component c)
```
   Remove a `Component` from this `Container`'s list. In the version 1.1 variant, the `Container` to be removed is specified by its index in the list. These methods look only at the top-level list and do not search down the containment hierarchy. Thus, in Figure 4.2, the call `panelA.remove(button2)` would do nothing. The call `panelA.remove(panelA2)`, however, would remove `panelA2` from `panelA`'s list and hence would also remove `button2` and `list2` from the hierarchy.

```
void removeAll()
```
   Removes all Components from this Container.

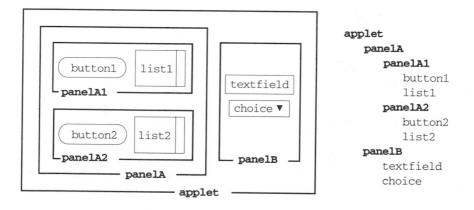

Figure 4.2 Visual organization of an applet and its containment hierarchy.

The Containment Hierarchy

The containment hierarchy is not determined by the order in which you add `Components` to a `Container`, but rather by which ones you add to which. Consider the example in Figure 4.2. From the top level down, note that `applet` (which, being an `Applet`, is a `Panel`, and hence a `Container`) contains panelA and panelB. panelA itself contains panelA1 and panelA2, each of which contain a Button and a List. The actual look on the screen would be determined by the LayoutManagers of the separate Containers, so, if you run this applet as it is, the odds are that it won't look like Figure 4.2. In any case, we would build the containment hierarchy as follows.

```
public class applet extends Applet
{
    // These declarations could be done in any order.
    Panel panelA = new Panel();
    Panel panelB = new Panel();
    Panel panelA1 = new Panel();
    Panel panelA2 = new Panel();
    Button button1 = new Button();
    Button button2 = new Button();
    List list1 = new List();
    List list2 = new List();
    TextField textfield = new TextField();
    Choice choice = new Choice();

    public void init()
    // Now we build the containment hierarchy, from the
    // bottom up.
    {
        panelA1.add(button1);
        panelA1.add(list1);        // done with panelA1

        panelA2.add(button2);
        panelA2.add(list2);        // done with panelA2

        panelA.add(panelA1);
        panelA.add(panelA2);       // panelA is now done

        panelB.add(textfield);
        panelB.add(choice);        // panel B is complete

        add(panelA);               // add panels to the applet
        add(panelB);               // finished!
    }
}
```

The Panel Class

The Container of choice for arranging Components is the Panel class. It's simple, small, and easy to use, as you saw in the preceding example. It has a default constructor, Panel(), that builds a Panel object with its layout set to FlowLayout, and in version 1.1 there is a constructor

Panel(LayoutManager layout)   // version 1.1 only

that allows you to set the LayoutManager the constructed Panel will use. We'll get to layouts immediately.

A Panel has no additional methods of interest to us here, beyond those it inherits from Container, Component, and Object.

4.2   LAYOUTS

The four layout classes we'll discuss in this section all implement what is known as the LayoutManager interface.[1] In simple terms, this means they are all responsible for positioning the Components within a Container; they differ only in how they accomplish this positioning. Some arrange the Components in rows, from left to right in each row, some divide the display of a Container into separate regions and allow you to specify within which region a Component will be drawn. Although it's beyond the scope of this book, it is even possible to design a class of your own that performs custom layouts.

All the layout classes we will mention[2] have access to the minimum and preferred sizes of the Components and may or may not use this information to decide where things should be placed. When a Component is resized, the layout is recomputed to compensate for the new size.

Container Layout Methods

As we mentioned earlier, every Container has its own LayoutManager, along with some methods that can be used to access and modify the layout.

void **doLayout**()   // version 1.1 only
Instructs this Container's LayoutManager to lay out the Components. Generally, you won't have to call this, but you could if you wanted to force layout to take place, rather than waiting for it to be done for you. This method replaces the version 1.0 method layout().

LayoutManager **getLayout**()
Returns the current LayoutManager for this Container.

Dimension **getMinimumSize**()   // version 1.1 only
Dimension **getPreferredSize**()   // version 1.1 only
These are overrides of the Component methods of the same names. They ask the LayoutManager to compute the minimum or preferred sizes,

---

[1]We'll talk about interfaces in Chapter 5. For now, you can think of an interface as a class and not be too far from the truth.

[2]The only AWT layout class we won't cover here is GridbagLayout.

respectively, necessary to hold all of this `Container`'s `Components`. They replace the 1.0 methods `minimumSize()` and `preferredSize()`.

void **layout**()   // may vanish
    This 1.0 method corresponds to version 1.1's `doLayout()`.

Dimension **minimumSize**()   // may vanish
Dimension **preferredSize**()   // may vanish
    These 1.0 methods are equivalent to the 1.1 `getMinimumSize()` and `getPreferredSize()` methods.

void **setLayout**(LayoutManager layout)
    Allows you to change the `LayoutManager` of this `Container`. You'll use this method quite often to switch from the default layout provided for a particular `Container`.

The `FlowLayout` Class

A `FlowLayout` positions `Components` in much the same way a word processor displays its text: from left to right by rows, arranging the rows from top to bottom. If you look back at Figure 3.3 you'll see an example of twelve `Components` positioned by a `FlowLayout`, using two different `Container` dimensions. As with all the layout classes, `FlowLayout` will do the best it can to fit all the `Components` in the visible portion of their `Container`. However, if the minimum sizes of all the `Components` can't be fit in the available space, there's nothing the layout can do—some parts of the `Components` simply won't appear. You can see this result if you run either the `Gigobite` or the `Ovenator` Lablet from this chapter in an applet runner and manually resize the window.

    `FlowLayout` contains three class constants: `FlowLayout.LEFT`, `FlowLayout.CENTER`, and `FlowLayout.RIGHT`. They correspond to the three possible alignments a `FlowLayout` can have. If the alignment is LEFT or RIGHT, the `Components` in each row are aligned flush left or flush right, respectively, and, if the alignment is CENTER, the `Components` of each row are centered in the row. In addition, a `FlowLayout` has two private variables that specify the horizontal gap between objects in each row and the vertical gap between rows. They may be negative integers, if you want the `Components` to overlap.

    `FlowLayout` is the default layout for `Panel` (and hence, by inheritance, for `Applet`), so if you don't set the layout for these objects, they will be set automatically to `FlowLayout`'s defaults (center alignment, gaps of five pixels).

    The `FlowLayout` class has three constructors.

FlowLayout()
    Creates a `FlowLayout` object with center alignment and horizontal and vertical gaps of five pixels each.

FlowLayout(int alignment)
     Constructs a `FlowLayout` with the specified alignment and the default gaps of five pixels in each direction.

FlowLayout(int alignment, int hGap, int vGap)
     Constructs a `FlowLayout` with the specified alignment and gaps. For example, you might change the layout of an applet with six buttons from its default alignment by making the following call in its `init()` method:

```
this.setAlignment(new FlowLayout(FlowLayout.RIGHT, 20, 10);
```

If you did, the result might look something like this (depending on the size of the applet panel, of course).

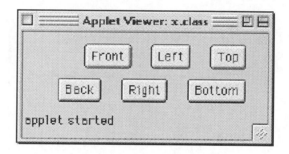

     There are three `FlowLayout` methods of interest to us in version 1.0, and version 1.1 adds six more.

int **getAlignment**()   // version 1.1 only
     Returns an integer corresponding to the alignment of this `FlowLayout`. This integer could then be compared against one of the three class constants to determine the current alignment of this object, for example.

int **getHgap**()   // version 1.1 only
int **getVgap**()   // version 1.1 only
     Returns the current horizontal or vertical gap, respectively, for this `FlowLayout`.

void **layoutContainer**(Container c)
     Draws the argument's `Components` on the screen, using this `FlowLayout`'s alignment and gaps.

Dimension **minimumLayoutSize**(Container c)
Dimension **preferredLayoutSize**(Container c)
     Return the width and height necessary to place all of c's `Components` in a single row, using the `Components`' minimum and preferred sizes, respectively.

```
void setAlignment(int alignment)          // version 1.1 only
```
Sets the alignment of this FlowLayout to one of the three class constants.

```
void setHgap(int h)                        // version 1.1 only
void setVgap(int v)                        // version 1.1 only
```
Sets the horizontal or vertical gap, respectively, of this layout.

The BorderLayout Class

In a BorderLayout, the Container is divided into five regions: North, East, West, South, and Center. Here's an example of an applet with the layout set to BorderLayout, to which we added five labeled Buttons.

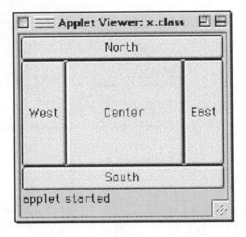

To add Components to a Container that has a BorderLayout, use the version of the add() method that takes an additional String argument,

```
void add(String location, Component c)
```

The location is specified by using the String literals "North", "East", "West", "South", or "Center". For example, if p is a Panel whose layout had been set to BorderLayout (rather than its default FlowLayout), we could add a Button to its East region by calling p.add("East", myButton). In version 1.1, this class is provided with five class constants,

```
BorderLayout.NORTH
BorderLayout.EAST
BorderLayout.WEST
BorderLayout.SOUTH
BorderLayout.CENTER,
```

so in version 1.1 you could call `p.add(BorderLayout.EAST, myButton)` to add `myButton` to the East region of p. You don't have to add Components to each region—any missing region will be treated as a Component of size 0.

In common with `FlowLayout`, a `BorderLayout` allows you to specify horizontal and vertical gaps between regions, though in this layout their values will be 0 unless you specify otherwise. This layout is the default for the containers `Window`, `Frame`, and `Dialog`, which we'll discuss shortly.

This layout does a fair amount of work behind the scenes. When a `Container` is laid out, the North and South `Components` are given their full heights and any remaining vertical space will be allotted for the East, Center, and West regions. In the horizontal direction, the East and West regions are given their full widths and any remaining width is given to the Center region. The North and South `Components` are given the full `Container` width. In all these calculations, the appropriate gaps are also figured in. Unlike `FlowLayout`, `BorderLayout` will resize the `Components` (particularly the Center) to fill the available space. This explains why the `Buttons` completely filled the regions in the preceding illustration.

If you don't want your `Components` to be resized during layout, you can place them in `Panels` and add the `Panels` to the `Container`.

We did just that to get the following picture, adding the Center `Button` to a `Panel` and then adding the `Panel` to the Center region. Now, the `Panel` fills the Center, but the `Button` does not fill the `Panel`.

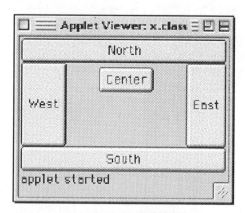

There are two BorderLayout constructors.

BorderLayout()

Creates a `BorderLayout` object with center alignment and horizontal and vertical gaps of 0 pixels.

BorderLayout(int hGap, int vGap)
> Constructs a BorderLayout with the specified gaps.

The methods of this class are quite similar to those of FlowLayout.

int **getHgap**()   // version 1.1 only
int **getVgap**()   // version 1.1 only
> Return the current horizontal or vertical gap, respectively, for this layout.

void **layoutContainer**(Container c)
> Draws the argument's Components on the screen, using the procedure described previously.

Dimension **minimumLayoutSize**(Container c)
Dimension **preferredLayoutSize**(Container c)
> Return the width and height necessary to place all of c's Components, using the Components' minimum and preferred sizes, respectively.

void **setHgap**(int h)   // version 1.1 only
void **setVgap**(int v)   // version 1.1 only
> Sets the horizontal or vertical gap, respectively, of this layout.

The GridLayout Class

When you need a "graph paper" layout, with all regions of the same size, use a GridLayout. In this layout scheme, you specify a number of rows and columns and, when adding Components, they will be placed in the same order you're reading this paragraph: left to right within rows, and top to bottom in row order.

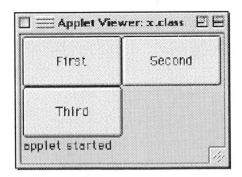

You can construct a GridLayout by specifying the number of rows and columns it will have. When the time comes to do a layout, the Components will be placed in cells of equal size (resizing them, if necessary, to fill the cells) in the order in which they had been added. A portion of a row may be left unfilled, as we showed, and if more items are added to the Container than there are cells, the layout will allocate enough columns to fit all the Components.

In the Exercises, we will explore exactly how a GridLayout determines the number of rows and columns needed. For now, it's enough to advise you to have enough Components to result in placing at least one in the last row. For example, with three rows of four columns each, you shouldn't expect any surprises if you add nine, ten, eleven, or twelve Components.

As you might infer from the preceding screen shot, GridLayout will resize the Components to fill its cells. In common with FlowLayout and BorderLayout, this layout also allows you to specify the horizontal and vertical gaps between cells (with the default value 0).

There are three constructors for this class, depending on how much information you want to provide.

GridLayout()
Creates a new layout with one row, an unlimited number of columns, and no horizontal and vertical gaps between cells.

GridLayout(int rows, int columns)
This method is like the default constructor, except that you can set the number of rows and columns in the layout.

GridLayout(int rows, int columns, int hgap, int vgap)
Here, you get to set everything.

If FlowLayout, BorderLayout, and GridLayout were the only LayoutManagers that Java had and would ever have, you could factor out almost all the methods of these three classes into a single superclass. That's an indication that you're going to see quite a few methods in GridLayout that you've already seen.

```
int getColumns()                          // version 1.1 only
int getRows()                             // version 1.1 only
```
Returns the number of columns or rows, respectively, in this layout.

```
int getHgap()                             // version 1.1 only
int getVgap()                             // version 1.1 only
```
Returns the current horizontal or vertical gap, respectively, for this layout.

```
void layoutContainer(Container c)
```
Draws the argument's Components on the screen, using the procedure just described.

```
Dimension minimumLayoutSize(Container c)
Dimension preferredLayoutSize(Container c)
```
These two methods return the width and height necessary to place all of c's Components, using the Components' minimum and preferred sizes, respectively.

```
void setColumns(int columns)          // version 1.1 only
void setRows(int rows)                // version 1.1 only
```
Sets the number of columns or rows, respectively, of this layout.

```
void setHgap(int h)                   // version 1.1 only
void setVgap(int v)                   // version 1.1 only
```
Sets the horizontal or vertical gap, respectively, of this layout.

The CardLayout Class

Unlike the other LayoutManagers we've discussed, CardLayout displays its Components one at a time, in much the same way you'd use a stack of index cards or a flip book. You add Components to the parent Container in more or less the usual way, but only one is visible at a time.

To add Components in this layout, you can use the one-argument method, add(Component c), but we don't advise it. Instead, we recommend the add() method with an additional String argument:

```
void add(String name, Component c)
```

The String argument will assign a name to the Component, allowing you to pick a Component for display by using its name. We recommend this style for two reasons: First, it's required in Java 1.1, and, second, we've discovered that adding a nameless Component to a CardLayout-equipped Container will sometimes cause bizarre behavior in version 1.0. When you add Components in a CardLayout, they are displayed in the order added—the first Component added will be the first in visibility order.

There are two constructors you can use for a CardLayout, depending on whether you want to specify horizontal and vertical gaps or not.

CardLayout()
Creates a new layout with no gaps.

CardLayout(int hgap, int vgap)
Allows you to specify the horizontal and vertical gaps. Since the Components are never displayed together, the gaps in this case serve to specify the horizontal and margins around each Component when it is drawn on the screen.

As you might expect, along with the usual layout methods, this class has methods to determine which of the "cards" will be displayed.

void **first**(Container parent)

Displays the first Component of the parent Container in visibility order. Note that this method requires as its argument the Container with this layout. Also, you will need the CardLayout object itself to make this call. This means that instead of using an "on-the-fly" declaration like

```
myContainer.setLayout(new CardLayout());
```

you'll have to set aside a variable for the layout, as follows.

If you intend to use first(), last(), next(), previous(), or show() with a CardLayout (which is really the only reason to use this layout), you should declare a layout variable such as

```
CardLayout cd = new CardLayout();
myContainer.setLayout(cd);
...
cd.first(myContainer);
```

---

int **getHgap**()   // version 1.1 only
int **getVgap**()   // version 1.1 only

Returns the current horizontal or vertical gap, respectively, for this layout.

void **last**(Container c)

Displays the last card in visibility order. See the discussion of first() for how to use this method.

void **layoutContainer**(Container c)

Draws the argument's Components on the screen. Initially, all the Components are visible and don't vanish until one is selected by first(), last(), next(), previous(), or show().

Dimension **minimumLayoutSize**(Container c)
Dimension **preferredLayoutSize**(Container c)

Return the width and height necessary to place all of c's Components, using the largest width and height among the Components' minimum and preferred sizes, respectively.

void **next**(Container c)

Displays the next card in visibility order, wrapping from last to first as necessary. See the discussion of first() for how to use this method.

```
void previous(Container c)
```
Displays the preceding card in visibility order, wrapping from first to last as necessary. See the discussion of `first()`.

```
void setHgap(int h)                    // version 1.1 only
void setVgap(int v)                    // version 1.1 only
```
Sets the horizontal or vertical gap, respectively, of this layout.

```
void show(Container parent, String name)
```
Displays the card with the given name. If there is no `Component` with the specified name, this method does nothing.

Here's an applet that uses the `CardLayout` class. We gave the applet `Panel` a `BorderLayout`. In the North region of the applet, we placed a `Panel` with two control `Buttons`, and in the Center region we placed a `Panel` with five `Labels`, arranged with a `CardLayout`. The North Panel `Buttons` control the visible card: If the "<<" `Button` is clicked, the preceding card is displayed in the Center region, and if the ">>" `Button` is clicked, the Center panel displays the next card.

We encourage you to enter and run this applet to see how the Center `Panel`, with its `CardLayout`, works. It should look something like this when running.

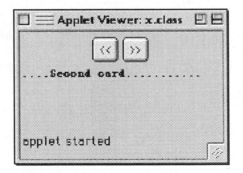

```
public class CardTest extends Applet
{
    // the North Panel and its Buttons
    Button nextBttn = new Button(">>");
    Button previousBttn = new Button("<<");
    Panel bttnPanel = new Panel();
    // the Center Panel and its layout
    Panel cardPanel = new Panel();
    CardLayout cdLayout = new CardLayout();
```

```
public void init()
{
      // Build the North control Panel.
      bttnPanel.add(previousBttn);
      bttnPanel.add(nextBttn);

      // Build the Center card Panel
      cardPanel.setLayout(cdLayout);
      cardPanel.setFont(new Font("courier", Font.BOLD, 10));
      cardPanel.add("1", new Label("First card.............."));
      cardPanel.add("2", new Label("...Second card........."));
      cardPanel.add("3", new Label("......Third card......."));
      cardPanel.add("4", new Label(".........Fourth card..."));
      cardPanel.add("5", new Label(".............Fifth card"));

      // Place the control and card panels in this applet.
      setLayout(new BorderLayout());
      add("North", bttnPanel);
      add("Center", cardPanel);
}

public boolean action(Event e, Object arg)
// We won't be able to explain this method until Chapter 6.
// For now, just accept that it catches a mouse click,
// determines which button was clicked, and calls the
// appropriate CardLayout method in consequence.
{
      if (e.target == nextBttn)
            cdLayout.next(cardPanel);
      else if (e.target == previousBttn)
            cdLayout.previous(cardPanel);
      else
            return false;
      return true;
}
}
```

No Layout

There's no long list of methods here, we promise. In fact, the last layout we'll discuss has no constructors and no methods, since it isn't a class at all. The layout classes we've discussed so far are powerful and easy to use, but they do so much behind the scenes that they take a lot of control out of our hands. Most of the time, that's a good idea—most of us wouldn't want to have to deal with the differences of display among a dozen or more different platforms, browsers, and Java development environments, nor do we want to worry about possibly losing sight of a Component when an applet is resized.

Still, there are times when you might want to take the reins and lay out widgets to a precise and unvarying specification. To do so, indicate that no LayoutManager should be used in a Container by using the null layout. We'll have more to say about null in Chapter 5: It's the only Object constant, and it is often used as a signal to mean "nothing" in various contexts. For example, if we say

```
myContainer.setLayout(null);
```

we are indicating that we don't want to use any LayoutManager to place the Components of myContainer, but rather want to position and size them ourselves, using the Component methods move(), resize(), and reshape() (particularly reshape()). This approach can be handy if we're using widgets in combination with on-screen graphics. If, for example, we wanted to group two buttons within an enclosing rectangle, we would want to anchor the buttons in place with respect to the underlying graphic. Let's suppose that we want to achieve the following look, with two buttons on a yellow rectangle, all surrounded by a 2-pixel-wide black border:

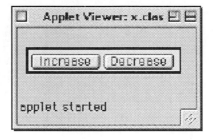

Here's a first cut at the program. Cover the screen shot, pretend you never saw it, and look the program over carefully. How clear is it?

```
public class Fixed extends Applet
{
    Button increase = new Button("Increase");
    Button decrease = new Button("Decrease");

    public void init()
    {
        setLayout(null);
        add(increase);
        add(decrease);

        increase.reshape(12, 24, 70, 16);
        decrease.reshape(86, 24, 70, 16);
    }
```

```
    public void paint(Graphics g)
    {
        // Draw the 2-pixel-wide border
        g.drawRect(7, 19, 156, 26);
        g.drawRect(8, 20, 154, 24);
        // Now fill it with yellow.
        g.setColor(Color.yellow);
        g.fillRect(9, 21, 152, 22);
    }
}
```

It works, more or less, but note that the program has no less than *twenty* magic numbers! Of course, we could cut through some of this fog by declaring extra instance variables, like ANCHOR_X, ANCHOR_Y, BTTN_HEIGHT, BTTN_WIDTH, VSPACE, and HSPACE. Even if we do that, we would wind up with something that is, at best, a lot of work to code and, at worst, incomprehensible. The moral is clear:

The null layout can be useful, but generally it's better to leave the work to a real LayoutManager.

4.3   OTHER CONTAINERS, OTHER DETAILS

The Containers we've discussed so far all "live" in the applet Panel. There are also some Containers that are far more mobile—in fact, they can be placed anywhere on the screen. In this section, we introduce the Window, Frame, and Dialog classes. We will also talk about using Frames to make Java *applications*—programs that aren't invoked by a browser but are more like traditional "free-standing" programs. Before we get to either of these topics, though, we need to introduce one more class that addresses some of the problems created by mixing graphics and widgets.

The Canvas Class

If you want to paint on the screen, there's a Component that's made specifically for the purpose, namely, Canvas. Unless you're using a null layout, there's no possible way for any LayoutManager to know where you've placed your graphics, so an applet that looks good when you're designing it may be a horrible mess when you run it in a different system.

Java Design Tip:

It's a good idea to try a program in as many different environments as possible. Not only might the appearance vary considerably, but you might even find that a Java program that runs as expected on one system may produce entirely unexpected results in another.

The `Canvas` class, as we'll show in Chapter 6, also responds to all events, which, when combined with its drawing prowess, makes it the ideal candidate for creating custom `Components`. Want a visual thermometer, a dial, or a fancy button? Make your own subclass of `Canvas` to do the job.

This class has a single default constructor,

`Canvas()`

Creates a `Canvas` object of size 0. As with most other `Components`, a `Canvas` will generally be used within some `Container`, like a `Panel`. If it is, the `LayoutManager` of the parent `Container` will size the `Canvas` for you. If you want to specify the size, you can always use one of the `Component` size methods, like `reshape()`, or its version 1.1 replacement, `setBounds()`.

Canvas also has a `paint()` method, that provides you with a `Graphics` argument which you can use for all of your drawing calls.

Let's see how we can use `Canvas` to produce a class of our own. We'll invent a class, `WarningMessage`, that will display an attention-grabbing message, provided by the user of the class. The message will be drawn in bold italics, and will be preceded by three red exclamation marks:

!!! *Really erase hard drive?*

(Trust us, the exclamation marks really are red, however black they might look here.)

Let's investigate the class definition, by looking first at its structure.

```
class WarningMessage extends Canvas
{
    private String myMessage;        // We save the message here.

    public WarningMessage(String message)
    {
        . . .
    }

    public void paint(Graphics g)
    {
        . . .
    }
}
```

The header indicates that this class is named `WarningMessage` and that it is a subclass of `Canvas`, and so inherits all of the available `Canvas` methods (along with all those of `Component`, too). The body of the definition contains one instance variable, where we store the message to be displayed, along with a constructor and an override of the `Canvas` `paint()` method.

Now let's fill the pieces in. Here's the constructor:

```
public WarningMessage(String message)
{
    myMessage = message;
    resize(60, 25);
}
```

As you've seen, a constructor is invoked when a new object is created. This is the place to do any initialization, and in this case we get the message provided for us and store it in the instance variable `myMessage`. Having done that, we set the size of our `WarningMessage`.[3]

A constructor almost always has `public` access (so it can be called in declarations in other classes). It has no return type (not even `void`), and must *always* have the same name as the class. Constructors are intended for any initializations that must be done to build a new object.

---

[3]We used magic numbers to set the size of the `WarningMessage`. It would have been better to have found the dimensions of the message and used them to set the size. Look up the `FontMetrics` class to see how that might be done.

The paint() method override is simple enough: We set the current color and font of the Graphics context g, draw three exclamation marks in different locations, change the color and font, and draw the message.

```
public void paint(Graphics g)
{
    g.setColor(Color.red);
    g.setFont(new Font("Helvetica", Font.BOLD, 18));
    g.drawString("!", 10, 20);
    g.drawString("!", 16, 24);
    g.drawString("!", 22, 16);
    g.setColor(Color.black);
    g.setFont(new Font("Helvetica",
                       Font.ITALIC + Font.BOLD, 10));
    g.drawString(myMessage, 32, 18);
}
}
```

Now you can see why we bothered with the instance variable myMessage. We had to have it, since we needed to set it in the constructor and use it in the paint() method. If we had made it a local variable in either the constructor or paint(), it would have been accessible in only one place and would have had no meaning in the other.

An instance variable is accessible by any method in its class, so it provides a convenient way of sharing information between methods. Instance variables should almost always have private access (so other objects can't inspect or modify them without the class's permission).

That's it—we've built a class all on our own. This is really the heart of almost all "real" programming tasks, and especially so in object-oriented programming. The designers of Java clearly couldn't possibly have made classes to handle every programming situation. Instead, they gave us a powerful suite of fundamental classes and provided us with the ability to make classes of our own. In essence, designing classes allows us to *extend* Java to meet our own needs. If we ever need a graphic warning message in a program, all we have to do is write our own WarningMessage class and save it for use whenever we need it. As a matter of fact, this wasn't an empty exercise—we'll use this class shortly.

At a fundamental level, programming in Java is nothing more than designing and using classes.

Windows

It's time to return to our discussion of Containers. The Window class is the superclass of two other classes we'll discuss in this section: Frame and Dialog. A Window appears as a rectangular area that is displayed on top of any existing applet, browser, or, in fact, anything that is already showing on the screen. In that respect, a Window object acts visually like the windows you're used to seeing on your system, except that a Window doesn't have any of the ornaments you're used to, like scroll bars, a title, and "grow" and "go away" boxes. Because a Window is, visually, a naked rectangle, it is most often subclassed to create custom pop-up Components. We won't have much to say about the Window class here, since it is rarely used on its own. Instead, you'll be much more likely to use the Window subclasses Frame and Dialog.

There are three useful Window methods we should mention before we leave, particularly since they are often used in the Window subclasses Frame and Dialog.

void **dispose**()
Once it has been created, a Window consumes quite a few system resources. You can't necessarily be sure that these resources will be released when the window vanishes from sight, so it's good programming practice to free up all resources by calling this method after you've finished with the Window.

void **pack**()
This method resizes this window to fit the Components it contains. You would call this method if you didn't want to call resize() to set the dimensions of a Window.

void **show**()
Creating a Window (or any of its subclasses) and even adding it to some other Container won't make it appear on the screen. To do that, you need an explicit call to show().

Frames

A Frame is a Window with all the dressing that's appropriate to the system in which it is running. It will have a title, and it may have scroll bars, a menu bar, its own cursor, and system-specific widgets to hide it, minimize it, grow it, and so on. A Frame is a Container subclass (with default BorderLayout), so we can add to it any Components we want.

The default size for a `Frame` is (0, 0), so a `Frame` should call `reshape()` to size itself and place itself appropriately on the screen. The anchor position is measured in screen coordinates, relative to the upper left corner of the whole display. In addition, a `Frame` is initially invisible, so you'll need to have it call `show()` to make itself visible.

There are two `Frame` constructors you can use, depending on whether you want to specify a title.

Frame()
Creates a new `Frame` with the title "Untitled" in version 1.0 or no title in version 1.1.

and

Frame(String title)
Creates a new `Frame` with the specified title.

`Frame` has the usual `Container` and layout methods and just two others that are of interest to us here.

boolean **isResizable**()
void **setResizable**(boolean canResize)
The first method returns `true` if the `Frame` can be resized by the user, and `false` if it cannot. The second allows you to set whether the `Frame` is resizable or not.

The following is an example of an applet that pops up a `Frame` asking for information from the user. The North region (remember, `Frames` default to `BorderLayout`) contains instructions, the Center region contains a `Panel` with two `Labels` and two `TextFields`, arranged in a grid, and the South region contains a `Panel` with a `Button`.

```
public class Framer extends Applet
{
     Frame myFrame = new Frame("Entry");
     Label explainLbl = new Label("Fill in the fields below,
                                        then click OK");
     Label label1 = new Label("User ID:", Label.RIGHT);
     Label label2 = new Label("Password:", Label.RIGHT);
     TextField field1 = new TextField(15);
     TextField field2 = new TextField(15);
     Button okayBttn = new Button("OK");

     public void init()
     {
          // Set the background color of the frame, the
          // font used in the label, and the password echo char.
          myFrame.setBackground(Color.white);
          explainLbl.setFont(new Font("Helvetica", Font.BOLD, 10));
          field2.setEchoCharacter('*');

          // Add the explanation label to the frame.
          myFrame.add("North", explainLbl);
          // Build the center panel and add it to the frame.
          Panel pc = new Panel();
          pc.setLayout(new GridLayout(2, 2, 8, 2));
          pc.add(label1);
          pc.add(field1);
          pc.add(label2);
          pc.add(field2);
          myFrame.add("Center", pc);
          // Put the OK button in a panel and add it, too.
          Panel ps = new Panel();
          ps.add(okayBttn);
          myFrame.add("South", ps);

          // Finally, set the location and the size of the frame,
          // and make it visible.  We need both of these calls.
          myFrame.reshape(50, 150, 220, 100);
          myFrame.show();
     }
}
```

If you run this applet in a Web browser, you might find that the browser adds an alert message to the frame. This is a security precaution, since it would be fairly easy for an unscrupulous programmer to write an applet that "spoofs" some other program, asking for information that it would then save for later use. In this example, for instance, users might think they are interacting with their own mail server and thus unwittingly reveal all the information necessary to get into their e-mail account.

```
┌─────────────────────────────────────────────┐
│ ▣ ═══════════════ Entry ═══════════════ ▤ │
├─────────────────────────────────────────────┤
│      Fill in the fields below, then click OK  │
│                                               │
│              User ID : ┌──────────────────┐   │
│                        └──────────────────┘   │
│                                               │
│            Password : ┌──────────────────┐    │
│                        └──────────────────┘   │
│                                               │
│                  ╭──────────╮                 │
│                  │    OK    │         ·       │
│                  ╰──────────╯                 │
│                                               │
├─────────────────────────────────────────────┤
│ ▨ │ Unsigned Java Applet Window    │ ▨ │ ◢  │
└─────────────────────────────────────────────┘
```

Dialogs

A `Dialog` is a `Window` that is intended for simple input and output. In fact, the `Frame` example we just finished really would be better as a `Dialog`, since it only gets two pieces of text and responds to a button click (well, it would if we had put in the code to handle mouse events).

If you've spent any time at all using computer applications, you've probably seen dozens of dialogs. You may have also observed that some dialogs are *modal,* meaning that while they're up they hog the incoming events. Selfishly, a modal dialog acts as if it, and it alone, should get all the attention—no moving windows, clicking on other buttons, or using menus while the dialog is open. `Dialogs` in Java can be modal or *modeless,* they may or may not be resizable, and they may or may not be given a title. As we mentioned, each `Dialog` is also a `Window`, and hence also a `Container` (and a `Component`, as well). As we also mentioned, a `Dialog` has a `BorderLayout`, unless you set its layout to something else.

A `Dialog` must be associated with a `Frame`, known as its *parent* frame. This presents a small difficulty for `Dialogs` associated with applets, since an applet may not have a `Frame` to act as parent for its `Dialogs`. Somewhere, either in the browser or applet runner, there may be a `Frame`, but getting it isn't easy. Fortunately, there's an easy solution: Simply create a dummy `Frame` in the applet whose sole purpose is to provide a `Frame` for the dialog. Using a `null` parent sometimes also works.

As with Frame, you must set the size and location of a `Dialog`, and you must also call `show()` to make it appear. In addition, it's a good idea to call `dispose()` when you're finished with a `Dialog`, to free up its system resources.

Dialog has four constructors.

Dialog(Frame parent)   // version 1.1 only
   Creates a new, untitled, modeless Dialog with the specified parent.

Dialog(Frame parent, boolean isModal)   // may vanish
   Allows you to specify whether the Dialog is modal (true argument) or
modeless (false argument).

Dialog(Frame parent, String title)   // version 1.1 only
   Creates a modeless Dialog with the given title.

Dialog(Frame parent, String title,
         boolean isModal)
   Creates a Dialog with the specified properties.

   There is a fairly small collection of Dialog methods of interest to us here.

boolean **isModal**()
void **setModal**(boolean isModal)
   The first method returns true if the frame can be resized by the user and false
if it can't. The second allows the user to set whether the frame is resizable.

boolean **isResizable**()
void **setResizable**(boolean canResize)
   The first method returns true if the Dialog is currently modal and false
if it isn't. The second allows you to set whether the Dialog is modal.

   We give an example of using a Dialog in Figure 4.3. When the program
opens, it immediately presents a Dialog with a warning message and a pair of
Buttons that the user may click. It's a good thing this is just an example, since it's
not exactly what we would call user-friendly (in fact, "user-hostile" might be a
better description). In the screen shot, note that the Dialog isn't tied to the rest of
the display. We deliberately set the location of the Dialog to extend beyond the
application Frame and, in fact, could have placed the Dialog completely outside
the Frame, had we wanted to.
   The program is interesting not only for its use of a Dialog, but also for the
fact that it is an application, not an applet. As we mentioned earlier, an application
is a program that doesn't need an enclosing program like a browser or applet runner
in which to run. In fact, it's quite possible to compile the classes, link them

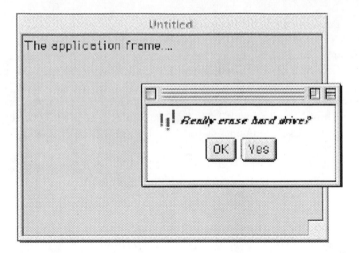

Figure 4.3 A Dialog

appropriately, and turn a Java application into a stand-alone program just like your favorite word processor or Web browser.[4]

    As we did before, let's begin by looking at the structure of the file "DialogAppTest.java." We see immediately that the file contains three class definitions: `DialogAppTest`, `WarningDialog`, and—lo and behold!—our old friend, the `WarningMessage` class we invented a few pages back.

A Java program is nothing but a collection of class definitions, perhaps spread over several files. Every Java source code file must have a `public` class definition, and the name of the file must be the same as that of the `public` class (with the extension ".java" added).

    In this example, the first class, `DialogAppTest`, depends on the second, and the second, `WarningDialog`, obviously uses `WarningMessage`. This ordering was for purposes of readability only.

The order in which class definitions appear in a file need not have anything to do with dependencies among the classes.

---

[4]Sun's *HotJava* Web browser is just that—a Web browser written entirely in Java. It was one of the earliest Java applications, and the first Java-aware Web browser. This provides ample evidence that Java isn't just for "toy" programs.

We'll look at the organization of the `DialogAppTest` class first.

```
public class DialogAppTest extends Frame
{
    public DialogAppTest()
    {
    }

    public static void main(String[] args)
    {
        ...
    }
}
```

First, note that `DialogAppTest` is defined to be a subclass of `Frame`. Making it so gives the application a window for display and also provides a parent for the `Dialog`, in the bargain. While we don't have to build an application by subclassing Frame, it's commonly done.

This class has a constructor with no arguments (and no statement body, either), along with a method we haven't seen before, `main()`. Since the constructor does nothing, we could have left it out, but we've gotten into the habit of putting at least one constructor in almost every class we write. Doing so makes it less likely we'll forget to put a constructor in when we really do need one, and an empty constructor adds negligible overhead to the size or speed of a program. Roughly speaking, the constructor for a class does the same first-time initializations that the `init()` method does in an applet.

The `main()` method is the important one here. In a Java application, execution starts at the first statement of `main()` and continues until the method returns (or disaster strikes). In some Java programming environments, you need to specify the "startup file" to be the one containing the `main()` method that controls execution.

Every Java application must have a `main()` method. Its header must look like

```
public static void main(String[] args)
```

for reasons we'll explain later.

We'll finish this class definition by looking at the `main()` method. After the header, we see a local declaration of a `Frame`, `f`. Most applications will want to display something on the screen, so we declare a `Frame` object for that purpose. In this case, as often happens, the class is a `Frame` by inheritance, so we initialize `f` to be a new instance of `DialogAppTest`. We didn't need to do it this way in this simple example, but it serves as a good protocol in many cases.

The rest of the method is simple enough: we add a `Label` to the `Frame`, set the size and location of the `Frame`, and show it. The last thing the method does before expiring is to create and show a new `WarningDialog`. Note that we didn't need to add the `Dialog` to the application `Frame`. Can you figure out why?

```
public static void main(String[] args)
{
        Frame f = new DialogAppTest();
        f.add("Center", new Label("The application frame...."));
        f.reshape(20, 20, 300, 200);
        f.show();

        WarningDialog wd =
            new WarningDialog(f, "Really erase hard drive?");
        wd.show();
}
```

The next part to explore is the `WarningDialog` class. This class contains a `WarningMessage` widget of our own design and two `Button`s. The constructor for the class is mostly the sort of thing we've seen before: a bunch of calls to `add()` to place the `Component`s in the object, followed by a `reshape()` call to place this `Dialog` where we want it. Excising that lot leaves us with

```
public WarningDialog(Frame parent, String message)
{
        super(parent, false);

        // ...
}
```

The constructor has two arguments: the parent `Frame` and the message `String` (which gets sent to `WarningMessage` via its constructor). That's clear enough, but what's that `super()` thing? Is it a method we haven't seen before? It sure looks like one, having a parenthesized argument list, but it's not—it's a constructor call. You see, `WarningDialog` doesn't need a parent `Frame`. In fact, since it's a class we invented, it needs only whatever we decide it needs. However, `WarningDialog` is a `Dialog` by inheritance, and `Dialog` most definitely needs a parent `Frame`. That's why our constructor contains a `Frame` argument—so we can use it to initialize the inherited `Dialog`. The `super()` call is just a call to the appropriate `Dialog` constructor!

In a class that extends another class, you can use a call to `super()` to invoke the constructor of the superclass. Here, "super" is just a synonym for "the next class up in the class hierarchy," just as "this" is a synonym for "this object."

Caution: If you use a `super()` constructor in a subclass constructor, it *must* be the first statement.

We haven't had to do this before, because Java has always done it for us—the first thing that happens in a subclass constructor is always a hidden call to the no-argument superclass constructor. We needed an explicit `super()` call here precisely because there is no such thing as a no-argument constructor for Dialog.[5]

Finally, we're done. The only part of the file that remains is the definition of the `WarningMessage` class, and we've already been through that. Here's the complete file, with comments restored.

```
//---------------- File DialogAppTest.java -----------------

import java.awt.*;     // Notice, no java.applet.* import!

public class DialogAppTest extends Frame
// This is an application, not an applet.  It extends Frame
// so there's some place for it to be displayed
// and has a main() method, which is where execution begins.
{
    public DialogAppTest()
    // In this simple application, the constructor
    // has no work to do.
    {
    }

    public static void main(String[] args)
    // Set up the application frame and the warning dialog
    {
        Frame f = new DialogAppTest();
        f.add("Center", new Label("The application frame...."));
        f.reshape(20, 20, 300, 200);
        f.show();

        WarningDialog wd =
            new WarningDialog(f, "Really erase hard drive?");
        wd.show();
    }
}


//----------------------------------------------------------
```

(continued)

---

[5]If this seems confusing, rest easy. We'll go over it in more detail in Chapter 5.

```
class WarningDialog extends Dialog
// This class is an extension of Dialog.  It has a graphic display
// and two buttons.
{
    WarningMessage warn;
    Button okayBttn = new Button("OK");
    Button yesBttn = new Button("Yes");

    public WarningDialog(Frame parent, String message)
    // Our constructor for this class.  We need a Frame argument,
    // since a dialog must know its parent frame.
    {
        // First, call the Dialog constructor and then
        // set some of the properties of this object.
        super(parent, false);
        setBackground(Color.white);
        setResizable(false);

        // Initialize the warning message and add it
        // to this dialog.
        warn = new WarningMessage(message);
        add("North", warn);

        // Add the two buttons in a panel of their own
        Panel p = new Panel();
        p.add(okayBttn);
        p.add(yesBttn);
        add("Center", p);

        // Finally, set the size and location of this dialog.
        reshape(140, 130, 190, 75);
    }
}


//----------------------------------------------------------


class WarningMessage extends Canvas
{
    // To save space, we've deleted the class definition
    // here, since we discussed it at the start of this section.
}
```

Menus

We've all seen and used menus that drop down with a list of choices when we click on them. Java has menus, even though the class structure that implements them is a bit complicated.

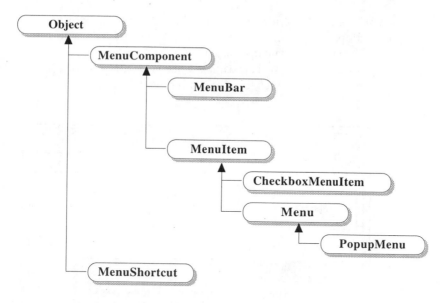

Figure 4.4 The Menu class hierarchy.

For all the complexity of the class hierarchy, menus have a straightforward logical structure.

- A MenuBar holds a collection of Menus, and must be associated with a Frame.
- A Menu holds a collection of MenuItems and separators.
- A MenuItem may be enabled or disabled, and it may be checkable.
- A Menu may also be a MenuItem, leading to hierarchical menus.

In Figure 4.5 the MenuBar is at the top of the Frame. This MenuBar contains two Menus, "File," in the default location and "Help!" in a special location set aside for help menus. The "File" Menu contains six MenuItems: "New," "Open," "Save," "Lose," "Randomize," and "Scatter," along with a *separator* between the "Open" and "Save" items. The "Save" item is *disabled,* meaning that it is displayed in a distinguishing way and will not respond to the mouse. The "Lose" item is actually another Menu (which is why Menu is a subclass of MenuItem) containing four items, "Some File," "This Directory," "Hard drive," and "Mind." The "Mind" item is a CheckBoxMenuItem: It initially looks like any other item and it toggles between a checked and unchecked state each time it is selected.

MenuShortcut is a version 1.1 class that allows you to associate key combinations with menu items so that, for example, pressing the Control and Z keys simultaneously might have the same result as selecting the "Undo" item from the "Edit" menu. We won't discuss this class in depth.

You can designate a Menu as being a *tear-off menu.* On the systems that support this option, you can drag a selected Menu off the menu bar to another location, where it will remain open as a floating *palette.*

Where a `MenuBar` will appear and what its `Menus` will look like depends, of course, on the system in which the program is running.

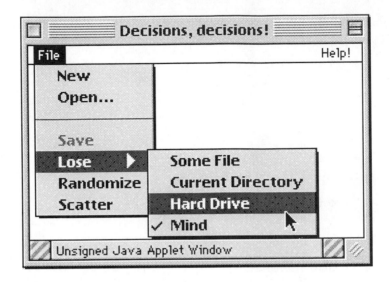

Figure 4.5 The parts of a menu.

MenuComponents

This is an abstract class and it's the superclass, directly or indirectly, of all the menu classes except `MenuShortcut`, meaning that its methods can be called by any of the other menu classes. The only methods of concern to us here are two get/set pairs.

```
Font getFont()
void setFont(Font f)
```
Gets or sets the `Font` used for the name of this component. Setting a Font for a Menu will set the Font for all its items. You can use the `setFont()` method creatively to make strikingly ugly menus.

```
String getName()
void setName(String name)
```
Gets or sets the name used for this component.

MenuBars

The `MenuBar` class holds `Menus`. You use the `add()` method to add a `Menu` to the `MenuBar` and you associate a `MenuBar` with a `Frame` by using the `Frame` method `setMenuBar(MenuBar mb)`. This class has a single default constructor, `MenuBar()`, and the following methods, among others.

Menu **add**(Menu m)
>   Adds a `Menu` to this `MenuBar`. `Menus` are added in the order in which they appear in the program. You can't add a `MenuItem` to a `MenuBar`. `Menus` (and `MenuItems`) are distinguished by name, so a `MenuBar` can have only one `Menu` with a given name.

int **countMenus**()   `// may vanish`
>   Returns the current number of `Menus` in this `MenuBar`. This count does not include any submenus; it counts only the top-level ones whose names appear in the bar. This method may be replaced in the future by `getMenuCount()`.

Menu **getHelpMenu**()
>   Returns the `Menu` designated as a help menu by `setHelpMenu()`, if any.

Menu **getMenu**(int index)
>   Returns the `Menu` at the given position in this bar. The index value must represent a valid position in this bar and, as usual, positions are counted from 0 up.

int **getMenuCount**()   `// version 1.1 only`
>   This method is the version 1.1 equivalent of `countMenus()`.

void **remove**(int index)
>   Removes the `Menu` with the given index from this bar. The index must be a valid, so you must have 0 ≤ index < *menu count.*

void **remove**(MenuComponent m)
>   Removes the given `MenuComponent` from this bar. You'll pass this a `Menu`, rather than a `MenuItem`. If the argument is not present in this bar, nothing happens.

void **setHelpMenu**(Menu m)
>   Designates a `Menu` in this bar to be set in a special location (usually on the far right of the bar, for those systems that support help menus). The `Menu` in the argument must have been previously added to this bar, otherwise nothing will happen.

Menus

The Menu class has three constructors.

Menu ()   `// version 1.1 only`
Menu (String name)
Menu (String name, boolean canTearOff)
    The first constructor creates an untitled Menu that can't be torn off. The second allows you to provide a name (like "File") for a nontearable Menu. The last permits you to provide a name and indicate whether this Menu will be tearable (true argument) or not (false argument).

    The methods of this class are similar in many ways to those of MenuBar. You use the add () method to add MenuItems (which can be Menus, recall) to the Menu. Items are added in order and are indexed from 0.

void **add** (String name)
    This useful method creates a new MenuItem with the specified name and adds it to this Menu. Remember, MenuItem names must be distinct—if the argument string has already been used in this or another Menu, the existing item is first removed.

MenuItem **add** (MenuItem m)
    Adds a MenuItem to this Menu.

MenuItem **addSeparator** ()
    Adds a graphic separator to this Menu. Separators do not respond to mouse events but are figured in the item count. See also insertSeparator ().

int **countItems** ()   `// may vanish`
    Returns the current number of MenuItems in this Menu. This count doesn't include items in any submenus. This method may be replaced in the future by getItemCount ().

MenuItem **getItem** (int index)
    Returns the MenuItem at the given position in this Menu. The index value must represent a valid position in this Menu.

int **getItemCount** ()   `// version 1.1 only`
    This method is the version 1.1 equivalent of countItems ().

void **insert** (MenuItem item, int index)   `// version 1.1 only`
    Inserts the item in the given position in this Menu. The index argument must be greater than or equal to 0.

```
void insert(String name, int index)      // version 1.1 only
```
      Creates a new `MenuItem` with the specified name and inserts it in the indicated position in this `Menu`. The index argument must be greater than or equal to 0.

```
void insertSeparator  (String name,
                            int index)      // version 1.1 only
```
      Inserts a separator in the indicated position in this `Menu`. The index argument must be greater than or equal to 0.

```
boolean isTearOff()
```
      Returns `true` if this `Menu` has the "tear-off" property, whether or not the system supports tear-off menus, and returns false if this `Menu` doesn't have that property.

```
void remove(int index)
```
      Removes the `Menu` with the given index from this bar. The index must be a valid position number, so we must have 0 ≤ index < *menu count*.

```
void remove(MenuComponent m)
```
      Removes the given `MenuComponent` from this bar. The argument should be `Menu`, rather than a `MenuItem`. If the argument is not present in this bar, nothing happens.

```
void removeAll()                            // version 1.1 only
```
      Removes all items from this Menu.

MenuItems

This class describes the items that live in menus. Bear in mind that `MenuItem` is a superclass of `Menu`, so all the methods we describe here are available to `Menus`, too.

      Of the three constructors for this class, two are of interest to us.

```
MenuItem()                                  // version 1.1 only
MenuItem(String name)
```
      The first method constructs an unnamed `MenuItem`, and the second constructs a new `MenuItem` with the specified name. In both, the items start in an enabled state.

      The `MenuItem` methods deal primarily with enabling/disabling items and inspecting/modifying their names.

```
void disable()                              // may vanish
void enable()                               // may vanish
```
The first method sets this item so that it will not respond to mouse events. Disabled items are often dimmed. The second enables the item, so it can be selected. You can use these methods to disable or enable an entire menu. They may be replaced by setEnabled().

```
String getLabel()
```
Returns the name of this item.

```
boolean isEnabled()
```
Returns true if this item is enabled and false otherwise.

```
void setEnabled(boolean isEnabled)      // version 1.1 only
```
If the argument is true, this item is enabled, and, if it is false, this item becomes disabled.

```
void setLabel(String name)
```
Sets the name of this item.

CheckboxMenuItems

A CheckboxMenuItem is a MenuItem, by inheritance. It maintains a state and a corresponding visual representation. An object of this type starts in the false, unchecked state, and changes its state each time it is selected.

This class has three constructors.

```
CheckboxMenuItem()                          // version 1.1 only
CheckboxMenuItem(String name)
CheckboxMenuItem(String name,
                boolean state)          // version 1.1 only
```
The first constructor creates a new, unnamed, item in false (unchecked) state. The second creates a named item in the false state. The third allows you to set both the name and the state.

Along with the inherited MenuItem methods, this class includes the following methods of its own.

```
boolean getState()
void setState()
```
Gets or sets the state of this item.

PopupMenus (version 1.1 only)

A `PopupMenu` is a `Menu`, with all the `Menu` features, that can appear when you click in a `Component`.

There are two `PopupMenu` constructors.

```
PopupMenu ()                              // version 1.1 only
PopupMenu (String name)                   // version 1.1 only
```
The first creates a new, unnamed menu. The second creates a menu with the indicated name.

At this stage, all we can do is describe the single method of interest to us here. We can't describe how to use the method, though, until we've had a chance to discuss some other events, in Chapter 6.

```
void Show (Component c, int x, int y)    // version 1.1 only
```
Causes the menu to appear at the given location, measured in the local coordinates of the `Component` argument. In practice, a `PopupMenu` usually appears in response to a mouse click in the `Component` argument. It is then the job of the program to determine the `Component`, calculate the coordinates, and then call this method, placing the menu where desired.

A Menu Sample

The menu classes are a lot easier to use than they are to describe. The process is really quite simple.

1. Construct a `Menu`.
2. Add items and separators to the `Menu`, disabling as necessary.
3. Repeat steps (1) and (2) as desired.
4. Construct a `MenuBar`.
5. Add all the `Menus` to the `MenuBar`.
6. Use `setMenuBar ()` to attach the `MenuBar` to some `Frame`.

Take a look at the following applet, and you'll see what we mean. It creates a `MenuBar`, named mb, with two `Menus`, m and h. `Menu` m contains six items, "New," "Open...," "Lose," "Randomize," and "Scatter," and `Menu` h has one ("None"). The item "Lose" is a submenu with four items of its own. By the way, we've adopted a somewhat nonstandard indentation scheme, to make the organization of the multiplicity of menu-related statements a bit clearer.

```
public class MenuTest extends Applet
{
    Frame myFrame = new Frame("Decisions, decisions!");

    public void init()
    {
        myFrame.setBackground(Color.white);

        //----------------------------------------------------

        Menu m = new Menu("File", true);
            m.add("New");
            m.add("Open...");
            m.addSeparator();
            MenuItem item = new MenuItem("Save");
            m.add(item);
            item.disable();
            Menu sub = new Menu("Lose");
                sub.add("File");
                sub.add("Directory");
                sub.add("Hard drive");
                sub.add(new CheckboxMenuItem("Mind"));
            m.add(sub);
            m.add("Randomize");
            m.add("Scatter");

        Menu h = new Menu("Help!");
            h.add("None");
        MenuBar mb = new MenuBar();
        mb.add(m);
        mb.add(h);
        mb.setHelpMenu(h);
        myFrame.setMenuBar(mb);

        //----------------------------------------------------

        myFrame.reshape(40, 130, 250, 130);
        myFrame.show();
    }
}
```

4.4   HANDS ON

The Lablet for this chapter displays a simulation of a microwave oven. The design contains two graphics, one for the oven door and one for the time display. It also contains ten buttons, arranged as shown in Figure 4.6.

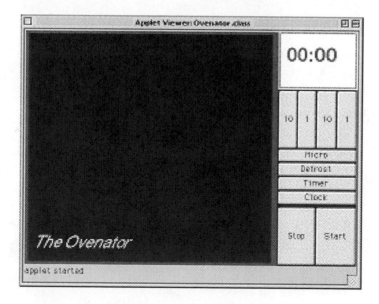

Figure 4.6 The Ovenator applet in action.

Designing the Lablet

When we were setting up the design, we decomposed it into a collection of logically related units, and then decomposed those units as needed. This is a good overall approach.

Design Tips:

1. Design from the top down.
2. Don't worry about the details until you have clarified the organization.
3. Defer low-level decisions as long as possible.

These tips apply equally well to GUI design and programming.

The visual hierarchy quickly became clear. Within the applet, we would place a control panel on the right side. The control panel would be further divided into four regions, one each for the time display, the four time buttons, the four cook mode buttons, and the two start/stop buttons. This gave us a total of five conceptual units, not counting the applet itself. Figure 4.7 illustrates the containment hierarchy, often called the *GUI hierarchy*.

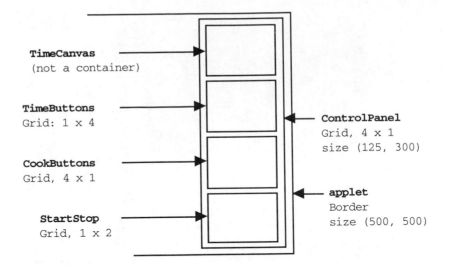

Figure 4.7 The GUI hierarchy of Ovenator.

It seemed that ten buttons, five container areas, and two graphics areas were entirely too many to lay out in one `init()` method. Even without counting up all the statements that would be required, we were certain that putting them all in one place would make `init()` too difficult to understand at first glance.

Programming Tip:

Make life easy for the readers of your programs. Try to hold method definitions to a screen's worth of code, at most.

We could have broken the `init()` method into a collection of smaller methods and then called each of these from `init()`, but there was an even better solution. The GUI hierarchy seemed to be crying out for us to impose the obvious structure on it by breaking it into separate classes, and that's exactly what we did.

Programming Tip:

Think of design in terms of classes. Whenever you see a clearly related "chunk" of design, consider encapsulating that chunk into a class of its own.

Let's see—where does that leave us? It looks as if we'll have six classes:

- The applet itself, using a variable to hold a `ControlPanel`.
- `ControlPanel`, which contains `TimeCanvas`, `TimeButtonsPanel`, `CookButtonsPanel`, and `StartStopPanel` instance variables.
- `TimeCanvas`, containing nothing but a picture.
- `TimeButtonsPanel`, with four instance variables for the four buttons.
- `CookButtonsPanel`, also containing four buttons.
- `StartStopPanel`, with its two buttons.

The Lablet Code

Now we'll walk through the Lablet, pointing out sites of interest along the way. As usual, we begin with a comment block and a collection of `import` declarations.

```
/* ********************************************************
              CHAPTER 4 LABLET:  OVENATOR

This class uses a combination of widgets and containers to
display the front panel of a microwave oven.  The oven doesn't do
any actual cooking, of course, but it's better to look good than
to be good.

************************************************************ */



import java.awt.*;
import java.applet.*;
```

The applet class definition comes next. The instance variables all make sense: We have the `ControlPanel` variable we expected and a `Font` that we'll use when we paint the door logo.

Did these *have* to be instance variables? No—myControls could have been local to `init()`, and the `logoFont` could have been local to `paint()`, just as `myAppletDim` is. We put `myControls` up among the instance variables solely to make it easy to find, and we put `logoFont` there since, unlike `myAppletDim`, it was computed just once and never changed thereafter. In that sense, `logoFont` is a *constant,* so it's slightly more efficient to initialize it once, rather than each time `paint()` is called by the system.

Before we leave this class, we should point out that the applet is initialized to a fixed size, using a `BorderLayout` to place its `ControlPanel` on the right side. Note, also, how we use the dimensions of the applet when painting the door and its logo.

```
public class Ovenator extends Applet
{
      ControlPanel myControls;
      Font logoFont = new Font("Helvetica", Font.ITALIC, 24);

      public void init()
      {
            // Set the general properties of the applet
            // We use a border layout so that we can position the
            // control panel to one side
            setBackground(Color.darkGray);
            resize(500,350);
            setLayout(new BorderLayout());

            // Create and add the control panel to the right side
            // of the applet
            myControls = new ControlPanel();
            add("East", myControls);
      }

      public void paint(Graphics g)
      // Paint the oven door and logo, using the current size
      // of the applet
      {
            Dimension myAppletDim = size();
            g.setColor(Color.black);
            g.fill3DRect(5, 5, myAppletDim.width - 135,
                        myAppletDim.height - 10, true);
            g.setColor(Color.yellow);
            g.setFont(logoFont);
            g.drawString("The Ovenator",10, myAppletDim.height - 25);
      }
}
```

The `ControlPanel` class comes next. As we mentioned before, we can put the class definitions in any order in their file, so this choice is just for our convenience in reading the program. This class extends `Panel`, the usual choice when we're doing visual design. As before, we put the four objects it contains up as instance variables simply to make them easy to find.

Note that we use a `GridLayout`, arranging the four data members in a single column, and that we also set the size to avoid surprises. Since `ControlPanel` isn't an applet, we do all our initialization in the constructor. Not only don't we have an `init()` method available, we wouldn't use one even if we did—initializations belong in constructors.

```
class ControlPanel extends Panel
{
     TimeCanvas timeDisplay;
     TimeButtonsPanel myTimeButtons;
     CookButtonsPanel myCookButtons;
     StartStopPanel myStartStop;

     public ControlPanel()
     {
          // This panel uses a grid layout to line the components
          // up in a single column
          setBackground(Color.black);
          setLayout(new GridLayout(4,1));
          resize(125,300);

          // Create the components of the control panel
          timeDisplay = new TimeCanvas();
          myTimeButtons = new TimeButtonsPanel();
          myCookButtons = new CookButtonsPanel();
          myStartStop = new StartStopPanel();

          // Add the components in the desired order
          add(timeDisplay);
          add(myTimeButtons);
          add(myCookButtons);
          add(myStartStop);
     }
}
```

We're now down to the bottom of the GUI hierarchy. The `TimeCanvas` class is simplicity itself; all the real work is done in our override of `Canvas`'s `paint()` method. In an applet that actually did something, this class would probably be a `TextField`, so that we could change the time in a realistic way.[6]

```
class TimeCanvas extends Canvas
{
     // This class is just a graphics area containing no widgets
     Font timeFont = new Font("Helvetica", Font.BOLD, 30);

     public TimeCanvas()
     // To Construct a TimeCanvas object, all we have to do
     // is set the background color.
     {
          setBackground(Color.white);
     }
```

(continued)

---

[6]That, by the way, is a surprisingly difficult task. We won't be able to make a working timer until Chapter 11.

```
public void paint(Graphics g)
{
    // Here is where we draw our "time",
    // and position it based on the canvas size
    Dimension myCanvasDim = size();
    g.setColor(Color.black);
    g.draw3DRect(2, 2, myCanvasDim.width - 5,
                  myCanvasDim.height - 5, true);
    g.setColor(Color.red);
    g.setFont(timeFont);
    g.drawString("00:00", 12, 45);
}
}
```

All that's left are the definitions for the classes `TimeButtonsPanel`, `CookButtonsPanel`, and `StartStopPanel`. These are nearly identical, and are all easy to understand. In each, the contained buttons are instance variables, constructed in the class's constructor and then added to the class. It's worth noting that we're using a form of the declaration you haven't seen so far. If you have several variables of the same type, you can declare them all in one statement, by following the type name with a comma-separated list of the variables.

```
class TimeButtonsPanel extends Panel
{
    // This panel consists of four buttons arranged in a
    // single row (hence, the grid layout)
    Button b10Minutes, b1Minute, b10Seconds, b1Second;

    public TimeButtonsPanel()
    {
        setLayout(new GridLayout(1,4));

        // Define the buttons that will go in the panel
        b10Minutes = new Button("10");
        b1Minute = new Button("1");
        b10Seconds = new Button("10");
        b1Second = new Button("1");

        // Add them to the panel using the panel's
        // grid layout scheme
        add(b10Minutes);
        add(b1Minute);
        add(b10Seconds);
        add(b1Second);
    }
}
```

```
//-----------------------------------------------------------------

class CookButtonsPanel extends Panel
{
    // This panel holds the four "cook" buttons in a
    // one-column grid
    Button      bMicro, bDefrost, bTimer, bClock;

    public CookButtonsPanel()
    {
        setLayout(new GridLayout(4,1));

        // Define the buttons that will go in the panel
        bMicro = new Button("Micro");
        bDefrost = new Button("Defrost");
        bTimer = new Button("Timer");
        bClock = new Button("Clock");

        // Add them to the panel using the panel's
        // grid layout scheme
        add(bMicro);
        add(bDefrost);
        add(bTimer);
        add(bClock);
    }

}

//-----------------------------------------------------------------

class StartStopPanel extends Panel
{
    // This panel holds a pair of buttons in a single row
    Button bStop,bStart;

    public StartStopPanel()
    {
        setLayout(new GridLayout(1,2));

        // Define the buttons that will go in the panel
        bStop = new Button("Stop");
        bStart = new Button("Start");

        // Add them to the panel using the panel's
        // grid layout scheme
        add(bStop);
        add(bStart);
    }
}
```

4.5   SUMMARY

❧ We discussed the following classes:

```
BorderLayout
CardLayout
Canvas
CheckboxMenuItem
Container
Dialog
FlowLayout
Frame
GridLayout
LayoutManager  (an interface, briefly)
Menu
MenuBar
MenuComponent
MenuItem
Panel
PopupMenu
Window
```

❧ A `Container` is used to group `Components` for visual display. A `Container` is a `Component`, by inheritance, so `Containers` can hold other `Containers`.

❧ It's quite common to have a hierarchical GUI organization, with containers nested within containers, nested within containers, and so on.

❧ `Components` are added to a `Container` by using the `Container add()` method. A `Container` cannot contain itself, either directly or indirectly.

❧ For graphic purposes, each `Component` (hence, each `Container`) has a local coordinate system, relative to its anchor point (the upper-left corner of its bounding rectangle).

❧ `Container` is an abstract class. The instances of `Container` must, consequently, come from the AWT `Container` subclasses `Panel`, `Window`, `Frame`, or `Dialog`, or from user-defined subclasses of `Container` or its subclasses.

❧ `Panel` is a commonly used subclass of `Container`. `Panel` exists for the purpose of grouping `Components` in the GUI hierarchy. `Panel` is often subclassed for custom purposes. `Applet` is a subclass of `Panel`.

❧ Each `Container` has its own `LayoutManager`, describing how its `Components` will be displayed. The `LayoutManager` of a `Component` may be changed by the `setLayout()` method.

❧ The AWT classes that implement `LayoutManager` are `FlowLayout`, `BorderLayout`, `GridLayout`, `CardLayout`, and `GridBagLayout` (which we didn't discuss). With the exception of `GridBagLayout`, all these classes have two integers that specify the horizontal and vertical gaps between the `Components` being laid out.

❧ The `FlowLayout` class is the default layout for `Panel` (and hence for `Applet`). In a `Container` with `FlowLayout`, the `Components` are arranged in the order in which they were added, left to right within rows, with the rows arranged top to bottom.

❧ `BorderLayout` is the default layout for `Window`, `Frame`, and `Dialog`. In a `BorderLayout`, the `Container` is arranged into five regions, identified by the names North, East, South, West, and Center. In this layout, `Components` are added by specifying the name (as a `String`) in the `add()` method call.

❧ In a `Gridlayout`, the `Container` is divided into a rectangular array of cells of equal size, arranged in rows and columns. The number of rows and columns may be specified in the layout constructor.

❧ Using a `null` argument in `setLayout()` will result in the `Container` having no `LayoutManager` at all. Used with the `Component` methods `move()`, `resize()`, and `reshape()`, this permits precise and unvarying arrangement of the `Components`, at the expense of flexibility and possible platform-dependence.

❧ The `Canvas` class is a `Component` subclass (but not a `Container`) used for drawing. It is the common choice for designing custom `Components`. `Canvas` has a `paint()` method, which can be overridden for drawing.

❧ `Window` is a subclass of `Container` and a superclass of `Frame` and `Dialog`. A `Window` object appears as an unadorned rectangle that "floats" above the underlying applet or application. `Window` is rarely used by itself—it is much more common to use one of its subclasses or to use `Window` as the base for a user-defined custom class.

❧ A `Frame` is a `Window` with all the ornaments of the windows of the underlying system, like a title and a close box.

❧ A `Dialog` has some of the `Frame` ornaments, but not all. A `Dialog` is most often used to inform the user of some condition or to get a limited amount of information. A `Dialog` must have a parent `Frame`.

❧ While an applet must be run in a program like an applet runner or Web browser, a Java application is capable of executing on its own. Any class can serve as the basis for an application (though its most common to subclass `Frame`). To serve as an application, a class must have a `main()` method.

❧ A Java program may have menus. The `MenuBar` class, which must be associated with a `Frame`) contains `Menus`. `Menus` contain `MenuItems`.

❧ `Menu` is a subclass of `MenuItem`, permitting a `Menu` to have submenus.

❧ A `MenuItem` may be enabled, so that it responds to mouse events, or disabled, so that it doesn't.

❧ A `CheckboxMenuItem` has two states, which are indicated when the item is displayed. The state (and its visual representation) changes each time the item is selected.

4.6   EXERCISES

1.   Why would you ever need to call either of the `Container` methods `countComponents()` or `getComponentCount()`? Hint: think about changing the layout of the `Container` or adding another `Component`.

2.   In Figure 4.2:
     a.   Name all the `Containers`.
     b.   Name all the `Components`.
     c.   In this method call: _____`.isAncestorOf(List2)`, which `Container` names could you put in the blank to make the method return `true`?

3.   Assuming `myPanel` is of type `Panel`, what does this code fragment do?

```
int n = myPanel.countComponents();
Component c = myPanel.getComponent(n - 2);
myPanel.remove(c);
```

     Give your answer in simple terms; don't just tell what each statement does.

4.   Which has more methods available for its use, an `Applet` object or a `Window` object?

5.   What's the default alignment for `FlowLayout`? How would you change it?

6.   Of the four layouts we discussed, one stands out from the others for having default horizontal and vertical gaps that are different from the others. Which is the odd one?

7.   What are the default layouts for `Panel`, `Window`, `Applet`, `Dialog`, and `Frame`, respectively?

8.   Take a look at Figure 4.2 and the applet below it. Run the applet and note that it doesn't look like the figure. Obviously, the difference is due to the fact that we used the default `FlowLayout` for each `Panel`. Rewrite the applet, inserting the necessary `setLayout()` calls and modifying the arguments to the calls to `add()`, where necessary, to make the applet look like the figure.

9.   Do (or redo) Exercise 19 of Chapter 3, knowing what you do now.

10.   Here's the skeleton of an applet.

```
public class Layouts extends Applet
{
       Button    bA = new Button("A"),
                 bB = new Button("B"),
                 bC = new Button("C"),
                 bD = new Button("D"),
                 bE = new Button("E"),
                 bF = new Button("F");
       Panel     p1 = new Panel(),
                 p2 = new Panel(),
                 p3 = new Panel(),
                 p4 = new Panel(),
                 p5 = new Panel(),
                 p6 = new Panel();

       public void init()
       {
              ...
       }
}
```

For each of the parts below, fill in the init() method so that the applet looks like the picture. There may not be just one way to make these layouts; in each part, try to find the most elegant or efficient solution.

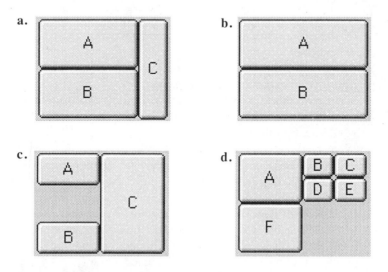

e.    **f.**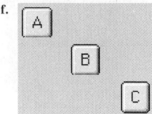

11. Write an applet that produces a display that looks *exactly* like the entire collection of pictures in Exercise 10, with part letters and gray backgrounds included. Don't use a `null` layout. (This is quite a challenging problem.)

12. Rewrite the Chapter 3 `Gigobite` Lablet so that it doesn't get weird when the applet window is resized. (This is time-consuming, but nowhere near as difficult as Exercise 11.)

13. Do Exercise 20 in Chapter 3. This time, you don't have to be especially careful to make the calculator look exactly like the screen shot. Don't waste your time with a `null` layout, and don't worry about the drop shadow.

14. Suppose you were designing a `LabeledTextField` class containing a `Label` and a `TextField`. It should look something like this.

(You don't have to paint the gray background—some background will be provided by the browser or applet runner).

a. What constructors would you want? You can't write the constructors, since you haven't designed the class yet—all we want are the arguments you would want for them.

b. What methods would you want? As in part (a), just give the method *signatures,* describing the name, return type, and arguments. In doing this part, try to anticipate what a user of your class might want. You might find it helpful to look at the methods for similar classes.

c. What member data would the class require?

d. What class should you subclass to make `LabeledTextField`?

e. Once you've answered the questions in parts (a) and (c), you can write the definitions of the constructors you designed. Do so.

f. (You'll have to do some digging here, if any of your methods in part (b) have non-`void` return types.) Write the definitions of your methods and then write an applet that uses a `LabeledTextField` to test your class.

15. When time comes to do a `GridLayout`, Java computes the number of columns needed without regard for what you said in the constructor. The formula it uses is as follows, where *rows* is the number of rows specified in the constructor:

    number of columns = (*number of components* + *rows* – 1) / *rows.*

    In doing the division, the remainder is discarded, so 8 / 3 yields 2 and 9 / 3 is 3.
    a. Let the pair (*c, r*) denote the number of `Components` to be laid out and the number of rows specified, so (8, 3) would mean trying to lay out 8 `Components` in 3 rows. How many columns does Java allocate in the following situations? (8, 1), (9, 3), (10, 3), (2, 6).
    b. Draw the layouts for (9, 3), (10, 3), (11, 3), . . . and describe in simple terms what happens in general.

16. Put yourself in the shoes of a `LayoutManager` and describe what you would do when asked to compute the minimum layout size of a `Container` that was using a `GridLayout`. To make life easier, assume that the number of rows and columns were already known.

17. Exercise your creativity and come up with a specification of a useful new layout class. Try to be as detailed as we were in our descriptions of the AWT layouts.

18. Suppose you wanted to design an electronic phone directory. You could use the `CardLayout` example we presented, replacing each `Label Component` with a panel containing fields for name, address, and phone number. For a directory with a lot of names, though, clicking the ">>" or "<<" buttons to find a name could be quite tedious.
    Suppose we grouped the cards alphabetically, so that the "A" group would contain all the cards for Able, Kathy; Allanson, Otto; Axelrod, J.T., and so on. We might then have ">" and "<" buttons for moving within groups, and use "<<" and ">>" to move between groups (from the "P" group to the "Q" group, for instance). How would you organize such a program? In other words, specify the design by indicating what `Containers` and layouts you would use, and tell (without writing any code) what the buttons would do.

19. Why does the `MenuBar` method `add(Menu m)` return a `Menu`? Is there any good reason why it shouldn't have a `void` return type?

20. `add()` is a popular method name.
    a. Name two classes that have an `add()` method.
    b. Name *all* the classes we've discussed so far that have `add()` methods.
    c. (Only for the compulsive.) Among all the classes we've discussed so far, what's the most frequently occurring method name? You're allowed to count methods that differ only in their signatures (return type or argument)

as being distinct, but you should limit yourself only to those methods we've actually mentioned in the first four chapters.

    d.   (Only for the *extremely* compulsive.) Among *all* Java classes and methods, which method name is most popular? Hint: It's not one we've talked about so far.

21.   Every Java program needs a `main()` method. Where's the `main()` hiding for applets?

22.   It might be useful to have an Undo choice in both the File and Edit menus in a program. Can a Java `menuItem` appear in two `Menus` at the same time? Explain.

23.   Which of these are supported by the Java environment(s) in your system?
    a.   Help menus.
    b.   Tear-off menus.
    c.   Modal dialogs.

In Exercises 24–28, we'll take a first look at some GUI design principles. We'll continue these investigations in the chapters that follow.

GUI design gives you tremendous power and flexibility. Using a language like Java, you can produce programs that communicate with the user in a clear, efficient, and intuitive fashion. Power always comes with the responsibility of using it properly, though—GUI design allows you to design a program that is inefficient, unintuitive, ugly, and irritating.

    We designed the `Gigobite` Lablet for the pedagogical purpose of showing off as many of Java's widgets as we could. For a similar reason, we deliberately avoided or violated GUI design principles, so that we could discuss them later (like here, for instance).

24.   An interface should be *transparent,* meaning that the purpose of all of its parts should be immediately obvious. Remember, what may be obvious to you may be completely opaque to someone who's never heard the acronym AWT.
    a.   Which parts of `Gigobite` wouldn't necessarily be obvious to the user?
    b.   Are there any obvious widgets that are obscurely identified? How would you fix them?
    c.   How logical is the placement of elements? What changes would you make in the design to make it clearer?
    d.   Is the use of color helpful or irritating? What changes would you suggest?

25.   When you've completed Exercise 24, rewrite `Gigobite` to incorporate your changes.

26.   When writing any program, especially one with a complicated interface, you should *design for use*. Think carefully about all the things a user may want to do, and see that your program is capable of doing them all.
  a.   What tasks might a customer want to perform that would be difficult or impossible in `Gigobite`?
  b.   While you can't change the action of `Gigobite` right now (since it's just a layout for now, and incapable of any actions), how would your answers to part (a) affect the interface?

27.   A program, whether graphically oriented or not, should be *forgiving*. That means that, with very few exceptions, the user should always be able to undo any action and revert to a previous state. A consequence of this guideline is that the user should never have to guess what the current state is.
  a.   How good is the original version of `Gigobite` at letting the user know where things presently stand? Suggest any improvements.
  b.   Design is an iterative process. Often, making changes to one aspect will require changes in another. If you've answered any of Exercises 24–26, have your changes influenced the forgiveness or user awareness of the program? If so, make any necessary corrections.

28.   Whether or not you've completed Exercises 24–27, go back through them and do one more refinement, producing the best `Gigobite` you can.

CHAPTER FIVE

Java Language Basics

You've seen all you need to know about laying out the parts necessary to make the visual portion of an applet or application. Along the way, you've learned quite a lot about the Java language itself. You know what a class is (the *semantics,* or meaning, of classes) and what a class definition looks like (the *syntax,* or rules of Java grammar). You know about variables and their declarations, and you've seen scores of method definitions and the calls necessary to invoke them. By now, you should be hankering to get to the next stage, making all the widgets in a Java program actually *do* something. Before we can teach you how to do that, though, we need to make sure you have a solid grasp of the Java language itself, and that's what we'll do in this chapter. You've seen some of this material before, so you can best think of this chapter as a combination of instruction and reference.

OBJECTIVES

In this chapter, we will
- Review the structure of a Java program.
- Discuss the *primitive types* that Java provides for your use.
- Complete our discussion of variables, talking about *access* and *scope.*
- Introduce a few statements that you haven't seen so far.
- Talk about some of the principles that guide efficient programming.

5.1   PRIMITIVE TYPES

In Java, as in many other programming languages, every piece of information has an associated *type.* The type of an object determines how much space the object will occupy in memory and how the object may be used. For example, a `Panel` object takes more space than an `int`, and it obviously makes no sense to add 2 to a

`Panel`, even though addition makes perfect sense for `int`s. Each class is a type of its own, so a `Panel` object is considered to be a different type from a `Button` object or an `int`. In addition to all the types in the class hierarchy and those you make by extending existing types, Java provides a collection of eight *primitive types* for things like numbers and characters.

The Eight Java Simple Types:

`byte, short, int, long`	Integers
`float, double`	Floating-point numbers
`char`	Characters
`boolean`	Logical values

As we'll see shortly, there are fundamental differences between the primitive types and the class types.

Integers

Java has four types available for representing whole numbers like 2, −54, and 3677009. These *integral types* are, in order of the sizes of numbers they represent, `byte`, `short`, `int`, and `long`. A `byte` takes up very little room in the computer's memory, only eight binary digits, but in consequence is capable of representing only numbers in the range −128 to 127. A `short` integer uses twice as much space and can represent numbers in the range −32768 to 32767. When we want to represent whole numbers, we usually use the `int` type, which is four times as long as a `byte` and can represent any whole number from −2147483648 to 2147483647. Clearly, then, the `int` type should be sufficient for most of the programs you're likely to write, but if you need to use really big integers, the `long` integer type uses sixty-four binary digits. We'll leave as an exercise the problem of discovering where these ranges come from and the maximum and minimum `long` integers.

For the primitive types, a *literal* expression is the way a specific value is written in a program. For the integral types, the rule governing the way a literal is written is quite simple.

Syntax:

An integer literal must be written as [*optional sign*]*stringOfDigits*. Literals of type long are distinguished by a trailing L.

The following are all legal integral type literals:

```
0    3L    -200    5556556665656565L    +343
```

These numbers are not Java integral-type literals:

```
1,000            (can't use commas)
two              (can only use digits, + or −)
```

All of the primitive types have a *default value* when they are declared, unless you initialize them to some other value. For instance, the default value for integral-type variables is 0, so if you declare an `int` variable by writing

```
int total;
```

Java will set `total`'s initial value to 0, just as if you had written

```
int total = 0;
```

Caution:

We don't advise making a habit of declaring a variable without setting its initial value. It's a bad habit to get into, since you might some day forget to set the initial value when you most emphatically don't want it to be 0.

Floating-Point Numbers

As useful as integers are, there will be times when you need to use numbers with fractional parts, like 3.14159 or −0.000675. The two *floating-point* types, `float` and `double` are designed for such problems and, like the integral types, they are distinguished by the number of bits in their internal representations and, hence, the accuracy and sizes of numbers they can represent.

To save typing when writing numbers like 0.00000000000000000012, Java allows you to use *scientific notation,* by following a number with e and an integer. The integer after the e indicates how many places to the right to shift the decimal point, if the integer exponent is positive, and to the left if the integer is negative. Thus, the preceding number could be written more compactly as `0.12e-18`, or `1.2e-19`, or even `1200.0e-22`. The e actually represents multiplication by the indicated power of 10, so `3.245e2` represents 3.245×10^2, or `324.5`.

A `float` number has approximately seven decimal digits of accuracy and can represent numbers as small as `1.4e-45` and as large as `3.4e+38`. For really big or small numbers, the `double` type will give you about ten decimal places of accuracy and a range of `4.9e-324` to `1.7e+308`. As with integers, floating point numbers have a default value of zero (0.0).

Syntax:

Floating-point literals must be written in one of the following eight forms:

digitString	*digitString* e *integerLiteral*
digitString .	*digitString* . e *integerLiteral*
. *digitString*	. *digitString* e *integerLiteral*
digitString . *digitString*	*digitString* . *digitString* e *integerLiteral*

`float` literals are distinguished by following the literal with the letter `f`. All floating-point numbers may have a leading + or - sign.

The following are all legal floating-point literals:

```
0    3f    .34    0.34    40.f    -12e8    -12e+8    -10.08e-23f
```

Characters

There will be times when we need to manipulate information other than numbers. Java provides the `char` type to represent individual characters. Characters are written literally as a single character within single quotes, like 'X' or 'x' (which are considered as two different characters). Internally, characters are stored using the 16-bit coding scheme known as *Unicode,* the details of which need not concern us here. Some nonprinting characters are used so often that they have been given special representations: '\b' is the backspace, '\n' is the linefeed, '\r' is the carriage return, and '\t' is the tab. Since the single quote, backslash, and (as we'll see in a moment) the double quote characters have special meanings, they also have their own representations: '\'', '\\' and '\"', respectively. Strings of more than one character may also be written in a program, by enclosing them in double quotes (not two single quotes), like "This is a string". We'll have much more to say about character strings in Chapter 8.

   Strictly speaking, the `char` type is an integral type, since `char`s are stored by their Unicode representation, a 16-bit value. For example, the character that appears to us as 'A' is stored in Java as the number 65. The default value for the `char` type is the character with code zero, written '\0'. This is a nonprinting character.

The boolean Type

The boolean type has just two values, expressed by the literals true and false. We'll see shortly that just as the numeric types come with *operators,* like +, that allow us to perform arithmetic, the boolean type has a collection of operators that allow us to perform logical computations. The default value for boolean variables is false.

5.2   IDENTIFIERS, KEYWORDS, AND VARIABLES

Names of variables, methods, classes, and packages are known collectively as *identifiers.* The syntax of identifiers is simple enough.

Syntax: Identifiers

Identifiers must all have the form *letter* or *letter letterNumberString,* where *letter* is any of the characters 'A' .. 'Z' or 'a' .. 'z' and *letterNumberString* is any collection of letters, digits ('0' .. '9'), or underscores ('_').[1] In addition, an identifier cannot be a Java *keyword.*

Java keywords are the built-in parts of the language. There are fifty Java keywords, all but three of which we'll cover in this text.[2]

Syntax: Java Keywords

abstract	default	goto	null	synchronized
boolean	do	if	package	this
break	double	implements	private	throw
byte	else	import	protected	throws
case	extends	instanceof	public	transient
catch	false	int	return	true
char	final	interface	short	try
class	finally	long	static	void
const	float	native	super	volatile
continue	for	new	switch	while

---

[1] You can also use the dollar sign, '$', in the letterNumberString, but we don't advise it.

[2] For the "language lawyers," true, false, and null are actually literals, not keywords.

For example, the following are all valid identifiers in Java

```
x  foo  Int  button2  the_message  identifiersCanBeAsLongAsYouLike
```

We threw in the "`Int`" identifier to serve as a reminder that identifiers in Java are case-sensitive. We couldn't have used "`int`" as one of our identifiers, since "`int`" is a keyword. Since Java considers the lower- and uppercase versions of a letter as different (since they have different Unicode representations), "`Int`" is a perfectly legitimate identifier, although it's so close in look to a keyword that we wouldn't recommend using it.

None of these are valid identifiers:

`2fold`	(Doesn't start with a letter.)
`my Panel`	(Contains an invalid character, the space.)
`final`	(It's a keyword.)

Variables

You've already seen quite a few variables in the examples we've used so far. You know that a variable is used to store information for later use, and you've seen two different kinds of variables. *Instance variables* are declared at the class level and represent the data "owned" by an object of that class, and *local* variables are declared in a method and have meaning only within that method.

Figure 5.1 illustrates the distinction between instance and local variables.

```
class Triple
// Stores and manipulates triples of floating-point numbers.
{
  double x, y, z;            instance variables:  can be used
                             here, or
  Triple()                   here, or in any method in this class.
  {
   x = 0.0;
   y = 0.0;
   y = 0.0;
  }

  double sum()
  {
    double theSum = 0.0;       local variable:  can only be used
    theSum = x + y + z;        here, in this method.
    return theSum;
  }
}
```

Figure 5.1 Instance and local variables.

An instance variable "belongs" to any object that is an instance of a class. If the *access* of an instance variable permits, we can inspect and modify an instance variable by using the name of the object, a dot, and the name of the variable.[3] For example, if we had made the following declaration in the method of another class,

```
Triple origin = new Triple();
```

we could then set the x variable of `origin` to 2.3 by writing

```
origin.x = 2.3;
```

in much the same way as we could invoke `origin`'s sum() method by using the "dot notation,"

```
double value = origin.sum();
```

Syntax: Instance Variables

Instance variables of a class may be accessed by using *objectName.variableName*. (The last dot is the end of the sentence, and wouldn't be part of a program.)

Each instance of a class has its own collection of instance variables. If `origin` and `translate` were two `Triple` instances, `origin.x` and `translate.x` would be entirely different things—one might contain 2.3 and the other might have the value 0.0, for example.

Scope

The *scope* of an identifier is that portion of the class where the identifier may be used. As we've mentioned, a class variable, instance variable, or method name can be used anywhere in the class. A local variable, on the other hand, may only be used within the closest pair of braces { and } that enclose the declaration, and then only in those statements within the braces that occur *after* the declaration. The following code is an example.

---

[3]We'll discuss access shortly.

```
class MyClass
{
    int inst;               // INSTANCE VARIABLE
    ...                             // can use inst here
    void someMethod()
    {
        ...                         // can use inst here, but not loc
        {
            ...                     // can use inst here, but not loc
            int loc = 3; // LOCAL VARIABLE
            ...                     // can use inst or loc here
        }
        ...                         // can use inst here, but not loc
    }

    void someOtherMethod()
    {
        ...                         // can use inst here, but not loc
                                    // could also call someMethod() here
    }
}
```

Let's make a minor change to this example, using the *same* name for both the instance and local variables.

```
class MyClass
{
    int huh = 2;
    ...
    void someMethod()
    {
        int huh = 3;
        ...             // Is huh 2 or 3 here?
    }

    void someOtherMethod()
    {
        ...             // Is huh 2 or 3 here?
    }
}
```

In `someOtherMethod()`, the answer is pretty clear—we're referring to the instance variable (since we can't see the local variable in `someOtherMethod()`), and so its value is 3. In `someMethod()`, though, it's not clear which variable we're using at the indicated place. Should the local variable or the instance variable be more important?

Java's rule for these situations is common in other languages: *The most local variable is the one in force.* In this case, we say that in the indicated line the local (value 3) variable *shadows* the less local (value 2) one, meaning that in that particular location it is as if the less local variable isn't even defined.

Syntax: Resolving Scope

Java has no difficulty dealing with identically named variables. The syntactical rules are

1. You cannot declare two variables of the same name at the same scope level.
2. Any variable declared strictly within the scope of another with the same name will shadow the outer named variable.

This rule holds for method arguments, as well. Method arguments have local scope, so they have no meaning outside of the method, and they are defined throughout the body of the method. This implies that you can't have a local variable in a method that has the same name as one of the method's arguments.

The Modifiers `static` and `final`

There are times when it is either more efficient or makes better sense to associate a variable with an entire class, rather than have a separate copy of the variable for every instance of that class. For example, we may have a class `Circle` whose instances were intended to represent circles and perform certain computations, like calculating areas. We'd probably need the value for π to do this, but it would be silly to waste space in each `Circle` object for a copy of that value. Much better would be to set this value once and associate it with the class, rather than with all the instances of the class. We do that by using the `static` modifier:

```
class Circle
{
     static double PI = 3.1415926535;
     . . .
}
```

Now, just as with an instance variable, every method in this class has access to the variable `PI`. You can access a class variable from outside the class, using the dot notation, but this time you don't put an instance name in front. Rather, you use the class name itself, `Circle.PI`, in this case. Look familiar? It should—think of `Color.red` or `FlowLayout.RIGHT`, for some examples of class variables you've already seen.

Syntax: `static` Variables

Class variables are distinguished from instance variables by the use of the modifier `static` at the start of their declarations. Within the class, such a variable may be accessed by its name. Outside the class a class variable may be accessed by using the dot notation, *className . variableName.*

Methods may be `static`, too. This is commonly done in classes like `java.lang.Math` that are used only to hold methods and aren't subclassed. Such classes often have no constructors and all their methods are `static`. We'll discuss the `Math` class in the next section.

Even if you don't know much mathematics, you probably realize that `PI` shouldn't really be a variable. After all, π is fixed, and we shouldn't give users of our `Circle` class the opportunity to change it. We can fix an instance of a variable forever by using the modifier `final`. In our `Circle` example, we should say

```
class Circle
{
    final static double PI = 3.1415926535;
    ...
}
```

to indicate that the class variable `PI` shouldn't act like a variable, but rather as a *constant*. When we have declared `PI` this way, modifying it by later writing an expression like the following would be illegal.[4]

```
Circle.PI = 3.2;    // ERROR: PI is final, so can't be changed.
```

You can define a class as `final`, too. While it's not often done, a `final` class cannot be subclassed. The `Math` and `Color` classes are `final`.

---

[4]This actually happened. In 1897, the Indiana State Legislature, in a 67–0 vote, passed a bill legislating the value of pi to be 3.2. By more or less dumb luck, the bill failed in the Indiana Senate. For details, see

```
http://www.urbanlegends.com/legal/pi_indiana.html.
```

Syntax: `final` Variables

A class variable or instance variable may be declared to be `final`, making it an error to change its value. The declaration of a `final` variable must include an initialization so that the declaration

```
final int ZERO = 0;
```

would be legal and

```
final int ZERO;
```

would not, in spite of the apparent default initialization of `int`s. It's common to identify final variables by using ALL_CAPS for their names.

Brief Interlude: Packages

Java allows you to group files into *packages*. The AWT classes, for example, are defined over dozens of separate files, but they're all part of the package `java.awt`. You can make packages of your own, if you wish, and import their names the same way you import the names from the `java.awt` package.

To indicate that a file is part of a package, all you need to do is include the package declaration

```
package packageName;
```

as the *very first* line in your file (except, perhaps, for blank lines and comments) and then make sure that this file is in a directory or folder with the same name as the package. Suppose, for example, that we had made a couple of widgets of our own, say, a `GraphicButton`, and a `Slider`. For convenience, we might have put each of them in a separate file, so we might have the following file for our `GraphicButton` class definition.

```
//--------------- File GraphicButton.java ----------------
package myWidgets;

import java.awt*;   // so we can use the name "Canvas"

public class GraphicButton extends Canvas
{
    . . .
}
```

Similarly, the `Slider` class might reside in its own file, "Slider.java," and might look like

```
//--------------- File Slider.java ----------------
package myWidgets;

import java.awt*;

public class Slider extends Canvas
{
    . . .
}
```

Both of these files would be placed in the directory "myWidgets," and we could then use them in another file by `importing` them:

```
//--------------- File Test.java ----------------
import java.applet.*;
import java.awt.*;
import myWidgets.*; // NOTE: we get both class names here

public class Test extends Applet
{
    GraphicButton myButton;
    Slider mySlider;
    . . .
}
```

Finally, note that our applet file doesn't have a `package` declaration. In fact, if you look back, you'll see that none of the applets we've made so far have had `package` declarations. Throughout, we've been making use of the fact that Java always sets aside an *anonymous package,* into which go all of the files that don't have `package` declarations. We've been using packages all along—we just haven't generated one with a name. We haven't mentioned packages so far, but we need them now, so that we can talk about *access.*

Access Modifiers

An important consideration in good programming is *information hiding.* The old observation, "There are two things you don't want to watch being made: sausages and laws" could be amended with equal truth to include program design. We want to make life easy for the users of our classes, so we don't want to burden other programmers (or ourselves, for that matter) with the need to remember all the details of how we implement a class. What we'd like to do is let the users know how to use our classes in their programs, without ever giving them access to the dirty details of the variables and methods we use along the way. Doing this, we not only reduce the mental effort on the part of our fellow programmers, but, perhaps even more important, we can guarantee that outsiders won't derange the actions of our classes by mucking about with things that are better left alone.

Consider, for instance, the Container class. Every Container has to know how many Components it contains, so it keeps an instance variable that we might call numComponents. This variable is increased by 1 every time the user of the class calls add() and is reduced by 1 in every remove() call. There's an important *class invariant* at work here: "numComponents represents the number of Components in the Container." Imagine the chaos that could result if this variable was accessible from outside the class—a user might inadvertently set it to 0 or increase it by 7. What would happen then when time came to lay out the Container? We can't say for sure, but we can almost guarantee that it wouldn't be pleasant.

Java provides us with three declaration modifiers that allow us to specify the levels of access we will grant to *members* (class variables, instance variables, and methods).

private Access

The private modifier completely hides a member from outsiders. A private variable or method can be accessed by name *only within the class's methods*. The identifier is unknown to other classes, even those that extend the class in which it is defined.

A good rule of thumb is to make all the instance variables of a class private. If they need to be inspected, provide the class with *accessor methods* and if they need to be modified, provide the class with public *mutator methods*. Here's an example, obtained by second-guessing how the Container class is defined.

```
class Container extends Component
// Our implementation of Container--not the real one.
{
    private int numComponents;
    private LayoutManager ourLayout;

    ...

    public int countComponents()
    // Accessor: The outside world can look, but not touch.
    {
        return numComponents;
    }
```

```
        public LayoutManager getLayout()
        // Accessor
        {
            return ourLayout;
        }

        public void setLayout(LayoutManager layout)
        // Mutator: Allow the user to change ourLayout
        {
            ourLayout = layout;
        }

        . . .

    }
```

Syntax: `private`

A member can be declared to have `private` access, by placing the modifier private in front of its declaration. Thus, `private` access means that the identifier is defined only within the class and can be used only in methods of this class. `private` members are *not* inherited by subclasses.

This doesn't imply that there's no way of getting to the value of a `private` variable. It just means that there's no *direct* way. In the preceding example, if `c` were some `Container` object, we could never legally refer to `c.numComponents` outside the class, but we could still get to that value by using the accessor method call, `c.countComponents()`. In the preceding example, the class designer is saying, in effect, "I've provided a method that allows you to look at `numComponents`, but I don't want you changing it, so I haven't given you a way to do that."

Programming Tip:

Design classes on a "need to know" basis. Unless there's a compelling reason for a member to be accessed from outside a class, make the member `private`.

As with the rest of our programming tips, you can violate this guideline if you have a good reason for doing so. In the `Point` class, for instance, the two instance variables x and y are `public`, meaning that for a `Point` p, the data `p.x` and `p.y` can be accessed anywhere. This makes sense in this situation, since the

`Point` class is little more than a way of gathering two `int`s into one object. In `Point`, accessor and mutator methods would be overkill.

Package Access

If we don't place any of the `private`, `protected`, or `public` modifiers in front of a member declaration, we are giving that member what is known as *default* or *package* access. A member with default access is visible within its own class, of course, and is visible in methods of any class in the same package.

Syntax: Package Access

A member without any access modifiers is visible anywhere within its own package, but cannot be seen outside of the package where it is declared.

Until now, we've given many of the members in our example classes package access, simply so we wouldn't have to explain the modifiers. Most of these members should have been given `public` or `private` access. From here on, we'll be more careful about specifying access (except in the Lablet, where we've left it for you to determine the appropriate accesses for its members).

`protected` Access

If a member is given `protected` access, it is accessible anywhere within the same package, and cannot be seen outside of the package, exactly as if it had default access. The difference between `protected` access and default access is that `protected` members of a class are inherited by subclasses, even if the subclass is defined in another package.

Syntax: `protected`

Declaring a member to be `protected` means that the identifier is defined within the package and within any subclass, whether or not the subclass is in the same package.[5]

---

[5]You might see a related form of access, `private protected`. This access is allowed in version 1.0, but not in 1.1, so you shouldn't use it.

If you design a class and suspect that it may eventually be subclassed, you can declare as `protected` any variables or methods that a subclass will need but that should be hidden from outsiders.

There is one minor quirk to this form of access that we should mention for the sake of completeness. The problem comes up only when a subclass is declared in a different package from the base class. In that case, the subclass inherits any `protected` members of the base class and can use them as its own. What it *cannot* do, though, is access any of the `protected` members *of an instance of the base class.* We'll give an example, and then leave, since this situation is fairly uncommon.

Here's the base class defined in the package `utilities`:

```
package utilities;

class Triple
{
    protected double x, y, z;
    . . .
}
```

and here's a subclass defined in a different package:

```
package myOtherUtilities;

import utilities*; // so we can recognize the name "Triple"

class AlgebraicTriple extends Triple
{
    . . .
    void add(Triple t)
    {
        this.x = this.x + t.x;    //NO!
        . . .
    }
}
```

The problem here is that `AlgebraicTriple` can certainly look at its own x variable (which it inherits from `Triple`) when we use `this.x`. It *can't,* however, inspect the x member of any superclass instances, like t. This is a cause for confusion in some rare situations, but we just have to live with it.

`public` Access

The least restricted access is `public`. If a member is given `public` access, that member is visible anywhere, in or out of the class.

Syntax: `public`

A member with `public` access is visible anywhere. Constructors are almost always `public`, and methods are generally `public` as well, except for those "helper" methods that are called only within the class. The `public` members are inherited in subclasses.

Putting it all together, we have the following table.

Access	Class	Subclass	Package	Everywhere
`private`	✔			
(default)	✔		✔	
`protected`	✔	✔	✔	
`public`	✔	✔	✔	✔

Syntax Review: Modifiers

We've discussed five modifiers in Java: `public`, `protected`, `private`, `static`, and `final`.[6] The order in which they appear is unimportant, as long as they appear before the declaration they modify. In any declaration, only one of `public`, `protected`, or `private` may be used.

Local variables cannot be modified.

For example, the following declarations are all equally acceptable in Java, and they all have the same result: setting the class variable `PI` to the fixed value `3.1415926535` and allowing it to be accessed by any other class, no matter where the other class is defined.

```
public static final double PI = 3.1415926535;
public final static double PI = 3.1415926535;    // our preference
static public final double PI = 3.1415926535;
static final public double PI = 3.1415926535;
final public static double PI = 3.1415926535;
final static public double PI = 3.1415926535;
```

---

[6]There are two other modifiers, `transient` and `volatile`, that are outside the scope of this book.

5.3 OPERATORS AND EXPRESSIONS

In this section, we find ourselves back on familiar ground, looking at the operations Java provides for doing things like arithmetic. We'll discuss the operators first, then use the operators to produce complicated expressions, and finally, in the next section, discuss how to use these expressions to write the statements that make up programs.

Numeric Operators

Scattered among the example classes we've shown so far, you'll find the basic operators for manipulation of numeric information: + for addition, – for subtraction, * for multiplication, and / for division. Each of these takes an *operand* on the left and one on the right, performs the operation, and returns the value to the program. These operations, and all others, for that matter, can be combined to make *expressions* as complicated as you need, using parentheses as necessary to group subexpressions together.

Here are some examples. Let's suppose we've already declared

```
int n = 3, m = -1;
```

Then, all of the following are legitimate expressions:

```
n                    // value 3
2 + n                // value 5
4 * n + m            // value 11
4 * (n + m)          // value 8
2 - n - 4            // value -5
```

Hmm. There seems to be more to this than appears at first glance. Consider the expression 4 * n + m. We have two operators here, multiplication and addition. If we do the multiplication first, 4 * n evaluates to 12 and the resulting expression, 12 + m, gives us 11. But, doing the addition first gives us 2 for the value of n + m and then multiplication by 4 yields 8. There's a genuine ambiguity here and Java adopts a time-honored solution—it simply legislates the problem away. Each of the Java operators has an associated *precedence*. In cases where there are no parentheses to force a different order of evaluation, the operator with higher precedence is performed first. In this case, since multiplication has a higher precedence than addition, the multiplication is performed first. The summary section at the end of this chapter has a complete precedence list.

What about the expression 2 - n - 4, though? Should we evaluate it as if it were written (2 - n) - 4 or should we do it in the order 2 - (n - 4)? In the first order, the result is –5 and in the second the steps would be $2 - (3 - 4)$, then

2 – (–1), for a result of 3. Precedence is clearly no help here—we need another rule, for the way the implicit parentheses are placed. This rule is known as *associativity*, and in Java it's simple: two-operand arithmetic operators are grouped from the left.

Semantics: Precedence and Associativity

Every Java operator has a precedence. Unless an expression is parenthesized to indicate a different order of evaluation, the operators are evaluated in order of their precedence.

If an expression contains operators of the same precedence, the order of evaluation is governed by the operators' associativity. The operators +, – , *, and / all group from the left.

As a rather complicated example, consider the expression

```
2 * 4 - 3 + 5 * 4
```

First, the two multiplications have higher precedence than the subtraction and addition, so we have an expression with three terms:

```
(2 * 4) - 3 + (5 * 4)
```

Finally, since the operators + and – have the same precedence, we rely on their associativity to group the expression from left to right:

```
(((2 * 4) - 3) + (5 * 4))
```

Here's how the expression would be evaluated

```
(((2 * 4) - 3) + (5 * 4))
((   8  -   3) + (5 * 4))
(      11      + (5 * 4))
(      11      +    20  )
                31
```

There are forty-six Java operators, grouped into thirteen levels of precedence, with each operator having a defined associativity. It seems like a daunting exercise in memorization to keep all that straight, but fortunately there's an easy way out.

Programming Tip:

When dealing with any but the simplest expression, *completely parenthesize it.* Not only will parentheses make it less likely you'll specify the wrong order of evaluation, but it will make the expression considerably easier to read.

We haven't used division in any of our examples in this section. There are actually two different division operators, one for integers and one for floating-point numbers. Integer division is used when both operands are integral types, and it returns the quotient, discarding any remainder and, effectively, rounding towards zero. For example, (8 / 4), (9 / 4), (10 / 4), and (11 / 4) all evaluate to 2 and (-9 / 4) yields -2. You can use the operator % to get the remainder of integer division, so (8 % 4) is 0, (9 % 4) is 1, (10 % 4) is 2, and so on. The % operator is often used to test whether one integer is evenly divisible by another, since n % m is 0 only when m divides n evenly.

Floating-point division uses the same symbol, /, but this time the quotient and fractional part are both retained, so 9.0 / 4.0 evaluates to the floating-point number 2.25.

There are no "mixed" arithmetic operators. In an expression like 9.0 / 4, the integer 4 is first *promoted* to the floating-point equivalent, 4.0, and then the floating-point version of division is performed, yielding 2.25. Promotion is always done from "shorter" forms to longer: byte, short and char are all promoted to int, and the promotions int → long → float → double are performed as needed to make the operands match.

There are times when you might want to do these conversions yourself. For example, the red, green, and blue components of a Color are implemented as integers in the range 0 to 255. Suppose you had a double value, amount, in the range 0.0 to 1.0, which expressed the relative amount of a color component (so 0.0 would mean none of that color and 1.0 would represent the full 255 amount). The actual color component value, then, would be an int and would have value 255 * amount. Unfortunately, arithmetic promotion of such an expression would yield a double, not the int we want. To make the value an int we use the *cast operator,* (*typeName*) to force the result to be an int:

```
(int)(255 * amount)
```

Syntax: Type Casts

To convert an expression to a given type, place the cast class operator in front of the expression, like this: (*typeName*)*expression*.

Caution: This may lose data, and is never allowed to convert a primitive type to a class type.

In the preceding example, we needed the second set of parentheses because the cast operator has the highest of all precedences. Without the second parentheses, we would just convert 255 to an int, which it is already. Be careful when type-casting—remember that you are in effect asking Java to place a value in a chunk of memory where the value may not fit, so you run the risk of losing information if you "narrow" a value from double to int, for example.

Programming Tip:

Use type-casts sparingly. When you must convert types, make sure that the expression you're converting will always fit in the intended type.

There are only two more numeric operators we need to discuss, the *increment operator,* ++, and its sibling, the *decrement operator,* --. These are *unary* operators, like the negation operator, –, and the cast operator, which means that they take a single operand, rather than two.

The increment operator *may be applied only to a numeric variable* (never to an expression or a literal), and causes the value of the variable to be increased by 1. For example, if the int variable i had the value 4, after applying i++, the value of i would be increased to 5. There are two different forms of the increment operator. Placing the operator *after* the variable causes the value of the variable to be incremented only after it is used in an expression. Placing the operator *before* the variable causes the variable to be incremented before its value is used. The decrement operator works in a similar way, except that it decreases the value of its operand by 1.

To see this in action, suppose the int variable i had the value 4. Then,

```
2 * i++
```

would evaluate to 8 and would leave i with the value 5 (since the old value, 4, would be used in the expression before i was incremented). But

```
2 * ++i
```

would evaluate to 10 and would leave i with value 5. This can lead to considerable confusion. What, for instance, are we to make of an expression like the following?

```
i++ + ++i
```

Programming Tip:

To lessen confusion, avoid using the increment or decrement operators in any but the simplest expression and *never* use more than one in an expression.

As with all unary operators, the increment and decrement operators are in the highest precedence level and they group from the right.

The Math Class

The Math class contains, as you would expect, a number of methods that come in handy for mathematical calculations. This class is part of the package java.lang, which is automatically imported for you in every Java program. The Math class is final, so it can't be subclassed, it has no constructors, so you can't construct a Math object, and all of its methods are static, so they must be called by using the class name before the method name, as in the expression p + Math.max(q, 0).

There are two constants in this class:

```
final static double E
final static double PI
```

Math.E is the base of the natural logarithms, 2.718281828... and Math.PI is 3.141592653... .

We'll describe the common Math methods here. If there's a mathematical function you need (like the arctangent) that's not mentioned here, there's a good chance you'll find it if you look through the complete documentation.

```
int abs(int x)
long abs(long x)
float abs(float x)
double abs(double x)
```

Each method returns the absolute value of its argument: Math.abs(3) is 3 and Math.abs(-4.009) is 4.009.

```
double ceil(double x)
```
Rounds its argument to the next highest integer: `Math.ceil(3.4)` is `4.0`, `Math.ceil(3.0)` is `3.0`, and `Math.ceil(-2.67)` returns `-2.0`. See also `floor()`, `rint()`.

```
double cos(double x)
```
Returns the cosine of its argument, where the argument is understood to be measured in radians: `Math.cos(PI / 3.0)` returns `0.5`. See also `sin()` and `tan()`.

```
double exp(double x)
```
Returns e^x, where e here represents `Math.E`. See also `log()`.

```
double floor(double x)
```
Rounds its argument down to the next lowest integer: `Math.floor(3.4)` is `3.0`, `Math.floor(3.0)` is also `3.0`, and `Math.floor(-2.67)` returns `-3.0`. See also `ceil()`, `rint()`.

```
double log(double x)
```
Returns the natural log of its argument. The argument must be greater than 0. See also `exp(x)`.

```
int max(int x, int y)
long max (long x, long y)
float max (float x, float y)
double max (double x, double y)
```
Return the larger of their two arguments. See `min()`.

```
int min(int x, int y)
long min (long x, long y)
float min (float x, float y)
double min (double x, double y)
```
Return the smaller of their two arguments. See `max()`.

```
double pow(double x, double y)
```
Returns the value of x^y. The argument x must be greater than 0.

```
double random()
```
Returns a number randomly chosen in the range 0.0 (included) to 1.0 (excluded), with a uniform distribution.

```
double rint(double x)
```
Returns the double value of the integer closest to the argument. If two doubles are equally close to x (for example, if x were `10.5`), the even one is returned (10.0, in this case).

```
int round(float x)
long round(double x)
```
Round the argument to the nearest integral value, rounding up if the argument represents 0.5 plus an integer, so `Math.round(2.5f)` returns 3 and `Math.round(2.49)` returns 2L.

```
double sin(double x)
```
Returns the sine of its argument (in radians). See `cos()`, `tan()`.

```
double sqrt(double x)
```
Returns the square root of its argument. The argument must be greater than or equal to 0.

```
double tan(double x)
```
Returns the tangent of its argument (in radians). See `cos()`, `sin()`.

Bitwise Operators*

There are seven other operators available for use on integral types. For these operators, the integer isn't regarded as representing a number, but rather is considered to be just a collection of bits, and the operations apply to each of the bits in the number. These operations are useful in some special situations, and we will use them from time to time in subsequent chapters, but we'll admit that they are somewhat specialized. For that reason, you can skip this section on first reading without losing any continuity in what's yet to come in this chapter.

In Java, `int`s are represented in a form known as *32-bit, two's complement.* The "32-bit" part means that each int uses 32 binary digits in memory (the `byte` and `short` types use eight and sixteen digits, respectively, and `long` uses sixty-four). As with the decimal numbers we're all accustomed to using, each position in the number represents a different value. Just as the decimal number 438 means "4 hundreds, 3 tens, and 8 ones," the digits in a *binary* representation indicate powers of some base. The only difference is that in decimal notation, the positions represent powers of ten, (1, 10, 100, 1000, . . .), while in binary they represent powers of two (1, 2, 4, 8, 16, 32, 64, 128, . . .). For example, the 8-bit binary number 00001101 represents what we call 13 in decimal, as you can see by adding the position values:

```
  0    0    0    0   1    1   0    1
128   64   32   16   8    4   2    1
                     8  + 4     + 1 = 13
```

Addition in this representation is easy, since there are only two "digit" values, 0 and 1. Figure 5.2 illustrates the addition table for binary arithmetic.

+	0	1
0	0	1
1	1	10

Figure 5.2 All you need to know about binary addition.

The 1 + 1 = 10 entry is just the way of saying 1 + 1 = 2 in binary, since 10 is the binary equivalent of our decimal 2. In school terms, then, we have "1 plus 1 is 0, carry 1." The addition *algorithm,* or the steps you use to add, is exactly the same as it is in decimal, except you use a different addition table. Here's an example, adding 25 + 13 in binary, with carries indicated:

```
      1 1 0 0 1
    0 0 0 1 1 0 0 1    (16 + 8 + 1 = 25)
  + 0 0 0 0 1 1 0 1    (8 + 4 + 1   = 13)
    0 0 1 0 0 1 1 0    (32 + 4 + 2 = 38)
```

The "two's complement" part of the description comes from the way negative numbers are represented. In this scheme, to negate a number, you first invert its bits, changing every 0 to a 1 and *vice versa,* and then add 1 to the result. To negate 13, for instance, in 8-bit two's complement, we would do this:

```
Original: 00001101
Invert:   11110010
Add 1:    11110011
```

So –13 would have the representation 11110011. This is a very logical scheme—take a look at the eight numbers that we can represent in 3-bit two's complement:

```
100     -4
101     -3
110     -2
111     -1
000      0
001      1
010      2
011      3
```

Note that the numbers change from top to bottom just as they would on a "binary odometer" (so 111 "rolls over" to 000, just as 999 would roll over to 000 on a decimal odometer) and that all the negative numbers are distinguished by having a 1 in the leftmost position. Note, also, that when we add 3 to −3 we get 0, as expected. (There's a final carry, which would go into the fourth bit, if there was one. Such "overflows" are ignored in this representation.)

The unary operator ~ is the *complement* operator that inverts the bits in its argument. If b is the byte with value 00001101, ~b will yield 11110010. The operators &, |, and ^, known as AND, OR, and XOR (for "eXclusive OR) take two operands and act on the bits according to the following tables.

&	0	1
0	0	0
1	0	1

|	0	1
0	0	1
1	1	1

^	0	1
0	0	1
1	1	0

      AND   **OR**   **XOR**

Figure 5.3 The AND, OR and XOR bitwise operators.

Let's take two 8-bit bytes, mask and sample, and apply the bitwise operations to them. We've separated the bits into two groups in each computation, the groups with all 0s and all 1s on top.

```
   0 0 0 0   1 1 1 1    mask
 & 1 0 1 0   1 1 0 1    sample
   0 0 0 0   1 1 0 1    result


   0 0 0 0   1 1 1 1
 | 1 0 1 0   1 1 0 1
   1 0 1 0   1 1 1 1


   0 0 0 0   1 1 1 1
 ^ 1 0 1 0   1 1 0 1
   1 0 1 0   0 0 1 0
```

Look at what happens: In the AND (&) example, any pattern paired with a group of 0s in the mask became all 0s and any pattern matched with a group of 1s in the mask stayed just as it was. *This* is why we took the time to explain the bitwise operations: They can be used to extract or set groups of bits in a number!

This idea of extracting bits using a mask can be combined with the remaining *shift* operators to perform useful tasks. The operator << takes two integral operands and returns the bits in the left operand, shifted left by the amount in the other operand, filling the resulting "holes" with 0s. For example, if b was a byte with bit pattern 00001101, the operation b<<3 would result in 01101000. Similarly, the operator >>> returns the bit pattern shifted right by the indicated amount, again padded with 0s. Finally, the operator >> shifts the bits left, but this time it pads with whatever was in the leftmost bit (it "sign-extends," in the jargon). Here are examples of how these operators work, with b having the pattern 10001101:

```
b << 2     returns the result   00110100
b >> 2     returns the result   11100011
b >>> 2    returns the result   00100011
```

Using the bitwise operators, we can break an integer into pieces. Suppose that instead of thinking of a 32-bit integer as a number in the range −2147483648 … 2147483647, we wanted to think of it as four 8-bit numbers, A, R, G, and B, collected into one chunk:

31 … 24	23 … 16	15 … 9 8 … 0	
A	R	G	B	source

To get the number in the R byte, for example, we would perform the following steps.

Step 1, build a mask:
```
byte ALL_ONES = -1;        // do you see why this is all 1s?
int mask = ALL_ONES << 16;
```

31 … 24	23 … 16	15 … 9	8 … 0	
00000000	11111111	00000000	00000000	mask

Step 2, mask out all but R:
```
int result = mask & source;
```

31 … 24	23 … 16	15 … 9	8 … 0	
00000000	R	00000000	00000000	result

Step 3, shift R down:
```
byte R = result >> 16;
```

31 … 24	23 … 16	15 … 9	8 … 0
00000000	00000000	00000000	R

This may seem like a lot of work, but we could always shorten it by eliminating some of the intermediate declarations, simply writing

```
byte ALL_ONES = -1;
byte r = ((ALL_ONES << 16) & source) >> 16;
```

Boolean Operators

We can compare numbers in Java, testing whether one is larger than or equal to another, for instance. The *comparison operators*, <, <=, ==, ! =, >=, and > take two numeric expressions as operands, evaluate them, and return a `boolean` value, indicating the result of the comparison. For example,

Expression	**Returns `true` if and only if**
f < g	f is strictly less than g
f <= g	f is less than or equal to g
f == g	f and g have the same value
f != g	the values of f and g are unequal
f >= g	f is greater than or equal to g
f > g	f is strictly greater than g
f < g	f is strictly less than g

For example, if n had the value 3 and x had the value 4.8f, we would have

```
n < 3                    // evaluates to false
n <= 3                   // true
n < x                    // true (n is promoted to float)
(n + 3) == 2             // false
(2 * n) != (f - 1.0)     // true
n >= n                   // true, of course
(n / 4) > 0              // false (do you see why?)
```

The comparison operators have fairly low precedence, below those of any of the arithmetic operators. This means we can dispense with the parentheses in the preceding examples, since we can be sure the arithmetic will be done before any comparisons. The comparison operators group from the left, as do most of the binary operators.

Syntax Cautions:

1. The order of the multicharacter operators is important: <= is a meaningful operator; =< is not.[7]
2. You cannot put spaces in any multicharacter operator, any m ore than you ca n in wo rds: < = and + + won't be interpreted as <= and ++ and will produce syntax errors in most contexts.

As we did with the numeric operators, we can use the comparison operators in complex expressions. For example, if `sample` was a `double` variable, it might be useful to test whether `sample` was in the range 0.0 .. 1.0. A mathematician would use the notation $0.0 \leq sample \leq 1.0$, but that would be completely unacceptable in Java. Do you see why? Think about it a moment.

*　　　　　　　*　　　　　　　*

Got it? Java would evaluate the expression `0.0 <= sample <= 1.0` as

```
(0.0 <= sample) <= 1.0
```

since the comparison operators are left-associative. The first comparison would be okay, but the second would involve a comparison of a `boolean` value with 1.0, and the comparison operators only take *numeric* operands.

Java has several logical operators that take `boolean` operands and return a `boolean` value. Here they are, assuming that p and q are boolean expressions, variables, or literals:

Expression	Returns `true` if and only if
`!p`	p is `false`
`p & q`	p and q are both `true`
`p && q`	p and q are both `true`
`f	g`	either p or q are `true` (or they both are)
`f || g`	either p or q are `true` (or they both are)
`p ^ q`	p and q have different values

The unary operator ! is called "not," & and && are called "and," | and | | are called "or," and ^ is called "exclusive or" ("xor," for short), because of their similarities to the logical operators of the same name. Now we see how to do the range-checking w wanted in the preceding example: `sample` is in the range 0.0 ..

---

[7]Though =< makes a nice "frowny face" for e-mail messages.

1.0 only when it is *both* greater than or equal to 0.0 and less than or equal to 1.0, so we could do the test by using the expression

```
(0.0 <= sample) && (sample <= 1.0)
```

The binary boolean operators have precedence below the arithmetic and comparison operators, so we could leave out the parentheses in this example (though we don't recommend it). Among the boolean operators, ! has the highest precedence (as so all unary operators), and the binary operators have precedence order, from highest to lowest, &, ^, |, &&, ||.

To test your understanding of the comparison operators and the boolean connectives, you should take the time to verify the following assertions. In these examples, assume that we've made the declarations

```
int sum = 45;
int index = 30;
double r = 2.5;
boolean done = false;
```

```
(sum > 0) && (index != 0)   // true, since both subexpressions are
!(r < 10.04)                // false (equivalent to r >= 10.4)
(sum == 45) || done         // true, since one subexpression is
done & !done                // false (for any value of done)
(2 == 2) | done             // true (for any value of done)
```

It may appear that there's some redundancy here, since & and && seem to do the same thing, as do | and ||. The difference between the two is that & and | act like other boolean operators—Java evaluates both operands before applying the operator. In the case of AND and OR, though, that may be more work than is necessary. Since false AND p is false, no matter what p is, we could evaluate the first argument in an AND expression and, if it is false, stop right there, in much the same way that we know 0 * x is 0, regardless of the value of x. Similarly, knowing that the first operand of an OR expression is true means that the whole expression is true, regardless of what comes later.

The operators && and || do just this sort of "short-circuit" evaluation.

Semantics: && and ||

1. If the left operand of && evaluates to false, the expression evaluates to false and the right operand isn't evaluated.
2. If the left operand of || evaluates to true, the expression evaluates to true and the right operand isn't evaluated.

This might seem like a minor time-saver and nothing more. It's much more than that, though. Suppose, for instance, we needed to take some action if an average, `sum / numScores` was greater than `85.0`. We could evaluate the expression `sum / numScores > 85.0`, but that could lead to disaster if `numScores` were 0, since we're not allowed to divide by 0 in Java. We could, though, use a *guard* clause, to check for the potential bad case:

```
(numScores > 0) && (sum / numScores > 85.0)
```

Now, if `numScores` were 0, the first operand would evaluate to `false` and Java wouldn't even look at the second, thereby eliminating the chance of dividing by 0. We advise getting into the habit using `&&` instead of `&` and `||` instead of `|`.

Programming Tip:

Program defensively. Expect the worst to happen (since it will, we guarantee you), and write your program to be *robust* enough not to fail when it does.

Complicated `boolean` Expressions

We don't have too much trouble analyzing complicated arithmetic expressions, but a boolean expression like

```
(a < 100) || !((t == MAX) && ((a - MAX) > 0))
```

gives us pause. Because few of us have the depth of experience with boolean expressions that we do with numeric expressions, it'll be helpful for you to know some of the tricks for analyzing them and generating them when you need to.

Analyzing boolean expressions is relatively simple in principle. Since any boolean expression can only be `true` or `false`, all we have to do to analyze a complicated expression is to test all possible cases (something that would clearly be impossible with integer or real expressions). One of the simplest ways to do this is to use a *truth table*. In a truth table, you begin by making columns for all possible values of the variables involved, and then in subsequent columns use the known values to find the values of increasingly complicated expressions, until you find the value of the expression you want. There are three basic truth tables, and all the rest are made by suitable combinations of them. You already know these tables—they merely represent in tabular form what you know.

a	b	a && b		a	b	a || b		a	!a
T	T	T		T	T	T		T	F
T	F	F		T	F	T		F	T
F	T	F		F	T	T			
F	F	F		F	F	F			

To find the value of an expression for a particular combination of variable values, simply find the values of the variables in the left columns (we've used T to represent true and F to represent false, to make the tables easier to write) and read the value of the expression in its column. For example, (T && F) is F, (F \|\| T) is T, and !F is T. Note, by the way, that for n variables, 2^n rows will represent all possible combinations of values for those variables.

It's important to realize how simple life is for us when we're dealing with boolean expressions. To prove the identity $(x + y)^2 = x^2 + 2xy + y^2$ for numbers x and y, we have to resort to a moderately complex proof using algebra, since there's no possible way to test whether this equation is true for all of the infinitely many possible values of x and y. However, to show that the expression a && (a \|\| b) always has the same boolean value as a, all we do is write a truth table for the expression and then compare its values with those of a:

a	b	a || b	a && (a || b)
T	T	T	T
T	F	T	T
F	T	T	F
F	F	F	F

Note that the first and last columns are identical. In other words, we've shown that (a && (a \|\| b)) equals a, for any possible values of a and b. Things are simple in the world of logic precisely because there are only two possible values for any boolean variable. A truth table is nothing more than a mechanical way of evaluating all possible cases.

To build a truth table for a more complicated expression, all you have to do is write the expression as it would be evaluated, and evaluate each row by using the values of the variables. For example, the expression

```
(a < 100) || !((t == MAX) && ((a - MAX) > 0))
```

has the form p \|\| !(q && r), where, for ease of writing, p represents the term (a < 100), q represents (t == MAX), and r represents ((a - MAX) > 0). Building this up in the truth table, we obtain the following.

p	q	r	q && r	!(q && r)	p || !(q && r)
T	T	T	T	F	T
T	T	F	F	T	T
T	F	T	F	T	T
T	F	F	F	T	T
F	T	T	T	F	F
F	T	F	F	T	T
F	F	T	F	T	T
F	F	F	F	T	T

It's easy to see from the last column of the truth table that this expression is false only when p is false, q is true, and r is true, so that

```
(a < 100) || !((t == MAX) && ((a - MAX) > 0))
```

is false only when a >= 100, t == MAX, and a - MAX > 0.

Truth tables are very helpful when you're trying to analyze someone else's boolean expression, but what do you do when you want to build a boolean expression to correspond to conditions of your own? There are lots of logical identities, like !(!a) == a, that any good logic text can give you (and that we'll explore in the exercises). Two classes of identities are particularly helpful to programmers.

The Distributive Laws:

(p && q) || (p && r) is equivalent to p && (q || r).
(p || q) && (p || r) is equivalent to p || (q && r).

DeMorgan's Laws:

!(p && q) is equivalent to (!p) || (!q).
!(p || q) is equivalent to (!p) && (!q).

You've seen numeric versions of some of these. The distributive laws allow you to "factor out" a common expression, as you might do in algebra when you replaced $xy + xz$ by $x(y + z)$.[8] ($\leftarrow$ That's not an exponent, that's a footnote reference.) In other words, you can replace the expression

---

[8]We couldn't interchange the operators, though: $(x + y) \times (x + z)$ is *not* the same as $x + (y \times z)$. In algebra, multiplication distributes over addition, but addition doesn't distribute over multiplication. In logic, both AND and OR distribute over the other.

```
((t > 0) && (s <= g)) || ((t > 0) && (r != MAX + 1))
```

by a simpler one, obtained by factoring out the common expression `t > 0`:

```
(t > 0) && ((s <= g) || (r != MAX + 1))
```

The distributive laws allow you to simplify a complicated expression, but you could always leave the expression alone if you couldn't remember the distributive laws. Fortunately, DeMorgan's laws, often tell us how to do things that we might not think of doing otherwise. We've already seen how to test whether `sample` is in the range 0.0 .. 1.0. We can use

```
(0.0 <= sample) && (sample <= 1.0)
```

Now suppose we wanted to test whether `sample` was *not* in the desired range? We could write

```
!((0.0 <= sample) && (sample <= 1.0))
```

but this isn't particularly transparent, nor is it as simple as it could be. Realizing that DeMorgan's laws say that "The negation of an AND expression is the OR of the negation of its components," we could write the equivalent expression

```
(!(0.0 <= sample)) || (!(sample <= 1.0))
```

which is itself equivalent to the much simpler

```
(0.0 > sample) || (sample > 1.0).
```

Note that how we negated the comparison operators. We can summarize this by saying that

---

`!(a < b)` is equivalent to `a >= b`.
`!(a > b)` is equivalent to `a <= b`.
`!(a == b)` is equivalent to `a != b`.

5.4 ASSIGNMENTS AND STATEMENTS

We've discussed variables and primitive types, and the operators Java makes available for manipulating its primitive types. Before we go on to statements, though, there's one other collection of operators we need to discuss.

Assignments

One of the most important operators, if not the most important, is the assignment operator, =. This is the operator we use to set a variable. This operator takes two operands: The left operand *must* be a variable; and the right operand may be a literal, a variable, or an expression of a type that is *compatible* with the variable on the left (we'll explain assignment compatibility in a moment). Assignment has the lowest possible precedence, so in any expression, the assignment operator will always be the last to be performed, unless we use parentheses to force a different order of evaluation.

If the first argument is a variable *of primitive type,*[9] the action of v = e is to evaluate e, store that value in v, and return that value to the enclosing expression, if any.

Alone among the two-argument operators, assignment operators are evaluated right to left. This allows us to perform "multiple assignments," like

```
a = b = 3
```

where a and b are, for instance, int variables.

Consider what happens when this expression is evaluated. First, since = groups from the right, the expression would be evaluated as if it were parenthesized:

```
(a = (b = 3))
```

The expression b = 3 would be evaluated first: b gets the value 3 as a *side-effect,* and the expression returns the value 3 to the expression. Now it looks like

```
(a = 3)
```

and the process repeats: a gets the value 3 and that value is returned to the expression (where it promptly dies, since there are no further expression parts to evaluate). What has happened? In simple terms, both a and b have been set to 3.

Somewhere out there, we can hear the astute reader muttering, "Aha! I can set the value of a variable inside an expression—hubba, hubba!" Yes, you can do that, writing something like

```
i = 2 * (j = 3);
```

rather than the longer

```
j = 3;
i = 2 * j;
```

---

[9]Remember this proviso—it's vitally important, as you'll soon see.

Cute, eh? Don't do it. *Never* do it. If we ever hear of you doing it, we'll track you down and erase your hard drive. This trick, beloved of C programmers, is a Very Bad Idea and should only be attempted by experts. The problem is that while it makes nifty, compact code, it also (as a side-effect) makes code that can be exceedingly difficult to understand. If you have any doubts, tell us—in 3 seconds— what the values of i, j, and k are after executing

```
int i = 2, j = 5, k = -1;
i = j = 3 * j;
k = (j = 3) * j;
```

Once you understand assignments, they're really quite simple. You have to start with the right mental model, though. A fairly common wrong path some people take is to think that = has something to do with an assertion of equality. It doesn't. The assignment

```
index = index + 1
```

makes utterly no sense if you think of it as saying "index is one more than itself." Instead, what we're really saying here is "take index's value, add 1 to it, and store the new result back in index," or, simply, "increase index by 1." The operator == tests for equality; = is used for assignment.

This is a common source of confusion, using = where you intended ==. It crops up in boolean expressions like

```
(final = 100) || (extraCredits > 25)
```

The intent here might be to assign an A+ grade if the final score is 100 or if more than 25 extraCredits points have been amassed. The expression is wrong, though, since it *sets* final to 100, rather than testing it. The correct expression uses the equality operator, ==, rather than the assignment:

```
(final == 100) || (extraCredits > 25)
```

You'll probably make this mistake several times. Fortunately, the Java compiler will catch it for you.[10]

Syntactic Caution: = != ==

Don't confuse the assignment operator and the equality operator.

---

[10]The only time you might run into trouble is when you're assigning to a boolean variable, like (honors = true) || (extraCredits > 25). A smart compiler will still catch this and warn you about a "possible unintended assignment."

Expressions to modify the value of a variable, like i = i * 2, occur so frequently in programs that Java has a collection of shortcut assignment operators for just these situations. In each of the following examples, the expression on the left has the same effect as the one on the right.

```
v += e       is the same as        v = v + e
v -= e             "               v = v - e
v *= e             "               v = v * e
v /= e             "               v = v / e
v %= e             "               v = v % e
v <<= e            "               v = v << e
v >>= e            "               v = v >> e
v >>>= e           "               v = v >>> e
v &= e             "               v = v & e
v |= e             "               v = v | e
v ^= e             "               v = v ^ e
```

All of these operators have the same precedence and grouping as simple assignment.

Class Variables vs. Primitive Variables

We've implied before that primitive types are different from class types. We mentioned that it is illegal to type cast a primitive type to be a class type, and we threw a warning in Footnote 9 to the effect that what we said about assignments applied only to primitive types. In fact, there's a *fundamental* difference between class-type variables and primitive-type variables:

Primitive-type variables hold values, class-type variables hold addresses.

All variables are just names for storage locations in memory. The difference is what's stored in those locations. For a primitive-type variable, the associated memory location holds a value. If we execute the code shown, the result is easy enough to understand. In Figure 5.3, we show what's happening in memory.

```
int a = 3, b = 0;
a = b;                 // a and b both contain 0
b++;                   // a contains 0, b contains 1
```

Upon completion, we see that the comparison a == b would evaluate to false, since a and b obviously contain different values.

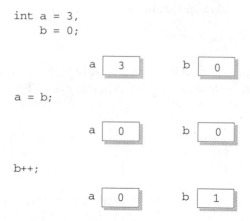

Figure 5.3 Memory snapshot of code using primitive types.

Now, let's do the same thing, using class-type variables. A class variable, recall, holds the *address* in memory where the object is located, so when we declare a new instance of that class,

```
Point a = new Point(3, 3),
      b = new Point(0, 0);
```

the variable just contains a reference to the object—the object itself is elsewhere in memory, at the address stored in the variable, as we indicate in Figure 5.4. This is why class types are also known as *reference types*.

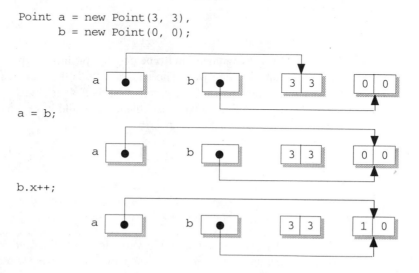

Figure 5.4 Memory snapshot of code, using class types.

If we now do an assignment,

```
a = b;
```

what happens? We've set the *address* in a to be the same as the one in b. In other words, a and b are now just two different names for the *same* object (and the original object originally referred to by a is lost)! Now, if we make a change to the b object, we're also changing the a object.

By making the assignment between two class variables, we've made them *aliases* for the same thing. Just as Batman gets a runny nose every time Bruce Wayne gets a cold, anything we do to a, we also do to b, since they're two references to the same thing.

Note that, unlike the situation with primitive type variables, the comparison a == b evaluates as `true`. Two class variables are equal if and only if they refer to the same object. If two class variables refer to different objects, they will be unequal under ==, even if the objects contain identical data.

Big Semantic Cautions:

1. Assignment behaves very differently for class types and primitive types. Assignment for primitive types makes the values the same, while assignment for class types makes the object references identical.
2. Equality testing also behaves very differently. Two primitive types are the same under == if their values are the same. For two class type variables, == is `true` only if the variables refer to the same object.

For the purposes of assignment and type casting, primitive types and class types work in somewhat the same way. The general rule is that you can perform assignment between different types if the variable on the left is "wider" than the term on the right. In the case of primitive types, then, we would have the following situations, where d is a `double` and i is an `int`:

```
d = i                  // OK: "wider" type on the left
i = d                  // NO: d might not fit into i
i = (int)d             // OK: you take the risk
d = true               // NO: double and boolean are incompatible
d = (double)(true)     // NO: can't even cast
```

In much the same way, you can assign a variable in a "narrower" class, that is, a subclass, to a superclass variable, but to assign in the opposite direction you need to make a type cast. In any case, you can't assign or cast across branches in the class hierarchy. For instance, suppose we made a class MyButton that extends

Button, that b was a variable of type Button, and that mb was a variable of type MyButton. We would then have the following legal and illegal assignments:

```
b = mb                       // OK: "wider" superclass on the left
mb = b                       // NO: mb "narrows" b
mb = (MyButton)b             // OK: you take the risk
b = new Point()              // NO:
b = (Button)(new Point())    // NO: can cast down, not across
```

Miscellaneous Operators

Before we leave operators, there are two more we should mention, just for the sake of completeness. The first is useful occasionally, and the second is a historical artifact, inherited from Java's grandparent, C.

You can test whether a variable is a particular type by using the instanceof operator. This operator takes a class variable on the left and a class name on the right and returns true if the variable is an instance of that type, or is an instance of a subclass of that type. If we continue the preceding example, all the following would be legal expressions, yielding the values shown:

```
b instanceof Button          // true: b is a Button
b instanceof MyButton        // false: wrong-way inheritance
bn instanceof Button         // true: bn is a Button by inheritance
bn instanceof MyButton       // true, of course
bn instanceof Object         // always true: any class is an Object
```

If the variable couldn't possibly be an instance of the indicated type, the compiler will generate an error message:

```
b instanceof Frame           // ERROR: No possible way for
                             // a Button to be a Frame
b instanceof int             // ERROR: must have a class type on right
```

The *conditional operator* is unique among the Java operators in that it is a *ternary* operator, taking three operands. It looks like this:

```
booleanExpression ? expression1 : expression2
```

When the time comes to evaluate this expression, the boolean value of the left argument is computed. If its value is true, expression1 is then evaluated and, as usual, its value is returned. On the other hand, if the boolean expression is false, expression2 is evaluated. The classic example of the conditional operator is

```
(a > b) ? a : b              // Evaluates to the larger of a and b
```

We rarely use the conditional operator. The `if` statement, which we'll cover in Chapter 6, can almost always be used as a replacement and is easier to read.

Statements

Statements are the fundamental units of execution in a program. There are several different kinds of Java statements. *Declaration statements,* like

```
Button clear;
private Point startpoint = new Point(45, 15), endpoint;
final int MAX = 10000;
int almostMax = MAX - 500;
```

identify new variables, specify the types they will be, indicate any other properties they may have (like `private` or `final`), and (optionally) set their initial values in an *initializer* part, occurring after the = symbol. As we mentioned, you may declare several variables of the same type in one declaration statement by placing the variables (and their initializers, if any) in a comma-separated list, after the type name.

Expression statements consist of an expression made into a statement by following it with a semicolon. An expression statement causes its expression to be evaluated and to perform any *side-effects,* like assigning a value to a variable or incrementing a variable. These are all legal expression statements:

```
clear = new Button("Clear");
i++;
p = q;
5;   // legal, but silly, since it does nothing but evaluate 5
```

Method calls to `void` methods are similar to expression statements, except that their execution consists of nothing but side-effects (namely, whatever happens when the object makes the call), as in

```
add(clear);
clear.SetLabel("Really clear");
```

You've seen *return statements,* but we haven't explicitly discussed them yet. A `return` statement is used in a method with non-`void` return type, to send the computed value back to the location where the method was called. For example, consider the method `magnitude`, which takes two `double` arguments and returns the square root of the sum of their squares.

```
double magnitude(double x, double y)
{
    double sqrSum = x * x + y * y;
    return Math.sqrt(sqrSum);
}
```

The right side of a `return` statement can be any expression of the type named in the header. When a `return` statement is encountered, it forces an immediate exit from the method. No subsequent statements in the method are executed.

A method with a non-`void` return type may be used anywhere in an expression where a variable of that type could appear, such as

```
double p = 0.0266, q = 0.0909, r;
r = 28.67 * (p / 2.8 + magnitude(p, q));
```

We'll mention *empty statements* for completeness. These statements do nothing. You generally won't see an empty statement, unless you make a typing error like

```
x = x + 1;;    // NOTE the two semicolons
```

This is actually two statements: the expression statement and an empty statement between the two semicolons. With some exceptions we'll mention in Chapter 6 and 8, empty statements are generally harmless.

The last of the statements we'll mention here (there are still a few we'll cover later) is the *group* or *compound* statement. This is any collection of statements enclosed in braces, { and }. The statement body of a method, for instance, must always be a compound statement, even if there's nothing between the braces. Unlike the other statements we've mentioned here, compound statements don't need to be terminated by a semicolon.

To see the importance of compound statements, we'll give you a teaser about a statement we'll explore in depth in the next chapter. The `if` statement looks like this:

```
if (booleanExpression)
    statement
```

This statement first evaluates the `booleanExpression`. If the expression evaluates to `true`, the `statement` part is then executed, and if the expression is false, the `statement` is skipped, and execution continues with whatever comes next.

We could use this to make a counter, for instance:

```
if (value > 0)
    numberOfPositives++;
```

Suppose, though, that we wanted to increment `numberOfPositives` *and* display some sort of message? The syntax of the `if` statement seems to allow for just one statement to be executed if the test succeeds. That's fine—from Java's point of view a compound statement *is* a single statement, so we could write our if statement in the following form.

```
if (value > 0)
{
    numberOfPositives++;
    messageBox.setText("Found another positive');
}
```

5.5 HANDS ON

This chapter's Lablet starts off in a familiar way—we design the user interface by laying out a collection of widgets, all placed in panels and positioned by the appropriate `LayoutManagers`. This time, though, to whet your appetite for what's to come, we add an event handler that deals with button clicks, so that our Lablet actually *does* something, rather than just sitting there.

Figure 5.5 The SodaPop Lablet, really in action this time.

In consequence, the Lablet is quite a bit more complicated than the ones you've seen, since we now have to decide how the parts of our program will communicate with each other to get the job done.

Designing the Lablet, I

As usual, we began by sketching the look of our applet, placing the widgets where we wanted them. We decided to have four buttons for drink selection, arranged on the right side. On the left, we wanted three buttons to simulate insertion of nickels, dimes, and quarters, along with a coin return button and an indicator that exact change would be required. Finally, we decided to have a text display along the bottom, to keep the user informed about what was going on. In short order, we came up with a design that looked like Figure 5.5.

At that stage, we already had an inkling of the logical, rather than just the visual, design, simply by the way things were arranged. It seemed reasonable to put the four drink selection buttons in one panel (with each button in a panel of its own, so they wouldn't get resized when they were laid out). The left side dealt with a single logical portion, money-handling, so we put everything on the right in a single panel. The three coin buttons were all closely related, so they deserved a sub-panel of their own. We wound up placing the ten widgets into a total of eight panels, as we illustrate in Figure 5.6.

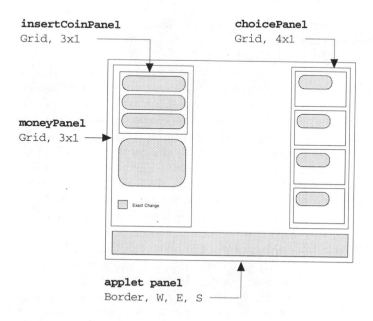

Figure 5.6 The GUI hierarchy of SodaPop.

We decided to make one of the major subcomponents, the `choicePanel`, a class of its own. We also decided not to make the left-hand `moneyPanel` a separate class, not because it wasn't a good idea (it was, in fact), but because we wanted to leave it as an exercise for you to do.

The visual layout was easy enough. In an earlier chapter, we could have stopped there, but now we wanted to add an event handler method, so the next task was to see whether we could get everything to work the way it should.

Designing the Lablet, II

The first question we asked in this phase of the design was, "What does a soda machine need to know, and where does it need to know it?" In other words, we had to decide on the instance variables for our two classes. Well, what *does* our soda machine need to know? In this simple instance, it seems to need only two things: the price of a soda, and the amount of money that has been inserted so far.

Design Tip:

It's often easier to start by thinking about data, rather than methods. Once you've decided on the data, you can think about how to manipulate it.

As a first approximation, we decided that we would need two `int` variables, which we named `amount` and `cost`, and that these should both be instance variables of our applet itself.

Now many of the methods we needed began to be clear. Clicking on the nickel, dime, or quarter buttons should activate methods that added the appropriate value to `amount` and updated the display text to indicate that a coin had been inserted. The coin return button was equally easy—it should call method that displays the amount returned and then set `amount` to zero. The exact change indicator was even easier—we decided to leave it as an exercise for you to do.

The only part that gave us pause was how to deal with the drink selection buttons. It wasn't that the action initiated by pressing a selection button was hard— far from it. Pressing a drink button would first cause a test to see whether the amount inserted so far was greater than or equal to the cost of a drink. If a sufficient amount had been inserted, we would simulate dispensing a soda by displaying an appropriate message and subtracting `cost` from `amount`. However, if `amount` was less than `cost`, all we'd have to do is display a message to the effect that not enough money had been inserted. How shall we do the test, though? Aha! This looks like a good time to try out the `if` statement that we introduced at the very end of the preceding section. You'll see how we did it when we dive into the code.

The Lablet Code

As usual, we begin with a comment block and a collection of `import` declarations. Since this portion will be part of every Lablet you'll see, we'll eliminate the description comments and the `import` declarations here and in the future.

The opening of the applet class declaration likewise holds no surprises. We declare the expected instance variables and then in `init()` we set up the GUI. Note, though, that at the very end of `init()` we initialize the `cost` variable, and one called `numberColas`, whatever that's supposed to be. (We don't want to give *everything* away here.)

```
public class SodaPop extends Applet
{
    Button      nickelButton,   //----------------------
                dimeButton,     // to simulate coin insertion
                quarterButton,  //----------------------
                returnButton;   // to return simulated coins

    TextField display;          // for status messages

    int       amount,          // amount available for purchase
              cost,            // price of a drink
              numberColas;     // colas currently on hand

    ChoicePanel    choices;    // for drink selection buttons

    public void init()
    {
        setLayout(new BorderLayout());
        setBackground(Color.red);
        resize(350,300);

        choices = new ChoicePanel();
        choices.setBackground(Color.blue);
        add("East", choices);

        Panel insertCoinPanel = new Panel();
        insertCoinPanel.setLayout(new GridLayout(3,1));
        nickelButton = new Button("Nickel");
        dimeButton = new Button("Dime");
        quarterButton = new Button("Quarter");
        insertCoinPanel.add(nickelButton);
        insertCoinPanel.add(dimeButton);
        insertCoinPanel.add(quarterButton);

        returnButton = new Button("Return Coins");
```

(continued)

```
Panel moneyPanel = new Panel();
moneyPanel.setBackground(Color.yellow);
moneyPanel.setLayout(new GridLayout(3,1));
moneyPanel.add(insertCoinPanel);
moneyPanel.add(returnButton);
add("West", moneyPanel);

display = new TextField();
display.setBackground(Color.white);
display.setForeground(Color.red);
display.setFont(new Font("Helvetica", Font.BOLD, 12));
add("South", display);

cost = 75;
numberColas = 5;
}
```

We need the `paint()` method, since we're painting on the applet's frame. We could have defined a Canvas subclass, perhaps named `logo`, with its own `paint()` method.

```
public void paint(Graphics g)
{
    Dimension d = size();
    g.setFont(new Font("TimesRoman", Font.BOLD, 36));
    g.setColor(Color.white);
    g.drawString("S",d.width / 2 - 20, d.height / 2 - 80) ;
    g.drawString("O",d.width / 2 - 20, d.height / 2 - 60) ;
    g.drawString("D",d.width / 2 - 20, d.height / 2 - 40) ;
    g.drawString("A",d.width / 2 - 20, d.height / 2 - 20) ;
    g.drawString("P",d.width / 2 - 20, d.height / 2) ;
    g.drawString("O",d.width / 2 - 20, d.height / 2 + 20) ;
    g.drawString("P",d.width / 2 - 20, d.height / 2 + 40) ;
    g.setFont(new Font("TimesRoman", Font.ITALIC, 12));
    g.setColor(Color.white);
    g.drawString("Insert 75 cents . . .",d.width / 2 - 20,
                    d.height / 2 + 90) ;
}
```

Now we're getting somewhere! Here's something new—an `action()` method. This, as we'll show in Chapter 6, is a way of detecting mouse clicks, among other events. Like `init()` and `paint()`, you don't call `action()` yourself—the system calls it for you whenever it has an event that it wants to give your program a chance to handle. As with `paint()` and `init()`, it's your job to make sure that this routine responds appropriately.

```
public boolean action(Event e, Object o)
{
    if (e.target == nickelButton)
    {
        processNickelButton();
        return true;
    }
    else if (e.target == dimeButton)
    {
        processDimeButton();
        return true;
    }
    else if (e.target == quarterButton)
    {
        processQuarterButton();
        return true;
    }
    else if (e.target == returnButton)
    {
        processReturnButton();
        return true;
    }
    else if (e.target == choices.colaButton)
    {
        processColaButton();
        return true;
    }
    else if (e.target == choices.dietButton)
    {
        processDietButton();
        return true;
    }
    else if (e.target == choices.liteButton)
    {
        processLiteButton();
        return true;
    }
    else if (e.target == choices.rootButton)
    {
        processRootButton();
        return true;
    }
    else return false;
}
```

You can probably make a pretty good guess about what's going on here. The system calls our `action()` method, passing it an `Event` and some sort of `Object` (the details of the latter don't seem particularly important here, since we never use it). We do use the `Event`, though. Its target data seem to be associated with the object that generated the event, and we use a cascade of if statements to determine where the Event came from.

For each of the eight buttons, the code is the same: Once we've determined the Event's target, we invoke a method of our own, and then return true (notice that the return type of action() is boolean). We'll discuss the purpose of the return value later, but for now we can say it's the way the action() method says to the system, "I'm done with this event; you can forget about it now."

We next come to a series of methods of our own, designed, as you just saw, to be invoked when a particular button is clicked. The processNickelButton() method, for example, does what we said should happen when the nickel button is pressed: it displays a message "Nickel inserted..." and then adds 5 to the current amount. The other two coin methods are the same. By the way—these methods all have default access. Which access would be more appropriate?

```
void processNickelButton()
{
    display.setText("Nickel inserted...");
    amount += 5;
}

void processDimeButton()
{
    display.setText("Dime inserted...");
    amount += 10;
}

void processQuarterButton()
{
    display.setText("Quarter inserted...");
    amount += 25;
}
```

The processReturnButton() method that is invoked when the coin return button is pressed has some interesting features. First, note that it has three local variables, amountString, dollars, and pennies. See if you can explain why we use / and % on the amount to initialize dollars and pennies.

```
void processReturnButton()
{
    String amountString;
    int dollars = amount / 100;
    int pennies = amount % 100;
```

The if .. else statement that follows acts as it appears to: if the boolean expression pennies < 10 is true, the first statement is executed, and, if it's false, the second is executed. All we're doing here is some minor cosmetic touches to make the display look like it should.

There's a + operator here you've seen only a few times before, and never quite in this context. You may recall that +, applied to Strings *concatenates* the Strings, joining them end to end into one new String. "But dollars isn't a String," you might say, "It was declared to be an int." Quite right—there's a nifty feature at work here. If + has one String operand, the other is converted to a String of the appropriate characters. Java "knows" how to convert values of primitive types to Strings, and if it sees a class variable, it calls that class's toString() method, if it has one. Almost all of the Java library classes have toString() methods.

```
    if (pennies < 10)
        amountString = new String("$" + dollars + ".0" +
                                        pennies);
    else
        amountString = new String("$" + dollars + "." +
                                        pennies);
    display.setText(amountString + " returned.");
    amount = 0;
}
```

Finally, when all the String manipulation is done, the amountString is sent to the display Textfield, and the amount variable is reset to 0, since we just gave back all the remaining money that had been inserted.

The drink selection methods all act in the same way—they use an if statement to check that amount >= cost (that is, if enough money has been inserted), and if the test returns true, the appropriate message is sent to display and the cost is deducted from the available amount.

The processCola() method is a wee bit more clever than its siblings. We'll ask you to explain it in the lab exercises.

```
    void processColaButton()
    {
        if(amount >= cost)
        {
            display.setText("COLA dispensed!!!");
            amount -= cost;
            numberColas--;
        }
```

(continued)

```
            if(numberColas <= 0)
            {
                    choices.colaButton.disable();
            }
    }

    void processDietButton()
    {
            if(amount >= cost)
            {
                    display.setText("DIET dispensed!!!");
                    amount -= cost;
            }
    }

    void processLiteButton()
    {
            if(amount >= cost)
            {
                    display.setText("LITE dispensed!!!");
                    amount -= cost;
            }
    }

    void processRootButton()
    {
            if(amount >= cost)
            {
                    display.setText("ROOT dispensed!!!");
                    amount -= cost;
            }
    }
}
```

We're done! The `ChoicePanel` class is just more good programming—we've split off the entire panel of drink choice buttons into a separate class so that it doesn't add further clutter to the applet's `init()` method. As the comments indicate, this class is just responsible for holding and laying out the four drink `Buttons`—no processing beyond that ever takes place.

```
//------------------------------------------------------------

class ChoicePanel extends Panel
// This class is only for display purposes in the SodaPop applet.
// It has no methods and serves only as a container for the
// drink selection buttons.
```

```
    {
        Button      colaButton,
                    dietButton,
                    liteButton,
                    rootButton;

        ChoicePanel()
        {
            setLayout(new GridLayout(4,1));

            Panel p1 = new Panel();
            colaButton = new Button("COLA");
            p1.add(colaButton);
            add(p1);

            Panel p2 = new Panel();
            dietButton = new Button("DIET");
            p2.add(dietButton);
            add(p2);

            Panel p3 = new Panel();
            liteButton = new Button("LITE");
            p3.add(liteButton);
            add(p3);

            Panel p4 = new Panel();
            rootButton = new Button("ROOT");
            p4.add(rootButton);
            add(p4);
        }
    }
```

5.6   SUMMARY

- We introduced only one new class in this chapter, the Math class. It contains a collection of useful math routines. It is part of the java.lang package, so you don't have to import it.
- The Java simple types are byte, char, short, int, long, float, double, and boolean.
- In order of size, the integral types are byte (8 bits), char, short (16 bits), int (32 bits), and long (64 bits). Each type is represented using two's complement notation, of the appropriate size.
- Integer literals have the form *optionalSign digitString,* where *digitString* is a string or one or more digits. Integer literals of long type have an L suffix.
- The floating-point numeric types are float (32 bits) and double (64 bits).
- Floating-point literals have the form *optionalSign digitDotString optionalExp,*

where *digitDotString* is a string of at least one digit, containing at most one decimal point and *optionalExp* has the form e*integerLiteral.*

❦ The char type is an integral type, since characters are represented internally using a 16-bit Unicode scheme. Character literals consist of a character between single quotes or an escape code, like \t for tab, enclosed in single quotes.

❦ The boolean type contains two values, represented by the literals true and false.

❦ Identifiers, the names for variables, methods, classes, and interfaces, all have the form *letter letterDigitString,* where *letter* is one of 'A' .. 'Z', 'a' .. 'z' and *letterDigitString* is any string of letters, digits ('0' .. '9'), or underscore characters ('_'). An identifier cannot be a Java keyword.

❦ Variables are identifiers associated with a single instance of a class or a single value of a primitive type.

❦ A variable must be declared in a class. If a variable is declared in a method, it is known as a local variable and has meaning only within the nearest pair of enclosing braces. If a variable is not declared within a method, it is known as a global variable (or instance variable) and has meaning throughout its class.

❦ A variable name may not be used in a file before the point of its declaration.

❦ The scope of a variable is that portion of its class where its name has meaning.

❦ If it has the proper access, an instance variable or method may be referred to outside of its class by the form *classInstanceVariable.memberName.* Within its class, a method or instance variable is referenced by its name.

❦ A method or variable declaration may be modified by preceding its declaration by any of the keywords static, final, private, protected, or public. In any collection of modifiers, only one of public, protected, or private may be used. Local variable declarations may not be modified.

❦ A static member (instance variable or method) is associated with a class, and not with any particular instance of the class.

❦ A final variable may not be modified. A class may be declared as final, meaning that it may not be subclassed.

❦ A package is a grouping of files into one logical entity. A file may declare its membership in a package by using the package *packageName*; declaration in the first line of the file. All files in a package must be in a single directory, with the same name as the package. All files in a Java program without package declarations are grouped in a single, unnamed, package, for purposes of determining access.

❦ Access determines the visibility of a member outside of its own class.

❦ A member with private access is only visible within its class. private members are not inherited by subclasses.

❦ A member declared without any of the modifiers public, protected, or private is said to have default or package access, and is visible anywhere within its package, but not outside.

❦ A member with protected access is visible throughout its package and cannot be accessed outside of its package, except within its subclasses.

❦ A `public` member is visible anywhere.

❦ Every one of the Java operators has a precedence, governing the order in which operators are evaluated. The operators and their precedences are as follows, listed from highest priority (done first) to lowest. In the descriptions, any operator not listed as (unary) or (ternary) is binary (two-argument).

Precedence	Operators	Descriptions
1.	`++   --`	Increment, decrement (unary)
	`+   -`	Plus, minus (unary)
	`~`	Bitwise complement (unary)
	`!`	Boolean negation (unary)
	`(type)`	Type cast
2.	`*   /   %`	Multiplication, division, remainder
3.	`+   -`	Addition, subtraction
	`+`	String concatenation
4.	`<<   >>   >>>`	Bit shifts
5.	`<   <=   >   >=`	Numeric comparison
	`instanceof`	Type comparison
6.	`==   !=`	Equality, inequality
7.	`&`	Bitwise AND, boolean AND
8.	`^`	Bitwise XOR, boolean XOR
9.	`|`	Bitwise OR, boolean OR
10.	`&&`	Short-circuit boolean AND
11.	`||`	Short-circuit boolean OR
12.	`? :`	Conditional (ternary)
13.	`=`	Assignment
	`*=   /=   %=`	Assignment with operation
	`+=   -=`	
	`<<=   >>=   >>>=`	
	`&=   ^=   !=`	

❦ Every one of the Java operators has an associativity, governing the order of grouping when evaluating expressions. The unary operators all group from the right. Except for the assignment operators, the binary operators all group from the left. The assignment operators and the conditional ?: group from the right.

❦ Don't rely on precedence when writing expressions. Use parentheses to make the order of evaluation clear.

❦ Numeric binary operators require both operands to be the same type. If they aren't, the narrower (smaller) type will be promoted to match the wider.

❦ Variables of primitive types store values, while variables of class type hold references to class instances.

❦ An expression of one type may be cast to be considered as another type by using the type-cast operator (*typeName*).

❦ An expression may always be cast to a wider type. For primitive numeric types, this means that it is always permissible to cast upwards in the sequence `byte`, `short`, `int`, `long`, `float`, `double`. For class types, it is always permissible to cast upward in any branch of the class hierarchy. For both, casts in the other direction are allowed, but some information might be lost.

❦ In no case may a primitive type be cast to a class type or vice versa, and class types may not be made across branches in the class hierarchy.

❦ Assignment to a variable of primitive type copies a value into the variable. Assignment to a variable of class type makes the variable an alias to the other argument.

❦ Assignment to a wider type is allowed. Assignment with a narrower type on the left requires a type cast.

❦ A frequent source of compile-time errors is to confuse assignment with equality.

❦ We covered the following statements: declaration, expression, method calls to void methods, return, empty, and group or compound (and `if`, briefly).

5.7   EXERCISES

1. Which of the following are legal Java literals? For those that are legal, tell what type they might be (there may not be unique answers, since `1` could be a `byte` or `int`, for example).

    a. `3`
    b. `2+3`
    c. `"2+3"`
    d. `5,280`
    e. `0L`
    f. `.333333...`
    g. `1e1`
    h. `-23.900e-0.5`
    i. `'\n'`
    j. `4f`

2. What is it about the `Math` and `Color` classes that makes it reasonable to

define them as `final`? Come up with a class of your own that might be a reasonable candidate for being defined as `final`.

3. This is a cute use for a `static` variable:

```
class RecordKeeper
{
    public static int hits = 0;

    RecordKeeper()
    {
        hits++;
    }
    ...
}
```

Why? What's going on here?

4. Go back over `Gigobite` and look at the access levels of its members. Fix them to the appropriate access.

5. Do Exercise 4 for the `SodaPop` Lablet. There are twenty-two members with package access. Fix all that need to be fixed and explain your reasons for each choice.

6. Consider the following class declaration.

```
class Whatever
{
    int x, y;                        // call these x1 and y1
    // A
    void someMethod()
    {
        // B
        int z;
        {
            // C
            int x;                   // call this x2
            // D
        }
        // E
    }
    // F
    void anotherMethod(int x)        // call this x3
    {
        // G
        int y;                       // call this y2
        // H
    }
}
// I
```

For each of the locations A–I, indicate whether the variables x1, x2, x3, y1, y2, and z would be visible, by placing a check in the appropriate cell.

	A	B	C	D	E	F	G	H	I
x1									
x2									
x3									
y1									
y2									
z									

7. Assuming that the following declarations aren't local, which are legal? For the illegal ones, explain what's wrong.
   a. `public int static x = 3;`
   b. `private boolean isDirty;`
   c. `static Button = new Button("Delete");`
   d. `public final private static int MARGIN = 15;`
   e. `public final double SCALE_FACTOR_X;`
   f. `final public double SCALE_FACTOR_Y;`
   g. `public restrooms;`
   h. `private static Point anchor = new Point(15, 15);`

8. For the following numeric expressions, place parentheses to indicate the order in which they would be evaluated. Assume that all variables have been declared as ints.
   a. `2 * 3 - 4`
   b. `p * q / r / 3`
   c. `-1 + p * (2 / q - r)`
   d. `p = p * 3 - 4`
   e. `7 / (double)q + 1`
   f. `p++ * 3`
   g. `q /= p * p << r / 2 ^ p - 1 >> q`

9. Give the Java versions of these algebraic expressions.

   a. $(3p + q)(p - 2q)$

   b. $\dfrac{1}{x + y} + \dfrac{1}{x - y}$

c. $x^4 - x^3 + x^2 - x + 1$

d. $1 + \cfrac{1}{1 + \cfrac{1}{1 + x}}$

10. The % operator is actually defined by p % q = p - (p / q) * q. This definition applies to floating-point values, as well. Use this definition to find the values of the following expressions.
   a. 13 % 3
   b. -13 % 3
   c. 13 % -3
   d. -13 % -3
   e. 13.0 % 3.0

11. Suppose that we have the following declarations.

    ```
    int p = 1, q = 3;
    long a = 31555750L;
    float f = 2.008f;
    double d = 6.023e+26;
    ```

    For the following expressions, tell the type of the result.
   a. p - 2 * q
   b. 2 * d
   c. 2.0 * d
   d. (a - 2f) / p
   e. p + q + a + f + d
   f. p + (long)q
   g. d - a

12. Which of the following expressions aren't correctly formed. For those that are incorrect, explain what's wrong with them. Assume that you have the variable declarations of Exercise 11.
   a. d << 2
   b. (p - a) * (d = 0)
   c. 8
   d. e < 0 && 0 < e
   e. f++ = 2.3f
   f. d << 2

13. Suppose you're interested in computing the average score for ten tests, each scored from 0–100 in integer amounts. Assume that the int variable sum contains the total of all ten scores. You want at least three decimal places of

accuracy, so you decide to cast the average to a double. Here's the code:

```
double average = (double)(sum / 10);
```

When you try it, though, you get a surprise. What's the surprise and what's your response?

14. **a.** By hand, convert 31847 seconds to the form *h* hours, *m* minutes, *s* seconds, with the usual conventions that both *m* and *s* are integers greater than or equal to 0 and less than 60.

   b. Remember what you did in part (a) and imagine that you were writing a Time class to store and manipulate times. Suppose that the class looked like this:

```
class Time
{
    private int h, // number of hours
               m,  // number of minutes (0 .. 59)
               s;  // number of seconds (0 .. 59)

    public Time(int startTime)
    // Sets h, m, and s to represent the
    // number of hours, minutes, and seconds
    // equivalent to startTime.
    {
        . . .
    }
    . . .
}
```

Write the constructor.

   c. Write the following Time method.

```
public void add(Time t)
// Adds t to this Time
{
    . . .
}
```

The intent here is that if this Time object held the values 30:47:15 (in hours:minutes:seconds) and if t held 2:24:50, the result of add(t) would be to set this time to 33:12:5.

   d. This class has a natural candidate for a final static int. What is it?
   e. Explain why we chose private access for h, m, and s.
   f. Describe two more constructors and three more methods that would be useful for this class.

15. Write an expression that evaluates to `true` if the `int` variable n is odd and evaluates to `false` if n is even.

16. Consider the following code segment, where a, b, and c are `ints`.

```
{
       c = a % b;
       a = b;
       b = c;
}
```

If you start with some positive values in a and b and repeatedly execute this block, stopping when c is 0, what can you say about the value that ends up in a? Hint: Try it with a = 120, b = 25; a = 128, b = 32; a = 720, b = 63.

17. Let d be a `double` variable. For what values of d is the following expression `true`?

```
Math.ceil(d / 3) == Math.floor(d / 3)
```

18. Write an expression that uses three `int` variables a, b, and c, and returns the largest of the values of a, b, and c.

19. If A and B are `ints` with A < B, what is the purpose of the expression

```
floor(A + (B - A + 1) * Math.random())
```

20. Explain why the `int` type represents values between –2147483648 and 2147483647. Where do these two numbers come from?

21. What's the largest possible `long` value in Java? Express your answer
   a. In binary.
   b. Using an expression involving a power of 2.
   c. In decimal.

22. Invent a good use for using the bitwise operators | and ^ (and, perhaps, ~) with a mask, as we did with &.

23. **a.** Represent –28 as an 8-bit two's complement number.
   b. What bit pattern is the result of -28 << 2? What number does this represent?
   c. What bit pattern is the result of -28 >>> 2? What number does this represent?
   d. Try parts (a) – (c) with enough samples to be able to make a reasonably simple description of what these shifts do to the values of numbers.

24. Use truth tables to verify DeMorgan's laws.

25. Express each of the following sentences as a boolean expression.
    a. *x* is greater than 10.
    b. Either *u* or *v* is smaller than 0.00001.
    c. *temp* is no farther than 1.5 away from *target*.
    d. *t* is no smaller than 3.7.
    e. Exactly one of *index* and *count* is 0.
    f. *sign* is positive, or both *x* and *y* are negative.
    g. *x* / *y* is defined and greater than 1.
    h. In binary.

26. Using DeMorgan's laws, show that you don't need AND in boolean expressions if you have NOT and OR available.

27. The operators AND, OR, and NOT are sufficient for any boolean expression. Exercise 26 shows that just two, OR and NOT, are sufficient. Show that you can get away with just one operation, NAND, defined below, by expressing p OR q and NOT p using only NANDs.

a	b	a NAND b
T	T	F
T	F	T
F	T	T
F	F	T

28. Assume that n and m are `ints` and p and q are `boolean`. For the following valid expressions, insert parentheses to show the order in which they would be evaluated. For the invalid ones, indicate what's wrong with them.
    a. `n => 0 || p`
    b. `p && ! q || p`
    c. `! 2 * n < m`
    d. `n && m < 0`
    e. `!p || n == m`
    f. `p = n == m`
    g. `2 * n - m >= 3 && -3 + p * q <= q / 2`
    h. `!!!!(m == n)`
    i. `n < 0 && m < 0 || p`

29. In Footnote 10 we mentioned that incorrectly using = instead of == might cause problems in expressions like

    ```
    (honors = true) || (extraCredit > 25)
    ```

Explain why this would not be a good way to test whether `honors` is `true` or `extraCredit` is greater than 25.

30. In the expression x = (x == x), there's only one possible choice for the type of x.
    a. What type must x be to make this expression legal?
    b. What is the result? Write an equivalent, simpler expression.
    c. Do parts (a) and (b) for the expression (x = x) == x. Is there now only one choice for the type of x? What's the value of the expression?
    d. Which of the two expressions in the Exercise statement and part (c) are equivalent to x = x == x under Java's rules for evaluation of expressions?

31. Consider the code

    ```
    temp = a;
    a = b;
    b = temp;
    ```

    a. Assume that `temp`, a and b have all been declared previously as `ints`. Do the kind of "memory snapshot" analysis we did in Figure 5.3 and tell, in simple terms, what this code does.
    b. Redo part (a), this time assuming that all three variables have been declared previously as `Buttons`. Do the same sort of thing we did in Figure 5.4. The picture for this part will, of course, look different from that of part (a), but does your "simple terms" answer change?

32. Which of the following are legal Java statements? As usual, for those that aren't, explain what's wrong with them. Make whatever assumptions about variables and methods you need to, to try to make the statements valid.
    a. `x++;`
    b. `public Point p;`
    c. `p = new Point(2, 4)`
    d. `p.x = Math.max(p.x, 0);`
    e. `p.move(2, 2)`
    f. `return (p.x < p.y);`
    g. `import java.awt.*;`
    h. `{5;;{int y = 0;};};`
    i. `x = y = x;`
    j. `if (x == 3)`
        `y++;`

CHAPTER SIX

Events and Actions

An important feature of many modern computer applications is that they are *event-driven*. An application like a spreadsheet or a Web browser, for example, not only spends its time doing its own work—computing new values, reading from files, and displaying information on the screen—but it also monitors keyboard activities, mouse moves and clicks, and so on. Java provides a rich collection of functions to monitor and report events. Making applets responsive to the demands of the user is the heart of event-driven programming.

OBJECTIVES

In this chapter, we will
- Introduce some Java programming constructs we'll need to handle events.
- Describe the events that are generated in the Java environment.
- Learn how to make an applet respond appropriately to events by including the necessary event-handling routines.
- Discuss event-driven programming in an object-oriented framework.
- Discuss the "delegation model" that Java 1.1 uses for handling events.

6.1   MORE JAVA PROGRAMMING

For the statement-level details of Java, we've adopted a "need to know" approach, discussing features as they become necessary, rather than starting off by dumping the whole lot on you at the start. In this chapter, you "need to know" two new Java features: the conditional statements, `if` and `switch`, and interfaces.

The if Statement

When we write applets that are intended to respond to actions, we need to be able to test things like an event's identification number, where it occurred, its target Component, and so on. That part isn't hard; in fact, we've already described the boolean operators we'll need to do such tests. Once we've made the tests, though, we also have to write our programs in such a way that they take different actions, depending on the test results. So far, all the methods we've written have embodied the computer equivalent of predestination: Do the first statement, then do the next, then do the one after that, and so on, with no way to depart from the path of executing statements in sequence from top to bottom. What we need are some other statements that allow our programs to take different actions, depending on the results of tests we make.

The if statement is written as

```
if (boolean expression)   // (the parentheses are required)
    statement             // the "controlled" statement
```

Semantics: The if Statement

When an if statement is encountered, the boolean expression is evaluated. If it evaluates to true, the controlled statement following is executed, and execution passes to any subsequent statement. If the boolean expression is false, the controlled statement is skipped, as if it weren't there.

For example, the statement

```
if (e.target == order)
    displayField.setText("Button order clicked");
```

first checks whether the target of the event e happens to be the Button object order. If it was, the message "Button order clicked" is displayed. If it wasn't, however, the setText() method call would be ignored and execution would continue with the following statement where, perhaps, another test would be tried.

Many times, we might need to select between doing or skipping several things. In those cases, we can use a compound statement as the controlled statement. As we mentioned in the last chapter, Java considers anything between paired braces to be syntactically equivalent to a single statement in constructs like an if statement. The following example is from the SketchPad Lablet for this chapter.

```
if (e.target == clear)
{
    Graphics g = getGraphics();
    g.setColor(Color.white);
    g.fillRect(theBounds.x, theBounds.y,
               theBounds.width, theBounds.height);
    g.setColor(currentColor);
    ...
}
```

Another version of the `if` statement allows us to execute one statement (simple or compound) if the test is `true` and a different one if the test is `false`. The `if..else` statement looks like this:

```
if (boolean expression)
    statement 1
else
    statement 2
```

Semantics: The `if..else` Statement

When an `if..else` statement is executed, several things happen in sequence.

1. The boolean expression is evaluated.
2. If the boolean expression evaluates to `true`, the first statement is executed.
3. If the boolean expression is `false`, the second statement is executed.
4. In either case, the program then continues with whatever comes after the `if..else` statement.

Here's a simple example:

```
if (e.target == colorButton1)
    currentColor = Color.red;            // e.target is
colorButton1
else
    currentColor = Color.black;   // e.target is anything else
```

The statement parts of an `if` or `if..else` statement can be anything, even another `if` statement. We often nest `if` statements when we need to base actions on several tests, such as

```
if (e.target == colorButton1)
    currentColor = Color.red;
```

```
else
    //----- We enter this part only if e.target isn't colorButton1
    if (e.target == colorButton2)
        currentColor = Color.blue;
    else
        // and we get here only if e.target isn't colorButton1
        // and also isn't colorButton2
        if (e.target == colorButton3)
            currentColor = Color.green;
        else
            // The only way we can get here is if all three
            // boolean expressions evaluated to false.
            currentColor = Color.black;
```

These successive levels of indentation give some people the screaming meemies. If you're one of them, remember that Java ignores carriage returns and tabs in source code, so you could write the preceding code like this:

```
if (e.target == colorButton1)
    currentColor = Color.red;
else if (e.target == colorButton2)
    currentColor = Color.blue;
else if (e.target == colorButton3)
    currentColor = Color.green;
else
    currentColor = Color.black;
```

While we're on the subject, we should mention that we always drop the statement part of an `if` statement down to the next line and indent it. Even though it's not required by the compiler, such indentation makes code far easier to read. For example, compare these two versions of the same statement.

```
// version 1
if (x > 0) if (y > 0) t = 1; else t = 2;

// version 2
if (x > 0)
    if (y > 0)
        t = 1;
    else
        t = 2;
```

Few people would deny that version 2 is far easier to understand. Version 2 also points out how Java deals with a potential ambiguity with the `if..else` statement. In version 1, it's not apparent whether the `else` should match the `if (y > 0)` part or whether it should be grouped like the following.

```
// version 3 (Bad! Misleading indentation)
if (x > 0)
    if (y > 0)
        t = 1;      // done when x > 0 and y > 0
else
    t = 2;          // done when x > 0 and y ≤ 0,
                    // even though it doesn't look that way
```

This is a genuine ambiguity, like the ambiguity we discussed earlier when Java evaluates an expression like 2 + 3 * 4, and the designers of Java solved it in the same way, by legislating the choice that would be made.[1]

An `else` clause is always matched to the nearest available unmatched `if`.

If we had wanted to force the statement to behave the way version 3 made it appear, we would "wall off" the inner `if` with braces, effectively terminating it before the `else`:

```
// version 4 (Different behavior from previous versions)
if (x > 0)
{
    if (y > 0)
        t = 1;      // done when x > 0 and y > 0
}
else
    t = 2;          // done when x ≤ 0, regardless of y's value
```

Common Problems with `if`

Because the `if` statement is more complex than the other statements we've seen so far, it leaves the door open for some common programming errors. These errors can be exasperating to track down and fix, so the best remedy we can suggest is to avoid them in the first place.

Take a look at the code below. It seems simple enough—it tests the variable x (which is probably a `double`), and if x is larger than `1e38` it displays a message on `displayField` (which is probably what sort of object?).

```
// WARNING: Bad programming here
if (x > 1e38);
    displayField.setText("My! What a big number!");
```

---

[1]Well, not exactly. Java was designed to have a syntax very much like C++, and C++ handles the `else` ambiguity that way. (Well, not exactly. C++ was designed to be syntactically compatible with C, so the decision really comes from C.)

The problem here is that this code doesn't behave as expected. In fact, it displays the message no matter how large or small x is! Before going on, see if you can spot the cause of the problem.

                    *   *   *

Find it? A smart compiler might find it for you, even though the example code is syntactically legal. The odd behavior is caused by the semicolon after the boolean expression (x > 1e38). A semicolon, recall, is a statement terminator. In this case Java expects a statement after the boolean expression and, indeed, finds one just where it should be. The only difficulty is that the statement it finds is the empty statement. In fact, the compiler treats our example code as if it were written

```
if (x > 1e38)
    ;                // Do nothing.
displayField.setText("My! What a big number!");   // Do always!
```

In this case, if x is larger than 1e38, the empty statement part is executed and control passes down to the method call. That's more or less what we wanted to happen. However, if x is less than or equal to 1e38, the empty statement is skipped and control still passes to the method call. We've inadvertently placed the wrong statement under control of the if statement.

Caution:

The if statement does not require a semicolon terminator. There's almost no reason for a semicolon in an if statement, except for those that are needed by the individual statements controlled by the if.

Now let's make a small modification to our example. Suppose that any x value larger than 1e38 will be too big for whatever processing we do later. We decide to guard against such "bad" values by setting x to 1e38 in those cases. As conscientious programmers, though, we don't want to surprise the user by doing something behind the scenes, so we first display an alert before we change the value. Our code becomes

```
// WARNING: More bad programming here
if (x > 1e38)
    displayField.setText("Amount too large. Using 1e38 instead");
    x = 1e38;
```

If we run the program, we discover to our dismay that x is *always* set to 1e38, no matter what its original value was. What went wrong?

                    *   *   *

We goofed again—we left off the braces. The only statement controlled by the `if` was the `setText()` call. As in the first example we showed, the next statement, `x = 1e38` is always executed. Indenting properly, our code would be

```
if (x > 1e38)
    displayField.setText("Amount too large. Using 1e38 instead");
x = 1e38;
```

Don't forget—indentation is only for humans. The compiler quite literally can't see extra spaces, tabs, or carriage returns, so don't be misled into thinking that indentation actually has anything to do with the workings of a program.

Caution:

Don't leave off braces. It's a good idea to get into the habit of typing a pair of braces immediately after typing the boolean test expression or the keyword `else`, and then going back and filling them in. It won't hurt to put a single statement inside the braces, and you'll be less likely to omit them accidentally if you adopt this habit.

Recall that with the exception of declarations, every statement must occur in some method. That means that we always have a `return` statement available to us if we ever need to make a hasty exit from the method. We can sometimes use this feature to dispense with a cascade of nested `if..else` statements.

Suppose, for example, that we are writing a tax-preparation program and that one of the methods, `taxOn()`, will take in an income amount and return the tax owed on that income. Suppose, further, that the tax laws dictate that incomes in the range 0 . . . 19,450.00 are taxed at a 15% rate, incomes in the range 19,450.01 . . . 47,050.00 are taxed at 28%, incomes in the range 47,050.01 . . . 97,620.00 are taxed at 33%, and that incomes larger than 97,620.00 are taxed at 50%. We could write this method definition as

```
private double taxOn(double income)
// Example 1: Using else to control execution
{
    double tax;              // the return value
    if (income <= 19450.0)
        tax = 0.15 * income;   // low income: 15% tax bracket
    else if (income <= 47050.0)
        tax = 0.28 * income;   // middle income: 28% tax bracket
    else if (income <= 97620.0)
        tax = 0.33 * income;   // well-off: 33% tax bracket
```

```
        else
            tax = 0.50 * income;   // rich: 50% tax bracket (ouch!)

        return tax;
    }
```

or we could do the following, using `return` to leave as soon as the appropriate test is satisfied.

```
private double taxOn(double income)
// Example 2: Acts like Example 1, but uses returns to break out
// of further testing.
{
    if (income <= 19450.0)
        return 0.15 * income;

    // Because of the return above, the only way way can get
    // here is if income > 19450.0.
    if (income <= 47050.0)
        return 0.28 * income;
    if (income <= 97620.0)
        return 0.33 * income;
    else
        return 0.50 * income;
}
```

This is a bit simpler than the first version, since we don't need to declare a variable to hold the amount to be returned, but it does require that we be aware of the fact that `return` forces an immediate break out of the method. We use this from from time to time, but we should alert you to the trouble you can get into if you combine these two paradigms:

```
private double taxOn(double income)
// Example 3: BAD mixture of Examples 1 and 2. This doesn't
// work as expected.
{
    double tax;
    if (income <= 19450.0)
        tax = 0.15 * income;
    if (income <= 47050.0)
        tax = 0.28 * income;
    if (income <= 97620.0)
        tax = 0.33 * income;
    else
        tax = 0.50 * income;

    return tax;
}
```

If you trace the execution of this method, you'll see that it won't make low-income taxpayers very happy, since the low, middle, and well-off taxpayers are all taxed at the 33% rate. An income of 10,000.00, for instance, passes all of the first three tests, so the tax is first set to 1500.00, then immediately reset to 2800.00, and finally to 3300.0.

Caution:

Until you're completely comfortable with the `if` statement, it's a good idea not to break out of an `if` statement by using `return`. Instead, make a cascade of `if..else` statements with a single `return` at the bottom.

The `switch` Statement

Programs use the "if *variable* == *constant*, do this, otherwise if *variable* == *constant*, do that, otherwise . . . " construct so often that it has become a feature of many programming languages, and Java is no exception. The `switch` statement is used to select one of several actions, depending on the value of some expression. It looks like

```
switch (expression)
{
case constant1:
    some statements
case constant2:
    some statements
...
default:
    some statements
}
```

The expression *must* evaluate to a primitive type, not a class type, and the constants must be literals or `final` variables. The default label may be omitted, but it's not a good idea, since failure of the expression value to match any of the constants will result in a run-time error.

Semantics: The `switch` Statement

When a `switch` statement is executed, the following steps are performed in order.

1. The expression is evaluated.
2. Control then passes to the statement following the first case label whose constant equals the value of the expression.
3. If none of the case constants match the expression value, control passes to the default label.
4. In either case, all the statements from the label to the end of the switch are executed.

It's important to note that this behavior differs from that of a collection of nested `if..else` statements. Although the look of a `switch` statement might mislead you into thinking that just the statements from one `case` label to the next would be performed, that's not so.[2] Carefully reread step 4, and you'll see why. Unless you take explicit action to force execution to leave the `switch` statement, *all* the statements from the `case` label to the end of the `switch` statement will be executed. If you want to separate the action of a `switch` statement into discrete units and avoid this "fall-through" behavior, you have to include a new statement, the `break`.

When a `break` statement is encountered, it forces an immediate exit from the entire `switch`, skipping any subsequent controlled statements. You will almost always write a `switch` statement with `break`s separating the case sections. Just about the only time you wouldn't have a `break` immediately before the next `case` label is if you want a labeled section to apply to several cases.

Semantics: The `break` Statement

The break statement forces an immediate `exit` from a `switch` statement.[3]

The following is an example of the `switch` statement in action. Suppose the variable `currentColor` contains a `Color` value, like `Color.red`, for instance, and we want the value of `currentColor` to cycle through the sequence black, red, and green. Suppose we also had three `int` constants BLACK, RED and GREEN, and an `int` variable `colorCode`, initially set to BLACK. We could then use `colorCode` to control a `switch` statement that cycles the colors.

---

[2]However much we'd like it to be that way, it just isn't. This peculiar behavior is inherited from C and has bedeviled novice programmers for decades.

[3]Or from a *loop,* which we'll discuss in Chapter 8.

```
// Local example: Don't look for this among the Lablets.
switch (colorColor)
{
case BLACK:     // cycle black -> red
     currentColor = Color.red;
     colorCode = RED;
     break;
case RED:       // cycle red -> blue
     currentColor = Color.green;
     colorCode = GREEN;
     break;
case GREEN:     // cycle blue -> green
     currentColor = Color.blank;
     colorCode = BLACK;
     break;
default:                // report error and abort the program
     System.err.println("Something went wrong in color cycle");
     System.exit(0);
}
```

To see the importance of the `break` statement, suppose we left them out of the example above and wrote, instead:

```
switch (colorCode)          // VERY BAD--give me a break!
{
case BLACK:
     currentColor = Color.red;
     colorCode = RED;
case RED:
     currentColor = Color.green;
     colorCode = GREEN;
case GREEN:
     currentColor = Color.black;
     colorCode = BLACK;
default:
     System.err.println("Something went wrong in color cycle");
     System.exit(0);
}
```

This is a terrible idea. No matter what value `currentColor` is, execution eventually will fall through to the last two statements, displaying an error message and aborting the program!

Caution:

Leaving out a `break` statement in a `switch` is a common cause of errors.

Abstract Classes and Interfaces

When we first mentioned inheritance in Chapter 1, we used an example of geometric objects, like rectangles, ovals, lines, rectangles, squares, and circles. Figure 6.1 reproduces the class hierarchy we invented and illustrated originally in Figure 1.9.

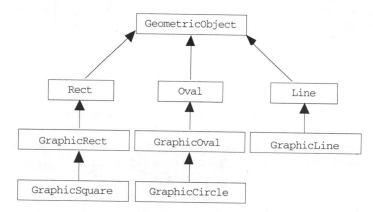

Figure 6.1 A hierarchy of geometric objects.

In this example, we have derived all of our classes from the class GeometricObject. This class might contain data members describing an object's bounding rectangle, for example, along with other properties and methods common to all geometric objects, like a move() method that would shift the object's anchor to another location, and an area() method that would compute the area of the object. It seems clear, though, that we would never want a direct instance of a GeometricObject in any of our programs (what, for instance, would it mean to compute the area of a general GeometricObject?). Instead, we'd construct rectangles, ovals, lines, and the like and use these specific classes in our programs.

Java provides a way to indicate that a class will serve as a template for its subclasses but will never exist as specific instances on its own. We declare an *abstract class* by using the modifier abstract in its declaration:

```
public abstract class GeometricObject
// Contains data and methods common to all its subclasses.
// Cannot be instantiated.
{
    protected Point anchor;
    protected Dimension bounds;

    public void move(int x, int y)
    {
        anchor.x = x;
        anchor.y = y;
    }
```

(continued)

```
    public double area();            // Note: Empty body.
}
```

In this declaration, we've defined the `move()` method because we have all
the information we need to implement it. We haven't provided a definition for
`area()`, though, because the body of that method will depend on the type of object
it's applied to (the code for finding the area of a rectangle, for example, is quite
different from that for finding the area of a circle).

Syntax:

Using the `abstract` modifier in a class declaration indicates that the class cannot
be instantiated. In other words, you cannot construct a new instance of an abstract
class. In an abstract class, you can declare a method with no body, indicating that
the method definition will be provided in the subclasses.

Any class with at least one empty method is automatically considered to be
abstract, though it's not a bad idea to emphasize the fact by using the `abstract`
modifier in the class header. A subclass of an abstract class is itself abstract unless it
provides implementations of all the abstract methods of its superclass. We might
want to do that in our example if we had wanted another abstract class to represent
one-dimensional objects like lines, arcs, and curves.

Now, of course, any class that extends `GeometricObject` will inherit the
`move()` method, and we can override the abstract `area()` method in each
subclass. For example, the subclass `Rect` might have the following declaration.

```
public class Rect extends GeometricObject
{
    // The anchor and bounds fields are inherited from the
    // superclass, as is the move() method.

    public double area()
    // Override of base class method, since we can now
    // compute the area of this object.
    {
        return (double)(bounds.width * bounds.height);
    }
}
```

This use of abstract classes is fairly common. In the AWT classes, for
example, `Component`, `Container`, and `MenuComponent` are all abstract.

After having made a collection of classes describing geometric objects, we
might decide to incorporate them into an illustration program. As soon as we do, we
see that we need to be able to draw things like rects and circles. Now we're faced

with a problem—how to integrate the capability for drawing into our existing class structure? In Figure 6.1 we did this by modifying five of the existing classes, adding new methods like `drawGraphicRect()` and `drawGraphicLine()` to the appropriate classes.

There's something inelegant about this solution, though—we're not making good use of the existing hierarchy. It would be much better to invent a new top-level class, `DrawableObject`, with an abstract `draw()` method, and then let our five lower-level classes override the `draw()` method they inherit from `DrawableObject`. Unfortunately, that won't work.

In Java, a class may only `extend` one other class. Multiple inheritance is not permitted.[4]

Java does, though, provide a simple means for doing what we want. An *interface* declaration looks a lot like an abstract class declaration and acts in much the same way. In our example, we might declare the `Drawable` interface like this,

```
public interface Drawable
{
    public void draw(); // Must have an empty body.
}
```

Syntax: interfaces

The declaration of an interface looks like the declaration of a class, except that the keyword `interface` is used in place of the keyword `class`. All methods of an interface must be abstract. An interface may have data fields, but they must all be `final` and `static`.

We would then use the `implements` clause in each of the class declarations that implement the `draw()` method. Our `Rect` class would then look like

```
public class Rect extends GeometricObject implements Drawable
{
    public double area()
    {
        return (double)(bounds.width * bounds.height);
    }
```

(continued)

---

[4]Multiple inheritance is permitted in some other object-oriented languages, like C++.

```
public void draw()
// Here's the method definition we promised when we said
// this class implements Drawable.
{
      drawRect(anchor.x, anchor.y, bounds.width, bounds.height);
}
}
```

Semantics: `interfaces`

A class may be declared to `implement` an interface. If it does, the class must provide implementations (i.e., statement bodies) for all the methods of the interface.

We may regard implementing an interface as a promise that we are going to provide definitions for all the interface's methods. In the AWT library, `LayoutManager` is an interface—you can invent your own layout scheme by writing a class that defines each of `LayoutManager`'s five abstract methods, like `minimumLayoutSize()`.

Unlike class inheritance, a class may implement as many interfaces as needed. We might, for example, define a `Scalable` interface that has an abstract method to change the shape of an object by scaling it horizontally and vertically. Then we could declare our `Rect` class to be drawable and scalable by writing the header

```
public class Rect extends GeometricObject
                implements Drawable, Scalable
```

Figure 6.2 shows how our class hierarchy would look if we used a `Drawable` interface. Compared to Figure 6.1 the structure is no less complicated, but the organization is cleaner and more obvious. When we talk about Java 1.1's event model, we'll see a dozen interfaces and nearly as many abstract classes.

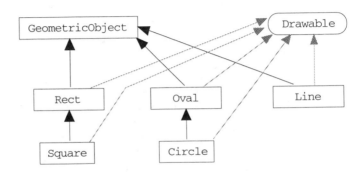

Figure 6.2 Using interfaces to clarify the `GeometricObject` hierarchy.

As we can with classes, we can declare a variable to be an interface type. A variable of interface type can be assigned to any other variable of a class that implements the interface. In our example, for instance, it would be perfectly legal to write

```
Circle c = new Circle();
Drawable d;
d = c;
d.draw(); // since c is a circle, it (and hence d, after the
          // assignment) knows how to draw itself.
```

This might be useful in a drawAll() method that had to display a collection of Drawable objects whose types we wouldn't know until the program was running.

6.2 EVENT-DRIVEN PROGRAMMING

Although you may not have been aware of it, you've already spent a considerable amount of time generating events for a program to respond to. In the labs, you've spent a lot of time generating, editing, and running Java applets. Every time you move the mouse, scroll the contents of a window up or down, or click on a button, you have generated an event that the text editor, applet runner, browser, or Java development environment had to recognize and handle appropriately. Each menu selection, keystroke, and mouse drag generates an event, and it is up to the program to decide how, or whether, to deal with it. In what follows, we will describe the Event classes and discuss the event-handling methods Java provides for our use.

Java 1.1 introduces a host of new methods to the AWT classes, as you've seen. It also introduces some new classes and packages, but most of the changes are more or less superficial, except for the changes in event handling. In event handling we see the most significant differences between Java versions 1.0 and 1.1. Here, the new version introduces a fundamental modification in the model itself—the version 1.1 model is quite a bit more complicated, but the proliferation of new classes and methods results in a model that is considerably cleaner and, eventually, easier to use. We'll discuss the 1.0 event model in Sections 6.2–6.4 and will cover the 1.1 model in Sections 6.5–6.7.

If you want to concentrate on just one model, you can base your decision on the following facts. First, a version 1.0 program should work in a 1.1 environment (no particular reason here for favoring one over the other); second, at the time of this writing, version 1.1 is not available on all Java-aware browsers (which temporarily works in favor of concentrating on 1.0); finally, there is no guarantee that future versions of Java will still support all of the version 1.0 features (which implies that learning 1.1 is a better long-term investment).

The Event Class

Most of the things a user does to an applet generate objects of the Event class. This class is quite a bit different from the Container and Component classes you've seen so far. First of all, the Event class contains a large collection of class constants, used to describe the nature of the event itself, along with other constants that provide additional information about the events.

Take a look at the online documentation for the java.awt.Event class. Along with three constructors that can be used to build new events and six methods (which you'll rarely use), you'll find a list of twenty-seven class constants (which you'll use regularly):

```
// The action event (for Buttons, Checkboxes, Choices, Lists,
// MenuItems, and TextFields)
    ACTION_EVENT
// Key events
    KEY_PRESS, KEY_RELEASE
    KEY_ACTION, KEY_ACTION_RELEASE
// Mouse events
    MOUSE_DOWN, MOUSE_UP
    MOUSE_DRAG
    MOUSE_MOVE
    MOUSE_ENTER, MOUSE_EXIT
// List events
    LIST_SELECT, LIST_DESELECT
// Scrollbar events
    SCROLL_ABSOLUTE
    SCROLL_LINE_UP, SCROLL_LINE_DOWN
    SCROLL_PAGE_UP, SCROLL_PAGE_DOWN
// Window events
    WINDOW_EXPOSE
    WINDOW_ICONIFY, WINDOW_DEICONIFY
    WINDOW_DESTROY
    WINDOW_MOVED
// File-related events
    LOAD_FILE, SAVE_FILE
// Input focus events
    GOT_FOCUS, LOST_FOCUS
```

Each of these names is declared to be public static final. The descriptor public, of course, means that they are accessible by objects of any class. They are static, which means they belong to the Event class, not to any particular Event object, so they would be accessed by using the class name, like Event.MOUSE_UP. They are final, and so their values cannot be modified. The actual integers they represent are completely immaterial to us: Event.MOUSE_UP might denote the number 3 or 4102, but since we just use its name, its number is of no interest except as trivia.

We'll describe most of these event types in complete detail shortly, but even now many of these descriptive constants should be familiar to you: MOUSE_DOWN is the code for the kind of event which is generated when the user presses the mouse button.[5] KEY_PRESS identifies an event generated when the user presses a key on the keyboard, and so on. In addition to the constants that describe event types, there are others that are used to describe multikey combinations like shift-k or ctrl-alt-delete, along with others that describe nonprinting keys like the f-keys, arrows, or the home and page-up keys that appear on some keyboards. The constants ALT_MASK, CTRL_MASK, META_MASK, and SHIFT_MASK are used, as you'll see, to determine whether one of four modifier keys was pressed as part of an event. The constants F1 through F12 refer to the function keys, and LEFT, RIGHT, UP, DOWN, HOME, END, PGUP, and PGDN refer to other special keys that may or may not be on the user's keyboard.

In addition to the class constants, each Event object has a number of public instance variables that provide further information about the event. As usual, we've flagged (with ❦) the most important or commonly used ones.

```
❦ Object arg           // Miscellaneous information, like the label
                       // String for a Button.
  int clickCount       // Only for mouse down events, this counts
                       // the number of multiple clicks.
  Event evt            // Generally not used for any event.
❦ int id               // What kind of event this is--one of the
                       // class constants above.
  int key              // The value of the key pressed, for keyboard
                       // events. Cast this to a char to get the
                       // character or check it against a class
                       // constant, like Event.PGUP.
  int modifiers        // Flags for the modifier keys that were
                       // pressed when this event occurred.
❦ Object target        // The object that generated this event.
  long when            // The time, in milliseconds, when this event
                       // occurred.
  int x                // The x coordinate of the event, in the
                       // component's local coordinates.
  int y                // The y coordinate of this event.
```

Not all these fields apply to all events. The arg field, for example, contains no useful information for any of the mouse events, like MOUSE_UP.

The Event Hierarchy

By now, you should be used to the notion that Java does a lot of things for you with no intervention on your part. For example, an object's paint() method is called

---

[5]In an attempt to apply to as many systems as possible, Java assumes it is dealing with a one-button mouse. You can identify the button in a multibutton mouse by looking at the key modifiers, which we'll describe in Section 6.4.

by Java when it needs to be, without any specific method call in your program. In much the same way, events are usually generated and tracked without any help from your code. Roughly speaking, what happens is that when Java detects an event, it constructs a new Event object and puts that object on an *event queue,* which is just a list of events waiting to be handled. In real-world terms, you can think of each new Event object joining at the end of a waiting line, patiently awaiting its turn for service at the front.[6]

When an Event object finally makes it to the head of the line, Java sends it off to the object it decides should have first crack at responding to the event. For example, a mouse click that happens when the pointer is over a Checkbox generates an ACTION_EVENT, so the Checkbox would be the first object to get that event. The Checkbox might have a handleEvent() method that would look at the event identification number, discover that it was an action event, decide that it was appropriate to deal with it, take whatever action its code dictated, and discard the event from further consideration by any other object.

However, it might have been that the Checkbox either didn't have a method for dealing with the action event, or detected it and decided that it didn't want to handle it. (You might have had such an experience at a store or a bank—you finally get the attention of a clerk only to be told, "I'm sorry, but that's not my job.") Whether the object takes any further action or not, the result is the same—the event gets passed up the line and gets sent to the next most appropriate object for attention. The next object is known as the *parent,* and is the container of the object that didn't handle the event. For example, the Checkbox might be contained in a Panel, as in Figure 6.3, in which case the Panel would get the event, and the whole process would begin anew. Eventually, either the event would find its way to an object in the GUI hierarchy that was willing to handle it, or it would never be handled and simply expire quietly.

It's important to note that the path an event takes, from object to parent, is not the upward path in the class hierarchy, but rather the path upward in the *containment,* or GUI hierarchy that comes from the way components are laid out on the screen. In fact, if you look at the class hierarchy with this example in mind, you'll see that there is no path upward from Button to Panel.

The path an event follows from component to component is governed by the GUI hierarchy.

Where to handle an event can be a delicate question. Good object-oriented programming dictates that an object should handle its own events whenever possible, but that's not always the most efficient course. In our example, for instance, we might decide that the Panel should be responsible for dealing with

---

[6]Although we won't discuss it here, a program can generate events of its own, by creating a new Event, e, and calling the Component method postEvent(e).

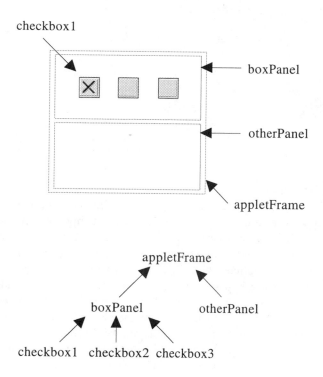

Figure 6.3 Passing an event through the hierarchy.

action events in any of its three Checkboxes. However, the Panel might have access to information that, because of the class structure of the GUI hierarchy, the Checkboxes couldn't easily access. In that case, it would make more sense to put the event handler in the Panel, rather than using an event handler in each of the three Checkboxes. In our store metaphor, this decision might reflect the store policy, "We can't expect you to be able to handle merchandise exchanges between departments, so pass all exchange requests up to the second assistant store manager."

6.3   EVENT HANDLING

We mentioned earlier that Java does most of the dirty work for us in terms of recognizing and keeping track of events. However, when it comes to making our program respond to events, it's up to us to write the code. The first step in recognizing events and acting on them is Component's handleEvent method. With the exception of menus, every widget you create will be derived, directly or indirectly, from the abstract class Component, so to deal with an event in a class of your own, you will override Component's handleEvent method by writing one of your own. The following is an example, taken from the SketchPad lablet.

```
public boolean handleEvent(Event e)
{
    if (e.id == Event.WINDOW_DESTROY)
    {
        System.exit(0);
        return true;
    }
    else
        return super.handleEvent(e);
}
```

Several things here deserve mention. First, note that `handleEvent()` is `public`, so it can be called by the system when needed, and it has a `boolean` return type. The return from a `handleEvent` method determines what happens to the event when you're finished with it: if `handleEvent(e)` returns `true`, the event `e` dies there and is not propagated any further, presumably because you have done everything you need with it. But, if your version of `handleEvent()` returns `false`, the event `e` is passed up the visual hierarchy, to be handled by the parent object's own `handleEvent` method. This option is useful in special cases, when you want an object to deal with an event and also have its containing component do something with it, but it's not an option you would choose very often.

This example also illustrates a commonly used third return choice, namely, to `return super.handleEvent(e)`. As you've seen, for any object, `super` refers to the class immediately above the object in the *class hierarchy*. For example, `SketchPad` extends `applet`, so in this case `super` refers to the Applet class. Thus, by writing `super.handleEvent()`, you are calling the `handleEvent` method belonging to `applet`, thus giving `applet` a crack at dealing with the event `e`, using its own `handleEvent` method. Why bother? Why not just default to returning `false` or `true` and not invoke the superclass method?

Most of the time, this tactic will work perfectly. There will be times, though, when you don't want to push off the event to the parent class by returning `false` from `handleEvent`. Because Java is doing quite a few method calls behind your back, you have to be careful not to skip a call to a `handleEvent` method in a base class that might do something you need. Even more important, though, is that by returning `false`, the event immediately gets passed out of the purview of the object that was the likely target of the event.

This wouldn't be a problem, except for the fact that Java gives each object *two* tries at handling an event. If `handleEvent` fails to terminate an event by returning `true`, Java will try again, looking among the target's *helper methods* like `mouseDown` or `action`. As Sun says in its documentation, "The default method [`handleEvent()`] calls some helper methods [like `action()`] to make life easier on the programmer," and this can make a serious difference in whether your program runs correctly.

Unless you're *sure* you don't want to pass an event to the parent of an object, your override of `handleEvent()` should either return `false` or return the result of calling `super.handleEvent(e)`.

Helper Methods

Many times, particularly in simple classes, using `handleEvent()` to catch all events can lead to a method that is long and cumbersome. If there are just a few events your program needs to respond to, you may find it more convenient to use one or more helper methods (also known as *convenience methods*) that are designed to catch specific events.

For instance, an `ACTION_EVENT` can be generated through a `Button`, `Checkbox`, `Choice`, `List`, `MenuItem`, or `TextField` object. If you are designing an event handler for one of these, or if your event handler is in an object that contains one of these objects, you can use the helper method `action()`, which responds only to ACTION_EVENTs. This is exactly what happens in the `GalaEvents` Lablet, where the applet has a handler:

```
public boolean action(Event e, Object arg)
{
    // This is the handler for events that occurred in
    // one of our four Lists, one Checkbox, a button,
    // or a Choice object.

    ...
}
```

The `action()` method takes two arguments—the event to be handled and another that has different meanings, depending on the type of event. Besides `action`, the `Component` class has helper methods to deal with many of the other types of events.

```
public boolean keyDown(Event e, int key)
public boolean keyUp(Event e, int key)
```

They are invoked by key events, and the `key` argument contains the code of the key that caused the event.

```
public boolean mouseDown(Event e, int x, int y)
public boolean mouseDrag(Event e, int x, int y)
public boolean mouseEnter(Event e, int x, int y)
public boolean mouseExit(Event e, int x, int y)
public boolean mouseMove(Event e, int x, int y)
public boolean mouseUp(Event e, int x, int y)
```

These helper methods are generated by the corresponding mouse events and the x and y values indicate the coordinates where the pointer was when the event was generated, measured in the Component's local coordinate system.

As with handleEvent, all these helper methods have a boolean return value, used to signal whether the method handled the event (return true) or decided to pass it up to the parent of the event's target (by returning false). The advice we gave with handleEvent() is also valid here: Unless you have a good reason to pass the event to the target's parent, you should give the superclass a chance at the event by returning super.action(e, arg), where arg is the second argument in the original action argument. The superclass may not have an action handler, but there's no guarantee that you won't eventually put one in.

Deciphering the Event

As we mentioned earlier, each Event object contains nine fields that describe it in full detail. They are used to provide additional information about the event. For example, target refers to the object, x, in which the event occurred, and y, which contain the coordinates in the target where an event like a mouse down originated, and clickCount records the number of clicks in a MOUSE_DOWN event.

As with the type constants we listed earlier, these fields of an Event object are public, so to refer to them all we need to do is use the object's name and the dot operator. For example, if thisEvent was an Event object, we would refer to its x-coordinate as thisEvent.x and its id code by thisEvent.id.

The arg field is the most complex, since what it contains depends on the type of event. For ACTION_EVENTs in buttons, choices, lists (activated by a double-click) or menu items, it's a string representing the button name, or the name of the selected item. If we have an ACTION_EVENT in a checkbox, arg is a boolean value representing the new state of the checkbox. In a LIST_SELECT or LIST_DESELECT event, arg is the index of the list element selected or deselected. This field is not used in key or mouse events.

Many times, we can decide what to do with an event simply by looking at its target field. We often use the target of an event and the boolean operator instanceof, described in Chapter 5, to categorize events for subsequent processing. In the action handler mentioned, we did this so that we could extract the event's arg string for later output.

```
public boolean action(Event e, Object arg)
{
    if (e.target instanceof List)
    {
        // Once we get here, we know the event was triggered
        // within one of our three lists.
        String c = (String) arg;    // get the list item's name
        if (e.target == sandwiches)
            System.out.println("Sandwich chosen: " + c);
```

```
            else if (e.target == drinks)
                System.out.println("Drink chosen: " + c);
            else if (e.target == sides)
                System.out.println("Side order chosen: " + c);
    }
    // The event wasn't triggered in a list, so we see if
    // it came from the superSize checkbox, the order button,
    // or the sizes choice.
    else if (e.target == superSize)
        System.out.println("Supersize box clicked!");
    else if (e.target == order)
        System.out.println("Order button clicked!");
    else if (e.target == sizes)
        System.out.println("Size choice made!");

    return true;       // We've handled all possible action events,
                       // so kill the event.
}
```

This handler deals with events that can occur in any of three `List` objects, a `Checkbox`, a `Button`, and a `Choice` object. Since we want to extract the name of any of the `List` objects for output, we first check whether the event occurred in one of the lists. We do that by testing whether `e.target` was an instance of a `List` type. If it was, we convert the `arg` object to a `String` and then continue with a collection of nested `if` statements to find which of the lists generated the event. If the target of `e` wasn't one of the lists, we continue with the cascade of `if` statements to find the appropriate event.

6.4 OTHER EVENTS

There are a few event-related topics we won't be dealing with in the Lablets for this chapter, but we include them here for the sake of completeness.

Masks, Key Modifiers, and Mouse Buttons

Earlier on, we mentioned that the `Event` class contains four constants, `SHIFT_MASK`, `ALT_MASK`, `META_MASK`, and `CTRL_MASK`, that are used with key events to determine whether the user had pressed a modifier key.[7] When a key event (`KEY_ACTION`, `KEY_ACTION_RELEASE` for the special keys like the f-keys and arrows, or `KEY_UP` or `KEY_DOWN` for the "ordinary" keys) is generated, the presence of a modifier key sets certain bits in the event's `modifiers` field. Once a handler has trapped a key event, the `modifiers` field can then be inspected to determine the presence of any of the modifier keys.

---

[7]Not all computers have all four of these keys. While you can probably count on any computer having a Shift key, you may not find a Meta key on every keyboard.

The way the modifier keys influence the `modifiers` field is really quite clever. It makes use of two logical operators we discussed in Section 5.3 but haven't used so far. Suppose, for the sake of efficiency, that we used four bits to indicate the presence or absence of a modifier key press. We might choose the bits to represent Shift, Alt, Meta, and Control, in that order. Then, 0000 would indicate that no modifiers had been used, 0100 would indicate that the user had pressed the Alt key, and 1101 would indicate a Shift-Alt-Control key combination (along with whatever other nonmodifier key might also have been pressed). With this ordering, we would then have `SHIFT_MASK` as 1000, `ALT_MASK` as 0100, `META_MASK` as 0010 and `CTRL_MASK` as 0001.

Now comes the clever part—using the masks to extract a single bit from the modifiers field. The operator `&`, recall, when used with integral operands, returns the number which is the bitwise AND of its operators, where we define b1 AND b2 to be 1 when both bits b1 and b2 are 1, and 0 otherwise. We perform this operation on all the bits of a number, so, for example, we would have

```
    00110011
&   11101111
    00100011
```

This is especially useful in cases where, as with the modifier masks, the mask has only a single 1 bit. Then, for instance, if e is an event, the expression

```
e.modifiers & Event.ALT_MASK
```

will be an integer which is 0 precisely when the Alt modifier key has not been pressed.

Similarly, we can check for the presence of two or more modifiers by using the bitwise OR operator, denoted by |. The OR of two bits is 1 when either or both are 1, and 0 only when both bits are 0. Using the masks described as examples, we would have `Event.SHIFT_MASK | Event.CTRL_MASK` equal to the pattern 1001. Thus, to test for the presence of either of these modifier keys, we could write

```
if ((e.modifiers & (Event.SHIFT_MASK | Event.CTRL_MASK)) != 0)
    // One or both modifier keys was pressed
else
    // Neither was pressed
```

To test for the presence of both simultaneously we could use the boolean operator `&&` and write

```
if ( ((e.modifiers & Event.SHIFT_MASK) != 0) &&
    ((e.modifiers & Event.CTRL_MASK) != 0) )
    // Both Shift and Control were pressed
else
    // One wasn't pressed (or neither was)
```

The Event class also has methods that can be used to detect the presence of a modifier key: `controlDown()`, `metaDown()` and `shiftDown()`. There is no test for the Alt key—you'll have to use masks for that. For example, to detect whether a mouse down event occurred with the meta key pressed (or, on a three-button mouse, whether the right mouse button was pressed) you might write a convenience method like this (in a `Canvas`, for instance):

```
public boolean mouseDown(Event e, int x, int y)
{
    if (e.metaDown())
    {
        // Take appropriate action
        return true;
    }
    return false;
}
```

One final helpful hint: These modifier keys also are tracked in MOUSE_DOWN, MOUSE_UP, MOUSE_MOVE, and MOUSE_DRAG events. They are also generated by the buttons on two- or three-button mice. On such devices, the left button doesn't set any modifier bits, but the right and center buttons act exactly as if the Meta and Alt keys, respectively, had been pressed.

Focus Events

The helper methods `gotFocus`, `lostFocus`, and `requestFocus` deal with focus events, which are generated when a component has received input focus (for example, when the user has clicked in a text field). This can be handy when you are trying to implement a user interface that allows the user to press the Tab key to move from one text field to another, or to allow keyboard equivalents to button presses (as, for example, in the case when you want pressing the Return or Enter key to have the same effect as clicking on the "OK" button). To do this, once a text field got focus, you would monitor key events and when you saw a Return or Enter key, you could then call `requestFocus` for the "OK" button, which would be equivalent to clicking on it. Be warned, though, that as of this writing not all Java environments implement these methods.

Scroll Events

Scrollbars, illustrated in Figure 6.4, are useful widgets, not only for controlling the contents of a `Canvas` or `TextArea`, but also in their own rights as controls. We can catch events that occur in scrollbars by trapping SCROLL_LINE_UP, SCROLL_LINE_DOWN, SCROLL_PAGE_UP, SCROLL_PAGE_DOWN, and SCROLL_ABSOLUTE events.

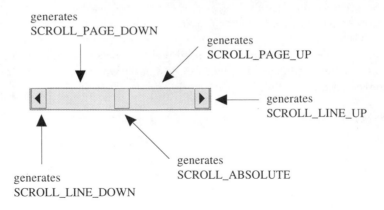

Figure 6.4 The parts of a scroll bar and the events they generate.

6.5   THE JAVA 1.1 DELEGATION MODEL

The version 1.0 event model relies on the GUI hierarchy of a program to determine where events will be sent for handling, as we showed in Figure 6.3. When the user takes some action, the Java environment generates a new `Event` instance, determines which `Component` should be the source of the event, and then sends the event up the containment (GUI) hierarchy in search of a `Component` that can handle the event.

This is a reasonable model in many respects, and has some precedents in other applications (Hypercard for the Macintosh and ToolBook for PCs both use this model), but it has some drawbacks. First, it seems somewhat inelegant to scatter events all over the place, in the hope that somewhere there is a waiting handler. Second, event handlers must be declared in `Components`, which inextricably links the event handling (the actions of a program) with the GUI portion (the look of a program). Because of this, there's no easy way to separate the code dealing with the logical model behind the program from the view that appears to the user. Finally, the 1.0 event model doesn't *scale* very easily to large programs. For example, we took a quick look at a popular spreadsheet and found twenty-three menus, thirty-seven buttons, six choice objects, and four scrollbars, arranged in what in Java terms would be ten or more panels, not to mention a dozen or more dialogs. Designing event handlers for all these components and placing them where they could have access to all the information they need could be a programmer's nightmare in version 1.0. Although such a task would still be complicated in version 1.1, the way events are handled in this model would make the programmer's life somewhat more pleasant.

Java 1.1 addresses these shortcomings with what is known as a *delegation model* of event handling. The salient features of this model are as follows.

❦ Any component can be the *source* of an event. A `Button`, for example, may

be the source of an action event, triggered by a click on the Button, just as it
would in the 1.0 model.

❦ Any class can be a *listener* for an event, merely by implementing the right
listener interface. For example, a class that was designed to handle a Button's
action event would merely have to implement the ActionListener interface,
declaring the interface methods to do whatever is appropriate in response to the
event.

❦ The event generated by a source Component isn't scattered throughout the
GUI hierarchy. Instead, the event is sent only to those listeners that have been
registered with the source object. In our example, we might have a doClose
object that dealt with a click on the "Close" Button. The Button, then, would
register this object by calling addActionListener(doClose).

The basic idea behind the 1.1 delegation model is that a source Component
generates events that are sent to registered listener objects for handling.

The details of this model may appear complicated at first, but the idea is
actually quite simple. We can illustrate how simple this model can be by
considering a single program in both models. Our Test applet consists of a custom
display with a red dot on a white background. The applet has two buttons, which
can be clicked to move the red dot left or right, respectively. In either model, the
applet looks like Figure 6.5.

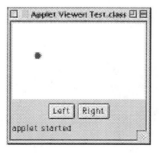

Figure 6.5 The Test applet.

We begin with the version 1.0 model of the applet. If you've read the
material in Sections 6.2–6.4, the code should hold no surprises. The applet has a
single action() handler that catches clicks on either of the two buttons and
responds by asking the display to move its dot to the left or right.

```
// Version 1.0 event model
import java.applet.*;
import java.awt.*;
```

(continued)

```
public class Test extends Applet
{
    private Button left, right;
    private Display myDisplay;          // custom component, defined
                                        // below
    public void init()
    {
        setLayout(new BorderLayout());
        myDisplay = new Display();
        add("Center", myDisplay);

        Panel p = new Panel();
        left = new Button("Left");
        p.add(left);
        right = new Button("Right");
        p.add(right);
        add("South", p);
    }

    public boolean action(Event e, Object arg)
    {
        if (e.target == left)
            myDisplay.shiftDot(-12);
        else if (e.target == right)
            myDisplay.shiftDot(12);
        else
            return false;
        return true;
    }
}


class Display extends Canvas
// A Display knows where its dot is, how to shift it left or right,
// and how to paint itself.
{
    private Point center = new Point(50, 50);

    public Display()
    {
        center = new Point(50, 50);
        setBackground(Color.white);
    }

    public void shiftDot(int xAmount)
    {
        center.x += xAmount;
        repaint();
    }
```

```
        public void paint(Graphics g)
        {
                g.setColor(Color.red);
                g.fillOval(center.x - 5, center.y - 5, 10, 10);
        }
}
```

Note the structure here: A button click is handled in the applet, by calling methods in class `Display`. Now, let's use the 1.1 event model to write the same applet.

```
// Version 1.1 model
import java.applet.*;
import java.awt.*;
import java.awt.event.*; // for the 1.1 Event stuff

public class EventTest extends Applet
{
    private Button left, right;
    private Display     myDisplay;

    public void init()
    {
            setLayout(new BorderLayout());
            myDisplay = new Display();
            add("Center", myDisplay);

            Panel p = new Panel();
            left = new Button("Left");
            p.add(left);
            right = new Button("Right");
            p.add(right);
            add("South", p);

            // Register myDisplay with each button
            left.addActionListener(myDisplay);
            right.addActionListener(myDisplay);
    }
}

class Display extends Canvas implements ActionListener
// Our Display class now can respond to action events.
{
    private Point center;

    public Display()
    {
            center = new Point(50, 50);
            setBackground(Color.white);
    }
```

(continued)

```
public void actionPerformed(ActionEvent e)
// This is the ActionListener method we must implement.
{
        String direction = e.getActionCommand();
        if (direction.equals("Left"))
            center.x -= 12;
        else if (direction.equals("Right"))
            center.x += 12;
        repaint();
}

public void paint(Graphics g)
{
        g.setColor(Color.red);
        g.fillOval(center.x - 5, center.y - 5, 10, 10);
}
}
```

This version is actually a few lines shorter than the 1.0 example, but not enough to be significant. The structure is quite a bit simpler here, though: events are generated by the buttons and sent to the listener myDisplay, where they are handled. The best feature of this version, however, is the separation of model and view. To change the applet so that it uses a Choice object instead of a pair of Buttons, all we would have to do is change the instance variables and make minor modifications to the init() method (the changes are indicated in boldface):

```
public class EventTest extends Applet
{
    private Choice myChoice;
    private Display      myDisplay;

    public void init()
    {
        setLayout(new BorderLayout());
        myDisplay = new Display();
        add("Center", myDisplay);

        Panel p = new Panel();
        myChoice = new Choice();
        myChoice.addItem("Left");
        myChoice.addItem("Right");
        p.add(myChoice);
        add("South", p);

        myChoice.addActionListener(myDisplay);
    }
}
```

That's all it takes—modifying six lines changes the look of the applet to that of Figure 6.6. The model, embodied in the Display class, needs no alteration.

That's what we meant earlier when we talked about a clean separation of model and view.

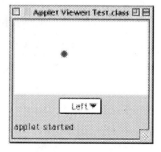

Figure 6.6 The modified Test applet.

6.6 THE AWTEvent HIERARCHY

There's only one Event class in version 1.0; the different kinds of events are distinguished by the Event class constants in the id field. In version 1.1, the different kinds of events are broken into a hierarchy of classes, as illustrated in Figure 6.7.

Although this hierarchy may appear intimidating, it's actually smaller than the twenty-seven events in the 1.0 model. There are only eleven event classes here that you would ever handle (AWTEvent and InputEvent are abstract classes, and you'll probably never deal with EventObject), and some of those, like FocusEvent and PaintEvent, are rarely used. In fact, in most Java programs you'll deal only with some of the ActionEvent, ItemEvent, KeyEvent, MouseEvent, and TextEvent classes, and these will be the ones we concentrate on in what follows. As usual, we'll flag (with 🍎) the methods that are particularly useful or common.

Upper Level Event Classes

The classes near the top of the event hierarchy will be of little use to you themselves. They do, however, contain some methods that will be useful when a listener needs to get information about the event it has received.

```
Object getSource()        // EventObject method
```
Returns the object that generated this event. Most of the time, the listener will probably already know the source object that generated the event, but this method could be useful in a listener that was responsible for handling events from several sources.

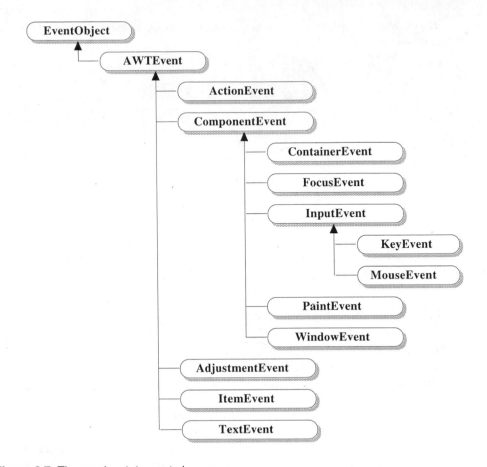

Figure 6.7 The version 1.1 event classes.

```
int getID()                    // AWTEvent method
```
      Returns the `int` constant corresponding to the type of the event. This method is sometimes useful for event classes like `MouseEvent`, which contain several different types of events. The `id` constants you might use are

```
// MouseEvent constants
MOUSE_CLICKED  MOUSE_DRAGGED   MOUSE_ENTERED   MOUSE_EXITED
MOUSE_MOVED    MOUSE_PRESSED   MOUSE_RELEASED

// KeyEvent constants
KEY_PRESSED    KEY_RELEASED    KEY_TYPED
```

As with `getSource()`, most of the time you won't need this method, since a `MouseListener`, for example, will have a `mouseClicked()` handler to deal with mouse events with `id` equal to `MOUSE_CLICKED`.

Action Events

An ActionEvent is generated when the user clicks a Button, double-clicks an item in a List, selects a MenuItem, or presses the <enter> key in a TextField.

🐾 String **getActionCommand**()

Returns a String identifying the source of the event. For Buttons, this is generally the Button's label, for List items and MenuItems, it is usually the text of the item selected, and for TextFields it is usually the contents of the field.

int **getModifiers**()

Returns the mask for any modifiers that accompanied this event, as, for example, if the user clicked a button while pressing the Alt key or clicked the button by using the middle button on a three-button mouse. See the following discussion of the InputEvent class for details.

Input Events

InputEvent is an abstract superclass of the KeyEvent and MouseEvent classes. It contains several useful constants and methods dealing with modifiers to key and mouse events. First, there are four class constants, ALT_MASK, CTRL_MASK, META_MASK, and SHIFT_MASK representing, respectively, presses of the Alt, Control, Meta, and Shift keys. To test for the presence of one of these modifiers, perform a bitwise AND of the event's modifiers and the appropriate mask. If the result is nonzero, the modifier is present. For example, to see if a mouse event e is accompanied by the user pressing the Alt key, we could write

```
if ((e.getModifiers() & InputEvent.ALT_MASK) != 0)
    // The Alt modifier is present.
else
    // The Alt modifier is not present.
```

Bitwise operators and masking are covered in more detail in Section 5.3. In deciphering key and mouse events, you don't need to use these mask constants, since the InputEvent class contains four boolean *predicates* that do the same thing.

```
boolean isAltDown()
boolean isControlDown()
boolean isMetaDown()
boolean isShiftDown()
```

These methods return true if the corresponding modifier key accompanied the event, and false otherwise. The preceding code, for example, could be replaced by the following code.

```
if (e.isAltDown())
    // The Alt modifier is present.
else
    // The Alt modifier is not present.
```

The only time you might need to use masks is to detect the presence of modifiers in an `ActionEvent`, since the four predicates listed aren't available to instances of `ActionEvent`.

int **getModifiers**()
As does the `ActionEvent` method of the same name, this method returns the mask for any modifiers that were in force when this event was generated.

We mentioned before that Java can distinguish between mouse events that came from a three-button mouse. On such a device, a click on the left button provides no modifiers, a click with the middle button sets the `ALT_MASK` bit, and a click on the right button sets the `META_MASK` modifier. For ease in readability, this class provides constants that are equivalent to the mask constants:

```
BUTTON1_MASK        // Currently unused
BUTTON2_MASK        // Equal to ALT_MASK
BUTTON3_MASK        // Equal to META_MASK
```

Item Events

An `ItemEvent` instance is generated when the user selects a `Checkbox`, a `CheckboxMenuItem`, a `Choice` item, or single-clicks a `List` item. Note that these are all two-state objects—they have either been selected or not. In Java 1.1, all these `Component` classes share an `ItemSelectable` interface, meaning that they implement the methods

void **addItemListener**(ItemListener il)
void **removeItemListener**(ItemListener il)

which we'll discuss in the next section, when we explore listeners.

There are actually two different events within the `ItemEvent` class, distinguished by whether the user selected or deselected the particular item. The class provides two class constants you can use to determine which subevent your listener method is using: `SELECTED` and `DESELECTED`.

ItemSelectable **getItemSelectable**()
Returns the `ItemSelectable` object that generated this event.

❦ Object **getItem**()

Returns the item selected. This is usually the `String` representing the item's text or label.

int **getStateChange**()

Returns one of the two class constants `SELECTED` or `DESELECTED`. To test whether an `ItemEvent` instance e had been selected, for example, you could write:

```
if (e.getStateChange() == ItemEvent.SELECTED)
    // The item is checked or highlighted
```

Key Events

Key events are generated when the user presses or releases a key on the keyboard. There are actually three different `KeyEvents`, a key press, a key release, and key typed, a combination of the first two. When the user presses and releases a key on the keyboard (as opposed to an *action key,* like a function or arrow key), all three of these events are sent. These subevents are handled by the `KeyListener` methods `keyPressed()`, `keyReleased()`, and `keyTyped()`, respectively.

There is a difference among the `KeyEvent` methods for those keys that represent characters, like 'A' or '$', and those action keys that do not. The "keyboard" events have the following available methods.

❦ char **getKeyChar**()

Returns the character corresponding to the key that generated this event. If the key doesn't correspond to a Unicode character (like Shift or an arrow key), this method returns the class char constant `CHAR_UNDEFINED`.

void **setKeyChar**(char c)

This method could be used to change the key value that generated this event. Any changes you make will appear in the Component (like a `TextArea`) in which the event was generated.

int **setModifiers**(int mask)

This method allows you to change the modifiers that accompanied this event. For example, you might want to do this to add a Shift modifier to this event, thereby changing the character to uppercase. Recall that the `KeyEvent` class inherits the method `getModifiers()` from its superclass `ItemEvent`.

❦ boolean **isActionKey**()

Returns true if this key is an action key, that is, a key that doesn't correspond to a Unicode character, and returns false otherwise.

Take a look at the keyboard on the computer you use. There's a good chance you'll find a host of action keys, like the arrows, the function keys F1 to F12, a Delete or Backspace key, and a Shift key. You might also find a keypad, often on the right, and keys for PageUp, PageDown, Home, End, NumLock, and so on. All of these keys are recognizable by Java, even though they might not be present on all keyboards, and they are each associated with a "virtual key code," represented by `KeyEvent` class constants. Here's a selection of the more common action key constants:

```
VK_ALT          VK_CONTROL      VK_META        VK_SHIFT
VK_F1    ...    VK_F12
VK_ESCAPE       VK_ENTER        VK_DELETE      VK_BACKSPACE
VK_LEFT         VK_RIGHT        VK_UP                 VK_DOWN
VK_PAGE_UP      VK_PAGE_DOWN    VK_HOME        VK_END
VK_NUMPAD0 ...  VK_NUMPAD9
VK_CAPS_LOCK    VK_NUM_LOCK
```

Once you've used `isActionKey()` to determine that the event is an action key event, you can use the following methods to detect and set the key code.

❦ int **getKeyCode**()

Returns one of the class constants corresponding to this key. This method can be used for keyboard keys, too, since there are codes for `VK_A .. VK_Z`, `VK_0 .. VK_9`, `VK_COMMA`, and so on.

void **setKeyCode**(int keyCode)

Sets the key code for this key to the argument.

Mouse Events

When the mouse is clicked, moved, or otherwise manipulated, a `MouseEvent` is generated by the `Component` where the pointer was at the time. This class contains a number of class constants describing the nature of the event, like `MOUSE_CLICKED` and `MOUSE_DRAGGED`. You won't have much use for them, since the seven kinds of mouse events all have corresponding methods in the `MouseListener` and `MouseMotionListener` interfaces, which we'll describe in the next section.

There are, though, some useful methods in this class.

❦ int **getX**()
❦ int **getY**()
❦ Point **getPoint**()

These return the *x*- and *y*-coordinates of this event, or the `Point` representation of the coordinates. All these are measured in the local coordinates of the originating `Component`. We would use these methods in a 1.1 version of the `SketchPad` Lablet, for instance.

```
int getClickCount()
```
> Returns the click count for this event (2, for example, for a double-click). There is no way to alter the time delay after which a multiple click is considered to be multiple instances of single clicks.

Text Events

`TextEvents` are triggered when the user has modified the contents of a `TextArea` or `TextField` or when the contents have been changed by a method like `setText()`. There are no methods of interest to us in this class—changes to text are trapped by the `textValueChanged()` method of the `TextListener` interface.

6.7   HANDLING EVENTS IN VERSION 1.1

In the version 1.1 event model, `Components` generate events that are handled by any listener objects that have been registered with the event source. A listener is any class that implements the interface that is appropriate for the event. For example, a class that is intended to deal with action events must implement the `ActionListener` interface and a class that deals with key events must implement the `KeyListener` interface.

> To produce a handler for an event, you will find or build an appropriate class and have that class implement the appropriate interface. That's just what we did in the Test applet example we discussed in Section 6.5. There, we had a custom component, `Display`, and we wanted it to monitor `ActionEvents` to know when to move its red ball. That was easy—all we had to do was declare `Display` to implement `ActionListener`, which in this case meant nothing more than providing an implementation of the interface's `actionPerformed()` method. Then, we declared an instance of our listener and registered the instance with the source. In this case, life was particularly easy for us, since the `Display` class already had all the information necessary to respond to action events. However, even in cases where we further separate the model from the view by declaring a separate class where the work goes on, the basic principle is the same.

To design a handler for an event, you will build a class that implements the listener that is appropriate for the event, and override the interface's methods

---

> The following example illustrates the interaction between an event generator, an event listener, and an object that the listener may need to do its work. This is certainly not the only form you'll use to link a listener to a source, but it is a common pattern.

```
class AClass
// This class has an event generator that registers
// a listener to handle its event.
{
    private NeededClass neededInstance = new NeededClass();
    private SomeClass eventGenerator = new SomeClass();
    private ListenerClass aListener;

    // Lay out and initialize, either an init() for
    // an applet or in the constructor for a non-applet.
    {
        ...
        aListener = new ListenerClass(neededInstance);
        eventGenerator.addAppropriateListener(aListener);
    }
}


class ListenerClass implements AppropriateListener
// This class may require information about neededInstance,
// so we pass a reference in via the constructor
{
    NeedfulClass myCopy;        // reference to neededInstance

    public ListenerClass(NeededClass ndInst)
    {
        myCopy = ndInst;
        // whatever else we need to initialize things
    }

    public void appropriateListenerMethod()
    {
        // Handle the event--may need to use myCopy here
    }

    // Other methods, as necessary
}
```

Listener Interfaces

We're almost at the end of our description of the 1.1 event model. With the exception of one minor but useful feature that we'll introduce in the next subsection, all we need to do is describe the listener interfaces. There are eleven of them, and we've flagged the ones we'll talk about:

```
❦ ActionListener        // for ActionEvents
AdjustmentListener      // for Scrollbars
ComponentListener       // for ComponentEvents
ContainerListener       // for ContainerEvents
FocusListener           // for tracking focus events
```

```
❦ ItemListener            // for ItemEvents
❦ KeyListener             // for KeyEvents
❦ MouseListener           // for all mouse events except:
❦ MouseMotionListener     // MOUSE_DRAG and MOUSE_MOVE
❦ TextListener            // for TextEvents
WindowListener            // for WindowEvents
```

ActionListener

This interface is implemented by any class that should respond to `ActionEvents`. To register an instance of `ActionListener al`, you would call the method `addActionListener(al)`. This interface has one method to override.

void **actionPerformed**(ActionEvent e)

     Here is where you deal with any `ActionEvents` generated by sources for which this object is registered. You saw an example of this in the `Test` applet we described in Section 6.5:

```
class Display extends Canvas implements ActionListener
{
    ...
    public void actionPerformed(ActionEvent e)
    {
        String direction = e.getActionCommand();
        if (direction.equals("Left"))
            center.x -= 12;
        else if (direction.equals("Right"))
            center.x += 12;
        repaint();
    }
    ...
}
```

ItemListener

This interface is used to implement listeners for the `ItemEvent` class. To register an `ItemListener` object, call `addItemListener()`. This interface has one method.

void **itemStateChanged**(ItemEvent e)

KeyListener

This interface is used to implement listeners for the three `KeyEvent` varieties. To register an `KeyListener` object, call `addKeyListener()`. This interface has three methods, corresponding to each of the varieties:

```
void keyPressed(KeyEvent e)
void keyReleased(KeyEvent e)
❦ void keyTyped(KeyEvent e)
```

Remember the nature of interfaces—to implement an interface, you must implement every one of its empty methods. If your event-handling class isn't interested in one of these cases, you still have to implement it, even if that means putting nothing within the braces of its body, like this:

```
void keyPressed(KeyEvent e)
// We're not interested in KEY_PRESSED events.
{}
```

MouseListener

This interface is used to implement listeners for the five MouseEvent varieties. To register a MouseListener object, call addMouseListener(). This interface has five methods:

```
❦ void mouseClicked(MouseEvent e)
void mouseEntered(MouseEvent e)
void mouseExited(MouseEvent e)
void mousePressed(MouseEvent e)
void mouseReleased(MouseEvent e)
```

MouseMotionListener

This interface should be folded into MouseListener. It's not, though, because MOUSE_DRAG and MOUSE_MOVE are fundamentally different from the other mouse events, if only because these two are far more computationally expensive than the others. To register a MouseMoveListener with a Component, call addMouseMoveListener(). This interface requires you to override two methods:

```
void mouseMoved(MouseMovedEvent e)
❦ void mouseDragged(MouseMovedEvent e)
```

TextListener

This interface is quite simple. It receives events that indicate that the text of a TextField or TextArea has been changed. To register a TextListener object, you will call addTextListener(). This interface has one method:

```
void textValueChanged(TextEvent e)
```

Adapters

As you know, when a class declares that it implements an interface, it is promising to provide implementations for all the interface methods. Some of the listener interfaces, like `MouseListener`, may contain several methods you wouldn't be interested in implementing. For such interfaces, Java provides seven abstract *adapter classes*. Each of these classes implements the appropriate listener interface, using methods with a no-statement body, { }, rather than an empty statement body. The advantage to this approach is that these classes allow you to subclass them and only implement the methods that are of interest to your listener.

For example, the following adapter subclass implements only the MOUSE_RELEASED event handler.

```
class Worker extends MouseAdapter
{
    public void mouseReleased(MouseEvent e)
    {
        // Do something
    }
}
```

The other mouse event handlers are available to this class, by inheritance, but they don't do anything, which, for our purposes is just fine. The adapter classes are

```
ComponentAdapter
ContainerAdapter
FocusAdapter
KeyAdapter
❦ MouseAdapter
MouseMotionAdapter
WindowAdapter
```

6.8   HANDS ON

There are two Lablets for this chapter; both are examples of event handling, using the Java 1.0 event model. The first, `GalaEvents`, tracks and displays the events that are generated by a typical GUI program. The second, `SketchPad`, makes use of the mouse events to implement a simple drawing program.

The `GalaEvents` Lablet

Chapter 4's Lablet, `Gigobite`, demonstrated the major widgets available to an applet. Of course, `Gigobite` was somewhat limited in that none of its lists, text areas, buttons, choices, or checkboxes did much of anything. In `GalaEvents` we extend `Gigobite` so that we can track the events that take place when the user interacts with its widgets.

The first part of the applet tracks the six mouse events. Whenever any mouse event is detected, the type of the event and its coordinates are displayed. We also include a handler for key events, as well as an `action()` method to detect and display any events generated by the three lists, the checkbox, button, and choice components. Note that we don't use a `handleEvent` method here—all the event handling is done by the convenience methods. As we mentioned before, we don't strictly need the convenience methods. If we had wanted, we could have done all event processing within a single `handleEvent()` method. The result, though, would have been a large and complex method, and it's almost always a good idea to break a complex method into several smaller ones.

Take the time right now for a quick scan of the code. Look how short it is—where are all the widgets? Aha! They're all declared in the `Gigobite` applet, so by declaring `GalaEvents` to be a subclass of `Gigobite`, we get all the widgets and methods of `Gigobite` for free. What we've done here is often called the *model/view* approach. We've made a clean separation between the GUI portion of our program (the view) and the active portion (the model). Adopting this approach allows us to modify the way a program *looks* without having to concern ourselves with the details of how it *acts,* and vice versa.

```
public class GalaEvents extends Gigobite
{
    public boolean mouseUp(Event e, int x, int y)
    {
        System.out.println("MOUSE UP event at " + x + "," + y);
        return true;
    }

    public boolean mouseDown(Event e, int x, int y)
    {
        System.out.println("MOUSE DOWN at " + x + "," + y);
        return true;
    }

    public boolean mouseDrag(Event e, int x, int y)
    {
        System.out.println("MOUSE DRAG at " + x + "," + y);
        return true;
    }

    public boolean mouseMove(Event e, int x, int y)
    {
        System.out.println("MOUSE MOVE at " + x + "," + y);
        return true;
    }
```

```
public boolean mouseEnter(Event e, int x, int y)
{
     System.out.println("MOUSE ENTER at " + x + "," + y);
     return true;
}

public boolean mouseExit(Event e, int x, int y)
{
     System.out.println("MOUSE EXIT at " + x + "," + y);
     return true;
}

public boolean keyDown(Event e, int x)
{
     System.out.println("KEYDOWN event: " + x);
     return true;
}

public boolean action(Event e, Object arg)
{
     if (e.target instanceof List)
     {
          String c = (String) arg;
          if (e.target == sandwiches)
               System.out.println("Sandwich chosen: " + c);
          else if (e.target == drinks)
               System.out.println("Drink chosen: " + c);
          else if (e.target == sides)
               System.out.println("Side order chosen: " + c);
     }

     else if (e.target == superSize)
          System.out.println("Supersize box clicked!");
     else if (e.target == order)
          System.out.println("Button order clicked!");
     else if (e.target == sizes)
          System.out.println("Size choice made!");
     return true;
   }
}
```

To be honest, we have departed somewhat from true object-oriented programming here, but we did so for good reason. Our separation of model from view is a step in the right direction, but it would still be conceptually cleaner if each of the Gigobite objects handled its own events, rather than having the applet itself decide what was going on in its Components. From a strict OOP point of view, it would be better to subclass the List type and make it a new class, perhaps named ActiveList, that would include its own action or handleEvent method. The result would be "purer" but would also be more complicated, since we would have to describe a total of five different classes—the applet itself and the extensions of the `List`, `Checkbox`, `Button`, and `Choice` classes. We opted for the less object-oriented "main event loop" style in this lablet because we deemed it simpler for you to understand. However, you would find it a profitable exercise to rewrite `GalaEvents` so that each of its widgets was responsible for its own events.

The `SketchPad` Lablet

In this Lablet, we go beyond simple reporting of events to using them in a constructive fashion. `SketchPad` is a simple drawing program that works in two different modes: The user can draw curves freehand, using the mouse, or can have more precise directional control over the drawing keys by extending the curve up, down, left, or right by using the arrow keys.

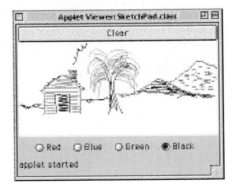

Figure 6.5 Drawing with `SketchPad`.

The curves the user draws are actually collections of line segments beginning at the point `startPoint` and ending at `endPoint`. In the lab exercises, you'll investigate how to use the `mouseDown` and `mouseDrag` handlers to draw a collection of lines made up of these smaller segments.

We begin the class declaration in the usual way, declaring the instance variables (all `private` to the class, notice) we will need. You should verify that none of these variables can be made local, since they all are used in more than one method.

```
public class SketchPad extends Applet
{
    private Button        Clear;
    private Checkbox      color1,         // drawing color choices
                          color2,
                          color3,
                          color4;
```

```
private Point          startPoint;      // the starting point for
                                        // each line segment
private Point          endPoint;        // the ending point for
                                        // each line segment
private Color          currentColor;    // current drawing color
private Rectangle      theBounds;        // bounds of this applet
```

The init() method holds no surprises—we initialize the widgets and lay them out. We also set the starting and ending points of the line segment we're drawing.

```
public void init()
{
    setLayout(new BorderLayout());
    setBackground(Color.white);
    theBounds = bounds();
    // Initialize the start and end points to inside
    // the upper left corner of the applet window
    startPoint = new Point(theBounds.x + 5,
                           theBounds.y + 20);
    endPoint = new Point(theBounds.x + 5,
                         theBounds.y + 20);

    Clear = new Button("Clear");
    add("North", Clear);

    // Set up the control panel to hold the color check boxes
    Panel colorControls  = new Panel();
    colorControls.setBackground(Color.lightGray);

    CheckboxGroup printColors;
    printColors = new CheckboxGroup();
    color1 = new Checkbox("Red", printColors, false);
    colorControls.add(color1);

    color2 = new Checkbox("Blue", printColors, false);
    colorControls.add(color2);

    color3 = new Checkbox("Green", printColors, false);
    colorControls.add(color3);

    color4 = new Checkbox("Black", printColors, true);
    colorControls.add(color4);

    currentColor = Color.black;
    add("South", colorControls);
}
```

Almost all of the event handling here is done by convenience methods. We do have a handleEvent() method, but its only purpose is to deal with the

WINDOW_DESTROY event, for which there is no convenience method. We'll explore what this does in the lab exercises.

```
public boolean handleEvent(Event e)
{
        if (e.id == Event.WINDOW_DESTROY)
        {
                System.exit(0);
                return true;
        }
        else
                // Give the helper methods a chance.
                return super.handleEvent(e);
}
```

The action() handler is where we deal with clicks on the Clear button (by erasing the current drawing) and the Checkboxes that set the drawing color.

```
public boolean action(Event e, Object arg)
{
        if (e.target == Clear)
        {
                // Clear the sketch pad by painting over the entire
                // applet in the background color.
                Graphics g = getGraphics();
                g.setColor(Color.white);
                g.fillRect(theBounds.x, theBounds.y,
                             theBounds.width, theBounds.height);
                g.setColor(currentColor);

                // Reset the start and end points
                startPoint.x = theBounds.x + 5;
                startPoint.y = theBounds.y + 20;
                endPoint.x = theBounds.x + 5;
                endPoint.y = theBounds.y + 20;
        }
        else if (e.target instanceof Checkbox)
        {
                // Set the color to be used in drawing
                if (e.target == color1)
                    currentColor = Color.red;
                else if (e.target == color2)
                    currentColor = Color.blue;
                else if (e.target == color3)
                    currentColor = Color.green;
                else
                    currentColor = Color.black;
        }
        return true;
}
```

In the `keyDown()` method we trap presses of the arrow keys. For example, if the user presses the right arrow key, we extend the current curve to the right by five pixels and then redraw the picture to reflect the change.

```
public boolean keyDown(Event e, int thisKey)
{
    // Change the end point based on which key was hit
    switch (thisKey)
    {
    case Event.LEFT:
        endPoint.x -= 5;
        break;
    case Event.RIGHT:
        endPoint.x += 5;
        break;
    case Event.UP:
        endPoint.y -= 5;
        break;
    case Event.DOWN:
        endPoint.y += 5;
        break;
    default:                // Some other key was pressed,
        return false;       // so pass the event up and leave.
    }
    repaint();
    return true;     // Eat the event--we're done with it.
}
```

The two mouse event handlers do the background work of setting things for the `paint()` method to draw the curve. When we detect a MOUSE_DOWN event, we know the user has clicked on the starting point of a new curve, so we set the coordinates of the new starting point. When we detect a MOUSE_DRAG event, we know the user is extending the existing curve, so we generate a new ending point and call `repaint()` to draw the new segment.

```
public boolean mouseDown(Event e, int thisX, int thisY)
{
    // Set a new start point at where the mouse was clicked
    startPoint.x = thisX;
    startPoint.y = thisY;
    return true;
}

public boolean mouseDrag(Event e, int thisX, int thisY)
{
    // Update the end point to wherever we drag
    endPoint.x = thisX;
    endPoint.y = thisY;
    repaint();
    return true;
}
```

Finally, we come to the painting methods. We have to override `update()` here, since the default `update()` erases the applet and then calls `paint()`. In this case, we don't want to erase the drawing, so we just call `paint()`. In the paint() method, all we do is extend the curve by drawing a new line segment. Note, by the way, that at each call to `paint()` we've effectively "forgotten" any earlier segments in the curve. This means that in this applet we would have a difficult time implementing an Undo operation. Once we talk about arrays in Chapter 8 you'll see that they provide a means by which we could store all prior start and end points, allowing us to "back out" of the drawing we've made so far.

```
public void update(Graphics g)
{
    paint(g);
}

public void paint(Graphics g)
{
    // Connect the start point to the end point
    g.setColor(currentColor);
    g.drawLine(startPoint.x, startPoint.y,
            endPoint.x, endPoint.y);
    // Update the start point so that the next
    // line picks up where we left off
    startPoint.x = endPoint.x;
    startPoint.y = endPoint.y;
}
}
```

6.9   SUMMARY

❧ The `if` statement has the form

```
if (boolean expression)   // (the parentheses are required)
    statement             // the "controlled" statement
```

In execution, the boolean expression is evaluated, and, if its value is `true`, the controlled statement is executed. If the boolean expression evaluates to `false`, the controlled statement is not executed.

❧ The if statement may also have an `else` clause:

```
if (boolean expression)
    statement1
else
    statement2
```

In this variant, `statement1` is executed if the boolean expression is `true`, and `statement2` is executed if the boolean expression is `false`.

❦ In either of the `if` statements the controlled statement or statements can be any Java statement, including compound statements or other if statements.

❦ The `else` clause is always logically associated with the nearest unmatched `if` (much like open and close braces).

❦ The `switch` statement takes the form

```
switch (expression)
{
case constant1:
    some statements
case constant2:
    some statements
...
default:                 // optional
    some statements
}
```

The expression is evaluated, and execution skips down to the first `case` label with a matching constant. Execution then proceeds through all subsequent statements to the end of the statement.

❦ In a `switch` statement, the expression must evaluate to a primitive type and the `case` constants must be literals or `final` variables of a type compatible with the value of the expression.

❦ The `break` statement causes an immediate exit from a `switch` statement and is commonly used to avoid "falling through" the rest of the controlled statements.

❦ It is also possible to break out of a `switch` statement by using `returns`. This option should be used with care.

❦ The `default` label in a `switch` statement indicates a default match for values of the expression that fail to match any of the `case` constants. The `default` label is optional, but it is a good idea to have one in any `switch` statement, since failure to match a `case` constant in the absence of a `default` label will generate a run-time error.

❦ A class may be declared to be abstract by using the `abstract` modifier. Abstract classes cannot be instantiated. Generally, abstract classes are used as templates and are intended to be subclassed.

❦ Whether the `abstract` modifier is present or not, any class having a method with a missing body (or any class that inherits a method with missing body) is automatically considered abstract. A method is declared to have a missing body by following its signature with a semicolon, as, for example,

```
void draw();
```

❦ A Java class can only `extend` one other class. Multiple inheritance is not allowed in Java.

❦ An interface is declared as follows:

```
optionalModifiers interface Name
{
        final static variable declarations

        declarations of methods with empty bodies
}
```

❦ A class may implement an interface by using an `implements` clause in its declaration, like this:

```
class MyClass implements MyInterface
{
        . . .
}
```

A class that implements an interface must provide overrides of all the interface methods, even if their bodies have no statements, using { } for the method body.

❦ A class may implement an arbitrary number of interfaces, using a comma-separated list of interface names in the `implements` clause.

Java 1.0 Event Handling

❦ An `Event` object contains ten public instance variables, describing the nature of the event:

```
Object arg          int clickCount
Event evt           int id
int key             int modifiers
Object target       long when
int x               int y
```

❦ The `id` field of an `Event` object contains one of the following `Event` class constants:

```
ACTION_EVENT
KEY_PRESS            KEY_RELEASE          KEY_ACTION
KEY_ACTION_RELEASE
MOUSE_DOWN           MOUSE_UP             MOUSE_DRAG
MOUSE_MOVE           MOUSE_ENTER          MOUSE_EXIT
LIST_SELECT          LIST_DESELECT
SCROLL_ABSOLUTE      SCROLL_LINE_UP       SCROLL_LINE_DOWN
SCROLL_PAGE_UP       SCROLL_PAGE_DOWN
WINDOW_EXPOSE        WINDOW_ICONIFY       WINDOW_DEICONIFY
WINDOW_DESTROY       WINDOW_MOVED
LOAD_FILE            SAVE_FILE
GOT_FOCUS            LOST_FOCUS
```

❦ The `Component`s that generate events of a specific type vary with the system, unfortunately.

❦ ACTION_EVENTs are generated within `Button`, `Checkbox`, `Choice`, `List`, `MenuItem`, or `TextField` objects.

❦ KEY_ACTION and KEY_ACTION_RELEASE events are initiated by pressing or releasing, respectively, a function or keypad key. They are generally targeted to `Canvas`, `TextField`, and `TextArea` objects.

❦ KEY_PRESS and KEY_RELEASE events are initiated by pressing or releasing, respectively, an ordinary keyboard key.

❦ The mouse events are generally targeted to `Canvas`, `Panel`, `Window`, and `Frame` objects. On most systems, the mouse events are *not* generated by `Button`s or other `Component`s that generate ACTION_EVENTs.

❦ It should come as no surprise that the `Scrollbar` events are generated by `Scrollbar`s.

❦ When an event is detected by the system, a new `Event` instance is created and is placed on a queue of pending events. When the instance reached the head of the queue, it is sent to the target `Component` that generated the event.

❦ If an event is not handled by a Component, it will be sent to the next Component in the GUI (visual) hierarchy.

❦ The `handleEvent()` method of `Component` is overridden to deal with the consequences of an event. If there is no contingency in `handleEvent()` for a particular event, the event is passed to a convenience method.

❦ `handleEvent()` returns a `boolean` value. Return `true` indicates that the event should not be propagated upwards (i.e., the event has been handled), and `false` propagates the event up the GUI hierarchy.

❦ In general, `handleEvent(e)` should return `true` to kill the event from further consideration and otherwise should return `super.handleEvent(e)` to give the convenience methods a chance at the event.

❦ The convenience methods of `Component` are

```
action(Event e, Object arg)        // arg is often the label
gotFocus(Event e, Object arg)
lostFocus(Event e, Object arg)
keyDown(Event e, int key)          // cast key to char
keyUp(Event e, int key)            // cast key to char
mouseDown(Event e, int x, int y)   // (x, y) is location
mouseDrag(Event e, int x, int y)   // of the event, in the
mouseEnter(Event e, int x, int y)  // local coordinate
mouseExit(Event e, int x, int y)   // system.
mouseUp(Event e, int x, int y)
```

❦ As does `handleEvent()`, the convenience methods have `boolean` return types. The return value is interpreted in the same way as in `handleEvent()`.

Java 1.1 Event Handling

❦ There is no event hierarchy in the 1.1 model. An event source registers one or more listeners, and these listeners implement the appropriate interface methods to handle the source's events.

❦ Any `Component` can be the source of an event and any class can be a listener.

❦ There are fourteen Event classes:

```
EventObject
    AWTEvent
        ActionEvent
        ComponentEvent
            ContainerEvent
            FocusEvent
            InputEvent
                KeyEvent
                MouseEvent
            PaintEvent
            WindowEvent
        AdjustmentEvent
        ItemEvent
        TextEvent
```

❦ The `MouseEvent`, `KeyEvent`, and `ItemEvent` classes are further broken into subsidiary events:

```
// MouseEvents
MOUSE_CLICKED   MOUSE_DRAGGED   MOUSE_ENTERED   MOUSE_EXITED
MOUSE_MOVED     MOUSE_PRESSED   MOUSE_RELEASED
// KeyEvents
KEY_PRESSED     KEY_RELEASED    KEY_TYPED
// ItemEvents
SELECTED        DESELECTED
```

❦ An `ActionEvent` is generated when the user clicks a `Button`, double-clicks an item in a `List`, selects a `MenuItem`, or presses the <enter> key in a `TextField`.

❦ `InputEvent` is an abstract superclass of the `KeyEvent` and `MouseEvent` classes. This class has methods and constants that can be used to detect the presence of the modifier keys Alt, Control, Meta, and Shift.

❦ An `ItemEvent` instance is generated when the user selects a `Checkbox`, a `CheckboxMenuItem`, a `Choice` item, or single-clicks a `List` item.

❦ Key events are generated when the user presses or releases a key on the keyboard.

❦ There are two classes of key events—keyboard events are associated with the alphanumeric keys on the keyboard, and action keys, like the arrows, do not have `char` equivalents.

❦ There are seven MouseEvents:

```
MOUSE_CLICKED   MOUSE_DRAGGED   MOUSE_ENTERED   MOUSE_EXITED
MOUSE_MOVED     MOUSE_PRESSED   MOUSE_RELEASED
```

❦ There are eleven listener interfaces:

```
ActionListener          // for ActionEvents
AdjustmentListener      // for Scrollbars
ComponentListener       // for ComponentEvents
ContainerListener       // for ContainerEvents
FocusListener           // for tracking focus events
ItemListener            // for ItemEvents
KeyListener             // for KeyEvents
MouseListener           // for all mouse events except:
MouseMotionListener     // MOUSE_DRAG and MOUSE_MOVE
```

```
TextListener              // for TextEvents
  WindowListener          // for WindowEvents
```
❦ Each listener interface contains empty methods that can be used to deal with
events of a particular kind.

6.10 EXERCISES

1. Fill in the blanks. We haven't indented the statements so as not to give you any
    extra clues.

    ```
    if (a > 1)
    if (m <= 0)
    ```
    This is executed when _____.
    ```
    else
    ```
    This is executed when _____.
    ```
    else
    ```
    This is executed when _____.

2. In the following code fragments, there are a number of boxes. Into which boxes
    could you put semicolons without causing syntax errors? Of the "legal" boxes,
    which are unlikely to receive semicolons and which *must* have semicolons?
    a.   `if ❑ (x != 0 ❑) ❑`
    `     a /= x ❑`
    b.   `if ❑ (n % 2 == 1) ❑`
    `       n = 3 * n + 1 ❑`
    `     else ❑`
    `       n = n / 2 ❑`

3. In Exercise 2(b), if you put the semicolons where they "should" be and execute
    the statement repeatedly for various starting values of n, what happens? Try it
    repeatedly for n = 32, 7, and 25. This is known as the *Collatz function,* and
    nobody has yet been able to show that it eventually reaches 1 for any starting
    value of n. If you'd like a chance at fame, try showing that it does, or finding a
    value of n for which it never reaches 1.

4. Suppose E1 and E2 are `boolean` expressions and S is a statement. What is the
    difference between these two statements, if any?

    ```
    if (E1 && E2)              if (E1)
        S                          if (E2)
                                       S
    ```

5. If we use the `return` statement to break out of a related collection of tests, we
    must be careful to order the tests from most restrictive to least. What would be
    the action of this version of the `taxOn()` method?

```
private double taxOn(double income)
{
        if (income <= 47050.0)
             return 0.28 * income;
        if (income <= 19450.0)
             return 0.15 * income;
        if (income <= 97620.0)
             return 0.33 * income;
        else
             return 0.38 * income;
}
```

6.   Write the body of the method

```
boolean isOrdered(int x, int y, int z)
```

that returns `true` if x, y, and z are in numeric order, namely, if $x \leq y \leq z$, and returns `false` if they are not.

7.   Write the body of the method

```
boolean isSum(int x, int y, int z)
```

that returns `true` if any one of x, y, and z is equal to the sum of the other two, and returns `false` if they are not.

8.   In a quadratic equation, such as $ax^2 + bx + c = 0$, we are given the coefficients *a, b,* and *c,* and are to find all values of *x* that make the equation true. The nature of the solution depends on the values of *a, b,* and *c* as follows.

> If $a = 0$ and $b \neq 0$, there is one solution.
> If $a = 0$ and $b = 0$, then there are no solutions if $c \neq 0$, and all *x* values are solutions if $c = 0$.
> If $a \neq 0$, let *d* denote $b^2 - 4ac$. If $d < 0$, then there are two complex solutions. If $d = 0$, then there are two identical real solutions, and if $d > 0$, then there are two unequal real solutions.

Write a method

```
void quadratic(double a, double b, double c)
```

that will take three coefficients and display the nature of the solutions of the quadratic equation having these coefficients.

9. Look at the `action()` handler in `SketchPad`. This portion,

    ```
    // Set the color to be used in drawing
    if (e.target == color1)
        currentColor = Color.red;
    else if (e.target == color2)
        currentColor = Color.blue;
    else if (e.target == color3)
        currentColor = Color.green;
    else
        currentColor = Color.black;
    ```

    looks like a natural candidate for a `switch` statement. Why didn't we use one?

10. Which `Components` can generate `ACTION_EVENT`s?

11. The `ACTION_EVENT` has a convenience method, `action()`, that is called when an `ACTION_EVENT` occurs. Which of the `Event`s don't have convenience methods? How would you handle such events?

12. In the `SketchPad` applet, we used the `handleEvent()` method to trap a `WINDOW_DESTROY` event. This event is triggered when the user clicks (or double-clicks, depending on the system) the window's "go-away" box. This box is located in the upper left corner of the window in most systems.

    For most applets, we don't need to trap a window destruction event, since the applet runner or browser will handle that for us. For example, in the lab exercises we ask you to remove the `handleEvent()` method from `SketchPad` and see what effect it has on the applet. The answer is: no effect.

    We do need to trap `WINDOW_DESTROY` events, though, whenever we make windows of our own. Here's an example, using just about the simplest application we can write:

    ```
    import java.awt.*;
    public class WinTest extends Frame
    {
        public WinTest()
        {
            add("Center", new Label("Just a label"));
        }

        public boolean handleEvent(Event e)
        {
            if (e.id == Event.WINDOW_DESTROY)
                System.exit(0);

            return super.handleEvent(e);
        }
    ```

(continued)

```
public static void main(String[] args)
{
      Frame f = new WinTest();
      f.reshape(50, 50, 100, 100);
      f.show();
}
}
```

Run this application, first as it's written and then again without the
`handleEvent()` method. In both cases, do whatever is necessary in your
environment to kill the window. What happens? Explain.

13. Take a look at the `Colors` Lablet from Chapter 1. Explain what's going on in
the `action()` handler. What is the purpose of the two expression statements
controlled by the `if` statements?

14. Enter and run this applet.

```
public class EventTest extends Applet
{
      private Button btn;
      private TextField msg;

      public void init()
      {
            btn = new Button("Hi!");
            add(btn);

            msg = new TextField(8);
            add(msg);
      }

      public boolean handleEvent(Event e)
      {
            if (e.id == Event.MOUSE_ENTER)
                  msg.setText("In");
            else if (e.id == Event.MOUSE_EXIT)
                  msg.setText("Out");

            return false;
      }

      public boolean action(Event e, Object arg)
      {
            if (e.target == btn)
            {
                  msg.setText("Hi, yourself");
                  return true;
            }
            return false;
      }
}
```

Why doesn't the Button respond by placing a message in the TextField? Fix the applet so it does.

15. For the applet with GUI hierarchy illustrated in Figure 6.3, answer the following.
    a. Name all the Components where you could place a mouseUp() handler to detect mouse clicks in otherPanel.
    b. Where would you put the mouseUp() handler if a mouse click in otherPanel was supposed to set the states of all three Checkboxes to false?

16. Write an applet with a List and a TextField. Each time the user double-clicks on a List item, the name of that item will appear in the TextField and the item will be deleted from the list. Recall that double-clicking on a List item generates an ACTION_EVENT with arg field containing the text of the item.
    a. Try this exercise by placing the action() handler in the applet itself.
    b. Try this exercise by subclassing List to make a new class, DiminishingList, and placing an action() handler in your new class that will do the item deletion and then pass the event up the GUI hierarchy.
    c. Do both of parts (a) and (b) and discuss which was easier to write and which was easier to understand. Would your answers be different if the applet contained ten such lists?

17. Write an applet that draws a filled green circle at the pointer location each time the mouse is clicked.
    a. First, try using an action() handler to trap the mouse click.
    b. Now try it with a mouseUp() handler.
    c. You'll probably find that only one of parts (a) and (b) works. Explain why.

18. a. Expand the applet in Exercise 16 with a Choice object that allows the user to select the color in which the circle will be drawn.
    b. Add another Choice object that will allow the user to select whether a circle or a rectangle will be drawn at the click location.
    c. Add a "Cycle" Button that will cycle through several background colors, as we did in the Chapter 1 Colors Lablet.

19. Change the applet of Exercise 16 so that it draws a filled rectangle while the mouse button is held down, as a paint program might. In other words, if the user clicked the mouse at point p and held the button down while dragging southeast to point q, the applet would draw a filled rectangle with upper left corner at p and lower right corner at q. Note: Getting this applet to act like a real paint program is rather tricky.

20. Build a working `ToggleButton`. A `ToggleButton` will act exactly like an ordinary `Button`, but it will change its label each time it is clicked. There will be one constructor,

```
public ToggleButton(String initial, String other)
```

that will set the initial label `String` and the `String` for the other state label (both of which will be used to set some instance variables where the `Strings` are stored). The class will also have an `action()` handler that will change the label `String` in an appropriate way and will then pass the event along. Here's a skeleton class declaration—you fill in the `action()` method. You might find it useful to use the `String` method `equals()`.

```
public class ToggleButton extends Button
{
    private String initial, other;

    public ToggleButton(String initial, String other)
    {
        this.initial = initial;
        this.other = other;
    }
    public boolean action(Event e, int x, int y)
    {
        // Fill in this part.
    }
}
```

You'll probably want to test your `ToggleButton` by placing an instance in an applet and trying it out.

21. We mentioned that different Java environments post events differently. Whether you're using the 1.0 or 1.1 model, augment the `GalaEvents` Lablet so that it tracks *all* Java events. For a particular environment, do you see any events that could be posted but are not? If you can, run your augmented program in several environments and see if there are any differences. With luck, we will be able to eliminate this question from subsequent editions of this book, but for now you'll just have to be patient with the inconsistencies, and test your applets in as many environments as possible if you intend to release them to the public.

22. Make a table, where the columns correspond to the the Java `Components` and the rows to the 1.1 events. In each cell of the table, put a check if the `Component` can generate the event.

23. Modify the `Test` applet of Section 6.5 so that it uses a `List` to control the `Display`. The `List` will have two items, "Left" and "Right." Double-clicking on one of the items should move the dot in the indicated direction. Remember that double-clicking a `List` item generates an `ActionEvent`.

     a. Modify the version 1.0 program (`arg` will contain a `String` equal to the item name).

     b. Modify the version 1.1 program (`getActionCommand()` will return the name of the item).

24. Change the `Test` applet of Section 6.5 so that it uses the left and right arrow keys to control the Display. This requires a more substantial change than the modification we made in the text.

25. Produce a Java 1.1 version of the `SketchPad` Lablet. You might find it useful to use the `Test` applet of Section 6.5 as a source of inspiration.

26. Produce a Java 1.1 version of the `GalaEvents` Lablet. This can be fun—if you add a `TextField` to the applet and have all event reporting go to that field, you can use the model we suggested at the start of Section 6.7.

CHAPTER SEVEN

Methodical Programming

You've seen a lot of Java details so far. You know that a Java program is made up of a collection of classes, that classes contain instance variables for storing information and methods for manipulating this information. You know that an object communicates with another by asking the recipient to invoke one of its methods. You've seen a significant portion of the AWT class hierarchy and you've seen how to use these classes and interfaces to produce the visual design of an applet or application.

In other words, you have a large collection of tools. In fact, with the exception of a few features we'll cover in Chapter 8, you have almost everything you need to build all but the most arcane Java programs.

Having the tools is necessary for writing programs. However, it's not sufficient. As with other crafts, to become proficient you need to know how to use the tools. Having a complete collection of classes, methods, and statements won't make you a programmer, any more than having a complete collection of brushes, paints, palette knives, and solvents will make you an artist. In both cases, you need to have a plan to guide you when you find yourself staring at that blank canvas, wondering, "Where do I go from here?" In this chapter, we'll design a complex program and show you how we got from imprecise description to working program.

OBJECTIVES

In this chapter, we will
- Use an extended programming exercise to illustrate the strategies of effective program design.
- Discuss designing from the top down, starting with a decision about what classes to use.
- See how decisions about classes suggest what methods to include in the classes.
- Talk about the nature of methods, their arguments, their return values, and their statement bodies.
- Show how decisions about methods suggest what statements they require.

7.1   METHOD RECAP

Since we'll be building quite a few methods in what's to come, it would be a good idea to review what we know about methods and lay down some of the syntactic and semantic rules governing methods.

Method Signatures

The *signature* of a method is what you see in the first line of the method declaration. Here are some examples:

```
void disable()                          // from Component
boolean isEnabled()                     // also from Component
void addItem(String name)               // from List
void addItem(String name, int index)    // also from List
String toString()                       // from Color, Event, and
                                        // over forty other classes
```

The signature of a method consists of the *name* of the method and the *argument list.* The signature of a method is used by the compiler to determine which method to call. A class may not have two methods with the same signature.

The return type is either a primitive type name (like `boolean`), a class name (like `String`), or the literal `void`. The return type tells the compiler the type of information that will be returned by the method. If the return type is `void`, the expression does its thing when called and then returns, not passing anything back to the program. If the return type is not `void`, the method sends back some information to the program, to be used where it was called, just as a variable of that type would be. For example, `isEnabled()` has a `boolean` return type, so could be used in any expression that expects a `boolean` value, like

```
if (myButton.isEnabled())   // okay: A boolean is returned here.
    myButton.disable();
```

The controlled statement in this example illustrates how we use a method with a `void` return type. The `disable()` method couldn't be used in a complex expression that expected some value, but it can be called by a simple expression statement. In effect, the expression statement

```
myButton.disable();
```

is like

```
index++;
```

in that both statements tell the system: Do this, and don't do anything with the value that's returned, if any.

The name that appears in the method signature can be any legal Java identifier, as long as it isn't a keyword, like `if` or `class`. In the samples above, you'll notice that two methods in `List` have the same name. That's perfectly acceptable—the compiler will be able to tell which is which by the fact that the two methods have different signatures (since their argument lists are different).

The argument list of a method consists of a pair of parentheses containing either nothing or one or more *TypeName argumentName* pairs, separated by commas. These argument descriptions look a lot like variable declarations. As you'll see shortly, they look like declarations because they act that way. However, you can't use the shortcut form you can with variable declarations. The signature

```
double average(double x, y)   // NO!
```

is illegal, since each argument must be paired with a type name. In Java, you can't set an initial value for an argument, either, so this would be unacceptable to the compiler.[1]

```
void sleep(int x = 0)          //NO!
```

Calling Methods

Every method belongs to a class. In Java there are no "free methods" that are declared outside of classes. This means that every instance of a class has a set of methods it can call into action, just as we did above when the `Button` instance `myButton` called the `Component` method `disable()`. As in the preceding example, an instance of a class can call one of its methods, or any accessible method of a superclass, by using the form *instanceName.methodName(arguments)*. For example, the following are all legal calls (to methods with `void` return types).

```
myButton.disable();   // disable() belongs to superclass Component
myButton.setLabel("OK");   // setLabel() is a Button method
```

The following are not legal calls.

```
myButton.add(x);       // NO.  There are add() methods in Container,
                       // Menu, MenuBar, and Rectangle, but these
                       // aren't Button superclasses.
myButton.erase();      // NO.  Who ever heard of erase()?
```

As you would expect, access plays a role here. An object can call any methods of its own class, the `public` methods of any other class, and the `protected` methods of any of its superclasses. An object cannot call a `private` method of any class but its own.

---

[1]This is known as a *default argument,* and is legal in some languages, like C++.

If a method has a non-`void` return type, a call to it can be used anywhere in an expression where a value of that type could be used, as we mentioned. For example, `getLabel()` is a `Button` method that returns a `String`, so we could use a call to `getLabel()` in any expression where a `String` would be allowed, like

```
myButton.getLabel() + " is the label"
```

Similarly, `myButton` has access, by inheritance, to the `Component` method `location()` that returns a `Point`. Since the `x` field of `Point` is `public`, and hence accessible everywhere, we could write the expression

```
3 + myButton.location().x
```

This is a little complicated, so let's unpack it. The dot notation isn't, strictly speaking, an operator in Java, though it acts like one.[2] If we think of the dot as an operator, it would have the highest possible precedence and would group from the left. With that in mind, the compiler would evaluate the expression above as

```
( 3 + ( ( myButton.location() ).x ) )
```

which would become

```
( 3 + ( someAnonymousPoint.x ) )
```

and then something like

```
( 3 + 78 )
```

which would finally yield

```
81
```

This order of evaluation works equally well for cascaded method calls, like this mess,

```
myButton.getParent().countComponents()
```

which gets the `Container` of `myButton` and then calls that `Container`'s `countComponents()` method, thus finding how many other widgets share `myButton`'s container. It's not a good idea to string too many method calls together with dots—it's pretty hard to read. Much better is to introduce temporary local variables, as follows.

---

[2]The dot *is* an operator in C and C++.

```
Container c = myButton.getParent();
int numComponents = c.countComponents();
```

However, if you ever see a sequence like that one, just start grouping from the left and keep going until you run out of dots.

For the sake of simplicity, a call to a method *from within the same class* doesn't need an instance name in front. If you want to make it obvious that you're calling one of the class's methods, you can use the synonym this, which means "this object." Here's an example, strangely including both ways of calling a method from the same class.

```
class PairOfInts
{
     private int x, y;

     public PairOfInts(int x, int y)
     // We need "this" here, to distinguish between the instance
     // variables and the constructor arguments.
     {
          this.x = x;
          this.y = y;
     }

     public void flop()
     // Changes (x, y) to (-y, x)
     {
          int temp = -y;
          y = x;
          x = temp;
     }

     public void flip()
     {
          flop();             // Note: no object name in front of call.
          this.flop();        // Same effect, but emphasizing we're
                              // calling the flop() method of
                              // this class.
     }
}
```

Arguments

The arguments of a method provide the means by which information may be sent from the calling context to the method.

Definition:

The *formal arguments* of a method are the ones that appear in the method definition. The *actual arguments* are the ones that are used in the method call. The actual arguments must match the formal arguments in number and order, and the types must be compatible (which we'll explain).

Consider, for example, the `Point` method,

```
void translate(int x, int y)
```

We can "second guess" what the definition of this method must look like:

```
void translate(int x, int y)
// Remember, Point has two int instance variables, x and y.
{
    this.x += x;    // Add the x argument to this x value
    this.y += y;    // Add the y argument to this y value
}
```

When this method is called, perhaps like this,

```
int deltaY = 10;
myPoint.translate(5, deltaY);
```

What happens, in effect, is that there are invisible initializations for the formal arguments that are done first:

```
void translate(int x, int y)
{
    x = 5;          // Initialize the first argument.
    y = deltaY;     // Initialize the second argument.

    this.x += x;    // Add the x argument to this x value.
    this.y += y;    // Add the y argument to this y value.
}
```

When a method is called, the first thing that happens is that the actual arguments in the call are used to initialize the corresponding formal arguments in the method declaration.

This hidden initialization has some important consequences. The first consequence is that the actual arguments don't have to be the same type as the corresponding formal arguments. As long as the formal argument type is "wider" than the actual argument, the initialization will work just fine. For example

```
byte dY = 10;
myPoint.translate(5, dY);
```

is perfectly acceptable, since we can always initialize the int argument y by using a byte with no loss of information. However, we can't use a wider type in the actual argument, like,

```
double largeDY = 1.0098;
myPoint.translate(5, largeDY)
```

since the hidden initialization

```
x = largeDY;
```

wouldn't be allowed (since we can't force a double into an int).

A formal argument may be initialized with an actual argument of another type, as long as the formal argument is "wider" than the actual argument.

To help you remember this, just keep in mind that a method with a double argument may be called by using any numeric type, since double is wider than any of the other numeric types. Refer to Section 5.4 for more information on this kind of type compatibility.

For arguments of class type, we have similar considerations: A formal argument of a given class type can be called by using actual arguments of that class or any subclass. For example, the Container method

```
void add(Component c)
```

could be called by myPanel (which is a Container, of course) in any of the forms

```
myPanel.add(theButton);    // Button is a Component
myPanel.add(theLabel);     // Label is a Component
myPanel.add(theWindow);    // Window is a Container is a Component
```

However, none of these calls would be allowed, unless you made a type cast:

```
myPanel.add(theMenu);    // Menu isn't a Component subclass
myPanel.add(theObject);  // Object is a Component superclass
myPanel.add(theInt);     // int isn't even a class type
```

The memory aid here is that if the formal argument is `Object`, you can use an instance of any class in the method call.

Value Arguments and Reference Arguments

Another consequence of the "hidden initialization" that takes place at the start of any method invocation is that methods act differently on *value arguments* (that is, arguments of a primitive type) than they do on *reference arguments* (arguments of class type). Remember, variables of primitive type hold values, while variables of class type hold addresses in memory where member data may be found.

Let's see how methods act on value arguments first. Consider a class with a helper method `swap(int x, int y)`. Interchanging two values is a common operation in many programs, and that's what `swap()` is supposed to do. If `swap()` is called with two variables containing 3 and 2, for example, after the call we want the variables to contain 2 and 3, respectively

```
class SomeClass
{
    public someMethod()
    {
        int a = 3;
        int b = 2;
        swap(a, b);
        // Now what are a and b?
    }

    private void swap(int x, int y)
    // Interchange the values of the arguments.   NOT!
    {
        int temp = x;
        x = y;
        y = temp;
    }
}
```

Figure 7.1 shows what happens when `swap(a, b)` is called, with a containing the value 3 and b containing the value 2. The first thing that happens is that the formal arguments, x and y, are initialized to the corresponding value of the actual arguments in the "hidden initialization" step. Then, in the three statements of the method, the local variable `temp` is set to x's value, 3, x gets the value, 2, of y, and finally, y is set to the value saved in `temp`. Perfect! The values in x and y are indeed interchanged.

However, this swapping never shows up in a and b. As far as we can tell, `swap()` has no effect! That's because all the work `swap()` does is performed on the *local* copies, x and y, of its arguments. The actual arguments are never touched. Indeed, this is always the case.

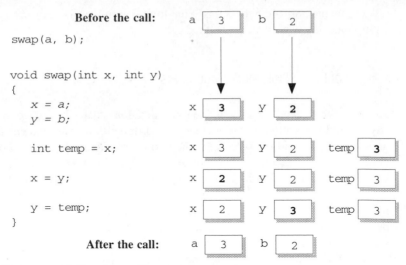

Figure 7.1 Trying, and failing, to modify value arguments.

A method *cannot* modify the values of primitive type arguments.

When the method returns, the arguments x and y, and the local variable temp are lost, and the variables a and b used in the method call have their original values. You can think of value arguments as *read-only*: they pass information in to the method, but that's all.

The situation is quite different for reference arguments. In Figure 7.2 we illustrate the action of a slightly different swap() method. In this case, the method has an argument of type Point and is designed to interchange the values of the Point's x and y fields. When this method is called, with some Point q as its actual argument, the "hidden initialization" sets the formal argument p to refer to q. Now p and q are *aliases* for the same object, since the addresses they contain are the same.

The method statements then interchange the values of the x and y fields, just as they did in our first example. This time, though, when the method returns, p and temp both vanish, as usual, and q persists, *with its fields changed*! Note that we really haven't changed q—it still has the same address it did before. We have, though, modified the data in the object to which q refers. You can think of the fields of a reference argument as *read-write*: they can be used to pass information both in and out of a method.

A method *can* modify the fields of class type arguments.

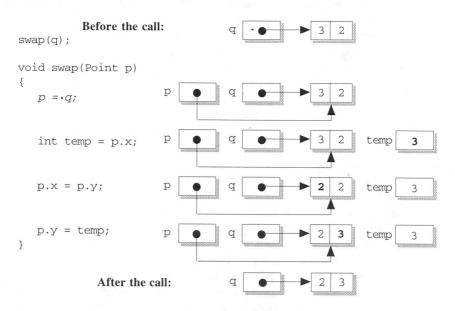

Figure 7.2 Successfully modifying the fields of a reference argument.

7.2   STEP 1: SPECIFICATION

The task that will occupy us throughout this chapter can be stated simply enough: Build an ATM. Hmm . . . that's not much of a description. Most of the time, you'll be given more details than we have here, but we're making a point. No matter how precisely a programming problem is phrased, the description will almost always be incomplete. Invariably, there will be questions that need to be answered: Should this ATM be a simulation, or is it intended to control a real piece of equipment? When writing our program, should we consider saving and retrieving account information, or should we just design the "front end" that the user will see? What *is* an ATM?

Advice: Look Before You Leap

Before you start doing anything with a programming task, be sure you know what you're supposed to do.

If the programming task occurs in a professional environment, you'll probably want to meet the client and clarify what he or she expects; in a classroom setting, your instructor will be your client; and for a program task you set yourself, you'll be the client, of course. In this case, we are the clients, so we need satisfy only ourselves, with only one constraint: What we do must provide you with a useful experience. Let's see how we can fill in the details of our project.

An automatic teller machine (ATM) is basically a remote terminal connected to a bank's computer. It has a store of cash that is used to fulfill requests for withdrawals, and it can also be used to accept and record deposits from bank customers. Since you don't yet know how to store information in files that persist after the program quits, we decided to do a simulation of just the front end and to produce an applet that will look like the real ATMs you find in banks, stores, and parking lots.

The next thing we did was go around our town and take a look at some actual ATMs. We were ready for a break, anyhow, and this "field research" was a good excuse. We discovered that all four ATMs in Clinton, New York[3] looked pretty much the same: Each had a display window and a numeric keypad for entering cash amounts, and most had a control panel of buttons labeled "Clear," "Enter," "Deposit," and Withdrawal." Of course, they had other parts, like the slot where the cash came out, which we noted but didn't intend to simulate.

We finally had a reasonably good idea of what we were trying to accomplish. In a more complicated task, we would certainly write down the specifications rather than rely on our memory. This precaution goes unspoken in the world of commercial programming. Not only is it an aid to design, but it eliminates some nasty surprises down the road when, after nine months of work, you show your design to the client, only to be told "This isn't anything like what we agreed on."

Look and Feel

To specify our program, we need to describe how it will look and also how it will work. We generally concentrate on the look first—not only is it generally the easier of the two tasks, but it also often serves to clarify questions about how the program can be organized and how it should behave.

Advice: First Impressions Are Most Important

Design the visual aspect of your program first, then describe how it will act.

In this example, for instance, we can stare at the picture of our program and pretend we are using it, asking questions like "What should happen in the other components when the user presses the Deposit button?"

After not too much thought, we arrived at the layout illustrated in Figure 7.3. It seems to have all the features we need, including the last-minute addition of a `TextArea` for instructions to the user. We decided to add that, rather than placing instructions in the `TextField`, since we thought that we might need more than a single line for some instructions.

---

[3]If you deduce from this that Clinton is a small town, you're quite right.

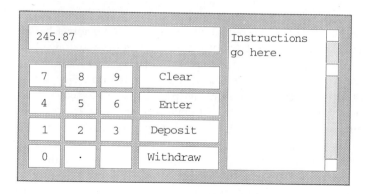

Figure 7.3 ATM visual design.

Things get a little more complicated when it comes to specifying the action of our program, but it's still not to hard to get started.

1. Opening: Show instructions, "Press Deposit or Withdraw buttons to make a transaction. Press Clear to end this session." Disable Enter button. Go to (2).
2. **a.** If Clear button pressed, show instruction "Thank you for doing business with us. Have a nice day." and then append opening instructions from (1).
   b. If Deposit button pressed, go to Deposit mode (3).
   c. If Withdraw button pressed, go to Withdraw mode (5).
   d. Ignore any keypad events.
3. Deposit mode: Show instructions, "Please key in amount of deposit and then press Enter to confirm. If you make a mistake, press clear and re-key the amount and then press Enter to complete your deposit." Enable Enter button, disable Deposit and Withdraw buttons. Go to (4).
4. **a.** If Clear button pressed, clear display.
   b. Send keypad presses to display.
   c. If Enter button pressed, and display is 0 or blank, show instruction, "You must enter a nonzero amount for your deposit," and append original deposit instructions.
   d. If Enter button is pressed and there is a nonzero amount in display, show confirmation message and go back to opening mode (1).
5. Withdrawal mode: Show instructions, "Please key in amount of withdrawal and then press Enter to confirm. If you make a mistake, press clear and re-key the amount and then press Enter to complete your deposit." Enable Enter button, disable Deposit and Withdraw buttons. Go to (6).
6. **a.** If Clear button pressed, clear display.
   b. Send keypad presses to display.
   c. If Enter button pressed, and display is 0 or blank, show instruction, "You must enter a nonzero amount for your withdrawal," and append original withdrawal instructions.
   d. If Enter button is pressed and there is a nonzero amount in display, show confirmation message and go back to opening mode (1).

Once we finished the action description, we found we also had a list of questions: Should we keep track of the amount the customer has available? Should we check the available amount before allowing a withdrawal? In a real ATM, withdrawals must be in multiples of some minimum amount, like ten dollars. Should we enforce that here, too? and Should we allow the user another option, to check his or her available funds? These are all good questions—the answer to all of them should probably be *yes*, but none of them seem to stand in the way of our design, so we leave them for later. We might actually do the same thing in a commercial project—get things partially up and running, so we could verify with the client that our design is acceptable so far. Since we are the clients, we'll allow these questions to go unanswered for the moment, but we put them on a list so we don't forget to come back to them.

Advice: Know Where You Are

At each step, go back over what you have and note any changes that should be made. Don't be afraid to suggest changes that seem worthwhile.

7.3   STEP 2: DETERMINE THE CLASSES

With a GUI design, the next step is to decide on the classes you need to achieve the look you've decided on. In our program, we have eleven keypad buttons, four control buttons, a field for numeric amounts, and a text area for instructions.

The first thing we notice is that the keypad seems to be a single logical unit. In addition it is not only the most complicated part of our program, but it also seems to be something we might want to use in other programs. Well, well, well—it seems like we might be best served by making a separate `Keypad` class. This has two important advantages: It gives us a widget we could reuse, and it allows us to think of it as a single conceptual unit, rather than having to keep track of eleven separate buttons.

Advice: Clump Logically

If you have a collection of objects that serve similar purposes, consider collecting them into a single class. If you think the collection might be useful in other programs, don't just *consider* collecting them into a class—do it.

Remember, a Java program is just a collection of classes. In the first pass, *let the visual design suggest the classes.*

Layout

Now comes the time to take a close look at our design and see how we can make it look the way we want it to look. We're down to seven widgets: The four control buttons, the `Keypad`, the numeric field, and the instruction text area. Keeping in mind the advice about grouping, it's clear that the control buttons should be grouped, but it's not clear that it's worth placing them in their own class. Instead, we'll use a `Panel` with a `GridLayout` to place them in our program.

Advice: Clump, Clump, Clump Visually

Do GUI design from the bottom up, collecting widgets in containers, collecting the containers in larger containers, and so on.

We now have just four things to deal with: A `Keypad` instance, a `Panel` with the control buttons, a numeric field and an instruction `TextArea`. See how easy design is when we clump things? Now go back to the visual design in Figure 7.1 and start drawing nested rectangles to collect things. It seems that we want to place the `Keypad` and the control button `Panel` in another `Panel`, and since they won't necessarily be the same size, we'll use a `BorderLayout` for that `Panel`.

Now we're down to just *three* objects: (1) The `Panel` containing the `Keypad` and the control `Panel`, (2) the number field, and (3) the `TextArea`. The number field and the other `Panel` seem to need a `Panel` of their own, with `BorderLayout`, again, since the objects almost certainly won't be the same size. Finally, we take our big `Panel` and the `TextArea` and lay them out in the applet. Note that this is the first time we used the word "applet." Since this program was a natural candidate to show in a browser, we decided to make it an applet. Figure 7.4 shows our design, laid out in `Panel`s.

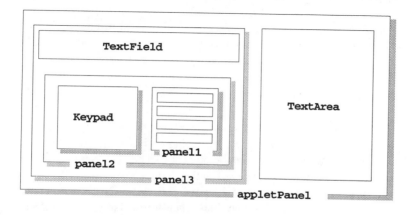

Figure 7.4 ATM GUI hierarchy.

Now, for the first time, we can sit down and write code. We know how tempting it is to hop right in and start coding, but we strongly discourage it. Unless you are *very* good at keeping track of a host of details or you are doing a "toy" program, coding without having first considered design is a prescription for disaster.

Advice: Design, Then Code

The longer you can put off coding, the better off you'll be in the long run.

The first pass through the code went quickly enough. It took perhaps ten minutes to write our applet and compile it. The expected compile errors greeted us, since we had typed `KeyPad` in a couple of places, instead of `Keypad`. Those were easy enough to find, since we were expecting errors from typing.

Advice: Let the Compiler Help

If you haven't already, get into the compile/catch errors/fix errors/compile cycle. Many times, the compiler will point you directly to the error. If that fails, start looking backward in the code from the point where the error finally surfaced.

Once the applet compiled, we ran it, only to discover that the `TextArea` filled the entire applet. Not only had we not specified the number of columns in the TextArea, but we had also set the size of the applet too small. We noted that, fixed the errors, and tried again.

Advice: Consider Keeping a Bug Log

It may slow you down a bit, but it is generally useful to note the errors you found and how you fixed them. This is a useful learning device and it's vitally important for larger programs, so you can keep track of the changes from one version to the next.

We fixed the `TextArea` constructor call and compiled the applet again. This time there were no errors (good typing on our part) but when we ran it, we discovered that the widgets were too closely packed. That was an easy fix—we just added some `hgap` and `vgap` values in the layout constructor calls.

Finally, our code looked like the following. Note, by the way, that we initialized all of our instance variables when we declared them, rather than using `new` in the `init()` method. We could have done the initialization in either location, but we decided that initializing the widgets inside init() would make that method even more cumbersome than it already was.

Advice: Keep Methods Short

If you have to scroll to get from the top to the bottom of a method, it's probably too long to be understood at first glance. Consider writing some private helper methods to pull out some of the code.

```java
import java.applet.*;
import java.awt.*;

public class ATM extends Applet
{
    private TextField  display = new TextField();
    private Keypad     pad = new Keypad();
    private Button     clear = new Button("Clear"),
                       enter = new Button("Enter"),
                       deposit = new Button("Deposit"),
                       withdraw = new Button("Withdraw");
    private TextArea   help = new TextArea(6, 20);

    public void init()
    {
        // Build the control button panel.
        Panel p1 = new Panel();
        p1.setLayout(new GridLayout(4, 1, 0, 3));
        p1.add(clear);
        p1.add(enter);
        p1.add(deposit);
        p1.add(withdraw);

        // Put the keypad and the control panel together
        Panel p2 = new Panel();
        p2.setLayout(new BorderLayout(3, 0));
        p2.add("Center", pad);
        p2.add("East", p1);

        // Put the display field with the keypad-control
        // panel
        Panel p3 = new Panel();
        p3.setLayout(new BorderLayout());
        p3.add("North", display);
        p3.add("Center", p2);

        // Put the TextArea with everything we've included
        // so far.
```

(continued)

```
           // Note, we use the optional "this." here to make
           // it clear that we're dealing with this applet.
           this.setLayout(new BorderLayout(5, 0));
           this.add("Center", p3);
           this.add("East", help);
           this.setBackground(Color.lightGray);
           this.resize(400, 150);
    }
}


//-------------------------------------------------------------

class Keypad extends Panel
// This will eventually be a panel of numeric buttons.
{
    private Label message;

    public Keypad()
    {
        message = new Label("The keypad");
        add(message);
        setBackground(Color.white);
    }
}
```

Finally, note that our `Keypad` class is just a *stub*. We didn't need to concern ourselves with its details just yet, so we simply wrote a class that did nothing but serve as a placeholder.

Advice: Write What's Necessary, and No More

If a class isn't absolutely required yet, just write a stub. (See "Design, then Code.")

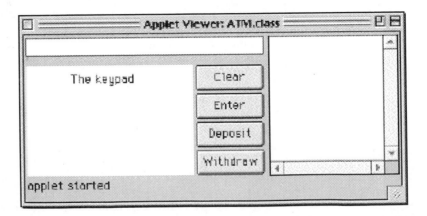

Figure 7.5 The ATM applet, stage 1.

After swatting all the design bugs, typos, and logic errors, we finally came up with a layout that reflected our original specification. To see how close we came, compare Figures 7.3 and 7.5.

Filling in the Details

Once the large-scale design was satisfactory, it was time to go back and do the layout part of the Keypad class. We declared the eleven buttons as instance variables and laid them out in the constructor, using the GridLayout we had decided on previously.

```
class Keypad extends Panel
{
    private Button b0, b1, b2, b3, b4, b5, b6,
                   b7, b8, b9, bPoint;

    public Keypad()
    {
        setLayout(new GridLayout(4, 3, 2, 2));
        b7 = new Button("7");
        add(b7);
        b8 = new Button("8");
        add(b8);
        b9 = new Button("9");
        add(b9);
        b4 = new Button("4");
        add(b4);
        b5 = new Button("5");
        add(b5);
        b6 = new Button("6");
        add(b6);
        b1 = new Button("1");
        add(b1);
        b2 = new Button("2");
        add(b2);
        b3 = new Button("3");
        add(b3);
        b0 = new Button("0");
        add(b0);
        bPoint = new Button(".");
        add(bPoint);
    }
}
```

We were on a roll—the applet compiled without errors the first time we tried. Unfortunately, it looked all wrong, since we had not only reversed the numbers for rows and columns in the GridLayout constructor, but we also had added the buttons in the wrong order. Fortunately, both of these logic errors were easy to identify and fix. It took several more iterations of fiddling to get the width of the applet and the number of columns in the `TextArea` to be such that the keypad buttons weren't too narrow or too wide. Finally, though, everything looked right, as we show in the screen shot in Figure 7.6, and we were ready to make our applet *do* something.

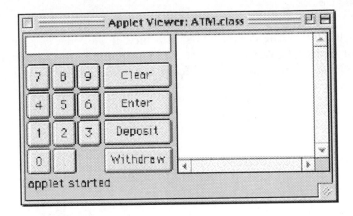

Figure 7.6 The ATM applet, layout complete.

7.4 STEP 3: DETERMINE THE METHODS

The next step in the process of making our program is the most time-consuming and, we'll admit, the trickiest. The visual arrangement suggested some of the classes we would need, like the `Keypad` class. The next step was to look closely at the classes and see what they suggested about the methods (and member data) we needed.

The best place to start this process is, of course, at the action specifications. In our example, it seemed that there was a clear division into *modes*: The applet behaves in one way at the start, it behaves in another way when a deposit is being made, and it behaves in another way (though much like it does in deposit mode) when the user is making a withdrawal. With this in mind, we can think of the control buttons as initiating transitions between modes.

We won't make a big deal about this part of our design, since it's somewhat specialized. With experience, you'll find that this modal behavior is common to many programs but is certainly not a universal feature.

Top Level Decomposition

In our case, it seems that the program needed to "know" what mode it was in (since, for example, the help message that is displayed will differ depending on the current mode). How did we do that? It seemed clear that we would need an instance variable to keep track of the current mode. If there were just two modes, we could use a `boolean` variable, `inModeA`, but in our program we needed to have a data member that's capable of expressing one of *three* values, and not just two. A common way of dealing with this is to establish three constants and make a variable of the appropriate type that will only be given these constants as its value. This is a technique that you've already seen in some of the AWT classes. The alignment of the text in a Label, for instance, is always one of the integer values given by `CENTER`, `LEFT`, or `RIGHT`.

That's what we did here—we declared three `int` constants `START_MODE`, `DEPOSIT_MODE`, and `WITHDRAW_MODE` and used them to set and modify the value of the instance variable `mode`:

```
public class ATM extends Applet
{
    private final int    START_MODE = 0,
                         DEPOSIT_MODE = 1,
                         WITHDRAW_MODE = 2;
    private int mode;


    . . .

}
```

We could do even more, though. It was fairly clear that, when the program started, the first thing we'd need to do after laying out the components was display the introductory message, set the mode to START_MODE, and disable the Enter button. Those activities were obviously related—they'd all be performed in an indivisible unit. This should set off a mental bell, since that's a clear requirement for collecting the statements into a method.

Advice: Clump Activities

If you find a collection of activities that are always performed as a unit, put them in a method and call the method to perform the activities.

We collected all the opening preamble into a method, `introStart()`, and put a call to it at the end of our `init()` method. Since `introStart()` was just a "helper" method and wouldn't ever be called from outside the applet, we gave `introStart()` private access. Finally, as long as we were at it, we made some similar methods, `introDeposit()` and `introWithdraw()` to handle entries into deposit or withdrawal mode. Here's the applet as it looked at that stage.

```
public class ATM extends Applet
{
    private final int    START_MODE = 0,
                         DEPOSIT_MODE = 1,
                         WITHDRAW_MODE = 2;
    private int mode;
```

(continued)

```
...

public void init()
{
    ...
    introStart();     // NEW: Enter start mode when we begin
}

public boolean action(Event e, Object obj)
// Just a stub, for now.
{
    return false;
}

private void introStart()
// Do the initialization needed to enter start mode.
{
    help.setText("          W E L C O M E\n\n");
    help.appendText("Press the Deposit or Withdraw ");
    help.appendText("buttons to make a ");
    help.appendText("transaction.\n\n");
    help.appendText("Press Clear to end this session.");

    mode = START_MODE;
    clear.enable();
    enter.disable();
    deposit.enable();
    withdraw.enable();
}

private void introDeposit()
// Do the initialization needed to enter deposit mode.
{
    help.setText("          D E P O S I T\n\n");
    help.appendText("Key in the amount of your deposit ");
    help.appendText("and then press Enter to finish.\n\n");
    help.appendText("If you make a mistake, press Clear, ");
    help.appendText("key in the amount again, ");
    help.appendText("and then press Enter. ");

    mode = DEPOSIT_MODE;
    clear.enable();
    enter.enable();
    deposit.disable();
    withdraw.disable();
}

private void introWithdraw()
// Do the initialization needed to enter withdrawal mode.
```

```
    {
        help.setText("         W I T H D R A W A L\n\n");
        help.appendText("Key in the amount of your withdrawal ");
        help.appendText("and then press Enter to finish.\n\n");
        help.appendText("If you make a mistake, press Clear, ");
        help.appendText("key in the amount again, ");
        help.appendText("and then press Enter. ");

        mode = WITHDRAW_MODE;
        clear.enable();
        enter.enable();
        deposit.disable();
        withdraw.disable();
    }
}
```

Note also that we included a stub for the `action()` handler. We weren't ready to deal with it, so we just marked it for later refinement.

Advice: Write What's Necessary, and No More (II)

"Use stubs while designing" applies to methods, as well as to classes.

Of course, we tested our applet. The first time, the introductory message wasn't spaced well and it all ran together, so we added some '\n' newline characters in the message strings, to force the text to drop to the next line. We also replaced the `introStart()` call in `init()` with calls to the other two methods so that we could verify that they displayed as they should.

Advice: Never Stray Too Far from a Working Program

Try to write your program so that after every few additions and changes you'll be able to compile and run it.

The reason we always try to test our program after making a few changes is that this strategy *localizes* the inevitable errors. If you test after adding a method and suddenly find that the program doesn't work correctly, the odds are excellent that you'll be able to blame the errors on your new code and will be able to find them quickly. It's common to get so involved in coding that hours pass before you do a test run. You'll certainly encounter some errors, and then you'll have to try to find their source among hundreds of lines of code, scattered in dozens of locations throughout your program. Trust us, this is *not* fun.

Filling in the Details, Again

With the top level actions complete, we could now start to fill in any stubs we left. In this case, that meant the `action()` handler. This was complicated, since the results of clicking on the various buttons depended on the current mode. We decided to use our top-level organization to organize the `action()` handler, breaking it into three distinct parts depending on the mode.

Initially, the `action()` handler looked like this:

```
public boolean action(Event e, Object obj)
{
    switch (mode)
    {
    case START_MODE:
        // Deal with clicks on the Deposit, Withdraw,
        // and Clear buttons
        return true;
    case DEPOSIT_MODE:
        // Deal with clicks on the Enter and Clear
        // buttons, and the keypad
        return true;
    case WITHDRAW_MODE:
        // Deal with clicks on the Enter and Clear
        // buttons, and the keypad
        return true;
    }
    return false;
}
```

Note how closely this organization reflects the action specification we wrote originally. The form of this method looks like an outline, as it should.

Advice: Make Your Code Self-Documenting

The organization of a method's code should be so logically coherent that the organization makes the purpose clear, even without comments. If you find that you need extensive comments to understand what's going on, you should probably rethink your design.

Again, note that we had arranged things so that we could fill in each part and test it before going on to the next. The START_MODE section just involved checking whether the Deposit or the Withdraw button was clicked, and then switching to the appropriate mode by calling either `introDeposit()` or `introWithdraw()`, respectively.

The other two modes, though, had some details that we wanted to defer considering until later. We couldn't have handled a press of the Enter button in either mode because we hadn't implemented the keypad, so there was no way of checking whether the amount entered was greater than 0. As usual, then, we just invented some new stub methods and put calls to them in the appropriate locations, arriving at the following code. This use of calls to stub methods is very convenient—when the time came to fill in the stubs, we'd never even have to look at the `action()` handler.

```java
public class ATM extends Applet
{
    // (Declarations and init() deleted for clarity.)

    public boolean action(Event e, Object obj)
    {
        switch (mode)
        {
        case START_MODE:
            if (e.target == deposit)
                introDeposit();
            else if (e.target == withdraw)
                introWithdraw();
            else if (e.target == clear)
                // FILL IN LATER
            return true;
        case DEPOSIT_MODE:
            if (e.target == enter)
                handleDeposit();
            else if (e.target == clear)
                display.setText("");
            else if (e.target == pad)
                // FILL IN LATER
            return true;
        case WITHDRAW_MODE:
            if (e.target == enter)
                handleWithdrawal();
            else if (e.target == clear)
                display.setText("");
            else if (e.target == pad)
                // FILL IN LATER
            return true;
        }
        return false;
    }

    // (introStart(), introDposit(), and introWithdraw() deleted
    // for clarity.)
```

(continued)

```
        private void handleDeposit()
        // A deposit request has been made.  Check whether the amount
        // in display is nonzero.  If so, just go back to start mode.
        // If not, display a help message.
        {
              introStart();     // FILL IN LATER
        }

        private void handleWithdrawal()
        // A withdrawal request has been made.  Check whether the
        // amount in display is nonzero.  If so, just go back to start
        // mode. If not, display a help message.
        {
              introStart();     // FILL IN LATER
        }
}
```

Did we test the new changes? You bet. We must have been getting better with practice, since there were no compile errors, and everything worked exactly as we expected it to.

7.5   STEP 3, CONTINUED

We had put off completing the Keypad class as long as we could. The applet was running perfectly, but it didn't respond to keypad events. We needed a way of passing keypad button clicks on to the applet's action() handler so that we could then send the appropriate digit or decimal point to the display field.

Here was where we encountered the first real problem, one that's fairly common when communicating between classes. The applet action() handler should have been able to look for the keypad button that was clicked by using the usual dot notation to find the button within the pad object:

```
if (e.target == pad.b0)
    // the b0 button in the pad was clicked
```

But it couldn't because we made the buttons private members of the Keypad class. Of course, we can easily fix this—just change the access of the eleven buttons to public. That's just what we'd do if we had no intention of ever using the Keypad class in another program. However, Keypad seemed to be useful enough that we might want to save it for future use, so we had to think about making it useful and robust enough that we'd be willing to put our names on it.

If we had changed our design and made the buttons public, we would leave the door open for some programmer to write

```
Keypad myPad = new Keypad();
...
myPad.b0.setLabel("zero");
```

Suddenly, the class would no longer work as specified. The `Keypad` class is supposed to have buttons with labels consisting of the digits "0" through "9" and the decimal point, ".". The intention is that a program using this class would be able to send the label string to another object, to represent part of a number. Now, though, the program might result in setting a numeric string to "37zero", rather than the "370" that was expected. This, clearly, could lead to all sorts of unpleasant errors.

The fix was surprisingly easy and appealingly clever, and used a feature we mentioned in the Method Recap in Section 7.3. Recall that we said a method could modify any accessible field of one of its reference arguments. We did just that, intercepting a button click and changing its `target` field (which is `public`) from the button to the `Keypad` object itself! To do so, we put an `action()` handler in the `Keypad` class and wrote the handler so that it would change the `target` field of the event and then just pass the event along. Any object that subsequently caught the event, then, would see the event as originating from the accessible `Keypad` object, rather than from one of its inaccessible buttons. That's all it took:

```
class Keypad extends Panel
{
    // (Button declarations and constructor omitted)

    public boolean action(Event e, Object obj)
    {
        e.target = this;      // Change the target,
        return false;         // and pass the event along.
    }
}
```

After patting ourselves on the back for being so clever, we tested our changes by putting in a call to `setText()` in the appropriate place in the applet's `action()` handler. It worked like a charm.

```
    else if (e.target == pad)
        display.setText((String)(e.arg));
```

Would it be reasonable to have expected you to discover this trick on your own? Of course not. Would it be reasonable to expect you to recall having seen this trick when you need it in the future? Yes, indeed, just as we would expect an athlete or actor to learn by studying what others do.

Advice: Learn from Others

Coming up with something brand new is *hard*. It's much easier to acquire a stock of patterns and techniques that you can apply when you need them.[4]

---

[4]The fact that experience can substitute for brilliance is one of the comforts of aging.

A New Class

Only one major task remained: designing the interactions of the applet with its `display` field. This occurred in four places, all originating within the applet's `action()` handler. The pair of methods `handleDeposit()` and `handleWithdraw()` both needed to check whether `display` contained a positive number and the two places where an event originating from the keypad needed to append the new string to the end of the display.

What, exactly did the display have to do? Thinking about it, we came up with a list.

1. Initialize itself to contain the empty `String`.
2. Append a digit or decimal point to the right end of its text.
3. Be able to recognize whether it contained the representation of a positive number.
4. Clear itself to contain the empty `String`.
5. At all times, contain either the empty `String` or the representation of a legal number (nothing like "`34.2.117`", for example.)

The last item in the list made us pause and think. It seemed we were looking at something that was like a `TextField`, but more specialized. It seemed, in fact, that we had come across another candidate for a class of its own. Thinking some more, it struck us that a numeric field class could be put to good use in other applications. That settled it—we would invent a new `NumField` class and use it in our applet.

How should we design our new class? The same way we design any new class, by first deciding what methods it should have. It's convenient to ask two questions at this stage: What would users like to know? and What kind of modifications would users want to make? The nice part about the early stage of class design is that we can let the class declaration serve as our outline. Here's what we came up with—a compileable class declaration full of method stubs.

```
class NumField extends TextField
{
    // Member data will go here

    // Constructors will go here

    //------------- Accessor -----------

    public double getValue()
    // Returns the double value represented by the text.
    {
        return 0.0;     // FIX.  We only have this here
                        // because a method with a non-void
                        // return type must return something.
    }
```

```
//------------ Mutators -------------

public void clear()
// Set the text to be the empty String.
{
}

public void setValue(double d)
// Set the text to represent the double value of the argument.
{
}

public void append(char c)
// Append the character c to the end of the text.
// We'll need to first check that this method will result
// in a legal number representation.
{
}

public void append(String s)
// Append the first character of s to the end of the text.
// As above, we should make sure that the result will be legal.
{
}

public void setText(String s)
// Override of TextComponent method.  We don't want to
// allow the user to change the text arbitrarily.
{
}
}
```

You may have noticed that we included methods here that wouldn't be used in our applet, like `setValue()`. We could have left them out if we were never going to use this class anywhere else, but we wanted to make this class useful in a potentially wide range of settings.

Advice: Build in Generality

When designing a class someone else might use, try to anticipate what the other programmer might want.

The flip side of this advice is that it's easy to go overboard here, designing in a host of methods that might be used only once in a hundred programs. This is a practice that in larger contexts leads to bloated commercial applications that require at least fifty megabytes of memory and five hundred megabytes of hard disk space.

Now we walked our way down the list of methods, filling them in as we went.

public double **getValue**(double d)

This method wasn't simple. How could we convert the text `String` to a `double`? We had to head to the documentation for this one. Eventually, though, we found what we needed. Each of the primitive types has an associated class, known as a *wrapper type.* They are intended for situations where we need to convert a primitive type into a reference type, but the important point here is that the `Double` wrapper class has a constructor that takes a `String` argument and converts it into a `Double`. The class also has a method, `doubleValue()` that converts a capital-D `Double` to a lowercase-d primitive `double`. We then had a two-step conversion that would do what we wanted. Finally, we had to remember that the text might be empty, and for those instances we decided to return 0.

```
public double getValue()
{
    if (this.getText().equals(""))
        return 0.0;
    else
    // Here's the two-step conversion, from String
    // to Double, and then from Double to double
    {
        Double d = new Double(this.getText());
        return d.doubleValue();
    }
}
```

Advice: Look It Up

If there's something you need to do, the chances are that Java has methods to do it. Rummaging through the documentation can be instructive, as well as useful.

---

public void **setValue**(double d)

This method took another trip to the documentation. The `String` class method `valueOf()` returns a `String` representing the value of its argument, and that was exactly what we needed.

```
public void setValue(double d)
{
    super.setText(String.valueOf(d));
}
```

public void **clear**()

Trivial. All we had to do was use the parent class's `setText()` method, with the empty string, "", as argument.

```
public void clear()
{
      super.setText("");
}
```

public void **append**(char c)

    This method seemed simple at first. All we needed was to get the text as a `String`, use the "+" concatenation operator to add the character to the end of the text and set the text to be the new value:

```
public void append(char c)
// NOT the final version--does no legality checking
{
      super.setText(this.getText() + c);
}
```

    The problem, as we noted in the comment, is that this did no checking for legality. The user could have appended 'g' just as easily as '7'. Keeping with our advice of putting off coding as long as possible, we invented a method, `isLegal(char c)`, that returns `true` if and only if the character c could be legally appended to the current text. Now our method became

```
public void append(char c)
// STILL NOT the final version
{
      if (isLegal(c))
            super.setText(this.getText() + c);
}
```

    The problem here was that `isLegal()` could check whether c was a digit or decimal point, but the decimal point is legal only if there's not already one in the text. We needed a `boolean` instance variable, `hasDecimalPoint`, to keep track of whether we've seen a decimal point. This will be used in `isLegal()` and we'll set it in this method, rather than in `isLegal()`, since the job of that method is only to test a character, and nothing more. Finally, we were done:

```
public void append(char c)
// FINAL VERSION (sort of, see the exercises)
{
      if (isLegal(c))
      {
            if (c == '.')
                  hasDecimalPoint = true;

            super.setText(this.getText() + c);
      }
}
```

Advice: Listen to the Code

Just as we let the design suggest the classes and the classes suggest the methods, often the methods can suggest the variables they will require.

public void **append**(String s)

This method does almost the same thing as the previous one, but it accepts a String argument, rather than a char. This method is the one we would use in our applet, since the Keypad-generated action event returns the button label as a String, like "4", for instance. We didn't know how to extract the first character from a String (well, all right, we did, but we pretended we didn't), so we went back to the documentation again and found the String method charAt(int i) that returns the character at position i, counted from 0, as usual. Now our method looked like this:

```
public void append(String s)
// NOT the final version
{
    char c = s.charAt(0);  // get the leftmost character
    if (isLegal(c))
    {
        if (c == '.')
            hasDecimalPoint = true;

        super.setText(this.getText() + c);
    }
}
```

What a waste! We had two methods that differed by a single statement. There's a much shorter way to write this, by calling the char version from within the String one:

```
public void append(String s)
// FINAL VERSION (perhaps, see the exercises)
{
    char c = s.charAt(0);  // get the leftmost character
    append(c);
}
```

Advice: Avoid Multiply Redundant Duplication

If you find you've written two chunks of code that are nearly identical, consider encapsulating them as methods. If they are already methods, see if you can call one to implement the other.

public void **setText**(String s)

Whenever you extend a class by inheritance, you are specializing it. There is always a chance that some methods of the parent class would give the user power to do something you don't want, and that's exactly what happened here. We certainly didn't want the user to be able to make arbitrary changes to the text in our display, so we overrode the parent[5] method here, turning it into a do-nothing method. This, by the way, is why we were so careful about calling super.setText() in the other methods in this class. If we hadn't, we would have been calling the Keypad version, which would do nothing:

```
public void setText(String s)
{
}
```

private boolean **isLegal**(char c)

We were down to the last of our methods, the one that tests for the legality of a character. We had two things to test: whether the character represented a digit (always legal) and whether it was the decimal point (legal only when hasDecimalPoint is false). Note that we made use of the Character wrapper class method isDigit() that returns true if and only if its argument is one of the digit characters.

```
private boolean isLegal(char c)
{
    if (Character.isDigit(c))
        return true;
    else if ((c == '.') && !hasDecimalPoint)
        return true;
    else
        return false;
}
```

All that remained was to fill in the constructors and any member data we discovered along the way. Filling the member data was easy—the only new variable we discovered we needed when designing the NumField methods was the boolean variable hasDecimalPoint. It needed to be an instance variable, since it was used in isLegal(), set in append() and—Oops!—needed to be reset to false in clear(). We were lucky to have thought of that, rather than having it turn up to bedevil us later.

The constructors are mirrors of those of the parent class. One is the default, and the other allows us to set the width of this field. Note how we did the same thing here that we did with append()—we implemented the simpler one with a call to the complex one.

---

[5]Grandparent, actually, since the setText() method belongs to TextComponent, not TextField.

```
public NumField()
{
    this(8);          // Call our other constructor.
}

public NumField(int cols)
{
    super(cols);    // Call the TextField constructor.
    this.setText("");
    this.setEditable(false);
    hasDecimalPoint = false;
}
```

It's worth mentioning that this isn't always a good idea. Method calls involve a fair amount of computational overhead, so if there is a very time-sensitive routine to implement, you would be better off duplicating code rather than making a method call. In this applet, though, a call to a `NumField` constructor will only be done once, and `append()` will have to wait eons (in computer time) for the user to hit a key. As you'll see if you continue your studies, this trade-off between space (of code in memory) and time (of execution) is quite common in many areas of computer science.

That's it—the `NumField` class was complete:

```
class NumField extends TextField
// A NumField stores (and displays) the text representation of
// a number.
{
    boolean hasDecimalPoint = false;

    //----------- Constructors -----------

    public NumField()
    // Default constructor--build a NumField eight columns wide,
    // initially empty.
    {
        this(8);          // Call the other constructor.
    }

    public NumField(int cols)
    {
        super(cols);      // Call the superclass constructor.
        this.setText("");
        this.setEditable(false);    // Don't let the user in.
        hasDecimalPoint = false;
    }

    //------------- Accessors ------------
```

```
public double getValue()
// Returns the value represented by this field's text,
// or zero, if the text is empty.
{
     if (this.getText().equals(""))
          return 0.0;
     else
     {
          Double d = new Double(this.getText());
          return d.doubleValue();
     }
}


//------------- Mutators -------------

public void clear()
// Set the text to be the empty String.
{
     super.setText("");
     hasDecimalPoint = false;
}

public void setValue(double d)
// Set the text to represent the double value of the argument.
{
     super.setText(String.valueOf(d));
}

public void append(char c)
// Append the character c to the end of the text.
// We check that this method will result in a legal
// number representation.
{
     if (isLegal(c))
     {
          if (c == '.')
               hasDecimalPoint = true;

          super.setText(this.getText() + c);
     }
}

public void append(String s)
// Append the first character of s to the end of the text.
// As above, we should make sure that the result will be legal.
{
     char c = s.charAt(0);
     append(c);
}
```

(continued)

```
public void setText(String s)
// Override of the TextComponent method.  We don't want to
// allow the user to change the text arbitrarily.
{
}


//------------- Utility -------------

private boolean isLegal(char c)
// Returns true if and only if c could legally be appended to
// the end of the text.  In other words, return true if
// c is a digit or if it would be the only decimal point
// in the text.
{
    if (Character.isDigit(c))
        return true;
    else if ((c == '.') && !hasDecimalPoint)
        return true;
    else
        return false;

}

}
```

We took a bit of a chance here, finishing up the whole class before trying it out, so before we went much further, we put it to the test. In fact, we were so close to the end that putting in the code to test our NumField class resulted in a substantially complete applet. All it took was to change TextField to NumField in the declarations, make a few modifications to the action() handler, and fill in the handleDeposit() and handleWithdrawal() methods:

```
public class ATM extends Applet
{
    // (Some declarations omitted.)

    private NumField        display = new NumField();

    // (More declarations and init() omitted.)

    public boolean action(Event e, Object obj)
    {
        switch (mode)
        {
        case START_MODE:
            // (Omitted.)

        case DEPOSIT_MODE:
            if (e.target == enter)
                handleDeposit();
```

```
                else if (e.target == clear)
                    display.clear();
                else if (e.target == pad)
                    display.append((String)(e.arg));
                return true;

        case WITHDRAW_MODE:
                if (e.target == enter)
                    handleWithdrawal();
                else if (e.target == clear)
                    display.clear();
                else if (e.target == pad)
                    display.append((String)(e.arg));
                return true;
        }
        return false;
}


// (introStart(), introDeposit(), introWithdraw() omitted.)

private void handleDeposit()
{
        if (display.getValue() == 0.0)
        {
                // display an error message
        }
        else
                introStart();
}

private void handleWithdrawal()
{
        if (display.getValue() == 0.0)
        {
                // display an error message
        }
        else
                introStart();
}
```

Cleanup

At this stage, the only part we had left undone was how to let the customer quit. The specifications stated that in Start mode the user could click the Clear button to leave. Since we didn't want to shut the applet down, we decided that clicking the Clear button would bring up another help message, thanking the user for his or her business and (the new part) indicating that clicking the Enter button would start the whole process up again. To implement this, all we had to do was add a call to a new method, doQuit(), defined as shown, and add a clause to the applet's action() handler to deal with the Enter button click.

```
public boolean action(Event e, Object obj)
{
    switch (mode)
    {
    case START_MODE:
        if (e.target == deposit)
            introDeposit();
        else if (e.target == withdraw)
            introWithdraw();
        else if (e.target == clear)
            doQuit();
        else if (e.target == enter)
            introStart();
        return true;

        ...

}
...


private void doQuit()
{
    help.setText("Thank you for your business.\n\n");
    help.appendText("Have a nice day.\n\n\n");
    help.appendText("Press the Enter button to start.");

    display.clear();      // So the next customer can't see
                          // what happened during this session.
    clear.disable();
    enter.enable();
    deposit.disable();
    withdraw.disable();
}
```

We did one final round of tests, first emulating an ordinary user making ordinary transactions and then trying to be as idiotic as possible. Everything seemed to work as it should. Of course, testing isn't going to guarantee that a program is correct. In the words of Edsger Dijkstra, "Testing can reveal the presence of errors, but never their absence." The parts of a program can interact in complicated and unexpected ways, but fortunately for us our design was solid from the start. The way we built our program resulted in a collection of more or less self-contained units: the applet itself and the Keypad and NumField classes. Each of these three classes was further comprised of methods, none of which was too large to comprehend at a glance. We had to make sure that the methods interacted smoothly, and that was only a major task in the ATM class, with its eight instance variables. We took the time to look at each place where the mode was changed, to be sure that the buttons were enabled and disabled as they should be, and we made sure that the transitions between modes were being made correctly.

Everything looked good, but while we were reading the code we noticed some unnecessary duplication. Several of the help messages contained exactly the same text:

```
and then press Enter to finish.

If you make a mistake, press Clear,
key in the amount again,
and then press Enter.
```

so we pulled those calls to `help.appendText()` out and placed them in a new method, `showGeneralMessage()`.

Finally, we went over the code one more time. There were some typos in the comments that the compiler didn't catch, of course. We had been putting comments in as we wrote the code, but we hadn't included a block of header comments at the beginning of the file, so we did that, too.

Advice: Writing Is Rewriting

Once your program is running satisfactorily, go back over the code. Is it clear? Is it well documented? Can it be streamlined? Can it be cleaned up? Edit, edit, edit!

Finally, we were done. From start to finish the project took three days to produce 336 lines of code. A hundred-plus lines of code per day is pretty good, especially considering that the program and the chapter were being written more or less in parallel. There were still lots of things that we could have done, some of which we mentioned at the end of Section 7.1.

- Keep track of the amount in the user's account.
- Don't allow withdrawals if the user doesn't have sufficient funds.
- Only allow withdrawals in multiples of some fixed minimum amount, like ten dollars.
- Allow the user to determine how much is in his or her account.
- Require the user to enter his or her PIN (personal identification number) before starting a session.

These are all interesting features and should all be part of the program. The real goal of the project, though, was to produce a program we could use as the centerpiece of this chapter, and we decided that what we had was sufficient.

Closing Advice

Programs are never finished, only released.

7.6   THE ATM APPLET

```
/* ***********************************************************
                  CHAPTER 7 EXTENDED EXAMPLE

This applet simulates the action of an automatic teller machine,
consisting of a keypad, a collection of control buttons, a
numeric display field, and a text area for instructions.

See _programming.java_, Chapter 7, for details and specification.
*********************************************************** */


import java.applet.*;
import java.awt.*;

public class ATM extends Applet
{
      private final int      START_MODE = 0,
                             DEPOSIT_MODE = 1,
                             WITHDRAW_MODE = 2;
      private int mode;

      private NumField       display = new NumField();
      private Keypad         pad = new Keypad();
      private Button         clear = new Button("Clear"),
                             enter = new Button("Enter"),
                             deposit = new Button("Deposit"),
                             withdraw = new Button("Withdraw");
      private TextArea       help = new TextArea(6, 18);

      public void init()
      {
            Panel p1 = new Panel();
            p1.setLayout(new GridLayout(4, 1, 0, 3));
            p1.add(clear);
            p1.add(enter);
            p1.add(deposit);
            p1.add(withdraw);

            Panel p2 = new Panel();
            p2.setLayout(new BorderLayout(3, 0));
            p2.add("Center", pad);
            p2.add("East", p1);

            Panel p3 = new Panel();
            p3.setLayout(new BorderLayout());
            p3.add("North", display);
            p3.add("Center", p2);
```

```
                    this.setLayout(new BorderLayout(5, 5));
                    this.add("Center", p3);
                    this.add("East", help);
                    help.setEditable(false);
                    this.setBackground(Color.lightGray);
                    this.resize(325, 150);

                    introStart();
              }

       public boolean action(Event e, Object obj)
       {
              switch (mode)
              {
              case START_MODE:
                    if (e.target == deposit)
                          introDeposit();
                    else if (e.target == withdraw)
                          introWithdraw();
                    else if (e.target == clear)
                          doQuit();
                    else if (e.target == enter)
                          introStart();
                    return true;

              case DEPOSIT_MODE:
                    if (e.target == enter)
                          handleDeposit();
                    else if (e.target == clear)
                          display.clear();
                    else if (e.target == pad)
                          display.append((String)(e.arg));
                    return true;

              case WITHDRAW_MODE:
                    if (e.target == enter)
                          handleWithdrawal();
                    else if (e.target == clear)
                          display.clear();
                    else if (e.target == pad)
                          display.append((String)(e.arg));
                    return true;
              }
              return false;
       }

       private void introStart()
       {
              help.setText("          W E L C O M E\n\n");
              help.appendText("Press the Deposit or Withdraw ");
```

(continued)

```
        help.appendText("buttons to make a transaction.\n\n");
        help.appendText("Press Clear to end this session.");

        mode = START_MODE;
        display.clear();
        clear.enable();
        enter.disable();
        deposit.enable();
        withdraw.enable();
}

private void introDeposit()
{
        help.setText("            D E P O S I T\n\n");
        help.appendText("Key in the amount of your deposit ");
        showGeneralMessage();

        mode = DEPOSIT_MODE;
        display.clear();
        clear.enable();
        enter.enable();
        deposit.disable();
        withdraw.disable();
}

private void introWithdraw()
{
        help.setText("            W I T H D R A W A L\n\n");
        help.appendText("Key in the amount of your withdrawal ");
        showGeneralMessage();

        mode = WITHDRAW_MODE;
        display.clear();
        clear.enable();
        enter.enable();
        deposit.disable();
        withdraw.disable();
}

private void handleDeposit()
// A deposit request has been made.  Check whether the amount
// in display is nonzero.  If so, just go back to start mode.
// If not, display a help message.
{
        if (display.getValue() == 0.0)
        {
                help.setText("*** oops!  The amount can't be ");
                help.appendText("zero\n\n");
                help.appendText("Key in the amount of your ");
                help.appendText("deposit ");
                showGeneralMessage();
        }
```

```
        else
                introStart();
    }

    private void handleWithdrawal()
    // A withdrawal request has been made.  Check whether the
    // amount in display is nonzero.  If so, just go back to start
    // mode. If not, display a help message.
    {
        if (display.getValue() == 0.0)
        {
            help.setText("*** oops!  The amount can't be ");
            help.appendText("zero\n\n");
            help.appendText("Key in the amount of your ");
            help.appendText("withdrawal ");
            showGeneralMessage();
        }
        else
                introStart();
    }

    private void doQuit()
    {
        help.setText("Thank you for your business.\n\n");
        help.appendText("Have a nice day.\n\n\n");
        help.appendText("Press the Enter button to start.");

        display.clear();
        clear.disable();
        enter.enable();
        deposit.disable();
        withdraw.disable();
    }

    private void showGeneralMessage()
    {
        help.appendText("and then press Enter to finish.\n\n");
        help.appendText("If you make a mistake, press Clear, ");
        help.appendText("key in your withdrawal again, ");
        help.appendText("and then press Enter. ");
    }
}

//-------------------------------------------------------------

class Keypad extends Panel
// A Keypad instance contains eleven buttons, representing
// the digits 0 through 9 and the decimal point.  A click on
// any of the buttons causes an event to be originated
// from the Keypad itself (and not one of the private
// buttons).  In effect, a Keypad acts like a Choice object,
```

(continued)

```
    // returning an event with arg field equal to the String
    // label of the button clicked.
    {
        private Button    b0, b1, b2, b3, b4, b5, b6,
                                    b7, b8, b9, bPoint;

        public Keypad()
        {
            setLayout(new GridLayout(4, 3, 2, 2));
            b7 = new Button("7");
            add(b7);
            b8 = new Button("8");
            add(b8);
            b9 = new Button("9");
            add(b9);
            b4 = new Button("4");
            add(b4);
            b5 = new Button("5");
            add(b5);
            b6 = new Button("6");
            add(b6);
            b1 = new Button("1");
            add(b1);
            b2 = new Button("2");
            add(b2);
            b3 = new Button("3");
            add(b3);
            b0 = new Button("0");
            add(b0);
            bPoint = new Button(".");
            add(bPoint);
        }

        public boolean action(Event e, Object obj)
        // When we get a click on any of the buttons, all we do is
        // pass the event on, but with this class as the target,
        // rather than the button.
        {
            e.target = this;
            return false;
        }
    }


    //-------------------------------------------------------------


    class NumField extends TextField
    // A NumField stores (and displays) the text representation of
    // a number.
    {
        boolean hasDecimalPoint = false;
```

```
//----------- Constructors -----------

public NumField()
// Default constructor--build a NumField eight columns wide,
// initially empty.
{
     this(8);            // Call the other constructor.
}

public NumField(int cols)
{
     super(cols);       // Call the superclass constructor.
     this.setText("");
     this.setEditable(false);    // Don't let the user in.
     hasDecimalPoint = false;
}

//------------ Accessors ------------

public double getValue()
// Returns the value represented by this field's text,
// or zero, if the text is empty.
{
     if (this.getText().equals(""))
          return 0.0;
     else
     {
          Double d = new Double(this.getText());
          return d.doubleValue();
     }
}

//------------ Mutators ------------

public void clear()
// Set the text to be the empty String.
{
     super.setText("");
     hasDecimalPoint = false;
}

public void setValue(double d)
// Set the text to represent the double value of the argument.
{
     super.setText(String.valueOf(d));
}

public void append(char c)
// Append the character c to the end of the text.
// We check that this method will result
// in a legal number representation.
```

(continued)

```
    {
        if (isLegal(c))
        {
            if (c == '.')
                hasDecimalPoint = true;

            super.setText(this.getText() + c);
        }
    }

public void append(String s)
// Append the first character of s to the end of the text.
{
    char c = s.charAt(0);
    append(c);
}

public void setText(String s)
// Override of the TextComponent method.  We don't want to
// allow the user to change the text arbitrarily.
{
}

//-------------- Utility -------------

private boolean isLegal(char c)
// Returns true if and only if c could legally be appended to
// the end of the text.  In other words, return true if
// c is a digit or if it would be the only decimal point
// in the text representation.
{
    if (Character.isDigit(c))
        return true;
    else if ((c == '.') && !hasDecimalPoint)
        return true;
    else
        return false;
}
}
```

7.7 HANDS ON

Design a four-function calculator. We'll give you some hints in the lab exercises, but it's high time you completed a real applet on your own. We've made it easy for you, though—note that the calculator contains some very familiar pieces that you might want to borrow from the ATM example. In general, of course, you would cite borrowed code, just as you would cite quoted material from other sources in a research paper. In a for-sale program, you'd go even further and get explicit permission from the author or owner. In this exercise, you have our blessing—use the `Keypad` and `NumField` classes and modify them as you see fit (since we don't want a flood of e-mail requests asking for permission).

Figure 7.7 The `Calculator` Lablet.

7.8   SUMMARY

- Every method is defined within a class. There are no "free methods" in Java.
- The signature of a method consists of the name of the method and the argument list. The name of a method can be any legal Java identifier that's not a keyword. The argument list is a pair of parentheses containing a (possibly empty) comma-separated list of the form "typeName identifier."
- The compiler uses signatures to determine which method is invoked by a method call.
- A class may not have two methods with the same signature.
- The return type of a method appears before the signature in a method declaration. The return type can be a primitive type, a class type, or the keyword `void`.
- A method is called by using an instance of the method's class (or a subclass), as in

  ```
  button1.hide();
  ```

- A method with a `void` return type is almost invariably called within an expression statement, like

  ```
  myPanel.add(button1);
  ```

- A call to a method with a non-`void` return type may be used anywhere a value of that type may appear.
- If a method returns a class type, the method call may be used where an instance of that type would be appropriate, as in

  ```
  myButton.getParent().countComponents();
  ```

❧ For syntactic purposes, the dot token acts as if it were a left-associative operator with precedence higher than any other.

❧ A call to a method from within the same class does not require an instance name and a dot before the call. To underscore the fact that the method call is being made by the instance itself, the word `this` is a synonym for the instance.

❧ The keyword this is used to distinguish members from nonmembers of the same name, as in

```
this.x += x;   // two different "x" variables in use here
```

❧ When a method call is made, the actual arguments in the method call are used to initialize the formal arguments in the method definition.

❧ The formal argument must be of a type that is at least as wide as the type of the actual argument. For the numeric primitive types, for example, `double` is wider than `float`, which is wider than `long`, which is wider than `int`. For class types, a class is wider than its subclasses.

❧ A method cannot modify the values of primitive-type arguments.

❧ A method can modify the fields of class-type arguments.

❧ For design of a Java program, a useful strategy is
  • Let the visual design suggest the classes.
  • Let the classes suggest the methods.
  • Let the methods dictate their statements.

❧ Before you begin writing a program, specify its look and its action as carefully as you can.

❧ Design the visual aspect of your program first.

❧ If you have a collection of objects that serve similar purposes, consider collecting them into a single class.

❧ Do GUI layout from the bottom up, collecting widgets into containers, collecting the containers into larger containers, and so on.

❧ The longer you can put off coding, the better off you'll be in the long run.

❧ Use the compiler as a tool for catching syntax errors.

❧ If you have to scroll to get from the top to the bottom of a method, it's probably too long to be understood at first glance. Consider writing some `private` helper methods to pull out some of the code.

❧ If a class or method isn't absolutely required at any stage in the design process, just write a stub.

❧ Test your program frequently while writing code. Try to write your program so that after every few additions and changes you'll be able to compile and run it.

❧ If you find a collection of activities that are always performed as a unit, put them in a method and call the method to perform the activities.

❧ Try to make your code as self-documenting as possible.

❧ Look at the code of other programs; try to learn from what others have done.

❧ When designing a class that someone else might use, try to anticipate what the other programmer might want.

☙ The primitive types all have associated wrapper classes, designed for situations when you need to use primitive types as if they were reference types.

☙ The wrapper classes are `Boolean`, `Character`, `Double`, `Float`, `Integer`, and `Long`. We'll discuss these classes in detail in Chapter 8. The wrapper classes have useful methods for converting from one type to another.

☙ Become familiar with the online documentation of the Java classes and methods. You can find the version 1.0 documentation at

```
http://java.sun.com/products/jdk/1.0.2/api/
```

and the 1.1 documentation at

```
http://java.sun.com/products/jdk/1.1/docs/api/packages.html
```

☙ Just as we let the design suggest the classes and the classes suggest the methods, often the methods can suggest the variables they will require.

☙ If you find you've written two chunks of code that are nearly identical, consider encapsulating them as methods. If they are already methods, see if you can call one to implement the other.

☙ Once your program is running satisfactorily, go back over the code. Is it clear? Is it well documented? Can it be streamlined? Can it be cleaned up? Edit, edit, edit!

☙ Writing a program needn't be an intimidating process if you approach it systematically and carefully.

7.9   EXERCISES

1.   Which of the following method headers are correctly formed? For those that are incorrect, tell what's wrong with them.
   a.   `real findInt()`
   b.   `char convert(x, y, z)`
   c.   `Point increase()`
   d.   `int return(double n)`
   e.   `void a()`
   f.   `function F(x : int): int`
   g.   `double randomNumber(void)`
   h.   `Component convert(Container c)`
   i.   `void convert(int x = 0)`

2.   For the method declared as `void check(Container c, int t)`, which of the following types could be used as actual arguments? For example, in part (a) the choice (`Button int`) means that we're asking if this method could be called with actual arguments (`myButton, 3`). For the arguments that are not allowed, explain what's wrong with them.
   a.   `(Button int)`
   b.   `(int Button)`

    c.   (Component int)
    d.   (Panel double)
    e.   (Container)
    f.   (boolean)
    g.   ()
    h.   (Label byte)
    i.   (Object byte)

3.   These two methods have different signatures, so they could be declared in the same class.

```
void sum(double x, int y)
void sum(int x, double y)
```

It wouldn't be a good idea to declare them both, though.

    a.   Which would be invoked if you called sum(r, s) with variable r of type long and s of type int?

    b.   Here's the problem: Suppose that you called sum(p, q) with p and q both of type int. Which of the methods *could* be called?

    c.   Try it—run the following applet. What happens? Why?

```
public class Test extends Applet
{
        private    int p = 3;
        private    int q = 2;

        private TextField display = new TextField(20);

        public void init()
        {
              add(display);
              sum(p, q);
        }

        public void sum(double x, int y)
        {
              display.setText("The double/int one");
        }

        public void sum(int x, double y)
        {
              display.setText("The int/double one");
        }
}
```

4.   Build the longest sequence of cascaded method calls you can, starting with the Button object myButton. Just to make this a challenging problem, you are allowed to use only one copy of each method, so you can't answer

```
myButton.getParent().getParent().getParent()
```

5. Consider the method declared as

```
Point pick(Point p, Point q)
{
    if ((p.y >= q.y) && (p.x >= q.x))
        return p;
    else
        return q;
}
```

Suppose that the following code were in another method in the same class.

```
// Assume Points a and b had already been declared.
Point origin = new Point(0, 0);
pick(a, b) = origin;
```

  a. Would this code be legal?
  b. What would it do?

6. Redo Exercise 5 with the method,

```
int pick(int p, int q)
{
    if (p >= q)
        return p;
    else
        return q;
}
```

and the code,

```
// Assume ints a and b had already been declared.
int origin = 0;
pick(a, b) = origin;
```

  a. Would this code be legal?
  b. What would it do?

7. One of these tasks can be done and one can't.
(1) Write a method `void stretch(int x)` that doubles the value of its argument.
(2) Write a method `void stretch(Dimension d)` that doubles the height and width of its argument.
  a. Which could be done and which couldn't? Explain.
  b. Produce the code for the method that could be written.

8. Change the layout of ATM, placing the TextArea *above* the `display` field, rather than on the right side of the applet.

9. In designing the ATM applet, we made an assumption that is quite common when moving a real-world task to the computer—we made our program look and act like the real thing. An important difference between physical objects and computer programs is the *plasticity* of programs: We can design programs to look and act any way we want them to. You have dozens of widgets available to you—use what you know to improve the user interface of the applet. In other words, draw and explain the action of a better interface, indicating why your design is better than the existing one.

10. Why didn't we make a separate class for the help text?

11. We could have pulled out much of the code of the ATM `action()` handler into three methods:

    ```
    private boolean startAction(Event e)
    private boolean depositAction(Event e)
    private boolean withdrawAction(Event e)
    ```

    a. Write these three methods and write the modified `action()` handler that would use them.
    b. Explain whether or not this is a worthwhile modification.

12. The `action()` handler of the ATM class must deal with clicks on the keypad and any of the four control buttons. It is currently arranged first by mode and then by the event targets within each mode.
    a. Change the organization so that the method first checks the target of the event and then bases its action on the mode. In other words, the handler should have five major divisions corresponding to the possible targets.
    b. Is the new organization clearer than the original? Explain.
    c. In which organization would it be easier to add a new button to the applet, say, a Funds button that checked the amount in the user's account?

13. Look at the visual appearance of the `Keypad` class. We have laid out the buttons in what might be called "calculator order," with 7, 8, 9 in the top row. Now take a look at the keypad of a telephone. You'll notice that the order is reversed—on telephones (and most ATMs, too)—the top row contains 1, 2, 3. It would be useful to implement either order, so let's do it.
    a. Make `Keypad` an abstract class and from it derive two new subclasses, `CalcPad` and `PhonePad`. For each of these, push as much functionality as you can up to the base `Keypad` class.
    b. Don't make `Keypad` a subclass. Instead, change the constructors so that they take a boolean argument, `calcOrder`, which causes the buttons to be arranged in calculator order when it is `true` and in phone order when it is `false`. You may also decide to have a default arrangement for use in constructors that don't use the `calcOrder` argument.
    c. Discuss the advantages and disadvantages of each approach. There are two important criteria here: Which is easier for another programmer to use, and which is easier for another programmer to read and modify?

14. Note that the `Keypad` class has room for twelve buttons, but only uses eleven. Add one or more constructors that take a `String` argument representing the label to be used on the twelfth button.

15. In many countries, the buttons on a telephone don't look like the default Java buttons. Instead, they have both letters and numbers, like this:

Design the class `PhoneButton` whose instances are phone buttons that act like ordinary buttons but that look like those shown. The one on the left has the usual look, and the one on the right is the way the button looks while the mouse is down over the button. As with most custom widgets, you should subclass `Canvas`, since `Canvas` generates all mouse events and also has a `paint()` method. Here's what the class skeleton should look like.

```
class PhoneButton extends Canvas
{
      // Dimensions of the button. You might need
      // to change these.
      private final static int WIDTH = 18,
                               HEIGHT = 18;
      private boolean isHilited = false;
      String letters, number;

      ...

      public Dimension MinimumSize()
      {
            return (new Dimension(WIDTH, HEIGHT);
      }

      public Dimension PreferredSize()
      {
            return (new Dimension(WIDTH, HEIGHT);
      }
}
```

a. Write the constructor or constructors for this class.
b. The `paint()` method should call two helper methods,

```
private void drawDefault(Graphics g)
private void drawHilited(Graphics g)
```

that draw the button in either its default or highlighted appearance. Write these two methods. Hint: You may want to use `WIDTH` and `HEIGHT`.

c. Write the paint() method. Hint: You may want to use isHilited.

d. Write the event-handling part of this class. Canvas generates the following event types: MOUSE_ENTER, MOUSE_EXIT, MOUSE_MOVE, MOUSE_DRAG, MOUSE_UP, and MOUSE_DOWN. A Button, in contrast, generates none of these events, so to make PhoneButton act like Button, you'll have to trap and consume all six of the mouse events. Button does generate an ACTION_EVENT, so when you get a MOUSE_UP event, you'll have to generate a new ACTION_EVENT:

```
public boolean mouseUp(Event e, int x, int y)
{
        // Draw this button in its default state.
        isHilited = false;
        repaint();
        // Construct a new ACTION_EVENT
        Event myEvt = new Event(this, e.when, ACTION_EVENT,
                                e.x, e.y, e.key, e.modifiers,
                                this.number);
        // Find out who to send it to.
        Container parent = this.getParent();
        // Send it off to the parent Container, if any.
        if (parent != null)
                return parent.postEvent(myEvt);
}
```

16. Many computer games use the keypad to control movement, with the 8 key for moving up, the 4 key for moving left, the 6 key for moving right, and the 2 key for moving down. Modify the Test applet of Section 6.5 so that the movement of the dot is controlled by a Keypad object.

17. The setValue() method of NumField could be written without using the String method valueOf(). How? Hint: +.

18. The append() methods of NumField allow the user to place the characters 04 in display. This is ugly. Fix the class so this can't happen.

19. Does append(String) work correctly if the argument is the empty string? If not, how would you guard against this eventuality?

20. We could augment NumField by adding a method

```
void addTo(double d)
```

that would add d to the number in the text, replacing it with the new sum.

a. Write this method and add it to the class.

b. Comment on whether this would be a change that *should* be made.

c. It would be silly to add this method without adding at least three more. What are they? Which of the three would be more complicated to implement than the others?

21. We could have added the following list of features to the ATM applet, but
didn't. Think about how you would add them to the program, and rank them in
increasing order of how difficult you think they would be to include.

    a. Keep track of the amount in the user's account. Assume that each user
    starts with five hundred (dollars, francs, lire, pesos, pounds, yen, or
    whatever your currency of choice happens to be).

    b. Don't allow withdrawals if the user doesn't have sufficient funds.

    c. Allow withdrawals only in multiples of some fixed minimum amount, like
    10.

    d. Allow the user to determine how much is in his or her account.

    e. Require the user to enter his or her PIN (personal identification number)
    before starting a session.

    f. Make the display show exactly two digits after the decimal point.

22. Implement (and test, of course) the modifications to the ATM applet we listed
in Exercise 19.

23. There are twenty-one Advice aphorisms in this chapter. If you had to pick the
five most important ones to impart to a novice programmer, which would they
be? Provide pithy and eloquent justifications for your choices.

CHAPTER EIGHT

Collections

Java's data types come in two forms. The primitive types, like int, float, char, and boolean, all represent single values, whereas a class is a *compound type,* in that an object of a class may have several data members, rather than just one. In this chapter, we will introduce a new compound type, the array. We'll also discuss the String class in more detail, since a String may be thought of as having the same sort of structure as an array of characters.

OBJECTIVES

In this chapter, we will
- Introduce some more Java programming constructs we'll need in order to manipulate arrays.
- Discuss Java's array type.
- Investigate some ways of sorting a list of numbers.
- Describe the String class and show how to use String objects.

8.1   LOOPS

Before we begin talking about arrays, we need to introduce some more Java programming details. In Chapter 5, we showed that we could use if and switch statements to control the order of execution of a program, based on information about the state of a program's variables at run time. When writing programs, we quickly become aware that it would be useful to be able to repeat a sequence of statements, something we can't do (at least not conveniently) with what we've developed so far. Fortunately, Java provides us with three different ways to perform such *loops,* as they are known.

Consider, for instance, a simple financial problem: If you invest some money at a given annual interest rate, how many years will it take for your money to double? Knowing just what we do now (and assuming that we didn't know how to solve the problem mathematically), this would be a forbidding task. Finding the amount of money at the end of a year for a given interest rate r is easy enough: If we start the year with an amount a, at the end of the year we have our original amount plus the interest, ar, for a total of $a + ar$, which is $a(1 + r)$. The problem, though, is that we have to keep repeating the "multiply by $1 + r$" step until we've at least doubled our original amount. We might have to write something like

```
// Assume we have a double variable, rate, containing the interest
// rate, like 0.05 for 5%

double amountSoFar = 1.0;
int years = 0;
// Compute the amount at the end of the first year
amountSoFar = (1 + rate) * amountSoFar;
years++;
if (amountSoFar >= 2.0)
    System.out.println("It took " + years + " to double");
else
{
    // Compute the amount at the end of the second year
    amountSoFar = (1 + rate) * amountSoFar;
    years++;
    if (amountSoFar >= 2.0)
        System.out.println("It took " + years + " to double");
    else
    {
        // Compute the amount at the end of the third year
        amountSoFar = (1 + rate) * amountSoFar;
        years++;
        if (amountSoFar >= 2.0)

            // ... and so on
```

Obviously, this is a Very Bad Idea, if for no other reason than we have absolutely no idea how many if tests we'd have to write. Clearly, what we need is a way to write code that does something like

```
double amountSoFar = 1.0;
int years = 0;

// keep doing this:
{
    amountSoFar = (1 + rate) * amountSoFar;
    years++;
} // as long as (amountSoFar < 2.0);

System.out.println("It took " + years + " to double");
```

The do Loop

Java has just what we need for cases like this. In fact, the language construct is almost an exact mirror of the "keep doing this . . . as long as some condition is satisfied" form we saw we would need in the preceding example. To express this in Java, we would write the fragment this way:

```
double amountSoFar = 1.0;
int years = 0;
do
{
    amountSoFar = (1 + rate) * amountSoFar;
    years++;
} while (amountSoFar < 2.0);
System.out.println("It took " + years + " to double");
```

The do loop is written

```
do
    statement                 // simple or compound
while (boolean expression);   // We need the semicolon here
```

It causes the statement to be executed repeatedly, as long as the boolean expression is `true`. The exit test is performed at the end of each loop iteration.

Two things are worth noting here. First, the statement *body* of the loop can be any statement, including a compound statement. In other words, if there are several statements you want to perform within the loop body, just group them with braces, as we did in the money-doubling example.

Second, note the location of the *termination* test—at the bottom of the loop. This means that the loop body of a do loop will always be performed at least once, prior to the first test. There are times, however, when we want the loop test to be performed first, rather than last. When that happens, we have a second loop form we can use.

The while Loop

Suppose we changed our financial problem slightly. This time, instead of finding out how long it would take to double our money, we want to determine how long it will take for an initial investment to grow to an amount greater than or equal a specific amount—our goal. This time we have to make the test before we add the interest and increment the year, since we have to allow for the possibility that the initial amount was actually larger than the goal. Here's the code to do that.

```
// assume we have the following double variables:
// amount, representing the amount at the start of any year
// goal, representing the desired amount
// rate, representing the interest rate

int years = 0;
while (amount < goal)
{
    amount = (1 + rate) * amount;
    years++;
}
if (years == 0)
    System.out.println("Lucky you, you already have your goal");
else
    System.out.println("It will take " + years + " to get there");
```

The `while` loop is written

```
while (boolean expression)
    statement                    // simple or compound
                                 // Note, no semicolon needed
```

It causes the statement to be executed repeatedly, as long as the boolean expression is `true`. The exit test is performed at the start of each loop iteration.

Note that, unlike the `do` loop, a `while` loop needs no terminating semicolon, since the termination at the end of the statement body already provides the compiler with all the information it needs (either from a semicolon or a brace) to determine where the statement ends.

The `for` Loop

The `do` and `while` loops are especially useful in cases where we don't know at the time of writing how many times the loop will be executed. Often, though, we will know exactly how many times we wish to loop. This happens so frequently that many languages include a special loop statement that uses a counter variable and increments the counter by one at each iteration, testing the counter value against an upper limit each time.

To see this in action, let's again modify our financial problem. This time, we want to produce a table that will tell, for a given interest rate and starting investment, how much money we will have at the end of each year, for a specified number of years. The code would be as follows.

```
// Assume we have the following double variables:
// amount, representing the amount at the start of any year
// rate, representing the interest rate
// and an int, numYears, indicating how many years
// we will run our simulation.


for (int y = 1; y <= numYears; y++)
{
    amount = (1 + rate) * amount;
    System.out.println("Year " + y + "    amount = " + amount);
}
```

The `for` loop is written

```
for (initStatement; testExpression; iterationExpression)
    statement                  // simple or compound
```

This does the following.
1. It performs the `initStatement` (if any) once, before starting the loop.
2. The `testExpression` is evaluated at the start of each pass through the loop. If it is `false`, control passes out of the loop, down to the next statement after the loop.
3. If the `testExpression` is true, the loop body statement is performed.
4. After performing the loop body, the `iterationExpression` (if any) is executed.
5. Finally, control passes back to step 2.

We could write the equivalent of the `for` statement using a `while` loop. (We'll explain the need for the extra braces in the "Problems" section that follows.)

```
{
    initStatement;
    while (testExpression)
    {
        statement;
        iterationExpression;
    }
}
```

While it is possible to do some fancy things in a `for` loop, in the vast majority of cases the three parts of the `for` statement (i.e., the `initStatement`, `testExpression`, and `iterationStatement`) take very simple forms:

```
for (int index = startValue; index <= finalValue; index++)
```

In this form, the loop iterates with index equal to startValue, startValue + 1, startValue + 2, . . . , and so on, to finalValue, just as it did in our financial example.

As with if statements, the statement body of a loop can be any statement, even another loop. For example, instead of compounding interest once a year, we could compound it monthly. To do so, we divide the interest rate by 12 and do the computations twelve times a year. In general, if interest is compounded periodsPerYear times each year our table-generating code would take the form

```
for (int y = 1; y <= numYears; y++)
// loop through the years
{
    for (int p = 1; m <= periodsPerYear; p++)
    // for each year, loop through the compounding periods
        amount = (1 + rate / periodsPerYear) * amount;

    System.out.println("Year " + y + "    amount = " + amount);
}
```

Remember that every statement in a loop is executed completely for each iteration. Thus if we have one loop within another, the inner loop gets executed completely for each pass through the outer loop. In simple terms, the inner loop iterates most rapidly.

In the preceding example, with numYears equals 5 and periodsPerYear equals 2, the (y, p) values that would be used would be, in order or execution, (1, 1), (1, 2), (2, 1), (2, 2), (3, 1), (3, 2), (4, 1), (4, 2), (5, 1), (5, 2).

Common Problems with Loops

Consider this seemingly perfectly reasonable code segment:

```
// computes the sum 1 + 2 + ... + n.   NOT!
int sum = 0;
for (int i = 1; i <= n; i++);
    sum += i;
```

What is the value of sum when this loop terminates? Surprisingly, this piece of code might not even compile! Can you spot the error? Take a close look—we'll wait.

*   *   *

There are two problems here, both caused by the semicolon immediately after the header of the loop. By placing the semicolon where we did, we were actually giving the loop an empty body. Indented to show what really was going on, we have

```
int sum = 0;
for (int i = 1; i <= n; i++)
    ;               // perfectly good statement: "do nothing"
sum += i;
```

Be careful not to place a semicolon at the end of a loop header. Doing so will give the loop an empty body, not the statement or statements you expect to be iterated.

If it were permitted to execute, this loop would iterate n times, doing nothing each time. It probably wouldn't execute, though, since there's another problem here. The variables declared in the `for` statement's header or body have meaning *only* within the loop itself. When the compiler got to `sum += i`, it would be out of the `for` loop and so it would look for the declaration of a variable named i. If it had seen one earlier in the same block of code, it would assume that i was the one to use and *not* the one declared within the loop. That would surely give an unexpected value for `sum`. If no variable i had been declared earlier, Java would generate an error during compilation, since every identifier has to be declared before it is used. (This explains why we needed the extra braces in the example at the bottom of page 334.)

Any variable declared within a `for` loop has meaning only within the loop.[1]

Another common problem is encountered in loops such as the following, a slight modification of the one we presented earlier:

```
double amountSoFar = 1.0;
int years = 0;
do
{
    amountSoFar = (1 + rate) * amountSoFar;
    years++;
} while (amountSoFar != 2.0);
System.out.println("It took " + years + " to double");
```

---

[1] C and C++ programmers, take note. This is different in Java.

Look at the loop test: `amountSoFar != 2.0`. The intent is that as long as the amount hasn't doubled, the loop will keep iterating. What will happen when this code executes? Think about it before going on.

*　　　　　*　　　　　*

It's very likely that it will look as if the program has frozen up. Nothing apparent will happen, since the loop will keep iterating and never satisfy the exit condition, namely, that `amountSoFar` will be *exactly* 2.0. This is a common source of error and is very hard to track down unless you know where to look.

Caution:

Whenever you design a loop, be very sure the test expression will eventually become `false`, no matter what happens. If your program gets hung up in the middle of processing, there's an excellent chance it has gotten stuck in what's known as an "infinite loop," never satisfying the exit condition.

8.2 ARRAYS

Like classes, arrays allow us to group information in a single logical unit. Arrays, however, differ from classes in three fundamental ways. First, the elements in an array must all be of the same type. Second, the elements in an array are *indexed* from 0 to some upper limit, so that the elements of an array are accessed by number, rather than by a distinct member name. Finally, although arrays have operations to inspect and manipulate their data like classes do, you cannot add methods of your own to the array type, since arrays cannot be subclassed. In a sense, then, arrays fall somewhere between primitive types and classes.

An array is nothing more than an indexed list of elements of the same type. The *base type,* that is, the elements stored in the array, can be any type. We can have an array of `doubles`, an array of `Buttons`, and even, as you'll see shortly, an array of arrays. In Figure 8.1 we show how an array of five `doubles` would be arranged.

0	1	2	3	4
3.01	-44.2	5.2e-9	0.0	0.0012

Figure 8.1 An array of five `double` values.

Note that the indices begin at 0. This may seem a peculiar way to enumerate the elements in a list, but it's simply one of those historical accidents we have to live with.

In any array of size `N`, the indices lie in the range `0, 1, . . . , N - 1.`

Declaring Arrays

As with any Java variable, we have to declare an array before we use it. Declaring array variables is a bit more complicated than declaring primitive types. We need to indicate to the compiler that the variable is an array, and we also need to specify the base type of its elements. We indicate the base type as we do in any declaration by putting it first, and we indicate that the variable represents an array by including a pair of square brackets. Java allows us to do this in two ways. We can place the square brackets after the variable name or place them after the type name:

```
double readings[];      // These declarations are both legal.
double[] readings;
```

Declaring an array, like declaring a class variable, simply tells the compiler the variable's type. It doesn't allocate any space in memory for the array, nor does it initialize any of the elements in the array. To initialize an array variable, we must do the same thing we do when initializing a class variable—use the `new` operator. In the preceding example, for instance, we could set aside space in memory for the array readings by writing

```
readings = new double[5];   // readings is an array with 5 zeros.
```

This initialization would set aside room in memory for five `double` values and would set them to the default value for `doubles`, namely 0.0. Most of the time, we would do the declaration and the initialization at the same time by writing

```
double readings[] = new double[5];
```

Caution:

It's a common mistake to declare an array without eventually initializing it. Get in the habit of doing the two at the same time whenever you can.

Of course, we may not be satisfied with the default values for the elements in an array. If we know in advance what the element values will be, Java allows us to specify them, in a manner similar to the way we can specify the initial value of a primitive type. The only difference is that we use braces to group a comma-separated list of values. For example, to initialize the array in Figure 8.1, we write

```
double readings[] = {3.01, -44.2, 5.2e-9, 0.0, 0.0012};
```

In this example, we don't use the `new` operator, and we don't specify the size of the array. Java will call `new` for us and will use the size of the list to determine the size of the array. Although we used constant values for the initialization list in the example, we could also compute the values on the fly:

```
final double PI = 3.1415926536;
double angles[] = {0.0, PI / 3, 2 * PI / 3, PI};
```

If we are using class elements for the base type of an array, we can do the same sort of initializing, placing in the list the expressions we would use to initialize any single variable of the base type, like this example.

```
Button controls[] = {new Button("Left"), new Button("Up"),
                     new Button("Down"), new Button("Right")};
```

Accessing Array Elements

Once we have declared and initialized an array variable, we may inspect and modify its elements by using the variable name followed by a pair of square brackets containing an integer expression. The integer expression is evaluated and the result will be the index value of the element to be accessed. For example, `readings[2]` will refer to the index-2 element of the array `readings` (the element containing `5.2e-9`, in our example). Remember that `readings[2]` will be the third element in the array, since indices start at 0.

Don't forget that arrays in Java begin with index 0. This means that an array declared by `int value[] = new int[3]` will have elements named `value[0]`, `value[1]`, and `value[2]` and that `value[2]` will be the third element in the array.

An element in an array can be used any way an ordinary variable of that type may be used. For example, given the declaration at the beginning, all subsequent statements are legal:

```
int value[] = new int[3];
value [0] = 34;
value [1] = 2 * value [0]++;
value [2] = 2 * value [1] - value [0];
```

```
if ((value [0] < value [1]) && (value [1] < value [2]))
    System.out.println("The list in in sorted order");
int sum = 0;
for (int i = 0; i < 3; i++)
    sum += value [i];
```

As the last line of code indicates, the contents of the square bracket can be any integer-valued expression. We could equally well write value[j + 2 * k], for instance, as long as the expression j + 2 * k evaluated to 0, 1, or 2. If it didn't, Java would detect that at run-time and generate an error. If you have C or C++ experience, you'll notice that Java is better behaved than you're used to, since it does *range-checking,* and will tell you if you are trying to access an element by using an index that's out of the allowable range for the array in question (like value[-1] or value[677], for example).

Arrays and Loops

Loops and arrays are natural companions. Often, we will use a loop to perform the same actions on each element of an array. We did that in the last two lines of the preceding example, where we computed the sum of all the elements in an array.

```
int sum = 0;                     // Initialize sum to zero.
for (int i = 0; i < 3; i++)      // For every element in the array...
    sum += value[i];             // add that element to the sum.
```

As a slightly more involved example, suppose we wanted to find the index of the smallest element at or after index start. To do so, we would keep track of the index, minIndex, of the smallest element to appear so far. For each element in the array from start to the end of the array, we would compare that element to the element in position minIndex. If the current element was smaller than the smallest obtained so far, we would mark its location as the next minIndex. Here's what it would look like as a method:

```
int Mindex(int[] theArray, int start)
// Returns the index of the smallest element at or after the
// index start.
{
    int minIndex = start;
    for (int i = start; i < theArray.length; i++)
    // For each index in the array...
        if (theArray[i] < theArray[minIndex])
        // Found a new smallest value, so record its index.
            minIndex = i;
    return minIndex;
}
```

A couple of things are worth noting here. First, you can see that we can pass an array as a method argument, simply by making what looks like a declaration in the argument list, as we did when we wrote `int[] theArray`. Second, in the loop header, we made use of a member datum, `length`, that every array has. The `length` field, as you might expect, contains the length of the array, namely, one more than the highest legal array index.

Arrays are like classes, in that if an array is used as a method argument, the elements of the array may be modified by the method.

When using loops in general, and particularly when using loops with arrays, we have to be especially careful. The smallest mistake in writing loops can lead to methods that don't work as we expect them to or, worse still, don't work at all. We'll point out some of the most common problems with loops by considering several attempts to solve the following problem.

> Write a method `int prefixSum(int[] a)` that will return the sum of the elements in `a`, up to but not including the first negative number. For example, if the array argument contains {0, 9, 4, 0, 4, –3, 2, 1, 1, –8, 3}, the method will return the sum $0 + 9 + 4 + 0 + 4 = 17$.

Here's our first attempt:

```
int prefixSum(int[] a)
// Attempt 1.   WRONG
{
    int  i = 0,
         sum = 0;
    do
    {
        sum += a[i];
    } while (a[i] >= 0);
    return sum;
}
```

This is dismal. Unless `a[0]` is negative, it will never leave the loop, since the index `i` never increases. We said it before, but it's important enough to bear repetition.

Caution:

When you design a loop, be very sure that there's *always* a way out.

It's a good idea to ask yourself, Under what conditions should I leave the loop? Then negating that condition will provide the loop control expression. In our case there are *two* conditions that will cause us to leave the loop: when we encounter a negative value for a[i] *or* when i is greater than or equal to a.length, indicating that we've run out of array elements to inspect. (Note that we missed the latter condition completely in Attempt 1.) Our exit condition is then

```
(a[i] < 0) || (i >= a.length)
```

so its negation, the expression that keeps us in the loop, is

```
(a[i] >= 0) && (i < a.length)
```

Or is it? Nope—we need i < a.length as a *guard* for the first clause, otherwise we'll run the risk of trying to access an element with a bad index. The correct control condition is

```
(i < a.length) && (a[i] >= 0)
```

Caution:

Unless you're certain that you're looking at a legal index in an array, guard the access with a test against the upper and lower possible index values.

Here's the next attempt, this time with the right control expression:

```
int prefixSum(int[] a)
// Attempt 2.   STILL WRONG
{
    int  i = 0,
         sum = 0;
    do
    {
        sum += a[i];
        i++;
    } while ((i < a.length) && (a[i] >= 0));
    return sum;
}
```

This is better, but it still won't work right. The problem here is that we added the element a[i] *before* we test whether it's negative. This is a classic "off by one" error—our sum will include the negative "sentinel" value, so it will be smaller than it should be. We need to rearrange the loop so that we test a[i] before we add it in.

```
int prefixSum(int[] a)
// Attempt 3.  CORRECT, finally
{
    int  i = 0,
         sum = 0;
    while ((i < a.length) && (a[i] >= 0))
    {
        sum += a[i];
        i++;
    }
    return sum;
}
```

Finally, let's take a look at one more attempt, this time using a for loop:

```
int prefixSum(int[] a)
// Attempt 4.  CORRECT but inelegant
{
    int  sum = 0;
    for (int i = 0; i < a.length; i++)
    {
        if (a[i] < 0)
             return sum;
        else
             sum += a[i];
    }
    return sum;
}
```

This is correct, but we're doing two things we shouldn't do. First, we're using an extra test inside the loop body, which makes our code that much less efficient and that much harder to read. Second, we're using a return statement to break out of the loop. Such an "emergency exit" is acceptable in some cases, but generally it should be reserved for just that—emergencies. It's much clearer if we write the loop so that the exit is controlled by the loop control.

Advice:

Loops that are controlled by counting (that is, that are known to iterate a fixed number of times) are best written with a for statement. Loops that are controlled by some logical condition (i.e., that will iterate as long as some condition is satisfied) should be written with while or do loops. If there is a possibility that the loop's body will never be executed, use a while loop. If the body must be executed at least once, consider using a do loop.

Multidimensional Arrays

In some programming languages, arrays are not limited to a single dimension. A two-dimensional array, for example, can be considered to be arranged in tabular form, with each element identified by two indices, one for the row and one for the column. Java, like its ancestors C and C++, does not provide direct support for multidimensional arrays, in part because it doesn't need to. Since the elements of an array can be any type, we can make a two-dimensional array, for example, by making an array of arrays. Consider, for instance, how we would make a 3 × 4 table. We could make the declaration

```
double table[][] = new double[4][3];
```

which would declare `table` to be an array of arrays and initialize it to a four-element array, each element of which was itself a three-element array, as we illustrate in Figure 8.2.

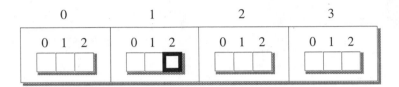

This is the way the array is arranged in memory

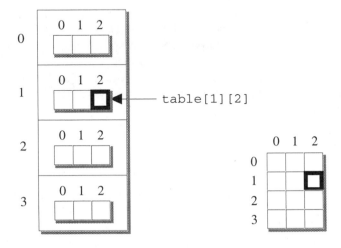

You can think of it this way ...   ... or this way.

Figure 8.2 Three ways to think of an array `double[4][3]`.

The initialization syntax is, we'll admit, a trifle confusing. You can take comfort in the knowledge that it really doesn't matter how you think of such declarations (is the 4 the number of rows or columns?), as long as you pick one interpretation and stick to it consistently.

We could, of course, do the same sort of thing to make three-dimensional arrays, or arrays with arbitrarily large dimensionality (though the pictures get pretty hard to draw beyond two dimensions). We can initialize multidimensional arrays with a list of values, much as we did with one-dimensional arrays. To fill the table above, for example, we could instead make the declaration–initialization

```
double table[][] = {{0.0, 0.1, 0.2}, {1.0, 1.1, 1.2},
                    {2.0, 2.1, 2.2}, {3.1, 3.0, 3.2}};
```

Finally, a potentially useful feature of Java arrays is that, because of the way they are declared, they need not be "rectangular." If we wanted to, we could defer the initialization of the "inner" pieces by not specifying their sizes. Making the declarations

```
double pyramid[][] = new double[4][];
pyramid [0] = new double[1];
pyramid [1] = new double[3];
pyramid [2] = new double[5];
pyramid [3] = new double[7];
```

would have created a structure with one element in the first row, three elements in the second, five elements in the third, and seven elements in the last row, as shown in Figure 8.3.

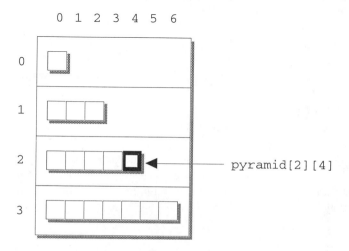

Figure 8.3 Java arrays need not be rectangular.

Heterogeneous Arrays

We said before that the elements of an array must all be of the same type. That's true enough, but it shouldn't stop you from making a *heterogeneous array,* whose elements are of different types, when you need to. Consider the following applet, for example.

```
public class Test extends Applet
{
    private Component[] c = new Component[3];

    public void init()
    {
        c[0] = new Button("button");
        c[1] = new Label("label");
        c[2] = new TextField("text");

        for (int i = 0; i < 3; i++)
            this.add(c[i]);
    }
}
```

Observe that the array c contains a Button, a Label, and a TextField. Well, that's the way it appears to us, at least. In fact, as far as the compiler is concerned, all the elements are the same type, Component. Since Component is a wider type than Button, Label, and TextField (i.e., since Component is a superclass of all three of these), we can initialize any of c[0], c[1], and c[2] to instances of the subclasses, which is exactly what we did in the applet.

In the preceding example, the only tricky part would come from trying to have one of the c[i]s call a method that wasn't a Component method. For example, if we wanted to set the label of the Button c[0], we couldn't make the call

```
c[0].setLabel("OK");
```

since setLabel() isn't a Component method. Instead, we'd have to make an explicit type cast,

```
((Button)c[0]).setLabel("OK");      // see footnote[2]
```

While you generally wouldn't use a heterogeneous array in a situation like this, they do come in handy. Suppose, for instance, that we were making a program to keep track of employee records. We might have a collection of classes like the following.

---

[2]We need the parentheses, since the dot binds more tightly than the cast operator, and we have to perform the cast *before* we can use the dot to call the method.

```
abstract class Employee
{
    static final double DEDUCTION = 35;      // applies to
everyone

    abstract double getPay();
    ...
}

class Salaried extends Employee
{
    private double salary;
    ...
    double getPay()
    {
        return salary - DEDUCTION;
    }
}

class Hourly extends Employee
{
    private double hourlyRate;
    private double hoursWorked;
    ...
    double getPay()
    {
        return hourlyRate * hoursWorked - DEDUCTION;
    }
}
```

We could then set up an array containing all the workers by declaring

```
Employee[] emps = new Employee[3];      // a small company
```

Then we could initialize `c[0]` to be a new `Salaried`, and `c[1]` and `c[2]` to be new `Hourly` employees, for instance, all in the same array. Now to compute the total payroll we could use a loop to iterate through the array:

```
double totalPayroll = 0.0;
for (int i = 0; i < 3; i++)
    totalPayroll += emps[i].getPay();
```

We don't need to do any type casting here. Since `Employee` is a class with an abstract `getPay()` method, the system will look at the type of each element at run-time and decide which `getPay()` method would be appropriate to call.

We could even do the same thing with the primitive types, but first we'd have to change them to class types by using the wrapper classes we mentioned briefly in Chapter 7. For example, if we wanted to put the `int 34`, the `double 6.2e+2`, and the `float 2.008f` into one array, we could use the wrapper classes

Integer, Double, and Float to make new class instances of these numbers, and then use the Number superclass to make our array:

```
Number[] nums = new Number[3];
Integer i = new Integer(34);
Double d = new Double(6.2e+2);
Float f = new Float(2.008f);
nums[0] = i;
nums[1] = d;
nums[2] = f;
```

Each of the numeric wrapper classes has a method doubleValue(), overriding Number's abstract doubleValue() method, so, just as we did with employees, we could add the elements of nums:

```
double sum = 0.0;
for (int i = 0; i < 3; i++)
    sum += nums[i].doubleValue();
```

8.3   SORTING

As long as we're doing examples of array processing, we may as well include one more, which illustrates a common task: sorting the elements in an array. The problems of sorting and searching an array for a particular value constitute a large research topic in computer science; the standard reference on these problems is more than 700 pages long!

Selection Sort

You've already seen a searching algorithm—Mindex() inspected each element in an array and returned the index where an element of minimal size is located. We can use the code of Mindex() to build a method that sorts. This method will take an array as its sole argument and will rearrange the array's elements so that they are in sorted order, from smallest to largest. The algorithm we will use is very simple—though not particularly efficient—and is known as *Selection Sort*. In this scheme, we assume that all the elements from indices 0 to i-1 are already in their final sorted order. We will then use Mindex() to find the index of the smallest element in the array from position i to the end. Having found the location of the smallest remaining element, we will swap it with the one in position i. Thus, at each stage we start with the sorted elements in positions 0 to i-1 and end with the sorted elements in positions 0 to i. Repeating this, we will eventually have the entire array in sorted order.

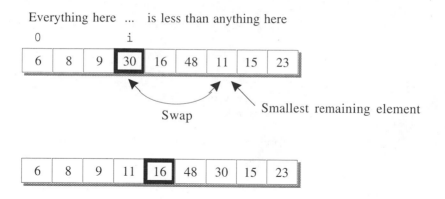

Figure 8.4 One pass of Selection Sort.

Figure 8.5 illustrates the action of Selection Sort on the array that initially contains the values (15, 23, 8, 30, 16, 48, 11, 6, 9). Note that after each pass, the highlighted element has been replaced with the smallest value at or after the highlighted location.

15	23	8	30	16	48	11	6	9

6	23	8	30	16	48	11	15	9

6	8	23	30	16	48	11	15	9

6	8	9	30	16	48	11	15	23

6	8	9	11	16	48	30	15	23

6	8	9	11	15	48	30	16	23

6	8	9	11	15	16	30	48	23

6	8	9	11	15	16	23	48	30

6	8	9	11	15	16	23	30	48

Figure 8.5 Selection Sort in action.

```
void selectionSort(int[] a)
// Sorts the array argument's elements in increasing order.
{
    for (int i = 0; i < a.length - 1; i++)
    {
        // Find the index of the smallest element in
        // a at or after position i.
        int minPos = Mindex(a, i);

        // Swap current element with the smallest remaining.
        int temp = a[i];
        a[i] = a[minPos];
        a[minPos] = temp;
    }
}
```

Insertion Sort

Selection Sort is by no means the only possible way to sort a list of objects. If you're a card player, think for a moment about the algorithm you use to sort a hand of cards. Many people use a manual version of Selection Sort, but another common way of arranging cards is to work from left to right and, for each card encountered, to place that card in its proper place among the cards to its left. In this scheme, as in Selection Sort, the elements to the left of the current position are in sorted order, but unlike Selection Sort, the elements in the left segment may not be in their final positions. This algorithm is known as *Insertion Sort*, and in Figure 8.6 we show what happens in one pass.

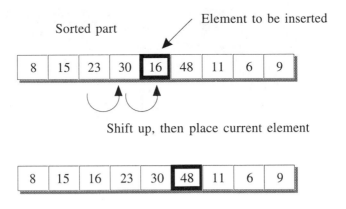

Figure 8.6 One pass of Insertion Sort.

At the start of the pass, we save the value of the current element. Then we walk our way down the array, shifting each element that is larger than the saved element up one position, and stop when we find an element that is smaller than the saved value (or find ourselves at the start of the array). Finally, we place the saved element where it belongs.

```
public void InsertionSort(int[] theArray)
// Sorts the array argument's elements in increasing order.
{
    for (int i = 1; i < a.length; i++)
    // For every element except the leftmost one,
    // insert it where it belongs in the sorted segment
    // to its left.
    {
        int  currentValue = a[i],
            index = i;
        // Walk down from the current position, i,
        // shifting up every element larger than temp.
        while ((index >= 1) && (currentValue < a[index - 1]))
        {
            a[index] = a[index - 1];
            index -= 1;
        }
        // Now we know where currentValue belongs,
        // so put it there.
        a[index] = currentValue;
    }
}
```

Figure 8.7 shows how Insertion Sort rearranges the same array we used in Figure 8.5. Note that some of the passes (the first, third, and fifth, in this example) have no work to do after the first comparison, since the element to be inserted happens to be larger than any of those to its left and so is already where it belongs. This "short-circuit" feature, where some passes have only one comparison to do, differs sharply from the situation in Selection Sort. There we always have to do the same number of comparisons to find the minimal element, regardless of how the data are arranged. Insertion Sort is particularly efficient when the initial array is very nearly sorted, as you can see by considering how it would act in the limiting case, when the initial array happens to be already arranged in sorted order. In that lucky case, for an array of size N, Selection Sort will make (as always) $1 + 2 + \ldots + (N - 1)$ comparisons (why?), whereas Insertion Sort will make only $N - 1$. To see what this means in practice, consider that on a perfectly sorted list of $N = 1000$ elements, Selection Sort will make 499,500 comparisons; in contrast, Insertion Sort will make only 999 comparisons.

Although Insertion Sort can use far fewer comparisons than Selection Sort (and, although it's beyond our scope here, uses about half as many comparisons in the "average" case), when we consider the number of data moves each of the algorithms make, Selection Sort clearly has the edge. At each pass, Selection Sort makes only one swap, to place the minimal element at the current position, but Insertion Sort may have to do a lot of data moves if the current element is smaller than almost all the elements to its left. As with many problems in computer science, there's no "best" choice in this case: If you have reason to believe the input data are nearly sorted to begin with, Insertion Sort is clearly the winner, but if the number of data moves is important (if, for example, the data elements were very large and hence would take significant time to copy) then Selection Sort would be preferred.

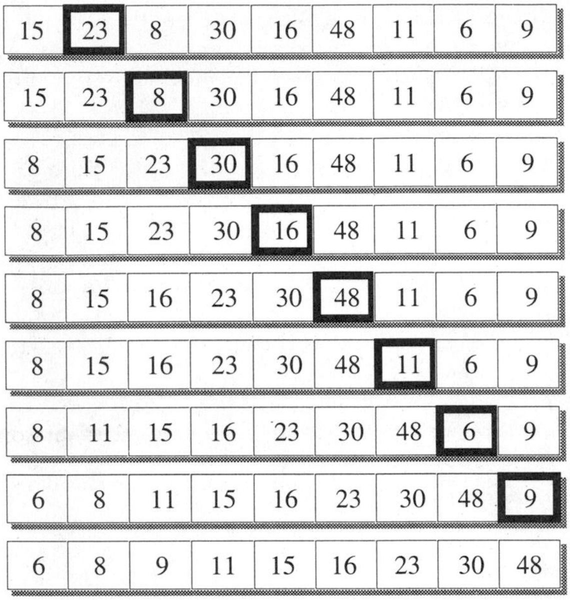

15	23	8	30	16	48	11	6	9
15	23	8	30	16	48	11	6	9
8	15	23	30	16	48	11	6	9
8	15	23	30	16	48	11	6	9
8	15	16	23	30	48	11	6	9
8	15	16	23	30	48	11	6	9
8	11	15	16	23	30	48	6	9
6	8	11	15	16	23	30	48	9
6	8	9	11	15	16	23	30	48

Figure 8.7 Insertion Sort in action.

Shellsort

While there may be no clear reason to pick either Insertion Sort or Selection Sort to sort an array, there are good reasons to choose *neither.* We'll conclude our introduction to sorting by considering one more sorting technique—one that generally runs far faster than either of the two we've covered so far. Let's begin with the observation that Insertion Sort is inefficient primarily because it moves the data so slowly, shifting an element by only one position per step. We'd be in much better shape if we could find a way, as we do in Selection Sort, of moving the data near their ultimate resting places more rapidly.

In 1959, D. L. Shell published a sorting method that does just what we need. The fundamental idea behind his technique is what is known as a *divide and conquer* scheme. We consider the list to be sorted as made up of several sublists whose elements lie in equally spaced positions and use Insertion Sort on each of the sublists. For example, if we chose an increment of 4, we could consider the array `a[0], a[1], . . .` to comprise the four sublists

```
a[0],                a[4],                a[8], ...

   a[1],                a[5],                a[9], ...

      a[2],                a[6],                a[10], ...

         a[3],                a[7],                a[11],
```

If we now sort each of the sublists separately, we won't necessarily have the data in their final order. But we will be moving each element much more rapidly toward its proper location, since each of the sublists will be in sorted order, as shown in Figure 8.8.

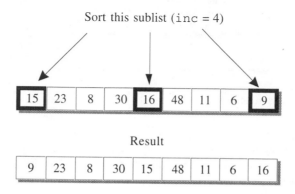

Figure 8.8 One pass of Shellsort.

The key to *Shellsort* is to use a decreasing sequence of increments, always finishing up with an increment of 1. Even with just two increments, 4 and 1, studies have shown a considerable improvement in average running time over either Insertion or Selection Sort. Although the data (in the form of sublists) are sorted several times, two facts work in our favor. First, the larger the increment is, the shorter the sublists will be and hence the faster they will be sorted. Second, since the early passes, with larger increments, move the data elements close to their ultimate—sorted—locations, the data quickly become "nearly" sorted, which is exactly when Insertion Sort is most efficient!

Figure 8.9 illustrates how Shellsort works for our sample array. First, with increment 4, we sort the sublists in positions {0, 4, 8}, {1, 5}, {2, 6} and {3, 7}. Then we reduce the increment to 2 and sort the sublist in positions {0, 2, 4, 6, 8} and the 1 in positions {1, 3, 5, 7}. Finally, we do one more pass with increment 1, sorting the entire list.

The nicest part of all this is that it's very easy to redesign Insertion Sort so that it sorts the sublists for a given increment. In fact, all that's needed is to replace every 1 in the function with the argument k (which we use instead of the more descriptive "increment" only because it makes the following code fit the page better).

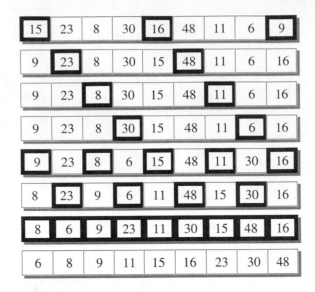

Figure 8.9 Shellsort in action.

For each index i, from k to the last index in the array, we place the element theArray[i] in its correct position in the sublist at positions i, i - k, i - 2 * k, and so on. The table shows how the new Insertion Sort method works in the first few iterations of the outermost loop.

Element at index	Insert among positions
4	4, 0
5	5, 1
6	6, 2
7	7, 3
8	8, 4, 0
9	9, 5, 1
10	10, 6, 2

Here's the new version of Insertion Sort. Compare it with the original to see how similar they are.

```
void insertionSort(int[] a, int k)
// Perform an Insertion k-Sort on the   argument array.
// When this completes, each k-separated sublist is sorted.
// Calling this with k equal to 1 results in ordinary
// Insertion Sort.
{
    for (int i = k; i < a.length; i++)
    {
        int currentValue = a[i];
```

```
            int index = i;
            while((index >= k) && (currentValue < a[index - k]))
            {
                a[index] = a[index - k];
                index -= k;
            }
            a[index] = currentValue;
        }
    }
```

Now it's easy to write Shellsort. In the example that follows, we have used Shell's original choice for increments, namely $N/2$, $N/4$, $N/8$, ...

```
void shellSort(int[] a)
// Perform a Shell Sort on the  argument array.
{
    int increment = a.length / 2;
    while (increment >= 1)
    {
        insertionSort(a, increment);
        increment /= 2;
    }
}
```

There are other possible choices for the sequence of increments, some of which are better than others. In the exercises, you will explore one of the most popular.

An interesting fact about Shellsort is that, although we know it's efficient, nobody knows exactly how efficient it is. For example, it has been known for years that both Selection Sort and Insertion Sort execute no more than a multiple of N^2 statements when sorting a list of N elements, no such bounds are known for Shellsort. Experiments with arrays filled with random numbers indicate that Shellsort runs far faster than either of the other algorithms we've introduced. Its time advantage gets more pronounced the longer the data list is, but four decades after Shell's invention, we still don't know exactly how good it is.

As a test, we coded and ran all three sorting functions for arrays of sizes 500, 1000, 1500, . . . , 4000, filled with randomly chosen integers. We found that Selection Sort was consistently 25% slower than Insertion Sort and that Shellsort was a clear winner: It was 7 times faster than Insertion Sort on arrays of size 500, 19 times faster on arrays of 2000 numbers, and a whopping 30 times faster on arrays of size 4000.

8.4 STRINGS

The `String` class is part of the `java.lang` package, meaning that it is already known to the compiler without the need for you to write a special `import` declaration to get its names into your programs. You've seen quite a few examples of the `String` class already. In the Lablets and the sample code in this book, we've used dozens of `String` literals, written as any sequence of characters between quotes, as, for example, "`This is a string`". Combining the appearance of a String literal with what you've learned in this chapter, you might guess that a `String` is represented internally as an array of `chars`, and you'd be exactly right. The `String` class, though, is both more and less powerful than an array of characters.

First, the `String` class contains a large collection of methods that allow you to do things with its instances. As you can with arrays, you can find the length of a String and inspect the character in a given position. This class also has methods with no corresponding array equivalents, like the ability to search a `String` for a match with another `String`. In spite of all this power, there are things you can do with arrays of characters that you can't do with Strings. One thing you can't do is change a `String`. Once a `String` instance has been created, there is no way to change its characters or its length. This is done primarily in the interest of efficiency—knowing that `String` objects cannot change gives the designers of Java compilers the ability to use internal data structures that optimize the efficiency of the `String` methods and conserve space in memory.

Unlike other classes, `Strings` are *immutable*—once a `String` instance has been created, it cannot be changed.

Another difference between the `String` class and most of the rest of the Java classes is that `String` is a `final` class—you cannot make `String` a subclass. Again, this is dictated largely by the need for efficiency.

The `String` Class

We won't cover all the details of the `String` class—it would be worth your time to read what we consider to be the most important and useful features of `String` and then take a look at the documentation for a taste of `String` arcana.

There are quite a few `String` constructors, most of which we won't discuss here. The first, and most common, does much of its work behind the scenes. You can construct a `String` simply by initializing it to a literal in a declaration, like this:

```
String myString = "Brand new string";
```

Note that there's no `new` operator in this declaration. The compiler will invoke whatever is needed to build a new string containing the literal and make sure that `myString` gets the right reference address. We should remark here that a string literal can't be broken over several lines in the source code. If you have a very long literal, you should break it into pieces, using the concatenation operator,

```
String myString = "This is an exceptionally long string.  In fact,"
                + " it won't even fit on a single line,"
                + " but rather has to be broken over three.";
```

The other constructors are more like the constructors you've seen and, like other constructors, are invoked in declarations by using new.

String(String s)

A copy constructor, this constructs a new String containing the same characters and having the same length as the argument.

❦ **String**(char[] c)

This is a conversion constructor. Given an array of chars, it constructs a new String containing those characters. For instance, if we had declared and filled an array of chars like

```
char[] myChars = {'A', ' ', 's', 't', 'r', 'i', 'n', 'g'};
```

we could then use this array to initialize a String by

```
String myString = new String(myChars);
```

This constructor is often used with toCharArray(), which we describe in the next subsection.

Access and Comparison

We'll begin our discussion of the String methods by looking at those that allow you to get information about a String and compare two Strings. In what follows, we'll use the example Strings

   s = "alphabet" and t = "answer".

char **charAt**(int i)

Returns the character at position i in this String. The argument must be a valid position in this String, so it must be greater than or equal to 0 and less than the length of this String. For our example, s.charAt(2) returns 'p'.

int **compareTo**(String s)

Compares this String with the argument String, using what is known as *lexicographic order*. This ordering is an extension of the underlying order on characters. For the standard characters we're used to in English (the ASCII ordering of characters, as it's called[3]), it is as follows.

---

[3]ASCII stands for "American Standard Code for Information Interchange."

```
<space> ! " # $ % & ' ( ) * + , - . / 0 1 2 3 4 5 6 7 8 9 : ; < = > ?
@ A B C D E F G H I J K L M N O P Q R S T U V W X Y Z [ \ ] ^ _ ' a b
c d e f g h i j k l m n o p q r s t u v w x y z { | } ~
```

This order is extended to `Strings` using the following rules.

1. Starting at the left, compare the strings character by character, stopping at the first pair of characters that differ, or when you run out of characters in one or both Strings, whichever comes first.
2. If you find two different characters, return the difference of their codes, so in the comparison `s.compareTo(t)` "alphabet" first differs from "answer" in the index-1 position and 'l' is two places earlier in character order than 'n', so the call `s.compareTo(t)` would return 2. Similarly, `t.compareTo(s)` would return –2.
3. If the method runs out of characters before finding a mismatch, it returns the difference in the lengths of the Strings, so `s.compareTo("alpha")` would return 8 – 5, or 3.

    If `compareTo()` returns a negative value, we say that this `String` is less than the argument. Some consequences of this ordering are (1) the empty string is less than any other, (2) "BRAIN" is less than "BRAWN" (unfortunately), and (3) "BEE" is less than "BEEKEEPER". See the discussion of `equals()`.

boolean **endsWith**(String st)
    Returns true if and only if this `String` ends with the argument `String`. For example, `s.endsWith("bet")` returns `true` and the method call `s.endsWith("beta")` would return `false`. See the companion method `startsWith()`.

❦ boolean **equals**(Object obj)
boolean **equalsIgnoreCase**(Object obj)
    The first method returns `true` if and only if this `String` and the argument (which must be a `String`) have equal contents (i.e., if `compareTo()` would return 0). The second method acts like equals() but counts upper- and lowercase letters as equal, so the call `s.equalsIgnoreCase("AlPhAbEt")` would return `true`.

void **getChars**(int start, int end, char[] c, int cStart)
    This is one of those uncommon Java methods that modifies one of its arguments. This fills the char array `c` with the characters in this `String`, from position `start` to (but not including) position `end`. The argument `cStart` specifies where in the `c` array the copying should begin. For example, if we were to make the call `s.getChars(2, 6, myChars, 3)`, the effect would be as if we had written

```
myChars[3] = 'p';
myChars[4] = 'h';
```

```
myChars[5] = 'a';
myChars[6] = 'b';
```

There is a complicated precondition for this method to work without error. For example, we must have `start < end`, and there must be enough room in c to place all the characters. We'll leave specification of the complete precondition as an exercise. See the simpler version `toCharArray()`.

❦ int **indexOf**(char c)
int **indexOf**(char c, int start)
int **indexOf**(String st)
int **indexOf**(String st, int start)

All of these methods return the index (counting from 0, of course) of the first location where the argument `char` or `String` is found, and return –1 if the indicated `char` or `String` isn't found in this `String`. If an `int` argument is specified, the search returns the first index where a match is found, at or after the start index. For example,

```
s.indexOf('a')          // returns 0
s.indexOf('a', 2)       // returns 4
s.indexOf("pha")        // returns 2
s.indexOf("pha", 4)     // returns -1
```

int **lastIndexOf**(char c)
int **lastIndexOf** (char c, int start)
int **lastIndexOf** (String st)
int **lastIndexOf** (String st, int start)

These methods act like `indexOf()`, except the search starts at the right of this `String`, rather than the left.

❦ int **length**()

Returns the length (the number of characters) of this String. For our example Strings, `s.length()` returns 8 and `t.length()` returns 6.

boolean **startsWith**(String st)

Returns true if and only if this `String` starts with the argument `String`. For example, `s.startsWith("alp")` returns `true` and the method call `s.startsWith(t)` would return `false`. See `endsWith()`.

❦ char[] **toCharArray**()

Constructs and returns a new array of chars, having the same length as this String and the same characters. This is commonly used to do String manipulations that aren't provided by the class, like this

```
String manipulator(String original)
{
    // First, build the array from the String
    char[] myChars = original.toCharArray();
```

```
// (Then, do something with the array myChars)

// Finally, build a new String from the modified array
// and return it.
return new String(myChars);

}
```

Builders

Although you can't modify a `String` instance, the class provides methods that allow you to make a new `String` from an existing one. These methods all have `String` return types.

String **concat**(String st)
> Returns a new `String` that is the concatenation of this `String` and the argument. For example, `s.concat("ical")` returns the String `"alphabetical"`. This method is equivalent in its action to the concatenation operator +.

String **replace**(char original, char replacement)
> Returns the `String` that results from replacing every instance of `original` in this `String` with `replacement`. For instance, a call to `s.replace('a', 'e')` would return the new String `"elphebet"`. If no instances of `original` are found in this `String`, a reference to this `String` itself is returned.

String **substring**(int start)
String **substring**(int start, int end)
> Return a new `String` containing the characters in this `String` from position `start` to the end of this `String`, or from position `start` to (but not including) position `end`, respectively. The index `start` must be nonnegative and it cannot be larger than the length of this `String`. The index `end` must satisfy the same conditions, and in addition must be greater than `start`. Here are some examples:

```
s.substring(5)      // returns "bet"
s.substring(8)      // returns "" (the empty String)
s.substring(0, 5)   // returns "alpha"
s.substring(2, 2)   // returns "p"
```

String **toLowerCase**()
String **toUpperCase**()
> Return a new String made by converting each letter in this String to lower- or uppercase, respectively These methods only convert the characters that have Unicode lower- or uppercase equivalents. For our purposes that means letters, not numbers or other characters.

```
String trim()
```
Returns a new `String` made from this one by removing all leading and trailing whitespace (blanks, tabs, and returns, for example).

Using Strings for Conversion

Programmers commonly store and display information in `String` form in a Java program—we do this all the time in the `TextFields` and the `TextAreas` of an applet. As a result, we often find ourselves in the position of having to convert an `int`, for instance, to a `String`, placing the result in a `TextField` for the user to see, and then later having to convert that `String` back to an `int`. The `String` class has methods for converting objects to `Strings`, but we have to look elsewhere for conversions in the opposite direction.

All Java classes have a method, `toString()`, that can be used to return a `String` representation of an instance, because the ultimate superclass, `Object`, has a `toString()` method. Object's `toString()` method doesn't do anything, but many of the built-in Java classes provide overrides of this method. Typically, calling `someInstance.toString()` will return a `String` that contains useful information about the object `someInstance`—perhaps its label, location, or size. For example, if `display` is a `TextField` and you write

```
Point p = new Point(10, 30);
display.setText(p.toString());
```

you'll find that `display` gets the text "`java.awt.Point[x=10,y=30]`". You don't even need the explicit call to `toString()` we used above—when the compiler sees a class instance as one of the operands of the concatenation operator `+`, it will automatically insert a call to `toString()`. In other words, we could have written this code as

```
Point p = new Point(10, 30);
display.setText("Information: " + p);
```

or, to accomplish exactly the same thing as the first example, we could have used the empty `String`,

```
Point p = new Point(10, 30);
display.setText("" + p);
```

It's not a bad idea for you to include an override of `toString()` in classes you write. This can be handy for providing debugging information.

The primitive types don't have `toString()` methods, of course, since they're not classes. However, the `String` class contains `static` methods that accomplish the same thing.

```
static String valueOf(boolean b)
static String valueOf(char c)
static String valueOf(int i)
static String valueOf(long l)
static String valueOf(float f)
static String valueOf(double d)
```

All of these methods return a `String` representation of their arguments, so we could execute the code

```
double d = 266.0909;
boolean b = (d > 0.0);
display.setText(String.valueOf(b) + "   " + String.valueOf(d));
```

and find that the display contains the text `"true 266.0909"`.

As with `toString()` for classes, Java will insert the necessary calls to `valueOf()` in `String` concatenation expressions, so we could equally well have written that code as

```
double d = 266.0909;
boolean b = (d > 0.0);
display.setText(b + "   " + d);
```

The only care you have to exercise when doing this kind of conversion is to be sure that you're forcing `String` concatenation by including at least one guaranteed `String` operand. For example, the call

```
display.setText(b + d);
```

would be wrong on two counts: We can't add a `boolean` and a `double`; and even if we somehow could, the result almost certainly wouldn't be a `String` and couldn't be used as an argument to `setText()`.

The easiest way to convert an object or a primitive type to a `String` is to use concatenation with the empty `String`, `"" + x`, and let the compiler insert the necessary call to `toString()` or `valueOf()`, as appropriate.

To convert in the other direction, from `String` to a primitive type, we need to use the wrapper classes `Boolean`, `Character`, `Integer`, `Float`, `Long`, and `Double`. All of these classes have their own `static valueOf()` methods, each of which returns a class instance corresponding to a `String` argument. Once a wrapper class object has been created, we can then use the appropriate `booleanValue()`, `charValue()`, `intValue()`, `floatValue()`, `longValue()`, or `doubleValue()` method to convert to the corresponding primitive type. For example, if we assume that `display` contains the `String` "2048", we could extract that `String`, convert it to an `int`, and store the result in an `int` variable i by following this two-step process:

```
String s = display.getText();
Integer classyInt = Integer.valueOf(s);    // String --> Integer
int i = classyInt.intValue();              // Integer --> int
```

The result would be that i would contain the value 2048.

This process, by the way, is both sufficiently common and opaque that it would make sense to encapsulate it in a descriptively named method:

```
int intFromString(String s)
// Remember, the dot groups from the left, so we're doing
// Integer.valueOf() first, and then intValue().
{
    return Integer.valueOf(s).intValue();
}
```

8.5   HANDS ON

This chapter's Lablet is an example of what is known as *algorithm visualization*. Knowing how to code a sorting routine is a far cry from having an intuitive understanding of how it works. The analytical part of your brain can think of sorting in terms of making comparisons and moving data, but we shouldn't neglect the part that sees patterns in the data movements. Thanks to Java's graphic features, we can design an applet that shows how a sorting algorithm looks in action.

Figure 8.10 shows what it looks like when running. The main portion of the applet is a collection of `TextFields` that hold the values of the data, along with a related collection of lines drawn so that their length is proportional to the size of the data. At the bottom are three controls: a Reset button, which generates new random data values, a Sort button, which starts the sorting process, and a `Choice` object, which allows the user to select a particular sorting algorithm to observe.

Designing the Lablet

By now, you should have no problem coming up with the layout for `Sortmeister`: We group the display `Textfields` in one `Panel`, the control widgets in another, set the applet's layout to `BorderLayout`, and add the display `Panel` to the West and the control `Panel` to the South, thereby reserving a large open region in which to draw the lines.

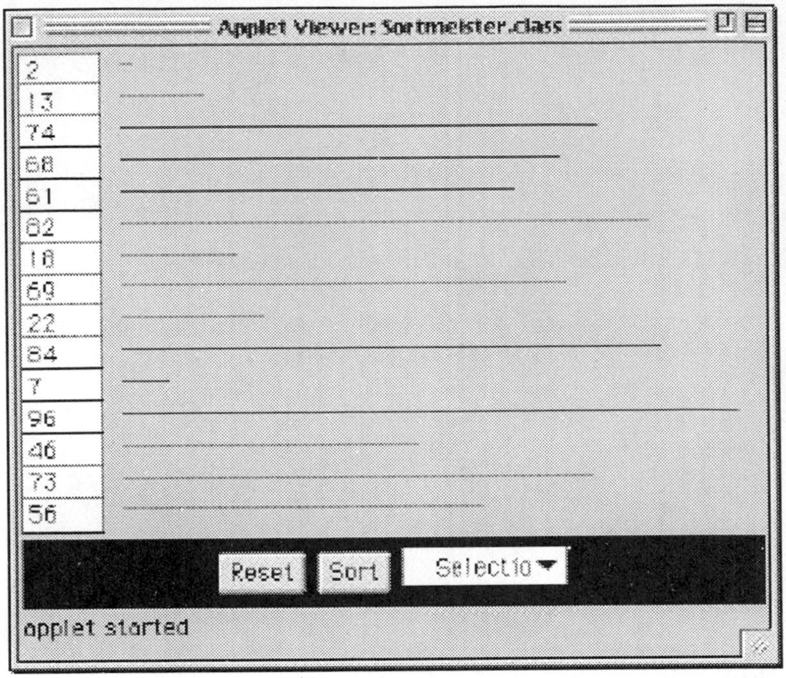

Figure 8.10 `Sortmeister`, ready to go.

Because we have a collection of logically related objects of the same type—namely, the `TextFields`—it makes good sense to group them by using an array. In addition, we keep all the data to be sorted in an array of `ints`, as you can see in the following declarations in the `Sortmeister` class.

```
TextField display[];
int data[];
```

The action part of the applet is a bit more complicated than the visual design, but not intimidatingly so. We invent two constants, `SELECTION` and `SHELL`, and use these as values for an instance variable `currentSortMethod` that indicates which of the two sorting schemes we'll use to sort the data array. The `Choice` object `sortChoice` will be used to set `currentSortMethod`.

The `reset Button` will fill the data array with random integers and clear the drawing rectangle. We'll encapsulate these tasks in a `private` utility method `doReset()`.

The `sort Button` will simply check the value in `currentSortMethod` and use that value to call the corresponding sort method.

The most complicated method in this class is `paint()`. When we have to repaint the applet, often as a result of `repaint()` calls we've made, we have several things to do. For each row (display `TextField` and corresponding line), we have to update the text in the display, erase the old line, and draw the new one. This isn't too bad, but the drawing parts are complicated by the fact that we have to determine the starting point of the line and its length, based on the value of the corresponding data element and the size of the applet and the display `Panel`. You'll see what we mean when we investigate the `paint()` method.

Exploring the Lablet

As usual, we won't discuss the `import` declarations and the opening comments, since they have nothing new to show us. The declaration of the applet class begins with the usual collection of constant and instance variable declarations.

```
public class Sortmeister extends Applet
{
        private final int      SELECTION = 0;
        private final int      SHELL = 1;

        private final int      SIZE = 15;        // number of data values
        private final int      DATA_MAX = 100;   // largest possible data
        private final long     DELAY = 100000;   // ADJUST: delay amount

        private TextField      display[];        // to display the data
        private int            data[];           // the data to be sorted
        private int            currentSortMethod;
        private Button         reset,
                               sort;
        private Choice         sortChoice;
        private Rectangle      appletDim,
                               dataDim;
```

We mentioned the `SELECTION` and `SHELL` constants—they set the sort mode. We wanted to make the applet as general as we could, so we declared an `int` constant `SIZE` to hold the sizes of the `data` and `display` arrays. In simple terms, `SIZE` determines how many lines we'll have in our applet. `DATA_MAX` contains the upper bound for the data elements to be sorted—if you wanted the data elements to range from 0 to 500, for instance, you would set this constant to 500. The constant `DELAY` controls the delay between updates of the applet—the larger this value is, the slower the sorting routines will appear to run. Because of the awkward way we have to produce the delay, you might find you have to tweak this value, depending on how fast your computer is.

The instance variables are the ones you would expect. We've already mentioned the `display` and `data` arrays—note that we have set aside space only for references to the arrays, and haven't yet provided any space in memory for the arrays themselves. We've also mentioned `currentSortMethod`, which will hold one of the constants `SELECTION` or `SORT` to indicate the algorithm we'll use to do the sorting. The widgets `reset`, `sort`, and `sortChoice` will, as we indicated, control the action of the applet. Finally, the two `Dimension` objects, `appletDim` and `dataDim`, will hold the dimensions of the applet and the display panel. They will be initialized in the `init()` method and used in `paint()`.

The init() method should be familiar enough. The only things we do here that you haven't seen in other applets is initialize the two arrays with

```
data = new int[SIZE];
display = new TextField[SIZE];
```

and use a loop to add the display array elements to the Panel p1.

```
public void init()
{
    setLayout(new BorderLayout());
    resize(400,300);

    // Create the two arrays to be the right SIZE.
    data = new int[SIZE];
    display = new TextField[SIZE];

    Panel p1 = new Panel();
    p1.setLayout(new GridLayout(SIZE,1));
    // Create SIZE different text fields and add them to
    // the display panel.
    for (int i = 0; i < SIZE; i++)
    {
        display[i] = new TextField(3);
        p1.add(display[i]);
    }
    this.add("West", p1);

    Panel p2 = new Panel();
    p2.setBackground(Color.blue);
    reset = new Button("Reset");
    sort = new Button("Sort");
    sortChoice = new Choice();
    sortChoice.addItem("Selection");
    sortChoice.addItem("Shell");
    p2.add(reset);
    p2.add(sort);
    p2.add(sortChoice);
    this.add("South", p2);

    // Force layout, so we can get the dimensions
    // of the applet and the display panel.
    this.layout();
    appletDim = this.bounds();
    dataDim = p1.bounds();

    currentSortMethod = SELECTION;
}
```

The last few lines of init() deserve some mention. In Chapter 4 we mentioned briefly that the Components of an applet don't have reliable dimensions until they are first painted. We used a call to the inherited `Component` method `layout()` to force layout to take place, thereby giving us useful values for the dimensions of the applet and the display `Panel p1`.

The next thing we see is an override of the update() method. We've already mentioned that the `Component` method `update()` erases the entire `Component` (in this case, the whole applet) and then calls `paint()`. If `repaint()` is called frequently, as it is in this applet, the default `update()` can result in an irritating flicker. By overriding `update()` to eliminate the erasing step, we can eliminate the flicker. You'll get a chance to explore this in the lab exercises.

```
public void update(Graphics g)
{
     paint(g);
}
```

In order to paint the lines representing the data, we have to know how much space we have available for painting. This is why we had to save `appletDim` and `dataDim`. The width available for painting is

`appletDim.width - dataDim.width`

(minus ten pixels, to give a little space between the line and the display `TextField`) and the height is `dataDim.height`, as shown.

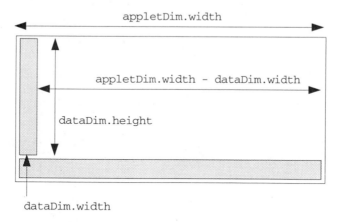

We establish a local variable, `unitY`, that equals

`dataDim.height / SIZE,`

to give us the approximate vertical spacing between lines, and we set the `double` variable `unitX` to

`(appletDim.width - dataDim.width - 10.0) / DATA_MAX`

to give us the width in pixels of a single unit of data.

```
public void paint(Graphics g)
{
        // Determine the approximate height of each
        // data field and the size of each unit of data.
        int unitY = dataDim.height / SIZE;
        double unitX = (appletDim.width - dataDim.width - 10.0) /
                            DATA_MAX;
```

We update the display by using a loop that iterates over all lines, from top to bottom. Within the loop, we first update the data TextField, and then we use unitX and unitY to erase the old line (by drawing a line the full width of the painting region in the background color) and draw the new one in red.

```
for (int i = 0; i < SIZE; i++)
{
        // Update the i-th display,
        display[i].setText("" + data[i]);

        // Erase the old i-th line.
        g.setColor(this.getBackground());
        g.drawLine(dataDim.width + 10,
            unitY / 2 + i * unitY,
            dataDim.width + 10 + (int)(unitX * DATA_MAX),
            unitY / 2 + i * unitY);

        // Draw the new i-th line.
        g.setColor(Color.red);
        g.drawLine(dataDim.width + 10,
            unitY / 2 + i * unitY,
            dataDim.width + 10 + (int)(unitX * data[i]),
            unitY / 2 + i * unitY);
    }
}
```

The heart of this applet is the action() handler. Note how we've factored out all the real work into the helper methods doSortChoice(), doReset(), and doSort().

```
public boolean action(Event e, Object arg)
{
    if (e.target == sortChoice)
    {
        String whichSort = (String)arg;
        doSortChoice(whichSort);
        return true;
    }
    else if (e.target == reset)
    {
        doReset();
        return true;
```

```
        }
        else if (e.target == sort)
        {
            doSort();
            return true;
        }
        return false;
    }
```

In the doSortChoice() method, we handle a selection of the Choice widget by simply setting currentSortMethod to one of the two applet constants, based on the String we got from the arg argument of action().

```
private void doSortChoice(String s)
// Choose the selected sorting algorithm by setting
// currentSortMethod to the appropriate constant.
{
    if (s.equals("Selection"))
        currentSortMethod = SELECTION;
    else if (s.equals("Shell"))
        currentSortMethod = SHELL;
}
```

The doReset() method handles the response to a click on the reset Button. We reset each data element by calling the Math class method random(). As we showed in Chapter 5, this method returns a double value, randomly chosen in the range 0.0 to 1.0. We multiply this by DATA_MAX to get a random double in the range 0.0 to DATA_MAX, and we cast that to an int and place it in data[i]. Having reset the data, all we have to do is erase the entire line drawing area and force our changes to appear by calling repaint().

```
private void doReset()
// Reset all data items to random values (0-100), and
// clear the drawing area.
{
    for (int i = 0; i < SIZE; i++)
        data[i] = (int) (Math.random() * DATA_MAX);

    Graphics g = getGraphics();
    g.clearRect(dataDim.width + 1, 0,
            appletDim.width - dataDim.width - 1,
            appletDim.height - dataDim.height);
    repaint();
}
```

The last of the action() helper methods is doSort(), called into action when the user clicks the sort Button. All we do here is look up the currentSortMethod variable and use it in a switch statement to invoke one of the two sorting methods.

```
private void doSort()
// Call the chosen sorting routine.
{
     switch (currentSortMethod)
     {
     case SELECTION:
          selectionSort(data);
          break;
     case SHELL:
          shellSort(data);
          break;
     }
}
```

The class declaration concludes with the two sort methods and the helper method insertionSort() that we use to define shellSort(). We've described these methods in Section 8.3—the only added features are the calls to the method redrawAndPause(), the last method declared in this class. As originally written, these sort methods work far too rapidly for us to watch them in action; redrawAndPause() causes the applet to delay long enough for us to watch what happens. To get a fair comparison, we call this method after every comparison and after every data move.

```
private void selectionSort(int[] a)
// Perform a Selection Sort on the argument array.
{
     for (int i = 0; i < a.length - 1; i++)
     {
          int minPos = i;
          // Find the smallest remaining element.
          for (int j = i + 1; j < a.length; j++)
          {
               if (a[j] < a[minPos])
                    minPos = j;

               redrawAndPause();
          }
          // Swap current element with the smallest remaining.
          int temp = a[i];
          a[i] = a[minPos];
          a[minPos] = temp;

          redrawAndPause();
     }
}

private void insertionSort(int[] a, int k)
// Perform an Insertion k-Sort on the  argument array.
// When this completes, each k-separated sublist is sorted.
```

```
        // Calling this with k equal to 1 results in ordinary
        // Insertion Sort.
        {
            for (int i = k; i < a.length; i++)
            {
                int currentValue = a[i];
                int index = i;
                while ((index >= k) && (currentValue < a[index - k]))
                {
                    a[index] = a[index - k];
                    index -= k;

                    redrawAndPause();
                }
                a[index] = currentValue;

                redrawAndPause();
            }
        }


    private void shellSort(int[] a)
    // Perform a Shell Sort on the  argument array.
    {
        int increment = a.length / 2;
        while (increment >= 1)
        {
            insertionSort(a, increment);
            increment /= 2;
        }
    }
```

The `redrawAndPause()` method first forces a repaint and then enters a loop whose sole purpose is to waste time. It iterates DELAY times and at each iteration does a dummy statement, copying the index value into a variable.

This is an inelegant way of making an applet delay. In fact, you may discover that it doesn't work at all on your system—you may not see any changes until the sorting is finished. When we talk about threads in Chapter 11 you'll see a much more reliable way of animating this applet. In the lab exercises, we'll give you a taste of what's to come.

```
    private void redrawAndPause()
    // Redraw the applet and pause in a "busy wait" loop.
    {
        repaint();
        long s;
        for (long t = 0; t < DELAY; t++)
            s = t;
    }
}
```

8.6   SUMMARY

❦ We discussed the following classes.

```
Boolean
Character
Double
Float
Integer
String
```

❦ The do loop is written

```
do
      statement
while (boolean expression);          // We need the semicolon here
```

It causes the statement to be executed repeatedly, as long as the boolean expression is `true`. The exit test is performed at the end of each loop iteration.

❦ The `while` loop is written

```
while (boolean expression)
      statement
```

It causes the statement to be executed repeatedly, as long as the boolean expression is `true`. The exit test is performed at the start of each loop iteration.

❦ The `for` loop is written

```
for (initStatement; testExpression; iterationExpression)
      statement
```

It does the following things.

1. It performs the `initStatement` (if any) once, before starting the loop.
2. The `testExpression` is evaluated at the start of each pass through the loop. If it is `false`, control passes out of the loop, down to the next statement after the loop.
3. If the `testExpression` is true, the loop body statement is performed.
4. After performing the loop body, the `iterationExpression` (if any) is executed.
5. Finally, control passes back to step 2.

❦ In each of the loop statements, the statement body can be any statement, simple or compound.

❦ If the statement body of a loop is another loop, the inner loop iterates most rapidly.

❦ There's almost never a good reason to place a semicolon immediately after a loop header.

🐛 Any variable declared within a `for` loop has local scope: It has meaning only within the loop.

🐛 Whenever you design a loop, make very sure the test expression will eventually become `false`, no matter what happens.

🐛 Loops that are controlled by counting (i.e., that are known to iterate a fixed number of times) are best written with a `for` statement. Loops that are controlled by some logical condition (i.e., that will iterate as long as some condition is satisfied) should be written with `while` or `do` loops. If there is a possibility that the loop's body will never be executed, use a `while` loop. If the body must be executed at least once, you should consider using a `do` loop.

🐛 An array is an indexed list of elements of the same type.

🐛 Java arrays always begin with index 0.

🐛 An array in Java may be declared in two equivalent forms:

```
typeName variableName[];
typeName[] variableName;
```

🐛 An array declaration does not allocate space in memory for the array. To do that, the array must be initialized by

```
variableName = new typeName[integerValue];
```

🐛 It's a good idea to combine declaration and initialization of arrays, like this:

```
double[] myArray = new double[10];
```

🐛 Remember, array indices begin at 0. Declaring

```
int[] nums = new int[4];
```

constructs an array with elements `nums[0]`, `nums[1]`, `nums[2]`, and `nums[3]`.

🐛 An array's elements may be initialized by providing their values within a comma-separated list enclosed within braces, as in

```
nums = {2, 100, -3, 8};
```

🐛 You can initialize an array and let the compiler determine its size, as in

```
int[] nums = {2, 100, -3, 8};
```

🐛 The initialization form works for classes, as in

```
Button controls[] = {new Button("Left"), new Button("Up"),
                new Button("Down"), new Button("Right")};
```

❦ Once you have declared and initialized an array variable, you may inspect and modify its elements by using the variable name followed by a pair of square brackets containing an integer expression.

❦ Java will check the legality of array indices at run-time and will generate an error if the value of the expression within the square brackets is less than 0 or greater than or equal to the length of the array.

❦ Every array has a public field, `length`, that contains the number of elements in the array.

❦ An array element may be used anywhere a variable of the base type may be used.

❦ An extremely common use of loops is to iterate through the elements of an array.

❦ Arrays are like classes, in that if an array is used as a method argument, the elements of the array may be modified by the method.

❦ In Java you can implement a multidimensional array by using an array of arrays, like

```
double table[][] = new double[4][3];
```

❦ To initialize a multidimensional array, you can use nested initializations, like

```
double table[][] = {{0.0, 0.1, 0.2}, {1.0, 1.1, 1.2},
                    {2.0, 2.1, 2.2}, {3.1, 3.0, 3.2}};
```

❦ Using inheritance, you can make an array of objects whose elements are of different types, as long as all types are subclasses of the element type.

❦ In Selection Sort, the element in position i is found by searching all the elements in positions $j \geq i$ for the smallest. This smallest element is then swapped with the element at position i.

❦ The invariant property of Selection Sort is that at at the end of iteration i, all the elements in positions at or before i are in their corect locations.

❦ Insertion Sort is performed by inserting the element in position i in sorted order among the earlier positions.

❦ The invariant property in Insertion Sort is that at the end of iteration i, all the elements in positions at or before i are in sorted order.

❦ Selection Sort and Insertion Sort both require no more than a fixed multiple of N^2 steps to sort a list of N elements.

❦ Shellsort uses Insertion Sort on sublists where each element is a set distance from the next. At the end of each pass, all of the k-separated lists are in sorted order. The increments k decrease at each pass, ending with 1 (which is just ordinary Insertion Sort).

❦ Shellsort is, in general, more efficient than either Selection Sort or Insertion Sort.

❦ A `String` instance is a list of characters. Once it has been created, a `String` cannot be modified. The `String` class is a `final` class—it cannot be subclassed.

❦ There is an order on `Strings`, derived from the underlying order on Unicode characters. In this lexicographic order, the empty `String` is less than any other, "BRAIN" is less than "BRAWN", and "BEE" is less than "BEEKEEPER".

❦ `Strings` may be manipulated by generating an array of `chars` from the `String`, manipulating that array, and creating a new `String` result from the array.

❦ Every class has a method `toString()` that can convert an instance of that class to a String representation. For primitive types, the `static String` method `valueOf()` will convert a primitive type valuye to a `String` representation.

❦ The wrapper classes `Boolean`, `Character`, `Integer`, `Float`, `Long`, and `Double` contain methods that can be used to convert appropriately formed Strings to instances of the corresponding wrapper class type.

8.7 EXERCISES

1. In the following segments, identify and correct any syntax errors. Don't worry about whether the code does anything useful—you're interested here only in whether the segments will compile. You may assume that all variables have been declared and initialized.

   a.
   ```
   while n != -1
       sum = sum + n;
       n--;
   ```

   b.
   ```
   do
   {
       n--;
   } while ((n > 0) && (n % 2 != 0))
   ```

   c.
   ```
   do
       g += g;
   while (h <= 0);
   ```

   d.
   ```
   for (int i = 0; i < 10;)
       s *= 2;
   ```

2. Once you've made the necessary corrections in the segments of Exercise 1, tell which loops, if any, may never terminate.

3. The `for` loops you've seen so far all increase the index variable by 1 at each iteration. There are times, though, that you might want other sequences. Write `for` loops where the index variable takes the following values.
   a. 10, 9, 8, 7, 6, 5, 4, 3, 2, 1
   b. 1, 2, 4, 8, 16, 32, 64, 128, 256, 512
   c. 1, 4, 13, 40, 121, 364, 1093

4. Assume that S is a statement and that b is a boolean expression.

    a. Using a `while` statement and anything else you might need, write the equivalent of

```
do
    S
while (b);
```

    b. Using a `do` statement and anything else you might need, write the equivalent of

```
while (b)
    S
```

5. Write a method `double power(double x, int n)` that returns x^n.

    a. Assume that n will always be greater than or equal to 0.

    b. Don't assume that n will always be greater than or equal to 0.

6. Write a method `int sumOdds(int n)` that will return the sum of the first n odd integers. For example, if n is 4, the method would return $1 + 3 + 5 + 7 = 16$. If n is less than or equal to 0, the method should return 0.

7. (Tricky) Do Exercise 6 without using a loop.

8. Look at the attempts to write `prefixSum()` on pages 340–343. For the following new attempts, comment on whether they are correct and, if so, whether they are clearer or less clear than Attempt 3.

    a.
```
int prefixSum(int[] a)
{
    int sum = 0;
    for (int i = 0; (i < a.length) && (a[i] >= 0); i++)
        sum += a[i];
    return sum;
}
```

    b.
```
int prefixSum(int[] a)
{
    int    i = 0,
           sum = 0;
    boolean done = false;
    do
    {
        if ((i < a.length) && (a[i] >= 0))
            sum += a[i];
        else
            done = true;
    } while (!done);
```

```
                    return sum;
            }


    c.      int prefixSum(int[] a)
            {
                    int   i = 0,
                          sum = 0;
                    while (true)
                    {
                            if ((i < a.length) && (a[i] >= 0))
                                    sum += a[i++];
                            else
                                    return sum;
                    }
            }
```

9.   In the following loops, how often is the statement s executed?
     a. `for (int i = 0; i < 5; i++)`
             `    for (int j = 0; j < 5; j++)`
             `        s;`

     b. `for (int i = 0; i < 5; i++)`
             `    for (int j = i; j < 5; j++)`
             `        s;`

     c. `for (int i = 0; i < 5; i++)`
             `    for (int j = i; j < 5 - i; j++)`
             `        s;`

10. You can find the square root of a nonnegative number n without using the
     Math routine `sqrt()` by performing the segment

```
double a = n;
while (Math.abs(a * a - n) < 1.0e-8)
        a = a - (a * a - n) / (2.0 * a);
```

     In this segment, we do the loop until the answer a has a square that is within
     0.00000001 of n. This technique is known as *Newton's method,* and the nice
     part about it is how fast it works. Try it, writing the current value of a at each
     iteration and see how many iterations it takes to compute the square root of 100
     to eight places. Try it again, this time to find the square root of 10000.

11. (Tricky) The *harmonic series,* $1 + 1/2 + 1/3 + 1/4 + \ldots + 1/n$ increases
     without limit as n increases. Eventually, for example, it will become larger
     than 30. You could find out how many terms it would take for the series to
     become larger than 30 by writing the following code.

```
double sum = 0.0;
int n = 0;
do
{
     n++;
     sum += 1.0 / n;
} while (sum < 30.0);
System.out.println("It took " + n + " terms to get over 30.");
```

This won't work, though. Why?

12. The following loop takes a number, n, assumed to be composed only of the digits 0 and 1, and sets num equal to the decimal equivalent of n, so if n was 1101, the loop would set num to 13. Fill in the boolean expression to control the loop.

```
int num = 0;
int power = 1;
while (_____)
{
     digit = n % 10; // Get the rightmost digit of n.
     num += power * digit;
     power = 2 * power;
     n = n / 10;      // Remove the rightmost digit from n.
}
```

13. Write the method int digits(int n), that counts the number of digits in n. Hint: look at Exercise 12.

14. **a.** Write the method

```
int reverse(int n)
```

that reverses n, so that reverse(4723) returns 3247. This is a tricky problem. It involves extracting the digits from the right of n and building the reverse by using these digits as they come in. Look at Exercise 12 for a hint.

b. Use reverse() to write the method

```
boolean isPalindrome(int n)
```

that returns true if and only if n is a *palindrome* (i.e., reads the same left to right as right to left, as do 454 and 3333).

c. An interesting problem that appeared on *Square One* (a Public Broadcasting System show about mathematics for kids) is the following.

Take a starting number, *n,* add it to its reverse, and continue this process until the result is a palindrome. For example, starting with 95, we add it to its reverse to get 95 + 59 = 154. Add this to its reverse and we get 154 + 451 = 605. Add this to its reverse and we have 605 + 506 = 1111, which is a palindrome, after three iterations. Write a program to count the number of iterations this process takes to produce a palindrome and try it for some starting values. You might want to use the `long` type, instead of `int`s, since the numbers can get pretty big. For example, starting with value 98 takes 24 iterations and results in the palindrome 8813200023188, which won't fit in an `int`. Don't even think about trying it on 295—if that ever results in a palindrome, the result is at least 3200 digits long. Does the process always result in a palindrome for any starting value?

15. The following method is supposed to return the index of the first instance of repeated numbers in an array of `int`s. For example, when give the array {2, 8, 6, 6, 10, 6, 7, 7, 7, 3, 9}, the method would return 2, the index of the start of the (6, 6) pair. The method is to return −1 if there are no adjacent equal numbers. The following method doesn't work correctly. Why?

```
int firstRepeat(int[] a)
{
    int i = 0;
    while ((i < a.length - 1) && (a[i] != a[i + 1]))
        i++;

    if (a[i] != a[i + 1])
        return -1;
    else
        return i;
}
```

16. A sequence of increments for Shellsort that has been shown to perform well is 1, 4, 13, 40, 121, 364, . . . , where each term is three times the preceding term, plus 1. To use this version of Shellsort for a list of size *N,* you add a preliminary step, computing the sequence and stopping as soon as the value is greater than or equal to *N*. Then, drop back to the previous value of the sequence (that's easy, once you see the trick) and use that for your first increment. Subsequent increments are just the earlier terms in the sequence. Write this new version of Shellsort.

17. Here are two lists of integers. One is 2-sorted, and the other isn't. Which is which? Explain.
    a. 4, 2, 19, 21, 24, 23, 35, 48, 44
    b. 6, 7, 11, 28, 29, 31, 22, 32, 36

18. If a list is 2-sorted, is it necessarily 4-sorted? If so, explain why; if not, give an example of a 2-sorted list that's not 4-sorted.

19. Suppose that $k > n > 0$. If a list is n-sorted, is it necessarily k-sorted? If so, explain why; if not, give a counterexample.

20. For any list of numbers, we can measure how far each element is from its correct location by simply taking the absolute value of the difference between its index and its place in the sorted order. For example, in the list 15, 23, 8, 30, 16, 48, 11, 6, 9, element 15 is in index 0 and would be in position 4 when the list was finally sorted, so 15 is $|0 - 4| = 4$ places from where it should be.

We can extend this to a measure of the "unsortedness" of a list by adding the differences we computed for each element. For example, here's a list and the "misplacement numbers" for each element.

```
element:        15    23    8     30    16    48    11    6     9
index:          0     1     2     3     4     5     6     7     8
sorted index:   4     6     1     7     5     8     3     0     2
difference:     4     5     1     4     1     3     3     7     6
```

Adding the bottom row, we can say that the list has unsortedness $4 + 5 + 1 + 4 + 1 + 3 + 3 + 7 + 6 = 34$.

a. What's the unsortedness of a sorted list?

b. For a list with nine elements, like the one shown, what is the largest possible value the unsortedness number can be?

c. (Hard) Prove that the unsortedness number of a list of size n is always less than or equal to $n^2 / 2$.

21. For the illustrations of Selection Sort and Insertion Sort in Figures 8.5 and 8.7, give the unsortedness (defined in Exercise 20) of the list at each step. Generally speaking, both sorting methods reduce the unsortedness number, but they do so in different ways. In one of the methods, for instance, the unsortedness number of the list tends to decrease slowly at first and then much more rapidly at the end. Come up with some "high-level" descriptions of how each of Selection Sort and Insertion Sort effect the unsortedness number of a list.

22. Suppose that s is the `String` "flabbergasted" and that t is the `String` "berg". What are the values of the following expressions?

a. `s.indexOf('s')`

b. `s.indexOf(t)`

c. `s.lastIndexOf('e')`

d. `length(s.concat(s))`

e. `s.indexOf(s.substring(1, 4))`

f. `s.compareTo(s)`

g. `s.compareTo(t)`

h. `t.compareTo(s)`

i. `s.compareTo(s.concat(t))`

j. `valueOf(s.equals(t))`

k. `s.substring(0, 2) + s.substring(2)`

23. Each of the following pictures illustrates a sorting algorithm at an intermediate stage, as we might see while watching the Sortmeister Lablet. Identify each as Selection Sort, Insertion Sort, or Shellsort. Explain the reasons for your choices.

a.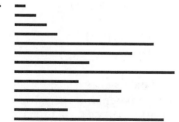

b.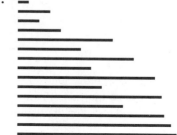

c.

24. For the String method

```
getChars(int start, int end, char[], int cStart),
```

what conditions on start, end, the length of the string, the length of the array, and the value of cStart must be satisfied for the call to succeed?

25. Rewrite Insertion Sort so that it sorts an array of Strings.

26. *Planit reduction* transforms English words into a coded form by using the following rules, in order.

(1) Replace each character in the word, using the following rules:

A, E, I, O, U, Y → A
B, F, P, V → B
C, G, K, J, Q, S, X, Z → C
D, T → D
H, W → H
L → L
M, N → M
R → R

(2) For any consonant that's followed by an H, eliminate the H, so that DH would be replaced by D, for instance.

(3) Replace any repeated sequence of consonants by a single instance. For example, MM would be replaced by M.

(4) Finally, eliminate all the A's. For example, the planit reduction of THINNING is

$$\begin{aligned} \text{THINNING} &\rightarrow \text{DHAMMAMC, after step (1)} \\ &\rightarrow \text{DAMMAMC, after step (2)} \\ &\rightarrow \text{DAMAMC, after step (3)} \\ &\rightarrow \text{DMMMC, after step (4)} \end{aligned}$$

Planit reduction is useful in automated dictionaries, since variant spellings often have the same Planit reduction. Write a program to perform Planit reduction and test it on the strings THEIR, THERE, THEYRE, and EITHER.

27. Write a program that will take a text string and produce a classified ad by deleting all lowercase vowels. For example, given the source string (in a `TextArea`, for instance)

> 1989 Ferrari Testarossa. Auto, air, awesome stereo.
> Some minor body damage, mostly small holes.
> Contact Sonny, this paper, box MH1765.

the program will produce

> 1989 Frrr Tstrss. At, r, wsm str.
> Sm mnr bdy dmg, mstly smll hls.
> Cntct Snny, ths ppr, bx MH1765.

(Clearly, this algorithm needs some fixing. We particularly like what happens to "Ferrari" and "air.")

28. **a.** Write a method,

```
String numToWord(String s)
```

that takes a `String` argument representing an integer between 0 and 9999 and returns the word equivalent. For example, for s = "423", the method would return the `String` "four hundred twenty-three".

b. Use `numToWord()` in an applet that gets a `String` from the user and replaces the numbers with words. For example, the sentence "John had 130 hogs that he traded for 4091 guinea pigs." would produce the output "John had one hundred thirty hogs that he traded for four thousand ninety-one guinea pigs."

29. Write the method `String reverse(String s)` that returns the reverse of its argument, producing "rotagilla" from "alligator," for instance.

30. a. Write a method,

```
boolean isPalindrome(String s)
```

that returns `true` if and only if the argument is a *palindrome*—that is, it is the same as its reverse, like "pop" and "toot."

b. Extend `isPalindrome()` so that it ignores all nonletters and isn't sensitive to case, so, for example, it would recognize "Madam, I'm Adam." as a palindrome.

31. A simple way of encoding a message is the *railfence cypher.* In this scheme, we first make a string from the original by extracting all the characters in the even positions and then append the string we get from the original's odd-index characters. For example, in the string "FOOLEDYOUDIDNTI" we have the even-position characters "FOEYUINI" and the odd-position characters "OLDODDT". Concatenating these character sets gives the encoded string "FOEYUINIOLDODDT."

a. Write a method that takes a `String` argument and returns the string that results from applying the railfence cypher.

b. The railfence cypher has the interesting property that, if it is applied repeatedly to a string, eventually the original string is produced. The number of repetitions needed to get back to the original depends on the length of the string. For instance, for strings of length 2, one iteration of the cypher obviously leaves the string unchanged; for strings of length 32, five iterations suffice, whereas strings of length 30 take 28 iterations. Write a program to investigate the number of iterations of the railfence cypher it takes to bring a string back to its original form. What conclusions can you draw?

CHAPTER NINE

Exceptions

An inescapable fact of life is that *things go wrong*. This fact raises its ugly head so often during the execution of programs that we seriously considered adding a subtitle to the title of this chapter: "When bad things happen to good programs." Even if you design a program with utmost care, verifying that every method works exactly as it should and that all the classes coordinate their actions smoothly, there will still be things that can cause your beautifully wrought code to go down in flames. For example, you have no control over how your classes will be used (or misused) by other programmers, and you can't possibly guarantee that all the users of your program will know precisely what you expect them to do. Fortunately, Java provides powerful error-handling facilities that can be used to make your programs respond gracefully when the inevitable excrement hits the ventilator.

OBJECTIVES

In this chapter, we will
- ❦ Introduce the `Exception` classes.
- ❦ Review some methods that can generate exceptions.
- ❦ Discuss Java's techniques for dealing with exceptions.
- ❦ Show you how to invent exceptions of your own.

9.1 EXCEPTIONAL CONDITIONS

Things can go wrong during the execution of a program that can't possibly be detected at compile-time. Suppose, for instance, that your program includes the statement

offset = x / n;

for `int` variables `offset`, `x`, and `y`. Now, there's not a thing wrong with this statement from the compiler's point of view—it's a garden-variety expression statement. However, during execution of the program, n might have the value 0. This is an exceptional state of affairs, since there's no reasonable way to define int division by zero. Java then indicates that something unusual and problematic has happened by *throwing an exception*. In effect, what then happens is that an internal alarm bell goes off, indicating to the run-time system that emergency action must be taken. The system then immediately halts its normal mode of execution and goes looking for help. With luck, the system will find some code in your program that will *catch* the exception and deal with it, perhaps by displaying an error message or taking some other action, like setting offset to some default value. Once the exception has been caught, the alarm bell is silenced and the system picks up execution at a location after the block that contained the offending statement.

Note how this technique differs from the error handling you're used to. In the old way, you would write code to head off the error before it occurred, probably by writing a guard like this:

```
if (n > 0)                  // Guard against division by 0.
    offset = x / n;         // normal action
else
    offset = 10;            // error-state action
```

Using exceptions, you would allow the unusual situation to be noted and take steps elsewhere in your program to deal with it. As so often happens in programming, there's no simple reason to prefer one strategy over the other. You'll see shortly that both techniques for dealing with exceptional situations have their advantages and disadvantages.

Exception Subclasses

There are thirty-three kinds of exceptions in Java 1.0, and version 1.1 adds nearly twenty more. All these classes are derived from the class Exception, which is itself a subclass of Throwable, as we illustrate in Figure 9.1. The Throwable class is also a superclass of Error and its subclasses. We won't discuss dealing with errors, since they usually arise from situations, like running out of memory, that are beyond the power of your program to handle.

Exceptions, however, are used to indicate situations that you generally will be able to handle, like trying to access a character in an illegal String location. A list of some of the more common Exception subclasses follows.

java.lang.**ArithmeticException**
Indicates that something, like division by zero, has gone wrong in an arithmetic expression.

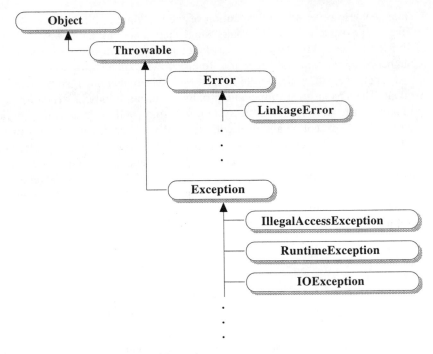

Figure 9.1 Part of the `Throwable` hierarchy.

`java.lang.`**`ArrayIndexOutOfBoundsException`**
Indicates that an attempt has been made to access an element in an invalid index in an array (less than 0 or greater than or equal to the array length, for instance).

`java.lang.`**`ArrayStoreException`**
Indicates that an attempt has been made to place an element of the wrong type into an array.

`java.io.`**`EOFException`**
Indicates that an end-of-file mark has been seen. We'll talk about files and the `java.io` package in Chapter 10.

`java.io.`**`FileNotFoundException`**
Indicates that a reference has been made to a file that could not be found.

`java.lang.`**`IllegalArgumentException`**
Indicates a method call with an invalid argument. This is the parent class of `IllegalThreadStateException` and `NumberFormatException`.

`java.lang.`**`IllegalThreadStateException`**
Indicates that a thread is in an inappropriate state for some method call. We'll explain threads in Chapter 11.

`java.lang.`**`IndexOutOfBoundsException`**
> Indicates that an index is out of bounds. This is the parent class of `Array-IndexOutOfBoundsException` and `StringIndexOutOfBoundsException`.

`java.lang.`**`InterruptedException`**
> Indicates that a thread has been interrupted.

`java.io.`**`InterruptedIOException`**
> Indicates that an input or output operation has been interrupted.

`java.io.`**`IOException`**
> Indicates a general input/output exception.

`java.net.`**`MalformedURLException`**
> Indicates an improperly formed URL. We'll discuss the `java.net` package in Chapter 12.

`java.lang.`**`NegativeArraySizeException`**
> Indicates that an attempt has been made to declare an array with a negative size specification.

`java.lang.`**`NullPointerException`**
> Indicates that a class method is being called by an instance that is currently `null`.

`java.lang.`**`NumberFormatException`**
> Indicates that an illegal number format is being used, often as the argument to a method.

`java.lang.`**`StringIndexOutOfBoundsException`**
> Indicates that an attempt has been made to use an inappropriate `String` index.

The `Exception` class itself is very simple. It consists of only two constructors.

`Exception``()`
`Exception``(String message)`
> Both construct a new `Exception` instance. The second constructor allows you to specify a message string as part of the instance. This string could be used to provide details about the nature of the exception, for example. To retrieve the message, you can use the parent class `Throwable`'s method `getMessage()`, which returns the message, if any, associated with the exception. You generally won't construct a new `Exception`—instead, you'll use one of the subclass constructors, with or without a message `String`. As you'll see shortly, you can subclass `Exception` to make exceptions of your own, defining your own constructors.

Methods That Throw Exceptions

Many of the methods we've discussed throw exceptions. Since we've not made use of that fact so far, it's clear that a Java program doesn't have to deal with exceptions. Now that you know they exist, we'll provide a fairly complete list of the methods we've covered that do throw exceptions.

Choice:
```
void add(String s)                          // version 1.1
void addItem(String s)
```
       Throw a `NullPointerException` if the argument is `null` (i.e., hasn't been initialized).

```
String getItem(int index)
void insert(String item, int index)     // version 1.1
void remove(String item)                // version 1.1
void select(int index)
```
       Throw an `IllegalArgumentException` if the index is out of range or the argument of `remove()` isn't in this `Choice`.

Container:
```
void add(Component c)
```
       Throws an `IllegalArgumentException` if you attempt to add this `Container` to itself. All the `Component add()` methods have this property.

Dialog:
```
Dialog(Frame parent)
```
       All the `Dialog` constructors throw an `IllegalArgumentException` if the `parent` argument is `null`.

Double:
```
static Double valueOf(String s)
```
       Throws a `NumberFormatException` if the argument doesn't represent a valid `double`.

Float:
```
static Float valueOf(String s)
```
       Throws a `NumberFormatException` if the argument doesn't represent a valid `float`.

Integer:
```
static int parseInt(String s)
static Integer valueOf(String s)
```
       Throw a `NumberFormatException` if the argument doesn't represent a valid `int`. We haven't talked about `parseInt()` yet, though we will shortly.

Label:
```
void setAlignment(int alg)
```
Throws an `IllegalArgumentException` if the argument isn't one of the class constants `Label.LEFT`, `Label.CENTER`, or `Label.RIGHT`.

List:
```
void remove(String item)                    // version 1.1
```
Throws an `IllegalArgumentException` if the `item` argument isn't in this `List`.

Long:
```
static long parseLong(String s)
static Long valueOf(String s)
```
Throw a `NumberFormatException` if the argument doesn't represent a valid `long`.

String:
```
String(String s)
String(char[] c)
int compareTo(String s)
String concat(String s)
boolean endsWith(String s)
int indexOf(String s)
int lastIndexOf(String s)
boolean startsWith(String s)
```
Throw a `NullPointerException` if the argument is `null`.

```
char charAt(int index)
void getChars(int start, int end, char[] c, int cStart)
String substring(int index)
String substring(int start, int end)
```
Throw a `StringIndexOutOfBoundsException` if one or more of the arguments doesn't represent a valid index in this `String`. In addition, `getChars()` will throw a `NullPointerException` if the array argument is `null`.

TextArea:
```
void setColumns(int c)                       // version 1.1
void setRows(int r)                          // version 1.1
```
Throw an `IllegalArgumentException` if the argument is negative. The `TextField` method `setColumns()` also does this

9.2   HANDLING EXCEPTIONS

The process of dealing with exceptions in Java includes some nitpicking details, but the basic idea is simple: You indicate your intention to handle an exception by marking the block where the exception could be raised. Then you include some code that will only be called into action when the need arises to deal with the exception. If the exception doesn't arise, Java simply ignores the extra code.

`try` and `catch`

The keyword `try` is used before a *block* of statements (i.e., a collection of zero or more statements within braces) that can throw an exception. Putting `try` before a block of code indicates that you have the intention of handling some or all of the exceptions that are thrown within the block. If no exceptions are raised while the statements are executing in the block, no special action is taken, as if the `try` weren't there.[1]

Syntax: `try` Block

A `try` block is written as

```
try
{
    // Code that might raise an exception.
}
```

Once you've indicated by a `try` block that you intend to handle some exceptions, the next step is to follow the `try` block with one or more `catch` clauses. A `catch` clause consists of a segment of code that looks very much like a method declaration, with a formal argument and a statement body enclosed in braces.

Syntax: `catch` Clause

A `catch` clause is written as

```
catch (ExceptionType variable)
{
    // code to handle the exception, perhaps using variable
    // The variable has meaning only within this block.
}
```

If no exception is raised during execution of a `try` block, its associated `catch` clauses are skipped. However, if an exception is raised in the `try` block

---

[1]We're simplifying things a bit here. You'll see why when we talk about the `finally` clause at the end of this section.

and a subsequent `catch` clause is compatible with the exception type, control immediately passes out of the `try` block to the appropriate `catch` clause. The statements in the `catch` block are then executed and control passes to the first statement after the `try` block (ignoring any subsequent `catch` clauses). The division by zero example we used in Section 9.1 would be handled as follows.

```
try
{
    offset = x / n;
    // anything from here down will be ignored if n is 0.
}
catch (ArithmeticException e)
{
    offset = 10;
}
// Here's where execution picks up again after handling the
// exception.
```

A couple of important facts are worth mentioning here. First, because of the semantics of `try..catch`, you can assume that, if a statement in the `try` block is executed, none of the previous statements raised any exceptions because once control passes out of a try block it doesn't return.[2] Second, the `catch` clauses are examined from the top down, stopping at the first one that has an argument compatible with the exception thrown (in the usual sense of argument compatibility) and skipping all subsequent clauses. Thus you should list your `catch` clauses in order from most to least specific. For example, the following code would be a waste of effort, as the second `catch` clause would never be executed.

```
try
{
    ...
}
catch (Exception e)                  // This argument type is assignment
                                     // compatible with every exception,
{
    ...
}
catch (ArithmeticException e)        // so this would never be used.
{
    ...
}
```

A `try` block must be followed immediately by one or more `catch` clauses, and neither can exist on its own. You can't write a `try` block without following it with a `catch` clause, and you can't write a collection of `catch` clauses without an immediately preceding `try` block.

---

[2]Unless control enters the block from the top later in the usual course of execution, as it might in a loop, for example.

Exception Propagation

Suppose an exception occurs outside a `try` block or within a `try` block that's not associated with a `catch` clause of a compatible kind. What happens to the exception then?

If an exception is raised within a `try` block, the system first looks for an associated `catch` clause that can handle it. If none of the `catch` arguments are assignment compatible with the exception (i.e., none are superclasses of the exception), the system looks for an enclosing `try..catch` pair. For example, since any statement can appear in a `try` block, the program might look like this:

```
try
{
    ...
    try
    {
        // exception raised here
    }
    catch (SomeException e)
    {
        // but not caught here
    }
}
catch (SomeOtherException e)
{
        // so look here
}
```

This search continues until it comes to the block enclosing the entire method body. If no compatible `catch` clause is found, the search is widened to include the block containing the method call:

```
void oops()
{
    try
    {
        // exception generated
    }
    catch (SomeException e)
    {
        // but not caught
    }
}

...
```

```
// We're in some other method here, where the original
// call was made to oops(), the method that caused the exception
// in the first place.
try
{
    oops();              // Exception generated by this call
                         // wasn't caught in oops(),
}
catch (SomeOtherException e)
{
                         // so look here, after having looked in
                         // the code of oops().
}
```

If there still isn't a match, the process continues, outward through blocks and backward through method calls (and their enclosing blocks), until a `catch` clause can be found. The same sort of behavior applies to an exception that isn't raised within a try block—the search begins at the block enclosing the offending statement and continues outward and backward through method calls until the system finds a handler for the exception.

Eventually, a handler for the exception will be found. Where? In the Java environment itself. The reason is that, if you trace backward through the method calls that got you to a statement, sooner or later you'll find a method that Java itself called, since *it is impossible to run an applet or application except through a call made by Java.* Think about it—an application begins execution at `main()`, and an applet begins with `init()` (or a similar call, to `paint()`, for instance). Do you make those calls? Nope—the Java environment does.

Of course, if you haven't provided an exception handler somewhere along the line, Java will terminate the program. That's not always a bad idea—if a method is called by an object that hasn't been initialized, for example, there's really nothing you can do about the resulting `NullPointerException`, so it's best not to catch it at all and simply let the program die a horrible death.

Throwing Exceptions

There will be times when you want to generate an exception under your control, rather than passively sitting back and letting Java generate them for you. You can do that by using a `throw` statement.

Syntax: throw Statement

A `throw` statement has the following form:

throw *exceptionInstance;*

When a `throw` statement is executed, the `exceptionInstance` is sent off to the runtime environment, in the same way an exception is generated by Java when it encounters something like an array index out of bounds. Your program could then use a `try..catch` collection to deal with the exception in the usual way. Suppose, for instance, that you had a sequence of statements that required the variable n to be even in order to work correctly. You might deal with this precondition by throwing an appropriate exception:

```
// n gets set to some value here
try
{
    if (n % 2 == 1)              // n is odd
            throw new ArithmeticException();
    else
            // The code that requires n to be even is here
}
catch (ArithmeticException e)
{
    // Deal with odd values of n here.
}
```

This is a somewhat contrived example, we'll admit. It would be far simpler to place the code dealing with odd n right inside the first `if` clause, replacing the `throw` statement, and eliminate the `try..catch` construct entirely. You still might want to do it as shown, though, if the "odd n" case was rare and the code for dealing with it was extensive. In that case, putting the exceptional part within the `if` statement would just obscure the sense of what goes on in the vast majority of situations, forcing the reader to wade through dozens of lines before realizing, Oh, this stuff will almost never be done—why did I have to waste time reading it here?

A good use for exceptions is to isolate complicated code that deals with unlikely occurrences. Doing so can make a program easier to read.

When you are designing a method that may throw an exception, you have two choices: You can use a `try..catch` to deal with the exception within the method, or you can let the exception go uncaught and rely on the propagation mechanisms to catch the exception elsewhere. If you take the latter course and let the exception propagate out of the method you should (and in some cases you *must*) indicate to the compiler that your method may perhaps throw an exception that it isn't going to catch itself. To do so, use a `throws` clause in the method header.

Syntax: throws Clause

A `throws` clause may be appended to a method header, like this:

```
void myMethod() throws ExceptionType1, ExceptionType2
```

A `throws` clause may name as many `Exception` types as necessary, separating their names by commas.

Here's an example, a method that indicates it could throw one of two kinds of exceptions, either an `IllegalArgumentException` that is explicitly thrown by one of the statements or a `NullPointerException` that is thrown by `equals()` if the invoking `String` instance is `null`.

```
String wantCookie(String s) throws IllegalArgumentException,
                                    NullPointerException
{
    if (s.equals("Cookie"))
        return "Thanks!";
    else
        throw new IllegalArgumentException("Me want Cookie!");
        // Don't need a return, since you can't get here.
}
```

In fact, this method doesn't actually need the `throws` clause. Java makes a distinction between what are known as "checked" and "unchecked" exceptions and has different requirements for each. A checked exception is one that *must* be declared in a `throws` clause if it could be thrown and not caught within the method. If the method does not declare that the exception will be thrown, the statement that could cause the exception must be placed in a `try` block with an appropriate `catch` clause later. Of the checked exceptions, the ones that you'll be likely to see are

- `InterruptedException`,
- the file exceptions, that is, the subclasses of `IOException`, and
- those that you invent yourself by subclassing `Exception`.

The subclasses of `RuntimeException`, which constitute the most common exceptions, are unchecked and do *not* have to be mentioned in a `throws` clause or thrown from within a `try` block. These include

- `ArithmeticException`,
- `IllegalArgumentException`,
- `NumberFormatException`,

- `IndexOutOfBoundsException` and its two subclasses,
  `ArrayIndexOutOfBounds` and `StringIndexOutOfBounds`,
- `NullPointerException`, and
- those that you invent yourself by subclassing `RuntimeException`.

In making this distinction, the designers of Java were guided by the fact that it would be a major hassle for a programmer to have to remember every possible exception that could be thrown by every statement in a method and then include all of them in a `throws` clause. Therefore they reserved compile-time checking for those that were both rare, easy to locate, and serious.

Advice:

Make life easy on yourself—use a `throws` clause only if a method will throw (and not catch) one of the checked exceptions.

Here's an example of *not* using a `throws` clause. We've designed a subclass, `IntTextField`, of `TextField`. Our intention here is that an `IntTextField` object will contain only a text string that could represent a legal integer. Thus we have to override the superclass's `setText()` method, to check that the user of this class won't try making a call to the `setText()` method of this class by using an argument like "two."
We use the `Integer` wrapper class method:

```
static int parseInt(String s)
```

This method checks the `String` argument to determine whether it is a legal representation of an `int`, like "278." If it is, the method returns the corresponding `int` value, and if it's not, the method throws a `NumberFormatException`. Note that we don't catch the exception, first since it's not clear what we'd do with it if we did catch it, and second because a bad number format is such a serious violation of the `IntTextField` specification that the user of this class should probably be informed that a mistake had been made.

```
class IntTextField extends TextField
{
    . . .

    public void setTheText(String s)
    // NOTE: This method will throw a NumberFormatException if
    // the argument string does not represent a legal int.
    {
        int dummy = Integer.parseInt(s);
        super.setText(s);    // Okay--set the text
    }
}
```

This method, by the way, is an example of *not* being able to use a `throws` clause, even if we wanted to. Doing so would produce a compilation error, for somewhat subtle language design reasons which we won't explain here.

A method override cannot be declared with a `throws` clause that names exceptions not thrown by the parent method.

In our example, the superclass `setText()` method doesn't throw any exceptions, so it would be a syntax error for us to have a `throws` clause in our override.

Prophylactic Programming

A good program is *robust,* which is to say that it handles unusual situations by taking appropriate action, rather than going down in flames. As we mentioned, there are basically two ways to deal with run-time problems—make sure they don't happen in the first place, or let them happen and then deal with the problem.

The first strategy is often implemented by the programmer recognizing a potential problem and guarding against it, often by using a test in an `if` statement. The second strategy, of course, is to write a program so that the problem situation will raise an exception and then to catch the exception and handle it. We'll illustrate the difference between these two approaches by considering the method `mindex()` that we introduced in Chapter 8.

```
int mindex(int[] theArray, int start)
// Returns the index of the smallest element at or after the
// index start.
{
    int minIndex = start;
    for (int i = start; i < theArray.length; i++)
        if (theArray[i] < theArray[minIndex])
            minIndex = i;
    return minIndex;
}
```

Whenever we design any method we should always ask, What is expected to be true when this method is called? The statement of what must be true at the start of a method, or any section of code for that matter, is known as the *precondition.* In the case of `mindex()`, the precondition is simple—the array argument must represent a valid array, and `start` must be a valid index within the array.

The next question we should ask is, Is there any action this method can take to recover if the precondition is violated? In our example, the answer is both yes and no. If the array argument hasn't yet been initialized, there's nothing `mindex()` can do to recover. Because a method with a non-void return must return a value no matter what, there's not even a way to return a default value, like 0. Doing so would violate the *postcondition,* which is to say the condition that is assumed to be true when the method is complete. In our case, the postcondition is that the int returned is the position in the array where a smallest element is to be found. As there is no legal position in a null array, no possible return value could satisfy the postcondition. In short, if the array argument is null, we can't even complete the method. In this case, it's best to let the NullPointerException occur, thereby aborting the method.

Advice:

If there's no possible way of handling a potential error, raise an exception.

In our example, the NullPointerException will be thrown for us. We could throw one ourselves, if we wanted to, providing a diagnostic error message:

```
int mindex(int[] theArray, int start)
{
    if (theArray == null)
        throw new NullPointerException("null array in mindex()");
    ...
}
```

For the other part of our precondition, if the argument start isn't a valid index in the array, we can recover, although we have to change the precondition slightly. If the start index is negative, we can simply set it to 0. If start is greater than the last array index, we can simply make start the last index. We don't need exceptions for this—we can handle everything internally. Our method now looks like the following, where we have also specifically listed the pre- and postconditions:

```
int mindex(int[] theArray, int start)
// Pre: theArray has been initialized.
// Post: (1) if start < the length of the array, returns the index
// of a minimal element at or after position start. (2) if
// start >= the length of the array, returns the last index in the
// array.
{
    // NEW--make sure the index is valid
    if (start < 0)
        start = 0;
    if (start >= theArray.length)
        return theArray.length - 1;        // can leave immediately
```

```
        int minIndex = start;
        for (int i = start; i < theArray.length; i++)
        // For each index in the array...
            if (theArray[i] < theArray[minIndex])
            // Found a new smallest value, so record its index.
                minIndex = i;
        return minIndex;
}
```

Advice:

If you can handle an error simply, do so without raising an exception.

One of the most important reasons for using exceptions sparingly is that, compared to using an `if` statement to detect and handle the bad situations, throwing and catching exceptions is *slow,* often extremely so. In many environments, throwing and catching an exception takes hundreds of times longer than using an `if` statement to do the same thing locally. We'll explore this difference in the exercises.

Advice:

Reserve exceptions for exceptional circumstances.

Finally, `finally`

The `finally` clause is used for activities that should be performed whether or not an exception was thrown and caught.

Syntax: `finally`

The `finally` clause looks like this:

```
finally
{
    // Cleanup code.
}
```

A `try` block can have at most one `finally` clause, and it must appear immediately after the last `catch` clause. If a `try` block has a `finally` clause, it need not have any `catch` clauses. As with `catch`, a `finally` clause must be associated with a `try` block.

The block of a `finally` clause will be executed, no matter how control leaves its `try` block. If none of the `catch` clauses are executed, the `finally` clause is executed after the `try` block. If one of the `catch` clauses is executed, the `finally` clause is executed after completion of the `catch`. The `finally` clause is executed even if the `try` or `catch` portions contain `break` or `return` statements.[3]

A `finally` clause is generally used for cleanup purposes. For example, a `Graphics`, `Frame`, or `Window` object ties up a considerable amount of system resources, so it's sound programming practice to explicitly free those resources by calling the `dispose()` method:

```
void myMethod()
{
    Graphics g = this.getGraphics();
    try
    {
        ...
    }
    finally
    {
        g.dispose();
    }
}
```

Sooner or later g would be disposed by the Java environment, no matter what we did—all we're doing here is making sure it gets freed up as soon as possible.

9.3   YOUR VERY OWN EXCEPTIONS

In spite of the wealth of exception types Java provides, there will be times when you want to invent exceptions of your own, to signal situations not covered by any of the predefined `Exception` classes. To do so, make `Exception` a subclass, if you want a checked exception, or make `RuntimeException` a subclass if you want to invent an unchecked exception.

Programmer-defined exceptions are treated like any others, except, of course, that you have to throw them yourself. In the Lablet for this chapter we have two exception types of our own design. One of them, `MissingData`, is intended to be thrown when one or more of the applet's `Textfields` are empty. The declaration is simple enough.

---

[3]Or a `continue` statement, which causes execution to skip to the bottom of an enclosing loop.

```
class MissingData extends Exception
// Thrown by the processSubmitButton() method when one or more
// of the data fields are empty.
{
    public MissingData()
    {
        super();
    }
    public MissingData(String s)
    {
        super(s);
    }
}
```

In both the constructors, all we need to do is call the appropriate superclass constructor. (We actually don't need the first constructor, since Java will call the default superclass constructor for us, but we include it to make our intent obvious to the reader.)

The `MissingData` exception is thrown within a utility method:

```
private void processSubmitButton() throws MissingData
// Make sure all data is filled in before submitting the order.
{
    if ((custName.getText().equals(EMPTY))          ||
        (custStreet.getText().equals(EMPTY))        ||
        // (six more clauses omitted here)
        (order.getText().equals(EMPTY))  )
    {
        throw new MissingData ("Must enter data in all fields");
    }
    else // Data is all there, so submit the order.
    {
        order.appendText(CRLF + "   ***  ORDER PLACED  ***");
        repaint();
    }
}
```

Note that we had to use a `throws` clause in the header, since `MissingData` is a checked exception.

Finally (no pun intended), the exception that was generated and thrown in `processSubmitButton()` is caught within the applet's `action()` handler.

```
...
else if (e.target == bSubmit)
{
    try
    {
        processSubmitButton();
    }
```

(continued)

```
    catch (MissingData ex)              // Some data were missing
    {
        order.appendText("*** " + ex.getMessage() + CRLF);
        repaint();
    }
    return true;
}
```

You can see here how we make use of the message field of `Exception`, by calling `getMessage()` to retrieve the message "Must enter data in all fields" and display it to the user.

9.4 HANDS ON

This chapter's Lablet, `OrderPlease`, is an online ordering program quite similar in purpose to Chapter 2's `Gigobite`. The main difference is that here we also get information about the customer (name, address, credit card data, and the like), and, as a well-behaved electronic order form should, we check for errors in customer information before processing the order.

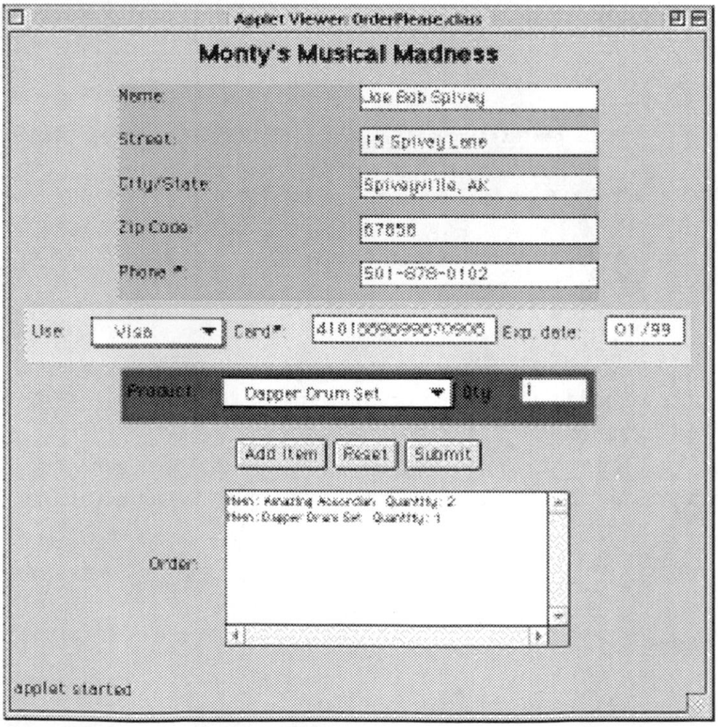

Figure 9.2 The `OrderPlease` applet.

As you would expect, we'll use exceptions to handle correctness checking. As an added pedagogical bonus, we'll also use an auxiliary class to manage the complexity of this applet in a way you'll find useful in other situations.

Designing the Lablet

The visual design of our applet is simple, once we've collected the various parts into functional units. We have five main parts: customer information (name, address, phone number, and so on); the usual credit card information (card type, number, and expiration date); a unit for ordering items (item description and quantity ordered); three buttons to add a new item to the order, clear the order form, and submit an order; and, finally, a text area where information about the current order is displayed.

The action of the applet is concentrated entirely in the three buttons. The Add Item button will add the name of the current selection in the `productChoice` widget and the number of such items desired to the `order` display. The Reset button will cause all the text in the customer information part and in the order display to be cleared. Finally, the Submit button will display a message that the order has been submitted. Of course, in a real order form this last action would be much more complicated, since we would have to get all the customer, credit card, and order information and send it back to the host computer.

We will deal with button clicks in an `action()` handler where each button click will invoke one of the utility methods `processAddItemButton()`, `processResetButton()`, and `processSubmitButton()`.

The bulk of the work done by each of these three methods will deal with handling possible errors on the part of the customer.

Arrogant, Patronizing, and Syntactically Incorrect Definition Which, in Spite of its Faults, Still Contains a Grain of Truth:

"User" == "Idiot."

In spite of the fact that error detection will require some extra work on our part, we should always keep in mind that a program serves the user, and not the other way around. Good user interface design is, fundamentally, nothing more than good manners embodied in code—we should never forget that one of the most important parts of a user-centered program is to make the user feel comfortable, no matter what he or she might do. For our part, the design process should always include consideration of what might go wrong and how the program will deal with problems.

In `processAddItemButton()`, we will need to check that the user has indicated a valid number of items in the `custQuantity` field. The Reset button will require no special checking on our part. However, the method `process-SubmitButton()` will at least have to verify that all the fields have been filled before submitting the order. In a real application, we might even devote the time necessary to verify that the fields have valid information. Verifying a name or address is probably beyond the current state of programming art, but we could certainly check that a zip code, telephone number, or credit card number is correctly formed. These latter checks, in fact, make good lab exercises, as you'll see.

Exploring `OrderPlease`

We begin the "OrderPlease.java" file by declaring two subclasses of `Exception`: `IllegalQuantity` and `Missing Data`. We will throw an instance of the former when our program discovers that the quantity of a certain item has been specified to be zero or less, and we'll throw a `MissingData` exception if we discover that the user has neglected to fill in a field like name or credit card number. As usual with `Exception` subclasses, these declarations consist of nothing more than definitions of the two possible constructors.

```
class IllegalQuantity extends Exception
// This is thrown by the doAddItem() method when the number
// of items isn't positive.
{
    public IllegalQuantity()
    {
        super();
    }
    public IllegalQuantity(String s)
    {
        super(s);
    }
}


// -----------------------------------------------------------


class MissingData extends Exception
// Thrown by the processSubmitButton() method when one or more
// of the data fields are empty.
{
    public MissingData()
    {
        super();
    }
    public MissingData(String s)
    {
        super(s);
    }
}
```

The next class has nothing to do with exceptions, but illustrates a tidy way of dealing with a complicated collection of widgets. Our design contains ten labels, not counting the title. We could have included each of them in the applet itself, making them local to `init()`, since they're never used anywhere else. However, `init()` is complicated enough already, with seven `TextField`s, two `Choice`s, three `Button`s, and a `TextArea`.

Instead, we collected all the `Label` instances into a single class, `Labels`, and then generated a new instance of that class, which we named `label`, in `init()`. The result was that `init()` was shortened by nine lines, and the only price we had to pay was to remember to refer to each label by using the instance name and a dot, as in `label.name` and `label.street`. Skip down to the applet's `init()` method to see what we mean.

```
class Labels
// The sole purpose of this class is to encapsulate the labels used
// in the OrderPlease applet.
{
    // Since this class is private within the applet, we can get
    // away with giving these variables package access.
    Label name,
            street,
            cityState,
            zip,
            phone,
            ccName,
            ccNum,
            ccExp,
            product,
            quantity,
            order;

    public Labels()
    // All the constructor has to do is initialize the labels.
    {
        name =          new Label("Name:", Label.RIGHT);
        street =        new Label("Street:", Label.RIGHT);
        cityState =     new Label("City/State:", Label.RIGHT);
        zip =           new Label("Zip Code:", Label.RIGHT);
        phone =         new Label("Phone #:", Label.RIGHT);
        ccName =        new Label("Use:", Label.RIGHT);
        ccNum =         new Label("Card#:", Label.RIGHT);
        ccExp =         new Label("Exp. date:", Label.RIGHT);
        product =       new Label("Product:", Label.RIGHT);
        quantity =      new Label("Qty:", Label.RIGHT);
        order =         new Label("Order:", Label.RIGHT);
    }
}
```

Now we come to the applet itself. We begin with the declaration of two `String` constants, for an empty `String` and a carriage return/line feed combination, and follow with declarations of the various widget instances.

```
public class OrderPlease extends Applet
{
     // two string constants
     private final String   EMPTY = new String(),
                            CRLF = new String("\n");

     // the textfields and a textarea
     private TextField      custName = new TextField(20),
                            custStreet = new TextField(20),
                            custCityState = new TextField(20),
                            custZip = new TextField(20),
                            custPhone = new TextField(20),
                            custCC = new TextField(15),
                            custExp = new TextField("  /  ",5),
                            custQuantity = new TextField(4);
     private TextArea       order = new TextArea(6,30);

     // a couple of choice boxes
     private Choice         ccChoice = new Choice(),
                            productChoice = new Choice();

     // three buttons to process the information
     private Button         bAddItem = new Button("Add Item"),
                            bReset = new Button("Reset"),
                            bSubmit = new Button("Submit");

     // a title for the applet
     private Label    title = new Label("Monty's Musical Madness");
```

The init() method does nothing but lay out the various widgets. Here you can see how we used the Labels class to replace ten Label declarations by a single initialization of a Labels object. This method is longer than we would have liked, but there's not much we can do about that for an applet as complicated as this one.

```
public void init()
{
     resize(520,480);
     title.setFont(new Font("Helvetica", Font.BOLD, 18));
     add(title);

     // lots of labels for the fields, declared in the
     // utility class Labels
     Labels label = new Labels();

     // p1 is the panel that holds the basic
     // customer information
     Panel p1 = new Panel();
     p1.setBackground(Color.cyan);
     p1.setLayout(new GridLayout(5,2, 2, 2));
```

```
p1.add(label.name);
p1.add(custName);

p1.add(label.street);
p1.add(custStreet);

p1.add(label.cityState);
p1.add(custCityState);

p1.add(label.zip);
p1.add(custZip);

p1.add(label.phone);
p1.add(custPhone);

add(p1);

// p2 is the credit card information panel
Panel p2 = new Panel();
p2.setBackground(Color.yellow);

ccChoice.addItem("Visa");
ccChoice.addItem("AMEX");
ccChoice.addItem("MasterCard");
ccChoice.addItem("Discover");

p2.add(label.ccName);
p2.add(ccChoice);

p2.add(label.ccNum);
p2.add(custCC);

p2.add(label.ccExp);
p2.add(custExp);

add(p2);

// p3 is the product panel
Panel p3 = new Panel();
p3.setBackground(Color.red);

productChoice.addItem("Amazing Accordion");
productChoice.addItem("Harmonious Harmonica");
productChoice.addItem("Dapper Drum Set");
productChoice.addItem("Going Going Gong!");
productChoice.addItem("Trump No Trumpet");
productChoice.addItem("Kabloowie Kazooie!");
productChoice.addItem("Power Panflute");
productChoice.addItem("Supersizer Synthesizer");
productChoice.addItem("Zany Zither");
```

```
        p3.add(label.product);
        p3.add(productChoice);

        p3.add(label.quantity);
        p3.add(custQuantity);

        add(p3);

        // Panel p4 is the button panel
        Panel p4 = new Panel();
        p4.add(bAddItem);
        p4.add(bReset);
        p4.add(bSubmit);

        add(p4);

        // p5 holds the information about the current order
        Panel p5 = new Panel();
        p5.add(label.order);
        p5.add(order);

        add(p5);
    }
```

The heart of the applet, as so often happens, is the `action()` method. Here we respond to clicks on any of the three buttons by calling a helper method. You'll see that the `processSubmitButton()` might throw a `MissingData` exception if one or more of the fields have not been filled in. We catch that exception here and deal with it by displaying an error message in the `order` TextArea. Since `order` is an applet instance variable, and hence accessible within `processSubmitButton()`, we could also have dealt with the missing data problem within the method itself, not using an exception. That, in fact, would have been a better choice, but we chose to ignore our own advice to show you how exceptions are raised and handled.

```
public boolean action(Event e, Object arg)
// This action routine not only responds to the button clicks
// for processing the order information, but also catches the
// possible MissingData exception thrown by method
// processSubmitButton().
{
    if (e.target == bAddItem)
    {
        processAddItemButton();
        return true;
    }
    else if (e.target == bReset)
    {
        processResetButton();
        return true;
    }
```

```
             else if (e.target == bSubmit)
             {
                  try
                  {
                        processSubmitButton();
                  }
                  catch (MissingData ex) // Some data was missing
                  {
                        order.appendText("*** " +
                                          ex.getMessage() + CRLF);
                        repaint();
                  }
                  return true;
             }
             else
                  return false;
      }
```

The `processAddItemButton()` method handles its own exceptions and illustrates two points. First, we find ourselves in a situation where not using an exception would entail a considerable amount of extra work, namely, checking that the text in the `custQuantity` field represents a legitimate integer. Although we could write the code necessary to check that a `String` represents a legal `int`, it wouldn't be pleasant to write, especially when the `Integer` class method `parseInt()` will do it for us.

Second, we have a `try` block with two associated `catch` clauses. The first catches a `NumberFormatException` and the second catches the possibility that the quantity is less than nor equal to zero (since it would make no sense for the customer to request –3 accordions, for example). In both cases, the `catch` clause displays an error message, forces the message to be displayed by calling `repaint()` (which isn't necessary in some environments), and returns from the method.

```
  private void processAddItemButton()
  // Before adding a new item to the order, this method first
  // checks that the quantity entered in the custQuantity
  // Textfield is (1) an integer and (2) greater than zero.
  {
        try
        {
              // This might throw a NumberFormatException
              int quantity =
                        Integer.parseInt(custQuantity.getText());
              // This might throw our own IllegalQuantity
              // exception
              doAddItem(quantity);
        }
        catch (NumberFormatException ex)          // not an integer.
        {
```

(continued)

```
        order.appendText("*** Must provide an integer value"
                              + CRLF);
        order.appendText("*** in the quantity field"
                              + CRLF);
        repaint();
        return;
    }
    catch (IllegalQuantity ex)              // not positive.
    {
        order.appendText("*** " + ex.getMessage() + CRLF);
        order.appendText("*** in the quantity field"
                              + CRLF);
        repaint();
        return;
    }
}
```

The doAdditem() method is a helper for processAddItemButton(). It verifies that the quantity of items is 1 or more and throws one of our IllegalQuantity exceptions if it isn't. If the quantity is positive, the method appends the item and its quantity to the order text. Take a look back at the processAddItemButton() method—you'll see that by placing a call to this method within a try block, after a call to Integer.parseInt(), we have guaranteed that this method will be called with a valid integer argument.

```
private void doAddItem(int quant) throws IllegalQuantity
// Try to add the current item to the order, checking that the
// number entered was positive.
// Called by processAddItemButton().
{
    if (quant < 1) // Scream if it isn't!
    {
        throw
        new IllegalQuantity("Must have a positive amount");
    }
    else // Quantity is OK, so go ahead and add the item.
    {
        order.appendText("Item: "
                    + productChoice.getSelectedItem()
                    + "  Quantity: " + custQuantity.getText()
                    + CRLF);
        repaint();
    }
}
```

The processResetButton() method is trivial—it only has to clear all the TextFields.

```
private void processResetButton()
// Reset all the data fields.
{
    custName.setText(EMPTY);
    custStreet.setText(EMPTY);
    custCityState.setText(EMPTY);
    custZip.setText(EMPTY);
    custPhone.setText(EMPTY);
    custCC.setText(EMPTY);
    custQuantity.setText(EMPTY);
    custExp.setText("  /  ");
    order.setText(EMPTY);
}
```

The last method in this class is `processSubmitButton()`, called by the `action()` handler. This first determines whether all the `Textfields` have some data. If one or more don't, it terminates abruptly by throwing a `MissingData` exception. If all the fields have data, this method simply displays a message that the order has been submitted.

```
private void processSubmitButton() throws MissingData
// Make sure all data is filled in before submitting the order.
{
    if ((custName.getText().equals(EMPTY))            ||
            (custStreet.getText().equals(EMPTY))      ||
            (custCityState.getText().equals(EMPTY))   ||
            (custZip.getText().equals(EMPTY))         ||
            (custPhone.getText().equals(EMPTY))       ||
            (custCC.getText().equals(EMPTY))          ||
            (custQuantity.getText().equals(EMPTY))    ||
            (custExp.getText().equals("  /  "))       ||
            (order.getText().equals(EMPTY))    )
    {
        throw
        new MissingData("Must enter data in all fields");
    }
    else // Data is all there, so submit the order.
    {
        order.appendText(CRLF + "    ***   ORDER PLACED   ***");
        repaint();
    }
}
}
```

9.5 SUMMARY

❦ We discussed the following classes.

```
Throwable
Exception, and its subclasses
    EOFException
    FileNotFoundException
    InterruptedException
    InterruptedIOException
    IOException
    MalformedURLException
    RuntimeException, and its subclasses
        ArithmeticException
        ArrayIndexOutOfBoundsException
        ArrayStoreException
        IllegalArgumentException
        IllegalThreadStateException
        IndexOutOfBoundsException
        NegativeArraySizeException
        NullPointerException
        StringIndexOutOfBoundsException
```

❦ The Exception class has no methods and only two constructors One constructor takes no arguments and the other takes a String argument specifying a message that can be retrieved by using the method getMessage(), belonging to Exception's superclass Throwable.

❦ When an exception is thrown, the Java run-time environment immediately suspends its normal mode of execution and looks for a way of dealing with the exception.

❦ To indicate that a block of code may throw exceptions that your program will attempt to handle, preface the block with the keyword try:

```
try
{
    // Code that might raise an exception.
}
```

❦ A try block must be followed immediately by one or more catch clauses (or a finally clause) of the form

```
catch (ExceptionType variable)
{
    // code to handle the exception
}
```

❦ If no exception is raised during execution of a try block, its associated catch clauses are skipped. If an exception is raised in the try block and there is a subsequent catch clause that is assignment compatible with the exception type, control immediately passes out of the try block to the appropriate catch clause.

❧ Once control leaves a try block, it doesn't return after executing a catch or finally clause.

❧ If an exception is thrown, the system looks for catch blocks by moving outward through enclosing blocks until the entire method has been searched. It then moves back to the location of the method call and through its enclosing block structure, and so on. If no catch that is compatible with the exception is found, the exception will eventually be caught by the run-time environment.

❧ A finally clause is executed when control passes out of a try block, whether through an exception or a return, break, or continue statement. As with catch, a finally clause must be associated with a try block. A finally clause must appear after the last catch clause associated with its try block.

❧ finally clauses are generally used for cleanup purposes.

❧ The throw statement throws an instance of an exception. It has the form

    throw *exceptionInstance*;

❧ If a method doesn't catch an exception, you can indicate that to the compiler by using a throws clause at the end of the method header:

    returnType methodSignature throws *listOfExceptionTypes*

❧ RuntimeException and its subclasses do not need to be mentioned in a throws clause and do not need to be thrown within a try block. All other exceptions do.

❧ A method override cannot be declared with a throws clause that names exceptions not thrown by the parent method.

❧ If there's no possible way of handling a potential error, raise an exception.

❧ If you can handle an error simply, do so without raising an exception.

❧ Reserve exceptions for exceptional circumstances—do not use them for routine checking that could be done better with an internal test, using an if statement, for example.

❧ You can declare your own exceptions, usually by subclassing Exception (for a checked exception) or RuntimeException (if you don't care whether the exception will be checked by the compiler for an enclosing try block or throws clause).

9.6 EXERCISES

1. We mentioned that there's no meaningful way to define int division by zero. Why? Pick one or more ways of defining division by zero and show that each eventually leads to an inconsistency in the way you would expect arithmetic to work.

2.   If you were to write the declaration

```
int[] myArray = new array[5.5];
```

would that statement raise an exception at run-time, or could it be caught earlier, during compilation?

3.   Unfortunately, at the time of this writing, some Java runtime environments don't raise all the exceptions we listed in Section 9.1. Write an applet that deliberately raises exceptional conditions, like division by zero and out of range indices in arrays and strings. Which are caught by your system and which are ignored?

4.   You've gotten all the way to Chapter 9 and haven't yet seen a true/false exercise. Just for variety, here's one. Indicate whether each of the following statements is true or false. Warning: Some are tricky.
   a.   Every `try` block must be followed by at least one `catch` clause.
   b.   Every `catch` clause must be associated with a `try` block.
   c.   A `try` block may have two associated `catch` clauses.
   d.   A `try` block may have two associated `finally` clauses.
   e.   If a `try` block controls just one statement, that statement doesn't need to be enclosed in braces.
   f.   A `try` block may be nested within another `try` block.
   g.   A `catch` clause may appear within another `catch` clause.

5.   In Section 9.1 we listed a number of exceptions that are thrown by methods we've discussed. Which of them are checked exceptions and which aren't?

6.   Complete the definition of the `IntTextField` class.

7.   What's wrong here?

```
try
{
    // something
}
catch (StringIndexOutOfBoundsException e)
{
    ...
    int errorCount = 1;
}
finally
{
    if (errorCount > 0)
        // do something
    else
        // do something else
}
```

8. Here's a method that takes an array, `source`, and fills another array, `destination`, with all the nonzero elements in source, in their original order. For example, if `source` contained {34, 0, 0, 9, 17, 0, 22}, `destination` would contain {34, 9, 17, 22} when the method completes. Upon completion, the method will return the number of nonzero elements it saw.

```
int copyNonzero(int[] source, int[] destination)
{
    int j = 0;
    for (int i = 0; i < source.length; i++)
        if (source[i] != 0;
        {
            destination[j] = source[i];
            j++;
        }
    return j;
}
```

a. What is the precondition for this method?
b. Which parts of the precondition can the method handle itself, and which are beyond the method's ability to handle?
c. Write the method so that it handles all the problems it can and throws appropriate exceptions for the ones it can't.
d. Describe the best postcondition you can for this method.

9. Here's the method we used in the text to illustrate the use of the `finally` clause.

```
void myMethod()
{
    Graphics g = this.getGraphics();
    try
    {
        ...
    }
    finally
    {
        g.dispose();
    }
}
```

There may be a problem here that we didn't mention. Suppose that some statement in the `try` block generates a `NullPointerException` that the method is incapable of handling. We still want to dispose of the Graphics object g, but after having done so, the exception hasn't gone away. Do we need to take any special action to pass the exception out of the method and if so, what do we have to do?

10. Suppose that any of `method1()`, `method2()` and `method3()` might throw an `ArithmeticException` and that we want to take different actions to handle the exception, depending on its source. If our error-handling was done like this,

```
try
{
      method1();
      method2();
      method3();
}
catch (ArithmeticException e)
{
      ...
}
```

how could we identify the method that threw the exception? You're not allowed to take the easy way out and enclose each of the method calls in its own `try` block. Hint: Consider modifying the methods, too.

11. We mentioned that exceptions take much longer to raise and handle than equivalent local tests—let's see how large the difference is. Try the following applet, which uses the `Date` class to measure the time, in milliseconds, it takes to handle several thousand out-of-bounds `String` accesses.

```
import java.applet.*;
import java.awt.*;
import java.util.*;      // for the Date class

public class Test extends Applet
{
      private TextField display = new TextField(10);

      public void init()
      {
            add(display);
            char c = 'a';
            String s = "Sample";
            Date dStart = new Date();
            long timeStart = dStart.getTime();
            for (int i = 0; i < 50000; i++)
            {
                  try
                  {
                        char c = s.charAt(i);
                  }
                  catch (StringIndexOutOfBoundsException e)
                  {
                  }
            }
```

```
        Date dEnd = new Date();
        long timeElapsed = dEnd.getTime() - timeStart;
        display.setText("" + timeElapsed);
    }
}
```

Now replace the body of the `for` loop with the following equivalent block and compare the running times of the two versions. Do this exercise in several different Java environments, if possible. If you can, you'll see why doing so is instructive.

```
{
    if (i < s.length())
        c = s.charAt(i);
}
```

CHAPTER TEN

Input/Output

Until now, none of the programs you have written have any long-term memory. When your programs complete their intended tasks and quit, all the information they have saved is lost forever, gone to that great bit bucket in the sky. Clearly, if computers are to have any real practical use, there must be some way to store their results in a more or less permanent form. Consider the Java compiler that you have been using, for instance. In this case, two things need to be stored permanently: your source code and the resulting object code. You could dispense with the object code and recompile the source code every time you need it, but it would be an incredible bother to enter your source code, test and run it, quit for the day, and have to reenter the same source code the next day.

All modern programming languages have the ability to save the output of a program in an external file that may reside on a hard disk, for instance. Once the file has been written to the disk (or tape, or compact disk, or any of a number of other media), it may be read later and used as input for a program—either the same program that generated the file in the first place or an entirely different program. In this chapter, we will discuss the classes Java provides for file input and output.

OBJECTIVES

In this chapter, we will
- ❦ Introduce Java's stream types.
- ❦ Use streams to read from and write to files.
- ❦ Discuss Java's security measures and show how they determine the amount of access to be provided to the environment's file structure.
- ❦ Use what we've discussed to build a functional word processor.

10.1 STREAMS

Java input and output are accomplished through the use of the *stream* classes
`InputStream`, `OutputStream` and their subclasses, some of which we
illustrate in Figure 10.1. These classes, along with the `File` class, are all found in
the `java.io` package. A stream in Java is an ordered sequence of objects and a
collection of methods that allow you to extract an object from the stream (*read* it
from the stream) and add a new object to the stream (*write* it to the stream).
Although we'll be primarily concerned with reading from and writing to files that
reside on an external source, like a floppy disk or a hard drive, Java streams may be
associated with other data sources, like a `String` or an array of bytes in memory.

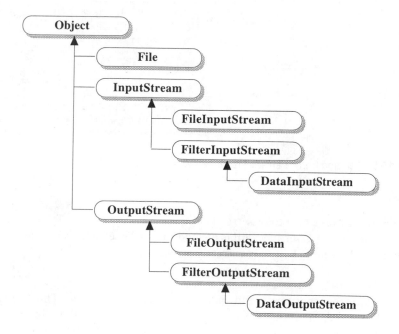

Figure 10.1 Part of the stream hierarchy.

The Classes `InputStream` and `OutputStream`

The basis for input and output in Java is the pair of abstract classes `InputStream`
and `OutputStream`. Because they're abstract, you can't construct an instance of
either class, but they provide the basic operations common to all their subclasses.
These classes reside at the top of their respective hierarchies, so they provide
limited functionality for input and output—more sophisticated methods are provided

by their subclasses. In fact, the input and output methods of these two classes are limited to reading and writing single bytes or arrays of bytes.

An `InputStream` object provides a source of bytes that your program may read. All the methods described may throw an `IOException`. That might happen in response to a number of conditions, as, for example, if the source of bytes has become unavailable because a disk has been ejected or has become corrupted.

`InputStreams` differ from most other Java data structures, in that the access methods `read()` have the side-effect of removing the byte or bytes read, rather than just copying them, as shown in Figure 10.2.

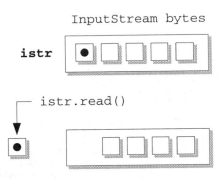

Figure 10.2 Reading from a stream removes what was read.

```
int available() throws IOException
```
     Returns 0. Overrides of this method in subclasses may return an integer that indicates how many bytes are currently available to be read.

```
void close() throws IOException
```
     Streams consume a fair amount of system resources. This method frees resources and, in consequence, makes further input operations impossible. You should always close an `InputStream` object when you've finished using it.

```
int read() throws IOException
```
     This abstract method is intended to be overridden by subclasses of this class. Where it is implemented, it extracts and returns the next available byte from this stream. The byte value is a number from 0 to 255, and if no bytes are currently available in this object, the method returns −1.

```
int read(byte[] bArray) throws IOException, NullPointerException
```
     Reads bytes from this stream and transfers them into the argument array. This method attempts to fill the entire array and returns the actual number of bytes read. It throws a `NullPointerException` if the array has not been initialized.

```
int read(byte[] bArray, int offset, int length)
     throws IOException, NullPointerException,
          IndexOutOfBoundsException
```
Reads bytes into the array, starting at bArray[offset] and continuing until length bytes have been transferred, or no bytes remain. This method returns the actual number of bytes transferred. It's not hard to come up with the conditions that would cause this method to throw an IndexOutOfBoundsException— we leave that as an exercise.

```
long skip(long n) throws IOException
```
Discards the specified number of bytes from this stream, just as if they had been read. This method returns the actual number of bytes discarded, since, for instance, there may not be n bytes available in this stream.

The OutputStream class is the companion class to InputStream. An instance of OutputStream provides a destination to which your program may write one or more bytes, as illustrated in Figure 10.3. By the way, you can think of bytes being written to one end of a stream and read from the other. This viewpoint will be useful when we discuss files because you can use the same sequence of bytes for both input and output streams.

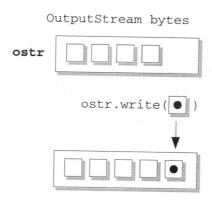

Figure 10.3 Writing to an OutputStream (compare with Fig. 10.2).

```
void close() throws IOException
```
As does the InputStream method of the same name, this method closes this OutputStream. Once it has been closed, no further operations may be performed on this stream. You should close an OutputStream as soon as you've finished with it.

```
void flush() throws IOException
```
This method does nothing. In some subclasses of OutputStream, though, objects are stored temporarily in a *buffer* before being written to the stream. For

those classes, flush() causes all buffered objects to be immediately written to the stream.

void **write**(int n) throws IOException
      Writes the low-order eight bits of n to the stream, ignoring the other twenty-four bits. For example, write(781) would write the byte 00001101 to the stream, since 781 is 00000000 00000000 00000011 00001101 in binary.

void **write**(byte[] bArray) throws IOException, NullPointerException
      Writes the bytes bArray[0], bArray[1], . . . in that order, to the stream.

int **write**(byte[] bArray, int offset, int length)
      throws IOException, NullPointerException,
         IndexOutOfBoundsException
      Writes the bytes bArray[offset], bArray[offset + 1], . . . , bArray[offset + length - 1] to the stream.

The Classes DataInputStream and DataOutputStream

The DataInputStream and DataOutputStream classes are so useful that you'd probably write them yourself if they hadn't already been provided in the java.io package. In almost all applications that need input or output, you will want to do much more than simply read and write bytes. For example, it would be far easier to be able to read an int from a stream by calling one method, readInt(), than it would be to read four bytes from an InputStream and convert them into an int yourself.

      The two classes we'll discuss in this section may be regarded as wrapper classes for InputStream and OutputStream. DataInputStream and DataOutputStream have access to all the methods of their parent classes, and they add the extra functionality necessary to read or write any of Java's primitive types.[1]

The class DataInputStream has a single constructor.

DataInputStream(InputStream in)
      Constructs a new DataInputStream, using the InputStream argument as the source of its bytes.

      DataInputStream provides a complete suite of methods for reading primitive types. These methods are all final, so you can't override them if you make your own subclass of DataInputStream. As with the InputStream methods, all of these methods may throw an IOException (if they're called on a closed stream, for example). Although we don't mention it in the individual

---

[1]Though we needn't go into details here, the wrapper class methods implement the interfaces DataInput and DataOutput.

descriptions, all of these methods (except `skipBytes()`) will throw an `EOFException` if the end of file is reached before all the needed information has been read.

All of these methods are compatible with the `write()` methods of `DataOutputStream`. For example, the bytes written by `writeInt()` will be converted correctly when read by `readInt()`.

We won't bother to flag any of these methods with 💀, since they're all useful.

boolean **readBoolean**() throws IOException

Values of `boolean` type are stored in streams as a single byte, with value 0 representing `false` and any nonzero value representing `true`. This method reads a single byte from the stream and returns the corresponding boolean value.

byte **readByte**() throws IOException

Reads and returns a single byte. The byte value is considered to be signed, so it may represent any value between −128 and 127.

char **readChar**() throws IOException

Extracts two bytes and returns the corresponding Unicode character.

double **readDouble**() throws IOException

Reads eight bytes and returns the corresponding `double` value.

float **readFloat**() throws IOException

Reads four bytes and returns the corresponding `float` value.

int **readFully**(byte[] bArray)
                    throws IOException, NullPointerException
int **readFully**(byte[] bArray, int offset, int length)
                    throws IOException, NullPointerException,
                    IndexOutOfBoundsException

These methods read data from this stream into an array of bytes. See the descriptions of the `read()` methods of `InputStream` for details.

int **readInt**() throws IOException

Reads four bytes and returns the corresponding `int` value.

String **readLine**() throws IOException

Reads individual bytes, converting each to a character, until the newline character '\n' is encountered, or until there are no further bytes to read. It then discards the newline character, if any, converts the characters to a `String`, and returns the result.

`long` **`readLong`**`() throws IOException`
Reads eight bytes and returns the corresponding `long` value.

`short` **`readShort`**`() throws IOException`
Reads two bytes and returns the corresponding `short` value.

`void` **`skipBytes`**`(int n) throws IOException`
Discards n bytes from this stream. This method may discard fewer than the desired number of bytes, if there aren't enough available in the stream. In any case, it will return the number of bytes discarded.

As we mentioned, the `DataOutputStream` class provides writing methods that are compatible with the reading methods of `DataInputStream`. Thus you don't have to worry about how `writeInt()` actually stores an `int` in four bytes—all that matters is that, if the `int` was written by `writeInt()`, those four bytes will give the same value when `readInt()` is called.

There is a single `DataOutputStream` constructor.

`DataOutputStream``(OutputStream out)`
Constructs a new `DataOutputStream`, using the `OutputStream` argument as the destination of its bytes.

Some of the descriptions of `DataOutputStream` methods are self-evident and have been omitted. For details about the number of bytes each type requires, see the descriptions of the corresponding `read()` methods of `DataInputStream`.
As with `DataInputStream`, most of these methods are `final`.

`void` **`flush`**`() throws IOException`
As with the `OutputStream` method of the same name, this method causes immediate writing of any buffered output.

`int` **`size`**`()`
Returns the number of bytes written to this stream so far.

`void` **`write`**`(int n) throws IOException`
This method is an implementation of the abstract `write()` method of `OutputStream`. It writes the low-order eight bits of the argument.

`int` **`write`**`(byte[] bArray, int offset, int length)`
`        throws IOException, NullPointerException,`
`        IndexOutOfBoundsException`
Writes the bytes `bArray[offset]`, `bArray[offset + 1]`, . . . , `bArray[offset + length - 1]` to the stream. This method is an override of the similar method in `OutputStream`.

void **writeBoolean**(boolean b) throws IOException

void **writeByte**(int n) throws IOException
    Writes the low-order eight bits of n to the stream.

void **writeBytes**(String s) throws IOException
    Writes s to this stream, using one byte for each character in the argument String. To use this method with readLine(), be sure that the argument is terminated by a newline character. You'll often call this method like this:

```
ostr.writeBytes(myString + "\n");
```

void **writeChar**(int n) throws IOException
    Writes the low-order two bytes of the argument to this stream. Most of the time, you'll call this method with a char argument, which is of course compatible with the wider int type.

void **writeChars**(String s) throws IOException
    This method acts much like writeBytes(), except that it uses two bytes for each character in the String argument. If you use this method in conjunction with readLine(), which expects a single byte for each character, you may get strange results.

void **writeDouble**(double d) throws IOException

void **writeFloat**(float f) throws IOException

void **writeInt**(int n) throws IOException

void **writeLong**(long l) throws IOException

void **writeShort**(int n) throws IOException
    Writes the low-order two bytes of n to this stream.

10.2 FILE I/O

The term "file" is an abstraction representing the information that's physically stored on some device, like a floppy disk. You can think of a file as any collection of information that is logically related, like the text and formatting tags in an HTML document or the bytes in a compiled program. Fortunately, the hardware-specific details of how the information in a file is stored on a device and how it may be located is handled by the *operating system* of the computer, so we can blithely go our way without concerning ourselves with any of the messy bits.

    Java further isolates us from the details of the operating system by providing two fundamental stream classes, along with a few other classes that make file input and output fairly painless.[2] In this section and the next, we'll start with a simple problem in file input and output, and gradually introduce and add features that illustrate the way a well-behaved program deals with files.

The `FileInputStream` and `FileOutputStream` Classes

To use a file as a source of bytes for reading or as a destination for writing, Java provides the `FileInputStream` and `FileOutputStream` classes. These are subclasses of `InputStream` and `OutputStream`, respectively, and provide the same primitive reading and writing capabilities as their parent classes.

FileInputStream has three constructors, two of which are of interest to us here.

```
FileInputStream(String filename)
      throws FileNotFoundException, SecurityException
FileInputStream(File f)
      throws FileNotFoundException, SecurityException
```

The first method creates a new `FileInputStream` attached to the file with name specified by its argument; the second creates a new instance attached to the specified `File` argument. We'll talk about the `File` class shortly. We'll discuss the `SecurityManager` class and `SecurityExceptions` in Section 10.4.

This class has the following methods, which are either implementations or overrides of methods in `InputStream` (where you should look for the method descriptions).

```
int available() throws IOException

void close() throws IOException

int read() throws IOException

int read(byte[] bArray) throws IOException, NullPointerException

int read(byte[] bArray, int offset, int length)
        throws IOException, NullPointerException,
        IndexOutOfBoundsException

long skip(long n) throws IOException
```

---

[2]At least when we can do file I/O at all. You'll see what we mean in Section 10.4.

FileOutputStream is defined in a way that's quite similar to FileInputStream. It has two constructors, and its methods are implementations or overrides of the similarly named methods of the parent class OutputStream.

```
FileOutputStream(String filename)
      throws FileNotFoundException, SecurityException
FileOutputStream(File f)
      throws FileNotFoundException, SecurityException

void close() throws IOException

void write(int n) throws IOException

void write(byte[] bArray) throws IOException, NullPointerException

int write(byte[] bArray, int offset, int length)
        throws IOException, NullPointerException,
        IndexOutOfBoundsException
```

A FileInputStream is an InputStream by inheritance, so we can use it as the actual argument in the constructor of DataInputStream. By wrapping a FileInputStream in a DataInputStream, we can use the methods of DataInputStream to read any of the primitive types from a file. To open a file with a specified name this way, all you need do is write

```
FileInputStream fstr = new FileInputStream(name);
DataInputStream in = new DataInputStream(fstr);
```

or you could eliminate the step of making a FileInputStream variable and simply fold the two constructors together:

```
DataInputStream in = new DataInputStream(new FileInputStream(name));
```

If you want to write to a file, you can do the same sort of thing to wrap a FileOutputStream inside a DataOutputStream:

```
FileOutputStream fstr = new FileOutputStream(name);
DataOutputStream out = new DataOutputStream(fstr);
```

I/O for Primitive Types

After you have constructed a FileOutputStream and used it to construct a DataInputStream, you have all the write() methods of the latter class. For example, the following method shows you how to make a new file named "Sample," write a double, an int, and a String to it, and then close the file that was created.

```
void buildMyFile(double d, int n, String s)
{
    // First, attach the file to a DataOutputStream.
    FileOutputStream fstr = new FileOutputStream("Sample");
    DataOutputStream out = new DataOutputStream(fstr);
    // Now, write the information.
    out.writeDouble(d);
    out.writeInt(n);
    out.writeBytes(s + "\n");
    // We're done, so close the stream.
    out.close();
}
```

After all the preliminaries it took to get to this point, we suspect that you'd agree that this process is pretty simple. Once we're done, our file looks like

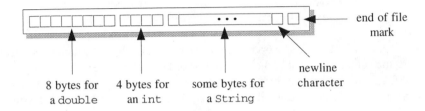

The end of file mark in this picture is just a conceptual convenience, indicating that Java has a way of knowing where the file ends, either by counting bytes or by using a special character. It's not a "real" byte in the sense that you could read it or, in fact, inspect it in any way.

If you were to use a text editor to open the file "Sample," you'd see the string, preceded by a bunch of unrecognizable junk. The junk would be the double and the int, since those values are stored in a DataInputStream in their binary representations, not in their character equivalents.[3] This condition makes inspecting the file once it has been built somewhat difficult, but it actually makes our job easier. Suppose that a DataOutputStream stored numbers as strings of characters. How would you interpret the string "34.091667" if you knew that it represented a double followed by an int? Should it be interpreted as 34.0 and 91667 or 34.091 and 667? The nice part of using a *fixed length representation* for all primitive types is that there is no ambiguity—the first eight bytes are the double and the next four are the int.

Reading the file "Sample" is equally easy. Conceptually, we write to a file by

---

[3]If you ever need to write primitive types as strings of characters, you can use the PrintStream class. It is an OutputStream subclass that provides methods for writing information in textual, rather than binary, form.

appending new material to the right, and we read by removing data from the left. Thus we would read the `double` first, followed by the `int`, and finally by the `String`.

Fundamental Principle of File I/O:

Read 'em in the order they were written.

Here's how we would read the data from the file:

```
double d;
int n;
String s;
...
void readMyFile()
{
    // First, attach the file to a DataInputStream.
    FileInputStream fstr = new FileInputStream("Sample");
    DataInputStream in = new DataInputStream(fstr);
    // Now, read the information, in the order it was written.
    d = in.readDouble();
    n = in.ReadInt();
    s = in.ReadLine();
    // We're done, so close the stream.
    in.close();
}
```

In the example where we wrote "Sample," we really didn't need to add the newline character to the `String` we were writing. The reason is that `readLine()` reads up to the first newline character (which is then discarded) or the end of the file, whichever comes first. We would most certainly want the newline character, though, if we intended to write anything after the `String`. Without it, Java would continue past the end of the `String`, valiantly trying to make characters out of whatever followed, to the end of the file (or a subsequent newline character).

Advice: String Output

When writing a `String` to a file, you should get in the habit of appending a newline character. That way, you'll never have problems using `readLine()` to get the `String` back.

I/O for Class Types

It's not much more difficult to read and write class types than it is to do I/O on the primitive types. All you do is apply the appropriate `DataInputStream` or `DataOutputStream` methods to the class's member data. It's often convenient to provide a class with methods that can be used to do the reading and writing, as we do here with the methods `readFrom()` and `writeTo()`.

```
class Record
{
    private double   d;
    private int      n;
    private String   s;

    public Record(double d, int n, String s)
    {
        this.d = d;
        this.n = n;
        this.s = s;
    }

    public void readFrom(DataInputStream in) throws IOException
    // Try to read the data from "in."  If something goes wrong,
    // we can't handle it, so just pass the IOException along.
    {
        d = in.readDouble();
        n = in.readInt();
        s = in.readLine();
    }

    public void writeTo(DataOutputStream out) throws IOException
    // Try to write the data to "out."  As with reading, if
    // something goes wrong, pass the exception to the calling
    // routine.
    {
        out.writeDouble(d);
        out.writeInt(n);
        out.writeBytes(s + "\n");
    }
}
```

Then we could use this `Record` class in an applet or application by constructing the appropriate stream and using it for input or output. To write a file "Sample2" containing one `Record` object, we could write

```
Record myRecord = new Record(34.09, 1667, "Thursday");
...
private void doSave()
```

```
{
    try
    {
        FileOutputStream = new FileOutputStream("Sample2");
        DataOutputStream out = new DataOutputStream(fstr);
        myRecord.writeTo(out);
        out.close();
    }
    catch (IOException ex)
    // Just display the exception.
    {
        System.err.println(ex);
    }
}
```

To get the saved value from the file "Sample2" and use it to set the fields of myRecord, we could call the method defined as

```
private void doOpen()
{
    try
    {
        FileInputStream = new FileInputStream("Sample2");
        DataInputStream in = new DataInputStream(fstr);
        myRecord.readFrom(in);
        in.close();
    }
    catch (IOException ex)
    {
        System.err.println(ex);
    }
}
```

Headers

Suppose now that we wanted to write and later read not just a single Record object, but rather an entire collection of such objects. We might, for instance, have set up an array of Record objects like

```
Record[] rArray = new Record[10];
rArray [0] = new Record(3.00787, 442, "first");
rArray [1] = new Record(0.02768, -5, "second");
rArray [2] = new Record(-4.30117e2, 0, "third");
int numRecs = 3;
```

It certainly wouldn't be hard to write these to a file—all we'd have to do is have each of the three array elements call its own writeTo() method. The problem, though, comes when we try to read the elements back, perhaps in another program. How do we know how many `Records` are stored in the file?

An elegant solution is to store the number of records in the file itself, using a single `int` at the start to hold the number of `Records` that follow. What we've done is make a file *header*—some extra data in the file that provides information about the file itself, as illustrated in Figure 10.4.

A `Record` object

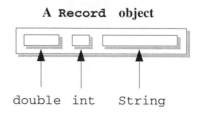

double   int   String

A file of `Record`s, with header

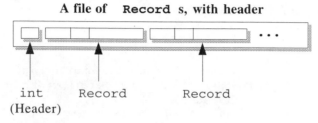

int   Record   Record
(Header)

Figure 10.4 A typical file structure.

Using a file with a header that stores the number of records, our `doSave()` and `doOpen()` methods now would look like this:

```
private void doSave()
{
    try
    {
        FileOutputStream = new FileOutputStream("Sample3");
        DataOutputStream out = new DataOutputStream(fstr);

        // Write the header.
        out.writeInt(numRecs);

        // Write the rest of the Records
        for (int i = 0; i < numRecs; i++)
            r[i].writeTo(out);
        out.close();
    }
    catch (IOException ex)
    {
```

```
                    System.err.println(ex);
            }
    }


    private void doOpen()
    {
        try
        {
            FileInputStream = new FileInputStream("Sample3");
            DataInputStream in = new DataInputStream(fstr);

            // Read the header value.
            numRecs = in.readInt();

            // Read the Records, now that we know how many we have.
            for (int i = 0; i < numRecs; i++)
                r[i].readFrom(in);

            in.close();
        }
        catch (IOException ex)
        {
            System.err.println(ex);
        }
    }
```

Using a header to store the number of records in a file is indeed elegant, but you can't guarantee that every program that would make a file of Records will be that helpful. If the file just consisted of a collection of Records, how would you know how many elements the file contained? Actually, you don't need to know. A simple way of reading all the elements from such a file is just to keep reading until you run out of things to read. If any of read() methods of DataInputStream encounter the end of the stream before they have enough bytes to complete their operation, they will throw an EOFException. All we have to do is catch that exception and realize that it means we've read everything there is in the file. Our doOpen() method would then take the form

```
private void doOpen()
{
    try
    {
        FileInputStream = new FileInputStream("Sample4");
        DataInputStream in = new DataInputStream(fstr);

        numRecs = 0;

        while (true)
        {
```

(continued)

```
                    r[numRecs].readFrom(in);
                    numRecs++;
            }
            in.close();
    }
    catch (EOFException ex)
    {
            // Nothing needed here, since we expected this exception
            // to be thrown eventually.
    }
    catch (IOException ex)
    // Catch any other unexpected behavior.
    {
            System.err.println(ex);
    }
}
```

10.3 ADVANCED FILE I/O

As you just saw, writing to files and reading from files is basically quite simple. There are, though, some things we'd like to be able to do with files that go beyond the basics. In this section, we'll introduce some new classes that permit us to do the things with files that a robust and sophisticated program should do.

Filtering File Names

You may have seen some applications that limit the files you can open to a certain type. A paint program, for example, might restrict you to opening only files that contain graphic images. The FilenameFilter interface provides you a way of doing so. A class that implements FilenameFilter will provide the code for a single method:

boolean **accept**(File directory, String name)
        Returns true if the file in the given directory and having the given name is one that should appear in a list of files or a file dialog box.

When we talk about the File and FileDialog classes, you'll see how they can use a class that implements FilenameFilter. Here's an example of such a class, which filters out any file whose name doesn't end with a ".txt" extension.

```
class TxtFilter implements FilenameFilter
{
    // Doesn't need a constructor, since we let Java
    // provide a default constructor for us.
```

```
        public boolean accept(File dir, String name)
        {
              if (name.endsWith(".txt")
                    return true;
              else
                    return false;
        }
}
```

The File Class

Lots of things can go wrong when we try to open a file. The filename we provide in the FileInputStream or FileOutputStream may not be the name of any file, it might be the name of a directory (rather than a data file), or it might be the name of a file to which we are denied access for security reasons. The constructors for these two streams will throw a FileNotFoundException if the associated file can't be opened, but we might want to know about the validity of a file *before* we attempt to open it.

The File class has several methods that allow us to get information about a file. To construct a new File object, we give the constructor the String representing the name of the file.[4] The File instance will be created, even if the name doesn't represent a valid file—this is handy, since we can then use methods of the File class to test whether the name really does refer to a file.

In the following list of File methods, we omitted some that are beyond the scope of this discussion. Each of the methods listed may throw a SecurityException if the current SecurityManager won't permit the operation. We'll talk about security in Java in Section 10.4.

❦ boolean **canRead**()
> Returns true if this file can be read; otherwise, returns false.

❦ boolean **canWrite**()
> Returns true if this file can be written; otherwise, returns false.

boolean **delete**()
> Attempts to delete this file. This method returns true if the deletion succeeded and returns false if the file wasn't deleted. You might use it in a program if you were trying to write a file with a name that already existed. The program might then ask something like, "A file with this name already exists. Delete it?"

---

[4] Actually, the string is the *path name* of the file, relative to the directory where the Java interpreter is located. We won't discuss the intricacies of path names in any detail.

```
boolean equals(Object ob)
```
Returns `true` if the argument is a file with the same name as this one; otherwise, returns `false`.

❦ `boolean exists()`

Returns `true` if this object exists (i.e., there is a file or directory with the same name as this file); otherwise, returns `false`.

```
boolean isDirectory()
```
Returns `true` if this object is a directory; otherwise, returns `false`.

❦ `boolean isFile()`

Returns `true` if this object is a data file; otherwise, returns `false`.

```
long lastModified()
```
Returns a number representing the last modification time of this file. This number may have no correspondence to clock time. All you can be sure of is that, if you compare the numbers for two files, the one with larger number was modified more recently.

```
long length()
```
Returns the number of bytes in this file.

```
String[] list()
String[] list(FileNameFilter f)
```
If this file is a data file, these methods return a `null` array. If this file is a directory, they return an array containing the names of all the files the directory contains. These methods list only the top-level entries in this directory—they don't look in any directories that this directory might contain.

The second of these methods allows us to specify a `FileNameFilter` to limit the files that appear in the list. For example, we could use the filter we declared at the start of this section to limit the list of files to those with names ending in ".txt."

```
String[] items;
File myFile;
...
TxtFilter filter = new TxtFilter();
items = myFile.list(filter);
```

In the following example, we use some of the `File` methods. The primary task of `makeInputStream()` is to encapsulate the construction of a new `FileInputStream` and wrap it in a `DataInputStream`. As a bonus, this method also first determines whether the `FileInputStream` constructor should be able to complete its task, by seeing if a file with the given name exists, is a data file, and can be read. If any of these conditions are not met, the method throws a

FileNotFoundException of its own, providing a diagnostic message about the reason for failure.

```
private DataInputStream makeInputStream(String name)
            throws FileNotFoundException
{
    // Get information about the file, if any,
    // with the specified name.
    File f = new File(name);

    if (!f.exists())    // Does the file exist?
        throw new FileNotFoundException("\"" + name
                                + "\" doesn\'t exist");

    if (!f.isFile())    // Is it a data file?
        throw new FileNotFoundException("\"" + name
                                + "\" isn\'t a file");

    if (!f.canRead())    // Can we read from this file?
        throw new FileNotFoundException("\"" + name
                                + "\" can\'t be read");

    // If we get this far, we can attach a new
    // DataInputStream to the file,
    // and that's just what we do.
    FileInputStream fs = new FileInputStream(name);
    DataInputStream source = new DataInputStream(fs);
    return source;
}
```

Now we could modify our doOpen() method so that it begins by calling makeInputStream(). If that call doesn't throw an exception, we know that we can try to read from the file. If makeInputStream() happens to throw one of our FileNotFoundExceptions, we can take some action based on the message we gave the exception when we threw it.

```
private void doOpen()
{
    try
    {
        DataInputStream in = makeInputStream(name);

        numRecs = in.readInt();
        for (int i = 0; i < numRecs; i++)
            r[i].readFrom(in);
```

(continued)

```
            in.close();
      }
      catch (FileNotFoundException ex)
      {
            String s = ex.getMessage();
            if (s.endsWith("doesn\'t exist"))
                  // Take some action.
            else if (s.endsWith("isn\'t a file"))
                  // Take some other action.
            else if (s.endsWith("can\'t be read"))
                  // Take yet another action.
            else
                  System.err.println(ex);
      }
      catch (IOException ex)
      {
            System.err.println(ex);
      }
}
```

The `FileDialog` Class

In the footnote at the bottom of page 434 we said we weren't going to discuss the details of how to deal with the native file system's path conventions. We don't have to, since for most user-oriented programs we can use Java's `FileDialog` class to provide users with the familiar file selection dialog boxes. We thereby eliminate any need for them (or you, for that matter) to know how to specify the location of a file. Figure 10.5 illustrates a typical file dialog box. While the look of a file dialog will depend on the system in which it appears, all file dialogs do the same thing: They allow the user to find or specify a file and they then return the path name of the chosen file for the program to use.

The `FileDialog` class is part of the `java.awt` package. It is a subclass of `Dialog`, which we discussed in Section 4.3. File dialogs are modal, which you may recall means that they trap all events the user might generate until the dialog is put away.

The `FileDialog` class has two constants: `FileDialog.LOAD` and `FileDialog.SAVE`. They are used in one of the constructors to indicate whether the dialog is to be used for locating a file for reading, like the example in Figure 10.5, or whether it is to be used to specify a file for writing, like the one illustrated in Figure 10.6.

There are three constructors for a `FileDialog`. All three require a `Frame` argument, specifying the parent of the `FileDialog`. As a result, it is easier to construct a `FileDialog` from within an application, rather than an applet, since a Java application is generally made by subclassing `Frame`. This, as you'll see in Section 10.4, isn't much of a hardship; file access from applets is problematic, at best.

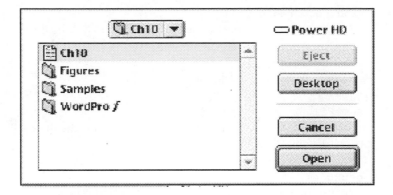

Figure 10.5 A LOAD file dialog box.

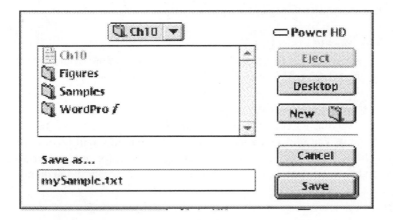

Figure 10.6 A SAVE file dialog box.

```
FileDialog(Frame parent)                    // version 1.1 only
FileDialog(Frame parent, String mssg)
FileDialog(Frame parent, String mssg, int mode)
```

The first constructor creates a new `FileDialog` with no message string (which would appear as the dialog title or as a label within the dialog), in LOAD mode. The second constructor allows you to specify the message for a LOAD dialog, and the third allows you to specify both the message and the mode. The mode must be one of `FileDialog.LOAD` or `FileDialog.SAVE`.

The `FileDialog` methods allow you to get the file information the user provided and to set the initial information displayed in the dialog. All of the `set()` methods must be called before the dialog is shown.

❦ String **getDirectory**()
    Returns a String representing the directory selected by the user.

❦ String **getFile**()
    Returns the name of the selected file.

FilenameFilter **getFilenameFilter**()
    Returns the FilenameFilter associated with this dialog. This method
returns null if this dialog has no FilenameFilter.

int **getMode**()
    Returns the current mode of this FileDialog. The returned value will be
one of the constants FileDialog.LOAD or FileDialog.SAVE.

void **setDirectory**(String dir)
    Allows you to set the opening directory, that is, the one the user will see
when the dialog comes up.

void **setFile**(String name)
    Allows you to set the opening file name. You would use this method to
produce a default file name in a SAVE mode dialog.

void **setFilenameFilter**(FilenameFilter filter)
    Set the FilenameFilter of this dialog to be the one specified in the
argument. The files that appear in the dialog window will be only those for which
the filter's accept() method returns true. Unfortunately, you may find that
your Java environment won't filter the names that appear in the dialog.

void **setMode**(int mode)   // version 1.1 only
    Allows you to set the mode of this dialog.

    If we were interested only in reading and writing files in the current directory
(i.e., where the Java interpreter resided), we wouldn't have to bother with the
directory information. However, since we can't guarantee that the user won't choose
to open a file elsewhere in the file system, we need to use the directory to construct
the complete file name. For example, as this chapter is being written, it is located in
the directory

/power HD/Books/programming.java/text

and has the name Ch10, so the complete name for this chapter would be made by
concatenating the directory, the separator character (which can be found in the
File class constant File.separator), and the file name:

"/power HD/Books/programming.java/text" + "/" + "Ch10"

Fortunately, we never have to see these details. We can get the information from the `FileDialog` and use it to build the file name and then use the name to construct a `FileInputStream` or `FileOutputStream`. The following code might be executed after the user selected Open from the File menu, for example.

```
// Build the dialog.
FileDialog fd = new FileDialog(this, "Open...", FileDialog.LOAD);

// Bring it up.  As with any modal dialog, execution blocks at this
// point, until the user puts the dialog away.
fd.show();

// Make the complete file name.
String fdir = fd.getDirectory();
String fname = fd.getFile();
String name = fdir + File.separator + fname;

// Be polite and free the dialog's system resources.
fd.dispose();

// Now we can use the name to make a FileInputStream.
FileInputStream = new FileInputStream(name);
```

We should actually be more careful here, since the `getFile()` method returns a `null String` if the user puts the dialog away by clicking the Cancel button. Safer would be to test first, like this:

```
FileDialog fd = new FileDialog(this, "Open...", FileDialog.LOAD);
fd.show();
String fdir = fd.getDirectory();
String fname = fd.getFile();
fd.dispose();
if (fname != null)
{
    String name = fdir + File.separator + fname;
    FileInputStream = new FileInputStream(name);
    ...
}
else
    // Take some action in response to a user cancellation.
```

10.4 SECURITY, APPLETS, AND APPLICATIONS

Almost from the beginning, Java was designed with the Worldwide Web in mind. The operating assumption was that a Java applet would reside on a *host* system and would be downloaded over the Net to a *client* computer. Once it had been copied to the client system, the applet would then be run by a Java-enabled Web browser. The last thing in the world the Java design team wanted was to put a loaded gun in the hands of a malicious applet designer, so Java was designed from the start with security in mind.

Consider some of the things that could happen if a hostile program were allowed to execute on the client system. The program might do any of the following things.

- Destroy or alter files.
- Damage the client system's directory structure.
- Get information about the client system, like user name, e-mail account information, or passwords, and pass it back to the host system.
- Get file system information, like directory contents, and send it to the host system.
- Damage other executable programs, causing them to malfunction or not work at all.
- Introduce viruses into the client system.
- Consume so many system resources that the client machine slows to a crawl or can't do anything.
- Steal data or programs from the client.
- "Spoof" the client by appearing to be a trusted program and then acting in a dangerous or annoying fashion.

As you'll see, Java does quite a lot to protect against these and other forms of dangerous behavior by applets. Web browsers typically add their own security measures to the precautions Java takes. The resulting protections aren't perfect—it's theoretically impossible to protect against every eventuality—but we can say that Java is at least as secure as other programming languages—and far more secure than many. The theme of this section, though, is not so much security in Java, but rather the implications these security measures have on what your applets are allowed to do with files and what they're forbidden to do.

Java Security

People have known for centuries that security is enhanced by adopting a multilayer approach: If a potential danger slips through one level, there's still a chance it will be caught at the next. Java embodies this approach by providing four levels of protection, which we'll explain by using metaphors from a hypothetical action movie.

First, *the Java language itself is safe.* By not having explicit access to pointers, Java programs cannot search arbitrary locations in memory. This same memory protection is enforced by array bounds checking. If a program could set up an array and then access array indices far outside the array bounds, a program could do what is known as "core fishing," making probes into memory locations outside those allocated to the program to see what's stored in memory. In our movie, this means that access to the top-secret government installation is restricted to humans only—no ultrapowerful alien cyborgs that can bash down the doors and no supernatural beings that can phase through walls are permitted.

Second, before running an applet, Java passes the compiled code through a *bytecode verifier,* to make sure that the code is legitimate Java and doesn't contain any viruses, for instance. The next scene in the movie shows the visitor passing through a metal detector and being subjected to ID checks, fingerprinting and retina scans to make sure that Doctor Jones isn't carrying any weapons and is who she claims to be.

Third, applets that come across the Net are handled by the *applet class loader,* which assigns the applet its own limited area of memory and makes sure it obeys access restrictions. The class loader also makes sure that an applet doesn't replace any of the standard Java classes with versions of its own. Doctor Jones has gotten in from the outside, but she is restricted to visiting only Level Five—all the doors to the other levels are locked.

Finally, every applet runs under a *security manager,* which monitors any attempts to access the rest of the system and throws a `SecurityException` when the applet attempts an action that is deemed to be insecure. Having gotten into Level Five, Doctor Jones finds herself accompanied by an armed guard wherever she goes. She can walk around Level Five to her heart's content, but the guard will block any attempt she makes to open one of the closed doors or look in a locked file cabinet.

We'll be interested mainly in the last level, since the `SecurityManager` instance assigned to an applet controls access to the file system. We'll show that our movie metaphor, like all metaphors, is only a partial reflection of reality.

Applet Security

When an applet is loaded, either by an applet viewer or a Web browser, the application uses its own `SecurityManager` instance to monitor the applet while it is running. In general (though not always) the `SecurityManager` is initialized to make a distinction between applets that come across the Net, assuming that they aren't to be trusted, and applets that are loaded from the client's local file system, which are treated as being somewhat more trustworthy.

If an applet is loaded from the Net, it is generally not allowed to

- read or write files on the local file system,
- delete any files on the local file system,
- get any information about local files or directories, or even check whether they exist,
- make a new directory on the local system, and
- rename or move any files on the local file system.

Some applet viewers allow you to establish an *access control list* that names files and directories to which applets may have access, but you can usually be guided by the following observation.

Advice: Local File Access

Assume that any applet you write will be denied access to the client's file system.

Applet viewers are designed with an eye toward applet development, so for applets that reside on the same system as the applet viewer, the rules are often relaxed. If you write an applet that accesses files on your own computer, you will probably discover that you can do most of the file operations you want.[5]

However, Web browsers generally don't distinguish between local applets and applets that they load over the Net and so keep both from any access to the local file system. This constraint, of course, makes a Web browser a less than ideal vehicle for testing applets that do any file access. For example, you shouldn't expect an applet to be able to put up a `FileDialog` within a Web browser. Doing so would allow the applet to get information about the local file system from a trusting but naive user.

Note that nothing we've said would have any impact on an applet like `Gigobite` or `OrderPlease`. Both get information from the user (but *not* from the user's file system) and could be expanded to send the order information back to the host file system, from which the applet originated. Denying access to the host file system would severely limit the usefulness of many applets, so such access is generally allowed.

Advice: Access to the Host System

You may usually assume that an applet will be allowed access to files on the host system.

Everything we've said so far concerns applets, rather than Java applications. There's a good reason for that, since the security restrictions imposed on applets differ markedly from those on applications.

Security of Java Applications

A Java application is a stand-alone program, has the same access to the system on which it is running as any other program, and thus has no security. For an application, the client system is the same as the host system, and the user takes the same chances with a Java application as he or she would with any "off the shelf" software like a Web browser, a spreadsheet, a word processor, or a game. The safety features of the language itself are still in place, but as far as files are concerned, an application can do whatever it wants.

---

[5]Though you will probably not be allowed to use the `File` class's `delete()` method.

For programs that must deal with files, the conclusion is obvious. Unless you're writing a program that must be run from within a browser, like our ordering Lablets, write it as an application, rather than an applet.

This restriction isn't burdensome, for there's very little difference between the code that makes up an applet and the code that makes up an equivalent application. Although there are some minor details to take care of, you can usually change an applet to an application and vice versa by using the following equivalences.

1. An application extends `Frame`; an applet extends `Applet`.
2. An application is initialized within its constructor; an applet does its initialization in its `init()` method.
3. An application has a `main()` method; an applet doesn't.

You can see the equivalences in each line of the following parallel lists of an applet and an application.

```
       APPLET VERSION                 APPLICATION VERSION

public class Foo extends Applet  public class Foo extends Frame
{                                {
   // Variables                      // Same variables

   public void init()               public Foo()
   {                                {
      // Code                           // Same code
   }                                }

   // Methods                           // Same methods
}
                                    public static void
                                       main(String[] args)
                                    {
                                       Frame f = new Foo();
                                       f.show();
                                    }
                                 }
```

As an example, we'll provide an application that uses `FileDialogs` and shows the complete path name of the file the user selected. You should recognize much of this code from the example we provided at the end of Section 10.3—all we've done here is wrap the code in an application with some widgets.

```
import java.awt.*;
import java.io.File;
```

(continued)

```
public class Test extends Frame
{
      private TextField      display;    // to display path information
      private Button         loadBttn,   // brings up LOAD dialog
                             saveBttn;   // brings up SAVE dialog

      public Test()
      // Lay out the widgets.
      {
            display = new TextField(20);
            add("Center", display);
            Panel p = new Panel();
            loadBttn = new Button("Load");
            p.add(loadBttn);
            saveBttn = new Button("Save");
            p.add(saveBttn);
            add("South", p);
      }

      public boolean action(Event e, Object arg)
      // Handle clicks on either of the buttons.
      {
            if (e.target == loadBttn)
            {
                  FileDialog fd = new FileDialog(this, "Open...",
                                                FileDialog.LOAD);
                  fd.show();
                  String fdir = fd.getDirectory();
                  String fname = fd.getFile();
                  fd.dispose();
                  if (fname != null)
                  {
                        String name = fdir + File.separator + fname;
                        display.setText(name);
                  }
                  return true;
            }
            else if (e.target == saveBttn)
            {
                  FileDialog fd = new FileDialog(this, "Save...",
                                                FileDialog.SAVE);
                  fd.show();
                  String fdir = fd.getDirectory();
                  String fname = fd.getFile();
                  fd.dispose();
                  if (fname != null)
                  {
                        String name = fdir + File.separator + fname;
                        display.setText(name);
                  }
                  return true;
```

```
                }
                else
                        return false;
        }

        public boolean handleEvent(Event evt)
        {
                if ((evt.id == Event.WINDOW_DESTROY) &&
                                        (evt.target == this))
                        System.exit(0);
                return super.handleEvent(evt);
        }

        public static void main(String[] args)
        {
                Frame f = new Test();
                f.reshape(20, 20, 400, 200);
                f.show();
        }
}
```

10.5   HANDS ON

Perhaps the most surprising part of this chapter's Lablet is how short it is. It's a tribute to the power of Java that, in under three hundred lines, we've managed to build a functioning word processor. Admittedly, WordPro lacks many of the features we've come to associate with its commercial cousins—it has no formatting capabilities like tab and margin settings, the text is limited to a single typeface in a single style, and we can't embed graphics in a WordPro document. However, it does have the ability to open any text document and save a document to a file, and it can do the usual cut, copy, and paste operations. If you wanted, you could use WordPro to write and edit your Java programs or compose a letter to a friend. As you'll see when you do the lab exercises, you can even use WordPro to inspect its own source code!

Designing the Lablet

As Figure 10.7 shows, the WordPro application is visually quite simple.[6] It has two Menus, File and Edit, a central TextArea where the text is displayed, and a TextField at the bottom that is used for status messages.

---

[6]When you run WordPro, it won't look exactly like this. First, the screen shot is from a Macintosh system with a few enhancements a standard Mac doesn't have, and we've also resized the application frame so that its picture will fit on the page.

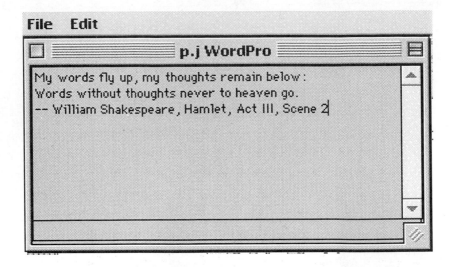

Figure 10.7 The WordPro interface.

You've had enough experience by now that you can probably anticipate what we did to make the WordPro interface. We constructed two Menus and added the necessary MenuItems (as Figure 10.8 shows), we used the default BorderLayout of Frame to put the TextArea in the center and the TextField in the south region. The Frame, of course, came from the fact that WordPro is an application, not an applet.

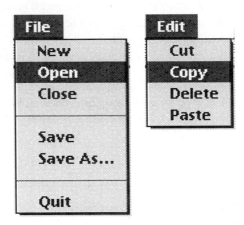

Figure 10.8 WordPro's File and Edit menus.

The action part of the Lablet is based entirely on the items in the two menus, so we can begin this stage by specifying what should happen when the user selects each of the menu items. Specifying these actions was easy—all we had to do was look at what a real word processor does. In the following list we've described the actions `WordPro` currently takes, along with some hints about what a good program should do.

File Menu Items

New: Clears the text in the `TextArea` and clears the current file name, if any. *Enhancements*: A user-friendly application should first ask the user if he or she wants to save the current text. A sophisticated program would keep the current text and bring up a new editing frame for the new text.

Open: Brings up a `FileDialog` in LOAD mode. On the one hand, if the user cancels the dialog, a message to that effect is displayed in the status box and no further action is taken. On the other hand, if the user selects a file to open, the text is cleared and replaced by the contents of the opened file. The number of characters read is displayed in the status field. *Enhancement*: As with New, we should first give the user a chance to save the current text before it's replaced or take the sophisticated option of opening the file in a new frame.

Close: Not implemented in `WordPro`. *Enhancement*: A sophisticated program would close the front frame, after first asking the user whether he or she wants to save the frame's contents to a file. A really sophisticated program would keep track of whether the text in the frame was "dirty," that is, whether it had been modified since the last save. It wouldn't bother the user by asking whether to save text that wasn't dirty.

Save: First, checks whether we have a name for the current file. If we do, just write the text to the current file. If we don't have a current file name, we bring up a `FileDialog` in SAVE mode and allow the user to select a file where the text should be saved. The number of characters written is displayed in the status field. *Enhancement*: We should be sure that we have write permission and that we're not trying to write to a directory. Most of the time, the latter condition won't happen because of the way `FileDialog` works on most systems.

Save As: Not implemented. We leave to you the task of figuring out what choosing this item should do.

Quit: Exit the application. *Enhancement*: If there's any text, we should give the user the option of saving it before quitting. A sophisticated program would ask only whether to save the text if it was dirty. A very sophisticated program with multiple frames would ask this question for every dirty frame.

Edit Menu Items

Cut: Copy the selected text to a clipboard `String` and then delete the selected text.

Copy: Replace the clipboard text with the current selection, without changing the text in the `TextArea`.

Delete: Delete the selected text, without saving it to the clipboard.

Paste: Insert the text in the clipboard, if any, at the location of the cursor in the text area.

To implement these actions, we'll design `private` utility methods for nearly every menu choice. In fact, if you stop to think about it, the only portions of

WordPro that have to be `public` are the `action()` handler, the `handleEvent()` method that an application needs to deal with closing its frame, and the `main()` method (which must be `public`). We made the constructor `public` out of habit—it doesn't have to be, since it will never be called from outside the WordPro class, but it might be if we ever made a subclass of this application.

Exploring `WordPro`

We begin with the usual collection of instance variables. The `String` `clipboard` will be used to save text that is cut or copied, so that we'll have it for subsequent paste operations.

  The `init()` method does the usual layout—we build the menus and add their items, and we add the `text` and `display` widgets.

```
public class WordPro extends Frame
{
    String clipBoard = new String();
    String fileName = new String();
    TextArea text = new TextArea(20,80);
    TextField display = new TextField(15);

    public WordPro()
    {
        setTitle("p.j WordPro");
        MenuBar mbar = new MenuBar();

        // Define and add the File menu to the menu bar.
        Menu m = new Menu("File");
        m.add(new MenuItem("New"));
        m.add(new MenuItem("Open"));
        m.add(new MenuItem("Close"));
        m.addSeparator();
        m.add(new MenuItem("Save"));
        m.add(new MenuItem("Save As..."));
        m.addSeparator();
        m.add(new MenuItem("Quit"));
        mbar.add(m);

        // Define and add the Edit menu to the menu bar.
        m = new Menu("Edit");
        m.add(new MenuItem("Cut"));
        m.add(new MenuItem("Copy"));
        m.add(new MenuItem("Delete"));
        m.add(new MenuItem("Paste"));
        mbar.add(m);
```

```
        // Attach the menu bar and add the text area and display
        // to our frame.  Remember, frames use Border layout.
        setMenuBar(mbar);
        add("South", display);
        add("Center", text);
    }
```

The real work begins with the `action()` handler. As we mentioned when discussing the design of this Lablet, we respond to most of the menu selections by invoking one or more appropriate helper methods.

```
public boolean action(Event evt, Object arg)
{
    if (evt.target instanceof MenuItem)
    {
        if (arg.equals("Quit"))
            System.exit(0);
        else if (arg.equals("New"))
        {
            clearText();
            fileName = "";
            return true;
        }
        else if (arg.equals("Open"))
        {
            doOpen();
            return true;
        }
        else if (arg.equals("Save"))
        {
            doSave();
            return true;
        }
        else if (arg.equals("Cut"))
        {
            doCopy();
            doDelete();
            return true;
        }
        else if (arg.equals("Copy"))
        {
            doCopy();
            return true;
        }
        else if (arg.equals("Delete"))
        {
            doDelete();
            return true;
```

(continued)

```
            }
            else if (arg.equals("Paste"))
            {
                    doPaste();
                    return true;
            }
      }
      return false;
}
```

When the user selects Open from the File menu, the action() handler invokes the doOpen() method. You've seen this method in several guises already. We put up a LOAD FileDialog and when control returns from the dialog we check that the user selected a file. If not, we leave immediately.

```
private void doOpen()
// Display a file dialog box to allow the user to specify an
// input file.
{
      FileDialog myFD = new FileDialog(this,"Open...",
                                        FileDialog.LOAD);
      myFD.show();
      // Get the file name chosen by the user.
      String name = myFD.getFile();
      String dir = myFD.getDirectory();
      fileName = dir + File.separator + name;
      if (name == null)
      // User canceled the open dialog, so return without
      // doing anything.
      {
            display.setText("Open operation cancelled");
            return;
      }
```

If the user hasn't canceled the operation, we assume (dangerously) that the selected file is valid, so we clear the current text and read from the file into the text. We do our reading one line at a time, using the DataInputStream method readLine(). Recall that readLine() reads up to a newline character and discards the character. When we place the line in our text area, we replace the discarded newline. Note that we also keep a local variable, charsRead, to count the total numbers of characters read. Once we've finished reading, we use charsRead as part of the status message in the display field.

```
      clearText();
      try
      {
            // Create an input stream and attach it to the
            // chosen file.
            FileInputStream fis = new FileInputStream(fileName);
            DataInputStream inStream = new DataInputStream(fis);
```

```
                // Read from the file one line at a time.
                String textLine = inStream.readLine();
                int charsRead = 0;
                while (textLine != null)
                {
                        text.appendText(textLine + '\n');
                        charsRead += textLine.length() + 1;
                        textLine = inStream.readLine();
                }
                inStream.close();
                display.setText(charsRead + " chars read from "
                                + fileName);
        }
        catch (IOException e)
        {
                display.setText("" + e);
                return;
        }
    }
```

The doSave() method is very similar to the doOpen() method. We do a
little more here than we did in doOpen(), though, since we first check whether
fileName is the empty String. If it is, the user hasn't gotten the text from a file,
so we put up a SAVE dialog to get a name for the file to be saved. As we did in
doOpen(), we also check whether the user has canceled the save operation and
leave this method if that happened.

```
private void doSave()
// Copy the contents of the TextArea into a file.
{
        if (fileName.equals(""))
        // If we don't have a file name, get one.
        {
                FileDialog myFD = new FileDialog(this,"Save as...",
                                                FileDialog.SAVE);
                myFD.show();
                // Get the file name chosen by the user.
                String name = myFD.getFile();
                String dir = myFD.getDirectory();
                fileName = dir + File.separator + name;
                if (name == null)
                // User canceled the save dialog, so return without
                // doing anything.
                {
                        display.setText("Save operation cancelled");
                        return;
                }
        }
```

If the user hasn't canceled the operation, we assume (again, dangerously) that
the selected file is suitable for writing. We get the entire text String and write it

to the file, newline characters and all, using the `DataOutputStream` method `writeBytes()`.

```
String theText = text.getText();
try
{
    // Create an output stream and attach it to the
    // chosen file
    FileOutputStream fos =
                    new FileOutputStream(fileName);
    DataOutputStream outStream =
                    new DataOutputStream(fos);

    // Write the entire contents of the text to
    // the file.
    outStream.writeBytes(theText);
    outStream.close();
    display.setText(theText.length() +
                    " chars written to " + fileName);
}
catch (IOException e)
// Report any problem with output.
{
    display.setText("" + e);
    return;
}
}
```

The `clearText()` utility is called by `doOpen()` and by the New choice of the `action()` method. We encapsulate it as a method so that we can use a descriptive name in the two locations where it's called. This makes the code somewhat easier to read, at the expense of another method call. Since this operation will occur so infrequently, we judged that the expense of a method call was justified in the interest of clarity.

```
private void clearText()
// Empty the text area.
{
    text.setText("");
}
```

We've finished with the file operations, so we can turn our attention to the actions that take place when the user selects an option from the Edit menu. We get a lot of help from Java here, since a `TextArea` automatically handles the details of highlighting any selections we make, recording the positions of the start and end of the selected text. As we have mentioned, several of the editing operations use a `String`, which we called `clipBoard`, to hold selected text for copying and pasting.

The doCopy() method is called when the user selects the Cut or Copy items from the Edit menu. All we have to do here is copy the selected text to the clipBoard.

```
private void doCopy()
// Place the current selection of the clipboard.
{
     clipBoard = new String(text.getSelectedText());
}
```

The doDelete() method is called when the user selects Cut or Delete from the Edit menu. We delete the selected text in a three-step process. First, we use the String methods getSelectionStart() and substring() to make a temporary copy of everything before the selected portion. Second, we use getSelectionEnd() and substring() to get everything after the selection. Finally, we concatenate these two substrings and replace the text with the result, thereby removing the selected portion. Clever, eh?

```
private void doDelete()
// To delete a selected portion of text, we get the
// following strings:
//     s1: the part before the selection
//     s2: the part after the selection
// and then we simply set the text to be s1 + s2.
{
     // String "all" holds our text temporarily so that we can
     // operate on it
     String all = new String(text.getText());
     String s1 =
          new String(all.substring(0,text.getSelectionStart()));
     String s2 =
          new String(all.substring(text.getSelectionEnd()));
     text.setText(s1 + s2);
}
```

The doPaste() method is simple. All we have to do is replace the selected text with the contents of the clipboard, using the replaceText() method of the String class.

```
private void doPaste()
// Replace the current selection with the contents of
// the clipboard
{
     text.replaceText(clipBoard, text.getSelectionStart(),
                         text.getSelectionEnd());
}
```

We finish our class declaration with the usual boilerplate code that's part of most Java applications. We need to override the `handleEvent()` method so that this application responds correctly when the user clicks the frame's go-away box. In this application, all we do is exit the program. Things would be slightly different if we were doing the sophisticated version, since we would want to destroy the frame and not exit from the program.

The `main()` method here is more or less standard for applications. We construct a `Frame` for the application by invoking the `WordPro` constructor, size the frame suitably, and show it. Then, all the program has to do is wait for the `action()` handler to deal with events triggered by menu selections.

```java
public boolean handleEvent(Event evt)
{
    if ((evt.id == Event.WINDOW_DESTROY) &&
                  (evt.target == this))
        System.exit(0);
    return super.handleEvent(evt);
}

public static void main(String args[])
{
    Frame myFrame = new WordPro();
    myFrame.resize(400,300);
    myFrame.show();
}
}
```

10.6 SUMMARY

❦ We discussed the following classes.
```
    DataInput    (interface)
    DataOutput   (interface)
    File
    FileDialog
    FilenameFilter   (interface)
    InputStream   (abstract)
        FileInputStream
        FilterInputStream
            DataInputStream
    OutputStream   (abstract)
        FileOutputStream
        FilterOutputStream
            DataOutputStream
```
❦ A stream is an ordered sequence of objects and a collection of methods that allow the user to extract an object from the stream (*read* it from the stream) and add a new object to the stream (*write* it to the stream).

- The abstract class `InputStream` is the basis for all streams that serve as a source of data to be read. This class contains methods for byte-level input.
- The abstract class `OutputStream` is the basis for all streams that serve as a destination for data to be written. As with InputStream, the methods of this class support byte-level output.
- Conceptually, information is read from one end of a stream and written to another.
- The streams we've discussed may be opened for reading or writing, but not both. (The `RandomAccessFile` stream can be opened in both modes.)
- The `DataInputStream` subclass of `InputStream` provides methods for reading all of Java's primitive types.
- A `DataInputStream` is constructed by supplying any `InputStream` instance. The resulting `DataInputStream` then provides all of its operations in addition to those of the `InputStream` instance it encloses.
- The `DataOutputStream` class is a companion to `DataInputStream`, in that any value written by a `DataOutputStream` method can be read by the corresponding `DataInputStream` method.
- Because of the way streams are read and written, the information in any stream constructed by a sequence of write operations can be extracted by the corresponding sequence of read operations.
- A file is any collection of information that is logically related and stored on a physical device, like a floppy disk, hard drive, magnetic tape, or compact disk.
- File input is accomplished through the `FileInputStream` class. This is a subclass of `InputStream`, so a `FileInputStream` can be used in the constructor of a `DataInputStream` instance, to provide routines for reading any primitive type from a file.
- The class `FileOutputStream` is the companion of `FileInputStream`. As with input, it is common to wrap a `FileOutputStream` inside an instance of `DataOutputStream`.
- When writing a `String` to a stream using `writeBytes()`, you should get in the habit of appending a newline character. That way, you'll never have problems using `readLine()` to get the `String` back.
- It is generally easy to perform I/O on class instances, by reading or writing the primitive types that comprise the instance's member data.
- A header is a collection of information at the start of a stream. A typical use of headers is to store the number of records that follow in the stream.
- Most of the stream read methods will throw an `EOFException` if they reach the end of the stream before completing the read operation. A common way of reading from files is to keep reading until the `EOFException` is thrown.
- The `FilenameFilter` interface includes a single method, `accept()`. A class that implements `FilenameFilter` provides an implementation of `accept()`, to determine whether a file name will be accepted. This interface is used with the `File` method `list()` and (perhaps, depending on the Java environment) the `FileDialog` method `setFilenameFilter()`.
- An instance of the `File` class is constructed by supplying a file name. This class contains a number of useful methods for finding information about files.

❦ FileDialog is a subclass of Dialog. It allows the user to select a file and to return the name of the file and the name of the file's directory.

❦ A FileDialog instance may be in one of two modes, LOAD and SAVE. The only difference is in the appearance of the resulting dialog.

❦ In most cases, applets have no access to the client file system.

❦ It is usually safe to assume that an applet will have access to its own host file system.

❦ There are no limitations on the file system access a Java application has, save for those that are in force for all other programs on the system.

10.7 EXERCISES

1. Under what circumstances will the InputStream method

   ```
   int read(byte[] bArray, int offset, int length)
   ```

   throw an IndexOutOfBoundsException?

2. Suppose that the bytes in a stream object out are written by calling

   ```
   out.write(a);
   out.write(b);
   out.write(c);
   ```

   Then, suppose that those bytes are later used as the basis of another stream, in, and are read by the segment

   ```
   x = in.read();
   y = in.read();
   z = in.read();
   ```

   What are the values of x, y, and z?

3. To give you an idea of how useful the wrapper classes DataInputStream and DataOutputStream are, consider what you'd have to do if you were limited to byte-level operations.

   a. Suppose that you read four bytes into an array b[0], b[1], b[2], b[3]. Write a code segment that would convert these bytes to an int, with b[0] as the high-order eight bits and b[3] as the low-order bits. You might make good use of the bit-level operations we mentioned in Section 5.3.

   b. Reverse the process and show how you would convert an int to four bytes and write them to a stream, in such a way that the result would be compatible with the read operation of part (a).

4.   Here's the last doOpen() method from Section 10.3. Recall that it reads Records until it runs out of things to read. There's nothing syntactically wrong with this method, but it could cause problems at runtime. What could happen, and how would you prevent it?

```
private void doOpen()
{
      try
      {
            FileInputStream = new FileInputStream("Sample4");
            DataInputStream in = new DataInputStream(fstr);

            numRecs = 0;
            while (true)
            {
                  r[numRecs].readFrom(in);
                  numRecs++;
            }
            in.close();
      }
      catch (EOFException ex)
      {
      }
      catch (IOException ex)
      {
            System.err.println(ex);
      }
}
```

5.   Write the method

```
void copy(FileInputStream src, FileOutputStream dest)
```

that will copy src into dest. You may assume that the two file streams have been constructed and that both are valid. Note that neither of the arguments is wrapped in DataInputStream and DataOutputStream classes, so you're just copying bytes.

6.   Modify the copy() method of Exercise 5 so that before copying it checks whether the argument streams are valid for reading and writing. If either or both of the files are invalid, throw a FileNotFoundException with an appropriate message.

7.   Change the copy() method of Exercise 5 to

```
void append(FileInputStream src, FileOutputStream dest)
```

that will append the bytes of src to the end of dest.

8. Give the class declarations for each of the following data structures and describe briefly how you would write instances of these classes to a file. You might find it helpful to use some auxiliary classes.

    a. A class list of students, including their names and scores (integers in the range 0 . . . 20) on each of five quizzes, two exams (integers in the range 0 . . . 100) and a final (integer in the range 0 . . . 300).

    b. The current state of a game of chess (those of you who aren't chessplayers will have to do a little more work than those who are).

    c. A black and white picture. You may assume that the picture is 200 pixels wide and 150 pixels high and that each pixel is either black or white.

    d. A black and white picture of arbitrary size.

9. Suppose that you had a file of `doubles` that had been generated by using the method `writeDouble()` from `DataOutputStream`. If you needed to read all the elements from the file, how could you tell how many `doubles` the file contained?

10. How would you sort a file of `ints`, assuming that there was enough room in memory to store the entire file in an array?

11. How would you sort a file of `ints`, assuming that only half of them would fit in memory? This is a hard problem, and there are several correct answers.

12. Suppose you had two files of `ints`, each of which was sorted in order from smallest to largest. Write a method that would *merge* the two files into one, sorted in increasing order. For example, the merge of files containing 3, 15, 18, 25, 39 and 4, 7, 22, 41, 44 would be 3, 4, 7, 15, 18, 22, 25, 39, 41, 44.

13. Write an application that will open a file (which you may assume contains text only) and count the number of instances of each letter, treating upper- and lowercase letters as identical. The method should ignore any character that is not 'A' . . . 'Z' or 'a' . . . 'z'.

14. Suppose that the `OrderPlease` Lablet of Chapter 9 was to be modified to write a completed order to a file. We haven't discussed the naming conventions for files on remote machines, so just describe the structure of the file for an order and how you would write it.

15. Assume that you had three classes, A, B, and C, and that each had its own `readFrom()` and `writeTo()` methods. What would you do to create a file containing a mixture of instances of these classes in such a way that it could be read by a program that didn't know ahead of time the types of the elements in the file, except that they would be A, B, or C? A typical file, for example, might contain

    ```
    b1, b2, a1, b3, c1, a2, c2, c3, c4, b4, c5, a3
    ```

    where the as are of type A, the bs are of type B, and the cs are of type C.

16. Write a method `long size(File f)` that acts like the following.

- If f doesn't exist, it returns 0.
- If f is a data file, it returns the length of the file.
- If f is a directory, it returns the sum of the sizes of all files in the directory.

You will make use of the `File` methods `list()` and `length()`, among others. This is an exceptionally difficult problem. A true understanding of the fact that a method definition can include calls to itself changes the problem from exceptionally difficult to almost trivial.

CHAPTER ELEVEN

Threads

"Time," it is said, "is what keeps everything from happening at once." Few domains are more rigidly time-constrained than the activities that take place within a computer. A single processor executes the instructions of a program sequentially, employing what is known as the *fetch–execute cycle*. At each iteration of this cycle, the next program instruction is fetched from memory, and that statement is used to determine the action of the machine. Having fetched and executed one statement, the cycle begins again at the next instruction and continues in the same way until the program halts. The fetch–execute cycle is implemented in an orderly manner by endowing the computer with a sense of time.

Each computer includes a clock at the heart of its circuitry, marking off the steps of the fetch–execute cycle like an electronic metronome. Thus we can envision the action of the computer as an elaborate dance with thousands of performers, choreographed by the program, and conducted by the clock, at a rate of millions of steps per second.[1]

The problem with this approach is that we often want several things to happen in our programs simultaneously. For instance, we would like to be able to click buttons while our program is doing other processing, like updating the screen. Oh—we already can, can't we? We can because the Java environment provides the *illusion* of simultaneity by slicing two or more tasks into small pieces, executing one task for a moment, then executing part of another, and returning its attention to the first, and so on. The computer is still doing one thing at a time, but it works so fast that several things appear to be going on concurrently.

Modern languages like Java provide the capability to exploit this time-slicing feature in our programs, by specifying *threads* of execution. Using threads, we'll be able to split off the execution of parts of our programs and imagine that the separate parts are capable of executing simultaneously, without ever having to concern ourselves with the invisible details of how this *multiprogramming* or *multithreading,* as it's called, is actually being implemented by the underlying system.

---

[1]With the right equipment, it's actually possible to hear or see this dance, since the circuits of a computer emit faint but detectable radio signals.

OBJECTIVES

In this chapter, we will
- ❦ Discuss the concept of independent threads of execution in a program.
- ❦ Introduce the `Thread` class and the `Runnable` interface.
- ❦ Show how threads may be grouped.
- ❦ Discuss some problems that may arise from concurrent execution and introduce techniques for synchronizing threads.
- ❦ Build a digital alarm clock.

11.1   THREADED EXECUTION

You've gotten through ten chapters so far and haven't seen any threads. You might be tempted to think that a programmer could lead a happy and productive life without ever worrying about separating execution into several pieces. Well, take a look at a simple task and try to do it knowing what you do now. Here's the assignment:

> *Write an applet that draws an animated picture of a ball bouncing back and forth across the screen. Provide a toggle button that will allow the user to start and stop the animation.*

That sounds simple enough. First, set up a `Canvas` for the drawing and a `Button` to control the animation, as shown in Figure 11.1. The button will begin life with the label "Start" and each time it is clicked, it will toggle its label between "Start" and "Stop." Good object-oriented practice calls for making a separate `Ball` class that will know how to `draw()` itself on the `Canvas` and `move()` to another location.

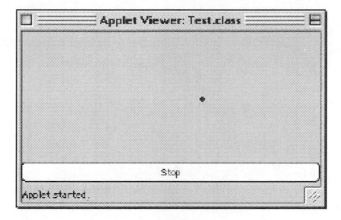

Figure 11.1 The bouncing ball applet, as it should appear.

The initial part of the applet is simplicity itself.

```
// BOUNCING BALL APPLET, VERSION 1
public class Bouncer1 extends Applet
{
    private Canvas  display = new Canvas();
    private Button  startStop = new Button("Start");
    private Ball    ball;

    public void init()
    {
        resize(300, 150);

        setLayout(new BorderLayout());
        add("South", startStop);
        add("Center", display);
    }
```

The `action()` handler is only slightly more difficult. The only event it deals with is a click on the `startStop` button. If its label is "Start," change it to "Stop" and start the ball bouncing, by constructing a new Ball instance and moving it, as long as the button label is "Stop." When you click on the "Stop" button, it will change its name, thereby stopping the loop.

```
    public boolean action(Event e, Object arg)
    {
        if (e.target == startStop)
        {
            if (startStop.getLabel().equals("Start"))
            {
                startStop.setLabel("Stop");

                // Bounce the ball.
                ball = new Ball(display);
                ball.draw();
                while (startStop.getLabel().equals("Stop"))
                    ball.move();
            }
            else
            {
                startStop.setLabel("Start");
            }
            return true;
        }
        else
            return false;
    }
}
```

The `Ball` class likewise has few surprises. A `Ball` knows what `Canvas` to use to draw itself, and its *x*- and *y*-coordinates, along with how far to move at each step. The only new part is to draw the ball in what is known as XORMode. This painting mode has the property that drawing an object over itself will erase the object. Note that the move() method checks for collisions with invisible boundaries at $x = 10$ and $x = 290$ and reverses the direction variable increment if it detects a collision.

```java
class Ball
{
    // a reference to where the ball can do its drawing (set in
    // the constructor)
    private Canvas   theCanvas;
    // the ball coordinates
    private int            x,
                           y;

    // the amount we move at each step
    private double         velocity;

    public Ball(Canvas c)
    // Record the Canvas on which drawing will take place
    // and start the ball at a random location, with
    // random velocity.
    {
        theCanvas = c;
        x = (int)(Math.round(10 + 280 * Math.random()));
        y = (int)(Math.round(10 + 100 * Math.random()));
        velocity = 0.6 + Math.round(2.5 * Math.random());  }

    public void draw()
    // Draw a filled circle at (x, y).  Since we've set
    // the drawing mode to XOR, drawing a ball twice at
    // the same location will erase it.
    {
        Graphics g = theCanvas.getGraphics();
        g.setXORMode(Color.red);
        g.fillOval(x, y, 5, 5);
        g.dispose();
    }

    public void move()
    {
        // Do a "nothing" loop to slow the ball down.
        for (int i = 0; i < 10000; i++)
            ;
        // Erase the old image,
        draw();
        // move the ball, checking for bounces,
        if (x >= 290)
            velocity = -Math.abs(velocity);
        if (x <= 10)
            velocity = Math.abs(velocity);
```

```
        x = (int)(Math.round(x + velocity));
        // and draw the ball in its new location.
        draw();
    }
}
```

We encourage you to take a moment to enter and run this applet. Be advised, though, that it's likely to misbehave. The result will depend on the system you're using, but there's a very good chance that once the ball starts up, you won't be able to stop it. Not only won't the button work, but you may not even be able to quit the applet runner or browser you're using.

The problem is that the "tight loop" we highlighted in the `action()` handler is hogging all the computer's attention. As long as the ball is bouncing in the loop, nothing else can happen. All the button clicks are piling up in the event queue (if they're even being received), and the system simply can't find the time to get to them. In technical terms, the processor and the GUI resources are *shared resources,* needed by the applet and the environment within its running. The applet is *starving* the system by not letting it in to the resource it needs.

If you stop to think about it, you'll see there's not even a good place to put the loop. The `action()` method clearly isn't a good choice—as long as the loop is running, control never gets out of the first `if` clause, so you never get a chance to change the button label in the second clause. You can't put the loop in the `init()` method, either—if the loop ever were to finish, control would pass out of the method and never return. Where else could the loop go? In a `paint()` method? No, that wouldn't work either, for reasons we'll leave to you. It seems that you're stuck—with the tools you have at your disposal, it seems that there simply is no way to write a program to do what you need. Basically, you need another place for the animation to go, and you need to be able to iterate the loop in such a way that the rest of the program can still have an occasional chance to do its own work.

The Basics of the Thread Class

A thread represents an independent sequence of action in a program. If you're used to thinking of the execution of a program as if you were running your finger down the code from statement to statement, perhaps jumping backward to the start of a loop, or jumping from one place to another in response to a method call, you'll have a good model of a thread, the applet thread. You can, however, have several fingers following the action. In practice, the fingers never move simultaneously—one finger may execute several statements and then pause while another traces through the code—but this alternation happens so rapidly that you may as well think of them both working at the same time.

The `Thread` class is part of the `java.lang` package. It has a moderate number of constructors and methods, many of which we'll have to defer discussing until later. For now, one constructor and four methods are of interest to us. First, let's look at the constructor:

Thread()

Creates a new thread. Using our finger metaphor, a new finger has been raised, but it hasn't yet pointed at any location in the code.

The Thread methods that we'll use now include one class method and three instance methods.

❦ static void **sleep**(long ms) throws InterruptedException

Halts the execution of the current thread for approximately the given number of milliseconds. This method is useful, since it gives other threads a chance to execute while the current thread is sleeping. The Thread.sleep() method throws an InterruptedException in case the sleeping thread is interrupted by another. That won't often happen (and will never happen in version 1.0), but since InterruptedException is a checked exception,[2] we have to use a try/ catch pair whenever we call Thread.sleep(), even though we don't do anything in the catch clause. There's no guarantee that sleep() will cause a thread to pause for *exactly* the indicated number of milliseconds—the runtime system will do the best it can, but it may be a bit off.

❦ void **start**() throws IllegalThreadStateException

Starts this thread, including any initialization that has to take place before the thread begins running. This method calls run() when it is finished with the initialization you've given it. The finger has been set down in the code of this method, and almost immediately hops to the next. This method may throw an IllegalThreadStateException. This is an unchecked exception—we'll talk about thread states in Section 11.3.

❦ void **run**()

Begins execution of this thread. This method is the heart of any thread—it is where the thread does its work. Here's the home for the finger, as you'll soon see. You'll rarely call run() yourself, instead, you'll call start() and let it call run() for you.

final void **stop**() throws SecurityException

Stops the execution of the thread. Metaphorically, the moving finger stops here and goes away. Note that this method is final—you can't override it for your own purposes. You won't see the unchecked SecurityException unless you do something the SecurityManager determines is forbidden, like trying to stop a thread that doesn't belong to you.

For simple threads, you may not need to call stop(), but you will certainly need to call start() and write your own run() method.

---

[2]See pp. 395–396 for a review of checked and unchecked exceptions.

Fundamental Principle of Threads:

A thread executes in a run() method.

There are two standard ways of dealing with threads in a program. The first is to make a subclass of Thread and provide a run() method in the class. The second is to create an instance of Thread and provide an external run() method in which the Thread instance may execute. Let's apply the first technique to our bouncing ball exercise. The only modifications needed in the Ball class are to make it a subclass of Thread and give it a run() method.

```
// BOUNCING BALL APPLET, VERSION 2 MODIFICATIONS
class Ball extends Thread
{
    // No changes in the instance variables and the constructor.

    public void run()
    {
        draw();
        while (true)
        {
            move();
            try
            {
                sleep(10);
            }
            catch (InterruptedException e)
            {
            }
        }
    }

    // No changes in draw() and move().
}
```

We've taken the animation loop out of the applet and put it in our run() method. Doing so solves the "Where do we put the loop" problem we mentioned before—the loop has a natural home in the run() method. The only other part worth mentioning here is that we used the Thread sleep() method to cause this thread to pause for 10 milliseconds. This solution is a much better way of slowing the motion of the ball than the "do nothing" loop we had in Bouncer1. Now the Ball thread actually surrenders control for a hundredth of a second in each loop iteration, which is plenty of time for any other threads to get useful things done. In particular, it allows the applet thread to call the stop() method for this thread, terminating its execution. This explains why we could get away with the neverending while(true) loop in the run() method—we let the thread run until it is stopped externally by the user pressing the "Stop" button.

A well-mannered thread will always call the class method `Thread.sleep()` in its `run()` method to give other threads a chance to execute.

The applet also requires very few changes. In fact, all we have to do is change the `action()` handler, by moving the animation loop out and replacing it with calls to the `Thread` methods `start()` and `stop()`. Note that the `Ball` class doesn't override these two methods—we're using the `start()` and `stop()` methods of the `Thread` superclass.

```
// BOUNCING BALL APPLET, VERSION 2 MODIFICATIONS
public boolean action(Event e, Object arg)
{
    if (e.target == startStop)
    {
        if (startStop.getLabel().equals("Start"))
        // Start the animation
        {
            startStop.setLabel("Stop");

            ball = new Ball(display);
            ball.start();
        }
        else
        // Stop the animation and clear the canvas.
        {
            startStop.setLabel("Start");
            ball.stop();
            display.repaint();
        }
        return true;
    }
    else
        return false;
}
```

The `Runnable` Interface

Suppose that for some reason `Ball` was a `final` class so that we couldn't make it a subclass or that `Ball` needed access to private information in the applet. How would we find a home for the animation loop then? The other standard way of using threads is to provide an external `run()` method, using the `Runnable` interface, declared in the `java.lang` package.

This interface contains a single method:

void **run**()

By declaring a class to implement `Runnable`, we're promising to provide an implementation of that method, so that any threads declared in that class will have a place to execute.

Two Ways of Running Threads:

1. Declare a class that is a subclass of `Thread` and override the `Thread` method `run()` in the class. Run instances of that class.
2. Declare a class that implements `Runnable`, provide an implementation of `run()`, and use that to run any threads you declare.

You can think of these two strategies as if you (a class) were looking for a place to change clothes and get a night's sleep (perform some actions). In the first strategy, it's as if you're a camper carrying your own tent (your own `run()` method). In the second you're checking into a hotel room (using an external `run()` method). We can illustrate the second strategy by again modifying our bouncing ball example.

In this version, the applet class implements `Runnable` and provides a `run()` method, in which we bounce the `ball` instance. We must declare a `Thread` for the animation in this version, since our modified `Ball` class isn't a `Thread` itself.

```
// BOUNCING BALL APPLET, VERSION 3 MODIFICATIONS
public class Test extends Applet implements Runnable
{
    // no changes to other instance variables
    private Thread ballThread;

    // init() is unchanged

    public void run()
    {
        ball.draw();
        while (true)
        {
            ball.move();
            try
            {
                Thread.sleep(10);
            }
            catch (InterruptedException e)
            {
            }
        }
    }
}
```

Note that we use a different version of the `Thread` constructor in the `action()` method. This version requires a `Runnable` object as an argument so that the new `Thread` will know where to look for its `run()` method. In this example, the `run()` method is in the applet, so we use the applet's synonym `this` for the argument.

```
public boolean action(Event e, Object arg)
{
    if (e.target == startStop)
    {
        if (startStop.getLabel().equals("Start"))
        {
            startStop.setLabel("Stop");

            ball = new Ball(display);
            ballThread = new Thread(this);
            ballThread.start();
        }
        else
        {
            startStop.setLabel("Start");
            ballThread.stop();
            display.repaint();
        }
        return true;
    }
    else
        return false;
}
}

class Ball
{
    // no other changes
}
```

Before we leave this example, we should point out that we don't have to limit ourselves to a single animation thread. In fact, we can have as many threads in a program as we want. We could modify our bouncing ball applet so that it has several balls on screen at once, by spawning a new thread each time the user clicked the button. We'll change the version 3 applet by changing the start/stop button to one that simply creates a new thread. In the new version, we remove the `ball` and `ballThread` instance variables, constructing a new thread in the `action()` handler and a new ball at the start of the `run()` method.

In the new version, we don't have to modify the `Ball` class. Aside from removing the two instance variables, the only changes that we make are in the applet's `run()` and `action()` methods.

```
// BOUNCING BALL APPLET, VERSION 4 MODIFICATIONS
public void run()
{
    Ball ball = new Ball(display);
```

```
        ball.draw();
        while (true)
        {
            ball.move();
            try
            {
                Thread.sleep(10);
            }
            catch (InterruptedException e)
            {
            }
        }
    }

public boolean action(Event e, Object arg)
{
    if (e.target == newBttn)
    {
        Thread ballThread = new Thread(this);
        ballThread.start();
        return true;
    }
    else
        return false;
}
```

Grouping Threads

It's quite possible for a moderately complicated program to have dozens of threads alive at any time. It would be very useful in such cases to be able to provide some overall organization to the mass of threads, and Java does just that with the ThreadGroup class, which is part of the java.lang package. By collecting threads into a ThreadGroup, we can apply some operations to the entire group, rather than having to apply the operation to each thread individually.

Every thread is contained in exactly one ThreadGroup. With the exception of the top-level "system" ThreadGroup, every group is contained in another, known as its *parent*.

There are two constructors for this class:

```
ThreadGroup(String name) throws SecurityException
ThreadGroup(ThreadGroup parent, String name) throws
                                NullPointerException,
                                SecurityException,
                                IllegalThreadStateException
```

Construct a ThreadGroup containing no threads. The first constructor makes a ThreadGroup whose parent is the group containing the current thread. The second constructor allows you to specify the ThreadGroup in which this new ThreadGroup will be contained. The second constructor will throw a NullPointerException if the parent ThreadGroup hasn't yet been initialized and will throw an `IllegalThreadStateException` if the parent has been destroyed. Both constructors allow you to specify a name for the new `ThreadGroup`.

```
Thread(ThreadGroup parent, Runnable target) throws
                              SecurityException,
                              IllegalThreadStateException
Thread(ThreadGroup parent, String name) throws
                              SecurityException,
                              IllegalThreadStateException
```
Construct a new thread belonging to the specified parent `ThreadGroup`. The `target` argument in the first constructor specifies the object that contains the `run()` method for this `Thread`. The second constructor is used for thread subclasses that contain their own `run()` methods. The `name` argument allows you to give this new `Thread` a name (see the `Thread` summary in Section 11.4 for details about naming threads). If you don't specify a group to which a new `Thread` belongs, Java will put it in a default group.

There are quite a few methods for this class, especially since it has been hit hard by the transition from Java version 1.0 to version 1.1. As usual, we'll flag the most important or useful methods.

```
int activeCount()                         // may vanish
```
Returns the total number of threads in this group and all its subgroups. This method will eventually be replaced by `allGroupsCount()`.

```
ThreadGroup[] allGroups()               // version 1.1 only
```
Returns an array containing the `ThreadGroups` in this group and its subgroups. To find the size of the array, you could call `allGroupsCount()`. This method replaces the 1.0 method `enumerate()`.

```
int allGroupsCount()                    // version 1.1 only
```
Returns the total number of threads in this group and all its subgroups.

```
Thread[] allThreads()                   // version 1.1 only
```
Returns an array containing the `Threads` in this group and its subgroups. To find the size of the array, you could call `allThreadsCount()`. This method replaces the 1.0 method `enumerate()`.

```
int allThreadsCount()                   // version 1.1 only
```
Returns the total number of threads in this group and all its subgroups.

```
int activeGroupCount()                    // may vanish
```
This method is the 1.0 equivalent of `allGroupsCount()`.

```
int destroy() throws SecurityException,
        IllegalThreadStateException
```
This method destroys this group. Before you call it, you must have stopped

all the threads it contains or an `IllegalThreadStateException` will be thrown.

```
void enumerate(Thread[] threads)          // may vanish
void enumerate (Thread[] threads,
               boolean recurse)           // may vanish
void enumerate (ThreadGroup[] groups)     // may vanish
void enumerate (ThreadGroup[] groups,
               boolean recurse)           // may vanish
```

These methods are equivalent to the 1.1 versions `allThreads()`, `threads()` (if `recurse` is `false`), `allGroups()`, and `groups()` (if `recurse` is `false`), respectively.

final ThreadGroup **getParent**()

Returns the parent `ThreadGroup` of this group or `null` if this group is the top-level system group.

ThreadGroup[] **groups**()   // version 1.1 only

Returns an array of all `ThreadGroups` in this group. This method replaces the 1.0 method `enumerate()`.

int **groupsCount**()   // version 1.1 only

Returns the number of `ThreadGroups` directly contained in this group. To get a count of all groups in this group and its subgroups, use the version 1.1 method `allGroupsCount()` or the 1.0 equivalent `activeGroupsCount()`.

boolean **parentOf**(ThreadGroup g)

Returns `true` if and only if the argument is equal to this `ThreadGroup`, or is a parent of this group.

❦ final void **resume**() throws SecurityException

Calls `resume()` on all threads in this group and its subgroups.

❦ final void **stop**() throws SecurityException

Stops all threads in this group and its subgroups. Note that `ThreadGroup` doesn't have a matching `start()` method.

❦ final void **suspend**() throws SecurityException

Suspends all threads in this group and its subgroups.

Thread[] **threads**()   // version 1.1 only

Returns an array of all threads directly contained in this group. This method replaces the 1.0 method `enumerate()`.

Finally, there is a `Thread` method that deals with `ThreadGroups`.

ThreadGroup **getThreadGroup**()

Returns the group to which this thread belongs. Recall that every `Thread` belongs to some `ThreadGroup`.

We've included a new `ThreadGroup`, to contain all the ball threads, in version 5 of our bouncing ball applet. The Stop button kills all threads in the Balls `ThreadGroup`. If you try to run this applet, you may discover that the `SecurityManager` under which the applet runs won't let you construct a new `ThreadGroup`.

```
// BOUNCING BALL APPLET, VERSION 5 MODIFICATIONS
public class Bouncer5 extends Applet implements Runnable
{
    private Canvas display = new Canvas();
    private Button newBttn = new Button("New"),
                          stopBttn = new Button("Stop");

    private Thread ballThread = null;
    private ThreadGroup tg = new ThreadGroup("Balls");

    // init() and run() omitted

    public boolean action(Event e, Object arg)
    {
        if (e.target == newBttn)
        {
            ballThread = new Thread(tg, this);
            ballThread.start();
            return true;
        }
        else
        if (e.target == stopBttn)
        {
            tg.stop();       // Kill all threads in this group
            display.repaint();
            return true;
        }
        else
            return false;
    }
}
```

11.2 THREADS AND APPLETS

Try running `Bouncer4` or `Bouncer5`. In particular, run the applet in a browser and create a dozen or so balls. Then, without quitting the browser, switch to a program with which you're familiar, like a word processor, and see if you notice any difference in its behavior. There's a good chance you will—your program may seem quite sluggish. The reason is pretty clear: The dozen ball threads are still running in the background and your program has to share computational resources with all of them. You might notice the same problem even if you didn't open a new program and just went to another page in the browser. What we need is a way to stop a thread from running once the browser leaves the page containing the applet.

Two `Applet` methods will help us do what we want. Like `init()` and `paint()`, you can't call these methods yourself. They are called for you by the browser.

❦ void **start**()

This method is called each time the page containing the applet appears. Unlike `init()`, which is done only once, when the applet is loaded, `start()` may be called many times during the life of the applet. Be careful here—in spite of the name similarity, this method has nothing to do with the `Thread` method `start()`.

❦ void **stop**()

Called when the page containing the applet is replaced by another. You would usually override this method to suspend or stop any threads that are currently active. The earlier warning applies here, too—don't confuse this method with the `Thread` method `stop()`.

The usual way of using these two methods is to do something like this:

```
public class MyApplet extends Applet implements Runnable
{
    ...
    Thread myThread = null;
    ...
    public void run()
    {
        // Do something.
    }

    public void start()              // the Applet method
    {
        if (myThread == null)
        {
            myThread = new Thread(this);
            myThread.start();    // the Thread method
        }
    }

    public void stop()               // the Applet method
    {
        if (myThread != null)
        {
            myThread.stop();     // the Thread method
            myThread = null;
        }
    }
}
```

Here, we're using `null` for two purposes: It serves as a flag to indicate whether a thread has been started (since we'd get a `NullPointerException` if we tried to stop a `null` thread) and it hastens reclamation of the dead thread's resources after it has been stopped.

If we didn't want to kill a thread when the applet page was replaced, we could use a gentler pair of `Thread` methods.

🐾 `final void` **`suspend`**`() throws SecurityException`

Stops the execution of this `Thread`. This method acts in a manner similar to `Thread.sleep()`, except that the thread stays suspended until a call is made to `stop()` (which will wake it up and kill it, if you'll permit a somewhat gruesome description) or to `resume()`. If a thread has already been suspended, calling `suspend()` has no effect.

🐾 `final void` **`resume`**`() throws SecurityException`

If this thread has been suspended, it starts execution again, at the place where it was suspended. If this thread is currently executing, this method has no effect. As we mentioned when we discussed the `Thread` method `stop()`, this method (and `suspend()`) may throw `SecurityExceptions`, but you don't have to check for them and you'll probably never see them.

Here's an example of the difference between start/stop and suspend/resume. We begin with a simple `Thread` extension that counts from 0 through 99, displaying the count in an external `TextField` and sleeping for a second between display updates.

```
class Counter extends Thread
{
    private TextField   theField; // where to write the value

    public Counter(TextField t)
    {
        theField = t;
    }

    public void run()
    {
        for (int i = 0; i < 100; i++)
        {
            theField.setText("" + i);
            try
            {
                sleep(1000);
            }
            catch (InterruptedException e) {}
        }
    }
}
```

In the applet, we set up an array of three Counters and three TextFields in which they will write. We start all three Counters in the init() method, but we take different actions for each thread in the applet's start() and stop() methods—the thread c[0] is started and stopped, the thread c[1] is suspended and resumed, and we take no special action for c[2], simply letting it run.

```
public class StartStopTest extends Applet
{
    private Counter[]    c = new Counter[3];
    private TextField[] t = new TextField[3];

    public void init()
    {
        for (int i = 0; i < 3; i++)
        {
            t[i] = new TextField(5);
            add(t[i]);
            c[i] = new Counter(t[i]);
            c[i].start();
        }
    }

    public void start()
    {
        if (c[0] == null)
        {
            c[0] = new Counter(t[0]);
            c[0].start();
        }
        c[1].resume();
    }

    public void stop()
    {
        if (c[0] != null)
        {
            c[0].stop();
            c[0] = null;
        }
        c[1].suspend();
    }
}
```

If you run this applet in a browser, you'll see that the three TextFields will be incremented more or less in step. After about fifteen seconds or so, they might have the values 15, 15, and 15. If you then direct the browser to another page and stare at that page for a while before returning to the applet's page, you might see the values 0, 15, and 45 in the fields for c[0], c[1], and c[2]. The 0 shows that the c[0] thread was killed and reborn, the 15 reflects the fact that c[1] was suspended at 15 while you were away, and the 45 would come from the fact that all the time you were looking at the other page the `c[2]` thread was still merrily counting away in the background.

It's generally a bad idea to let a thread keep running after an applet has stopped. An applet that declares threads should have a `stop()` method that either kills or suspends each of its threads.

11.3 SYNCHRONIZING THREADS

Once you have a program with threads, life can get a bit complicated. Consider the following seemingly simple description.

> *Thread* A *and thread* B *share a* `TextField, display`. *Thread* A *repeatedly does some calculation resulting in an* `int` *and places the text equivalents in* `display`. *Thread* B *repeatedly gets the text from* `display` *and converts it to an* `int` *for its own calculations.*

When the program is running, the system will swap execution between A and B. How this happens varies from environment to environment and is completely beyond your control.

Fundamental Principle of Thread Execution:

You cannot assume *anything* about the order of execution of two or more threads.

The system might run one thread to completion before starting the other; it might run one thread through three statements before running the other for one statement; and it might even let one thread get halfway through a statement, suspend it, and start the other. Once you realize that you can't know how execution will be interleaved between A and B, several ugly scenarios become possible.

1. A gets partly through updating `display` and then execution switches to B—the result is that B might get garbage when it tries to inspect `display`.
2. A puts new information in `display` before B has inspected the old value—the old value is lost.
3. B gets a value and then gets back to `display` before A has sent in a new value—the old value is used twice.

Scenario 1 calls for *mutual exclusion*—the two processes should not be allowed simultaneous access to the shared `display` resource, while scenarios 2 and 3 require *serialization*—that is, each process must wait until the other finishes using the shared resource.

It's important to note that these scenarios are problematic only because threads A and B both access the `display` object. If the code executed by A and the code executed by B never made reference to a common object, A and B could both go their way in any order the run-time system decided, and the order of execution would have no effect on the result of the program.

If two threads never communicate or share information, you don't have to worry about synchronizing them. If they do, you do.

Synchronization and Mutual Exclusion

The first problem we have to deal with is eliminating the possibility that two or more threads might try to access an object at the same time. Java deals with this problem by using what are known as *monitors*. We implement monitors by providing each object with a *lock*. Once a thread acquires a lock for an object, no other thread can acquire the lock until the original thread surrenders it. In Java, the keyword `synchronized` is used to identify a method or other segment of code associated with an object's lock.

To identify a method associated with an object's lock, we use the `synchronized` keyword in the method header:

```
class MyClass
{
    . . .
    public synchronized void doThis()
    {
        . . .
    }
    public synchronized void doThat()
    {
        . . .
    }
    public void doTheOther()
    {
        . . .
    }
}
```

`MyClass` has three methods, two of which are synchronized and one of which is not. Suppose that `foo` was an instance of `MyClass`, declared as

```
MyClass foo = new MyClass();
```

and suppose also that none of the `foo` methods had yet been called. Now, if `foo.doThis()` was called, the current thread would acquire `foo`'s lock and no other thread could complete a call to any of `foo`'s `synchronized` methods until the original thread left the `doThis()` method. Whether the lock had been acquired or not, any thread could enter the nonsynchronized `doTheOther()` method. In Figure 11.2, we illustrate a typical situation, using a heavy line to indicate which thread currently has `foo`'s lock.

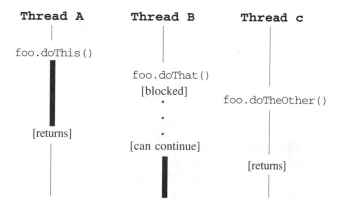

Figure 11.2 Acquiring and releasing locks on an object.

If a thread enters a `synchronized` method of an object, no other thread can enter any of that object's `synchronized` methods until the first thread leaves the method.

What makes this process work is that acquiring and releasing a lock are *atomic* actions—a thread cannot be preempted by the system while it is doing either of these operations. In other words, when a `synchronized` method is called, you can be sure that one of two things will happen: The thread will be able to enter the method, thereby acquiring the lock for the object, or the thread will block and not enter the method until the object's lock has been released.

You can synchronize a block of code, as well. The statement

synchronized (*expression*)
    statement or block of statements

requires that the *expression* evaluate to an object (not a primitive type). The thread executing this statement will then either acquire the object's lock and execute the controlled statements or will block its execution until it acquires the object's lock.

Synchronization solves the first of our problems—enforcing mutual exclusion.

To guarantee that two threads don't try to access an object simultaneously, `synchronize` the methods or code that access that object.

As you might expect, several of the methods of the standard Java classes are synchronized. The `Component` methods `disable()` and `enable()`, for instance, are synchronized, since we wouldn't want one thread to try to disable a `Button` while another was trying to enable it. Doing so might result in a button that was dimmed but still responded to mouse clicks, for instance. For similar reasons, the `add()` and `remove()` methods of `MenuBar` are also synchronized.

The `wait()` and `notify()` Methods

Synchronization allows us to deal with the mutual exclusion problem, but we haven't yet addressed the serialization problem—that a thread may have to wait for a resource until another thread has done something to it. Consider our example from the start of this section—thread A places integers in `display`, but before depositing a new value it should wait until B has had a chance to get the old one.

It would be easy enough for the two threads to communicate, once we realize that they could use the display field for more than just sending and receiving integers. One possible solution would be to use an empty text string:

1. The sender, A, would wait until `display` was empty before sending an `int`.
2. The receiver, B, would wait until `display` had a number. Then, it would get that number and empty the field.

This protocol wouldn't be hard to implement. We could just use a pair of empty loops so that the two threads would "spin their wheels" until `display` was in the necessary state.

```
public synchronized int getInt()
{
    while (display.getText().equals(""))
        ;
    // The only way we can get to this point is if there's
    // some text, so we get it and convert it to an int.
    int n = ...

    display.setText("");    // Signal that we've gotten the value,
    return n;               // and send it back
}

public synchronized void setInt(int n)
{
```

```
        while (!display.getText().equals(""))
            ;
        // The only way we can get to this point is if the
        // text is empty, so we can now send the int.
        display.setText("" + n);
}
```

Unfortunately, this may not work. Recall the fundamental principle of thread execution: *You can't guarantee anything about how the order of execution of two threads will be interleaved.* Suppose, for example, that thread B gets into getInt() before A gets into setInt(). Then, B will hog the processor while it loops, waiting for something to be placed into display. As long as B is looping, of course, A never gets a chance to put something in display, so there's a chance that B will never get out of its loop. As far as anyone could tell, it would appear that the program had locked up, which in fact would be the truth. It's not even a help if A gets in first—as an exercise, we ask you to come up with a scenario in which the program still wouldn't work as it should.

What we need is a way to make a thread block until some situation has occurred, and then wake up and continue execution. Three methods allow us to do this. They're found—of all places—in the Object class. All three may throw an unchecked IllegalMonitorStateException, which you won't have to worry about unless you call one of these methods without having acquired the object's lock.

Call wait(), notify(), and notifyAll() only within synchronized methods or code.

Since these three methods are called only within a synchronized method or block of code, they all deal with the associated object's lock.

❦ final void **wait**() throws IllegalMonitorStateException,
                                 InterruptedException

This method causes the current thread to suspend execution and give up its lock on the object where the call was made. The thread doesn't give up any other locks it may possess. The thread remains suspended until it is awakened by notify() or notifyAll(). It is then free to try to reacquire its lock. If it does, it picks up execution where it left off; if it doesn't, it remains blocked until it acquires the lock again.

❦ final void **notify**() throws IllegalMonitorStateException

Awakens some thread that has been suspended on this object by a wait() call. If several threads have been blocked by wait() calls for this object, you cannot predict which will be awakened.

❦ final void **notifyAll**() throws IllegalMonitorStateException

Awakens all threads suspended by wait() calls for this object.

If a thread has been suspended by `wait()` and then awakened by `notify()` or `notifyAll()`, it has to compete for a lock before it can continue execution.

In the following applet, we implement our reader/writer problem. We first declare a class `IntField` to serve as our display. The only reason we declare this class, rather than just using a `TextField`, is so that we could provide it with the synchronized methods `getInt()` and `setInt()`.

```java
class IntField extends TextField
{
    public IntField()
    {
        super("", 15);
    }

    public synchronized int getInt()
                    throws InterruptedException
    {
        while (getText().equals(""))
            wait();

        int n = -1;
        String s = getText();
        try
        {
            n = Integer.parseInt(s);
        }
        catch (NumberFormatException e)
        {
            System.err.println("???!!!");
            System.exit(0);
        }
        // Delay a second so we can see what's happening
        // before we clear the text.
        Thread.sleep(1000);
        setText("");
        notify();
        return n;
    }

    public synchronized void setInt(int n)
                    throws InterruptedException
    {
        while (!getText().equals(""))
            wait();
        setText("" + n);
        notify();
    }
}
```

The classes `Reader` and `Writer` are subclasses of `Thread`. The `run()` method of `Reader` just gets the values in the `IntField` and sums them, while the `run()` method of `Writer` just generates the successive odd integers 1, 3, 5, . . . , 19 and places them in the field. The only detail we haven't mentioned yet is that `Writer` signals the end of its task by placing the *sentinel* value –1 in the field, and `Reader` uses that as a signal for it to report the sum it has found.

```
class Writer extends Thread
{
    private IntField f; // the external display field

    public Writer(IntField f)
    {
        this.f = f;
    }

    public void run()
    {
        try
        // We enclose the whole block in a try, since
        // both setInt() and sleep() may throw an exception.
        {
            for (int i = 0; i < 10; i++)
            {
                f.setInt(2 * i + 1);
                sleep(500);
            }
            f.setInt(-1);   // Signal completion.
        }
        catch (InterruptedException e)
        {
        }
    }
}

class Reader extends Thread
{
    private IntField f;

    public Reader(IntField f)
    {
        this.f = f;
    }

    public void run()
    {
        int n = 0;
        int sum = 0;
```

(continued)

```
                    try
                    {
                        n = f.getInt();
                        while (n >= 0)
                        {
                            sum += n;
                            sleep(1000);
                            n = f.getInt();
                        }
                        f.setInt(sum); // Report the result.
                    }
                    catch (InterruptedException e)
                    {
                    }
                }
            }
```

We use these three classes in a very simple applet, containing an IntField and a Button that, when clicked, starts the two threads.

```
public class ReaderWriter extends Applet
{
    private IntField    display = new IntField();
    private Button      startBttn = new Button("Start");

    private Writer      w = new Writer(display);
    private Reader      r = new Reader(display);

    public void init()
    {
        resize(300, 150);
        add(display);
        add(startBttn);
    }

    public boolean action(Event e, Object arg)
    {
        if (e.target == startBttn)
        {
            w.start();
            r.start();
            return true;
        }
        else
            return false;
    }
}
```

Priorities

As you have seen several times so far, lots of things are going on in the background while a Java program is running. One of these background processes is the *thread scheduler.* It's the job of the thread scheduler to decide which thread to run when; for example, the current thread is suspended by wait() or sleep().

While the details of how the thread scheduler makes its decisions vary from one system to another, there are a few things you can count on. First, every thread in a Java program has a *priority,* expressed as an integer from 1 through 10. When deciding which thread to run, the thread scheduler will generally choose to run the thread with highest priority. This decision doesn't mean that the scheduler will wake up a sleeping thread, nor will it revive a thread that has been suspended by wait() but hasn't yet heard a notify(). It does, though, mean that if two threads are capable of being run, the one with the higher priority will be favored to run next.

The Thread class contains three class constants you can use to refer to priorities:

```
final static int MIN_PRIORITY = 1;
final static int NORM_PRIORITY = 5;
final static int MAX_PRIORITY = 10;
```

You can inspect or modify the priority of a thread by using a pair of Thread instance methods.

```
final int getPriority()
```
Returns the priority of this thread.

```
final void setPriority(int p) throws SecurityException,
                                      IllegalArgumentException
```
This method sets the priority of this thread to the value specified in the argument (assuming the SecurityManager will permit such an operation). If the argument is smaller than MIN_PRIORITY or larger than MAX_PRIORITY, this method will throw an IllegalArgumentException. The priority of a thread cannot be larger than the maximum permitted priority of its thread group.

Each ThreadGroup has a maximum priority value for all its threads. This value can be set and inspected by the following methods.

```
final int getMaxPriority()
final void setMaxPriority(int p) throws SecurityException,
                                        IllegalArgumentException
```

You can adjust the priority of a thread to suit the needs of your program. A thread that does some relatively unimportant task could be given a low priority, for instance. It's usually a bad idea to give a task a priority of MAX_PRIORITY, since doing so might lock out other important threads (like the applet thread itself).

The following applet inspects all currently active threads while it's running. Try running this applet in several different environments—the default priorities given to the applet thread and the thread "Mine" vary quite a bit from system to system. See Section 11.4 for a description of the `Thread` class method `activeCount()`.

```
public class Test extends Applet implements Runnable
{
    private TextArea display = new TextArea(10, 30);
    private Thread mine = new Thread(this, "Mine");

    public void init()
    {
        resize(300, 150);
        add(display);
        report();
    }

    public void run()
    {
    }

    private void report()
    {
        Thread[] t = new Thread[10];
        Thread.enumerate(t);
        for (int i = 0; i < Thread.activeCount(); i++)
        {
            display.appendText(t[i] + "\n");
        }
    }
}
```

11.4 SUMMARY OF THE Thread CLASS

Since we've scattered the `Thread` methods throughout Sections 11.2 and 11.3, we'll list here most of the constants, constructors, and methods of the `Thread` class, explaining only those we haven't mentioned before.

Class Constants

```
final static int MIN_PRIORITY = 1;
final static int NORM_PRIORITY = 5;
final static int MAX_PRIORITY = 10;
```

Constructors

Thread()

Thread(String name)
> Creates a Thread with specified name.

Thread(Runnable target)

Thread(Runnable target, String name)
> Creates a Thread with specified name and an object where the run()
> method for this Thread is located.

Thread(ThreadGroup parent, String name) throws
                                    SecurityException
                                    IllegalThreadStateException

Thread(ThreadGroup parent, Runnable target) throws
                                    SecurityException
                                    IllegalThreadStateException

Thread(ThreadGroup parent, Runnable target, String name) throws
                                    SecurityException
                                    IllegalThreadStateException

Class Methods

static int **activeCount**()   // may vanish
> Returns the number of threads in the ThreadGroup to which the current
> Thread belongs. Note that this method and the four that follow are static, so
> they would be called by using the prefix "Thread," unless called from within a
> subclass of Thread.

static Thread **currentThread**()
> Returns the current thread, that is, the one that was active when this method
> was called.

static void **enumerate**(Thread[] t)   // may vanish
> Sets the argument to an array containing all threads in this thread's group and
> any subgroups of the group.

☢ static void **sleep**(long ms) throws InterruptedException

static void **yield**(long ms)
> Causes the current thread to surrender its execution. Doing so may allow
> another thread to be selected for execution. All this method does is give other
> threads the possibility of running—the system may decide to run another thread or
> simply revive the old current thread. This method is another way a thread can be

polite—rather than calling `sleep()`, you can call `yield()` to give other threads a chance to execute.

Instance Methods

```
final String getName()
```
Returns the name of this `Thread`, or `null` if no name has been specified.

```
final String getPriority()
```

```
final ThreadGroup getThreadGroup()
```

```
final boolean isAlive()
```
Returns `true` if this thread has been started and has not yet died, either as a result of having called `stop()` or completing its `run()` method.

```
final void join() throws InterruptedException
final synchronized void join(long ms) throws InterruptedException
```
The first method causes the current thread to suspend its execution until this thread has finished, either by being stopped or by completing its `run()` method. The second method waits for the current thread until this thread has completed or the indicated number of milliseconds have elapsed. These methods are useful when the current thread spawns another and has to wait for the new thread to complete before it can continue.

```
❦ final void resume() throws SecurityException
```

```
❦ void run()
```

```
final void setName(String name) throws SecurityException
```
Sets the name of this `Thread`.

```
final void setPriority(int p) throws SecurityException,
                                     IllegalArgumentException
```

```
❦ synchronized void start(int p) throws
                                     IllegalThreadStateException
```

```
❦ final void stop() throws SecurityException
```

```
❦ final void suspend() throws SecurityException
```

Methods from `Object`

```
❦ final void notify() throws IllegalMonitorStateException
```

```
❦ final void notifyAll() throws IllegalMonitorStateException
```

☙ final void **wait**() throws IllegalMonitorStateException
                                     InterruptedException

11.5 HANDS ON

The `TickTock` Lablet is a simple digital alarm clock. It displays the system time in hours, minutes, and seconds and is updated often enough that it is never off from the system time by more than a second. As you'll see, we get a lot of help here from Java's `Date` class, part of the `java.util` package. This program also makes use of threads, but you probably already expected that from the fact that it's the Lablet for the thread chapter.

In addition to displaying the current time, our clock has an alarm feature, as well. We can set the time when the alarm is to go off and can turn off the alarm once it has been set.

Designing the Lablet, I: The `TickTock` User's Manual

Designing a consumer electronics device, even in simulation, can be surprisingly difficult. If you've ever struggled with programming a VCR, you've seen evidence that coming up with a good design isn't easy, even for experts. In fact, if you specify the action of a device for general use and find the process easy, there's a good chance that you're either *very* good or have missed the point somewhere. We'll shortly provide the user's manual for our clock, but before we do we should be honest and mention that we had trouble with the design ourselves. In fact, what you see is the third major revision of the Lablet. Each of the first two revisions worked, but we discarded them and started anew after asking ourselves, Would this be usable right out of the box, or would we have to hire extra people to answer the help lines?[3]

Finally, though, we settled on the final design and wrote the User's Manual.

☙ Welcome!

Thanks for using `TickTock`™, another fine product of Rick and Stu's Applet Mill®. `TickTock` is a fully functional digital alarm clock, and a lot more. Not only can you use `TickTock` as it comes, but you can also configure it to your own needs, just by following the simple guidelines in the Lab Manual that came with

---

[3]Authorial rant: Many companies would do well to ask themselves this question before their products hit the stores.

your purchase. In this User's Manual, we'll take a look at your new product and show you how you can get the most out of it. To learn how to change `TickTock` into a visual sorting demonstration or an online order form, just take a look at the Lab Manual.

Product Hint. If you want to become a true master of `TickTock`, we suggest you look at *programming.java* (PWS Publishing Co., Boston, MA). This book makes a tasteful gift, as well, for those hard-to-satisfy relatives and friends.

❦ System Requirements

`TickTock`™ is system-independent. You can run it on any computer that has a Java-aware Web browser or applet runner installed.

❦ Getting Started

When you start `TickTock`, it will look like this:

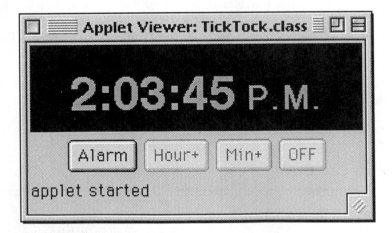

There are two basic parts to `TickTock`: the Time Display™, where the time is displayed, and the Control Panel™, which contains the control buttons.

`TickTock` starts in Time Mode: The Time Display shows the current system time. In Time Mode, `TickTock` is a clock—it's as simple as that! You'll notice that only one of the buttons in the Control Panel is active—clicking on the "Alarm" button will take you out of Time Mode and into Alarm Mode.

☙ The Alarm

When you press the "Alarm" button, the Control Panel changes to look like this:

When you see this configuration, you know you're in Alarm Mode and can set the alarm. To do so, click on the "Hour+" and "Minute+" buttons. Each of these advances the hour or minute portion of the Time Display. Once you've changed the Time Display to the time you want the alarm to go off, just press the "Set" button. You'll return to Time Mode and the Time Display will revert to showing the system time, as usual. That's all there is to it!

Back in Time Mode, you can tell that the alarm has been set, since the "Off" button will be active:

Once the alarm has been set, it will go off at the indicated time, turning the display from green to red.[4] To turn off the alarm, just click on the "Off" button—the display will turn back to green and the "Off" button will be disabled until you go back to Alarm Mode (by clicking the "Alarm" button) and set the alarm again.

Designing the Lablet, II: Meeting the Specifications

As amusing as it was to write the User's Manual, we had to settle down eventually and build the applet. The look of the applet dictated the first stage of design, as usual. We needed a display for the time and four buttons. We decided to write our own class for the display, since there was no way to get the look we wanted from a `TextField` (mainly because we couldn't have two sizes for text). Since we would be drawing the time string, we made our `Timer` class a subclass of `Canvas`.

The next step was to write the applet. We deliberately deferred writing the `Timer` class, since we wanted to let the applet design dictate the methods we would

[4]Our engineers plan to add an audible alarm, but first they need to find out how by looking in Chapter 12. When this feature is added to `TickTock` `2.0`, all registered users will be able to participate in our upgrade program.

include in `Timer`. We knew that we would need a thread to control the time display, since we wanted the time to be updated independently of whatever else the applet was doing. Deciding where to put the thread was more or less a matter of preference. We had two choices:

1. Make the thread an instance variable of the applet and put the thread's `run()` method in the applet itself. This choice would require that we declare the applet to implement the `Runnable` interface.
2. Put the thread and its `run()` method in Timer. This brought up a problem we hadn't encountered so far. We couldn't make `Timer` a subclass of `Thread`, since it was already a subclass of `Canvas`, and Java doesn't allow multiple inheritance. In this case, the solution is to do with `Timer` what we had done with the applet in the preceding option—we would declare `Timer` to implement the `Runnable` interface, give it its own thread and write a `run()` method for the thread.

Since the Timer wouldn't need access to any of the applet's data, there was no clear reason to prefer one solution over the other. Since you hadn't seen the second strategy in action, we opted for that one.

Now the applet started to take shape. Keeping in mind that this applet might be used in a browser, we wrote `start()` and `stop()` overrides to start and stop the timer when we visited or left the page containing the applet. Having done that, all we had to do was fill in the applet's `action()` method. Here's what we came up with for the four buttons.

bMode: The leftmost button. When clicked, we first look at its label.
    "Alarm": The user wants to set the alarm. Enable the "Hour+" and "Min+" buttons and change the label of this button to "Set." Tell the timer to go to alarm mode.
    "Set":   The user has set the alarm. Disable the "Hour+" and "Min+" buttons and enable the "Off" button. Tell the timer to return to time mode.
bHr: Tell the timer to increment the hour part of its display by 1.
bMin: Tell the timer to increment the minute by 1.
bOff: Disable the "Off" button. Tell the timer to turn its alarm off.

We now knew what the `Timer` class had to do. It needed its own thread, of course, and it needed to keep instance variables for the hour, minute, and second to display, along with the alarm hour and minute. It needed to know whether it was in time mode and whether its alarm had been set. It needed `start()` and `stop()` methods and a `run()` method for its thread. It needed a method to instruct it to switch between time and alarm modes, along with one to set its alarm. It also needed methods to set its alarm hour and minute and it needed to be able to `paint()` itself. In the words of the User's Manual, "That's all there is to it!" Let's take a look at the result.

Exploring `TickTock`

We begin with the usual `import` declarations. The `Date` class is one we haven't discussed yet. A `Date` object contains the system time, day, month, and year when it was created. To get our clock to reflect the time, we'll create new `Date` objects in the `Timer`'s `run()` method and use them to update the display.

```
import java.awt.*;
import java.util.Date;
import java.applet.*;
```

The start of the applet declaration is easy enough to understand. We declare the `Timer` instance we'll use, along with the four buttons, and lay everything out in the `init()` method.

```
public class TickTock extends Applet
{
    private Timer    timeDisplay;      // the clock

    private Button   bMode,            // sets the mode
                     bHr,              // increment the alarm hour
                     bMin,             // increment the alarm minute
                     bOff;             // turn off the alarm

    //--------------------- Applet Methods ---------------------

    public void init()
    // This is called when the applet is first loaded.
    // It is only done once.
    {
        resize(250,100);
        setLayout(new BorderLayout());

        Panel controlPanel = new Panel();
        bMode = new Button("Alarm");
        bHr = new Button("Hour+");
        bMin = new Button("Min+");
        bOff = new Button("OFF");
        controlPanel.add(bMode);
        controlPanel.add(bHr);
        controlPanel.add(bMin);
        controlPanel.add(bOff);
        add("South", controlPanel);

        bHr.disable();
        bMin.disable();
        bOff.disable();

        timeDisplay = new Timer();
        add("Center", timeDisplay);
    }
```

The start() and stop() methods just call the methods of the same names in the Timer class.

```
public void start()
// Called each time the browser returns to the page containing
// this applet.  In this program, we just start the timer.
{
      timeDisplay.start();
}

public void stop()
// Called when the browser leaves the page containing this
// applet.  In this program, we just stop the timer.
{
      timeDisplay.stop();
}
```

The applet does all its work in the action() method. We've described what it has to do—a click in the mode button does different things, depending on whether we're about to change the alarm settings or setting the alarm and returning to time mode. Aside from disabling and enabling the buttons as needed, this method just calls the setTimeMode(), incrementAlarmHour(), incrementAlarmMinute(), and setAlarm() methods of the Timer instance.

```
public boolean action(Event e, Object o)
{
      if (e.target == bMode)
      // The user has changed from time to alarm mode or
      // vice versa.
      {
            if (bMode.getLabel().equals("Alarm"))
            // Get things ready for the user to set the alarm.
            {
                  bMode.setLabel(" Set ");
                  bHr.enable();
                  bMin.enable();
                  timeDisplay.setTimeMode(false);
            }
            else
            // Set the alarm to the time the user set
            // and then return to clock mode.
            {
                  // Tell the timer to set its alarm,
                  timeDisplay.setAlarm(true);
                  // and reset our widgets back to time mode.
                  bMode.setLabel("Alarm");
                  bHr.disable();
                  bMin.disable();
                  bOff.enable();
```

```
                        timeDisplay.setTimeMode(true);
                }
                return true;
        }
        else if (e.target == bHr)
        // Increment the hour part of the display.
        {
                timeDisplay.incrementAlarmHour();
                return true;
        }
        else if (e.target == bMin)
        // Increment the minute part of the display.
        {
                timeDisplay.incrementAlarmMinute();
                return true;
        }
        else if (e.target == bOff)
        // Tell the timer to turn its alarm off.
        {
                timeDisplay.setAlarm(false);
                bOff.disable();
                return true;
        }
        return false;
    }
}
```

Note that the Timer class declaration begins with the instance variables for its thread of execution, the time display variables, and two boolean variables, describing whether the alarm has been set and whether we are in time mode. The constructor just sets the background color and sets the display thread to null so that it will be initialized in the class's start() method.

```
class Timer extends Canvas implements Runnable
// A Timer object displays the current system time in hh:mm:ss
// format, followed by "A.M." or "P.M.," as appropriate.
// A Timer has an alarm that can be set by the user.
// This class carries its own thread for updating the time.
{
    private Thread    clockThread;       // the thread
    private int       hour = 0,          // displayed hour
                      minute = 0,        // displayed minutes
                      second = 0,        // displayed seconds
                      aHour = 0,         // alarm hour
                      aMinute = 0;       // alarm minutes
    private boolean   alarmSet = false,
                      timeMode = true;

    public Timer()
    // All we do to construct a Timer is set its background color
```

(continued)

```
// and flag the clockThread as null.
{
     setBackground(Color.black);
     clockThread = null;
}
```

The start() and stop() methods are called externally when the applet needs to start and stop the clock.

```
public void start()
// Called to start the clock.  We make a new clock thread,
// if needed, and start it.
{
     if (clockThread == null)
     {
          clockThread = new Thread(this);
          clockThread.start();
     }
}

public void stop()
// Called to stop the clock.  We check that the thread
// exists, and if it does, we kill it.
{
     if (clockThread != null)
     {
          clockThread.stop();
          clockThread = null;
     }
}
```

The thread, of course, spends its time in this class's run() method. Depending on whether we're in time mode or not, we either use the Date class methods getHours(), getMinutes(), and getSeconds() methods to update the display, or we set the display to the current alarm values.

The updateTime() method we call here just sets the hours, minutes, and seconds of the display and then calls repaint() to show the new result.

```
public void run()
// This is the implementation we promised when we declared this
// class to be Runnable.  This is where the clockThread
// executes.
{
     while (clockThread != null)
     {
          if (timeMode)
          // We're in time mode, so just update the timer.
          {
               Date now = new Date();
               updateTime(now.getHours(),
```

```
                                       now.getMinutes(),
                                       now.getSeconds());
          }
          else
          // We're in alarm-setting mode now, so ask the timer
          // to show its alarm setting, for possible changes
          // by the user.
                updateTime(aHour, aMinute, 0);

          try
          // clockThread politely sleeps here, so that other
          // threads have a chance to do their things (like
          // painting and responding to button clicks).
          {
                Thread.sleep(250);
          }
          catch (InterruptedException e)
          {
          }
      }
  }
```

The paint() method is fairly complex. The Date class keeps hours in 24-hour format, so we use this to determine whether to paint "A.M." or "P.M." and adjust the hour to 12-hour format. We also use two local variables minSep and secSep to contain either just a semicolon separator or a semicolon and leading 0, if the minutes or seconds are less than 10.

We set the horizontal offset to compensate for a one- or two-digit hour, and we set the drawing color to red if the alarm has been triggered. Finally, we build a string representing the time and draw it in the appropriate color.

```
public void paint(Graphics g)
{
      String minSep = ":";   // separator for hh:mm
      String secSep = ":";   // separator for mm:ss
      String ampm = " ";         // "A.M." or "P.M."
      int adjHour = hour;    // conversion from 24-hour format.

      // Make the String for A.M./P.M.
      if ((hour >= 0) && (hour < 12))
            ampm = ampm + "A.M.";
      else
            ampm = ampm + "P.M.";

      // Set the hour displayed to reflect a 12-hour clock.
      if (hour > 12)
            adjHour = hour - 12;
      if (hour == 0)
            adjHour = 12;
```

(continued)

```
        // Insert leading zeroes into the time, if necessary
        if (minute < 10)
              minSep = minSep + "0";
        if (second < 10)
              secSep = secSep + "0";

        // Set the horizontal offset to compensate for a
        // one- or two digit hour.
        int x;
        if (adjHour >= 10)
             x = 10;
        else
             x = 30;

        // Finally, draw the time string in the
        // appropriate color.
        if (alarmTriggered())
              g.setColor(Color.red);
        else
              g.setColor(Color.green);
        g.setFont(new Font("Helvetica",Font.BOLD,36));
        g.drawString(adjHour + minSep + minute +
                              secSep + second, x, 50);
        g.setFont(new Font("Helvetica", Font.BOLD, 24));
        g.drawString(ampm, 155, 50);
}

private void updateTime(int h, int m, int s)
// Set the time shown to h hours, m minutes, s seconds.
{
        if ((s != second) || (m != minute) || (h != hour))
        // Only repaint if the time has changed.  Doing so, we
        // eliminate most of the annoying flicker that comes from
        // frequent calls to repaint().
        {
            hour = h;
            minute = m;
            second = s;
            repaint();
        }
}
```

The methods dealing with the alarm are all short and simple. We provide methods to set the time mode, enable or disable the alarm, and set the alarm hours and seconds. The private method `alarmTriggered()` is a utility called in `paint()`, to determine whether we should paint the display string in red or green.

```
public void setTimeMode(boolean timeMode)
{
        this.timeMode = timeMode;
}
```

```
    public void setAlarm(boolean isOn)
    // If the argument is true, enable the alarm.  If the
    // argument is false, disable the alarm.
    {
        alarmSet = isOn;
    }

    public void incrementAlarmHour()
    // Increase the alarm hour setting by 1, making sure
    // that 0 <= aHour < 24.
    {
        aHour++;
        if (aHour == 24)
            aHour = 0;
        updateTime(aHour, aMinute, 0);
    }

    public void incrementAlarmMinute()
    // Increase the alarm minute setting by 1, making sure
    // that 0 <= aMinute < 60.
    {
        aMinute++;
        if (aMinute == 60)
            aMinute = 0;
        updateTime(aHour, aMinute, 0);
    }

    private boolean alarmTriggered()
    // Detect whether the alarm should go off (i.e., alarm has been
    // set and the current time is later than the alarm setting)
    // and return the appropriate value.
    // Called in paint().
    {
        return alarmSet &&
                ((hour > aHour) || ((hour == aHour) &&
                                        (minute >= aMinute)));
    }
}
```

11.6 SUMMARY

❦ We discussed the following classes:
>   Applet (for the methods start() and stop())
>   Date
>   Object (for the methods wait(), notify(), and notifyAll())
>   Runnable (interface)
>   Thread
>   ThreadGroup

- ❦ A thread represents an independent sequence of action in a program. A program can have arbitrarily many threads.

- ❦ A thread requires a `run()` method. A thread executes in its `run()` method.

- ❦ There are two standard ways of dealing with threads in a program. The first is to make a subclass of `Thread` and provide a `run()` method in the class. The second is to create an instance of `Thread` and provide an external `run()` method in which the `Thread` instance may execute.

- ❦ The fundamental thread methods are `start()` (which you can override and call), `run()` (which you'll always override and never call) and `stop()` (which you may call, but can't override).

- ❦ The class method `Thread.sleep()` suspends the current thread for the specified number of milliseconds.

- ❦ A well-mannered thread will always call the class method `Thread.sleep()` or `yield()` in its `run()` method, to give other threads a chance to execute.

- ❦ If you declare a class to implement the `Runnable` interface, you must provide a `run()` method in the class (unless it's also declared to be `abstract`). The `run()` method may then be used for the class's threads.

- ❦ Threads may be declared to be part of a `ThreadGroup`. Each thread is in some `ThreadGroup`—if you declare a thread without specifying a `ThreadGroup`, the thread will be assigned to the group containing the currently executing thread. A thread may be a member of only one `ThreadGroup`.

- ❦ With the exception of the top-level group, every `ThreadGroup` belongs to another. A `ThreadGroup` may not belong to itself.

- ❦ The `Applet` method `init()` is called once, when the applet is loaded by the browser.

- ❦ The `Applet` method `start()` is called whenever the browser opens the page containing the applet. Unlike `init()`, `start()` may be invoked several times during the applet's life. Like `init()`, you don't call `start()` yourself—the system makes the call for you.

- ❦ The `Applet` method `stop()` is called when the browser leaves the page containing the applet.

- ❦ The `Applet` `start()` and `stop()` methods are often used to call the `Thread` methods `start()` and `stop()`, for the threads in the applet.

- ❦ The `stop()` method kills its thread. To keep the thread but stop it from executing, use the `suspend()` method to put the thread to sleep and `resume()` to wake it up.

- ❦ A thread may continue to execute long after the applet has quit. It's good practice to stop any thread you declare eventually, unless you are sure it will reach the end of its `run()` method.

- ❦ You cannot assume anything about the order of execution of two or more threads. That's up to the thread scheduler and is beyond your control.

- ❦ Every object has an associated lock. If a method is declared to be `synchronized`, or if a block of code is part of a `synchronized` statement. A thread that enters a synchronized method or block belonging to an object acquires the lock for the object. No other thread can enter any of the objects synchronized portions until the thread that has the lock leaves the synchronized segment.

❧ To guarantee that two threads don't try to access an object simultaneously, synchronize the methods or code that access that object.

❧ The wait(), notify(), and notifyAll() methods of Object must appear within code that has been synchronized.

❧ The wait() method suspends the action of the thread and forces it to give up its lock.

❧ The notify() method wakes up some waiting thread, allowing it to compete for the lock it surrendered. Once the thread has reacquired its lock, it continues from where it left off.

❧ The notifyAll() method wakes up all the threads waiting for the lock on the object.

❧ Every thread in a Java program has a *priority,* expressed as an integer from 1 to 10. When deciding which thread to run, the thread scheduler will usually choose to run the thread with highest priority.

11.7 EXERCISES

1.   In the Bouncer applets, versions 2–5, does increasing the argument of sleep() slow down or speed up the motion of the balls? Explain.

2.   Change Bouncer5 so that each ball's direction has a *y*-component, as well as an *x*-component. In other words, allow the balls to move in a diagonal direction and bounce off the top and bottom, as well as the left and right walls. This exercise has nothing to do with threads, but it makes the applet more fun to watch.

3.   Change Bouncer5 by assigning the second ball's thread a different priority than the others. Describe the changes, if any, you see and explain your findings.
      a.   Assign the second thread a priority that is 1 more than the priority of the first ball's thread.
      b.   Assign the second thread a priority of MAX_PRIORITY.
      c.   Assign the second thread a priority of MIN_PRIORITY.

4.   In Bouncer5, how could you determine whether a ball was about to collide with another?

5.   Change Bouncer5 so that the balls collide realistically. This exercise is best when combined with Exercise 2. This solution is quite difficult, even if you know about conservation of energy and momentum.

6.   Look at the StartStopTest applet at the end of Section 11.2. As written, it uses a Counter class, declared as a subclass of Thread. Rewrite it for our

other strategy, namely, have the applet implement `Runnable`, declare three threads in the applet, and declare a single `run()` method for all three threads. You won't need the `Counter` class. Compare your result with the original and comment on which is easier to understand.

7. Why are `wait()`, `notify()`, and `notifyAll()` methods of the `Object` class?

8. Look through the documentation of the `java.awt` package and find an example of a `synchronized` method that we didn't mention. Explain why the method you found is declared to be `synchronized`.

9. Generally, a `run()` method is not declared to be `synchronized`. Why?

10. Look at the `ReaderWriter` example applet we presented at the end of Section 11.3. Explain why it would not be a good idea to move the `getInt()` method into `Reader` and to move `setInt()` into the `Writer` class.

11. Would the `ReaderWriter` applet work correctly if we modified it by adding one or more additional `Writers`?
    a. Explain why or why not.
    a. Modify `ReaderWriter` so that it uses two `Writers`.

12. All of the communication between threads we've talked about use a shared resource, like the `display` field we used in `ReaderWriter`. Another way of communication is to have a thread call a method of another. For example, in `ReaderWriter` we didn't really need `display`, except to show the final result. Instead, we could have the `Writer` send its new value by calling a method belonging to `Reader`. Modify `ReaderWriter` so that the two threads communicate by calling each other's methods. There will still be problems of synchronization you'll have to address.

13. Suppose that three threads all shared a `run()` method and that within `run()` there was a call to a method `doSomething()`. Suppose also that the three threads were represented by the variables `thread1`, `thread2`, and `thread3`. The nature of `doSomething()` is that `thread1` is always allowed to enter the method, `thread2` cannot enter the method until `thread1` has entered and returned, and `thread3` cannot enter the method until `thread2` has entered and returned. Write `doSomething()`.

14. Simulate the action of a car wash with a single wash bay and a driveway capable of holding a fixed number of cars. The cars arrive at unpredictable intervals (perhaps by the user clicking a button to generate a new car), and each car will always spend the same amount of time in the wash bay. If the driveway is full, an entering car will simply leave. You don't have to write a complete applet, but you should describe the threads you will use and show what their

run() method or methods would look like. You should also describe any auxiliary variables you need.

15. A common thread problem is that of *deadlock,* when one thread has resource A and needs resource B to continue, while another thread has resource B and needs resource A to continue. Consider, for example, the problem of crossing a river on a series of stepping stones. If two people try to cross in different directions, they might arrive at the middle with each standing on a stone that the other needs.

    a. Come up with *two* strategies that the river crossers could use to avoid deadlock.

    b. For each of your strategies, tell whether they could lead to the possibility of *starvation,* that is, the chance that some person may never be able to cross the river.

    c. Come up with a strategy that avoids both starvation and deadlock.

16. Here's a possible way of simulating the river crossing problem of Exercise 15. We might represent the stones as an array of boolean values, along with two methods, moveEast() and moveWest(), that are to be used by the threads attempting to cross the river.

```
class SteppingStones
{
    private boolean[] stone = new boolean[10];

    public SteppingStones()
    {
        for (int i = 0; i < 10; i++)
            stone[i] = false;
    }

    public synchronized void moveEast(int n)
    {
        // If n equals 9, indicate that the thread has
        // successfully crossed to the east bank.
        // If stone[n+1] is false, set it to true and
        // set stone[n] to false, indicating that the thread
        // has moved one step east.
        // If stone[n+1] is true, the thread can't move,
        // since its destination stone is occupied.
    }

    public synchronized void moveWest()
    {
        // If n is 0, indicate that the thread has
        // successfully crossed to the west bank.
        // Otherwise, act like moveEast(), except that
        // we look at stone[n-1].
    }
```

A thread is constructed with an initial direction, 1 for an east destination and −1 for a destination on the west bank. The run() method for each thread is

```
public void run()
{
    int current, destination;
    if (direction == 1)
    {
        current -1;
        destination = 9;
    }
    else
    {
        current = 10;
        destination = 0;
    }
    while (current != destination)
        if (direction == 1)
            // try to call theStones.moveEast()
        else
            // try to call theStones.moveWest()
}
```

Implement your best strategy from Exercise 15. Before you start, here are a couple of questions you should ask yourself: Where should most of the decision-making go, in the move methods or in run()? How should the SteppingStones class communicate to the threads whether a move was successful?

17. A classic scheduling problem is the *dining philosopher's problem.* In this problem, *n* philosophers are sitting around a circular table. Each philosopher is sitting in front of a bowl of food. Between each pair of bowls is a single chopstick, as shown for the case *n* = 4.

At any time, a philosopher is eating, talking, or hungry. A talking philosopher eventually gets hungry. A hungry philosopher tries to pick up the chopsticks to her left and right (our philosophers are all women). These are two distinct actions and can't be done simultaneously. If a hungry philosopher gets both chopsticks, she eats for an unpredictable length of time, drops the chopsticks, and starts talking. If a hungry philosopher doesn't get both chopsticks, she stays hungry. The problem is to come up with a strategy that can be applied to all the philosophers so that each gets to eat eventually. For each of the following strategies, tell whether it will be successful. For those that aren't, give a sequence of philosophers' actions that will either result in a deadlock or starve one of the diners.

a. Each hungry philosopher will first try to pick up the chopstick on her left.

b. Each philosopher is assigned a number, 1, 2, . . . , n, arranged sequentially around the table. An odd-numbered hungry philosopher will first try to pick up the chopstick on her left and an even-numbered hungry philosopher will first try to pick up the chopstick on her right.

c. A hungry philosopher will pick up a chopstick only if both are available.

d. If more than one philosopher is hungry at any time, the waiters forceably restrain all but one from trying to pick up the chopsticks.

18. Write an applet that displays an animation of the dining philosophers' problem.

a. Use one of the strategies from Exercise 17.

b. Come up with a fair solution (if none of those strategies are fair) and implement it.

c. To see one solution, point your browser to
    `http://java.sun.com/applets/contest/DiningPhilosophers/`
    `index.html`

19. Go back to the Chapter 8 lablet, `Sortmeister`.

a. Modify it so that the sorting animation is threaded.

b. Modify it so that it shows two animations side by side, one running Selection Sort and the other running Shellsort on the same data. This exercise is moderately complicated, but you'll find it extremely instructive to watch the two sorting routines running in parallel.

CHAPTER TWELVE

Applets in Cyberspace

We've mentioned several times that applets are designed to be run in a Web browser, as part of an HTML document. As anyone with even a modicum of Net surfing experience knows, the Worldwide Web (the Web) is a vast collection of information, organized into millions of pages distributed among hundreds of thousands of computers. An applet can be as much a part of this world of information as the Web page in which it lives—it can access graphic images, sounds, and other data on remote computers, use and manipulate this data, and receive input information from the HTML document that calls it into action. In this, our final chapter, we'll show you how to make your applets into first-class Web citizens.

OBJECTIVES

In this chapter, we will
- ❦ Show how information can be sent to an applet, and how an applet can discover the context in which it is running.
- ❦ Demonstrate how applets can use sounds and images.
- ❦ Discuss image manipulation.
- ❦ Continue the discussion of animation that we began in Chapter 11.
- ❦ Complete the discussion of programming in general and Java programming in particular by investigating a Lablet that is as close to an "industrial strength" program as we can make it.

12.1 SETTING THE SCENE

If an applet is intended to be accessed from a Web page, the HTML document that describes the page will contain a reference to the applet, using the HTML tag <APPLET>. The applet doesn't really "live" in the HTML document, any more than an image does. Instead, the <APPLET> tag will contain the address of the location where the applet's .class file or files may be found.

When a user "goes to" a Web page, by clicking on a link, for example, what happens is that the user's local computer finds the host computer where the desired page is located and sends a request to the host computer to send a copy of the page to the local system. Once the HTML document reaches the local system, the local Web browser takes over and attempts to lay out the page by interpreting the embedded HTML tags. Some of these tags, like <HR>, instruct the browser to do layout actions that can be accomplished locally, like placing a horizontal rule on the display.

Some of the tags, though, might require the browser to send off a request for further information. This might happen if the tag contained a reference to an image or an applet that was stored on another computer. In that case, the browser would instruct the local system to do the same sort of thing it did when the page was first loaded—go off to another computer and ask it to send a copy of the necessary information, like the image or applet.

This process is fast, but you've probably seen that it's not instantaneous. You've almost certainly had the experience of waiting while your computer loads the images, sounds, movies, and applets needed by a Web page. What is amazing about this process, though, is that it works at all. At any instant, hundreds of thousands of computers throughout the world are doing the same thing, locating files on other computers and transferring them back and forth. What makes this process work more or less invisibly to the users is that every single file available on the Internet is uniquely identified by a name, known as its *Uniform Resource Locator,* or URL, for short.

URLs

The Uniform Resource Locator is a string divided into four parts: the *protocol,* the *host name,* the *path name,* and the *file name,* which identifies the resource.

A URL has the form

protocol://host name/path name/file name

The protocol identifies the format to be used for transfer of this information. The protocol you'll see most frequently is http, short for *hypertext transfer protocol.* This is the format for all Worldwide Web documents. Other formats include file, for a file on the local system, ftp, for files on an FTP (*file transfer protocol*) server, and gopher, for files using the Gopher protocol.

The host name is a hierarchical listing of *domains,* separated by periods, like www.hamilton.edu or java.sun.com. The domains that make up a host name are listed in increasing order of generality. For example, the host name www.hamilton.edu represents the computer named www in the wider domain of all systems at the hamilton location (all the computers at Hamilton College), which is itself located in the top-level `edu` domain of all educational institutions. You may find an optional *port number* as part of a host name, like

```
www.somewhere.com:8080
```

and you may have seen a host name in the *dotted quad* format, consisting of four integers (from 0 to 255) separated by periods, like

```
150.209.8.36
```

Once the host computer has been located, the path name describes where in the system's file structure the resource may be found. The path name is also hierarchical, but is listed in decreasing order of generality, that is, in the order of directory and subdirectory. For example, the path name for our department's Web pages is

```
HTML/academic/compsci
```

indicating that the pages are found in the top-level `HTML` directory, in the subdirectory `academic`, and finally within the `compsci` subdirectory contained in `academic`.

Finally, once the protocol, host name, and path name have been specified, the file within the lowest directory is identified by its name. Putting all the parts together, at the time of this writing, the home page of the Computer Science (CS) Department at Hamilton—`default.html`—has the URL

```
http://www.hamilton.edu/HTML/academic/compsci/index.html
```

This is quite a chunk of text, we'll admit. At times, though, you don't need the entire URL to specify a file. A *partial* or *relative* URL is a shorter form in which part of the address is implied, rather than stated explicitly. For instance, in the context of the URL just shown, the partial URL `faculty.html` would refer to the file of that name in the last-named directory, just as well as the full, or *absolute* URL

```
http://www.hamilton.edu/HTML/academic/compsci/faculty.html
```

We can also refer to files in subdirectories of the current directory by continuing the path and ending with the file name. In our department's file system, for example, there is a subdirectory, `cs149`, within the `compsci` directory. So to refer to the file `about.html` in `cs149`, we could use the relative URL

```
cs149/about.html
```

instead of the absolute URL

```
http://www.hamilton.edu/HTML/academic/compsci/cs149/about.html
```

Finally, we can also go upward in the directory structure, by placing one or more slash characters before a path name. For example, relative to the URL

```
http://www.hamilton.edu/HTML/academic/compsci/cs149/about.html
```

the partial URL

```
/cs343/notes.html
```

with an initial slash would indicate that the address begins one level higher in the directory structure, namely in the `compsci` directory, so the corresponding absolute URL would be

```
http://www.hamilton.edu/HTML/academic/compsci/cs343/notes.html
```

The URL class in the package `java.net` is used to construct and inspect URLs in an applet or application. This class is commonly used by applets that load images or sounds from the host computer. This class has four constructors; each throws a `MalformedURLException` if the information provided isn't sufficient to create a legal URL. As checked exceptions, you'll have to enclose calls to these constructors in a `try` block.

URL(String name)
>Constructs a URL object from the absolute name given in the argument.

URL(URL base, String relative)
>Constructs a URL object from the name given in the argument, relative to the specified base URL.

URL(String protocol, String host, String file)
>Constructs a URL from the information provided. For example, we might construct a URL by writing

```
URL theURL = new URL("http", "www.host.com",
"images/ball.gif");
```

URL(String protocol, String host, int port, String file)
>Acts like the preceding constructor, except that it also allows you to specify the port.

There are four URL methods you might find useful in case you want to extract one of the parts of a URL object.

String **getFile**()
>Returns the string describing the path and file name of this URL.

String **getHost**()
>Returns the string describing the host name of this URL.

```
int getPort()
```
Returns the port number of this URL.

```
String getProtocol()
```
Returns the string describing the protocol in use for this URL.

The Applet Class, Revisited

The java.applet package contains the Applet class and three interfaces: AppletContext, AppletStub, and AudioClip. An applet interacts with its environment by calling some Applet methods we'll discuss in this section. Many of these methods work by calling AppletContext methods of the same name, in effect asking the browser or applet runner to do the work. The AppletContext and AudioClip interfaces are implemented by the applet viewer or browser that's actually responsible for running the applet. Unless you are writing your own applet viewer, there's little chance that you'll ever need AppletStub, so we won't discuss it here.

The first two Applet methods we'll cover are used to get information about where the applet and its HTML document reside on the host file system. This information is important, since an applet often requires data, like sounds and graphic images, that are stored on the host system. When an applet is loaded into a local computer, then, the applet must have a way to request that the needed data be loaded from the host computer.

❦ URL getCodeBase()
Returns the URL of directory containing this applet's .class file.

❦ URL getDocumentBase()
Returns the URL of the current HTML document.

In the file structure illustrated in Figure 12.1, suppose that page1.html contained an <APPLET> tag referring to the applet whose compiled bytecode was in file Button1.class. Then, within the Button1 applet, the statement

```
URL appURL = this.getCodeBase();
```

would set appURL to correspond to the URL

```
http://www.server.edu/pub/fred/web/applets/
```

and the statement

```
URL docURL = this.getDocumentBase();
```

would set docURL to correspond to the URL

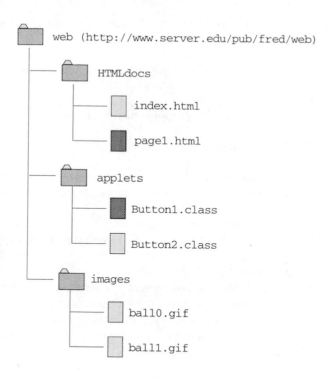

Figure 12.1 An example of a portion of a file structure.

```
http://www.server.edu/pub/fred/web/HTMLdocs/page1.html
```

The URL class is commonly used in combination with `Applet` methods to load images and sounds. These are often stored on the host computer and referenced by addresses relative to the applet or the HTML document that uses the applet.

```
AudioClip getAudioClip(URL absolute)
```
❦ AudioClip **getAudioClip**(URL base, String relative)

These methods return an `AudioClip` object that is located at the indicated URL. We'll discuss the `AudioClip` interface in Section 12.2. The first method takes a `String` argument representing an absolute URL. The second uses a base URL and an address relative to that URL to determine where the AudioClip is located.

```
Image getImage(URL u)
```
❦ Image **getImage**(URL base, String relative)

These methods return a reference to the `Image` stored at the specified absolute or relative URL.

In Figure 12.1, for instance, the image `ball0.gif` has a relative URL,

```
/images/ball0.gif
```

with respect to both the code and the document, so we could load the image `ball0.gif` into our applet by writing

```
URL ballURL = new URL(getCodeBase(), "/images/ball0.gif");
Image ball = getImage(ballURL);
```

or by using this shorter but perhaps more opaque statement

```
Image ball = getImage(getCodeBase(), "/images/ball0.gif");
```

There are seven more methods of interest to us in the `Applet` class. We'll list them here for completeness and discuss the two flagged ones in detail shortly.

❦ `AppletContext` **getAppletContext**`()`
Returns the `AppletContext` object associated with this applet.

`String` **getAppletInfo**`()`
You'll override this method to return a `String` containing information about this applet. Although most browsers and applet runners don't call this method at present, it is designed for potential use in an environment that would provide an "About this applet" menu choice. You might want to override this method to return copyright information, for example.

❦ `String` **getParameter**`(String name)`
The `<APPLET>` tag allows you to specify information that the applet might need. This list of *parameters* consists of certain named pieces of information, somewhat like variables. This method returns the `String` value of the parameter with the specified name, or the `null String` if no parameter with the given name has been supplied.

`String[][]` **getParameterInfo**`()`
Returns an arbitrarily long array of triples of strings, each consisting of the parameter name, its type, and its description. You'll override this method to provide a complete description of the parameters your applet uses.

`void` **play**`(URL absolute)`
`void` **play**`(URL base, String relative)`
Load and play the `AudioClip` at the given absolute or relative URL.

`void` **showStatus**`(String message)`
Displays the `String` argument in the applet runner or browser's status bar. This method is most commonly used to display the status of an operation, as, for example, "Image loading complete." Since the environment uses the status bar for its own purposes, you should use this method only for incidental information, understanding that it may vanish fairly rapidly. You may have seen the status bar used to irritating effect by an applet that hogs it for worthless messages like, This is my first applet. Isn't it way cool? Don't do that—users depend on the status bar for

information about links in an HTML document and will hate you if you parade your ego where they are looking for useful information.

The `AppletContext` Interface

The `AppletContext` instance of an applet is "owned" by the applet runner or browser in which an applet is running. This instance provides a means by which the applet can communicate with the outside world. The `AppletContext` interface is `abstract`—all the methods it names are implemented by the program that runs your applets. This interface contains some methods that have the same names as the `Applet` methods we've mentioned.

```
AudioClip getAudioClip(URL absolute)
Image getImage(URL absolute)
void showStatus(String message)
```

In addition, there are some methods that you might call, once you've associated the `AppletContext` instance with the environment, by using the `Applet` method `getAppletContext()`.

```
Applet getApplet(String name)
```
Returns a reference to an applet with the given name. The applet named must be on the same HTML page as the applet where the method call takes place. This method provides you with a limited amount of interapplet communication. Suppose, for instance, that an HTML page contains two applets, "Tick" and "Tock," and that "Tock" was of type `Timer` and had a `public` method `reset()`. Then, from within "Tick" we could make a call to "Tock" by using the appropriate type cast:

```
Timer otherApplet =
(Timer)getAppletContext().getApplet("Tock");
otherApplet.reset();
```

The name argument in this method can be either the class name or the name given by the NAME attribute of the <APPLET> tag (which we'll discuss when we review the <APPLET> tag later). This method returns `null` if the applet can't be found, so be sure to get the name right.

```
void showDocument(URL absolute)
void showDocument(URL base, String relative)
```
These request the environment to show the document with an absolute or relative URL specified. The environment is allowed to ignore this request, as might happen, for example, in an applet runner that's not equipped to display an HTML document. We could use this method in a Web browser, though, to tell the browser to load another page. We do so in the Lablet, where you'll find the code:

```
// destURL has previously been set to the URL of a Web page
getAppletContext().showDocument(destURL);
```

Applet Parameters, Applet Attributes

Communication between applets and the world of the Web can work in both directions. In particular, an HTML document can send information to any of the applets it contains. In the Lablet, for instance, we construct a `GraphicButton` class and use it in an applet that displays a widget that acts like a regular button, but looks nicer. Like an ordinary AWT `Button`, a `GraphicButton` has a `setLabel()` method, but it's of no use to the HTML document containing the applet, since HTML has no way of accessing the methods of its applets.

The <APPLET> tag, though, provides Web page designers with a way of sending information to an applet, as long as the applet has indicated that it is interested in the information. This method uses the <PARAM> tag within the <APPLET> element. The Lablet for this chapter, for example, appears within a Web page and is specified by the <APPLET> tag

```
<APPLET    CODE = "OldButtoner.class"
           WIDTH = 82
           HEIGHT = 27
           ALIGN = left>
    <PARAM     name = "pattern"     value = "bttn*.gif">
    <PARAM     name = "numPix"      value = "2">
    <PARAM     name = "label"       value = "Home">
    <PARAM     name = "destURL"     value = "http://www.bogus.edu/">
</APPLET>
```

Each <PARAM> element has two required attributes: the name of the parameter and a string representing its value. In the preceding example, for instance, the parameter name "label" is paired with the value "Home." The `OldButtoner` applet contains a `String` instance variable, `theLabel`, and this variable is set within the applet's `init()` method by the statement

```
theLabel = getParameter("label");
```

This method looks in the <APPLET> element for a parameter with the name "label" and, if it finds one, returns the `String` value of the parameter with that name. In this case, the value (and hence the `String` used for the button label) is "Home."

The `Applet` method `getParameter(String name)` looks for a parameter with the given name among the <PARAM> elements of the <APPLET> element. If it finds a matching name, the method returns the value of that parameter. If there is no parameter with the given name, `getParameter()` returns `null`.

This method can be extremely handy—a Web page author needs to know only the parameter names and can then match those names with values to customize the applet, without knowing any Java at all!

While we're on the subject, we should explain the rest of the <APPLET> tag, namely the attributes, like CODE, WIDTH, HEIGHT, and ALIGN, that appear in the example just discussed. Three attributes are required:

CODE = the name of the applet's class file
WIDTH = the width in pixels the browser allocates for the applet on its page
HEIGHT = the height in pixels the browser allocates for the applet

You can also include several optional attributes:

CODEBASE = the URL where the applet's class file is located
NAME = the name you give the applet, which is useful if you have two applets
     of the same type on a page.
ALT = a string that will appear if the browser can't load the applet or isn't equipped
     to deal with Java.
ALIGN = any one of these words: left, right, top, bottom, or middle, which
     determine the placement of the applet on the page.
VSPACE = the amount of vertical padding, in pixels, the browser will place above
     and below the applet.
HSPACE = the amount of horizontal padding, in pixels, the browser will place
     to the left and right of the applet.

12.2 LIGHTS, CAMERA, . . .

When you have learned how to locate resources on the Web, you're ready to load sounds and images and use them in your applets. We'll take care of sounds first, since they're fairly simple and then spend most of this section talking about creating, using, and manipulating images.

Audio Clips

There are a bewildering number of formats for storing sounds in digital form. Web browsers deal with this proliferation of formats by using *helper applications.* When a browser encounters a sound file it needs to play, it first looks in the header of the file to determine its format and then checks whether it has a program it can call to play the sound. If it can't find an appropriate helper application, the browser may put up a dialog box, asking the user to select a program that can play the file. If the user can't find the right program, the browser simply ignores the request and doesn't play the sound.

This strategy would clearly violate Java's design principle of platform independence, so in consequence there is only one sound format a Java environment is guaranteed to recognize: the AU format. That is, if you find a sound you want to use and it's in WAV or SND format, for example, you'll have to find a program that will convert the sound file into AU format before you can use it.

When you have obtained a file with the right format, though, playing it is simple. First, you will use the `Applet` method `getAudioClip()` to load the sound. This method returns an `AudioClip` instance associated with the sound file whose URL you specified in the method's argument. The `AudioClip` interface contains three methods that you will use for handling sounds.

❦ void **play**()

Plays this `AudioClip`, from start to finish.

void **loop**()

Plays this `AudioClip` continuously. Once it reaches the end of the file, it returns to the beginning and starts over.

❦ void **stop**()

Stops playing this `AudioClip`. It's important that you stop any sound you play, especially if you are looping it. Failure to do so will keep the sound playing, even when the user leaves the Web page containing the applet. Needless to say, that can be quite annoying.

Suppose, for instance, that you have a sound file, "gong.au," that's stored in the same directory as the class file for the applet. To play this sound, here's all you have to do:

```
AudioClip gongClip = getAudioClip(getCodeBase(), "gong.au");
if (gongClip != null)    // We were able to load it,
    gongClip.play();     // so now play it.
```

To be safe, you'd also stop the sound in the applet's `stop()` method:

```
public void stop()
{
    if (gongClip != null)          // It's still playing,
        gongClip.stop();           // so stop it.
    . . .
}
```

Image Basics

You've learned how to use `Graphics` class methods to do simple drawing. In theory, at least, you could use `drawRect()`, `drawOval()`, `drawLine()`, and the like to produce any picture you want. In practice, of course, you'd never want to draw the Mona Lisa this way—even if you had the necessary skill, it would require thousands of method calls. It would be far easier to render the picture in a paint program or use a scanner to convert an existing image to digital form and then somehow load the image and draw it where you wanted.

Java's Image class provides support for loading, manipulating, and displaying images. Fortunately, the problem of multiple formats we mentioned when talking about audio files is nowhere near as serious for images. The two widely used formats for images on the Web are known as GIF and JPEG, and Java supports both.

Although Java's support for sounds is quite limited, it provides an intimidatingly complex and powerful set of classes for image manipulation. Besides the Image class in java.awt, the package java.awt.image contains eleven classes and three interfaces devoted to image manipulation. Fortunately, if all you want to do is display an image in an applet, the process is quite simple. First, you use the Applet method,

```
Image getImage(URL base, String relative)
```

to associate an Image object with the GIF or JPEG file at the specified URL and then all you have to do is use the Graphics method,

```
boolean drawImage(Image im, int x, int y, ImageObserver ob)
```

to load and then draw the Image instance, anchored at (x, y). We'll have more to say about the ImageObserver interface later. For this simple illustration all we need to know is that the Component class implements ImageObserver, so we can use this applet as our ImageObserver. The following applet gets an image and displays it, as illustrated in Figure 12.2.

```java
import java.applet.*;
import java.awt.*;

public class ImageTest1 extends Applet
{
    Image asteroids;

    public void init()
    {
        asteroids = getImage(getCodeBase(), "aster.gif");
    }

    public void paint(Graphics g)
    {
        g.drawImage(asteroids, 10, 10, this);
    }
}
```

By the way, we're doing something a bit unusual here. The drawImage() method returns a boolean value, indicating whether it was able to load and draw the image. When we make the call, though, we never make use of the return value. In a fancier program, we might use the return value to discover whether the image was successfully drawn before we do something else.

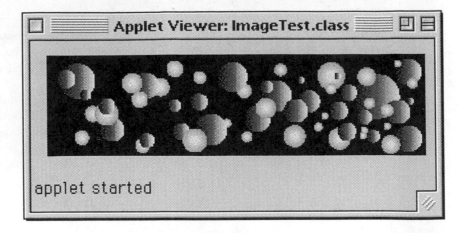

Figure 12.2 An image displayed in an applet.

The Graphics method drawImage() comes in quite a few forms. These methods allow you to place the image where you want, crop it, scale it, and perform other manipulations. Each method returns true if the image has been completely drawn, and false otherwise.

☙ boolean **drawImage**(Image im, int x, int y, ImageObserver ob)
    We've just used this method. It loads and draws the image, with its upper left corner at (x, y), measured in the Graphics object's local coordinates.

boolean **drawImage**(Image im, int x, int y, int width, int height,
                          ImageObserver ob)
    Acts like the preceding method, except that it scales the image to fit the given width and height. To do so may take a *long* time—if you're using version 1.1, you should instead use getScaledInstance() to scale the image first. We'll discuss this further when we cover the Image class.

boolean **drawImage**(Image im, int x, int y,
                          Color bgColor, ImageObserver ob)
    Some graphics formats, like GIF89A, allow you to specify that one color will be transparent. This method allows you to specify a background color that will show through any transparent parts of the image.

boolean **drawImage**(Image im, int x, int y, int width, int height,
                          Color bgColor, ImageObserver ob)
    Allows you to set the width, height, and background color.

boolean **drawImage**(Image im, int dx1, int dy1, int dx2, int dy2,
                  int sx1, int sy1, int sx2, int sy2,
                  ImageObserver ob)   // version 1.1 only
    The coordinates (sx1, sy1) and (sx2, sy2) determine the corners of a

rectangle in the image, and (dx1, dy1), (dx2, dy2) determine the corners of a rectangle in the Graphics drawing region. This method draws the portion of the image within the specified source (s-) rectangle in the destination (d-) rectangle in this Graphics object. If the corners don't correspond, the image will be reflected when drawn. If the source rectangle is larger than the destination rectangle, the image will be cropped to fit, and if the source rectangle is smaller than the destination rectangle (as it is in Figure 12.3), the image rectangle will be scaled to fit.

```
boolean drawImage(Image im, int dx1, int dy1, int dx2, int dy2,
               int sx1, int sy1, int sx2, int sy2, Color bgColor
               ImageObserver ob)       // version 1.1 only
```

Acts like the preceding method, but it also allows you to specify the background color that will show through any transparent parts of the image.

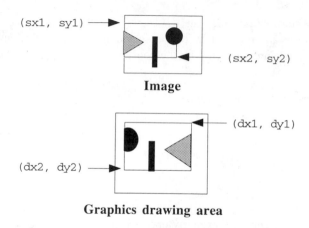

Figure 12.3 Scaling and reflecting with drawImage().

The Image class is fairly simple. It has no constructor you can call—you have to get an Image instance by calling the Applet method getImage() or the Component method createImage(). In version 1.1, this class contains five class constants that are used in getScaledInstance():

SCALE_AREA_AVERAGING: uses a particular slow but nice scaling scheme.
SCALE_DEFAULT: uses the default scaling algorithm.
SCALE_FAST: prefers speed over a nice result.
SCALE_REPLICATE: uses a particular fast but not pretty scaling scheme.
SCALE_SMOOTH: prefers a nice result over speed.

```
void flush()
```

Forces an image to be reloaded the next time it is drawn, rather than allowing the system to reuse the original image without reloading. You would use this method if you expected the source image to be changed over time, as it might be if the original was made from a real-time video source.

❦ Graphics **getGraphics**()

Returns a Graphics instance associated with an image. You can use this method only with an image that came from the Component createImage() method. You cannot use it with images that came from a remote source via getImage(). This method is useful for drawing on "offscreen images," as you'll see.

❦ int **getHeight**(ImageObserver ob)

Asks the ImageObserver for the height of an image. If an image hasn't been completely loaded, the ImageObserver may not yet have enough information to report the height and will so signal by returning −1.

❦ int **getWidth**(ImageObserver ob)

As with getHeight(), this method returns the width of this image if it's known; it returns −1 if the width isn't known yet.

Image **getScaledInstance**(int w, int h, int hints) // version 1.1

Returns an image made from an image, scaled to width w and height h, using the scaling scheme specified by the constant, like Image.SCALE_FAST, in the hints argument.

❦ ImageProducer **getSource**()

Every image is associated with an ImageProducer, as you'll see. This method returns the ImageProducer that is the source of bits in an image.

Drawing Offscreen

When drawing to the screen, we rely on Component's paint() method to be sure that the screen gets properly updated. If we're doing a complicated drawing, though, paint() may take a noticeable amount of time to refresh the screen completely. A common method for dealing with this problem is known as *double buffering*. In this technique, we use an Image instance to do the drawing. When the image is complete, we display the whole thing at once, by calling drawImage() within our paint() method. This approach generally makes the drawing process appear much smoother, which can be a big advantage in animation work.

Double Buffering:

1. Use the Component method createImage(int w, int h) to construct an Image instance of width w and height h.
2. Use the Image method getGraphics() to get a Graphics instance associated with the image.
3. Use the Graphics object to do all the drawing.
4. Call drawImage() to display the image on the screen.

In the following applet, we illustrate a simple use of double buffering. The result is pictured in Figure 12.4.

```java
import java.applet.*;
import java.awt.*;

public class ImageTest2 extends Applet
{
    Image offscreen;

    public void init()
    {
        // Step 1: Get an image for our drawing.
        offscreen = createImage(200, 50);

        // Step 2: Get a Graphics instance for the image.
        Graphics g = offscreen.getGraphics();

        // Step 3: Draw on the image.
        doComplexDrawing(g);

        g.dispose();     // Throw away the Graphics object,
                         // now that we're done with it.
    }

    public void paint(Graphics g)
    // Step 4: Copy the offscreen image to the screen.
    {
        g.drawImage(offscreen, 10, 10, this);
    }

    private void doComplexDrawing (Graphics g)
    {
        g.setColor(Color.white);
        g.fillRect(0, 0, 200, 50);
        // Draw a border.
        g.setColor(Color.black);
        g.drawRect(1, 1, 198, 48);
        g.setColor(Color.red);
        g.drawRect(2, 2, 196, 46);
        g.setColor(Color.pink);
        g.drawRect(3, 3, 194, 44);
        g.setColor(Color.black);
        // Draw some radiating lines.
        for (int i = 0; i < 11; i++)
            g.drawLine(5, 45 - 4 * i, 195, 5 + 4 * i);
    }
}
```

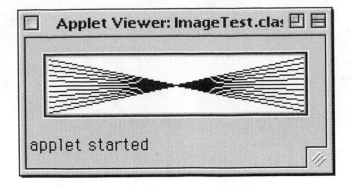

Figure 12.4 Offscreen drawing with `ImageTest2`.

Image Processing Prerequisites

Java provides extraordinarily powerful image processing facilities. Many of the operations that you can perform on images, though, are beyond the scope of this book. We'll give you a taste of what you can do with images by talking about one simple form of an *image filter* that can be used to modify an image's colors. You can do many more things with image filters, like rotate an image, blur it, or fade between one image and another. If that sort of thing sounds exciting, we encourage you to look at the online documentation and search the Web for samples.

Before we get to image filtering, we need to cover some preliminary topics. We'll first take a closer look at the `Color` class, which we introduced in Chapter 2, and while doing that we'll give a quick introduction to *hexadecimal* representation of integers.

An instance of the `Color` class represents a color, as you know. You can represent colors in a computer in many different ways, but all require the use of some sort of numeric code.[1] One of the color models Java uses is to divide a color into its red, green, and blue components, in much the same way a color television does. Each of these components is represented by an integer from 0 (component is turned off) to 255 (component is at maximum brightness). For example, the color with (R, G, B) components (0, 0, 0) is black, (128, 128, 128) represents a medium gray, and (255, 175, 175) represents pink, since we're adding some more red to the light gray that we'd have from (175, 175, 175).

Since we can represent the numbers from 0 to 255 in binary[2] using no more than eight bits (a `byte`, in other words), we can pack all three components into a single 32-bit `int` and still have eight bits to spare.[3] In this compressed

---

[1]Painting a bit in memory red, for instance, would be difficult.

[2]We introduced binary representation of integers in Chapter 5.

[3]The high-order eight bits are used to express *transparency,* as you'll see.

representation, the red component occupies bits 23 to 16, the green component is in bits 15 to 8, and the blue component takes up bits 7 to 0, as we illustrate in Figure 12.5. Pink, for instance, would have 11111111 in the red component, since 255 in binary is 11111111, and the green and blue components would both contain the bits 10101111, the representation for the decimal number 175 (= 128 + 32 + 8 + 4 + 2 + 1).

Components   (255,   175,   175)

Memory

31	24 23	16 15	8 7	0

00000000 | 11111111 | 10101111 | 10101111

Binary   00000000111111111010111110101111

Hex
0000	0000	1111	1111	1010	1111	1010	1111
0	0	f	f	a	f	a	f

Hexadecimal literal   0x00ffafaf

Figure 12.5 Representations of `Color.pink`.

The binary representation of pink, 11111111101011111010, is too cumbersome to use, even if we strip off the leading zeros. The decimal equivalent, 16756655, is tedious to calculate and hides all the information about the components. A more compact way of representing binary numbers is to collect the bits into groups of four and assign a code to each group. With four bits, we can represent the numbers 0 to 15, so we use the "digits" 0, . . . , 9, and a, . . . , f for each group. This approach is known as *hexadecimal* (or base-16) notation.

Hexadecimal "digits":

0000 –> 0	0001 –> 1	0010 –> 2	0011 –> 3
0100 –> 4	0101 –> 5	0110 –> 6	0111 –> 7
1000 –> 8	1001 –> 9	1010 –> a	1011 –> b
1100 –> c	1101 –> d	1110 –> e	1111 –> f

Now we can express a 32-bit number by using just eight hexadecimal digits. We can use this representation in a Java program, by appending "0x" in front of a hexadecimal number. That is, we can represent `Color.pink` by the hex (for short) literal 0x00ffafaf, or 0xffafaf, or, since we can use uppercase letters in this representation, OXFFAFAF. Note how easily we can determine the color components: there's ff of red, af of green, and af of blue.

The Color class has three constructors.

Color(int r, int g, int b)

Constructs a new Color instance with the given red, green, and blue components. These arguments should be integers in the range 0, . . . , 255.

Color(int rgb)

Constructs a new Color instance from the specified compressed integer. For example, Color(0xffafaf) and Color(16756655) will both construct a new Color.pink instance.

Color(float r, float g, float b)

Constructs a new Color instance from float values between 0.0 and 1.0 to represent the intensities of the components, where 0.0 represents none of the component and 1.0 represents the maximum value of the component. For example, since 175/255 is approximately 0.68627, we could construct a color close to Color.pink by calling Color(1.0f, 0.68627f, 0.68627f).

The Color methods allow you to inspect the components of a color, convert String names to the associated Color instances, and do some simple modifications to colors.

static Color **getColor**(String name)
static Color **getColor**(String name, Color default)
static Color **getColor**(String name, int default)

Return a Color instance corresponding to the name. The first method returns null if the name does not match one of the Color class constants black, blue, cyan, darkGray, gray, green, lightGray, magenta, orange, pink, red, white, or yellow (or a color defined among the system properties, which we won't discuss here). The second and third methods return the color or the color represented by the integer, if the name doesn't match a color constant name. Note that these are static methods, so would be called by using Color. in front, rather than a Color instance.

int **getBlue**()
int **getGreen**()
int **getRed**()

Return an integer in the range 0, . . . , 255, representing the value of the indicated component of this color.

int **getRGB**()

Returns an integer with the components in the low-order three bytes.

Color **brighter**()
Color **darker**()

Return a color that is somewhat brighter or darker than this color.

To illustrate using the Color class, we present a simple applet that allows the user to set the components of a color and see what the color looks like. Figure 12.6 shows the applet in action. The user enters the (R, G, B) component values in the three fields at the top and then clicks on the Set button to bring up a rectangle painted with the corresponding color. You'll have to take our word for the fact that (150, 50, 80) is a pleasant burgundy.

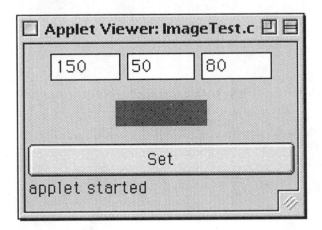

Figure 12.6 The color picker in action.

The applet is easy enough to understand that we can present it with almost no commentary. Do take note, though, of the last line,

```
return n & 0xff;
```

What we're doing here is using the hex value `ff` as a mask. Recall that `0xff` is the integer with twenty-four high-order 0s and eight 1s in the low-order byte. When we take the bitwise AND of this mask and the integer n, the result is the number in n with its topmost twenty-four bits set to 0. In other words, we're forcing the return value to be in the required range 0, . . . , 255. Bear this in mind—we'll do some more bit-level manipulation of color values when we talk about image filters.

```
public class ColorPicker extends Applet
{
        private TextField    redF = new TextField(4),
                             greenF = new TextField(4),
                             blueF = new TextField(4);
        private Button       setB = new Button("Set");
        private Color        paintColor = Color.white;

        public void init()
        {
            setLayout(new BorderLayout());
            Panel p = new Panel();
```

(continued)

```
        p.add(redF);
        p.add(greenF);
        p.add(blueF);
        add("North", p);
        add("South", setB);
    }

    public void paint(Graphics g)
    {
        g.setColor(paintColor);
        g.fillRect(65, 30, 70, 30);
    }

    public boolean action(Event e, Object arg)
    {
        int r = getComponent(redF);
        int g = getComponent(greenF);
        int b = getComponent(blueF);
        paintColor = new Color(r, g, b);
        repaint();
        return true;
    }

    private int getComponent(TextField t)
    {
        int n = 0;
        String s = t.getText();
        try
        {
            n = Integer.parseInt(s);
        }
        catch (NumberFormatException e)
        {
            return 0;
        }
        return n & 0xff;
    }
}
```

Image Processing, Behind the Scenes

The Image class contains seven methods, which makes it a small-to-medium-sized class, when measured against its AWT brethren. Image is larger than Panel, about the same size as Point and Dialog, and far smaller than Component. The relative simplicity of Image, though, is misleading. All the real work of dealing with images is handled by the classes within the java.awt.image package and that, as we mentioned earlier, is big, with eleven classes and three interfaces.

The complexity behind image processing is due, in part, to the fact that the java.awt.image package provides a rich collection of classes that we can use for image processing, but even more to the fact that the designers of Java had to deal with two inescapable constraints: images are big and the Net is slow. If you consider that a two-inch by one-inch picture might consume 40,000 bytes just for the raw pixel data, you can see that even a fast computer might take a while to manipulate every pixel of the image. In addition, with a 28.8Kbps modem commonly in use today and in the best of circumstances some eleven seconds would be needed just to get the information from a remote source.[4] We'll discuss some of what goes on when an image is loaded, processed, and displayed. Fortunately, Java takes care of most of the work for us.

An image begins with an `ImageProducer`. An object implementing this interface takes a source of data—from memory or a remote source over the Net, for instance—and produces an array of `int`s, representing the pixels of the image. When you call `getImage()` or `createImage()`, Java will generate an `ImageProducer` for you, whose job is to start gathering pixels.[5] Keep in mind here that the producer is almost certainly working faster than the data are arriving, so at any time not all the pixels of the image may be available. You'll need to use `ImageProducer`s, but you may never implement one.

If you've indicated that you want an image, you'll almost certainly want to do something with it, like draw it by calling `drawImage()`. When you do that, Java will designate an `ImageConsumer` for you. The responsibility of an `ImageConsumer` is to do something with the pixels an `ImageProducer` is generating. Every `ImageConsumer` is registered with some `ImageProducer`, and as the producer generates some more pixels it periodically calls one of the consumer's methods to pass the new data along. As in real life, the producer runs the show, notifying all its registered consumers as information about the image becomes available. You won't need to make much use of the `ImageConsumer` interface, and you'll almost certainly never implement one.

If you've called `drawImage()`, the system will spawn a new thread for loading and displaying the image. In that thread, the producer is generating new pixels from the source and calling the consumer's methods to pass them along. The consumer, in turn, is preparing the pixels for painting on the screen, often row by row. While this is going on, the consumer is being watched by an `ImageObserver`. The job of the `ImageObserver` is to observe what the consumer does and report to the rest of the program.

The `ImageObserver` interface consists of a single method:

```
boolean imageUpdate(Image, im, int flags, int x,
                     int y, int w, int h)
```

This method is called periodically by the `ImageConsumer`; you won't call it yourself. The consumer indicates the image it's preparing, the (x, y) coordinates

---

[4]Although images are typically compressed to take up less space (and hence be faster to load), loading images still takes time, as anyone who's waited for a Web page to load can attest.

[5]The `ImageProducer` won't start working until it's told to, often by a subsequent call to `drawImage()`, but you needn't be concerned about that.

of the upper left corner of the prepared part of the image, and the width and height of the portion of the pixel array it has prepared so far. The `flags` integer contains information about the status of the image being prepared. This method returns `true` if this `ImageObserver` is interested in getting further updates from the consumer and returns `false` if it knows everything it needs about the image.

The flags argument represents a collection of constants, chosen from the following list (where we've omitted some of the less important items).

ABORT	Loading has been halted, perhaps temporarily.
ALLBITS	All the bits of the image are now available.
ERROR	Loading has been halted and can't continue.
HEIGHT	The height of the image is known. A call to `im.getHeight()` will return the correct height of the image.
SOMEBITS	Part of the image has been loaded and prepared. If this flag is set, the `x`, `y`, `w`, and `h` arguments will contain the anchor, width, and height of the rectangle enclosing the prepared part of the image.
WIDTH	The width of the image is now known.

You can test these flags by forming the bitwise AND of the flags argument and the appropriate constant. For example, the expression

```
flags & ImageObserver.ALLBITS
```

will evaluate to 0 if all of the bits of the image haven't yet been processed and will be nonzero if all the bits are available.

The `Component` class implements `ImageObserver`, as we've said, so most widgets can be used as `ImageObservers`. The `Component` version just calls `repaint()`, to paint as much of the image as has been prepared. Thus `ImageTest1` (on page 520) might appear to take its own sweet time drawing the image. In fact, it's drawing as fast as it can—as soon as the default consumer has some more pixels prepared, it calls the applet's `imageUpdate()`, which forces a `repaint()` call.

You might want to wait until the image is completely loaded before trying to draw it. In that case, you could override the `imageUpdate()` method, as we do next.

```java
import java.applet.*;
import java.awt.*;
import java.awt.image.ImageObserver;

public class ImageTest3 extends Applet
{
    private Image    asteroids;
    private boolean  ready = false;   // true -> image is loaded

    public void init()
    {
```

```
        asteroids = getImage(getCodeBase(), "aster.gif");
        prepareImage(asteroids, this);
   }


   public boolean imageUpdate(Image img, int flags,
                              int x, int y,
                              int width, int height)
   {
        if ((flags & ImageObserver.ALLBITS) != 0)
        // All the bits have been loaded.
        {
             ready = true;     // Set the ready flag,
             repaint();        // force a call to paint(),
             return false;     // and tell the consumer we're done.
        }
        else
        // We still want to be called periodically.
             return true;
   }


   public void paint(Graphics g)
   // Don't even try to draw the image until it's been loaded.
   {
        if (ready)
             g.drawImage(asteroids, 10, 10, this);
   }
}
```

The `Component` method `prepareImage()` we called in the `init()` method forces loading to start. We need that here, since normally Java won't try to load an image until `drawImage()` is called, and we enclosed `drawImage()` within an `if` statement to guarantee that it wouldn't be called. Another way to deal with this problem is to realize that `drawImage()` returns `true` if the image has been fully drawn. We could eliminate the `ready` flag and just write

```
   public void paint(Graphics g)
   {
        if (!g.drawImage(asteroids, 10, 10, this))
             showStatus("Loading...");
        else
             showStatus("Loading complete");
   }
```

forcing `drawImage()` to be called in the `if` test. This method is less elegant than the first.

Delaying drawing by writing our own `imageUpdate()` is simple enough if we have only one image to handle. It's not so simple if we have multiple images. In Section 12.3 we'll discuss another way of waiting for images to load.

Image Filters

An image filter allows you to manipulate an image. With the appropriate `ImageFilter` object, you can fade or blur an image, scale or crop it, rotate or reflect it, and change its colors—in fact, you can do anything with an image your programming skill permits. As you might expect, some forms of image filter are quite complicated to write and, quite frankly, are beyond our scope here.

We can, though, do quite a lot with a class that is quite easy to use. The `RGBImageFilter` class is a subclass of `ImageFilter`, one in which the same operation is performed on every pixel of an image. The operations permitted in this class and its subclasses are purely local, in the sense that they may only modify the colors of each pixel, and may not inspect any other pixel while doing their modifications.

We can't use an `RGBImageFilter` to rotate or crop an image, but we can still do many interesting things. For example, we can *invert* the colors of an image like a photographic negative, as illustrated in Figure 12.7.

Figure 12.7 An image and its inverse.

To invert a color, we subtract each of its components from 255. A pure green, with components (0, 255, 0), would turn into magenta, with components (255, 0, 255). A medium gray, (128, 128, 128) would undergo almost no change except for an imperceptible darkening, as its components became (127, 127, 127). We can make an `InvertFilter` to do the inversions by making `RGBImageFilter` a subclass, as we do shortly.

You should note a few things about our new class. First, image pixels are slightly different from colors, in that the high-order byte is actually used. In the `int` representing one of an image's pixels, bits 24, . . . , 31 store the *transparency* (also called the *alpha* value). This storage determines how much of the background will show through the image—a value of 0 means that the pixel will be completely transparent, a value of 128 will let approximately half the background show through, and a value of 255 will make the pixel completely opaque.

Also, the helper method `flip()` is supplied with an `int` argument, a source, and an offset value. This method first gets the byte by shifting source down by the given offset and masking it with 0xff. It then subtracts that byte from 255 and shifts it back into its original position.

Once we've inverted the red, green, and blue bytes, we OR them together to produce the inverted pixel, and return it. That's all it takes—the parent class takes care of calling the filterRGB() method for each pixel in the image.

```
class InvertFilter extends RGBImageFilter
// An RGBImageFilter is a simplified filter that performs the same
// action on all pixels.
// To extend such a filter, all that's necessary is to add a
// constructor (if needed) and override the filterRGB() method.
{
    public int filterRGB(int x, int y, int pix)
    // The arguments x and y are needed by the base class filter,
    // even though they aren't used here.
    {
        int a = pix & 0xff000000;    // Just mask the alpha value.
        int r = flip(pix, 16);       // Invert each component.
        int g = flip(pix, 8);
        int b = flip(pix, 0);
        return a | r | g | b;        // Reassemble the components
                                     // into a pixel and return it
    }

    private int flip(int source, int offset)
    {
        int component = (source >> offset) & 0xff;
        return (255 - component) << offset;
    }
}
```

Defining an image filter, especially a simple one that is a subclass of the class RGBImageFilter, is conceptually much easier than using one. The applet ImageTest4 loads an image and displays it. When you press the mouse button, the applet displays the inverted image, and when you release the button, the original image is again displayed.

The complicated part of this applet is all in the init() method:

```
original = getImage(getCodeBase(), "start.gif");
ImageFilter f = new InvertFilter();
ImageProducer p =
        new FilteredImageSource(original.getSource(), f);
inverse = createImage(p);
theImage = original;
```

The class FilteredImageSource implements ImageProducer. It uses an ImageProducer, which we get from origin.getSource(), and an

ImageFilter, which in this case is an instance of our InvertFilter, to generate a new producer, p. We then make an image from this producer by calling the Component method createImage(), this time with the producer as argument.

In simple terms, the original image producer sends pixels to the filter (which implements ImageConsumer), and the filtered image is used to construct the producer FilteredImageSource.

```java
import java.awt.*;
import java.applet.*;
import java.awt.image.*;

public class ImageTest4 extends Applet
{
      private Image       original,
                          inverse,
                          theImage;

      public void init()
      {
            original = getImage(getCodeBase(), "start.gif");
            ImageFilter f = new InvertFilter();
            ImageProducer p =
                  new FilteredImageSource(original.getSource(), f);
            inverse = createImage(p);
            theImage = original;
      }

      public void update(Graphics g)
      {
            g.drawImage(theImage, 0, 0, this);
      }

      public boolean mouseDown(Event e, int x, int y)
      {
            theImage = inverse;
            repaint();
            return true;
      }

      public boolean mouseUp(Event e, int x, int y)
      {
            theImage = original;
            repaint();
            return true;
      }
}
```

If you run this applet, you'll probably discover that the first time you click the mouse button, the inverted image takes a while to appear. The reason is that the

InvertFilter takes quite a bit of time to produce the inverted image. You might also discover a noticeable amount of time is needed to load and display the original image. These delays aren't particularly bothersome in this applet, but they could be annoying in time-sensitive applications, like those that use animation, for instance. In the next section, we'll discuss some techniques for dealing with these delays.

12.3   ACTION!

Drawing static images is useful, but at times you will want your images to be more active. In this section, we'll discuss animation and give you some tips on making your programs draw as smoothly as possible. Before we do that, though, we'll introduce a custom widget that we'll use for all our drawing.

Preliminaries: Drawing on a Canvas

Many times, it's better for a program to do its drawing on a Canvas than to draw directly on the applet panel or application frame. First, it's good program design, since we're making a separate class for a collection of logically related operations. Second, doing all our drawing on a separate object simplifies the applet or application—the program's top level can concentrate on management and not be cluttered up with a lot of code for drawing. Finally, having a separate target for drawing provides us with a class we might want to use in other programs. In fact, that's just what we're going to do in this section. We'll write four different applets, but each of them will use the same class as a place for drawing.

Drawing Tip:

Except in the simplest programs, if you're going to do much drawing, it's a good idea to declare a Canvas or make a Canvas subclass of your own to draw on.

Our Display class is a subclass of Canvas. It will have a background image that it generates internally and will have the capability of drawing a foreground image on top of the background. We begin, as usual, with a collection of instance variable declarations.

```
class Display extends Canvas
{
    private Image     background,     // the background image
                      other = null;   // an image to be drawn on top
                                      // of the background
    private int       x, y;           // where to draw the
                                      // foreground image
    private boolean   initialized = false;
```

We need the `initialized` variable for a somewhat obscure reason. A `Component` instance has a height and width, but they aren't known at the time the object is declared. In fact, they aren't known until a layout is complete, and that may not be done until the applet or application is painted the first time. A `Display` object needs to know its height and width before that it can create the background image, so we defer creating the background until the `initialized` flag indicates that the height and width are known.

The `showImage()` method adds a new foreground image to this class and forces it to be drawn at a specified location. Note that extending this method would be easy enough that we could have an array of foreground images, rather than just one.

```
public void showImage(Image im, int x, int y)
{
      other = im;
      this.x = x;
      this.y = y;
      repaint();
}
```

The `paint()` method is about what you'd expect. After verifying that initialization is complete, it first draws the background and then draws the foreground image, if any, on top. If initialization hasn't been done, we determine whether we have the width and height; if so, we make the background image and set the `initialized` flag.

We override `update()` here, too, forcing it just to paint, rather than doing the default task, erasing-then-painting. This action is very important—with the default `update()`, the canvas would have an extremely annoying flicker as it was repainted, since almost none of the drawing is done in the background color.

```
public void paint(Graphics g)
{
      if (initialized)
      {
            g.drawImage(background, 0, 0, this);
            if (other != null)
                  g.drawImage(other, x, y, this);
      }
      else if ((size().width > 0) && (size().height > 0))
      {
            background = makeBackground();
            initialized = true;
      }
}

public void update(Graphics g)
{
      paint(g);
}
```

Drawing Tip:

When drawing a fixed background on a component, consider overriding that component's `update()` method so that it doesn't erase the background.

The `makeBackground()` method is called once, when we find that we know the width and height of this `Display` instance. This method draws `steps` rectangles, filling the canvas from top to bottom. Each band is filled with a shade of blue, ranging from darkest at the top to pure blue at the bottom. As a result, the background appears to shade smoothly from black to blue as you look down the display. Note that we're constructing an offscreen image here. As a result, we have to do the separate drawing calls only once: to construct the image in the first place. Then, all we have to do in the `paint()` method is to make a single call to `drawImage()`. If our background were more complicated, you'd notice a marked gain in smoothness, since the background would be repainted all at once, rather than through a sequence of separate drawing calls.

Drawing Tip:

If you have a complicated picture that has to be drawn repeatedly, draw it to an offscreen image first and then call `drawImage()` when you need to display the picture.

```java
private Image makeBackground()
{
    int      width = size().width,
             height = size().height,
             steps = 32,
             yIncrement = height / steps;

    Image img = createImage(width, height);
    Graphics g = img.getGraphics();

    g.setColor(Color.blue);
    g.fillRect(0, 0, width, height);
    for (int i = 0; i < steps; i++)
    {
        Color bg = new Color(0, 0, (255 / steps) * i);
        g.setColor(bg);
        g.fillRect(0, i * yIncrement, width, yIncrement);
    }
    g.dispose();
    return img;
}
}
```

Animation Preamble

Animation in Java is done as in other programming languages. The technique predates the computer by at least two hundred years—display a sequence of closely related images fast enough that the eye and brain blend them together to give the illusion of motion. Human physiology works in our favor here—ten images per second, more or less, is enough to fool the eye and brain into accepting the discrete images as a smooth stream. That's all you really need to know about the subject; all the rest is just technical details, with just enough programming thrown in to make the discussion worth pursuing here. Before we begin, though, we beg your indulgence while we make a short digression.

<RANT>
    Animation is a powerful, attractive, and—in Java—easy technique. It is also one of the principal reasons why some people have misgivings about Java. Mastery of a tool like animation should always include knowing when to use it and when to avoid its use. Jittering text and bouncing heads are perfectly fine if all you want to do is show off your mastery and share what you've learned (as we do in this book). When writing applications and applets for public consumption, though, you should never lose sight of the fact that computer programs are means of communication and that this communication can be irritating and annoying just as easily as it can be effective and engaging. If you write an applet and the animation detracts from the contents of the page, leave the animation out, no matter how nifty it is.
</RANT>

There—we feel much better. Now let's get back to work.

Loading Images: The `MediaTracker` Class

Since we do animation by displaying a sequence of images, we need to be sure that all the images are available before we start trying to display them. You've seen that we can use the `ImageObserver` method `updateImage()` to block execution until an image has been loaded. With some more work, we could modify this technique so that it applied to several images, but it's generally not worth the effort. The reason is that the `java.awt` package contains the `MediaTracker` class, which is specifically designed for watching the status of multiple images while they're being loaded.

    There are four class constants in `MediaTracker`. They are returned by the `statusAll()` and `statusID()` methods.

ABORTED	Loading of the image has been halted for some reason. It may be possible to continue later.
COMPLETE	The image has been loaded.
ERRORED	Loading has been halted, with no possibility of continuing.
LOADING	The image is being loaded.

There is one constructor in this class.

MediaTracker(Component c)

Creates a new MediaTracker instance. The argument is the Component that will serve as the destination of the images. You will almost always use this as the constructor argument.

This class has quite a few MediaTracker methods. We list those that will be of interest to us here.

❦ void **addImage**(Image im, int id)

Registers the argument image for observation by this MediaTracker. The id argument is used to assign the image to a group if you want to monitor the loading of different images in different ways. You can assign the same id to several images.

boolean **checkAll**()
boolean **checkAll**(boolean load)

Return true if all images registered with this tracker have completed loading, either successfully or in error. If the load argument is true, any image that hasn't begun loading yet will start to load.

❦ boolean **checkID**(int id)
boolean **checkID**(int id, boolean load)

Act like the checkAll() methods, except that they check only the images with a given id.

boolean **isErrorAny**()
❦ boolean **isErrorID**(int id)

Return true if any image (or any image with the given id) encountered an error while loading.

void **removeImage**(Image im)   // version 1.1 only
void **removeImage**(Image im, int id)   // version 1.1 only

Remove all instances of the specified image (or all instances with the given id). These methods were introduced in version 1.1 for efficiency, since a MediaTracker continues to monitor images even after they have been loaded.

int **statusAll**(boolean load)
int **statusID**(int id, boolean load)

Return the bitwise OR of the status constants for all registered images (or all images with the specified id).

❦ void **waitForAll**() throws InterruptedException
❦ void **waitForID**(int id) throws InterruptedException

These methods block the current thread until all images have been loaded (or until all images with the specified id have been loaded).

Here's an example of using a `MediaTracker`. We have four images in a directory "ships" that are named "ship0.gif," "ship1.gif," "ship2.gif," and "ship3.gif." We want to load them into an array of `Images`, named `ships[]`. We assign each image a separate `id` and we load them sequentially, using `waitForID()` to block until each is loaded. If any of the images fail to load, we display a status message to that effect, and return the value `false`. If all the images load successfully, we display a message and return `true`.

```
private boolean loadImages()
{
        showStatus("Loading images...");
        MediaTracker tracker = new MediaTracker(this);
        for (int i = 0; i < 4; i++)
        {
                ship[i] = getImage(getCodeBase(),
                                "ships/ship" + i + ".gif");
                tracker.addImage(ship[i], i);
                try{
                        tracker.waitForID(i);}
                catch (InterruptedException e){}
                if (tracker.isErrorID(i))
                {
                        showStatus("Failed to load image " + i);
                        return false;
                }
        }
        showStatus("Images loaded");
        return true;
}
```

Animation I: Starting Out

In our first animation example, we display a UFO in an evening sky. The UFO hovers while, in classic 1950s style, its lights cycle through a sequence of colors. Figure 12.8 illustrates one frame of the animation.

Figure 12.8 Visitors from Cydonia.

The applet that displays our visitor uses the `Display` class we discussed earlier and the `loadImages()` method.

```java
import java.applet.*;
import java.awt.*;

public class AnimationTest1 extends Applet implements Runnable
{
    private Image[]  ship = new Image[4];   // the ship images
    private Image    background;            // display background
    private Thread   animator = null;       // animation thread
    private int      x = 80, y = 40,        // where the ship is
                     currentShip = 0;       // the image index
    private Display  display;               // for drawing


    public void init()
    // Try to load the images.  Abort if any one couldn't
    // be loaded.  Otherwise, do layout as usual.
    {
        if (!loadImages())
        {
            showStatus("Couldn't continue");
            System.exit(0);
        }

        display = new Display();
        setLayout(new BorderLayout());
        add("Center", display);
    }

    public void start()
    // Start the animator thread.
    {
        if (animator == null)
        {
            animator = new Thread(this);
            animator.start();
        }
    }
}
```

As typically happens, we do the animation in a separate thread. All we have to do in the `run()` method for the `animator` thread is cycle through the indices of the `ships[]` array and call `display.showImage()` to draw the current ship image. Note that the animator thread is a good citizen and sleeps occasionally.

```java
    public void run()
    {
        while (animator != null)
        {
```

```
                    if (currentShip == 3)
                        currentShip = 0;
                    else
                        currentShip++;

                    display.showImage(ship[currentShip], x, y);
                    try
                    {
                        Thread.sleep(200);
                    }
                    catch (InterruptedException e)
                    {}
                }
            }


        public void stop()
        // Stop the animator thread
        {
            if (animator != null)
            {
                animator.stop();
                animator = null;
            }
        }


        public void update(Graphics g)
        // Remember, a call to paint() calls paint() on the components
        // contained in this applet.
        {
            paint(g);
        }


        // private boolean loadImages() omitted
    }
    // class Display omitted
```

Animation II: Better Design

The next pass at our program looks exactly like the first. The difference under the
hood is that we've split the ship off into a class of its own, running the animation,
rather than having the applet run the animation. Again, we're removing some of the
complexity from the animation and putting it where it belongs, in a Ship instance.
There's no need for the managing applet to know any of the details of what the ship
does with its running lights, after all—as far as the applet is concerned, the ship may
as well be a static image.

   The only tricky part about separating the ship from the applet is that the ship
needs to know where to draw itself. We provide this information to the ship via its

constructor, sending it a reference to the display, as well as an array of images and its location on the display canvas.

We take most of the Ship class code directly from the AnimationTest1 applet. Note that we've tried to make the class as general as possible, by allowing the use of an arbitrary number of images.

```
class Ship extends Thread
{
    Image[]     image;
    int         numImages,
                currentImage = 0,
                x, y;
    Display     display;

    public Ship(Image[] images, int numImages,
                Display display, int x, int y)
    {
        this.numImages = numImages;
        image = new Image[numImages];
        for (int i = 0; i < numImages; i++)
            image[i] = images[i];
        this.display = display;
        this.x = x;
        this.y = y;
    }

    public void moveTo(int x, int y)
    // We don't use this yet, but it seems reasonable that
    // sooner or later we'll want to move the ship.  After
    // all, we don't want to frighten the natives unnecessarily.
    {
        this.x = x;
        this.y = y;
        display.showImage(image[currentImage], x, y);
    }

    public void run()
    {
        while (true)
        {
            if (currentImage == numImages - 1)
                currentImage = 0;
            else
                currentImage++;

            display.showImage(image[currentImage], x, y);
            try
            {
                Thread.sleep(200);
            }
            catch (InterruptedException e)
            {}
        }
    }
}
```

By moving the animation to the `Ship` class, we've simplified the applet. It no longer needs to implement `Runnable`, so we remove the `run()` method and construct and start the `Ship` thread in the applet's `start()` method. The applet now has a more managerial air, as it should, since it delegates the display and animation operations to the `Display` and `Ship` classes.

```
public class AnimationTest2 extends Applet
{
    // other declarations omitted
    private Ship    theShip = null;

    // init() omitted--unchanged from old version

    public void start()
    {
        if (theShip == null)
        {
            theShip = new Ship(ship, 4,
                                display, x, y);
            theShip.start();
        }
    }

    public void stop()
    {
        if (theShip != null)
        {
            theShip.stop();
            theShip = null;
        }
    }

    // update(), loadImages() omitted--no changes
}
// class Display omitted
```

Animation III: Moving the Ship

In the third version of our program, the ship moves in response to mouse clicks. When the user clicks the mouse, the ship heads in the direction of the point where the mouse was clicked. Because of our design, changing the applet to move the ship requires no modification of the Display and Ship classes.

We change the applet back to implementing the `Runnable` interface, since the ship movement will be in a separate thread, `mover`.

```
public class AnimationTest3 extends Applet implements Runnable
{
    private Image[]    shipImg = new Image[4];
```

```
private int        destinationX = 80,
                   destinationY = 40;
private double     currentX = 80.0,
                   currentY = 40.0,
                   velocityX = 0.0,
                   velocityY = 0.0;
private Thread mover = null;
private Display    display;
private Ship       theShip = null;

// init() omitted
```

Since we have two threads at work here—one to animate the running lights and one to move the ship—we start and stop both threads in the applet's `start()` and `stop()` methods. In a more complex program, we could save some lines of code by placing all the threads in a single `ThreadGroup` and starting and stopping them as a group, but that's hardly worth the effort here.

```
public void start()
{
    if (theShip == null)
    {
        theShip = new Ship(shipImg, 4, display,
                                destinationX, destinationY);
        theShip.start();
    }
    if (mover == null)
    {
        mover = new Thread(this);
        mover.start();
    }
}

public void stop()
{
    if (theShip != null)
    {
        theShip.stop();
        theShip = null;
    }
    if (mover != null)
    {
        mover.stop();
        mover = null;
    }
}
```

The `run()` method for the mover thread repeatedly calls the helper method `computeNextMove()` and uses `moveTo()` to move the ship to its new location and draw it on the display.

```
public void run()
{
    while (mover != null)
    {
        Point p = computeNextMove();
        theShip.moveTo(p.x, p.y);
        try
        {
            Thread.sleep(125);
        }
        catch (InterruptedException e)
        {}
    }
}

// update() omitted
```

The sole event handler in this applet just records where the mouse event occurred and calls the helper method setVelocity() to determine the new values of the velocity components velocityX and velocityY.

```
public boolean mouseUp(Event e, int x, int y)
{
    destinationX = x;
    destinationY = y;
    setVelocity();
    return true;
}
```

To move the ship, all we do at each step is add velocityX to the current x coordinate, currentX, and likewise add velocityY to currentY.

```
private Point computeNextMove()
{
    currentX = currentX + velocityX;
    currentY = currentY + velocityY;
    int x = (int)Math.round(currentX);
    int y = (int)Math.round(currentY);

    return new Point(x, y);
}
```

The only tricky part of this applet is computing the new velocity components when the user clicks the mouse. As illustrated in Figure 12.9, we let deltaX and deltaY represent the differences in the x- and y-coordinates of the current point and the destination point. We then scale these distances, by multiplying them by 2.0 / distance, where distance represents the distance between the current and destination points. By doing so, we guarantee that the ship's velocity will always be 2.0 pixels per move, more or less.

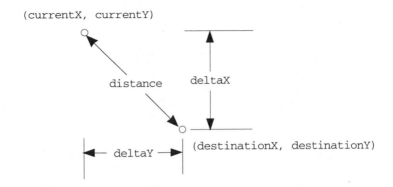

Figure 12.9 Computing the ship's velocity.

```
private void setVelocity()
{
      double deltaX = destinationX - currentX;
      double deltaY = destinationY - currentY;
      double distance = Math.sqrt(deltaX * deltaX +
                                   deltaY * deltaY);
      if (distance < 2.0)
      {
            velocityX = 0.0;
            velocityY = 0.0;
      }
      else
      {
            velocityX = 2.0 * deltaX / distance;
            velocityY = 2.0 * deltaY / distance;
      }
}

      // loadImages() omitted
}
// class Display omitted
// class Ship omitted
```

Animation IV: Clipping

If you stop to think about it, you'll realize that a lot of unnecessary drawing is being done in our applet. When the ship moves, we obviously have to erase the old image (which we do by painting over it with the background image) and draw the new image, but a lot of Display real estate never needs to be touched. In fact, all we really have to do at each ship move is repaint the rectangle that encloses the old and the new ship images, as illustrated in Figure 12.10. There, oldR is the bounding rectangle of the old image and newR is the bounding rectangle of the new image.

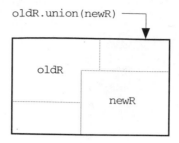

Figure 12.10 Computing the clipping rectangle.

The Graphics method clipRect() takes as its arguments the x, y, width, and height of a rectangle, and limits drawing to just the parts of that rectangle that lie within the total drawing area of the associated component.[6] In our final modification of AnimationTest, we changed Display's update() method so that it clipped the drawing region to the smallest rectangle that contained the changes.

Drawing Tip:

If your drawing is going to take place only on a small portion of the total drawing area, consider clipping the Graphics context to just the part of the region you need.

```
public void update(Graphics g)
{
        oldR = newR;
        if (other != null)
        {
                newR = new Rectangle(x, y, other.getWidth(this),
                                             other.getHeight(this));
                Rectangle clip = oldR.union(newR);
                g.clipRect(clip.x, clip.y, clip.width, clip.height);
        }
        paint(g);
}
```

The only thing you need to keep in mind when clipping is that, once you have set the clip rectangle for a Graphics instance, you can't increase its size. That isn't a problem here, since we're doing all our clipping in the update()

---

[6]Or it should, at least. When testing the animation applets on several platforms, we discovered that some run-time environments aren't as careful about clipping as they should be. By now, you may have noticed this lack of adherence to standards several times.

method and every time update() is called by the system, it is provided with an entirely new `Graphics` object.

12.4   HANDS ON

You've seen a lot of tools so far; some are specific to Java and many others are part of good programming in any language. In our culminating Lablet, we use almost every tool you've learned to use so far. Along with the customary language details, we have HTML, classes, inheritance, packages, arrays, exceptions, threads, graphics, URLs, applet parameters, and animation, to name a few. There are no file manipulation tools and no dialogs or menus, but those are just about the only tools we *don't* do. This multiplicity of features wasn't so much a deliberate choice on our part as it was a natural consequence of designing any moderately complicated program.

We've tried to make each of our Lablets and all of our example code models of good practice, and we took special care in this Lablet to make it as close to an industrial-strength program as we could. We'll need to explain a few of the programming techniques in this Lablet. A few omissions we left for you to fill in, in the lab exercises, but you can assess your mastery of programming by looking through the Lablet code to see if you can read and understand it easily.

Designing the Lablet

Our goal with this example was to design two applets and two classes that a Web page designer could use to place custom buttons on the page, as we illustrated in Figure 12.11.

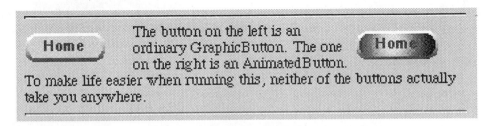

Figure 12.11 Two custom buttons embedded in a Web page.

One of the applets, `OldButtoner`, constructs and implements a static `GraphicButton`. A `GraphicButton` acts just like an ordinary button, but it uses two images to represent its normal up state and the down state that it takes when the user presses the mouse button while the pointer is over the button. The applet is responsible for getting the information necessary to construct the button, such as the two images, the button label, and the URL of the page where the browser will go when the button is clicked. Once the applet has gotten this information, it lays out the button and then just sits back and waits for a button click.

The other applet, Buttoner, acts just like OldButtoner, except that it produces an AnimatedButton instance. AnimatedButton is a subclass of GraphicButton, the only major difference being that an AnimatedButton cycles through several images when in its up state, to give an animated appearance.

Exploring the OldButtoner Applet

We've omitted most of the import declarations and comments in our Lablet explorations so far. This time, though, we kept them in. First, we wanted to point out that we used a package of our own, named "myWidgets," to organize our two button classes. Remember, to make a package of your own, all you need to do is head each class declaration with a package declaration and then put the compiled class file in the directory with the same name as the package.

We kept the comments in so that you could see what a moderately complete job of documentation looks like. When writing documentation for a program, you should write for someone who is a competent programmer but is seeing your program for the very first time. At the very minimum, the header comments should explain what the program does, indicate the information necessary to use it, and contain any notes about behavior that's not immediately obvious. It's not a bad idea, as well, to include a revision history and a "table of contents," listing the methods declared in the program.

```
import java.applet.*;
import java.awt.*;
import java.net.*;
import myWidgets.*;                    // for GraphicButton


public class OldButtoner extends Applet
/*   This applet is designed to place a custom button in a Web
     document.  To use this, place the file "OldButtoner.class" and
     "GraphicButton.class"with the HTML document along with two
     gifs, representing the down and up images of the button.  Then,
     embed the following HTML in the appropriate place in the main
     document:

     <APPLET CODE = "OldButtoner.class" WIDTH = 82 HEIGHT = 27>
          <PARAM name = "pattern"     value = "bttn*.gif">
          <PARAM name = "numPix"      value = "2">
          <PARAM name = "label"       value = "Home">
          <PARAM name = "destURL"
                      value = "http://www.some.destination">
     </APPLET>
```

```
PARAMETERS:
    pattern (REQUIRED): The name template of the button
        pictures.  In the example above, the pictures would
        be named "bttn0.gif" and "bttn1.gif".  The picture
        numbered 0 will be used for the down picture.
        For best results, these gifs should be the size
        specified in the WIDTH and HEIGHT arguments.
        If this argument isn't present or is malformed, the
        applet will default to using an ordinary button
        instead of a GraphicButton.
    numPix (OPTIONAL): The number of pictures.  This must be
        at least 2 and will default to 2 if missing,
        incorrectly written, or too small.
    label (OPTIONAL): The name that will appear in the
        button.  The label will be centered in the button,
        so if it is too long, you may have to adjust the
        WIDTH and HEIGHT arguments (the class will shrink
        the images to fit the label, but can't grow them
        beyond the applet size).
    destURL (OPTIONAL): If specified and valid, this is the
        destination the browser will go to when the button
        is clicked.
*/
```

The class declaration begins with declarations of the instance variables and the `init()` method. In `init()`, we get the applet parameters and lay out the single button. This method does most of its work by calling helper methods to decode the parameters and load the images. For example, `numPix` is an integer variable, but its parameter is, as all parameters are, a string. To avoid cluttering up `init()`, we wrote a method, `getIntParameter()`, that gets the value of the parameter with the specified name, converts it to an `int`, and returns the value. You've seen a simple version of `loadImages()` already. It returns `true` if all the images eventually load successfully. If they do, we construct a `Graphic-Button` and if they don't we default to constructing an ordinary button so that the applet always does something, even if it's not quite what we wanted.

```
{
    private GraphicButton        theButton;
    private Button               backupButton;
    private Image[]              images;
    private int                  numImgs;
    private String               theLabel;
    private URL                  destURL;

    public void init()
    {
        // Get all the parameters, sometimes using our own
        // utilities (see below).
        String pattern   = getParameter("pattern");
        numImgs = getIntParameter("numPix", 2);
```

(continued)

```
        if (numImgs < 2)
             numImgs = 2;
        theLabel = getParameter("label");
        destURL = getURLParameter("destURL", null);

        // Construct the button and add it to the applet.
        images = new Image[numImgs];
        Rectangle b = bounds();
        if (loadImages(pattern))
        {
             theButton = new GraphicButton(images, theLabel);
             theButton.resize(b.width, b.height);
             add(theButton);
             theButton.repaint();
        }
        else
        // Failed to make a GraphicButton, so default to an
        // ordinary Button.
        {
             backupButton = new Button(theLabel);
             backupButton.resize(b.width, b.height - 4);
             add(backupButton);
        }
    }


    public boolean action(Event e, Object arg)
    // Handle a mouse click in either of the buttons by sending the
    // browser to the URL given by the applet parameter.
    {
         if (((e.target == theButton) ||
              (e.target == backupButton)) &&
             (destURL != null))
         {
             getAppletContext().showDocument(destURL);
             return true;
         }
         return false;
    }
```

We do a little more in this version of loadImages() than we did in the version in Section 12.3. In this version we give the method a String argument representing the pattern of the image names. We require the user to ensure that all the button images have the same relative URLs, differing only by the image number, like "bttn0.gif" and "bttn1.gif," and to pass the pattern, with '*' where the numbers are, as a parameter. The method uses this pattern to generate the image URLs and then loads them, as usual.

```
    private boolean loadImages(String pattern)
    // Get the images with the given pattern name and load them
    // into the images[] array.
```

```
                // Return true iff all images were successfully loaded.
                {
                        // First, parse the pattern, splitting it into the base
                        // part, before '*', and the extension part, after '*'.
                        // For example, "bttn*.gif" would split into
                        // the base string "bttn" and extension string ".gif".
                        String      base,
                                    extension;
                        int starIndex = pattern.indexOf('*');
                        try
                        {
                                base = pattern.substring(0, starIndex);
                                extension = pattern.substring(starIndex + 1);
                        }
                        catch (IndexOutOfBoundsException e)
                        {
                                showStatus("Bad pattern parameter");
                                return false;
                        }


                        // Wait for the images to load, and signal by returning
                        // false if any are broken.
                        showStatus("Loading images...");
                        MediaTracker tracker = new MediaTracker(this);
                        for (int i = 0; i < numImgs; i++)
                        {
                                images[i] = getImage(getCodeBase(), base + i +
                                                                    extension);
                                tracker.addImage(images[i], i);
                                try
                                {
                                        tracker.waitForID(i);
                                }
                                catch (InterruptedException e)
                                {}
                                if (tracker.isErrorID(i))
                                {
                                        showStatus("Failed to load image " + i);
                                        return false;
                                }
                        }
                        showStatus("Images loaded");
                        return true;      // Indicate that loading was successful.
                }
```

We discussed the getParameterInfo() and getAppletInfo() methods in Section 12.1. The applet would work perfectly well without them, but they're methods that a well-constructed applet should have and not a lot of programming effort is required to put them in.

```
public String[][] getParameterInfo()
// Return an arbitrarily long array of three strings, one for
// each parameter.  The strings describe, respectively, the
// parameter name, its type, and its description.
{
        String[][] aboutParams = {
                {"pattern",      "String",    "base*extension"},
                {"numPix",       "int",       "number of images"},
                {"label",        "String",    "button label"},
                {"destURL",      "URL",       "destination"}};
        return aboutParams;
}


public String getAppletInfo()
// Returns a String giving information about the applet.  A
// browser might use this in an About box.
{
        return "Graphic Button applet. © 1997, Rick Decker ";
}
```

The applet concludes with the two helper methods that `init()` uses to get the parameters. Each tries to convert the `String` parameter value to the correct type and returns the value if it succeeds and a default value if conversion fails. As usual, we're trying to make our program as robust as possible, anticipating errors that might happen and dealing with them so that they don't cause disaster.

```
private int getIntParameter(String paramName, int defaultValue)
// Try to get the parameter with the given name.  If there's no
// such parameter or if the value is incorrectly formatted,
// return the given default value.
{
        try
        {       return (Integer.parseInt(getParameter(paramName)));}
        catch (NumberFormatException e)
        {       return defaultValue; }
}


private URL getURLParameter(String paramName, URL defaultValue)
{
        try
        {       return (new URL(getParameter(paramName))); }
        catch (MalformedURLException e)
        {       return defaultValue; }
}
}
```

Exploring the `GraphicButton` Class

Our `GraphicButton` has two images and a label. It generates `action` events when clicked, and its label can be set and inspected, just like a regular button. It also has a refinement that AWT buttons lack—moving the cursor over the button highlights its label in red and moving the cursor away sets the label back to its original color.

```
package myWidgets;

import java.awt.*;

public class GraphicButton extends Canvas
/*
    A GraphicButton has the same functionality as an ordinary AWT
    button.  The primary difference is that it uses images for its
    up and down displays.

    INITIALIZATION
        To construct a GraphicButton, supply the constructor with
        an array of two images and an optional label.
        In the array of images, image[0] should be the down image
        and image[1] the up.

        NOTE: While not required, it's a good idea for the images
        to be the same size.
        This class uses the size of the down image to center the
        label.

    EVENT HANDLING
        A GraphicButton object responds to MOUSE_ENTER and
        MOUSE_EXIT events by highlighting and de- highlighting
        its label. It responds to MOUSE_UP and MOUSE_DOWN events
        by redrawing the button in its appropriate state.

        The button consumes all four of these events and in the
        case of a MOUSE_UP, finishes by posting a new
        ACTION_EVENT, thus acting like an ordinary button.

    ACCESSORS, MUTATORS
        getLabel():     Returns the label string.
        setLabel():     Sets the label string to the argument.

*/
```

A `GraphicButton` needs references to the two images the constructor passes to it. It also needs to know its visible width and height, which it computes from the width and height of its label. Note that these are not the dimensions of the button canvas itself—the button may take up more space than it appears to.

```
{
        protected final static int  LABEL_INSET = 15;

        protected    Image[]       theImage;   // [0] -> down, [1] -> up
        protected    int           curImage = 1;
        private      String        theLabel;
        private      int           thisWidth,
                                   thisHeight,
                                   labelBase;

//--------- Constructors and initialization utility ---------

public GraphicButton(Image[] imgs, String label)
{
        theLabel = label;
        theImage = imgs;

        setFont(new Font("Helvetica", Font.BOLD, 10));
        fitLabel();
}

public GraphicButton(Image[] imgs)
{
        this(imgs, null);
}
```

To compute the height and width of the visible portion of the button, we need to know the width of its label text. The FontMetrics class keeps track of the sizes of the various parts of text in a particular font. A String is drawn when we give the coordinates of its *anchor,* which is a point on the *baseline* at the left edge of the text. A FontMetrics instance associated with a font has access to the methods getAscent(), getDescent(), and stringWidth(), among others.

The getAscent() method returns the maximum height, in pixels above the baseline, of any character in the font. Note that this might be larger than the height of a particular string (it wouldn't be the correct ascent of "stop," for example, since that string has no uppercase letters), but we can do nothing about that—no method gives the ascent of a particular string. Similarly, the method getDescent() returns the maximum height in pixels below the baseline that any character in the font can be. We're better off with respect to width. The method stringWidth() computes and returns the width of a given string in the font associated with the FontMetrics object. The fitLabel() method uses the height of the down button image, the LABEL_INSET constant, and the FontMetrics methods to decide the width and height of the visible portion of the button, along with the *y*-coordinate, labelBase, of the anchor. How this is accomplished we leave as an exercise.

```
protected void fitLabel()
// Size the button so that there is a LABEL_INSET pixel inset
// on each side of the label and the label is centered
// vertically in the button..
{
        thisHeight = theImage[0].getHeight(this) - 4;

        if (theLabel != null)
        {
                FontMetrics fm = getFontMetrics(getFont());
                thisWidth = 2 * LABEL_INSET +
                                    fm.stringWidth(theLabel);
                labelBase = (thisHeight + fm.getAscent() -
                                    fm.getDescent()) / 2;
        }
        else
                thisWidth = 3 * LABEL_INSET;
}
```

A GraphicButton deals with four mouse events and consumes all of them. A mouseDown event causes the button to be repainted in its down state, by setting curImage to 0 and then calling for a repaint, which will draw the down image theImage[0]. A mouseUp event will cause the button to be redrawn in its up state and send along a new action event, since that's the only event an AWT button triggers. The mouseEnter and mouseExit events redraw the label in its new colors.

```
public boolean mouseDown(Event e, int x, int y)
// Change the button state to down and consume the event.
{
        curImage = 0;
        repaint();
        return true;
}

public boolean mouseUp(Event e, int x, int y)
// Change the button state to down, eat the event and post an
// ACTION event.
{
        curImage = 1;
        repaint();

        postEvent(new Event(this, Event.ACTION_EVENT, theLabel));
        return true;
}
```

(continued)

```
public boolean mouseEnter(Event e, int x, int y)
// Deal with a MOUSE_ENTER event by highlighting the label of
// the button.
{
     Graphics g = getGraphics();
     g.setColor(Color.red);
     g.drawString(theLabel, LABEL_INSET, labelBase);
     return true;
}

public boolean mouseExit(Event e, int x, int y)
// Turn off highlighting.
{
     Graphics g = getGraphics();
     if (curImage > 0)
           g.setColor(Color.darkGray);
     else
           g.setColor(Color.white);
     g.drawString(theLabel, LABEL_INSET, labelBase);
     return true;
}
```

The paint() method scales the button image to the width and height that were calculated by fitLabel() and draws the label at the anchor point (LABEL_INSET, labelBase), in the appropriate color. We didn't need to override update() here, but doing so does no harm and we'll need the override in the subclass AnimatedButton.

```
public void paint(Graphics g)
{
     g.drawImage(theImage[curImage], 0, 0,
                      thisWidth, thisHeight, this);

     if (theLabel != null)
     {
          if (curImage > 0)
                g.setColor(Color.darkGray);
          else
                g.setColor(Color.white);
          g.drawString(theLabel, LABEL_INSET, labelBase);
     }
}

public void update(Graphics g)
// For flicker-free animation in the AnimatedButton subclass.
{
     paint(g);
}
```

The class declaration concludes with the accessor method `getLabel()` and the mutator `setLabel()`, neither of which need explanation.

```
public String getLabel()
// Return a copy of the label string.
{
        return new String(theLabel);
}

public void setLabel(String s)
{
        theLabel = s;
        fitLabel();
        repaint();
}
}
```

Exploring the `AnimatedButton` Class

The `AnimatedButton` class is very simple, since almost all of the work is done by the `GraphicButton` superclass. As a result, all this class has to do is handle the animation. It does so by implementing the `Runnable` interface, which means implementing a `run()` method for its animation thread.

The class has an instance variable, `delayTime`, that is supplied in the constructor and controls the speed of animation by setting the amount of time the animation thread sleeps at each iteration of the loop in `run()`. The only other thing we need to track is whether the animation is moving up or down through the images. For five images, for instance, the animation would cycle through image numbers 1, 2, 3, 4, 3, 2, 1, 2, 3, 4, ..., so even though we don't need to know what to do when the current image is at either end of the cycle, we do need to know what to do when we're in the middle of the image sequence. Note, by the way, that we animate only when the button is in its up state—that explains why we use image 0 for the down state.

```
package myWidgets;

import java.awt.*;

public class AnimatedButton extends GraphicButton
                                implements Runnable
// images[0] is the down picture--the rest are for the animated up
// state.
// Requires at least three images for animation.
{

    private long      delayTime;
    private Thread    myThread;
    private boolean   goingDown = false;
```

The constructors and the start() and stop() methods are simple and—by now—easy to understand. We'll leave explanation of the details of the run() method for the lab exercises.

```java
public AnimatedButton(Image[] imgs, String label, long delayMs)
{
        super(imgs, label);
        delayTime = delayMs;
        myThread = new Thread(this);
        myThread.start();
}

public AnimatedButton(Image[] imgs, long delayMs)
{
        this(imgs, null, delayMs);
}

//------------------ Thread handlers --------------------

public void start()
// This can be called by the parent applet's start() method.
{
        if (myThread == null)
        {
                myThread = new Thread(this);
                myThread.start();
        }
}

public void stop()
// This can be called by the parent applet's stop() method.
{
        if ((myThread != null) && myThread.isAlive())
                myThread.stop();
        myThread = null;
}

public void run()
// Cycle through the up pictures when needed.
{
        while (myThread != null)
        {
                try {
                        Thread.sleep(delayTime); }
                catch (InterruptedException e) {}

                // Do nothing this turn if button is down or no
                // animation.
                if ((curImage == 0) || (theImage.length == 2))
                        continue;
```

```
            if (goingDown)
                if (curImage == 1)
                {
                        curImage++;
                        goingDown = false;
                }
                else
                        curImage--;
            else
                if (curImage == theImage.length - 1)
                {
                        curImage--;
                        goingDown = true;
                }
                else
                        curImage++;

            repaint();
        }
    }
}
```

We didn't list the `Buttoner` applet that runs an `AnimatedButton`, since it's almost exactly the same as the `OldButtoner` applet. The only significant difference between the two is that they construct different types of buttons.

Finally, the HTML

To complete the Lablet, the chapter, and the book, all we have to do is show the HTML that the Web browser will use to display the two buttons and the text surrounding them. You can see that we use two <APPLET> tags, one for each button. In each we supply the necessary parameters.

```
<HTML>
    <HEAD>
        <TITLE>Button Test Page</TITLE>
    </HEAD>

<BODY>
<HR>
<APPLET CODE = "OldButtoner.class" WIDTH = 82 HEIGHT = 27
                                        ALIGN = left>
        <PARAM name = "pattern" value = "bttn*.gif">
        <PARAM name = "numPix" value = "2">
        <PARAM name = "label" value = "Home">
        <PARAM name = "destURL"
                value = "http://www.bogus.edu/">
    </APPLET>
```

(continued)

```
<APPLET CODE = "Buttoner.class" WIDTH = 82 HEIGHT = 27
                              ALIGN = right>
      <PARAM name = "pattern" value = "animate/ab*.gif">
      <PARAM name = "numPix" value = "11">
      <PARAM name = "label" value = "Home">
      <PARAM name = "destURL"
                  value = "http://www.alsobogus.org/">
</APPLET>
The button on the left is an ordinary GraphicButton.  The one
on the right is an AnimatedButton.  To make life easier when
running this, neither of the buttons actually take you
anywhere.
<HR>
<A HREF = "Buttoner.java">See the source.</A>
</BODY>
</HTML>
```

12.5 SUMMARY

❦ We discussed the following classes:

```
Applet
AppletContext    (interface)
AudioClip    (interface)
Color
Component
FilteredImageSource
FontMetrics    (briefly)
Graphics
Image
ImageConsumer    (interface)
ImageObserver    (interface)
ImageProducer    (interface)
MediaTracker
RGBImageFilter
URL
```

❦ A URL has the form `protocol://hostName/pathName/fileName`. The protocol identifies the file format (like `http`), the hostName identifies the computer (like `java.sun.com`), and the fileName identifies the location (like `products/jdk/1.1/docs/api/Package-java.awt.html`) of the file in the host's directory structure.

❦ URLs can be expressed as absolute or relative to a given directory.

❦ The URL class can construct a URL from a string and has methods for extracting the protocol, hostName, and fileName from a given URL.

❦ The `Applet` methods `getCodeBase()` and `getDocumentBase()` are used to get the URL of an applet's `.class` file or the URL of the HTML document referring to the applet.

- The `Applet` methods `getAudioClip()` and `getImage()` are used to initiate the process of loading a sound or an image into an applet.
- An applet may use parameters specified in the `<APPLET>` element of an HTML document. The `Applet` method `getParameter()` returns the value `String` of the parameter with the specified name.
- An applet has an `AppletContext`, referring to the context in which the applet is running. The `AppletContext` method `showDocument()` requests the context to load the document with the specified URL.
- The `<APPLET>` element requires the artibutes `CODE`, `WIDTH`, and `HEIGHT`, and may use the optional attributes `CODEBASE`, `ALT`, `ALIGN`, `VSPACE`, and `HSPACE`.
- An `AudioClip` file must be in AU format. The methods `play()` and `stop()`, respectively, play the sound and stop it.
- Once an `Image` has been identified by `getImage()`, it can be drawn by the `Graphics` method `drawImage()`. A call to `getImage()` does not initiate loading—loading will begin when a request comes to use the image, by drawing it, for example.
- To force an image to load, call the `Component` method `prepareImage()`.
- The Image methods `getGraphics()`, `getHeight()`, and `getWidth()` can be used to get a `Graphics` instance associated with the image and to get the height and width of the image. These methods might not yield reliable results if the image hasn't been fully loaded at the time of the call.
- To use an offscreen image, create a new instance by `createImage()`, get its `Graphics` context, and use the `Graphics` instance methods to draw on the image. The image can then be displayed by `drawImage()`.
- If you have a complicated picture that has to be drawn repeatedly, draw it to an offscreen image first and then call `drawImage()` when you need to display the picture.
- A `Color` instance represents a color by specifying its red, green, and blue componets. A value of 0 represents none of that component, and a value of 255 represents the maximum brightness of that component.
- It is often convenient to use hexadecimal notation to construct or manipulate a `Color`. A hexadecimal literal begins with the characters `0x`, so the literal `0xffafaf` could be used to construct `Color.pink`.
- When an image is drawn, an `ImageObserver` instance is created to monitor the loading of the image. `Component` implements `ImageObserver`, so you will generally use `this` to refer to the default `ImageObserver` in a `drawImage()` call. You can override the sole `ImageObserver` method `imageUpdate()` to do your own observing of the progress of an image.
- An `ImageFilter` object is used to modify the pixels of an image. The `RGBImageFilter` is a simple subclass of `ImageFilter` that performs the same color modification on each pixel of an image.
- To use an `ImageFilter`, supply one to a `FilteredImageSource`, along with an image producer (usually obtained by calling `getSource()`). A `FilteredImageSource` is an image producer, so you can then use it as an argument to `createImage()` to create a new filtered image.

❦ The high-order byte of an image pixel represents the amount of transparency of that pixel, with 0 denoting a transparent pixel and 255 representing an opaque pixel.

❦ It's generally a good idea to do drawing on a `Canvas` or a `Canvas` subclass.

❦ When drawing a fixed background on a component, consider overriding that component's `update()` method so that it doesn't erase the background.

❦ To do animation, display a sequence of closely related images fast enough that the eye and brain blend them together to give the illusion of motion. This is almost always done in a separate thread.

❦ The `MediaTracker` class is designed for watching the status of multiple images while they're being loaded. Calling `addImage()` registers an image with a `MediaTracker`. The methods `waitForAll()` and `waitForID()` block the current thread until all images (or the images with the specified id) are loaded.

❦ The `Graphics` method `clipRect()` takes as its arguments the `x`, `y`, `width`, and `height` of a rectangle, and limits drawing to just the parts of that rectangle that lie within the total drawing area of the associated component.

❦ If your drawing is going to take place only on a small portion of the total drawing area, consider clipping the `Graphics` context to just the part of the region you need.

❦ The `FontMetrics` class keeps track of the sizes of the various parts of text in a particular font, like the ascent, descent, and height of the text. The method `stringWidth()` can be used to compute the width of a `String` in a particular font.

❦ If you got this far, take a moment to reflect on what you've learned and congratulate yourself on your diligence and effort.

12.6 EXERCISES

1. With respect to the URL

    ```
    http://www.server.org/pub/docs/joubert/index.html
    ```

    give the absolute URLs corresponding to each of the following relative URLs.
    a. `page2.html`
    b. `art/rainbowBar.gif`
    c. `/misc/MyApplet.class`
    d. `//admin/recs/july92/index.html`

2. In the file structure of Exercise 1, how would `MyApplet` load the image `rainbowBar.gif`?

3. In the `SketchPad` Lablet of Chapter 6, resizing the applet window causes the drawing to vanish, since resizing the window forces a call to `paint()` and thus loses all the old drawing. You can fix this problem by double buffering,

using an offscreen image that mirrors what was drawn on the screen. In other words, you could write the program so that every drawing call was done twice, once to the screen and once to the offscreen image. Then, when time came to update the screen, all you would have to do is copy the offscreen image to the screen. Modify SketchPad so that it does this double buffering.

4.   What are the conventional names for the colors with the following (R, G, B) components?
   a.   (128, 0, 128)
   b.   (230, 230, 90)
   c.   (30, 90, 30)
   d.   (255, 0, 255)
   e.   (255, 255, 0)
   f.   (0, 255, 255)
   g.   (255, 128, 0)

5.   Convert each of the colors in Exercise 4 to their integer equivalents, expressed in hexadecimal form.

6.   Show that 16756655 is indeed the decimal representation of Color.pink.

7.   Come up with the best (R, G, B) values you can for the following colors. You may have to do a bit of research for this question.
   a.   Aubergine
   b.   Heliotrope
   c.   Taupe
   d.   Teal

8.   Consider the following method.

```
public Color mystery(Color c)
{
     int n = c.getRGB();
     int x = (n & 0x0000ff00) << 8;
     int y = (n & 0x000000ff) << 8;
     int z = (n & 0x00ff0000) >> 16;
     return new Color(x + y + z);
}
```

   a.   What color does this method return if the argument color corresponds to the integer 0x00ff8000?
   b.   What is the result of mystery(mystery(mystery(myColor)))?
   c.   We deliberately made this method incomprehensible, to make this exercise more challenging. Use the getRed(), getGreen(), and getBlue() methods to make mystery() less mysterious.

9.   If you look at ImageTest3, you'll notice that it consists of the methods init(), imageUpdate(), and paint(), none of which you call yourself.

Trace the action of `ImageTest3`, describing who calls the methods in what order. Remember, there are a lot of implicit players: the runtime system, an `ImageProducer`, an `ImageConsumer`, and an `ImageObserver`.

10. Remove the call to `prepareImage()` from `ImageTest3` and run it. Nothing will happen. Carefully explain why, including the circularity involved.

11. In `InvertFilter`, we used bitwise OR to combine the masked component values into a pixel. Could we have added them, instead? Explain why or why not.

12. Consider the problem of making an image filter that will take an image and gray it out. An easy way to do so is to take each of the red, green, and blue components of a pixel and average it with 128.
    a. Give the values that would result if you applied this scheme to the components 255, 128, and 0.
    b. Write a `FadeFilter` class that will do this task.
    c. Modify `ImageTest4` so that it uses your `FadeFilter`, rather than an `InvertFilter`.

13. Since a `FilteredImageSource` takes an `ImageProducer` as one of its arguments and returns an `ImageProducer` as a result, you should be able to chain two filters together to produce a new one.
    a. Try it. Modify `ImageTest4` so that it takes an image and applies an `InvertFilter` first and then applies the `FadeFilter` of Exercise 12.
    b. Would the result of part (a) be different if you applied the filters in the opposite order? Explain.
    c. What would happen if you chained two `InvertFilters` together?

14. You can't use an `RGBImageFilter` to blend two images, but you can simulate a blend by making a `TransparencyFilter` that sets the transparency of each pixel of an image to some value less than 255 and then drawing the filtered image on top of another. Try it.

15. At 72 pixels per inch and 4 bytes per pixel, how much memory would be required to store the pixels of a two-inch by one-inch image?

16. Run `AnimationTest1` with and without the override of the `update()` method in Display. Explain the differences you see.

17. We designed the `Ship` class used in the animation applets as a subclass of `Thread`. The other way of doing so would have been to have the `Ship` class contain a `Thread` and then have Ship implement `Runnable`.
    a. Rewrite `Ship` this way.
    b. Discuss the advantages or disadvantages of this approach, compared to the original.

18.   The `GraphicButton` and `AnimatedButton` classes don't quite have all the functionality of real buttons. In particular, we need some way of indicating visually what happens when we call the `Component` method `disable()` on our buttons.

   a.   Rewrite `GraphicButton` so that it has an override of `disable()`. Doing so should not only keep the button from generating action events (does it already?), but it should also dim the button (see Exercise 12 for a way to do that). Of course, you should also write an override of `enable()`, to make the button active and restore it to its original appearance.

   b.   Repeat part (a) for the `AnimatedButton` class. In this case, a call to `disable()` should also turn off the button's animation.

19.   Write the utility method

```
boolean getBooleanParameter(String name, boolean default)
```

   that will look for the parameter with the given name. If there is no parameter with the specified name, the method should return the `default` value. It should also return the `default` value if there is a parameter with the right name, but the value was neither of "false" or "true." If there is a parameter with the specified name and the value is "true" or "false," it should return the boolean value equivalent to the value string. Your method should treat value strings like "True," "true," and "TRUE" as corresponding to `true`. (Hint: use the `String` method `toLowerCase()`.)

20.   In the `fitLabel()` method of `GraphicButton`, explain what is being done in the calculation of `labelBase`. Suppose, for example, that `thisHeight` was 30, that the font's ascent was 8, and that the descent was 4. How much space would be above the label and how much would be below the label?

INDEX

Abstract class, 67, 227
Access control list, 443
Access modifiers, 165–170
  package, 168
  `private`, 166–168
  `protected`, 168–169
  `public`, 169–170
`ActionEvent`, 249
`ActionListener` interface, 253, 255
`action()` method, 237
Actual argument, 37, 281
Adapter classes, 257
`AnimatedButton` class, 559–561
Animation, 535–549
  clipping the rectangle, 547–548
  drawing on a `Canvas`, 535–538
  loading images, 538
`AnimationTest` applet, 541, 544–549
Applet, 15–18, 24, 31–58
  `Applet` class, 31–34, 512–515
  attributes, 517
  graphical programming, 39–52
  inheritance and overriding, 38
  methods, 35–38
  parameters, 516
  and threads, 475–479
  and Worldwide Web, 508
`AppletContext` interface, 515
Applet security, 443–444
Applications, 14–18
Arguments of a method, 35, 280
Arrays, 337–348
  accessing array elements, 339–340
  declaring arrays, 338–339
  heterogeneous, 346–348
  and loops, 340–343
  multidimensional, 344–345
Assembler program, 6
Assembly language, 6
Assignment operator, 44, 188–190
Associativity, 172
ATM applet, 314–320
Audio clips, 517–518
`AWTEvent` hierarchy, 247–253
  `ActionEvent`, 249
  `InputEvent`, 249–250
  `ItemEvent`, 250–251
  `KeyEvent`, 251–252
  `MouseEvent`, 252–253
  `TextEvent`, 253
  upper level event classes, 247–248

BASIC, 7
Binary representation, 3, 177
Bitwise operators, 177–181
Boolean operators, 181–187
  complicated boolean expressions,
    184–187
`boolean` type, 158
`BorderLayout` class, 108–110
`Bouncer` applet, 464, 468
`break` statement, 225
Browsers, 9, 10
`Button` class, 81–82

Byte, 8
Bytecode, 16
Bytecode verifier, 443

C++, 7, 12, 19–20
Calculator Lablet, 320–321
Call a method into action, 36, 55,
    278–280
Canvas class, 117–120
CardLayout class, 112–115
CardTest applet, 114
case-sensitive/-insensitive language, 17
catch clause, 390–391
char type, 157
Checkbox class, 82–84
CheckboxGroup, 84–85
CheckboxMenuItem, 136
Choice class, 85–86
Class
  ActionEvent, 249
  Applet, 476, 512–515
  AppletContext, 515
  Boolean, 362
  BorderLayout, 108–110
  Button, 81–82
  Canvas, 117–120
  CardLayout, 112–115
  Character, 362
  Checkbox, 82–84
  CheckboxGroup, 84
  CheckboxMenuItem, 136
  Choice, 85–86, 388
  Color, 45, 526–527
  Component, 66–71
  Container, 101–105, 388
  DataInputStream, 422–424
  DataOutputStream, 422, 424–425
  Date, 57, 499
  Dialog, 124–130, 388
  Dimension, 48
  Double, 362, 388
  Event, 232–233
  Exception, 385, 387
    subclasses, 385–387
  File, 435–438
  FileDialog, 438–441
  FileInputStream, 426, 427

FileOutputStream, 426–427
FilteredImageSource, 533–534
Float, 362, 388
FlowLayout, 106–108
Font, 46
FontMetrics, 556
Frame, 121–123
Graphics, 39–41, 520
GridLayout, 110–112
hierarchy, 38–39, 67, 101, 131, 248,
    386, 419
Image, 519–522
InputEvent, 249–250
InputStream, 419–421
Integer, 362, 388
ItemEvent, 250–251
KeyEvent, 251–252
Label, 72, 389
List, 87–90, 389
Long, 362, 389
Math, 175–177
MediaTracker, 538–540
Menu, 134–135
MenuBar, 133
MenuComponent, 132
MenuItem, 135–136
MouseEvent, 252–253
OutputStream, 419, 421–422
Panel, 104–105
Point, 47–48
PopupMenu, 137
Rectangle, 48–52
RGBImageFilter, 532–533
String, 356–363, 389
System, 57–58
TextArea, 76–78, 389
TextComponent, 73–74
TextEvent, 253
TextField, 74–75
Thread, 466–469, 488–491
ThreadGroup, 472–475
Throwable, 386
URL, 513
Window, 121
Classes, 15, 20–21
  determining, in GUI design, 288–294
Class loader, 443

Class variables, 190–193
Color class, 45
ColorPicker applet, 527
Colors Lablet, 24–26
Comment, 6, 14, 34
Comparison operators, 181
Compiler, 7
Component class, 66–71
    graphical methods, 67–71
Compound statement, 195
Computer language, 3
Concatenation of strings, 57
Conditional operator, 193–194
Container class, 100–105
    containment hierarchy, 103–104
    organization methods, 101–103
    Panel class, 104–105
Container layout methods, 105–106
Convenience methods, 237

Debug, 7
Declaration statements, 194
Decrement operator, 174, 175
Delegation model, 242–247
DeMorgan's laws, 186, 187
Dialog class, 124–130
Dijkstra, Edsger, 312
Dimension class, 48
Distributed hypermedia, 9
Distributive laws, 186–187
do loop, 332
Drawing offscreen, 522–524

Echo character, 75
Empty statements, 195
ENIAC (Electronic Numeric Integrator
        and Computer), 2, 5
Enough Rope to Shoot Yourself in the
        Foot (Holub), 19
Event-driven programming, 231–235
    Event class, 232–233
    event hierarchy, 233–235
Event handling, 235–239
    deciphering the event, 238–239
    helper methods, 237–238
    in version 1.1, 253–257
Exceptions, 384–411

exceptional conditions, 384–389
Exception class, 387
Exception subclasses, 385–387
handling exceptions, 389
    exception propagation, 392–393
    finally clause, 399–400
    handling run-time problems,
        397–399
    throwing exceptions, 393–397
    try and catch, 390–391
    methods that throw exceptions,
        388–389
    programmer-defined, 400–402
Excite, 10
Expressions, 171, 174
Expression statements, 194
Extending a class, 22

Fetch–execute cycle, 462
File class, 435–438
FileDialog class, 438–441
File I/O, 425–434
    FileInputStream class, 426, 427
    FileOutputStream class, 426,
        427
    headers, 431–434
    I/O for class types, 430–431
    I/O for primitive types, 427–429
Filtering file names, 434–435
finally clause, 399–400
final modifier, 163–164
Floating-point numbers, 156–157
FlowLayout class, 106–108
Focus events, 241
Font class, 46
for loop, 333–335
Formal argument, 37, 281
FORTRAN (FORmula TRANslator)
        language, 6
Frame class, 121–123
Framer applet, 123
FTP (file transfer protocol), 509

GalaEvents Lablet, 257–259
Gigobite Lablet, 90–92
Gosling, James, 12, 13, 19
GraphicButton class, 555–559

Graphics class, 39–41
  using, 42–45
GridLayout class, 110–112
Group statement, 195
GUI hierarchy, 139–140

handleEvent method, 235–237
Hello applet, 14
Helper methods, 237
Heterogeneous arrays, 346–348
High-level language, 7
Holub, Allen I., 19
HTML. *See* Hypertext Markup
        Language
http (hypertext transfer protocol), 509
Hypertext document, 9
Hypertext Markup Language (HTML),
        10–12, 561–562

Identifiers, 33, 158, 159
if statement, 195–196, 217–220
  common problems, 220–224
Image class, 519–522
  image filters, 532–535
  image processing, 524–531
ImageTest applet, 519, 523, 530, 534
import statement, 33
Increment operator, 174, 175
Inheritance, 21–22, 38
init() method, 54–55
InputEvent, 249–250
Input/output, 418–456
  file I/O, 425–434
    advanced, 434–441
  security, applets, and applications,
        441–447
  streams, 419–425
InputStream class, 419–421
Insertion Sort, 350–352
instanceof operator, 193
Instance variables, 53, 54, 120, 159, 160
Integral types, 155–156
Interface
  ActionListener, 253, 255
  FilenameFilter, 434
  Image, 522
  ImageConsumer, 529

ImageObserver, 529
Image Producer, 529
ItemListener, 255
KeyListener, 253, 255–256
MouseListener, 256
MouseMotionListener, 256
Runnable, 469–472
TextListener, 256
Interface declaration, 229–231
Interfaces, 32
Internet, 7–8
Internet Explorer, 10, 16
Interpreter, 7
Intranet, 9
ItemEvent, 250–251
ItemListener interface, 255

Java
  class, 20–21
  development of, 13
  inheritance, 21–22
  language basics, 154–205
    assignments and statements,
        187–196
    identifiers, keywords, and variables,
        158–170
    operators and expressions, 171–187
    primitive types, 154–158
  libraries, 22–23
  objects, 20–21
  syntax, 19
  and Web pages, 13–16
java.applet, 32
java.awt, 32, 39, 66

KeyEvent, 251–252
KeyListener interface, 253, 255–256
Key modifiers, 239–241
Keywords, 158

Label class, 72
Lablet, 24
Lablets
  ATM, 314–320
  Calculator, 320–321
  Colors, 24–26
  GalaEvents, 257–259

Lablets (cont.)
    GigoBite, 90–92
    OldButtoner, 550–554
    OrderPlease, 402–411
    Ovenator, 141–145
    SketchPad, 260–264
    Snapshot, 52–58
    SodaPop, 196–205
    Sortmeister, 363–372
    TickTock, 491–501
    WordPro, 447–456
Layout, in GUI design, 289–294
Links, 9
LISP, 7
List class, 87–90
Local variables, 53, 54, 159
Loops, 330–337
    arrays and, 340–343
    common problems with loops,
        335–337
    do loop, 332
    for loop, 333–335
    while loop, 332–333
Lycos, 10

Machine language, 2, 4, 5
main method, 14
Masks, 239–240
Math class, 175–177
MediaTracker class, 538–540
Menus, 130–138
    CheckboxMenuItem, 136
    MenuBar, 133
    Menu class, 134–135
    MenuComponent, 132
    MenuItem, 135–136
    PopupMenu, 137
    sample menu, 137–138
MenuTest applet, 138
Method calls, 194, 278–280
Methods, 14, 35–38, 277–285
    arguments, 280–285
    calling methods, 278–280
    determining, in GUI design, 294–300
    signatures, 277–278
Methods that throw exceptions, 388–389
Mouse buttons, 241

MouseEvent, 252–253
MouseListener interface, 256
Multidimensional arrays, 344–345

Netscape Navigator, 10, 14, 16
New class, designing, 302
notify() method, 483–484
null layout, 115–117
Numeric operators, 171–175

Object, 20–21
Object code, 6
OldButtoner applet, 550–554
Operand, 171
OrderPlease Lablet, 402–411
OutputStream class, 419, 421–425
Ovenator Lablet, 141–145
Overriding a method, 38

Package access, 168
Packages, 16, 22–23, 164–165
paint() method, 35, 37–38, 39, 54,
    67
Panel class, 104–105
Pixels, 36
Platform independent standard, 11
Point class, 47–48
PopupMenu, 137
Precedence, 171–172
Primitive types, 154
    boolean type, 158
    characters, 157
    floating-point numbers, 156–157
    integers, 155–156
Primitive types of information, 20
Primitive variables, 190–193
private access, 166–168
Programming, evolution of, 1–7
protected access, 168–169
public access, 169–170

ReaderWriter applet, 486
Rectangle class, 48–52
Reference arguments, 283–285
Reference types, 191
Return statements, 194–195
Runnable interface, 469–472

Scope of an identifier, 160–162
Scroll events, 241–242
Search engines, 10
Security
    applet, 443–444
    Java, 442
    of Java applications, 444–447
Security manager, 443
Selection Sort, 348–350
Self-documenting programs, 34
Semantics, 154
Shell, D. L., 352
Shellsort, 352–355
Signature of a method, 55, 277–278
SketchPad Lablet, 260–264
Snapshot Lablet, 52–58
SodaPop Lablet, 196–205
Sorting, 348–355
    Insertion Sort, 350–352
    Selection Sort, 348–350
    Shellsort, 352–355
Sortmeister Lablet, 363–372
Source code, 6, 16
Specification of programming problem,
        285–288
Statements, 194–196
static modifier, 162–163
Stored-program computer, 5
Streams, 419–425
Strings, 355–363
    access and comparison, 357–360
    builders, 360–361
    String class, 356–357
    used for conversion, 361–363
Stroustrup, Bjarne, 19
switch statement, 224–226
Syntax, 19, 154

Tag, 10, 17
TextArea class, 76–78
TextComponent class, 73–74
TextEvent, 253
TextField class, 74–75
TextListener interface, 256
Thread class, 466–469
    class constants, 488
    class methods, 489–490

constructors, 489
instance methods, 490
methods from object, 490–491
ThreadGroup class, 472–475
Threads, 462–501
    synchronizing threads, 479–480
        priorities, 487–488
        synchronization and mutual
            exclusion, 480–482
        wait and notify methods,
            482–484
    threaded execution, 463–475
        grouping threads, 472–475
        Runnable interface, 469–472
        Thread class, 466–469, 488–491
    threads and applets, 475–479
Throwable class, 385–386
throws clause, 394–395
throw statement, 393–394
TickTock Lablet, 491–501
Toggle button, 82
Truth table, 184–186
try block, 390–391

Unary operator, 174, 175, 179
Unicode, 157
Uniform Resource Locator (URL),
        509–512

Value arguments, 283–284
Variables, 43, 159–160
    declaring, 44, 53, 54
    scope, 160–162
Version 1.1 event model, 253–257
    adapters, 257
    listener interfaces, 254–256
Virtual machine, 6
Visual design, 100–145
    containers, 100–105
    layouts, 105–117
von Neumann, John, 5

wait() method, 483–484
Web page, 9, 10
    applet in, 16
    Java and, 13–16
Web server, 9, 11

while loop, 332–333
Whitespace, 17
Widgets, 66–95
  active widgets, 81–90
    Button class, 81–82
    Checkbox class, 82–84
    CheckboxGroup, 84–85
    Choice class, 85–86
    List class, 87–90
  Component class, 66–71
    graphical methods, 67–71
  textual widgets, 71–81

    Label class, 72
    TextArea class, 76–78
    TextComponent class, 73–74
    TextField class, 74–75
Window class, 121
WordPro Lablet, 447–456
Worldwide Web, 9–10, 12
  applets and, 508
Wrapper class, 304

Yahoo, 10